Getting Results with the
Object-Oriented Enterprise Model

(FM)

Page #s

① Interface between EM & OOA → 492

② Focus of Business Processes in → 499, 500
    EM & OO methodologies

Managing Object Technology Series

Charles F. Bowman
Series Editor
Editor
The X Journal
SIGS Publications, Inc.
New York, New York

and

President
SoftWright Solutions,
Suffern, New York

1. What Every Software Manager Must Know
to Succeed with Object Technology, *John D. Williams*

2. Managing Your Move to Object Technology:
Guidelines and Strategies for a Smooth Transition,
Barry McGibbon

3. The Object Primer: Application Developer's Guide to
Object-Orientation, *Scott W. Ambler*

4. Getting Results with the Object-Oriented Enterprise Model,
Thornton Gale and James Eldred

5. Deploying Distributed Business Software,
Ted Lewis, Ph.D.

Additional Volumes in Preparation

Getting Results with the Object-Oriented Enterprise Model

Thornton Gale
James Eldred

Future Strategies
Mercer Island, Washington

SIGS BOOKS

New York • London • Paris • Munich • Cologne

Thornton Gale and James Eldred are the owners of Future Strategies and offer professional consulting services internationally. For more information contact them at Future Strategies, 9404 S.E. 54th, Mercer Island, WA, or call (206) 232-1475.

Library of Congress Cataloging-in-Publication Data

Gale, Thornton, 1942–
     Getting results with the object-oriented enterprise model / Thornton Gale & James Eldred
        p. cm. — (Managing object technology series ; 4)
     Includes bibliographical references and index.
     ISBN 1-884842-16-X (pbk. : alk. paper)
     1. Enterprise modeling   2. Object-oriented modeling   I. Eldred, James, 1948– .
II. Title. III. Series.
QA76.64.G35   1995   95-46190
658.4'0352—dc20   CIP

PUBLISHED BY
SIGS Books
71 W. 23rd Street, Third Floor
New York, New York 10010

Design and composition by Kevin Callahan.
Cover design by Jean Cohn.
Printed on acid-free paper.

SIGS Books ISBN 1-884842-16-X
Prentice-Hall ISBN 0-13-242009-0

Printed in the United States of America
99 98 97 96   10 9 8 7 6 5 4 3 2 1
First Printing January 1996

Dedication

To Marty
— T. G.

To Dena
— J. E.

About the Author

THORNTON GALE IS A SENIOR SOFTWARE ENGINEER with over 30 years' experience in all phases of software engineering and has served as systems architect on a variety of high-profile projects in which computer technology empowered strategic business direction. He is a General Partner in Future Strategies, a Washington State consultancy. Gale specializes in object-oriented technologies, enterprise reengineering, information strategic planning, and Rapid Applications Development (RAD). He has personally tested and validated the claims of object-oriented technology by developing several GUI-based applications using object-oriented analysis (OOA), object-oriented design (OOD), and object-oriented programming (OOP) with Smalltalk.

During his career, Gale has relentlessly and successfully pursued his goal of shifting the paradigm from technology-focused systems to business-focused systems. Gale was the systems architect of the Bellingham Project, a corporate-sponsored US WEST reengineering project to provide alternative local exchange telephony. This strategic pilot project proposed and tested the complete reengineering and rediscovery of the local exchange business. Gale designed and established a Rapid Applications Development environment that accomplished the 24 months of work (standard approach) in 4 months (RAD approach).

James Eldred is an internationally recognized authority on the telecommunications industry and its evolution. Eldred is a general partner in Future Strategies, a Washington State consultancy. He has more than 25 years' experience in the areas of business transformation and information systems and services. He has particular expertise in strategic and tactical planning, business planning, operations management and performance, capacity and resource management, and applications development. Eldred spent 15 years in Pacific Northwest Bell's Data Systems organization; 4 years of this period were focused on strategic technology planning and architectures as a consultant to major corporations in the Northwest and as a Technical Director with US WEST Advanced Technologies.

Eldred's specific efforts in recent years have been directed toward establishing alternative ways to provide local exchange telephony. He was founder and director of US WEST's Bellingham Laboratory and project manager for a major alternative network provider project with US WEST International in Southeast Asia. As a General Partner in Future Strategies, Eldred continues to facilitate the deployment of a competitive global telecommunications infrastructure. It is the objective of Future Strategies to contribute significantly toward a communications environment that enables the realization of an information age in a manner that will benefit both industry and society.

Foreword

ALL TOO OFTEN, SYSTEMS DEVELOPERS INTERPRET THE TERM *system* to mean computerized information system (CIS). By assuming that all systems are computerized, they neglect the part that people and machines play in an enterprise. By recognizing only information, they fail to distinguish other corporate resources, such as technology, assets, and human effort. Without a fuller understanding of what a system is, analysts will not be able to model and reengineer an enterprise effectively. *Getting Results with the Object-Oriented Enterprise Model* is one of the first texts to embrace and adequately communicate this broader view.

This book helps system developers to take off their CIS blinders and gain a general systems view of an enterprise. The reader learns how to examine everything from the most atomic processes to the pragmatics of the global environment-as well as the ways in which the enterprise should interact with this environment. To accomplish this, *Getting Results with the Object-Oriented Enterprise Model* marries two important paradigms: General Systems Theory and Object Orientation. One paradigm provides a way of defining the general characteristics and properties of all systems, the other provides a way to organize and present our understanding of these systems. Together, they provide a powerful means of modeling enterprise systems.

Getting Results with the Object-Oriented Enterprise Model presents the underlying theory of general systems and OO in clear, concise language. It ties together foundations based on business, formal theory, modeling and methodology. Several well known OO modeling approaches have been selected, synthesized, and evolved. Various techniques ranging from chaos theory to value-chain analysis have been woven together to enhance the process. Finally, a detailed, cohesive methodology has been assembled, assisting the reader every step along the way. In short, the authors have produced a comprehensive treatment of enterprise modeling methods and techniques-one that will help us to develop effectively the next generation of enterprise systems.

— James J. Odell

Preface

THIS BOOK IS ABOUT A PROCESS FOR ESTABLISHING AND MAINTAINING a competitive results-optimizing view of an enterprise—an object-oriented enterprise model. We have observed a basic need for an enterprise-planning and leadership process that reflects the realities of the dramatically changing environments within which enterprises must operate. Current business-planning environments are, in the main, mechanisms for justifying budgets and organizational structure within enterprises. They are almost always focused on the internal processes and operations of the businesses themselves. Consistency among any vision, a competitive strategy, and the current plan is spotty if it exists at all.

Clearly, fundamental business planning must center on what is occurring in the global environment and on how an enterprise should best relate to, contribute to, and benefit from that environment. Like all individual enterprises, businesses need to focus on the world in which they exist more than upon themselves. Doing so requires a planning and leadership discipline that is a match for the complexities of today's competitive world.

The Nature of the leadership need

Enterprise planning and leadership don't need additional technology or tools to ingest information and generate directives to action. There are more than enough tools (although there could always be better ones) for performing specific tasks within the domain of leadership and planning. (We use the word planning here in the context of "vision"—that which establishes, characterizes, and "instantiates" some desired future and does so in a logical, convincing, and compelling manner.) What is lacking in enterprise planning and leadership is an approach that provides landmarks and guidelines for navigating the myriad competing enterprise issues and solutions. Every business leader is besieged by petitions to fund potential solutions originating from some narrow segment of the enterprise that promise to solve all of its problems. "Buy this approach to information systems, and it will increase shop floor productivity, improve morale, increase sales, and drive profits through the roof; buy this approach to business process design and regenerate your business. . . ."

What we need, then, is a framework for applying the appropriate tools, methods, and procedures—a structure within which the changing value conditions of the business environment can be effectively managed. We require a structure that helps identify these value conditions, establish—and retain—their appropriate meanings, influences, and relationships. That structure is a process—a "system" as defined in our theoretical foundations—for thinking about the future and for compelling others to bring that future to reality.

This process must reflect the pragmatic aspects of geopolitics, global economics, and competition as well as technology. We need a tool set that helps us to abstract from the most strategic and conceptual (e.g., competitive industry and market positioning strategies) to the most discrete levels of business operations (e.g., process use cases). Such a tool must also tangibly retain and reflect high-level esoteric business drivers and strategies for subsequent application to increasingly discrete and tactical planning—and ultimately operational—levels.

Such an approach provides a leadership system encompassing the global market, industry, and sociopolitical value systems within which an enterprise operates as well as effectively supporting the internal value-adding system that makes up the enterprise itself.

A systemic solution

A planning method or tool can be considered from two perspectives: (1) from that of the scope and nature of the elements and factors being used to plan, and (2) from that of the components of planning itself and how they are organized to achieve enterprise leadership. This section discusses some of both but is primarily focused upon presenting the appropriate content and context for "visioning," planning, and leading an enterprise.

The motivating concept for this book might be distilled down to the following:

> To instantiate a vision of a future state—to make it reality—requires that the vision be abstracted into concepts, terms, and semantics that are understandable to and manageable by those who will implement it, and that if this is so, the concepts and principles of general systems theory, and of the object-oriented paradigm should most efficiently support the requirements of abstraction.

Making vision into reality requires three things:

- The specifics of the concept or future condition can be articulated and communicated ubiquitously within the enterprise.

- The future state specifics can be correlated with current state specifics to enable creation of a plan for achieving the vision.

- Information about specific implementation actions and resources called for in the plan can be articulated and communicated effectively within the enterprise.

Translating this to the venue of business, tangible relationships, and dependencies among the following elements must be established and maintained:

- The definitive elements of the desired business future (business vision)

- The critical competitive success factors (business imperatives)

- The industry and market positioning strategies (external strategy)

- Operating strategies (implementation and operating plans).

The relationship between values and process

While this work speaks frequently from the perspectives of vision and planning, please keep in mind that what we present here is an approach to developing a model of an enterprise. The vision and planning perspectives are used liberally because, to the authors, they are the essence of what a model must reflect and communicate. Our working definition of model is "an artifact that describes or represents an entity or state of affairs that cannot be observed directly or completely." Such an artifact may represent the external relationship of some elements or parts within an entity, but it will always be incomplete—that is, it will leave room for speculation as to the reasons and values behind those relationships. Therefore, the artifact lacks the ability to help definitively in the repair and/or alteration of the relationships. However, by including as many "values" as possible in the model and providing a method that relates values to choices in structure, function, and behavior, the artifact combined with the process can provide significant help in determining such repairs and/or alterations to and/or among elements.

The object-oriented enterprise modeling method proposed in this book is designed to develop an artifact that is as complete as possible in all respects. The methodology and the resulting model are intended to be implementable, operable, and changeable tools. So, while they are critical to planning and reflect the approaches and content necessary for effective planning, these tools do not contain or represent all that is necessary in the visioning and planning processes. Please don't confuse object-oriented enterprise modeling with planning.

Blending disparate disciplines and experience

Our approach to establishing and communicating a leadership framework is a model, one that allows abstraction of an entire enterprise as a whole, in part(s), and at its most basic elements. The process and concepts associated with the modeling methodology developed in this book result from holistic consideration of four disparate intellectual areas. Object-oriented enterprise modeling borrows from, integrates, and "synergizes" existing theoretical work in these diverse areas. The four areas are represented graphically in Figure P-1 and include:

- **Business foundations**   Competitive business fundamentals

- **Theoretical foundations**   Abstract theory from formal academic disciplines

- **Modeling foundations**   Computer science and object-oriented theory

- **Methodology foundations**   Proven methods and procedures from leading experts

We don't pretend to represent the thoughts and ideas of these individuals. Rather, we attempt to convey the influence their combined work has had upon our thinking, upon the logical development of our work, and on the interpretation of our experiences in that work. Any errors in logic or fact regarding their work that the reader might conclude from the reading of this book should be attributed to our misinterpretation or miscommunication. Any serious student of the environment to which object-oriented enterprise modeling is applied should make it a point to study these ideas and concepts directly.

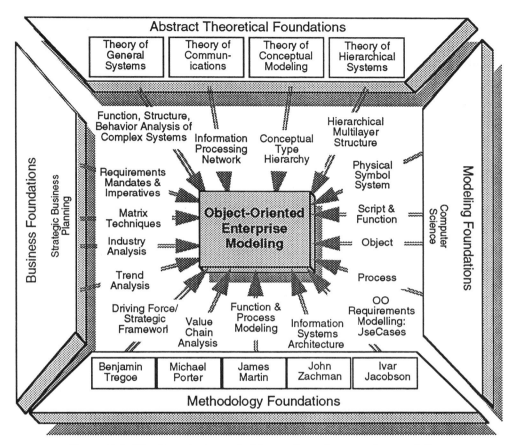

Figure P-1 *The foundations of object-oriented enterprise modeling.*

It's not the methodology—it's the people!

Finally, while we say a great deal about an approach and methodology for developing an enterprise model, we must admit that in the end this and all methods are futile without effective people making them work. It is our very real experience that empowering an appropriate collection of individuals is critical to the actual creation of an artifact representing what and/or how an enterprise does or should operate. While a methodology should be of great help to such a group, it alone is not sufficient in itself to ensure success. The members of the established team must be expected—and be allowed—to make decisions regarding the rationale, values, and processes of the enterprise.

People whose work and ideas have most significantly influenced our work include:

Business Foundations	Industries and Markets	Stanley Davis
		Michael C. Porter
		Benjamin Tregoe
		Lester Thurow
	Strategy and Vision	Kenichi Ohmae
		Michael C. Porter
		Peter Senge
	General Management	Joel Barker
		Peter F. Drucker
Theoretical Foundations	General Systems Theory	Nic Kramer
		Jacob de Smit
		John Sutherland
	Theory of Communications	Claude Shannon
		Warren Weaver
	Conceptual Modeling	John Sowa
		William Tepfenhart
		Heather Pfeiffer
		Robert Hartley
		Eileen Way
		Allen Newell
		Herbert Simon
	Theory of Hierarchical Systems	M. D. Mesarovic
		D. Macko
		Y. Takahara
		Steven Kim

People whose work and ideas have most significantly influenced our work include:

Modeling Foundations	Physical Symbol Systems	Allen Newell Herbert Simon
	Scripts and Functions	Allen Newell Herbert Simon
	Object-Oriented Paradigm	David Taylor Grady Booch Ivar Jacobson
	Processes	B. Curtis M. I. Kellner J. Over F. B. Vernadat P. J. Russel
Methodology Foundations	Value Chain Analysis	Michael Porter
	Function/Process Modeling	James Martin
	Driving Force/ Strategic Framework	Benjamin Tregoe
	Information Systems Architecture	John Zachman
	Object-Oriented Requirements	Ivar Jacobson

Acknowledgments

THE GENERAL CONCEPTS FOR THIS BOOK were gained over the span of the authors' careers. However, the book's concepts and principles coalesced during two significant team efforts. We owe a great deal to those who believed in us and our ideas enough to sponsor their pursuit. We owe still more to those who followed our ideas while simultaneously propelling us to a better understanding of those same ideas and how powerful they can be. For all those who supported and participated in the Living Lab and/or KL, you have our continuing appreciation and gratitude. May you continue to seek and then to act upon those "blinding flashes of the obvious."

Contents

Chapter 19   Market and Product Planning (Stage 2)   393

Chapter 20   Public Policy Strategy (Stage 3)   403

Chapter 21   Enterprise Model (Stage 4)   411

Contents

Part 1

The General System

Introduction to Part 1

As long as there has been business, there has been an effort to improve business—to methodically design and construct business to maximize profit. In this book, we call this *enterprise engineering*. From a historical perspective, enterprise engineering has changed in recent years. Probably the biggest difference today is that business terms permeate all parts of our business culture and being promoted and distorted, leaving one uncertain of what it all means. We see articles nearly every day in the *Wall Street Journal* and other business periodicals analyzing the efforts of American business to change itself. Today, business process reengineering is very hot, with the number of business process reengineering projects growing by leaps and bounds every year. Unfortunately, there is a big problem with all of this effort to improve business, a problem apparent to anyone who has attended a business conference recently. During the sessions on business process reengineering, a well-meaning presenter, usually a business consultant, will discuss in one form or another the concepts of enterprise engineering, using terms such as *business process, process flow, system,* or *information*. Then another business consultant will get up and give another presentation using these same terms but with different meanings. The presenters themselves do not agree on the meaning of the terms!

The problem is that there is no formal definition of the discipline of enterprise engineering. There is no coherent methodology, no standards, no theory, not even a set of terms agreed on by the practitioners of enterprise engineering, whom we call _enterprise engineers_. In particular, there is no formal definition of the enterprise as an empirical phenomenon that obeys a body of rules or principles. Scholars call this _formalism_. In short, there are no formalisms of the enterprise to which practitioners, scholars, and students can adhere. The first section of the book defines a set of formalisms to describe the enterprise.

Our two principal formalisms for enterprise modeling are general systems theory and the object-oriented paradigm. In the first part of the book, we will see that the enterprise is a general system consisting of business objects and that enterprise modeling can take advantage of the many results of the academic field of general systems theory. In the second part of the book, we will present the other major formalism, that of the object-oriented paradigm and related topics of modeling.

The first part of the book consists of five chapters that describe various aspects of general system theory as follows:

- Chapter 1 introduces the nature of modeling and its primary technique, abstraction. We discuss modeling as a tool to understand complex systems, but first we need to know just what a system is in the first place. We will define the word _system_ and introduce its important properties. We will see that not every collection of objects should be considered a system, although it's largely a subjective call of the modeler. To be a system, the collection of objects must pursue some overall objective.

- Chapter 2 continues our discussion of the system by introducing general systems theory. We introduce the major concepts of general systems theory. One of the main premises of this book is that the enterprise is an example of a general system and modeling can be done using the tools and concepts from general systems theory.

- Chapter 3 describes a very important organizational structure of complex general systems such as the enterprise, the hierarchical-multilayer system. We propose that the enterprise is a premier example of a hierarchical-multilayer system. The hierarchical-multilayer organization means the system has both a hierarchical aspect and a multilayer aspect. The hierarchical aspect means that the various subsystems will be arranged in hierarchies in which a coordination/control function is part of the larger system. The multilayer aspect means the division of the system into functional abstraction layers. In this chapter, we define the hierarchical-multilayer system and give examples of it.

◆ Chapter 4 introduces the information-processing network. An information-processing network is a general system with some specialized structural properties. It is made up of large networks of what we call *information-processing nodes,* which are connected in a lattice of communication channels. In this book, we propose that the enterprise is a premier example of the information-processing network. The information processing network is a unique example of a general system because it contains a significant property: information. The structure of the information-processing network is a communications infrastructure that transmits information between its subsystems, the information-processing nodes. Information processing nodes are agents that are capable of storing and processing information and include people, organizations, computers, and production machines. This will be one of our views of the enterprise, that of a general system consisting of a vast network of information-processing nodes.

Chapter 1

Modeling

1.1 Introduction

This book is about enterprise modeling. A reasonable question to start with, then, is, What is modeling? Anybody who builds things has an intuitive feel for what modeling is. We usually describe modeling as the construction of a small, inexpensive, and incomplete artifact that simulates some real-world domain in which we are interested. We use models to make predictions about the real world and then to test these predictions. By manipulating a model, we are in a sense testing those aspects of the real world that our model was designed to simulate.

Models are useful in any activity that designs and constructs things. This includes all of the engineering disciplines, including enterprise engineering. The noted systems scientist H. A. Simon puts it this way: "The engineer, and more generally the designer, is concerned with how things *ought* to be——how they ought to be in order to *attain goals* and to *function*" (Simon, 1981). Because models are inexpensive, they are very useful as a tool to test how something should work—in other words, how something should be designed. Thus, modeling is very much a tool for the engineer and designer for understanding complexity.

1.2 What is enterprise modeling?

Because this book is about enterprise modeling, another reasonable question to ask at this point is, What is an enterprise? An *enterprise* is a system of business objects that are in functional symbiosis. *Symbiosis* means that business objects work together to accomplish mutually beneficial goals. The business objects of the enterprise include people, machines, buildings, processes, events, and information that combine to produce the products or output of the enterprise. An enterprise is not necessarily a for-profit business and could include nearly any system of business objects.

Now we can put the terms together and ask the big question: What is enterprise modeling? *Enterprise modeling,* like any form of modeling, is the construction of a limited system that represents the larger system in question. The purpose of enterprise modeling is to understand and improve the enterprise, that is, to improve the symbiosis of the individual business objects. In this sense, *improvement* means any change in coordination among the business objects that increases the benefits of symbiosis. The methodology of enterprise modeling is the construction of a set of views of the enterprise considered as a system. The resulting enterprise model contains representations of facts, objects, and relationships that occur in the enterprise (Burkhart, 1992). Enterprise modeling is the tool of business reengineering.

During an enterprise-reengineering project, a model of the enterprise is constructed, usually in two views: present methods of operations and future methods of operations. The present methods of operations view of the enterprise model is used to diagnosis the enterprise. The future methods of operations view of the enterprise model is used to guide the reengineering of the enterprise. Thus the enterprise model first provides the big picture for prioritizing change (getting the most bang for the buck) and second, the big picture for changing the enterprise or portions of it.

1.3 What is a system?

We pointed out that the enterprise is a system, but just what is a *system?* The world is made up of sets of things we group together, such as parts into a machine or people into an organization. Are these groupings of things examples of systems? Scholars define a system in terms of a collection of related entities working as a whole to accomplish objectives. Thomas Athey uses this idea in his definition: "*Systems* are any set of components which could be seen as working together for the overall objective of the whole" (Athey, 1982).

Another aspect of the definition of a system is that the various parts of the system must somehow be related. In their definition of *system*, Nic Kramer and Jacob de Smit stress the importance of the relations among the components of the collection. According to Kramer and de Smit, a *system* is "a set of interrelated entities, of which no subset is unrelated to any other subset. This means that a system as a whole displays properties which none of its parts or subsets has" (Kramer and de Smit, 1977). Kramer and de Smit point out that when the individual entities enter into certain relations with one another, they form a system that has properties of the whole that the individual entities don't have.

Yet another aspect of the definition of a system is that it must accomplish objectives. For natural systems, accomplishing objectives often takes the form of achieving stability. For example, a natural system such as a weather system continues to exist and operate even when subjected to external influences. For human-made systems, accomplishing objectives means the system produces something useful by transforming input into output. For example, in a manufacturing plant, raw materials are transformed into products.

We have introduced several new words in the various preceding definitions: *objective, input and output, entity, relation,* and *property.* We define these in more detail in the following.

Objectives

Systems have objectives. We call an aggregation of objects a *system* if the aggregation meets objectives. Objectives are the results that a particular system achieves. They justify the system and are closely related to the *output* of the system (defined next). In the words of Arthur D. Hall, "A system has evolved, or has been designed, to satisfy or to tend toward at least one objective" (Hall, 1989). According to David O'Sullivan, system objectives tend to be either inner directed or outer directed. For example, the objectives of a biological system (e.g., an animal, a plant), are inner directed toward maintaining the life of the system. In human-made systems, objectives are both outer directed as products to customers as well as inner directed to continually improve the operation of the system (O'Sullivan, 1994).

Inputs and outputs

Systems exist in an environment. The environment of a system is the external world of the system under analysis and over which the system has no control. A system is either *open* (it has exchanges with its environment) or *closed* (it doesn't have exchanges with its environment). According to Derek Hitchins, closed systems do not exist in the real world but are considered closed to simplify their analysis. There is always some other system with which the system in question interacts and conducts exchanges (Hitchins, 1993). We refer to these exchanges of the open system with its environment as *input* and *output*.

The term *input* refers to any material, energy, or information that the open system receives from its environment. Inputs are required by the open system to accomplish its objectives. In the case of the manufacturing system, inputs include raw materials, orders, consumables, people, electricity, money, and fuel (O'Sullivan, 1994).

Like *input*, the term *output* refers to any material, energy, or information that the open system discharges to its environment. For the human-made open system, output represents the accomplishment of objectives. Robertshaw and his co-authors give guidelines for determining system outputs by asking: What is being accomplished? What is being produced? What is the goal? Function? Objective? They assert "the identity of a system lies in its *output*—in what it does. . . . . The uniqueness of a system lies in its function. The function is identified by the outputs" (emphasis added) (Robertshaw et al, 1978).

Entity (object)

Entities are the elements or parts of a system. An entity has objective or physical reality. In modern terminology, the term *entity* has given way to the term *object*. In this book, we will use *object*. Objects are intended to be the primitive components that make up a system at our level of analysis. An object may have internal complexity and could be analyzed as a system in its own right if we were concerned with that level of detail. We will return to this point when we discuss subsystems in the next chapter. Also, in later chapters, we will discuss the modern concept of *object* in some detail.

Relation

Earlier, we described a system as a set of interrelated objects. It is the relations between objects that cause the system to become a whole with its special system capabilities. What is a relation between objects? According to Kramer and de Smit, *relation* is defined as "the way in which two or more entities (objects) are dependent on each other. . . . It must be added that this definition uses entities more in the sense of their properties (attributes)" (Kramer and de Smit, 1977). According to them, relations between the objects of a system arise or depend on the individual properties of the objects. Changing the properties changes the relation.

Thus relations tie the objects of the system together. Arthur Hall defines *relations* as representing an energy bond that makes possible a bilateral flow "thus, attributing a direction of causality of the interaction." He lists the kinds of relations

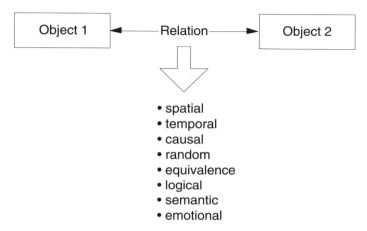

Figure 1.1 *Relation.*

as spatial, temporal, causal, random, equivalence, logical, semantic, and emotional (Hall, 1989).

We have summarized Arthur Hall's definition of *relation* in Figure 1.1.

1.4 Abstraction

The target of our enterprise-modeling efforts will be a complex system. The key word here is *complex*. The world around us, including the enterprise, is so complex that we, as designers, must somehow simplify it. This is not easy. When we focus on something with the purpose of modeling it, we want to separate the aspects that interest us from the ones that don't. This is called *abstraction,* which, according to the *Oxford Dictionary of Computing,* is "the principle of ignoring those aspects of a subject that are not relevant to the current purpose in order to concentrate more fully on those that are" (Oxford, 1986).

The use of abstraction has a very pragmatic aspect. If models are to be efficient, they must be inexpensive to develop. This means that models will have limitations in their capabilities. After all, if a model did not have limitations, it would, in fact, be equivalent to the complex reality that is being modeled. One big question, then, is how does the designer decide what the capabilities of the model will be? In short, the designer who is working on the larger design of the system must, in turn, design the model in order to design the larger system. In many ways, the designer has traded one design problem for another. However, the design of the model will be simpler because it is, by definition, limited in capability.

The problem then becomes one of achieving in the model the essence of the complex system being designed. In short, the designer must decide which capabilities to include in the model and not worry about any others. C. A. R. Hoare describes the act of abstraction as the "recognition of similarities between certain objects, situations, or processes in the real world and the decision to concentrate on these similarities, and to ignore, for the time being, their differences" (Hoare, 1972).

When we invoke the process of abstraction, what is it that we eliminate to make matters simpler? Brent Work and Ann Balmforth state it in terms of removing the nonpertinent relations that an object has: "Abstraction is a mental act which separates that which is characteristic of a thing from its accidental associations" (Work and Balmforth, 1993). We can conclude that one way to form an abstraction is not to worry about all of the incidental relations that an object has and focus on the relations important to the analysis we are conducting.

Thus what we are doing when we decide what few capabilities our model should include is the act of abstraction, a mental process we use to interpret the world around us. There is nothing intrinsically true about the abstractions we form. One abstraction of complexity is no more true or false than another. The only criteria in comparing abstractions would be their relative efficiency in helping one understand and work with a complex world.

1.5 Modeling

Now we are in a position to formally define *modeling*. In this section we will see that modeling is a mental process of abstracting the essence of a system of interest and then comparing those abstractions to a simpler system with which we are already familiar. We can formulate a definition of *modeling* in terms of abstraction.

Definition: Modeling

Brent Work and Ann Balmforth define *modeling* as an abstraction used as a tool to make sense of something we don't understand in terms of something we do understand. According to them, modeling is the construction of a relationship between two systems: "One is the system whose organization is unclear and the other is a system whose construction is well-understood." The former is the target system being analyzed, and the latter is the model. Since the model is well understood, it suggests an explanation of the target system's mechanisms by means of analogy. "Modeling postulates a similarity of structure between two items—the thing that is to be represented and the thing that serves as the model" (Work and Balmforth, 1993).

Figure 1.2 demonstrates the points made by Work and Balmforth. In this figure

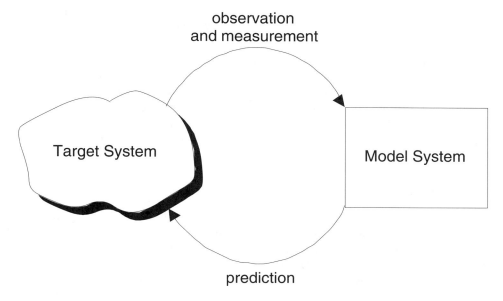

Figure 1.2 *Modeling.*

we see on the left the target system that is being studied. It is shown as an unstructured mass. On the right is the model constructed by the analyst to study the target system. It is a precise system that the analyst understands. The model system is constructed by observation and measurement as shown by the top arrow. Once constructed, the model system exhibits structure and behavior as it operates. These manifestations of structure and behavior in the model system will be used to predict the corresponding phenomena in the target system as shown by the bottom arrow.

Modeling is abstraction

We see in the preceding definition that constructing a model is a mental process that depends on abstraction. Recall that abstraction means drawing out the essence of a thing. Thus in constructing a model, we start with the familiar and draw out its essence. Then we use this picture that is very well known and familiar to us to analyze the unfamiliar target of our concerns. We apply the familiar abstraction to the unfamiliar to understand it. By constructing a model of the familiar, we abstract a set of principles or concepts that apply to that familiar world. We then use these principles and concepts against the unknown world we want to understand better. Our reasoning is that a principle or concept that applies in the familiar world should also apply in the unfamiliar world we are striving to understand.

For example, a model airplane is a simplified version of a real airplane. We could use the model airplane in many useful ways to understand the real-world airplane. We could put it in a wind tunnel to test its aerodynamics. We are assuming that the aerodynamic properties of a shape does not depend on size and that any conclusions we draw from the small model airplane will apply equally to the large real airplane, at least as it relates to aerodynamic properties. This assumption is not at all risky since the laws of aerodynamics do not mention size as a factor.

Decomposition

By breaking the target system into component objects and breaking those into subobjects, we can simplify the job of modeling. In the words of Subodh Bapat, "the model defines clearly separated components on which we can focus our attention separately and sequentially, because our minds can only deal with a small amount of information at any given time. The overall model of the complex system describes not only the components which result from such a decomposition but also the relationships of these components which describe how they interact to create the entire system" (Bapat, 1994).

On the other hand, modeling must provide a view of the global system. We call this the *architecture* of the system. According to Subodh Bapat, "an architecture imposes an organization on the elements of a problem domain—it provides a way of recognizing the major components of a system and the parameters under which they interoperate" (Bapat, 1994).

How much detail?

Because models are abstractions of systems from a complex world, they must be simpler and easier to work with than the systems they model. The trade-off for the model designer is defining the correct level of detail of the model. A simple model will be relatively easy to construct but will have limited value; one that is sophisticated will be difficult to construct but will be much more useful. In the words of Subodh Bapat, "a good model is one that strikes the correct balance in this inverse correlation between *versatility requirements* and the *efficiency requirements* of the system. Therefore, the design of the model, and the choice of the accuracy with which it represents the reality of the underlying system, is an exercise in *recognizing, evaluating, and selecting trade offs*" (Bapat, 1994).

For example, a map is a model of the real world. Maps can be simple or complex. A simple map might be the one you draw for your friends to show them how to get to your house for a social function. A complex map might show the detailed contours and geological features of the real world. The first type of map is very simple, but it can still be used to answer useful questions such as where the social function is relative to the freeway (e.g., on its left). The detailed contour map can be used to answer more sophisticated questions, such as what is the best route for building the freeway.

Putting the model to use

How are models used? One of the primary uses of models is as a communication tool during the design of a complex system. Two classical roles are necessary to design a system: the engineer and the owner who pays for the system. The engineer and the owner have completely different points of view not only because they are human beings but because of the differences in their roles. The owner determines the value of the proposed system and defines what the system would have to be like to be valuable. The engineer designs and constructs the proposed system but does not determine its value. The model represents a complete, albeit simplified, representation of the proposed system. The engineer and owner use it to understand the complex and expensive system prior to its construction. Both the engineer and the owner understand the model and frame all of their discussions in terms of it. The model is frequently changed to accommodate new ideas. In effect, the model serves as the external view of the proposed system and evolves into what the owner considers to be valuable. Once the model is complete and accepted, the owner makes a commitment to build the corresponding real system. The model then becomes a reference tool for the engineer to use in designing the system from a detailed, internal point-of-view.

Subodh Bapat identifies another very important use of models: to simulate and manipulate the real world. In this application, a model of the domain of interest is maintained which has communication links into key components of the real world. The model operates and simulates the real world. The communication links are used to gather information about the real world to update the model. The model is used to manipulate the real world by using the communication links to activate or change the components of the real world. In the words of Bapat, "By correlating objects in a model world based on their relevant relationships in the real world, we create a way of manipulating the system in an abstract manner. Providing that the model is reasonably accurate—that is, it closely approximates the behavior of the actual system in reality—we can then pretend to perform operations on the system by actually performing those operations on the model" (Bapat, 1994).

A related capability identified by Bapat is to use the model as a database to answer queries about the real world. For example, an updated model of some domain of the real world could be used to answer sophisticated queries about that domain. Since the model is a simulation of the real world, the answers to these queries can be very sophisticated revealing the subtleties of the domain in question (Bapat, 1994).

1.6 The state-process-event tricotomy

Modeling involves abstracting the essential characteristics of a complex system. What are these essential characteristics? What are we looking for? Are there any useful techniques for performing this abstraction? All systems can be described in terms of the three concepts: state, process, event. The essential characteristics of a system can be expressed in terms of these three. In this section, we discuss them and describe how they are used in modeling.

State-process-event

In Figure 1.3 we see the basic relationship between state, process, and event. This figure shows an event affecting a process. The event triggers the process which in turn causes State 1 (the initial state) to be transformed to State 2 (the final state). This is called a *state transition* and describes precisely the behavior of the system for a period of time.

Wait a minute! What are these things called *event, process, state, state transition*, and *behavior*? In this book, we will use these terms frequently. Let's define them now so we can use them freely in the rest of the book:

State

The two prominent systems theorists, Kramer and de Smit define *state* as the current condition of a system. The state of a system contains the effects of the accumulated history of the system: "The concept of state comprises, as it were, a part of the system's past. It can serve as a memory in which the relevant earlier history is stored so that, together with the input of the system, something can be said about the output" (Kramer and de Smit, 1977). The state of a system is caused by the operation of the system over a period of time. Put another way, the state of a system can only be changed by the operation of the system.

In this definition, an important aspect of state is the notion of storage of the state. We can assume that any system must be capable of internal representations of its state at any point in time. This representation of the state is called the *state*

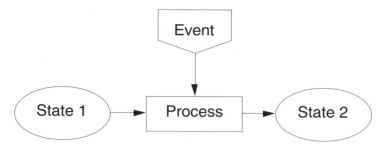

Figure 1.3 *State-process-event.*

memory. In simple systems, state memory may be just the unique configuration of internal objects at a point in time. An example of a simple state-memory would be a mechanical clock in which the state of the clock is stored in the internal configuration of gears, springs and other parts of the clock.

In complex systems, state memory may be a much more sophisticated representation actually involving the purposeful storage of physical symbol sequences representing information. An example of this type of state memory would be a calculator in which the intermediate numbers of the current calculation are stored internally within the calculator as number symbols. Notice that a mechanical calculator would store these symbols as physical phenomena (e.g., the configuration of gears and levers) and an electronic calculator would store these symbol as electrical phenomena (e.g., the magnetizing of a substance). However, these two examples of state memory of a calculator are equivalent for our definition of *state*.

Process

The term *process* is used extensively in the computer literature today as well as in daily speech. It is also an important term in enterprise modeling. To isolate its essential systems meaning, let's look at the academic definition of the term. Scholars define *process* as the dynamic property of a system. Externally, a process changes the state of the system. As observers, we can only detect a process by noting changes in the state of the system. Thus if there is a difference between our observations between one point in time and another, we conclude that the system has invoked a process. In this case, the process is defined and documented by this change in state and is called a *state transition*.

For open systems (i.e., systems that make exchanges with their environment), processes have an additional characteristic: transformation of input to output. Not only can we observe the processes of the open system by its state changes described earlier, we can also observe its processes by its transformations of input to output. As observers, we can detect a process of an open system by noting that certain input enters the system and result in output leaving the system. In this case, the process is defined and documented by the mapping between the input and the output.

Event

An *event* is a significant change in the environment of the system. It can be thought of as a change in the collective state of the environment. Events are considered to occur instantaneously and to have no internal structure. Events are a form of input to the open system and serve as the signals that cause processes to be started or stopped in the system. The system will react to an event by invoking a process. The process will cause a state transition from a beginning state to the ending state.

Stability

An open system may reach an equilibrium in which inputs and outputs are balanced. This is called *stability.* When an open system becomes stable, its state either does not change or its state cycles through a sequences of state transitions but always returns to an original state. According to Kramer and de Smit, "one of the primary functions of the (open) system is often the maintenance of stable conditions, since an unstable state is usually undesirable and frequently leads to catastrophes" (Kramer and de Smit, 1977).

Stability is much-valued as a system characteristic and a significant portion of the processes of a typical open system is devoted to maintaining it. However, there is a downside to stability. According to John Sutherland, the pursuit of stability limits the adaptability of a system to changes in its environment. The stable system is necessarily responsive to a very limited range of environmental changes. According to Sutherland, "A fully adaptive system, on the other hand, is one that constantly seeks to exploit new opportunities as they emerge, seeking always to maximize its efficiency rather than maintain its historical structure or preserve tradition" (Sutherland, 1975).

Problem solving: Achieving a desired future state

Not only are state and process important ways of describing a system, they also provide a way to describe how a system achieves a desirable state in the future. This we call *problem solving.* According to H. A. Simon, a problem is solved by first defining the state description of the solution: what would the world look like if this

Figure 1.4 *Problem solving.*

problem were solved? Then the task is to discover a sequence of processes that will produce the desired state from the initial state. According to Simon, "problem solving requires continual translation between state and process descriptions of the same complex reality. . . . Translation from the process description to the state description enables us to recognize when we have succeeded" (Simon, 1981).

In Figure 1.4, State 1 (the initial state) is transformed to State 2 (the final state) by the process. This is the basic state transition we have seen before. However, as a problem-solving sequence, State 1 represents the current state, and State 2 represents the desired state. Then the problem becomes one of defining the process to achieve the final state from the initial state.

Comparing state and process

State and process are different views of the real world. In many ways, state and process are intermingled. State is a side effect of process. Process is controlled by state. According to H. A. Simon, the concept of state is used to characterize the world as we sense it. State provides the criteria for identifying objects in the world. On the other hand, the concept of process provides the means for producing objects having the desired characteristics. Simon puts it this way: "A circle is the locus of all points equidistant from a given point. To construct a circle, rotate a compass with one arm fixed until the other arm has returned to its starting point. . . . The first sentence is a state description of a circle; the second, a process description" (Simon, 1981).

Comparing state, process, and event

John Sowa regards the three concepts of state, process and event as equivalent and differing only in the length of time in which they occur. Sowa regards these three as being derived from a single concept, which he calls a *situation*. A situation is a configuration of some aspect of the world in a limited region of space and time. According to Sowa, the concept of state describes a static situation that does not change noticeably over a long period of time. On the other hand, the concept of process describes a situation that makes a change during a specific period of time. Finally, an event is a situation that describes a change in a very short period of time.

The distinction between a long time and a short time depends on the amount of significant detail. According to Sowa, there is a characteristic time interval, called a *clock tick*, that distinguishes states, processes, and events: "A state is a situation that does not change appreciably during one or more clock ticks; an event is a situation that causes a significant change in less than a clock tick; and a process is a situation that causes a change over a period of several clock ticks" (Sowa, 1992).

The point is that if we have a long clock tick, a situation that causes change will be regarded as an event. This is because if our clock tick is long, our power of observation is much cruder and we can discern a change only as being associated with an event. On the other hand, if we have a shorter clock tick, our power of observation becomes more refined and the change will no longer be a single point in time but will occur over several of the shorter clock ticks. In this case, we no longer have to regard the change as the cruder event but have the observation power to regard it as a process.

Using states, processes, and events in modeling

Many scientific and business theories directly or indirectly use these three concepts. Much of our scientific tradition is based on them. For example, Newton's second law of motion defines how a material body will react when subjected to a force (see Figure 1.5). Newton's second law is founded on the idea that the state of a material body will not change until some external event happens to it. An object will not start to move on its own (i.e., *state*); a push or pull (i.e., *event*) is required to get it started. An external force (i.e., *event*) is required to slow down or to stop a material body already in motion (i.e., *state*). For inert material bodies what does *process* mean? For inert material bodies, the process is the innate nature of matter to react according to Newton's second law. We see that even inert material bodies can be modeled using these three concepts of state, process, and event.

In Figure 1.5, a material body has a starting acceleration (i.e., Acceleration 1) representing its initial state. The force is an external event to the material body. After the event (i.e., the application of the force) a new acceleration (i.e., Acceleration 2) is achieved representing the ending state of the material body.

1.7 Conclusion

In this chapter, we defined the *system* as a collection of related entities that work together as a whole to accomplish objectives. We can easily see that the enterprise is an example of a system. The enterprise consists of a collection of various business objects (i.e., people, machines, buildings, processes, events, and information) that work together to accomplish the objectives of the enterprise. An additional

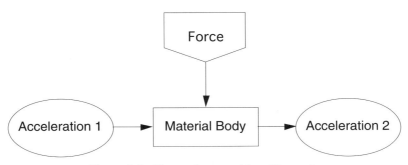

Figure 1.5 *Newton's second law* (F = ma).

aspect of the *enterprise* is that the collection of business objects are in functional symbiosis and accomplish mutually beneficial objectives. An enterprise is not necessarily a for-profit business and could include nearly any system of business objects.

This book is about constructing a *model* of the enterprise, which can be restated as constructing a model of a complex system. In this chapter, we saw that the task of any modeling project means we must construct a second simpler system (the model) that represents the complex system being modeled. The model is well understood and we use it to explain and reason about the complex system in question by means of analogy. That is, in constructing a model we make use of a set of familiar principles or concepts which we use against the unfamiliar system to understand it better. Constructing a model is a mental process that depends on abstraction. In this chapter, we learned that abstraction means drawing out the essence of the system in question.

Thus enterprise modeling involves abstracting the essential characteristics of the complex enterprise. What are these essential characteristics? In this chapter, we learned that any complex system can be described in terms of three concepts: state, process, and event. These concepts represent the essential characteristics of a system and are therefore useful types of abstractions in our model. They are our basic tools for modeling. We will make extensive use of these concepts in this book to model the enterprise.

In the next chapter, we will continue our discussion of the system and expand our horizon into what scholars call *general systems theory*.

Chapter 2

Introduction to General Systems Theory

2.1 Introduction

In Chapter 1, we introduced modeling and stated that modeling is used to explain and reason about systems of interest to us. We defined a system as a collection of related objects that work together for the overall objective of the whole. For the open system that makes exchanges with its environment, these objectives are manifested by the output from the system. In this book, we propose that the enterprise is an example of an open system.

Scholars refer to the study of systems as *general systems theory*. General systems theory is one major part of the formalisms we used to construct our theory of object-oriented enterprise modeling, the other being the object-oriented paradigm itself. In this chapter, we will introduce general systems theory as an academic discipline. General systems theory has produced a considerable body of knowledge defining the general characteristics and properties of all systems, including those found in nature as well as the human artifact type such as the enterprise.

2.2 System decomposition

An important question, especially to the modeler, is what does a system look like on the inside? We saw in Chapter 1 that systems are made up of elementary objects. For example, we know intuitively that the enterprise can be divided or decomposed into a collection of business objects such as people, machines, buildings, and so forth. Subodh Bapat makes the point that decomposition allows us to simplify a complex system: "Since we cannot mentally grasp at once the complete workings of the entire complex system, we can examine it to determine what its parts are. By examining the parts, we can determine what their subparts are. Clearly, we can continue this process until we have arrived at parts which are small enough for us to conceptualize and mentally manipulate in their entirety" (Bapat, 1994). In this section, we discuss the decomposition of a larger system into its subsystems.

Subsystem

When we decompose a system, we end up with what we consider to be a set of elementary objects. These constituent objects are considered elementary as a convenience to us as modelers. They are elementary because, at that point, they represent the limits of our analysis so far. The whole system is considered to be made up of elementary objects to simplify the depth and scope of our systems analysis. Once a system is decomposed to a lower level, we can then work with these elementary objects performing our analysis and modeling work on them. However, each elementary object is itself a subsystem consisting of its own elementary objects. Also, our system of interest is an elementary object of some larger system that is out of our view. Thus we have a new term, *subsystem,* which O. R. Young defines as "an element or functional component of a larger system which fulfills the conditions of a system in itself, but which also plays a role in the operation of a larger system" (Young, 1964).

Figure 2.1 shows the decomposition of a system into subsystems. We can conclude that every system is a subsystem of another system and that every system is made up of subsystems. In analyzing a system, we stay at a certain level of granularity to provide the appropriate amount of detail for our analysis. The problem becomes one of how much we want to limit the scope of our analysis so as to limit the amount of detail. We already have a word for this, *abstraction.*

Decomposition

The process of dividing a system into subsystems is called *decomposition.* A system is decomposed into a series of subsystems (see Figure 2.1) using one or more of the following differentiation criteria:

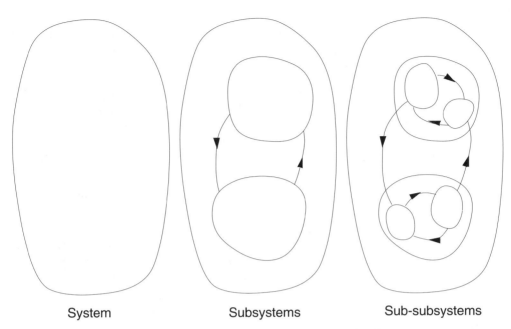

Figure 2.1 *System at various resolution levels.*

- **Functional** The system is decomposed into a set of elementary concepts or entities that are distinguished by their goals, their duties, or their actions. This type of decomposition takes advantage of the functional roles of the subsystems, each of which is specialized to specific capabilities or duties. John Sutherland calls these *differentiated systems:* "The fully differentiated system is evolved from the differentiation rule, which demands that each functionally unique task be performed by a subsystem that is structurally unique" (Sutherland, 1975). For example, a functional decomposition of an automobile might be locomotion, passenger comfort, safety, and so on.

- **Structural** Sutherland indicates that functional decomposition is often accompanied with structural decomposition in which the system is decomposed by its structure. In this type of decomposition, elementary objects are isolated and separated from each other based on their corporal aspects. Often, a structural decomposition will be equivalent to a functional decomposition because the elementary objects will correspond to the functions of the system as Sutherland points out. For a physical system, the structural decomposition is easy to understand. We look for its constituent parts. For an abstract system, the structural decomposition is based on the idea of corporal parts that are themselves abstract, such as ideas, concepts, or principles. For example, a structural decomposition of an automobile might be electrical, fuel, power train, body, wheels, and so on.

◆ **Spatial**   In this form of decomposition, the system is decomposed by a spatial criteria. Subsystems are identified by their position or locale. For physical systems, the spatial decomposition is based on geometry or geography. For an abstract system, the spatial decomposition is based on abstract spatial concepts such as position in a sequence. For example, a spatial decomposition of an automobile might be engine area, passenger area, trunk area, and so on.

◆ **Segmented**   Sometimes a system lends itself to being decomposed into a series of segmented subsystems in which the subsystems are similar, often identical. The subsystems look alike and perform alike and are distinguished only by their spatial position. An example of segmented subsystems would be an enterprise consisting of business franchises. For example, large franchise chains such as McDonald's or Wendy's consist of individual businesses that are similar if not nearly identical.

Wholeness

Even though we can decompose it, a system is nevertheless an inseparable whole. Decomposition is done to simplify the analysis of a complex system. Thus, we may choose to simplify our work by analyzing a system as a set of subsystems. However, we must eventually synthesize and combine our analysis of the individual subsystems to form the analysis of the whole. The idea of wholeness is very important to systems thinking. As Arthur D. Hall put it, "Systems methodology focuses on systems as wholes, and on their parts (subsystems) taken separately only insofar as they relate to properties of the whole" (Hall, 1989).

The term *wholeness* is used to describe this characteristic of a system. The idea of wholeness is more or less present in any system. Thomas Athey identifies the realization of the wholeness of a system as the major contribution of systems thinking. He states that "a distinguishing characteristic of systems thinking is the realization that (*a*) the whole is more than the sum of the parts and (*b*) what is best for the subsystems (components) is not necessarily what is best for the overall system and vice versa" (Athey, 1982).

Emergent properties

In Athey's comments on wholeness, there is the idea of synergy, that the whole is more than the sum of its parts. We refer to this as *emergent properties* in which the whole system displays capabilities that are not available from the collection of the properties of the individual parts of the system (i.e., if they acted individually and we combined their individual results). Thus emergent properties are global properties that exist at the system level and are not available in its decomposed subsystems. Only by integrating subsystems into the whole system will these emergent properties reveal themselves. Activating these emergent properties is the point of a system; it is why the system exists in the first place and why it will continue to exist. Emergent properties are made possible by the relations of the individual subsystems, a point we will return to later.

Optimization versus suboptimization

In Athey's comments on wholeness, there is a concern for the efficiency of the whole versus the parts. We refer to this as *optimization* versus *suboptimization*. Each subsystem will have its own purpose and goals. The subsystem can be made as effective and efficient as possible in its own right to achieve its individual objectives. However, the objectives of one subsystem may conflict with those of the other subsystems. Optimization of a subsystem may detract from the overall system.

If we are attempting to make a system more efficient or effective, we must focus on the optimization of the larger system and secondarily on the suboptimization of its subsystems. Sometimes a subsystem may appear to be very inefficient or wasteful when considered on its own, but the overall system is very efficient because of the configuration and performance of its subsystems. Changing the subsystem may cause the larger system to be less efficient or effective.

Optimization of the system and the avoidance of suboptimization of its subsystems is a well-known tactic of the systems analyst. However, it is problematic. In *Problem Solving: A Systems Approach*, Robertshaw, Mecca, and Rerick describe this potentially unending regression in the search for optimization to avoid suboptimization. They state that since every system is a subsystem to a larger system, it follows that all optimization of a system is actually suboptimization of a subsystem. This results in a problem of scope for the analyst since there is a tendency to keep expanding the boundary of the analysis to obtain optimization rather than the undesirable suboptimization. Robertshaw, Mecca, and Rerick conclude that we must "accept the fact that this will produce a suboptimization for a higher system. This is not a defect in our approach. It is the best we can do" (Robertshaw et al., 1978).

Nearly decomposable systems

As we saw earlier, complex systems are decomposed into subsystems using one or more of the decomposition criteria (i.e., functional, structural, spatial, segmented). The subsystems are in turn decomposed into their own subsystems and so forth.

H. A. Simon has pointed out an interesting characteristic of any systems decomposition: the frequency of interaction between subsystems will be sparse compared to the interactions of the objects of a given subsystem. Simon has developed these ideas in his famous essay "The Architecture of Complexity" reprinted in *The Sciences of the Artificial* (Simon, 1981).

According to Simon, the interaction within a subsystem is much more intense and frequent compared with the spurious interaction that a subsystem may have with other subsystems of the system. Simon has coined the term *nearly decomposable systems* to describe the interaction between subsystems versus the interaction within a subsystem. According to Simon, a nearly decomposable system is one in which "the interactions among the subsystems are weak but not negligible" (Simon, 1981).

In a nearly decomposable system, the short-term behavior of a subsystem will be more or less independent of the short-term behavior of the other subsystems. In the long term, the behavior of a subsystem of a nearly decomposable system depends on the other subsystems only occasionally. After all, if there were no interaction between the subsystems, the system would be completely decomposable. In this case, there would be no point in combining the subsystems into a system since they would have nothing to do with each other and would exhibit no emergent properties of wholeness (Simon, 1981).

2.3 Systems environment

In the previous section, we learned that the objects of a system can be regarded as systems in their own right, which we call *subsystems*. In this section we will describe the boundary of a system and consider systems as embedded in an environment. We already know from the previous section what the environment of a system contains: other systems. Also, our system in question and these other systems of the environment may be subsystems to yet a larger system out of view. This is because every system is a subsystem to some larger system.

System Boundary

The boundary of a system divides the system into an internal world and an external world. Scholars have presented several points of view on just what the systems boundary is:

- ◆ **Physical boundary of the system** This is the most obvious criterion for determining the boundary of a physical system. The walls surrounding a factory, a person's skin, or the city limits are examples of physical boundaries. However, not all systems are physical (some are abstract) and not all physical systems have obvious physical boundaries.

◆ **Nearly decomposable systems**   Another view of systems boundary is that expressed by H. A. Simon in his ideas of nearly decomposable systems. Simon would define the system boundary in terms of the concentration of relations where relations are sparse at the boundary of the system.

◆ **Objectives of the system**   From this point of view, to define the boundary, we must define the objectives of the system. Recall that a system is an inseparable whole consisting of a collection of objects that discharge a set of objectives. Once we have identified the systems objectives, we set the boundary to include the subsystems that directly participate in discharging that set of objectives.

◆ **Optimization versus suboptimization**   Another point of view that influences our definition of the system boundary is the scope of our modeling project. Recall the dilemma pointed out by Robertshaw, Mecca, and Rerick of the tendency to keep expanding the scope of our analysis to achieve total optimization of the system rather than its undesired suboptimization (Robertshaw et al., 1978). Thus setting the boundary of a system is often a decision on the scope of optimization with a tendency to error on the side of too much scope.

◆ **Purpose of research**   From this point of view, the criteria defining the boundary of a system will often depend on the intellectual purpose of our research in which we propose questions which we want to answer. In effect, we define the system boundary in terms of our research objectives. Then the system boundary is set to include the set of objects that seem to be involved or could participate in answering those questions. Kramer and de Smit use this idea in their definition of systems boundary: "It thus seems that a boundary can only be defined as something imaginary or conceptual inasmuch as everything within it can be considered as part of the system (for research purposes), and everything outside it as part of the environment" (Kramer and de Smit, 1977).

◆ **Pragmatic influence and control**   For systems that are human artifacts as opposed to natural systems, the boundary of the system may be defined pragmatically by the project to construct the system. Thomas Athey defines the system boundary for these type of systems as follows: "System boundaries comprise that set of components which can be directly influenced or controlled in a system-design" (Athey, 1982).

Environment

The idea of a system boundary divides the analysis into two focuses: that which is part of the system and that which is not. We use the term *environment* to describe the latter part, that which is not part of the system under consideration. Like the definition of systems boundary, there are also many points of view on the definition of a systems boundary:

◆ **Total environment versus relevant environment**   According to Kramer and de Smit, we can distinguish between a system's total environment and a system's relevant environment. According to them, it is important to limit the system environment to only that which seems to influence the system in question. They describe the method for selecting the environment as "that set of entities outside the system, the state of which set is affected by the system or which affect the state of the system itself" (Kramer and de Smit, 1977).

◆ **Influence and control**   Thomas Athey provides a succinct definition of environment: "Environment includes all those factors which have an influence on the effectiveness of a system, but which are not controllable" (Athey, 1982).

◆ **Relations**   Arthur D. Hall presents his definition of environment in more concrete terms of the relations of the system with its environment: "For a given system, the environment is the set of all objects outside the system, a change of whose attributes affects, and is affected by, the behavior of the system. . . . A system has at least one relation between an element of the system and an element of the environment" (Hall, 1989).

◆ **Common infrastructure**   Systems are decomposed into subsystems. If our focus is one of these subsystems, then its environment is the other subsystems, which are considered as a whole. That is, a subsystem can be thought of as being embedded in a common infrastructure that is provided by the global system. This supporting infrastructure is the environment of the subsystem in question. Frank Kowalkowski describes the parts of a system that are general facilities to its subsystems as "the commons." In many villages, especially in New England, there is a common tract of land usually at the center of the village that is available to citizens. The commons of a village is part of its infrastructure. If we regard the village as a general system, we see that it provides an environmental component, its common area, that is available to the subsystems of the village (i.e., its citizens) (Kowalkowski, 1994).

Open versus closed systems

As we have seen in previous parts of this book, an *open system* interacts and exchanges materials, energy, or information with the environment through the system boundary. The system boundary, which may be a physical or logical enclosure, restricts the access to the system. An *interface* is a point on the system boundary that permits flow into the system or out of the system. An interface does not necessarily have to provide both input and output capability and it is usually specialized to only one direction of exchange. An interface will typically filter (restrict) what enters the system from the environment or leaves the system to the environment.

A system with no interaction with the environment is called a *closed system*. No system is truly closed. Rather, a system is considered closed to simplify the analysis in which relations outside of a system are disregarded (i.e., they are considered irrelevant to the analysis).

Resource allocation

Within the environment are the resources the open system needs and consumes. These resources are the materials, information, or energy the system must consume to discharge its objectives. Several distinct profiles of resource competition and allocation can occur between the systems of an environment. John W. Sutherland provides the following classification of resource competition and allocation (Sutherland, 1975).

- ◆ **Institutionalized**   This is the simplest of the environments. Resources are scarce in this environment and are allocated to the systems by rigid rules or ritualistic algorithms. The systems of this environment must maintain a functional or structural status quo through time to survive. Competition among the systems is forbidden or is not a factor. There is little interaction among the systems of this environment. Systems in this environment are essentially closed because they are in a perpetual steady state. The critical success factor in this environment is conservation. An example of the institutionalized environment is a government (the environment) consisting of agencies (the systems).

- ◆ **Symbiotic**   This environment contains various differentiated resources and the systems of this environment are specialized to a particular resource. The systems enter into partnerships and compromises with each other such that the surplus or output of one becomes the input of another. This environment may appear to be complex, but it is highly programmed and predictable. The success of any particular system is dependent on the success of the others. Competition is either not a factor or voluntarily restricted. Systems in this environment are highly selective and wouldn't be considered open. The critical success factor in this environment is compromise. An example of the symbiotic environment is the factory (the environment) consisting of departments (the systems).

♦ **Competitive**   The systems of this environment compete with each other for resources. A system in this environment actively seeks to drive its competitors from the field by pursuing control of the resources of the environment. This environment would be considered complex because of its inherent unpredictability. Not only must a system pursue its own objectives, it must also consider the objectives of its competitors. A system in this environment that does not actively pursue dominance is likely to be quickly eliminated. Systems in this environment are moderately open. The critical success factor in this environment is exploitation. An example of the competitive environment is an industrial sector (the environment) consisting of enterprises (the systems).

♦ **Emergent**   The systems of this environment operate in an ever-changing, unstable environment that is the most complex of the four. Resource consumption is selective and often involves trade-offs among the various resources in which these trade-offs change over time. The aggregate behavior of the systems in this environment tends to continuously alter the environment and its resource configurations. In this environment, a premium is placed on quick adaptivity. Long-term survival depends on the ability to make adjustments and accommodations. Systems in this environment are wide open. The critical success factor in this environment is responsiveness. An example of the competitive environment is the technology industry (the environment) consisting of high-tech companies (the systems).

2.4 Systems analysis: Functionality, structure, behavior

Many professions or disciplines have a component of systems analysis integral to them. For example, the ecologist uses systems concepts to describe the biosphere; the aeronautical engineer uses systems concepts to describe an airplane; the psychologist uses systems concepts to describe the mind; the economist uses systems concepts to describe an economy. We can see that many professions have a systems-analysis component. Is there a common approach to systems that each profession uses? Put another way, we may ask just how are systems analyzed?

All general systems, both natural and human artifact, have certain common characteristics and can be analyzed using a common set of tools and vocabulary. These tools and vocabulary can be used in any systems analysis effort to quickly document and understand a system in question. The common tools and vocabulary are founded on three views of the system: a structural view, a functional view, and a behavioral view. Each of these views can be modeled using diagrams consisting of nodes with links connecting the nodes. For each view, the nodes and their links take on different meanings.

Let's look at the three views in more detail with a description of their node-link diagrams and some examples of each view. For our examples we will use both a physical system and an abstract system as follows:

- ◆ For our physical system example we will use an automobile engine.

- ◆ For our abstract system example we will use a financial model spreadsheet. The financial model spreadsheet is a system that models the financial dynamics of a business domain. Typically, a financial model spreadsheet compares two or more options by developing the inflows outflows of moneys for each option over time.

Structural view

The structure of a system is the configuration of its components (i.e., subsystems) at a particular point in time. The structure of a system evolves and changes by its behavior over time (discussed later). While the structure of a system changes over time, it usually has a characteristic steady-state configuration that endures. It is this steady-state structure that can be readily defined and is useful for analyzing the system. The transitional or temporary structural configurations resulting from the behavior of the system are better described by the behavior view described in the following.

The structural view of a system is documented and analyzed by the entity-relation diagram shown in Figure 2.2. In the entity-relation diagram, the nodes are called *entities* and represent the structural components of the system. The links are the *relations* between the entities of the system.

The entity-relation diagram shows the system at one point in time. It shows the enduring, stable view of the system since it would be impractical to draw an entity-relation diagram for multiple points in time. Construction of this stable view is usually not difficult since most systems have such a characteristic steady-state in which small changes can be disregarded. Of course, this depends on what we consider to be a "small change." The structural view of a system therefore is an abstraction.

Figure 2.2 *Portraying structure: entity-relation diagram.*

Let's look at the structure of our two example systems, the automobile engine and the spreadsheet financial model.

- ◆ *Example:* **Automobile engine structure**   When we look at an automobile engine (Figure 2.3) we readily see the structure of this system. The automobile engine system has many components that work together to accomplish the overall function of the engine of using fuel to produce usable force. The major entities of the automobile engine include the engine block, the cylinders, the carburetor, the valves, the pistons, and so forth. These entities have various relations including: contains, houses, connected, joined, touching, and so on.

- ◆ *Example:* **Financial model spreadsheet structure**   While the financial model spreadsheet has a physical representation such as when printed or displayed on a computer screen, that is not the structure in which we are interested here. The structure we must document and analyze is its configuration of abstract entities (Figure 2.4). At the systems level (i.e., the highest level), these abstract entities are the sections of the spreadsheet financial model. For example, there might be a section for assumptions or constants (e.g., the investment rate of return), another for portraying input of moneys over time, and another for portraying output of moneys over time. The financial model spreadsheet will typically have a final results section which provides a comprehensive summary of the whole model and can be used for decision making. A given section can be decomposed into a series of subsections representing the calculations which participate in the overall results of that section. A given subsection is decomposed into the various interconnected formulas and values that produce the intermediate results of that subsection. The various sections and subsections represent subsystems that are related to other subsystems by the flow of calculated results.

Functional view

The functional view of a system describes the overall objectives of the whole. Functionality relates to the collective purposefulness of the entities of the system

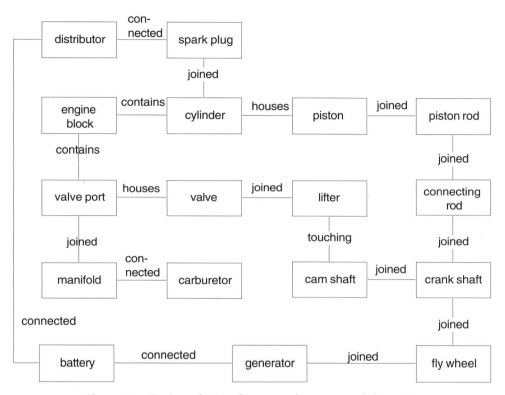

Figure 2.3 *Entity-relation diagram of an automobile engine.*

to accomplish its overall objectives. In analyzing functionality, we are not interested in how a function is performed but in what the functionality is from the standpoint of value or worth. For open systems (i.e., all real-world systems), functionality is described in terms of the overall transformations performed by the system. Thus any open system receives input from its environment in the form of materials, energy, or information. Any open system transforms at least one of these three to produce its output, which also takes the form of materials, energy, or information. The output represents the purpose of the open system, the reason it exists in the first place. We thus view the functionality of an open system in terms of these transformations of input to output with an emphasis on the usefulness of the output which we often describe as products.

The functionality of an open system is portrayed by the *transformation-flow diagram* shown in Figure 2.5. In this diagram, the nodes are transformations representing the components of functionality of the system (at that level of decomposition)

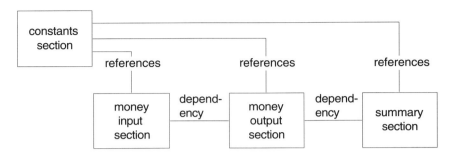

Figure 2.4 *Entity-relation diagram of a financial model spreadsheet.*

and the links are the flow of materials, energy or information from one transformation to the next.

Let's look at the functionality of our two example systems, the automobile engine and the spreadsheet financial model:

- *Example:* **Automobile engine functionality**   The overall functionality of the automobile engine system can be explained fairly simply. The automobile engine takes in input from its environment in the form of fuel and air and produces its output, that of a usable power and exhaust byproducts. The automobile engine can be decomposed into a set of subsystems shown in Figure 2.6. We could describe the collective functionality of its subsystems as a decomposition of the overall function of the automobile engine. For example, we can define the carburetor as a subsystem that participates in this overall function. In the case of the carburetion subsystem, its subfunction is to take in fuel and air and combine them to produce a combustible vapor which is directed to the cylinders of the internal combustion subsystem.

- *Example:* **Financial model spreadsheet functionality**   The financial model spreadsheet has input in the form of initial values or constants and produces output in the form of values representing the financial results of the model. The functionality of the spreadsheet is the transformation of the input values into the output values. The decomposition (Figure 2.7) of the

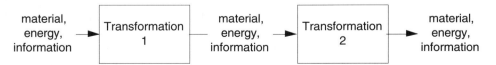

Figure 2.5 *Portraying functionality: transformation flow diagram.*

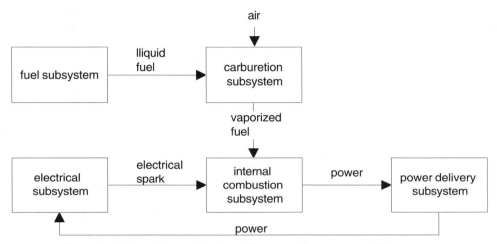

Figure 2.6 *Transformation flow diagram of an automobile engine.*

structure of a financial model spreadsheet into various sections matches the decomposition of its functions into subfunctions. For example, a typical subsystem of the spreadsheet would be a section which lists and calculates the outflow of moneys over time. This section would produce a set of bottom line results that would flow into other sections of the spreadsheet (e.g., the section that compares the input of money with the output of money for that option).

Behavioral view

Systems consist of subsystems, which at any point in time have a state. All of the individual states of its subsystems determine the global state of the system. The

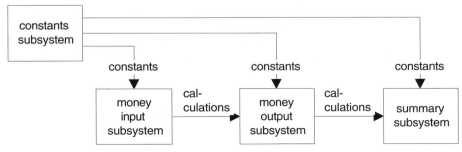

Figure 2.7 *Transformation flow diagram of a financial model spreadsheet.*

behavior of a system relates to the ordered set of state changes it traverses in time as determined by the ordered set of state changes of its subsystems. The state of a system is defined by attributes that we, as humans, assign to the system. We select attributes that lend themselves to analysis and comparison. For example, a typical attribute of a physical system is its position coordinates. We humans endow the physical system with its position coordinates; the physical system does not know it has them. A state-transition is the change of one of these attributes. For example, a physical system that is moved will undergo a state transition we acknowledge by the new values of its position coordinates.

Virtually all systems we will analyze are deterministic. A deterministic system can achieve a specific future state only if one or more state transitions will carry it to that state. For example, the position coordinates of a physical system when measured at a point in time limit the possibilities of its future position coordinates. The state of a system is defined at the level of detail of the time-granularity of the system. That is, any system has a characteristic clock-tick that is used to observe or describe the system. From one clock tick to the next, the system can be analyzed in terms of the state change it achieves in that clock tick. The clock tick depends on the domain being modeled and can be long (e.g., thousands of years for the analysis of geological systems) or short (e.g., nanoseconds for the analysis of atomic systems). The enterprise is an example of a deterministic system and can be analyzed using these concepts.

The behavior of a system is portrayed as a *state-transition diagram* as shown in Figure 2.8. The state transition diagram is defined for a subsystem or entity of the larger system. The state-transition diagram defines all the possibilities of its future states (and thus its future behavior, functionality or structure) without directly considering other entities or subsystems in the system. The state-transition diagram allows us to unbundle one part of a system so that we don't have to worry about its dependencies on other parts of the system to construct its state-transition diagram. The other entities and subsystems will certainly have their influence in the working system, but we do not need to define them to define and understand the state transition possibilities of one of its entities or subsystems. The state-transition diagram of a subsystem or entity is a definition of its life cycle. That is, the state-transition diagram generally defines the birth, life, and death of the subsystem or entity. It is usually not practical to define a state-transition diagram

Figure 2.8 *Portraying behavior: state-transition diagram.*

for each subsystem or entity and only the more important ones are diagrammed. In the state-transition diagram shown in Figure 2.8, the nodes represent the states and the links represent the transitions from one state to the next.

Let's look at the behavior of our two example systems, the automobile engine and the spreadsheet financial model:

◆ *Example:* **Automobile engine behavior**   The behavior of the automobile engine can be described in terms of states. Globally, the engine is in a state of either "running" or "off." Each subsystem or entity of the engine can also be described in terms of states and state transitions. For example, the states of a cylinder (Figure 2.9) are "off" state, "cylinder is empty" state, "cylinder has fuel vapor" state, "cylinder has compressed fuel" state, "combustion" state, or "cylinder has spent fuel state" state.

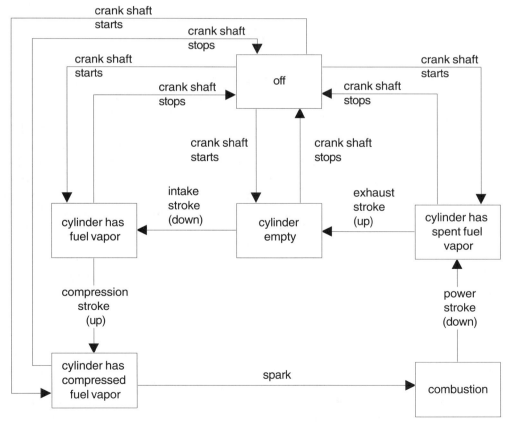

Figure 2.9   *Portraying behavior: state-transition diagram of a cylinder of an automobile engine.*

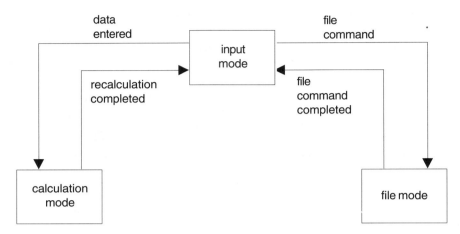

Figure 2.10 *Portraying behavior: state-transition diagram
of a financial model spreadsheet.*

◆ *Example:* **Financial model spreadsheet behavior** The behavior of the financial model spreadsheet can also be described in terms of states. The
spreadsheet considered as a system (Figure 2.10) is either in an "input
mode" state (accepting input or waiting for the user), "calculation mode"
state (performing its calculations), or "file mode" state (being printed or
saved to disk). The major sections of the spreadsheet considered as subsystems will have states depending on the application itself. For example,
error checking may be built into the spreadsheet to cross-check the results
of the financial model. In this case, a section might have the states of "correct" or "in-error." The final results section of a sophisticated financial
model spreadsheet might use rules, which are actually characterizations of
its state, to evaluate and make recommendations on the overall model. For
example, the states of the financial model might be "recommended" or
"notrecommended."

Comparing the views

The three views of structure, functionality, and behavior are interrelated and overlap, which may result in some confusion. Both structure and state are closely
related to the functionality of the system. If a function of the system is completed,
a new structure that defines a new state of the system results. That new state then
provides the opportunity for the future state transitions that it can make, which

also constrains the next opportunity for transformations to achieve the systems functionality. Let's compare these three and make sure we know the differences and uses of each of the three views:

◆ **The behavioral view versus the functional view**   One question that may arise is the difference between a behavioral view of a system and a functional view of a system. Each seems to cover some of the same territory. Recall that the functional description of a system is what the system does to accomplish the overall objectives of the whole. We use a transformation flow diagram to show the functions of the system to transform inputs to outputs. If we have a proper state-transition diagram of a system that shows its dynamic behavior, why do we need a transformation flow diagram? If we know the state transitions, can't we deduce the functionality? The answer lies in seeing a detailed view of the system dynamics (state transitions) versus a global view of the purpose of the system (transformations). The functional view is the answer to the classic problem of not being able to see the forest for the trees.

◆ **The structural view versus the behavioral view**   The structure of a system portrayed by the structural view is closely related to the state of the system portrayed by the behavioral view. The structure of a system is, in fact, the concrete representation of its state (Booch, 1991). The behavior of a system determines its structure, which in turn determines its behavior in the next time interval. Structure and state are related by a many-to-one relation. Thus a state can be achieved by many different structural configurations, but a particular structural configuration determines exactly one state (i.e., for a deterministic system).

◆ **Structural view versus functional view**   Any particular structural entity of a system can usually be described and analyzed as a proper subsystem, that is as a general system in its own right. Each subsystem can usually be decomposed into yet lower-level subsystems. We learned earlier in this chapter that any one of a number of differentiation criteria may be used to decompose a system including functional, spatial, segmented, as well as structural. Structural decomposition is the most obvious and widely used for physical systems.

Similarly, the overall functionality of a system as an input-transformation-output sequence can be readily decomposed into subfunctions. Each subfunction can also be described as an input-transformation-output sequence. The functionality of a subsystem is described by its role in discharging the overall objectives of the larger system.

As pointed out earlier in this chapter, the decomposition of a system into subsystems is often closely related to the decomposition of the function of the system into subfunctions. That is, a given subfunction will often be the purpose for the existence of a given subsystem. Thus structural decomposition and functional decomposition are equivalent for many types of systems. In fact, in a real-world system, subfunctions are often in one-to-one correspondence with subsystems: a given subfunction is discharged by a specific subsystem.

2.5 Classification of systems

We will close this chapter with a classification of systems. A useful classification hierarchy was provided by K. E. Bounding (Bounding, 1956). In Bounding's classification scheme, systems are classified by their complexity. Thus level 1 in the following is the simplest and level 6 is the most complex. Also, note that each level embodies all of the lower levels.

An important characteristic of Bounding's classification scheme is that complex systems at the higher levels can be described as lower-level systems if we are only interested in that level of abstraction. We make a model of the higher-level system using the concepts of a lower-level system. In this way, we avoid detail for the sake of insight. Admittedly, it may be crude and possibly incomplete but it simplifies the analysis.

Level 1: Framework system

A framework system (Figure 2.11) is a closed system that is used primarily as a first attempt at describing a more complex system. It is used as a tool in systems analysis to provide a quick model of the complex system. The framework system has only structure and function and has no internal behavior. Its function is implicit: the static configuration or relations of its parts we consider interesting. The frame-

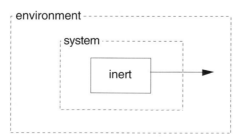

Figure 2.11 *Level 1: framework system.*

work system is a useful level to begin describing more complex systems in which we model the more complex system as if it were a level 1 framework. For example, we could model a complex organization of people (level 6) as an organization chart (level 1).

Level 2: Static (input-output) system

The static level (Figure 2.12) represents the simplest open system that takes input from the environment and produces output to the environment. A static system is analogous to a mathematical function in which an input set is mapped to an output set in a predicable, deterministic way. For this reason, the level 2 static system is sometimes referred to as the input-output system. The level 2 system has fixed goals and is not influenced by its environment. It has no means of internal control to insure that its systems objectives are meant. It has no complex behavior and is very constrained or limited, being a simple transformation of input into output. An example of the level 2 system is the mechanical clock. It has no internal mechanisms to make sure it is keeping accurate time. Also, the mechanical clock is incapable of dealing with changes in its environment such as being transported to another time zone. Any higher-level system can be described in terms of a level 2 system and for modeling purposes this is a useful abstraction level of a more complex system. For example, the economy (level 6) can be modeled at this level in which labor, resources, capital, management and energy are transformed into the GNP.

Level 3: Homeostatic system

The homeostatic system (Figure 2.13) represents the basic feedback control system. An example is the thermostat-controlled heating system of many houses, which attempts to maintain the temperature to which it is set. According to Kramer and de Smit: "Essential in these systems is the *transmission and interpretation of information*. As a

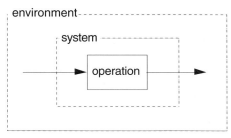

Figure 2.12 *Level 2: static system.*

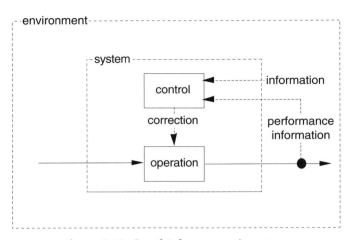

Figure 2.13 *Level 3: homeostatic system.*

rule, they are systems in which we attempt to reach a desired value or norm by means of feedback. The essential variable in such dynamic systems is the difference between observed and desired values" (Kramer and de Smit, 1977). The homeostatic system must obtain information on its performance to be used by its control process for making changes to its behavior. The behavior after receiving feedback can be either constrained or unconstrained. Two terms are used to describe this: *negative feedback* and *positive feedback.* Mesarovic and Takahara define these terms as follows (Mesarovic and Takahara, 1989):

- ◆ **Negative feedback**   The behavior of the system after feedback is more constrained. This means that the system is "closer" in an appropriate sense to a predetermined state or output. The system seeks a stable, predetermined state as it continuously corrects its behavior.

- ◆ **Positive feedback**   The behavior of the system is less constrained (even unconstrained). This means that the system deviates significantly from a predetermined state. At each point in time, feedback from the previous state or output causes the system to deviate further from the predetermined state.

The performance information is obtained from the environment either directly from its own output or from the general environment. We often use this level to describe the management functions of more complex systems. For example, budget-control (level 3) can be applied to an enterprise (level 6).

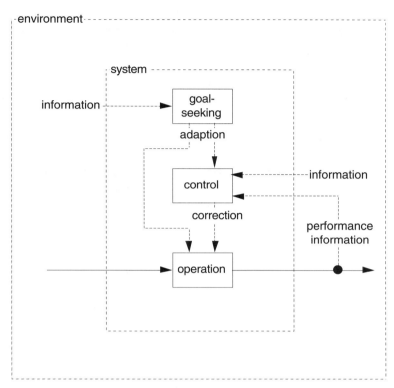

Figure 2.14 *Level 4: goal-seeking, adaptive system.*

Level 4: Goal-seeking, adaptive system

The goal-seeking, adaptive system continuously interacts with its environment and adapts its behavior to ever-changing conditions to accomplish ever-changing goals. According to Mesarovic and Takahara, a goal-seeking, adaptive system (Figure 2.14) can be described "as a system whose behavior. . . is explained in terms of an internal goal (reference, objective) and a process aimed at achieving that goal." They further explain that the goal-process is a decision-making activity that "on each occasion, determines the response of the system to external stimuli" (Mesarovic and Takahara, 1989). In our terminology, we usually refer to system goals as *system objectives*. These systems use feedback-control (level 3) to continue to meet systems objectives (goals). The big difference between level 4 and level 3 is the ability to change systems objectives. In the words of Thomas Athey, the systems objectives "are not rigidly fixed but are adaptable to changing conditions and responsive to new understanding. These systems gain from experience and thus, exhibit learning" (Athey, 1982). This is the basic information-processing node, which we will discuss in a Chapter 4.

Level 5: Intelligent system

Level 5 (Figure 2.15) represents systems that exhibit intelligence. Examples of this level are human workers as well as some computer systems that use artificial intelligence capabilities in their software. Figure 2.15 shows a typical intelligent system such as would be implemented by computer hardware and software. The level 5 system must have sophisticated input capabilities to obtain information from the environment, shown as sensors in the figure. Information received from the envi-

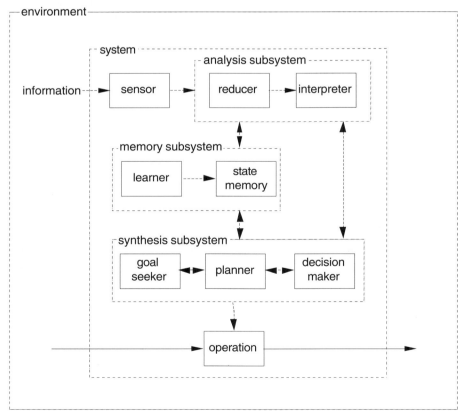

Figure 2.15 *Level 5: intelligent system.*

ronment is first reduced and then interpreted. The system shown in the figure has a separate analysis subsystem to perform these capabilities. A level 5 system is characterized by great information content and maintains an elaborate and complete internal model of its environment in its state-memory. Thus the intelligent system has the capability for learning, in which past experience is stored to be used for future decision making. The system in Figure 2.15 has a specialized memory subsystem that performs these learning and memory functions. The level 5 system is characterized by sophisticated goal-seeking, planning, and decision-making capabilities. The system shown in the figure has a synthesis subsystem for these functions that uses the memory subsystem. Like any system, the level 5 intelligent system takes in information, materials, and energy from the environment and transforms them by its operation function as shown in the figure.

Level 6: Complex-adaptive system

The complex-adaptive level (Figure 2.16) represents systems such as societies, human organizations, the biosphere, economies, ecosystems, as well as enterprises. M. M. Waldrop described the complex-adaptive system in his book *Complexity.* According to Waldrop, the complex-adaptive system consists of a network of agents, each acting independently and concurrently with each other. The environment of one of these agents is the collective interactions of the other agents. Each agent is constantly acting and reacting to the other agents. Control and coordination within a complex-adaptive system is highly dispersed. According to Waldrop, "if there is to be any coherent behavior in the (complex-adaptive). system, it has to arise from competition and cooperation among the agents themselves" (Waldrop, 1992).

The "agents" to which Waldrop refers are lower-level systems and can be any of the other levels. For example, a complex-adaptive system can be made up of level 5 intelligent agents in intricate, evolving relations such as a human organization. Therefore, complex-adaptive systems are indeed extremely complex. These systems are not approachable by any known modeling methodology. We usually model them using lower-level descriptions in the classification of systems. We will use these ideas in Chapter 4 in our discussion of information-processing networks. Figure 2.16 shows a grossly oversimplified example of a level 6 complex-adaptive system in which numerous agents are arranged in very complex relations with each other. The level 6 system, like any other system, takes in information, energy, and materials from its environment and transforms them as shown in the figure. The transformations performed by the level 6 system are often nondeterministic in the sense that a given input does not necessarily always produce the same output and it is usually impossible to trace the transformation using conventional analysis

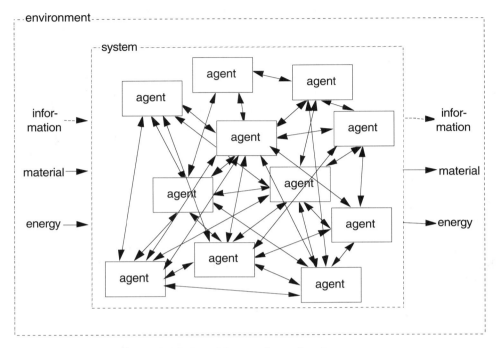

Figure 2.16 *Level 6: complex-adaptive system.*

tools. The internal subsystems of a level 6 system often act as agents with their own volition deciding on their own to act the way they do.

2.6 Conclusion

This chapter introduced many important concepts relevant to enterprise modeling. We saw that since the enterprise is a system, it can be decomposed into subsystems. In the modern enterprise, the decomposition is done by differentiated subsystems that are specialized by their function. We learned in this chapter that there is a tendency to focus on the efficiency of the subsystems and to make them efficient individually. This suboptimization of the subsystems may result in making the larger system (e.g., the enterprise) less efficient. Put another way, the point of the enterprise is wholeness, that of achieving system-level objectives. We also note that an enterprise is a subsystem of a larger system consisting of customers and suppliers. The optimization of this larger system can increase the economic rewards of the individual subsystems (the enterprises). These are important principles of enterprise management that can be understood as systems management principles.

We also saw in this chapter that open systems, such as the enterprise, exchange materials, information, and energy with their environment through interfaces in their system boundary. The environment contains the resources which the system must consume to survive. The relationship of the systems within the environment determines resource allocation profiles. We see many parallels here in the activities of the enterprise. In Sutherland's resource allocation classification introduced in this chapter, the enterprise would be part of a competitive or emergent environment. However, when we consider the enterprise as the environment and look at its subsystems, we see it as a symbiotic environment.

In this chapter, we learned about the three views of systems analysis: structural, functional, and behavioral. The structural view of a system is used to analyze the steady state configuration of its components and is documented with the entity-relation diagram. The functional view is used to analyze the accomplishment of the overall purposefulness of the system and is documented using the transformation-flow diagram. The behavioral view is used to analyze the ordered set of state changes that the system traverses in time and is documented using the state-transition diagram. The application of these three views will lead to an understanding of any system and can be used in any systems analysis project.

We closed this chapter with a presentation of K. E. Bounding's classification of systems. We saw that in Bounding's classification scheme there are six levels of systems in which each is more complex then the last. The levels are distinguished by the extent they possess an internal capability of adaptivity. In Chapter 3, we will see how this capability of adaptivity results in a sophisticated type of organization called the *hierarchical-multilayer system.*

We will also see in Chapter 3 that the structure of many complex systems is influenced by the organization of their subsystems. There we will see that the terms *organization* and *structure* describe different aspects of the configuration of subsystems, which often takes the form of a hierarchical-multilayer organization. That is, the entities of the system are arranged in a superstructure of layers that form a hierarchy.

Chapter 3

Introduction to Hierarchical-Multilayer Systems

3.1 Introduction

We saw in the previous chapters that a system is a set of objects with relationships between the objects. The objects that make up a system are considered primitive, atomic parts for purposes of analysis. However, these constituent objects are also systems in their own right and can be further decomposed depending on the needs of our modeling project. We concluded that decomposition is recursive: any system can be decomposed into subsystems that can, in turn, be decomposed into their own composite subsystems. At any given level, we have the view of the system of interest and its set of composite objects. If we are interested in more detail, we stop regarding a given object of the current system under analysis as an atomic object and start regarding it as a subsystem.

Thus when we open the black box of a system and look inside, we see a set of subsystems (objects) that interact with each other and exchange materials, energy, and information. These exchanges can be optimized to make the best use of limited materials, energy, and information. That is, the subsystems are not arranged arbitrarily but rather in some form of *organization*. In this chapter, we will define the most important organizational form: the hierarchical-multilayer system.

Many of the concepts of hierarchical-multilayer systems were first defined by M. D. Mesarovic, D. Macko, and Y. Takahara in *Theory of Hierarchical, Multilevel, Systems* (Mesarovic et al., 1970). In this classic work, hierarchical-multilayer systems are defined and explored in detail. There are actually two organizational concepts here: the concept of hierarchical organization and the concept of multilayer organization. Systems can be organized using either or both of these. We will define them shortly, starting with the hierarchical systems organization, followed by the multilayer organization. Then we will combine them to define the hierarchical-multilayer system that uses both of these organizational concepts. In later chapters, we will use the hierarchical-multilayer organization concept to describe the enterprise.

3.2 Hierarchical systems organization

The first form of systems organization we want to look at is the hierarchy. This is a very familiar form to most of us. We usually think of a hierarchy in terms of top-down control. In this section, we will make the point that systems that consist of complex arrangements of subsystems require a coordination/control function to keep the parts working together to accomplish the system objectives. Thus the point of a hierarchy is the constraint of subsystems to accomplish overall systems objectives. This is because subsystems have their own limited view of optimization and will know little about the global objectives of the whole system.

Classification of systems revisited

In Chapter 2, we outlined K. E. Bounding's classification of systems from the simplest system to the most complex. The classification scheme starts out with the level 1 "framework" system, which is used to model the static configuration or relations of objects we consider as interesting, such as pebbles on the beach. The classification scheme ends with the level 6 "complex-adaptive" system, which was used to model truly complex systems such as the biosphere.

At the "homeostatic" level 3 a very significant capability comes into the definition. Recall that a level 3 homeostatic system obtains information on its performance, which is used to make corrections to optimize its performance. In effect, the level 3 homeostatic system introduces a control layer not present in the simpler level 1 or level 2 systems. This control layer is present in all higher-level systems of the classification scheme and gets more and more sophisticated proceeding up the levels. We can conclude that the increasing levels of complexity relates to the emerging capabilities of this control layer. That is, the existence and

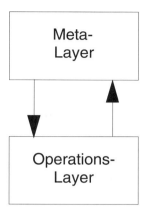

Figure 3.1 *The two basic layers.*

functionality of this control layer actually places a system in the classification scheme. Steven Kim describes these two basic layers as an operations-layer and a meta-layer as shown in Figure 3.1 (Kim, 1990).

The operations-layer provides the bread-and-butter output of the system. The meta-layer is where the objectives of the system are managed. Not all systems have both layers, but all systems have the operations-layer (Kim, 1990). Let's look at these two layers:

- ◆ **Operations-layer** This is the layer (see Figure 3.1) that produces the output of the system. It is unaware of the objectives of the overall system. In the words of Steven Kim, the operations-layer "performs its activities mindlessly without explicit knowledge of ultimate goals" (Kim, 1990). Kim characterizes the operations-layer as consisting of mechanisms and processes. The mechanisms consist of entities arranged in complex relations. The processes are the series of deliberate sequences that the mechanisms are capable of undergoing to produce the output from the system (Kim, 1990).

- ◆ **Meta-layer** The metal-layer monitors the operations-layer. Steven Kim describes the meta-layer as "the observer" and the operations-layer as the "observed." The meta-layer contains the objectives of the overall system. It monitors the operations-layer to make sure the objectives are being met and guides the operations-layer to meet them (Kim, 1990). Thus the meta-layer contains the state of the objectives that includes both what the objectives are and the current status to meet them. The meta-layer includes processes that can be invoked to control and monitor the operations-layer to meet the objectives. We see that meta-layer processes cause control/ coordination actions to be visited upon operations activities.

Definition: Hierarchical systems organization

A meta-layer providing a coordination/control function is inevitably part of most sophisticated systems because of the need to accomplish the overall objectives of the system. This is because subsystems are an unruly bunch. They have their own objectives that they discharge by their outputs, often by using their relations with the other subsystems around them. However, the global-level objectives are properties of the whole and are not apparent to the subsystems that discharge their duties more or less blind of the global objectives. The lower-layer subsystem objectives and corresponding outputs, as well as their relations, must be purposefully constrained to achieve the properties of the whole.

Figure 3.2 shows a typical hierarchical system. A hierarchical system consists of a series of levels in which higher levels control and coordinate lower levels. In the remaining paragraphs of this section, we will refer to this figure to describe the hierarchical systems organization.

In Figure 3.2, a three-level hierarchy is shown. We see in the figure that the operations-layer and the meta-layer define the relation between levels of a hierarchical system. We purposefully use the term *level* when we are referring to the structure of the hierarchy, whereas we use the term *layer* when we describe the functionality of a level. The structural levels of a hierarchy are related to the layered functionality as follows: an operations-layer and its meta-layer form an enduring relation between any two levels of a hierarchical system. Any hierarchical system, no matter how many levels it has, actually consists of the repetition of these two functional layers: the operations-layer and its metal-layer. Going down the levels, an operations-layer is the meta-layer of the level below. The difference between any two levels of the hierarchy is functional and relates to knowing about and managing systems objectives.

In the three-level hierarchy of Figure 3.2, the bottom level is strictly an operations-layer. It is made up of various subsystems. The middle level is the meta-layer of the bottom operations-layer. Also, the middle level is the operations-layer to the top level. It, too, is made up of various subsystems. The single subsystem of the top level is the ultimate meta-layer. In the figure, the system inputs and outputs are shown in their most general form as occurring at any of the levels. However, in actual hierarchical systems, it is usually the bottom operations-layer that conducts exchanges with the environment. In these cases, the inputs and outputs from the higher-level subsystems will be exchanged between the subsystems themselves at their own level or other levels.

Intervention and performance feedback

Notice in Figure 3.2 that the subsystems at a given level are connected to the upper level by lines labeled *intervention* and *performance feedback*. These lines represent communication between the levels that implements the hierarchical effect. The intervention lines extend downward from the meta-layer to its corresponding oper-ations-layer subsystems and the performance feedback lines extends upward from the operations-layer subsystems to their meta-layer. Mesarovic, Macko, and Takahara define terms for the relative relationship of upper-level subsystems versus the lower-level subsystems. The upper-level subsystems are referred to as "supre-mal," while the lower-level subsystems are referred to as "infimal." They describe the *intervention* and *performance feedback* in terms of *supremal* and *infimal*:

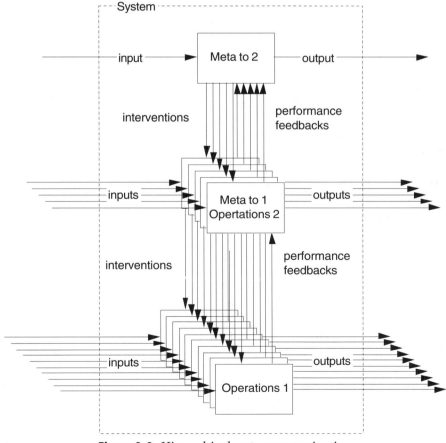

Figure 3.2 *Hierarchical systems organization.*

"There are two signals connecting the supremal unit with the infimal units. The downward signal representing intervention specifies the decision problems for the infimal units, which the upward signal furnishes (performance). information about the lower-level to the supremal unit. Due to priority of action, the supremal unit has the broad responsibilities of first instructing the infimal units how to proceed and second, influencing them to change their actions if needed" (Mesarovic et al., 1970).

Mesarovic, Macko, and Takahara define intervention as a system responsibility of the upper-level subsystems. Notice that in their definition of *intervention* two aspects are important: first, the upper-level subsystems instruct the lower-level subsystems in the sense that the lower-level knows less while the upper-level knows more about the overall objectives of the system; second, the lower-level subsystems are constrained by the influence of the upper-level subsystems. The lower-level subsystems are permitted only a limited number of selected actions out of their total repertoire.

Systems overhead

The meta-layer does not come free. It consumes its share of materials and energy that would otherwise be available to the operations-layer. The hierarchical systems organization introduces us to the idea of system overhead, that is, the expenditure of energy or materials needed to support the meta-layer to maintain the integrity of the system. John Sutherland puts it this way: "In broader terms, of the total energy or resources available to a system, a portion will be used to perform work, accomplish survival functions, etc. while the residual will be dedicated to coordinative, administrative, control, or integrative tasks. We may consider system resources or energy devoted to the latter tasks as constituting *system overhead*" (Sutherland, 1975).

Decomposition versus hierarchy

Decomposing a system into subsystems is not the same as organizing it into a hierarchy. While the two concepts result in a set of levels, they have completely different meanings. The term *decomposition* refers to an analysis tool that reveals a more finite and detailed set of subsystems, which are easier to understand than the system itself. The term *hierarchy* refers to the organization of a system in which the exchanges between its subsystems can be optimized to make the best use of limited materials or energy. While these two concepts have different purposes and meanings, the levels that result from them may in fact be similar. That is, the levels of decomposition may map to the levels of the hierarchy and vice versa.

Figure 3.3 shows a system S, which is decomposed (top) and organized into a hierarchy (bottom). As analysts, we decompose any system by first looking for its

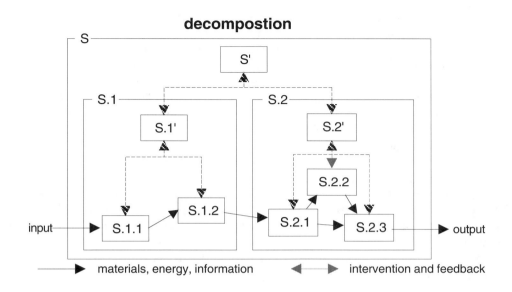

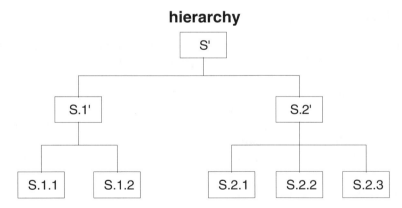

Figure 3.3 *Decomposition versus hierarchy.*

operations subsystems, which produce its bread-and-butter output. Next, we look for any meta-layer subsystems that conduct the intervention and feedback processes to the operations subsystems. For example, in Figure 3.3 (top) system S is decomposed into two operations subsystems S.1 and S.2 and the meta-layer subsystem S'. These three subsystems are peers. Subsystem S.1 is further decomposed into operations subsystems S.1.1 and S.1.2 and meta-layer subsystem S.1'. Similarly, subsystem S.2 is further decomposed into operations subsystems S.2.1, S.2.2, and S.2.3, and meta-layer subsystem S.2'.

The decomposition of system S shows two important points: first, all of the operations subsystems (S.1.1, S.1.2, S.2.1, S.2.2, and S.2.3) are connected by solid lines indicating the actual flow of materials, energy, or information between them from the initial system input to the eventual system output; second, the meta-layer subsystems S', S.1', and S.2' are connected by hashed lines indicating the flow of intervention and feedback information between them. Thus subsystem S' performs the meta-layer processes for the entire system S and is connected to S.1' and S.2'. Similarly subsystem S.1' performs the meta-layer processes for S.1; S.2' performs the meta-layer processes for S.2.

Figure 3.3 (bottom) shows system S organized as a three-level hierarchy. As analysts, we identify the hierarchy of a system by looking for any meta-layer subsystems that conduct the intervention and feedback processes to the operations subsystems. Then we arrange the meta-layer subsystems into a command-control hierarchy. For example, in Figure 3.3 (bottom) meta-layer subsystem S' is at the top level of the hierarchy, and meta-layer subsystems S.1' and S.2' are at the middle level. In each case, S', S.1', and S.2' are proper subsystems and peers of the operations subsystems at their level of decomposition.

3.3 Multilayer systems organization

The other typical form of systems organization besides the hierarchy is the multilayer organization. In multilayer systems organization the subsystems are layered in terms of abstraction. The total system is divided into functional layers, each consisting of an independent set of subsystems characterized by a definite set of properties and laws. The multilayer system organization is very compatible with the hierarchical organization and is often found with it. That is, the multilayer organization is combined with the hierarchical organization to form an integrated hierarchical-multilayer system. In this section, we will describe the unique features of the multilayer organization, and in a later section we will describe the hierarchical-multilayer organization itself.

Definition: Multilayer systems organization

In the multilayer systems organization, each layer consists of one or more subsystems that interact with each other. Mesarovic, Macko, and Takahara point out that the various layers represent different levels of abstraction. For each layer, "there is a set of relevant features and variables, laws and principles in terms of which the system's behavior is described" (Mesarovic et al., 1970).

A given layer is self-contained and functionally independent, although it may rely on lower layers to perform services or provide resources. The layers are often

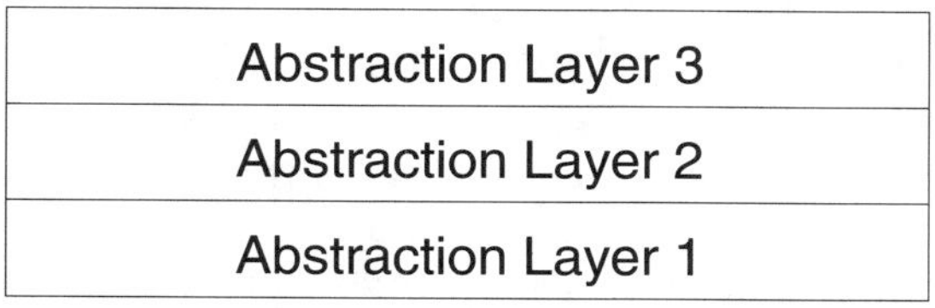

Abstraction Layer 3
Abstraction Layer 2
Abstraction Layer 1

Figure 3.4 *Multilayer systems organization.*

"what-how" pairs. That is, with any pair of layers, the upper layer expresses the "what" and the lower layer accomplishes the "how." The layers are usually in a top-down relationship starting with the most abstract or general top strata and descending to the most concrete or specialized bottom strata.

Figure 3.4 shows the general structure of a multilayer system. Notice that it is a series of layers of abstraction. We will describe the characteristics of the multilayer system in the following sections below.

Asymmetrical interdependence

In a multilayer system, the upper layers often rely on lower layers to discharge their objectives. However, lower layers do not depend on upper layers and, in fact, may not even be aware of them. This is not a hierarchical relationship but one of interdependence. For the system to function properly on a given layer, all the lower layers have to function properly. The requirements for proper functioning on an upper layer appear as constraints on the operations on the lower layers.

Stratification of information

The multilayered systems organization is characterized by a stratification of information: there is less information at the higher levels of the system; lower layers have a relative abundance of detailed information. Mesarovic, Macko and Takahara point out that this property can be used by the systems analyst to understand a multilayered system: "Understanding of a system increases by crossing the strata: in moving down . . . one obtains a more detailed explanation, while in moving up . . . one obtains a deeper understanding of its significance" (Mesarovic et al,, 1970).

Analysis of multilayer systems

Each layer tends to be founded on its own laws, rules, or concepts, which generally cannot be derived from the lower layers (e.g., by scientific or analytic methods). Since each layer has its own intellectual foundations, the study of a given layer must be done using the methodology of that layer.

The analyst studies a multilayer system from two perspectives. For each layer, the analyst must study both that layer itself as well as its lower layer. The analyst studies the interrelationships and operations of the subsystems on the lower layers to obtain a detailed or deeper understanding of the layer. On the other hand, the layer in question is studied from the standpoint of its meaning or significance. In effect, the lower layer cannot be used to understand its meaning or significance. Mesarovic, Macko, and Takahara describe the analysis sequence as follows: "Initially, one can confine his interest to one stratum, depending upon his interest and knowledge, and then increase his understanding of the system's significance or functioning by moving, respectively, up or down" (Mesarovic et al., 1970). Notice that this requires a mastery of the discipline of the layer in question and at least a working knowledge of the discipline of the lower layer (i.e., enough expertise to understand its interrelationships and operations).

Also, it should be noted that the studies of the lower layers are not necessarily better, more fundamental or more basic than those of higher layers. In the words of Mesarovic, Macko and Takahara: "One is able, by referring to lower strata, to explain more precisely and in more detail how the system functions so as to carry out a certain operation. On the other hand, by moving up . . . the description becomes broader and refers to larger subsystems and longer periods of time" (Mesarovic et al, 1970).

Example of a multilayered system: The computer

The computer is an example of a multilayered system. For simplicity, we can divide the computer into the three abstraction layers shown in Figure 3.5.

- ◆ **Top layer** The top layer of a computer is the world of the programmer. The principal abstraction at this layer is a programming language such as C or COBOL. To the programmer, this is a complete view, and the working programmer doesn't have to know anything about lower layers to use the computer. For example, at this top layer, the programmer has the view that the system receives input and produces output through the constructs of the programming language, although this actually takes place only at the

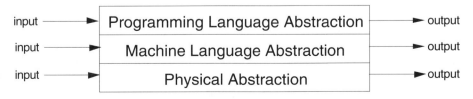

Figure 3.5 *The computer as a multilayered system.*

bottom physical layer. To obtain a deeper understanding of a program, the programmer must enter the world of the next lower level. However, this is normally not necessary since the programmer can usually work completely in the self-contained world of the upper layer.

◆ **Middle layer**   The middle layer is the machine-language abstraction. This is a technical world of the engineers who design and maintain the computer system. They work with the computer using primitive machine instructions that access and manipulate the bottom physical layer. The engineers regard this layer as a complete view of the computer, and they do not have to have any of the expertise of the top layer. While the programmer of the top layer does not need to know anything about this layer, he or she can obtain a deeper understanding of the program by looking at it from the standpoint of the middle machine-language layer.

◆ **Bottom layer**   At the bottom layer is the physical implementation of the computer as a set of electronic components that obey the laws of physics. This is the layer that ultimately implements the computer. It is the complete embodiment of the computer and accounts for all of its functions, structure, and behavior. For example, the physical processes of input and output actually occur here. It is the world of computer hardware engineering. The engineers who work at this layer do not need to have knowledge of the upper layers.

We see from this example that the layers of the computer are relatively independent and have their own discipline and expertise. While the computer is arranged in a top-down fashion, it is not really a hierarchy. Rather, each layer uses the services and resources of the next lower level. We also see that there is an asymmetrical interdependence as one moves down the layers. An upper layer depends on the lower layers to work correctly but not vice versa. Finally, there is a reduction of information as one goes from the bottom layer to the top layer. The bottom is the detailed world of electronic components, while the top layer is the abstracted world of computations.

3.4 Hierarchical-multilayer systems organization

From the previous discussion we see that the major distinction between a system organized as a hierarchy and a system organized as multiple layers is the meaning of the strata (i.e., levels versus layers) of the system. In a multilayer system, a strata is a world unto itself and completely accounts for the whole system seen through the eyes of the concepts that specialize that layer. Higher layers depend on lower layers, but it is not a hierarchy in the true sense. On the other hand, the hierarchy form of a system emphasizes control and the decomposition of goals. In any two levels of a hierarchy, the upper meta-layer contains the processes to decompose objectives and make sure they are accomplished.

In real systems, the distinction between the two is blurred, and a complex system such as the enterprise will exhibit characteristics of both the hierarchical and the multilayered organization. Since these two forms of organization are frequently found together, we can generalize the two into a special kind of system that we will call the *hierarchical-multilayer system*. In this section, we will discuss this special hybrid form of systems organization of which the enterprise is a premier example.

Definition: Hierarchical-multilayer systems organization

The hierarchical-multilayer system combines the best of hierarchical and multilayer organization. The authority echelons that make up the hierarchy are defined in terms of abstractions. In effect, the abstraction layers are "appliquéd" on top of the hierarchy. Figure 3.6 shows the hierarchical-multilayer system.

In Figure 3.6, a system consists of three layers, each made up of various subsystems. Each layer represents an abstraction strata, and the subsystems of a given layer will interact with each other to discharge the function or specialization of that layer. The subsystems of a particular layer may receive input from the environment and produce output to the environment although, as we pointed out earlier in the chapter, this often occurs only at the lower-levels of actual systems. Also, once output of a subsystem enters its environment, it is often consumed by another subsystem of the hierarchical-multilayer system.

Vertical arrangement

The first thing we notice about the hierarchical-multilayer system as shown in Figure 3.6 is the consolidation of abstraction strata and hierarchical levels into an integrated vertical arrangement. The total system is made up of several layers of subsystems that are arranged hierarchically. Each layer is formed around an abstraction concept similar to the multilayer system defined previously. Also, each layer contains subsystems that interact with one another and have subordination relationships with the upper layer.

Specialization of layers

In keeping with its hierarchical origins, the overall objectives of a hierarchical-multilayer system are subdivided into a series of subobjectives. A given subobjective is achieved by the capabilities of a layer of the system. The decomposition of objectives into subobjectives is matched by the existence of a lower layer to discharge those subobjectives. A subobjective is decomposed into its own sub-subobjectives

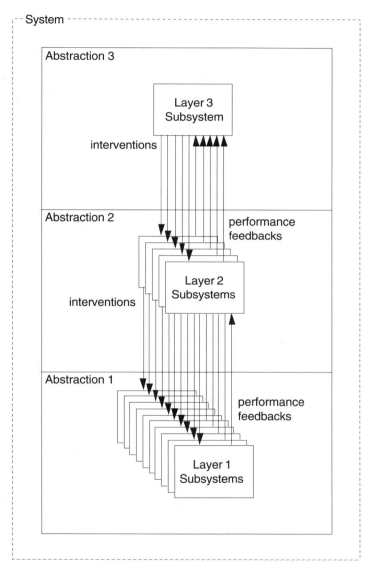

Figure 3.6 *Hierarchical-multilayer systems organization.*

that are, in turn, matched and discharged by yet another lower layer of specialization. This decomposition continues until the lowest layer.

The objectives of a layer help define the abstraction of that layer and vice versa. Thus any particular layer tends to be specialized around the objectives associated with that layer. The subsystems at a given layer work together to accomplish the objectives of that layer. The reason for the existence of a given layer is to discharge its objectives. The result is a system with a series of identifiable layers of functionality or specialization.

The subsystems of a layer tend to have concentrated relations with each other. That is, the subsystems that belong to a layer have relations with one another more frequently than they have relations with other subsystems of the system. This is because, as we saw above, the subsystems of a layer tend to exchange inputs and outputs to discharge the subobjectives of their layer.

Properties of the layers

The abstraction layers of a hierarchical-multilayer system are founded on an abstraction concept (i.e., they are similar to the multilayer system). However, the layers are in hierarchical relationships and are responsible for the attainment of subobjectives as presented from their meta-layer above. The layers of a hierarchical-multilayer system tend to have different scopes, time horizons, and levels of detail:

- ◆ The higher layers are concerned with broader aspects of the system, while the lower layers are concerned with more detailed aspects.

- ◆ The time-horizon of the higher layers is longer than the lower layers. The higher layers see the world in terms of relatively long time horizons while the lower layers see the world in shorter time horizons.

- ◆ Problems on higher layers are less structured with greater uncertainty than problems on lower-layers.

Right of intervention

The lower layer subsystems of a hierarchical-multilayer system are constrained so that the overall objectives of the system are achieved. We saw in the previous discussion of the hierarchy that this implies an authority relationship in which one or more subsystems function as "bosses." Mesarovic, Macko, and Takahara describe the authority relationship between the system and its subsystems of a hierarchical-multilayer systems as follows: "The operation of a subsystem on any level is influenced directly and explicitly from the higher levels, most often from the immediately superseding level. This influence is binding on the lower-levels and reflects a priority of importance in the actions and objectives of the higher levels" (Mesarovic et al., 1970).

Mesarovic, Macko, and Takahara describe the implementation of the authority relationship as the upper subsystem changing the parameters in the lower-level subsystem. They state that "intervention often takes the form of changing parameters in the lower-level systems" (Mesarovic et al., 1970). As we saw in Chapter 1, this means causing the state of a lower-level subsystem to change so that in the future it performs its various processes differently.

Need for autonomy of the lower layers

The subsystems of the lower layers must have some freedom to act autonomously in a hierarchical-multilayer system. Autonomy is necessary because of the amount of time it would take to rely on the decision-making capabilities of the upper layers coupled with the lack of detailed information at the upper levels. When a decision must be made, it cannot be postponed. The hierarchical-multilayer system must be designed to overcome the dilemma of decision making: the need for a quick decision versus the need to understand the situation better. Mesarovic, Macko, and Takahara clarify this point: "It can be shown that it is essential for the effective usage of the multilevel structure that the decision units be given a freedom of action; a suitable division of decision-making effort among the units on different levels should be established" (Mesarovic et al., 1970).

3.5 Examples of hierarchical-multilayer systems

Let's look at two examples of hierarchical-multilayer systems: the factory and the organization. Each demonstrates the properties described earlier.

Example of a hierarchical-multilayer system: The factory

The factory provides an ideal example of a hierarchical-multilayer system. A factory usually consists of three functional layers as shown in Figure 3.7. Notice that the bottom layer actually interfaces to the environment by accepting raw materials from suppliers and producing finished products for customers. The three abstraction layers of a factory are shown in Figure 3.8. A very important aspect of the factory is that the finished products, while physically the same items, are viewed differently on each layer. We will investigate this in more detail shortly.

- ◆ **Top layer** The top layer is the economics abstraction. It is the world of profit, loss, and business planning. This layer regards the finished product as a commodity. The main objective of this layer is to produce business decisions. Thus this layer produces the economic plan for the factory. The time-horizon of the top layer might be months or years. Also, this layer accepts customer orders and arranges them to increase profits within constraints of schedules and resources. This latter function in actual factories is usually called production planning. The intervention this layer presents

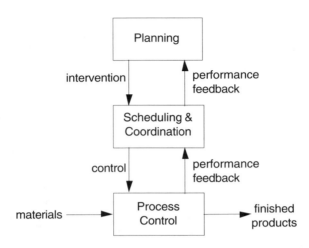

Figure 3.7 *Factory.*

to the next lower layer is initially a definition of products to produce as well as ongoing broad production schedules (e.g., weekly). The performance feedback which this layer receives from the middle layer includes information about actual production (i.e., broad results such as orders which have been filled). This layer maintains state information about the results of the business decisions and the progress being achieved for meeting business objectives.

◆ **Middle layer**   The middle layer is the world of information-processing and control. In this layer, the finished product is regarded as a variable to be controlled and coordinated. The main objective of this layer is the control and manipulation of the lowest (physical) layer. The middle layer monitors actual production and provides close coordination of the lower-layer resources. This layer receives broad workloads from above and breaks them down into local instructions for the lowest layer. The time-horizon of

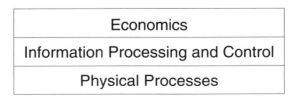

Figure 3.8 *Abstraction layers of a factory.*

the middle layer might be hours or days. This layer maintains state information on the goals and results of the production process and provides feedback to the upper layer on production status and results.

◆ **Bottom layer** The lowest layer is where products are actually manufactured. In this layer, the product is viewed as a physical object to be created or changed in accordance with physical laws. The principal functions of this layer are the supervisory control of manufacturing machines and processes. This layer receives control information from above that defines short-term work loads (e.g., measured in days). This layer attempts to optimize the various machine processes to control production costs (e.g., by batching products which require similar processes). The time-horizon of this layer might be hours, minutes, or even seconds. This layer provides feedback to the middle layer on current physical results and the status of physical processes.

Example of a hierarchical-multilayer system: The organization
The second example of the hierarchical-multilayer system is perhaps the most familiar: the human organization. Figure 3.9 shows a generalized organization such as would be found in enterprise.

The three abstraction layers of a human organization are shown in Figure 3.10. These three layers have been simplified. An actual organization may have more than three, but they would exhibit these three basic functional layers.

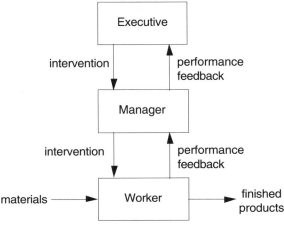

Figure 3.9 *Organization.*

Goals and Strategies
Learning and Adaption
Evaluation and Implementation

Figure 3.10 *Abstraction layers of an organization.*

◆ **Top layer**   The top layers must not only define the overall goals but specify the strategies of the lower layers as well as define their structure and functions. The feedback relations provide the status of the lower layers and the upper layers can change the behavior of the lower layers if the overall goals are not accomplished.

◆ **Middle layer**   The overall goals handed down from above are usually defined in terms that cannot be easily made operational so this layer must interpret them and break them down into attainable subgoals, which are then sent to the bottom layer. Also, the middle layer deals with uncertainty that continually changes as the human-organization operates. Thus a principal activity of this layer is to deal with uncertainty and adapt to an ever changing world by continually fine-tuning the subgoals sent to the bottom layer.

◆ **Bottom layer**   The people at the bottom layer of a human organization choose specific courses of action and then implement them. These people will be very deliberate and speedy in selecting their course of action and will use current information from the environment to make their selections. The bottom layer is under the direction of the upper layers, but the people at the bottom layer autonomously plug in their own processes to produce their courses of action. These processes include evaluation processes and implementation processes. That is, the lower layers decide on a course of action using a two-stage decision-making algorithm: evaluation and implementation.

3.6 Conclusion

In this chapter we introduced the concept of systems organization in which the various subsystems are arranged to optimize the operation of the whole system. For complex systems, a hierarchical organization is necessary to constrain the various subsystems to accomplish the objectives of the whole. Constraining subsystems means not only limiting their operation but changing their operations internally. We saw that complex systems are divided into two functional layers: the meta-layer, which monitors and changes an operations-layer. A hierarchical system is organized into levels in which the two-layered functionality is repeated for each adjacent level.

We also discussed the multilayered system. A multilayered system uses abstraction layers to implement various strata of specialization or use. In the multilayered system, each layer is self-contained but depends on lower layers for services or resources (usually the immediate lower level). Also, the subsystems on a layer depend on each other for services or resources. Each layer has its own concepts, theories, and methodologies and is studied by analysts with specialized expertise. To the analyst, each layer of abstraction is a different view of the whole system. That is, going up the layers consolidates and groups details into generalizations, which usually means the loss of detailed information about the lower layers.

These two forms of systems organization, the hierarchy and the multilayered system, can be combined into a hybrid organization, which we call the *hierarchical-multilayered system*. This hybrid form of systems organization is found in many complex systems, especially those constructed by humans. It is the form of organization of the enterprise and is thus very important to us.

Chapter 4

Information-Processing Networks

4.1 Introduction

In the previous chapters we defined the general system and saw that it consists of a set of related subsystems in the pursuit of common objectives. In this chapter, we will introduce a very special type of general system, the information-processing network. The information-processing network has subsystems called information-processing nodes that are interconnected in complex networks that exchange information. In addition to the classic properties of a general system, the information-processing network has a network infrastructure used by its subsystems to exchange information. This is a significant property. Any human organization, including the enterprise, is an information-processing network. Therefore, to understand the enterprise, we must understand the information-processing network that makes up its infrastructure.

The information-processing nodes that are the subsystems of the information-processing network are themselves a very special type of system. As systems, these nodes exhibit all of the properties of the general system defined in the previous chapters in addition to information-processing behavior. Examples of information-processing nodes are people and information-processing machines such as computers. These nodes are the basic building blocks of the information-processing network, much as the cell is a basic building block of living organisms. We will use it to model the "cellular" structure of the enterprise, with its vast networks of people and computers exchanging information.

In this chapter we will see that these subsystems of the information-processing network have a deeper significance. An information-processing node is an example of what Allen Newell and Herbert Simon call a physical symbol system. Newell and Simon are pioneers in such diverse fields as artificial intelligence, computer science, and psychology. They propose that a physical symbol system is the basic building block of any intelligent system (Newell and Simon, 1987). At the core of an information-processing node is a physical symbol system proposed by Newell and Simon. We will use these ideas to lay the groundwork for describing the information and intelligence of the enterprise as a physical structure of information-processing nodes.

4.2 Information-processing networks

In the introduction to this chapter, we used some new terms, information-processing network and information-processing node. In this section we will define these terms and discuss them in more detail. However, let's begin at a more fundamental level by asking a basic question.

What is information?

Information is a physical phenomenon that joins a sender and a receiver. According to Bernd-Olaf Küppers, "we can only speak of information when it has both a sender and a recipient" (Küppers, 1990). Information is not an absolute term but rather relative in the sense that the physical phenomena is somehow "understood" by both the sender and the receiver. Philosopher Carl Friedrich von Weizsacker says, "Information is only that which is understood" (von Weizsacker, 1980). Let's look at this in more detail.

In the real world, a sender is connected to a receiver by a physical substrate consisting of matter located between the two. Since this matter obeys the laws of physics, it can be purposefully excited by various physical phenomena. For example, to speak to another person, a speaker uses the substrate of air molecules to carry information to the listener. Thus to send information, the sender uses its physical connection to a receiver by exciting a physical phenomenon. However, physical phenomena are a common occurrence to the receiver because he or she is part of the real world. When do physical phenomena become information?

A physical phenomenon is elevated to the status of information by a convention between sender and receiver called *symbols*. A symbol has two properties: First, a given symbol has a physical implementation—it can be unambiguously and uniquely represented as a physical phenomenon such that it is not mistaken for another symbol. In effect, the physical phenomenon representing the symbol causes the symbol to become instantiated or real. Second, the symbol represents a concept meaningful to the sender and receiver. The sender and receiver consistently use that symbol to represent this concept; in short, they have established a mutual convention.

The sender has at its disposal a number of these symbols. Symbols may be strung together into a symbol sequence. An information exchange consists of one or more of these symbol sequences being physically transported from the sender to the receiver by the invocation of the physical phenomenon that implements the symbols. In order for the information to be useful, the receiver of the physical phenomenon must assign meaning to the sequence of symbols comparable to the meaning intended by the sender. Misunderstanding can take the form of anything from the receiver regarding the symbol sequence as meaningless physical phenomena to understanding it as a symbol sequence but not assigning the same meaning intended by the sender. However, the ultimate test of information is what the receiver does with it. For a physical symbol sequence to carry information, the receiver must alter its behavior or state in some noticeable way as a result of receiving the physical symbol sequence. In short, the definition of information requires that it is used in some way by the receiver.

Definition: Information-processing network

An *information-processing network* is a general system in which its subsystems discharge the objectives of the overall system by exchanging and processing information. A primary system objective of the information-processing network is to provide a communication infrastructure for information exchange among its subsystems, the information-processing nodes. In our classification scheme introduced in Chapter 2, we would classify the information-processing network as a level 6 (complex-adaptive system). Figure 4.1 shows the major components of an information-processing network.

Definition: Information-processing node

The information-processing network contains information-processing nodes connected to other information-processing nodes as shown in Figure 4.1. The information-processing nodes are the agents that make up this level 6 complex-adaptive system. Figure 4.2 shows a typical information-processing node embedded

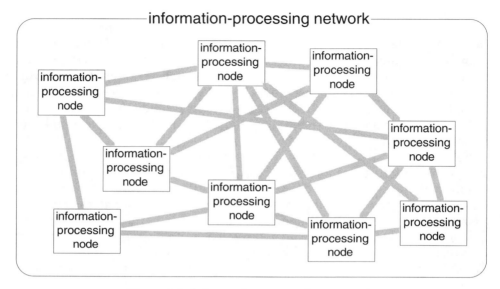

Figure 4.1 *Information-processing network.*

in its environment (i.e., the larger information-processing network). The information-processing node has ports that provide interfaces with its environment to receive or send information. Internally, the information-processing node contains a state memory, which we will discuss in a moment. The information-processing node may be one of the following:

◆ Person

◆ Information-processing machine (e.g., computer)

◆ Lower-level information-processing network

Functions of the information-processing node

Let's take a look at what an information-processing node must be capable of performing from an information standpoint. Information-processing nodes exchange information with each other. The environment of an information-processing node consists, in part, of other information-processing nodes. Information is exchanged when an information-processing node decides to present another information-processing node in the environment with some information.

Figure 4.3 shows the essential parts of two information-processing nodes. Information is physically transported from the sender information-processing node

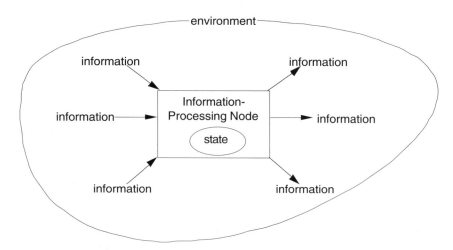

Figure 4.2 *Information-processing node.*

to the receiver information-processing node through a physical communication infrastructure that connects the two. The physical connection is called a *channel*. The channel is external to the information-processing node and is not part of it. While we regard the information-processing node as a black box, we conclude it must be internally capable of many fairly sophisticated information functions as follows:

- Receive information (i.e., accept external information from the communication channels of the environment and convert it to internal information. External information is represented as physical symbols encoded by a coding scheme known to the information-processing node. Internal information is also represented as physical symbols but possibly encoded using a different coding scheme).

- Use information (i.e., update its state memory based on internal information, possibly received recently from the external environment. We will discuss state memory in a moment).

- Select information (i.e., choose subsets of its internal information).

- Produce information (i.e., access its state memory and create consistent symbolic representations of the information using its internal coding scheme).

- Send information (i.e., produce external, physical symbols encoded by an appropriate coding scheme and cause the physical phenomenon to be excited on the communication channels).

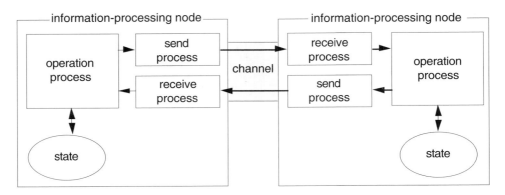

Figure 4.3 *Networking of information-processing nodes.*

While we are concerned here with the information aspects of the information-processing node, later in this chapter we will see an expanded view of the information-processing node in which we analyze it as a general system. Then we will see the information-processing node as a general system that takes in input and produces output. The input and output are energy or materials in addition to information. But for now, we want to focus on its information characteristics.

Message: Syntax, semantics, pragmatics

The symbol sequence sent from sender to receiver is called a *message.* For the message to be understood and used, the sender and the receiver must establish a convention. The convention is based on three levels of agreement as follows:

- **Syntax**   The syntax of a message relates to the symbols and their relationship in the symbol sequence. The symbol sequence must be encoded using rules that govern which specific symbols can be used and their physical representation (vocabulary). The symbols must follow rules of allowed combinations, order, and arrangements (grammar).

- **Semantics**   The semantics of a message relates to the meaning of the symbol sequence. The symbol sequence must be so constructed to stand for concepts mutually known to the sender and receiver. This implies a great deal of agreement between the sender and the receiver on these shared concepts. In effect, the sender and receiver must have a shared model of the environment. This agreement must be achieved prior to the transmission of the symbol sequence in question. According to Bernd-Olaf Küppers, "absolute information has no meaning since information only exists in relation to an idea" (Küppers, 1990).

◆ **Pragmatics** The "pragmatics" of a message relate to the effect that the symbol sequence has on the receiver. The sender has an expectation of the effect that the symbol sequence will have on the receiver and the subsequent behavior of the receiver.

Information content

Is there a way to measure the quantity of information of a message? There are two interpretations of the quantity of information of a symbol sequence. The first is at the syntactical level, considering the symbol sequence as a physical phenomena. Assume we have two symbol sequences in which their information is coded in the shortest means possible. The amount of information content of a symbol sequence is defined in terms of the probability of receiving (i.e., a measure of novelty) that symbol sequence as measured by the recipient. Thus if the recipient expects a 100% probability of receiving a given symbol sequence, then actually receiving it does not tell the recipient anything new. In this case, the information quantity is zero. Similarly, a completely unexpected symbol sequence, one that the recipient doesn't expect because it is so novel (i.e., it has a very low probability of being received as measured by the recipient), has a correspondingly higher information content. Some scholars call this the *measure of novelty* of a symbol sequence—the higher the novelty, the more information content.

The other way to measure information content is to consider how it actually affects the recipient. This is the pragmatic level of information content. Information content is higher when the sender actually causes the receiver to perform an action to change its state. In this case, state usually refers to the internal model of the environment that an information-processing node retains as part of its state. This means that the receiver is in a state of uncertainty; that is, the receiver either completely lacks suitable state information or at best may have formulated some limited and uncertain models of the environment. When the sender sends a symbol sequence, it makes one of these possibilities actual, excluding the others, and resolving the receiver's uncertainty. Thus, at the pragmatic level, a symbol sequence contains information when it removes uncertainty in some way, and the more uncertainty removed, the higher the information content.

State memory

As mentioned earlier, one of the functions of the information-processing node is to retain information in its state memory. The state of an information-processing node is represented internally as physical symbol sequences, that is, as physical phenomena configured using a symbol convention. This is a much more sophisticated storage of state than our previous description. Before, we regarded state as the configuration of the structure of a system. For example, the configuration of the gears and levers of a mechanical clock is its state. The information-processing node has a state-memory capability in which physical symbols representing its state are stored. Notice that we are focusing on information here. An information-processing node could also have physical parts whose configuration are also part of its state.

The state memory is capable of being accessed by the information-processing node and provides the source of information that the information-processing node may decide to communicate to the environment (e.g., to one or more other information-processing nodes in the environment). As discussed earlier, an information-processing node communicates with its environment by sending and receiving sequences of physical symbols. When information is received, an information-processing node performs internal actions such as accessing its internal state or changing its state appropriately as a response to the input information. Later, the information-processing node may decide to send its own information, possibly as a result of its new state caused by the original input information.

Decomposition of information-processing modes

An information-processing node can be atomic or complex. An atomic information-processing node is a person or a machine that does not require further decomposition. A complex information-processing node consists of people and computers and is, in fact, a lower-level information-processing network. Nevertheless, the complex information-processing node receives information, stores it, and transmits it, exactly like the atomic information-processing node.

An example of a complex information-processing node is the organization in an enterprise. The organization, which is actually a lower-level information-processing network, consists of people and computers. However, the organization is itself an information-processing node when regarded as an abstraction. An organization can be part of a larger organization, which can also be considered an information-processing node. At each level of decomposition, an information-processing node has the basic set of characteristics relating to the receipt, storage, and transmission of information.

Channel problems

The communication channel (see Figure 4.3) is problematic. First, it has limitations on its transmitting capacity due to limitations on the density of the physical phenomena used to transmit messages. If the sender produces more messages than the channel can physically transmit, then the receiver node receives only part of the messages, up to the channel's maximum capacity.

The second problem with the channel is noise. As the channel's properties are often not ideal, there is a risk of the signal being affected by interference in transmission that might distort the specific contents of the signal. This interference is called *noise* and is usually caused by the spurious activation on the channel of the physical phenomena used to carry messages. These spurious activations appear to the receiver as legitimate signals and may be mistaken as such.

Redundancy

The modern theory of information was developed by the mathematician Claude Shannon, who developed the theory while at Bell Telephone Laboratories and published two papers on the subject in 1948. At the time, Shannon was concerned with the engineering properties of radio transmissions. Jeremy Campbell described Shannon's papers and the implications of his findings in *Grammatical Man*: "Shannon's laws of information are universal, and in this way compel scientists and other thinkers to confront the fact that information itself is universal" (Campbell, 1982).

One of the achievements of Shannon's theory was it provided a systematic way to deal with the noise or interference on channels. The coding system of the signal can be used to endow the signal with redundant contents. Redundant contents means the signal has the same information encoded more than once and in more than one physical representation. In this way, if the symbol sequence is purposely made redundant, the receiver has an opportunity to cross check and verify it. In fact, Shannon proved mathematically that redundancy can be coded in such a way that the receiver can actually correct the symbol sequence if it is distorted. The only problem is that the symbol sequence becomes arbitrarily long depending only on the extent of precision desired. In the words of Jeremy Campbell, Shannon showed "that in any type of communications system, a (symbol sequence). can be sent from one place to another even under noisy conditions, and be as free from error as we care to make it, as long as it is coded (with redundancy). Nature does impose a limit, but the limit is in the form of the capacity of the communications channel. As long as the channel is not overloaded, the code guarantees as high a degree of accuracy as we choose" (Campbell, 1982).

The information-processing network as infrastructure

The lattice of channels between the various information-processing nodes forms a physical communications infrastructure. Thus the environment of an information-processing node at our level of abstraction actually contains two types of entities: not only does it contain other information-processing nodes but an infrastructure of information channels.

The infrastructure is external to a given information-processing node and is not functionally a part of it. The infrastructure must be maintained in a working state to make the flow of information between information-processing nodes dependable. This maintenance of the infrastructure is a system-level responsibility of the information-processing network, not the responsibility of the individual information-).processing node subsystems that use it. However, the information-processing network may assign one or more of the information-processing nodes to perform this infrastructure function including its operation and maintenance. Thus some of the information-processing nodes are specialized and dedicated to the infrastructure.

We can define the basic objectives of this infrastructure:

- ◆ **Ubiquity** The capability of the infrastructure to transmit information must be available anywhere in the environment.

- ◆ **Transparency** Using the infrastructure to transmit information must be simple to the information-processing nodes. Simplicity means minimizing processes or information an information-processing node must maintain and use to transmit information in the infrastructure.

Information explosion
In a typical information-processing network such as an enterprise, the networks of information-processing nodes are vast, consisting of thousands of nodes. This would be the view of the enterprise at the "cellular" level. The complexity of the information exchanges in these vast networks makes them difficult to analyze. Information might originate at one of the nodes, causing a cascading chain reaction of information being sent from node to node in the network. This information explosion is an example of a positive feedback system in which the information traffic in the network causes other information to be placed on the network. The information-processing network is seldom quiescent.

4.3 How does the information-processing node process information?

So far we have regarded the information-processing node as a black-box that processes information. A big question is, how does it do it? How does the information-processing node actually process information? In this section, we will present a generic model of the internal operations of the information-processing node. We will rely on the work of Allen Newell and Herbert Simon to provide the intellectual foundation of our model of the internal operations of the information-processing node. Our model will be an extremely simplified description of a very complex topic, but it will be quite sufficient for enterprise modeling. Here's our old friend abstraction again. We will use abstraction to draw out the essential characteristics of information-processing nodes for the purpose of modeling them.

Definition: Physical symbol system

The information-processing node is a hybrid example of what Allen Newell and Herbert Simon call a *physical symbol system*. Newell and Herbert have defined and described the physical symbol system in their study of intelligent action in artificial intelligence. The physical symbol system is their model of a machine that uses information to define its sequence of operations (Newell and Simon, 1987). We propose in this book that at the core of an information-processing node is a physical symbol system defined by Newell and Simon.

Figure 4.4 shows the essential components of a physical symbol system. In effect, this diagram is a model of the information-processing functions of a person or a computer. In the subsections below, we'll dissect this diagram of the physical symbol system in more detail:

How the physical symbol system uses symbol structures

As we saw earlier in this chapter, symbols are patterns implemented by physical phenomena. Symbol sequences are indicated in the Figure 4.4 as arrows. We can see

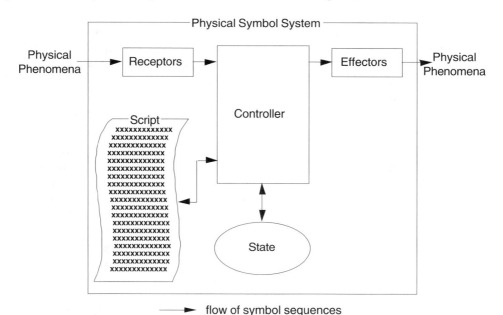

Figure 4.4 *Physical symbol system.*

in the figure that all of the components of the physical symbol system are involved with the flow of symbol sequences. Keeping in mind that we are describing an abstract machine, what do symbol sequences really represent to a physical symbol system? In general, the flows of symbol sequences are for the input, state, and output of the physical symbol system. Each of these is discussed in the following:.

◆ **Input** In Figure 4.4, the input to the physical symbol system are physical symbol sequences. They originate outside the physical symbol system and are produced by other physical symbol systems in the environment. The physical symbol system has receptors capable of receiving the physical phenomena representing the symbol sequence. The input process consists of creating internal symbol structures (i.e., via physical phenomena) that represent the original input physical phenomena.

◆ **State memory** In Figure 4.4, we see that the state of the physical symbol system is accessed and updated by its controller (described later). The state of a physical symbol system is implemented by a series of physical symbol sequences and stored in the state memory. The state memory is an identifiable physical component of the physical symbol system that is capable of storing, retaining, and retrieving physical symbol sequences.

◆ **Output** In Figure 4.4, we see that the output of a physical symbol system consists of physical symbol sequences represented as physical phenomena. The physical symbol system has effectors that are capable of converting internal symbol structures to the physical phenomena. The output physical phenomena will typically be directed to other physical symbol systems in the environment.

The controller

The physical symbol system contains a set of elementary processes that operate on these symbol sequences. According to Newell and Simon, "there must be a sufficiently general and powerful collection of operations to compose out of them all the macroscopic performance" of the physical symbol system (Newell and Simon, 1987). In effect, these elementary processes account for the behavior of the physical symbol system and its sophisticated functions are built-up from them. The elementary processes modify symbol sequences, create them, reproduce them, or destroy them. In the words of Newell and Simon, "A physical symbol system is a machine that produces through time an evolving collection of symbol structures" (Newell and Simon, 1987).

These elementary processes are realized by some physical mechanism that is capable of controlled manipulation of the underlying physical phenomena that implements the symbol sequences. In this book we call this mechanism the *controller*. In Figure 4.4, the controller is shown as the central component of the physical symbol system. The controller is capable of receiving input physical symbol sequences and by its operation producing physical symbol sequences.

To perform its duties, the controller implements the capability of *designation*—the formation of the correspondence between a symbol sequence and other internal symbol structures, internal processes, or external objects of the physical symbol system. Thus the controller uses the symbol sequences to designate processes to be performed and the corresponding entities that will be accessed or used by a process. In this way, access to an internal or external object is obtained by the controller by interpreting a symbol sequence for performing the designation function. Newell and Simon define this capability of interpretation: "The system can interpret an expression (symbol sequence). if the expression designates a process and if, given the expression, the system can carry out the process" (Newell and Simon, 1987).

Scripts: Sequences of orders

As we saw in the previous paragraphs, the behavior of the physical symbol system is implemented by the continuous act of interpreting symbol sequences by the controller. The behavior of the physical symbol system "consists of executing sequences of elementary information processes" (Newell and Simon, 1972). Symbol sequences designate these information processes executed by the controller. These symbol sequences are stored in the state memory of a physical symbol system and are extracted by the controller and interpreted as a series of orders that designate processes to be invoked.

In this book, this sequence of orders is called a *script*. In Figure 4.4, for clarity, the script is shown as a separate component from the state, but it should be regarded as part of it. In effect, the controller uses the state memory as one of its input sources, in this case, the symbol sequences representing the orders to be executed. The controller keeps track "of the current process being executed and after execution would find the next process to be executed" (Newell and Simon, 1972). For simplicity, we say that the controller "executes" a script.

The actual processes designated by the script are performed by lower-level components available to the physical symbol system. The controller constructs appropriate stimuli, which are transmitted to these components. The stimuli may itself consist of symbol sequences (i.e., they are messages) and be transmitted to the lower-level components using the communications capabilities of the physical symbol system. Figure 4.5 shows an example of a script for shopping at a supermarket. Notice that it could be executed by any kind of physical symbol system including a person or a robot.

As we see in Figure 4.5, a script consists of a series of orders that are specified using symbol sequences. We can say that the set of symbol sequences understood by the controller are the *language* of the physical symbol system. Like any language, the language of the controller is made up of symbol sequences expressed using symbols from the vocabulary and syntax that the controller of the physical symbol system is capable of interpreting.

Supermarket Script

```
Make shopping list
Enter supermarket
Do until shopping list completed:
        Shop
Checkout
Exit supermarket

Function:  Make shopping list
           Check for item at home
           If the item is missing
                   put item on shopping list

Function:  Enter supermarket
           Park car
           Enter supermarket building
           Take shopping cart

Function:  Shop
           Push shopping cart to next item
                   on shopping list
           Take item
           Put item in shopping cart

Function:  Checkout
           Wait in checkout line
           Greet checkout clerk
           Verify charge for each item
           Pay checkout clerk
           Take all purchased items

Function:  Exit supermarket
           Leave supermarket building
           Go to car
           Drive away
```

Figure 4.5 *Supermarket script.*

Defining the script is the key to defining the behavior of a physical symbol system. In effect, the script stored in the state memory of a physical symbol system defines the role of the physical symbol system. Changing the script changes its role. We will return to this point in a moment.

Functions: Reusable scripts

As we saw earlier, the controller of a physical symbol system is capable of a limited set of primitive operations, which make up its base vocabulary. Why not have the ability to define new operations of our own design that are executed by the physical symbol system as if these operations were part of its base vocabulary? These fabricated operations would be made up of the primitive operations of the controller as well as other fabricated operations. The term *function* is used to describe these fabricated operations. In effect, functions are scripts that are executed by the controller of the physical symbol system as if they were native operations.

Functions provide the ability to consolidate useful sequences of operations into scripts (i.e., symbol sequences) that can be identified and named by a single symbol sequence. Notice that this is just another use of the controller's capability of *designation*. In effect, functions are used to decompose a script into reusable sequences of orders that can be constructed separately and used in more than one script by designating them. For example, a cookbook contains recipes for cooking various dishes. The recipes are scripts executed by a physical symbol system, in this case the chef. A recipe will be made up of invocations of various functions such as "boil water" or "mix flour and sugar." The recipe does not explicitly specify the sequence of operations to "boil water" but rather uses the idea of a function. Human scripts are almost entirely made up of sequences of functions. Figure 4.6 shows the model of a function. This model of the function is based on the work of Peter Wegner (Wegner, 1989).

In the function of Figure 4.6, each input x determines a unique output *f(x)*. The output *f(x)* depends only on the input *x* and no other information. Thus the function does not maintain internal state and knows nothing of previous invocations. Another aspect of the function is that it is a black box; the script that invokes a function doesn't know anything about the internal workings of the function or how it accomplishes its mapping of the input *x* to the output *f(x)*.

Figure 4.6 *Abstract function.*

In the "Supermarket Script" of Figure 4.5, we see a series of script symbol sequences that designate functions at the top. These are followed by a series of functions that are defined by their own symbol sequences. For example, in the script there is the symbol sequence "Make shopping list" at the top. This symbol sequence designates a function below which would be recognized and executed by the physical symbol system as the designated symbol sequence. In the symbol sequence defining the "Make shopping list" function, there are lower-level processes such as "Check for item at home," which could either be primitive processes or designate even lower-level functions.

What elementary capabilities would a physical symbol system have to have to use functions? Newell and Simon propose that to keep track of the execution of a script consisting of a hierarchy of functions, the physical symbol system would use an internal list structure called a *stack*. The stack is a symbol sequence that is accessed and updated by the controller. When a function is to be executed, "its name is pushed on the stack; when execution is complete, popping the stack returns the prior symbol to the top and lets the system proceed to the next step" (Newell and Simon, 1972). This simple mechanism of the stack is all that the controller needs to execute a script consisting of complex hierarchies of functions.

Changing the behavior of the information-processing node

We saw earlier that scripts are specialized symbol sequences used by the controller of a physical symbol system to invoke a sequence of lower-level processes and thus specify the future events that will occur in the larger system. The controller is capable of performing a repertoire of elementary information processes that can be supplemented by functions. This means that the scripts used by a controller could be changed to cause different sequences of information processes to be performed. We now have an emerging concept of what we call *software* as distinguished from *hardware*. The script is "soft" because it can be changed to cause a different sequence of information processes, while the controller is "hard" because it is a physical machine capable of invoking any valid sequence of information processes specified in its current script.

A script causes the physical symbol system and thus the information-processing node to change its behavior. In effect, the information-processing node can be changed to perform a different *role*. The concept of role is very important to enterprise modeling. Roles provide us with a convenient modeling mechanism. When we model a complex domain, we acknowledge that there is a difference between the physical hardware of an information processing node and its various roles modeled as software scripts.

For example, employees are the most important information-processing node in an enterprise, the individual employee having a physical identity as an information-processing node. The employee performs different roles. For example, an employee has different tasks to perform on the job. Also, the employee may be the coordinator of a cross-functional team as well as a loaned worker to a charity supported by the enterprise. Each of these are different roles performed by the same information-processing node, that is, the employee in question. Roles must be defined in the enterprise model depending on our level of abstraction. We can see that a role played by an information-processing node can be modeled by the script for that role. In a later chapter, we will use these ideas of roles in object-oriented modeling.

Why do information-processing nodes exchange information?

Another big question is why would one information-processing node bother to exchange information with another information-processing node? The answer to this question relates the basic type of system that an information-processing network is. An information-processing network is an example of a level 6 complex-adaptive system (from Bounding's classification scheme outlined in Chapter 2). The information-processing nodes that are the subsystems of this special type of system are themselves classified on the classification scheme: an information-processing node would be either a level 5, intelligent system; a level 4, goal-seeking, adaptive system; or at least a level 3, homeostatic system.

The answer to why information-processing nodes do exchange information lies in the basic purpose of the level 6 system to discharge its objectives. According to Simon, it is adaptivity to its environment. Simon describes it this way: "Symbol systems are almost the quintessential artifacts, for adaptivity to an environment is their whole *raison d'être*. They are goal-seeking, information-processing nodes, usually enlisted in the service of the larger systems in which they are incorporated" (Simon, 1981).

Simon tells us that physical symbol systems that are our proposed way to model the minds of people or the controllers of information machines are often embedded as subsystems in larger systems. Since they have information-processing capability, the physical symbol system as a subsystem will extend their information-processing capabilities to the larger system. These larger systems are typically what we have called *information-processing nodes*.

Simon also tells us what special capability these symbol systems, people, or information machines present to the larger system in which they are embedded as subsystems. It is adaptivity. In effect, information makes adaptivity possible, and adaptivity requires information. Simon has given us a new way of thinking about information: it doesn't exist on its own; rather, it exists in the context of adaptivity. Simon has, in effect, stated that the purpose of information is adaptivity.

The computer as an information-processing node

Let's close this section by using our definition of the physical symbol system to describe the computer as an information-processing node. A computer directly implements the physical symbol system. It has a controller capable of accessing a script of orders that are stored in its state memory. In the case of the computer, the script is called a *program*. The orders are stored as symbol sequences that are capable of being interpreted by the controller of the computer. The invocation of an order is accomplished by the controller by interpreting the meaning of the symbol sequence representing the specified order. The controller, in turn, causes the meaning of an order to be carried out by using one or more of the components of the computer.

The controller of a computer is capable of a few simple operations on symbol sequences: storing symbol sequences, retrieving symbol sequences previously stored, making copies of symbol sequences, combining two symbol sequences using an algorithm (e.g., arithmetic), transforming symbol sequences using an algorithm, and comparing symbol sequences to see if they are identical. In this way, the sequence of orders, its program, is interpreted and executed by the controller of the computer. We see that a program is just an information symbol sequence that specifies the future processes of this special information-processing node.

The symbol sequences are stored in the memory of the computer and are there from previous operations of the controller. The controller has a scratch memory used to store the current symbol sequences being worked on as well as the symbol sequences of intermediate results. Originally, the symbol sequences must come from the outside so the controller has operations to retrieve symbol sequences from input components. Similarly, the controller must present results to the outside so it has operations to transfer symbol sequences to output components.

The modern computer was originally described by a team headed by John von Neumann. Figure 4.7 shows the architecture of the von Neumann computer as originally designed in EDVAC (1946). According to Michael Godfrey and David Hendry, the significance of the von Neumann computer was that it was the first machine (i.e., designed and constructed by humans) that clearly separated the control of the machine's processes from the implementation of the machine's processes. All previous machines "hard-wired" the implementation functionality, so that each machine was specialized to a specific set of objectives (Godfrey and Hendry, 1993). The control unit of a von Neumann computer is capable of general-purpose use that is not specific to any set of objectives. For this reason, the computer is sometimes called a "universal machine" because it is capable of emulating any other machine if it is given the necessary program and the various lower-level

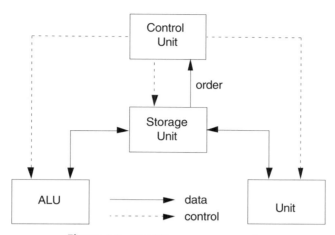

Figure 4.7 *von Neumann computer.*

components that actually perform the functions of the emulated machine. This general-purpose use is made possible by its hierarchical architecture centered around the central controller as shown in Figure 4.7.

In Figure 4.7, an order is being interpreted and executed by the controller. The current order is one of a series of orders of the program, which is created as a sequence of symbols understandable to the computer's central control unit. The sequence of orders (i.e., the program as a series of symbol sequences) is stored in the storage unit:

- The control unit interprets the order and directs the lower-level components to perform the order. Notice that the only information that the control unit uses to execute an order are the symbol sequence of the order itself and the current state of the controller due to the execution of previous orders. The control unit causes the lower-level electronic units (ALU, storage unit, I/O unit,etc. discussed in the following) to be activated by sending them physical symbol sequences. Usually several lower-level units are involved to complete the execution of one of the orders. Once the order is interpreted and executed, the control unit fetches another order from the storage unit and the process is repeated.

- The various electronic units (ALU, storage unit, I/O unit , etc.) are part of the lowest-level of the hierarchy. These electronic units are completely under the control of the control unit. They are capable of the simple and specific symbol manipulations required to effect the current order of the control unit. Each unit of the lowest level has very limited scope and no autonomy as it goes about its symbol manipulations. It is the control unit that knows that a specific sequence of manipulation by the lower-level units is a necessary part in the completion of the current order. These lowest-level units have no information about the larger world of the control unit and know only about their particular local operations, which are just subfunctions among the several needed to complete the current order. Also, note that while the control unit knows about the current order, it has no knowledge of the purpose of the current order. That is the province of the program.

4.3 The information-processing node as a physical symbol system

Newell and Simon's physical symbol system is an abstract machine that provides an effective model of information processing for both humans and machines. In this book, we propose that the physical symbol system can be used to model the information processing of the information-processing node and thus the enterprise. In effect, any information-processing node can be considered to have at its core a physical symbol system which performs the information processing of the larger system. While the information-processing node is a general system, when we focus on its information processing capabilities, we will be using Newell and Simon's physical symbol system as our model.

But is there really a physical symbol system?
Whether there is actually a component which resembles the physical symbol system inside of a given information-processing node such as a human is irrelevant. The only requirement is that the information-processing node behave in a manner that allows us to describe it as if it had a physical symbol system as its operational mechanism. Then we can use the physical symbol system with its corresponding scripts as a succinct and sufficient model of its information-processing capabilities.

However, as we saw above, at least one information-processing node—the computer—behaves exactly like this. To describe the human as a physical symbol system is much more difficult and controversial. Simon, however, does so: "The computer is a member of an important family of artifacts called *symbol systems,* or more explicitly, physical symbol systems. . . . Another important member of the family . . . is the human mind and brain" (Simon, 1981).

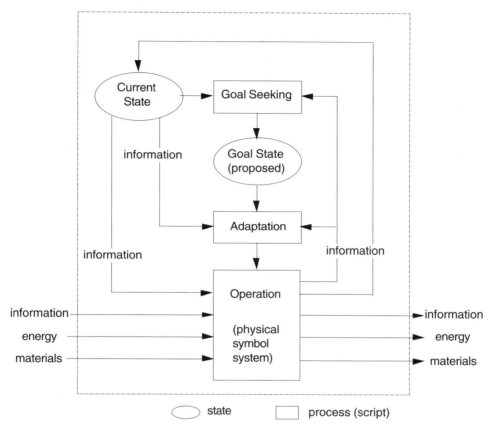

Figure 4.8 *Information-processing node as a general system.*

The information-processing node as a general system

We are now ready to present our model of the information-processing node (Figure 4.8). This model will be used throughout the remainder of the book. This model presents the information-processing node as a general system that incorporates information-processing capabilities as well as the other capabilities of a general system. This model shows the most general form of the information-processing node and specific instances may not have the full complement of capabilities shown in Figure 4.8. For example, only the most sophisticated computers would actually have the capabilities of Figure 4.8, but any human would.

In particular, our model highlights the hierarchical-multilayered organization of the information-processing node. Recall that in the Chapter 2, complex systems are organized into meta-layer/operations-layer pairs. In our case, the meta-layer implements the goal-seeking, adaptive processes of the information-processing node. The operations-layer consists of the systems processes that transform energy and materials, as well as information.

In the following, we will describe each of the internal functions of the information-processing nodes shown in Figure 4.8.

- **Input**   Similar to any other system, the information-processing node will take in energy, materials, and information from the environment. In particular, the information acquired from the environment must be passed through the boundary of the system and represented as physical symbol sequences.

- **Output**   Similar to any other system, the information-processing node produces outputs to fulfill the objectives of the system. These outputs include materials, energy, and information.

- **Processes**   The information-processing node continuously executes a number of processes. Figure 4.8 is a functional view that shows the processes as rectangles and state as ovals. The processes are implemented by scripts executed by the physical symbol system of the information-processing node. We will discuss the specific processes in a moment.

- **Current state**   The current state is used as a significant input to the various processes of the information-processing node. The current state undergoes transitions to a new state by the processes of the system.

  What information would make up the current state if the purpose of information is adaptation? For the most part, current state information serves as the internal representation of the environment in which the information-processing node is embedded. In effect, the state of the information-processing node allows it to model its environment as an abstraction containing much less detail and to reason about it. We see that these information-processing nodes are themselves using our old friends abstraction and modeling as a key part of their behavior. Thus the utility of symbol sequences is one of abstraction of the much more complex underlying meaning, which is usually very difficult or impossible to manipulate directly. In this way, the symbol sequences of the state-memory can be manipulated by the information-processing node as a shorthand way of referring to the underlying environment.

◆ **Goal-seeking process** To implement the goal-seeking imperative, the information-processing node has a goal-seeking process (i.e., script) executed by its physical symbol system. The goal-seeking process analyzes the current state and produces a proposed state called the *goal state*. The goal state is the internal representation of the future, the desired state the information-processing node wishes to achieve. Then the problem becomes one of defining the process to achieve this goal state from the initial state.

◆ **Adaptation process** To implement the adaptation imperative, the information-processing node has an adaptation process (i.e., script) executed by its physical symbol system. The adaptation process analyzes the current state and the proposed goal state and modifies the operation process to achieve the new goal state. Usually this takes the form of actually changing the script of the operation process. We recognize the goal-seeking process and the adaptation process as being part of the classic meta-layer discussed in Chapter 2.

◆ **Operation process** To implement the operation process, the information-processing node has an operation process (i.e., script) executed by the physical symbol system. The current state is transformed to the new state by the operation process. The operation process may include non–information-processing components that are under the direct control of the physical symbol system. These information-processing components collectively accomplish the objectives of the information-processing node to produce materials, energy, and information to the environment. The operation process may have recently been modified by the adaptation process to achieve new goals. As mentioned earlier, this takes the form of changing the script of the operation process that is executed by the physical symbol system.

4.5 Conclusion

In this chapter, we defined the information-processing network. The novelty of the information-processing network compared to other general systems is that the interaction between its subsystems (i.e., the information-processing nodes) is conducted by the actual exchange of information. We made the point repeatedly in this chapter that the enterprise is a premier example of an information-processing network in which people and machines are arranged in an infrastructure to exchange information in pursuit of the objectives of the enterprise. The design of the enterprise is in large part the design of this infrastructure. Thus the information-processing network is an important component of our work in enterprise modeling: to construct a model of the enterprise, we must construct a model of an information-processing network. We would do this at an appropriate level of detail depending on the level of abstraction we were after.

In this chapter, we also introduced the information-processing node, the basic cell of the information-processing network. The information-processing nodes are connected in vast information-processing networks and consist of people, information machines, or lower-level information-processing networks. The information-processing node has capabilities for receiving, storing, and sending information. Complex information-processing nodes can be decomposed into atomic information-processing nodes. The lowest-level atomic information-processing node, the person or machine, is the "living cell" of the information-processing "organism." Information-processing nodes are combined into more complex structures to make up higher level information-processing nodes much like cells form tissue or organs in a living organism.

In an enterprise, the information-processing nodes are the people, machines, or organizations (i.e., of people and machines) that combine to accomplish the objectives of the enterprise by the exchange of information. While the information-processing nodes will themselves be complex (e.g., people, organizations, machines), we are abstracting their essential characteristics in regard to information, that of receiving, storing, and sending information. This approach is perfect for modeling and serves our purpose of abstracting the essence of a complex world such as the enterprise.

In this chapter, we described in detail Newell and Simon's abstract machine, the physical symbol system. We proposed that the information-processing node can be modeled as having a physical symbol system at its core. This gives us the necessary intellectual tools to comprehend the information processing of the enterprise. As a modeling device, the physical symbol system allows us to model the behavior of the information-processing node as the execution of a script. The script implements the sequence of actions performed by the information-processing node. The script gives the information-processing node its behavior and defines its current role that it plays at that moment in the larger information-processing network. Whether a given information-processing node such as a person actually does have a component like a physical symbol system is irrelevant to our use of it as a modeling device.

Part 2

Modeling the Real World

Introduction to Part 2

THIS SECOND PART OF THE BOOK presents the modeling tools we will use to model the enterprise. The modeling tools we use will be capable of modeling any general system:

- ◆ Chapter 5 introduces the object-oriented paradigm. This will give us a very powerful tool, that of object-oriented modeling. While the object-oriented paradigm was originally conceived for software development, its ideas and methods can be extended to the domain of enterprise modeling.

- ◆ Chapter 6 introduces the subject of conceptual modeling; in particular, the conceptual type hierarchy, a tool that is used to structure the concepts of any modeling domain and thus can be applied to the domain of the enterprise. We will use conceptual modeling and the conceptual type hierarchy to define how the world, and especially the enterprise, really is. By basing our object-oriented class hierarchy on the conceptual type hierarchy. we will have a very solid foundation for defining the enterprise as a hierarchy of interacting objects.

◆ Chapter 7 focuses on one of the most important branches of the conceptual type hierarchy: the conceptual process and its subtypes. We will use the concept of the process extensively in enterprise modeling and this chapter explores its various characteristics.

◆ Chapter 8 presents an overview of object-oriented modeling. This will give us the vocabulary and concepts for discussing the enterprise as a system of objects for the remainder of the book. We will describe our two major abstract object classes: the abstract entity class and the abstract process class. We will also discuss object relations and describe a useful modeling tool, the class-relations diagram.

◆ Chapter 9 integrates the problem domain presented in the first part of the book and the modeling techniques of the second part of the book into a coherent whole. If we are to have a solid foundation to object-oriented enterprise modeling, we must be able map the theoretical underpinnings of the enterprise as a rather specialized general system to appropriate object-oriented modeling constructs. In this chapter, we will present a survey of these theoretical underpinnings of the enterprise, and then we will summarize the object-oriented modeling constructs that will be used to model them and comment on the implication of each theoretical underpinning to enterprise modeling in general.

Chapter 5

The Object-Oriented Paradigm

5.1 Introduction

In the preceding chapters, we discussed our first major formalism for enterprise modeling, the general system. We discussed its general characteristics, its organization as a hierarchical-multilayer system, and its special form as an information processing network made up of information-processing nodes. Each of those chapters presented another aspect of the enterprise considered as a general system.

This chapter introduces our second major formalism for enterprise modeling, that of the object-oriented paradigm. What is the object-oriented paradigm? In the words of Phil Sully, "An object-oriented approach is one in which we take the viewpoint that encourages the recognition of objects" (Sully, 1993). We will be using the object-oriented paradigm as a device to help us build models of real world domains, in our case the enterprise.

In this chapter, we will not regard objects in their traditional role as software structures but as a natural way to view the world. We focus on the properties of objects which make them ideal for real-world modeling.

5.2 The object-oriented paradigm

Using the object-oriented paradigm is very natural to us. Recognizing objects is what we human beings do anyway as we lead our daily lives. We will see in this section that the object-oriented paradigm takes advantage of a very natural mechanism that is built into all of us.

Episodic and semantic memory

We humans have a large database located at the upper end of our spinal cord. In this database we store information about the external world. In short, we have a state memory. John Sowa and others have classified these memories into two types: episodic and semantic (Sowa, 1984). We use episodic memory to store facts about entities and events in the real world and their relations. These are our memories of the mundane. Right now, my episodic memory contains such facts as *Outside, it's raining; my cat's name is Gracie; I have a meeting tomorrow.*

On the other hand, we use our semantic memory to store principles that we and others consider to be universal. These are our memories of laws, theories, and concepts. In my semantic memory, I store such universal principles as *All cats are animals; Diskettes are designed to hold digitalized data; matter falls to the earth when dropped.* According to John Sowa, "Semantic memory corresponds to dictionary definitions, and episodic memory corresponds to history and biography" (Sowa, 1984).

Intension and extension

These two categories of memory, episodic and semantic, relate directly to language and words. Words are encoded symbol sequences that are used by our brains to store and retrieve memories. Recall that we humans are information-processing nodes embedded in information-processing networks as explained in Chapter 4.

Any word in our memory has two aspects to its meaning, one episodic aspect and the other semantic. The episodic aspect of a word is called its *extension.* This is the set of all things to which the word applies. Thus my extension for the word *cat* includes all the cats I have known, such as my cat Gracie, my neighbor's cat Boris, or the cat I saw crossing the street yesterday. The semantic aspect of a word is called its *intension* and relates to its definition. Thus, my intension of the word *cat* is a small carnivorous, warm-blooded, furry animal that has a backbone, secretes milk to nourish its young, and spends a lot of time purring and sleeping.

How do we humans use intensions and extensions? We humans continually observe the external world, noting the various entities present in it. We continually look for how the entities in our world are similar or different. We then propose to ourselves that a given set of entities seems to share common properties. Alternatively, we are taught by our parents and teachers or we read that a given set of entities shares common properties; thus we don't personally have to discover it. Either way, we isolate those common properties into a definition that represents the common semantic aspects of the set of entities in question. We continually test and validate these generalizations of the common semantic aspects perfecting our emerging definition. In effect, we are establishing our intension of the entities in question relating to their common definition. Once we have a good definition of the set of entities in question, as we go through life we are able to classify new entities we encounter as being an example of the entity or not. In effect, we are expanding our *extension* of the entities to include the new examples we continually encounter in our daily living.

The world is made of objects

The formulation of the intension and extension of a set of entities is a natural mechanism of our thinking process as human beings. In the object-oriented paradigm, we will be using this concept to define objects. We will use the word *object* as a more down-to-earth concept when we discuss modeling. In other words, the formulation of the intension and extension of a set of entities is part of our fundamental human thinking skills, but the definition of an object is a mechanism we invoke in modeling. The point is that the definition of objects depends on that human mental capability of formulating the intension and extension of a set of entities. As such, object-oriented modeling is founded on natural human mental skills.

There are really two conceptual stages to object-oriented modeling: the first is to regard the world as being made up of objects; the second is to classify these objects into similar concepts by looking for their common characteristics. In a nutshell, the process of modeling a complex environment is nothing more than the process of decomposing that environment into a collection of objects. Stated another way, any domain we are modeling will be made up of objects, and the domain can be completely specified by the objects that make it up. In effect, the whole is made up of the sum of its parts.

Once we have a set of objects, we can look for their common characteristics. For every group of objects with common properties, we can define their intension by synthesizing their characteristics into a single concept and giving it a name. The naming of the concept, the act of formalizing the intension of the collection of similar objects, is a great boon to modeling. From then on, we can use the name of the concept as a shorthand way of referring to the underlying objects. When we discuss one of these objects, we don't have to keep restating its list of characteristics. In object-oriented terminology, we call the intension of a set of similar objects its *class*. We will return to the discussion of class in a later section. For now, we want to think about the basic idea of object.

Object identification

Objects have reality in the domain we are modeling. Our fundamental mental process of defining the intension and extension of a target set of entities helps us define objects with crisp boundaries. We define an object and its boundary with the rest of its domain by observing, comparing, and fine-tuning our concept of that object.

Objects in the modeling domain can have physical reality or abstract reality. Physical objects are the easiest to identify and define as all we need to do is look for physical things in the modeling domain. In an enterprise, they include the buildings, machines, documents, or people, all examples of physical objects. Abstract objects do not have physical reality but nevertheless are part of the domain being modeled. Grady Booch describes them as "something that may be apprehended intellectually. . . . Something towards which thought or action is directed" (Booch, 1991). In an enterprise, examples of abstract objects would be events (e.g., a delivery), interactions (e.g., a contract between two legal entities), or roles (e.g., a machine operator). We can see that abstract objects are every bit as real to the domain as physical objects.

Notice that in selecting the objects of the modeling domain, we are very selective about which objects are actually chosen for our analysis. Some of the objects will not make the final cut because they aren't really important to our analysis. How do we know which objects lying around the domain are important and which ones aren't? We are using abstraction here. Recall that abstraction means drawing out the essence of a domain. Thus as modelers, we depend on our abstraction skills to choose the objects of the domain we consider to be important.

5.3 Describing objects: Properties

Once we have selected an object from the modeling domain, we define its characteristics. Here again we use modeling and abstraction. David Taylor has pointed out that an object is itself a model of a target entity taken from reality. For example, a customer object is a model of a customer. It is an abstraction of a customer that has the essential properties of a customer (Taylor, 1994). In other words, in defining an object we are, in effect, choosing a subset of all the possible characteristics that an object might have. The subset of characteristics we use to define our target object are the ones we consider to be important for the purposes of our analysis. How do we describe these essential characteristics? We use the word *property,* which we will discuss in this section.

Abstracting object properties

An object has intrinsic properties, which are the superset of its definition. We abstract some of these intrinsic properties to serve as our definition of the intension of the object. Wand and Woo put it this way: "Properties are intrinsic to a thing (object), that is, the thing possesses the properties whether we know about them or not" (Wand and Woo, 1991). Another aspect of properties is that we as analysts assign them to the object. In effect, the object does not "know" that it has a given property. The analyst discovers and assigns the properties to the object. Wand puts it this way: "Properties do not exist on their own but are 'attached' to entities (objects)." (Wand, 1989).

The implication is that we can choose many different properties to define the object in question and that we purposefully select a limited subset appropriate to our analysis to make our analysis efficient and economical. We use this limited subset first to define the intension of our set of objects, that is, the defining set of characteristics all objects like that have in common. We later use this limited subset of properties as a filter to see if a given object we have encountered in the domain is a member of the extension of the objects, that is, the set of objects each of which has those common characteristics. In the words of Subodh Bapat, "The process of abstraction 'draws a line' around the object—it delimits it by enclosing it in a crisply defined conceptual boundary . . . inside the boundary are those *essential characteristics* of the object which—from the perspective of the application domain—make it different from every other object" (Bapat, 1994).

We choose the subset of characteristics that define a given object in our analysis by paying attention to our purpose in modeling the domain in the first place. A given object could be the subject of more than one modeling project, each having its own methodologies, concepts, and principles. In this case, each modeling project would probably select a different set of characteristics to define the same object. For example, the object representing "John Smith" would have a different set of characteristics if modeled by the discipline of accounting (e.g., "John Smith" as a customer) versus the discipline of psychology (e.g., "John Smith" as a person). Subodh Bapat comments that abstraction "is like a pair of blinders we purposely choose to use to limit our vision of the universe. There is no single correct abstraction—different application domains may abstract the same object in different ways, because the crucial aspects of interest may be different. . . . A correctly defined abstraction allows the same object model to be reused in various ways" (Bapat, 1994).

Figure 5.1 shows an example of how several different modeling disciplines would analyze and define their own abstractions of a target object. Each abstraction represents a different collection of properties and thus, a different view of the object. Each serves a different modeling client, each of whom is analyzing the object. Modelers measure the efficiency of an abstraction by the number of modeling clients it can serve. However, no single abstraction can serve all clients because a given client would have to contend with too many confusing and unneeded properties outside of their discipline, detracting from their individual effort.

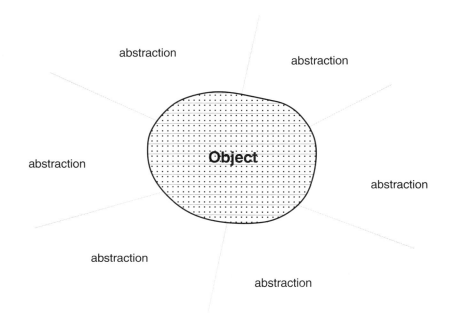

Figure 5.1 *Abstraction views of an object.*

Properties: State and behavioral

In describing an object in terms of its properties, two different types of properties emerge: state properties and behavioral properties. State properties describe both the structure of an object as well as its characteristics at a point in time. Here we are using an extended idea of *structure* as the description of the object. Structural properties of an object describe its relations with other objects. Also, the state properties describe the characteristics of the object, that is, its traits and qualities. The reason we notice the object in the first place is because of its state properties, both structural and descriptive.

On the other hand, behavioral properties define what it does, the dynamic aspect of an object. John W. Sutherland describes it this way: "Hence, on the behavioral dimension we speak in terms of purpose, work, change achievement, process . . . in short dynamic concepts" (Sutherland, 1975).

Together the state and behavioral properties of an object completely define the object from a modeling standpoint. In other words, to analysts contemplating an object, only its state and behavior are of interest. Any object will, more or less, have state properties and behavioral properties. If we have done our job as modelers, these properties will be the very reason an object is part of the system in the first place. That is, the properties we abstract of an object provide the system with needed capabilities or necessary characteristics to make the system achieve its objectives. In the following sections, we will clarify how state and behavior are defined in the object-oriented paradigm. In particular, we will define object behavior as the changing of the object's state over time.

Definition: Attribute

Let's first discuss the state properties. We'll discuss the behavior properties in a moment. State properties of an object make themselves known through their attributes. They represent potential capability while attributes represent the instantiation of the property in reality. For example, weight is a typical state property. Its specific values at a point in time is its attribute. Wand distinguishes the terms *property* and *attribute* as follows: "An individual (object). may have a (state). property that is unknown to us. In contrast, an attribute is a feature assigned by us to an object." According to Wand, we recognize a property because we assign an attribute to it. In other words, any property must have at least one attribute representing it (Wand, 1989).

We now have a more precise definition of the term *state*: in an object, each attribute has a value at each point in time. The state of an object at a point in time is the set of these attribute values at that point in time.

Wand and Woo conclude: "Attributes are characteristics assigned to things (i.e., objects). by humans. . . . For example, we attribute color (i.e., an attribute). to objects, however, the real property is the ability of the object to reflect certain wavelengths of electromagnetic radiation . . . for simplicity, we will assume that some attributes we assign to things represent observable properties. . . . Also, only some of the properties of a thing are of interest in a given context" (Wand and Woo, 1991).

Definition: Behavior

Next, let's discuss the behavioral property. Behavior of an object is closely related to state. In the words of Wand and Woo: "The *behavior* of a thing (object). in a given time interval is the ordered set of states that it traverses in this interval" (Wand and Woo, 1991).

Therefore, we define the behavior of an object empirically in terms of results. This definition of the behavior of an object is not unlike the definition of the behavioral view of the general system presented in Chapter 2. The object goes through various state changes as it pursues its objectives. Wand and Woo make an important observation about the limitations of these state changes using the idea of regularity: ". . . things do not behave arbitrarily, but according to some *law of behavior*. Without external stimuli, a thing will change its state if, and only if, there exists a transition to another state" (Wand and Woo, 1991).

Notice that we are not yet defining behavior as the workings of mechanisms of the object. This will be covered further on in the book. Rather we are defining behavior in terms of the change of the state of the object. Later, we will see that an object's behavior is implemented by mechanisms of the object, which we call object *services*.

State as system structure

As pointed out earlier, the state properties of an object can be both descriptive and structural. Let's focus on these structural properties for a moment. Structural properties of an object define how the object is made up. In the words of Subodh Bapat, "Any system of reasonable complexity is almost always an assembly of simpler components" (Bapat, 1994). We determine the structural properties of an object by decomposing it into its constituent parts. We then determine the relationships of these structural parts to each other. The parts of the object that are revealed by this decomposition are themselves objects. Thus the structural properties of an object consist of not only decomposed parts revealing yet other objects that can be further decomposed but the relationships among all of these decomposed objects.

We can conclude that the structure of an object is its predominant state at a point in time. Most objects change structurally over time. For example, if we decompose an object at two different points in time, we will probably see different configurations of the sub-objects that make up the object. The sub-objects may be created, distributed differently, or destroyed over time or the relationships among the sub-objects or the sub-objects and the object itself may change over time. Hence, the structure of an object at a point in time is the major manifestation of its state. If the structure of the object does change over time, then the behavior of the object "may be assumed to vary either as a function of the variances in inputs, or as a function of structural changes that have taken place during the sampling interval" (Sutherland, 1975). Accordingly, if the structure of the object does not change over time, then the "outputs are assumed to alter only as inputs alter " (Sutherland, 1975). The tip-off to object behavior is to look for a change in its structure.

5.4 Objects as encapsulations

Abstraction of a target domain as a system of objects is the basic modeling tool of many different disciplines. We perform this act of object abstraction from many different perspectives depending on if we are designing, investigating, or just using the domain. For example, if we are engineers designing a system, we use abstraction to endow the objects of our system with certain capabilities. If we are scientists investigating a domain, we use abstraction to simplify the domain of objects so that we can make predictions about it. If we are active participants in a domain (i.e., we live in it), we use object abstraction as an adaptation tool, considering the pragmatic limitations of achieving complete knowledge of the domain as we move through it. In each case, we identify objects in our domain and then abstract their essential properties. We make our objects well rounded and complete. In this section, we will discuss this process of isolating and identifying the capabilities of the objects of our domain, a process we call object *encapsulation*.

Isolating objects

When we abstract essential properties to define an object, we are picking a subset of the properties to include in our definition. To define our object, we have, in effect, drawn a line around it using what Subodh Bapat calls an *abstraction barrier* (Bapat, 1994). The abstraction barrier separates the essential properties of the object from the nonessential properties. It also simplifies the modeling project. Since no model can possibly capture the complete definition of an object, we select a set of properties considering the trade-off of accuracy in portraying the object versus the efficiency of modeling that domain. Isolating objects is primarily a mental skill.

Once we have defined an object, the question becomes one of how the object participates in the larger system. Let's take the example of engineering a new system such as an enterprise. The system will have a purpose—it must produce something or it won't exist for long. The component objects will accomplish the purpose of the larger system. As engineers, we must endow the component objects with the correct capabilities to produce the output of the system. Sounds simple, right? Wrong! In complex systems consisting of thousands of objects, we quickly lose sight of the overall purpose of the larger system as we design its thousands of constituent objects.

Once we identify an object for our system, we are faced with the difficult decision of going ahead and decomposing it into its component objects or just going on to the next object of our system. We know that once we go to that lower level of detail, we may lose our global view because it is difficult to hold both the detail view of individual objects and the global view of the system in our minds at the same time. We fear that when we are designing that lower level, we will inadvertently commit the overall system to inefficiencies that we do not recognize because of no longer having the global view. We must face this dilemma at any level of decomposition: the need for detailed design versus the need for understanding the overall system.

Definition: Encapsulation

We have a way of dealing with this dilemma. It is called *encapsulation*. We use encapsulation during design as a means to decouple the external use of the object from the object itself. In effect, the object is a black box that hides its internals from the outside world. Stephen Montgomery puts it this way: "Encapsulation provides a conceptual barrier around an object, preventing clients of an object from viewing its internal details" (Montgomery, 1994). The clients of an object are those who need to use it. For example, during system design, the clients are the designers of the larger system who need to incorporate the capabilities of an object into the larger system. On the other hand, during system operation, clients are the other objects of the system that need the capabilities of the object. The point of encapsulation is to limit the knowledge that these clients must have of the target object and make objects independent, stand-alone units.

What is actually encapsulated when we regard an object as a black box? It's the state of the object. The principle of encapsulated state is that a client object can never directly change the state of an object. Alan Snyder makes the point: "By preventing direct client contact with (state), you guarantee that objects satisfy certain integrity constraints. You can also insure that clients will not be affected by changes to object implementations" (Snyder, 1993).

Subodh Bapat describes encapsulation in terms of abstraction: "Encapsulation and abstraction, therefore, complement each other and together provide a powerful mechanism for specifying objects in our problem domain correctly and *orthogonally*—that is, ensuring that objects are defined to be as independent of other objects as possible" (Bapat, 1994).

Encapsulation is an engineering principle

The use of encapsulation is not new with the object-oriented paradigm and has always been a foundation principle of engineering. Engineers have always known that hiding the internal parts of objects is good engineering practice because it makes each object independent of the other objects in the system. Dependencies among objects are bad. Typically, various independent teams design the objects in a complex engineering domain (e.g., a Boeing 747). Each team produces the detailed internal design of their objects. However, client engineers working on other parts of the engineering domain regard these objects as black boxes.

In this way, the act of using any of the objects in the engineering domain does not depend on anything inside these objects. An object is a black box that provides a well-defined interface to its well-defined capabilities. An object is a reusable structure because a potential use depends only on having knowledge of its interfaces, how it is used. Therefore, a potential use of an object depends only on matching the requirements with the well-defined capabilities of the object. Once a local engineer identifies an object from the larger domain, meeting his or her needs, it is easy to integrate the object in the local design by designing the use scenario to the well-defined interface of the object.

Encapsulation also aids the engineer in another way, by making top-down design possible. Top-down design is a way of overcoming complexity in which the engineer defines the capabilities of an object from its external viewpoint. The engineer designs a system by specifying objects that he or she may not understand internally but does understand externally because of the object's well-defined external capabilities. In a later phase of the project, another engineering team will perform the actual internal design of these objects and then the team of engineers expert in that type of object will perform the internal design of them. They would work with the external definition of these objects to perform the internal design of them. Designing objects by defining their use is a point we will return to in a moment.

Object interface

We see from the preceding discussion that the interface to an object is all important. The responsibility of an object's interface is to encapsulate the object, to protect its internal state from the outside world. An object's interface must be selective and allow only certain inputs. John Sutherland describes the requirements of an interface in terms of integrity: An object "must be bounded in some way, having a perimeter which serves to define the domain of the system (object). Exogenous or external forces must pass through this perimeter to influence the (object's). structure or behavior. . . . In a sense, then, interface selectivity refers to the (object's). regulation of its interchanges with external entities" (Sutherland, 1975).

Thus the only way we can use an object is through its interface. The interface of an object can be an actual physical component of the object or just a modeling construct—an artificial boundary we impose and honor. A physical interface is fairly easy to understand. For example, every machine object has an interface implemented by physical components. An example of an interface implemented by physical components would be the various buttons which control a photostat-copy machine. On the other hand, the interface to an object may be a modeling construct. In this case, we are using the idea of an interface to model an object although the object does not really have a physical interface. An example of this type of interface would be a financial account object that is updated with debit and credit transactions. In this case, there are no physical buttons, but nevertheless, the account object must present an interface with the outside world to allow itself to be used and to protect itself.

As engineers, we incorporate existing objects (i.e., that have already been designed or actually exist) into our own design by designing into our target object the use-scenario to these existing objects. Thus to use an encapsulated object designed by another engineering team in our own design, all we have to do is follow the directions specified in its public interface. These directions to the public interface will specify the scenario about how we interact with the object to use it. That's all we have to know about it. As Steven Kim put it, "the interface of a system (object). relates to observable characteristics, whether in terms of physical or intangible qualities. In contrast, the interior aspect of the system (object).—its hidden components—refers to the mechanisms and processing requirements needed to support the interface" (Kim, 1990).

According to Steven Kim, the internals of an object exist to satisfy the demands from the outside world made through its interface. We can use this idea to design the object in the first place. In this view, the uses of an object completely define the object: we design our objects by defining the potential uses of them. Ivar Jacobson has formalized this idea and coined the term *use-cases* to describe the use-scenarios of an object. According to Jacobson, use-cases both encapsulate an object and serve as a mechanism for designing the object in the first place (Jacobson, 1992). We will return to this topic later in the book.

In Chapter 8, we will introduce the concept of system constraints. For now, we have an intuitive idea of constraints as the limitations placed on the accessing or operation of an object. We can note here that the major source of constraints is the interface of an object. The interface of an object constrains the access to the object. The level of constraint can be very restrictive or very flexible, in turn effecting the integrity of the object. The interface defines the level of flexibility in using the object. Restricting the interface makes the system less flexible but safer. Relaxing the interface makes the system more flexible but exposes its integrity.

Services

We mentioned earlier in this chapter that one of the ways of defining an object is through its behavior (the other being its state). We see from the preceding discussion that an object must hide the control or activation of its behavior behind its boundary of encapsulation. Behavior results in state changes in the object. Without a corresponding state change, we as observers wouldn't be able to detect behavior, nor would we care. The outside world stimulates an object via its interface, causing the corresponding behavior of an object.

As a modeling device, we can think of the behavior of an object as being implemented by what we will call *services*. A service is an individual "chunk" of behavior of the object. Firesmith describes services as a "discrete activity, action, or behavior performed by an object" (Firesmith, 1992). A service of an object receives input and, using the current state of the object, produces output coupled with a corre-

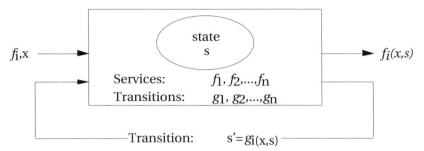

Figure 5.2 *Object services.*

sponding state change in the object. Figure 5.2 adapted from (Wegner, 1989). shows the way object services are modeled:

- In the figure, $f_1, f_2, \ldots, f_n$ are the set of services of the object; the potential user of the object would choose among these services. In the next section, we will describe the requesting of a service in terms of passing a message to the object. However, for now we will not worry about how a service is requested, rather we want to focus on the service itself. When a service is requested, the environment of the object is defined by x and can be thought of as input to the completion of the service. In its most simple form, x represents important properties of the environment that will affect the completion of the service. A more sophisticated form of x is that it is actually information provided by the requester of the service. In this case the requester provides a physical symbol sequence indicated by x in the diagram. In this case, the physical symbol sequence associated with a service represents information that the service will use to complete its operation. Either way, as important attributes of the environment or as actual information, we say that a service, f_i, has operands indicated by x.

- A service of an object is just an abstract function: an input operand x produces an output $f(x)$. The output $f(x)$ could be an information physical symbol sequence, but it is not limited to that. The output $f(x)$ could take the form of the object doing something useful or affecting the environment of the object in some way.

- However, unlike the simple abstract function, a service of an object has a side effect because of the internal state S of the object. The input operands, indicated by x, do not completely determine the effect of a service such as f_i. With an object, the effect of the service, f_i, depends on the internal state S in addition to the operands, x. Therefore, we use an s to represent the collective values of the internal state S and we say that a service such as f_i produces a useful output indicated by $f_i(x,s)$. The state indicated by s is an additional operand input to the function f_i.

♦ While the internal state S participates as an additional input to the services, such as f_i, it is also affected by them in the output sense of undergoing its own change as a side effect. We call this a *state transition,* which was introduced in Chapter 1 and discussed earlier in this chapter. To account for these state transitions, we see in the object model shown in Figure 5.2 a second series of functions, $g_1, g_2, \ldots, g_n$. These represent the state transition functions. In the model, a given service f_i has an associated state transition function g_i. The operation of a state transition function such as g_i depends on the old state s and the input operands x to produce a new state s'. We would then write $s'=g_i(x,s)$.

♦ To summarize, the user of the object selects a service f_i and directly or indirectly provides its input operands indicated by x. At that moment, the object has an internal state S represented by a collection of values shown as s. The user gets back $f_i(x,s)$, which is either actual information or a useful action or merely a change in the environment. As a side effect, the service f_i causes the state of the object to change using its associated state transition function g_i. Thus an additional output from the object besides $f_i(x,s)$ is a new state $s'=g_i(x,s)$.

Using these ideas, we can now model the interface to an object using the succinct concept of services. Also, we can model the internal behavior—its private business—in terms of services. These services originate inside the object rather than from the outside environment of the object. We conclude that we can define the total behavior of an object formally in terms of services whether they are requested from the outside or the inside of the object. Figure 5.3 shows our emerging view of a generic object as a state protected by its interface, which is made up of services.

Message passing

In the real world, objects interact with each other, causing the dynamics of a system. This is how the potential dynamics of a system becomes reality—by the interaction of its objects. As we saw earlier, the objects of the real world interact with one another through their interfaces and the invocation of service. However, the interaction of objects has a much deeper meaning—it is cause and effect, or simply causality. The theoretical physicist David Bohm describes the causality paradigm which is the foundation of our scientific tradition: "Any external disturbance

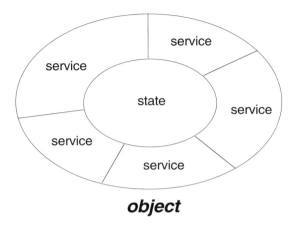

object

Figure 5.3 *Generic object.*

can be treated as a *cause*, which produces a specifiable *effect* that can in principle be propagated to every part of the system" (Bohm, 1980). In modeling the real world, we need a way of expressing these cause and effect dynamics. David Taylor describes it this way: "Real-world objects can exhibit an infinite variety of effects on each other—creating, destroying, lifting, attaching, buying, bending, sending, and so on. This tremendous variety raises an interesting problem—how can all of these different kinds of interactions be represented (in modeling)" (Taylor, 1990). The object-oriented paradigm presents a very elegant way of modeling causality called *message passing*.

We model the causality of the world by saying that an object sends a message to another object (see Figure 5.4). The sending object sends a message to the interface of the receiving objects, which then causes the receiving object to invoke a service and possibly undergo a state change. We saw earlier that a useful way to model this effect is to consider the behavior of the object as being implemented by a service expressed as a mathematical function such as "$y=f(x,s)$." Then message passing becomes the invocation of a function of the object.

The interface of an object receives these passed messages. Adele Goldberg characterizes an interface as three separate concepts that combine to form the overall concept of an interface. First, an interface is like a language. That is, there is a need for a formal definition of the grammar and vocabulary used in the messages to communicate with an object. We usually call this interface language a *protocol*. Second, an interface is an edge. It is a common boundary between the environment and the object in question. Third, an interface is a broker. Its enables an external system to select and properly access the internals of the objects

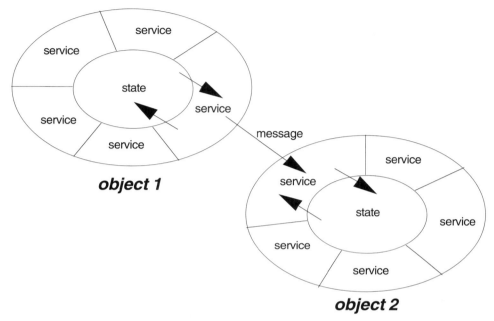

Figure 5.4 *Relationship between services, states, and messages.*

(Goldberg, 1994). When we describe the interface of an object, we will be using these three concepts of interface.

    Message passing can be literally true or merely a useful modeling device. The message could actually be information passed from one physical object to another, that is, a symbol sequence implemented by physical signals on a communication channel. For example, a customer object could send a message to a vendor object to purchase a product. In this case, there is an actual communication message. Alternatively, we could use the message to model the cause and effect between objects. For example, turning off a light could be modeled as sending a message from the light switch object to the lamp object to turn itself off. In this case, we are using the message as a way of identifying cause and effect without actually having to explain how.

Services as scripts
Chapter 4 introduced scripts as a modeling device to define a sequence of actions performed by a physical symbol system. The services of objects also perform sequences of actions and thus can be modeled using scripts. That is, the engineer

who designs an object can use the script as a way to model and document the internal actions of the object. In this way, the script of a service would specify the sequence of internal actions that the object would perform to discharge the service. The script that models a service can be thought of as being invoked by the message passed to the object to request the service. We will return to this in a later chapter.

Properties as state versus properties as process

One important use of a service is to ask the object to reveal one of its properties. We must always ask the object because it is a black box inside of which we as observers have no right to look. When we ask an object to reveal one of its properties via a service, we have no idea as to how it actually accomplishes the service. A service of an object that reveals a property can discharge its duties by either directly revealing the property or by invoking an internal service that derives the property.

The state of an object at a point in time is the accumulation of its behavior over time. For example, an account object maintains the property "balance." The account object could continually calculate the balance over time as part of the behavior of debit and credit events. Alternatively, the account object could calculate the balance from the various debit and credit events kept as objects associated with the balance object. In other words, when an account object is asked for its balance, the requester has no idea just how the request will be accomplished.

5.5 Object classes

In the first section of this chapter we introduced the idea of *intension* and *extension* of a set of objects. We saw that intension is our natural human mental skill of realizing that a set of objects has similar properties, thus examples of the same concept. On the other hand, *extension* is our natural human mental skill of categorizing an object as a member of an extension or not. The object-oriented paradigm incorporates these concepts and uses these natural human skills. In this section, we will focus on the definition of the intension of a set of objects that we will call the object's *class*.

Classification

We classify objects into named concepts based on the properties of the objects. The result of this classification process is the object's *class*. Dillon and Tan define object class as follows: "A class is a description of several objects that have similar characteristics" (Dillon and Tan, 1993). Thus the class of an object is the object-oriented modeling term we use for the intension of the set of entities.

Brent Work and Ann Balmforth put it this way: "Classification is a form of abstraction which allows a relationship among individual things, all of which have the same type of properties, to be thought of as a thing in its own right—a thing called a class. Once the class of an object is determined, then it can be assumed that the object will have specific properties which can be used (Work and Balmforth, 1993).

In classifying objects, we must give a name to the class of the objects. Then we can use that name when referring to the collective properties of the class. Work and Balmforth refer to the act of naming as the most fundamental abstraction. They state that "naming then is an abstraction which represents the relationship between a thing and a sign which signifies the thing" (Work and Balmforth, 1993).

In classifying a set of objects, we are doing more than matching the properties of a prospective object to our definition of the class. We saw in the earlier sections of this chapter that the properties of an object include both state properties and behavioral properties. Assigning an object to a class goes beyond merely matching its properties to the class definition. According to Subodh Bapat, "The notion of class . . . goes beyond structural and behavioral similarities into the realm of a common 'teleology'—all objects in a class have the same 'purpose'" (Bapat, 1994).

There is really no right way to classify a set of objects. As modelers we must select a classification scheme that matches the requirements of our modeling project. Once again, we see that there is no magic button that we can push and that our mental skill of synthesis coupled with good judgment are all important.

We see that a class is an implementation concept to make the implementation of a system easier by reusing concepts. On the other hand, an object is a modeling concept. It identifies an entity from the real world which we want to evaluate as a whole.

Generalization and specialization

Once we have defined a class for a set of objects, we have gone to a lot of trouble of identifying the various properties of those objects. Is there a way of reusing this intellectual work we have already performed? There is! We humans have a special mental skill to effect this reusability: *specialization* and *generalization*.

Specialization is a way of defining a new class in terms of one we have already gone to the trouble of defining. All we have to do is define how the new class is different from the original class. In this way we can reuse the intellectual concept of the original class in our new class. Figure 5.5 shows the efficiency of specialization, that is, defining a new class in terms of an existing class. In the figure, we have already gone to the trouble of defining Class 1 and have identified its properties labeled Property 1.1 and Property 1.2 in the figure. We can use this definition of Class 1 to define a new Class 2. We use all of the properties of Class 1 but add a new property labeled Property 2.1 in the figure.

The opposite of specialization is generalization. *Generalization* means synthesizing the common properties of lower-level classes into a higher-level abstraction. We use the terms *subclass* and *superclass* to describe these relationships. Thus in Figure 5.5, Class 1 is a superclass of Class 2 and Class 2 is a subclass of Class 1. Subodh Bapat makes the point that superclasses are simpler than subclasses: ". . . superclasses have fewer properties than subclasses, and actually represent a more primitive form of evolution" (Bapat, 1994). This leads to the idea of an inheritance hierarchy.

Inheritance hierarchies

The process of using specialization and generalization to define new classes shows that the modeler can arrange the classes in a hierarchy. An inheritance hierarchy is a very useful modeling tool. It gives us a road map to the properties of the classes we have defined in our modeling domain. A class near the top of the hierarchy will have common properties shared by all the classes under it. A class near the bottom of the hierarchy will have its own unique properties in addition to the common ones.

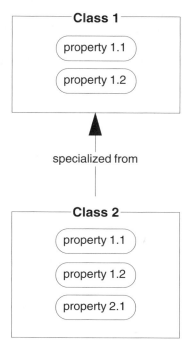

Figure 5.5 *Specialization of Class 2 from Class 1.*

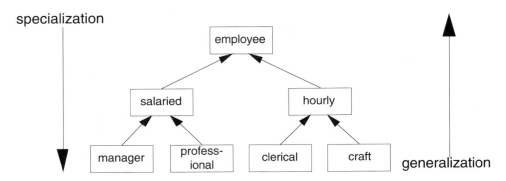

Figure 5.6 *Inheritance hierarchy.*

Figure 5.6 defines the employee hierarchy. When we use the term *craft employee,* we know we are talking about, first, one of our employees and, second, an hourly employee. In other words, "craft employee" inherits all the properties of "hourly-employee" as well as the "general employee" at the top of the class hierarchy. We see Subodh Bapat's point that a subclass is a more advanced form in the object hierarchy: "Subclasses are more complicated than their superclasses in terms of structure and more sophisticated in terms of function" (Bapat, 1994).

The inheritance hierarchy also will be an aid to abstraction. For example, in the preceding hierarchy, we can refer to "employee" as an abstraction of, say, "craft employee." The class "employee" captures the primitive characteristics of any employee in the domain and thus, we could use it anywhere in our model when we are analyzing employees. Any lower-level class of employee will have at least these properties. For example, we could substitute the class "employee" anywhere we use the class "craft-employee." As Subodh Bapat says, a superclass can always be safely used in any context in which an instance of the subclass is expected (Bapat, 1994).

Class libraries

We can place the classes of a modeling domain in a library to enhance their reusability as a design tool. We would arrange the library as a specialization/generalization hierarchy and document each class of the library with a focus on the following:

◆ Interface

◆ State properties

◆ Behavioral properties

For example, the class library would document the employee class hierarchy as follows:

Employee

Salaried Employee

Manager

Nonmanager

Hourly Employee

Clerical

Craft

Instantiation

Once we have defined a class, to use it we need to create some specific examples of that class. In the object-oriented paradigm, we call this *instantiation*. Instantiation creates the set of real objects that make up the extension of the class. In modeling, instantiation allows us to reuse the meaning of a class by declaring in our model specific examples of the class. In this way we can reuse the concept of the class without having to invent our own proprietary version of it. It's similar to buying a product out of a catalog. The object is called an *instance* of the class. An instance has its own identity that is different from the other instances of the same class. The instance will have its own existence that will take the form of evolving states through time as measured by the values of its attributes.

Generally, only the classes at or near the bottom of the class hierarchy are used to instantiate objects. Thus in Figure 5.6, the class "employee" would never be used to create an instance since the much more definitive "manager," "professional," "clerical," or "craft" are available. For this reason, we call a high-level class such as the "employee" class an *abstract class* because the primary use is in organizing and clarifying the concept of employee.

5.6 Conclusion

This chapter presented an introduction to the object-oriented paradigm. The object-oriented paradigm regards the world as being made up of objects—an object being an entity of the world we choose to regard as a whole. We construct a model by decomposing our domain of interest into objects. How do we identify and describe objects in our modeling domain? A given object has intrinsic properties some of which we use in our definition of it. There are two types of properties of an object: state properties and behavior properties. State properties describe the structure and qualities of an object at a point in time. Behavioral properties describe what the object does—its dynamic aspects. State properties make themselves known through their attributes—the actual values of the property at a point in time. Behavioral properties of an object are defined in terms of changes in its state attributes—we can't see a behavior property until something changes in the object.

In this chapter, we introduced the concept of object encapsulation. In addition to being a modeling discipline, encapsulation also captures the essence of an object. Encapsulation has two aspects: first, the state of an object is internal to the object and private to it; second, an object's state is changed only by the object itself through its behavior. The behavior of an object can be thought of as being implemented by a collection of services which are part of the object.

A given modeling domain is made up of objects that interact with each other. We can model object interaction as message passing between the objects. Both the services that implement the object's behavior and the messages that are passed between objects are really modeling devices—useful constructs invented to help us portray a complex world. These modeling devices of message passing and services portray exactly the way real world objects interact with each other. The services of an object cause the changes in its state. In this view, services are mechanisms. However, this, too, is just a modeling device. Whether a given real-world object has internal mechanisms that actually change its state is irrelevant to our use of these properties to model the object.

Finally, in this chapter we introduced object classes. An object class is a modeling device to classify various objects into a named concept. An object class is a generalization of a set of object properties. Every object that belongs to an object class has at least that set of object properties. In other words, we can use the class name when referring to the set of properties defining the class. Object classes can be arranged in an inheritance hierarchy. Object classes near the top of the inheritance hierarchy have fewer object properties, while object classes near the bottom have more object properties. Lower-level classes inherit all of the properties of the classes above them and can add properties of their own or change some of them. By arranging the object classes into an inheritance hierarchy, we have a road map of the properties of the classes we have defined in our modeling domain.

We readily see that we can use the object-oriented paradigm to model the enterprise. The enterprise is a set of business objects that interact with each other. To model the enterprise, we would isolate its objects and identify their properties. Then we would generalize these objects into a set of object classes that we would arrange into an object class-inheritance hierarchy. Our inheritance hierarchy would then be used to build a model of the enterprise.

Chapter 6

Conceptual Modeling

6.1 Introduction

In Chapter 5, we introduced the object-oriented paradigm and asserted that the world is made of objects. Since the enterprise is part of the world, it, too, must be made of objects. This means that a model of the enterprise should be developed and documented in terms of the object-oriented paradigm. We will devote the remainder of this book to stating how this requirement can be achieved.

However, before we continue our definition of object-oriented enterprise modeling, we have to discuss another foundation theory that will also be operational as we construct a model of the enterprise in terms of the object-oriented paradigm. It is the theory of *conceptual modeling*. The purpose of conceptual modeling is to construct a model of any kind of domain using a set of theoretical modeling constructs that capture the way the world really is.

Most of this chapter is devoted to a discussion of the central tool of conceptual modeling, the conceptual type hierarchy. The conceptual type hierarchy allows us to structure the concepts of any domain in the real world as an inheritance hierarchy of concepts. We can think of the conceptual type hierarchy as the forerunner of the object-oriented inheritance hierarchy introduced in Chapter 5. As such, it is an ideal starting point for developing our own object-oriented inheritance hierarchy for the enterprise, which is founded on strong theoretical grounds.

In this chapter, we will define a conceptual type hierarchy that we will use in enterprise modeling. Our conceptual type hierarchy is based on the work of several scholars and has four major subtypes: entities, scenes, situations, and relations. The assertion of the scholars is that these four major subtypes and their subtypes can be used to model any domain in the real world.

Next we will discuss the crux of the matter: how the typical modeling domain from the real world, such as the enterprise, is structured around these four concepts. We will define the conceptual activity as a subtype of the conceptual situation. Activities cause change to be visited on entities. This is a recurring and enduring relation between them. We will make extensive use of this basic relation between activities and entities in enterprise modeling.

6.2 Conceptual modeling

Conceptual modeling is the framework with which we humans interpret the world. That is, when we interpret the world, we in fact are using conceptual modeling or subsets of it. Therefore, as modelers, we must base our efforts in object-oriented enterprise modeling on conceptual modeling. By realizing that object-oriented enterprise modeling must be founded on conceptual modeling we can ground our modeling constructs on a rock-solid theoretical foundation. This section defines and discusses conceptual modeling.

History of conceptual modeling

The development of conceptual modeling comes from the artificial intelligence community and its goal of defining the processing of natural language by intelligent agents. John Sowa has been a pioneer in the field of conceptual modeling and has developed many of its concepts and ideas. Sowa's published his work on conceptual modeling in *Conceptual Structures—Information Processing in Mind and Machine* (Sowa, 1984). This classic, much-cited work served as a catalyst and popularizer of the field. Other scholars, including Roger Hartley, Allen Newell, Heather Pfeiffer, Herbert Simon, William Tepfenhart, and Eileen Way, have made their own significant contributions to the growing theory of conceptual modeling. In this chapter, we will use the ideas of these and other scholars.

What is a conceptual type hierarchy?

A *conceptual type hierarchy* is a way of organizing concepts in any modeling domain. The purpose of a conceptual type hierarchy is to provide the efficient structure of concepts and their relations. A conceptual type hierarchy takes advantage of the efficiency of inheritance to portray the increasing specialization of concepts as one moves down the hierarchy or increasing levels of generalization as one moves up the hierarchy. This is similar to the generalization-specialization of the object class inheritance hierarchy introduced in Chapter 5. In fact, a conceptual type hierarchy is the intellectual forerunner to the object class inheritance hierarchy. However, a conceptual type hierarchy is much more theoretical. Modelers use a conceptual type hierarchy to organize general knowledge found in any problem domain (i.e., that an intelligent agent might encounter), while an object class inheritance hierarchy is used to organize objects found in a modeling domain (i.e., that an analyst might encounter). An object-oriented inheritance hierarchy is a special case of a conceptual type hierarchy.

There is no single ultimate conceptual type hierarchy and, in fact, there are many different conceptual type hierarchies depending on which scholar you ask as well as the needs of the intelligent agent. As Eileen Way puts it: "Different beliefs and different knowledge about the world will generate a different hierarchy . . . language is inextricably interwoven with our knowledge and beliefs about the world" (Way, 1992).

From conceptual type hierarchy to object-oriented class hierarchy

Since our goal in this book is to construct an object-oriented approach to enterprise modeling, we need to define an object-oriented class hierarchy that we can use to model the enterprise. As modelers, we must base our object-oriented class hierarchy for enterprise modeling on the way the external world really is.

The reason we can use a conceptual type hierarchy as the starting point for our enterprise object-oriented class hierarchy is that at the higher levels, concepts that are common to any problem domain are revealed. William Tepfenhart observed that "at high levels of abstractions, the same concepts and conceptual relations have consistently occurred and reoccurred from problem domain to problem domain" (Tepfenhart, 1992).

6.3 Conceptual type hierarchy for enterprise modeling

Figure 6.1 shows the upper levels of the conceptual type hierarchy we will use in this book. Our conceptual type hierarchy is based on the work of Sowa, Tepfenhart,

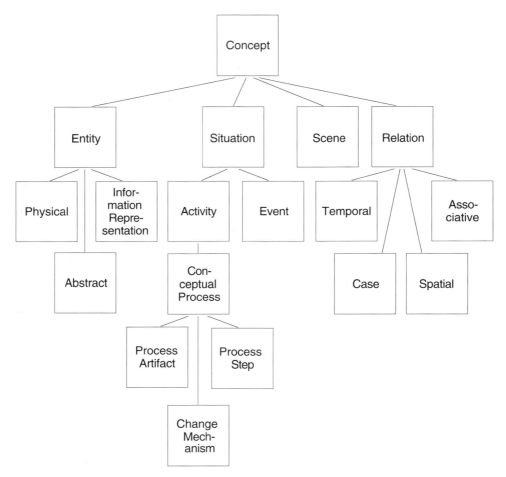

Figure 6.1 *Conceptual type hierarchy.*

Way, and others, but we have adapted it to the needs of enterprise modeling. Our adaptation simplifies some of the parts of the hierarchy that are not needed for enterprise modeling. Also, we have synthesized the ideas of these scholars into a specialized conceptual type hierarchy for enterprise modeling.

In the following sections, we will explain each node of our conceptual type hierarchy shown in Figure 6.1.

Concept
At the top of our conceptual type hierarchy (Figure 6.1) is the generic *Concept,* which is the common supertype of all the other nodes in the hierarchy. It is a place

holder. Its subtypes, *entity*, *scene*, *situation*, and *relation*, distinguish among existence, complexity, change, and connection. In effect, all of our concepts of enterprise modeling will spring from one of these four major subtypes.

Entity

The first major subtype (Figure 6.1) is *entity*. Entities are the "things" of a modeling domain and have separate and distinct existence. Entities are the corporal structure of a system and represent anything that we choose to evaluate as a whole. Entities have reality that may be objective or conceptual. In our conceptual type hierarchy, we have defined three entity subtypes:

- **Physical entity**   A physical entity is an entity with material reality. Physical entities "have physical properties, occupy a volume of space, and have a location determined by the region of space occupied by the object" (Tepfenhart, 1992). A physical entity has a distinct boundary separating it from its environment in which everything inside the boundary is part of the physical entity. Physical entities are constructed from other physical entities. In enterprise modeling we will have many examples of physical entities, including people, machines, buildings, and documents.

- **Abstract entity**   An abstract entity is an entity that has conceptual reality as opposed to physical reality. In other words, it is an idea or concept. Abstract entities are labels denoting a composite of physical entities and/or other abstract entities. That is, abstract entities can be traced to physical entities. Abstract entities have properties (like any other entity) tied to the underlying physical entities used to conceive of the abstract entity. For example, a purchase order is an abstract entity (a contract) that is related to physical entities (i.e., the items being purchased). The abstract entity endows the underlying collection of physical entities with properties normally not associated with them. Tepfenhart gives an example of a government as an abstract entity that "encompasses the individuals who rule, those individuals under that rule, and is bounded by the region of space over which that rule extends" (Tepfenhart, 1992). An enterprise model will contain many examples of abstract entities such as the representation of contracts, roles, procedures, locations, and so on.

- **Information representation entity**   An information representation entity is a symbol sequence that is a surrogate for a corresponding physical, abstract, or other information-representation entity. We originally introduced these terms (i.e., symbol and symbol sequences) in Chapter 4. In that chapter, we saw that symbol sequences are how an information-processing node stores its state and the physical phenomena in which information-processing nodes communicate with each other by sending each other symbol sequences. The information-processing node, particularly its physical symbol system component, has the basic capability of designation (Newell and Simon, 1987). According to Newell and Simon, designation is the formation of the correspondence between symbol sequence and its corresponding object. The information-representation entity is the embodiment of the concept of information being a surrogate to another entity.

An information-processing node such as a computer or person can store information representation entities in its state memory. Later, the information-processing node can retrieve the information from its state memory with exactly the same meaning to it. A very important point is that the information-processing node must represent all other entities (i.e., physical entities or abstract entities) as information-representation entity surrogates before the information-processing node can know or use them (Sowa, 1992).

Scene

The second major subtype of our type hierarchy (Figure 6.1) is the *scene*. Scenes represent structure and the complexity that exists between the entities and the relations between the entities. Tepfenhart defines *scene* as follows:

> A scene is "a state of the world described in terms of the entities and the relationships that hold among them at a particular point in time. Scenes are a means to denote with a single symbol a complex set of statements that define a state of the world. There are some necessary conditions which must be present in a description of the world in order for that description to constitute a scene. First there must be a location of interest present. . . . Second, a scene must describe the state of the world for one and only one temporal location. Third, every entity in the description must stand in relation to some other entity in the description. Finally, every relation that appears in a scene must be complete (no dangling relations)" (Tepfenhart, 1992).

Thus scenes represent complex aggregates of entities and the relationships that exist between them like a snapshot in time. The complex aggregate that makes up the scene has a common state derived from the aggregate entities and their relations. We will use the scene concept to describe complex aggregates such as the enterprise itself.

Situation

The third major subtype of our type hierarchy (see Figure 6.1) is the *situation* that models change. In analyzing the situation hierarchy, time becomes an important factor. Sowa defines the *clock tick* as the periodic interval of time that a modeler uses to analyze a system. The modeler defines the clock tick as appropriate to the system being analyzed (Sowa, 1992). A situation is closely related to the scene. In the words of Tepfenhart:

> A situation describes the world "as a sequence of scenes ordered such that a scene previous to it must have occurred earlier in time . . . every scene in the situation must be connected to some other scene in the description . . . every action must be complete" (Tepfenhart, 1992).

Thus a situation is a finite configuration of some aspect of the world in a limited region of space and time described at an appropriate level of detail. A situation may be a static configuration that remains unchanged for a clock tick or it may include activities and events that cause changes in a clock tick (Sowa, 1992). In this way, a situation is a set of scenes much like a sequence of frames in a movie. Each scene is the configuration of entities and relations for a clock tick. For each clock tick, a different configuration of the system may evolve (but doesn't have to). The clock tick and the corresponding change in the system define the subtypes of the situation hierarchy (Figure 6.1) as follows:

◆ **Activity** An *activity* is a subtype of situation that relates to a change over a period of several clock ticks (Sowa, 1992). Modelers define the activity in terms of a set of scenes that result and in which "each scene is linked to the preceding and following scene by an action" (Tepfenhart, 1992). The description of an activity includes a definition of the mechanism(s) that actually causes the change.

◆ **Event** An *event* is a subtype of situation that relates to a significant change in less than a clock tick (Sowa, 1992). William Tepfenhart describes an event as a situation "which consists of only three elements: an initial scene, a final scene, and an action which links the two" (Tepfenhart, 1992). Events are the signals that cause activities to be started or stopped. The definition of the event includes the mechanism that causes the event.

◆ **Conceptual process** The *conceptual process* is a subtype of activity. A conceptual process relates to an ordered set of actions that results in reaching goals. The major distinction between the conceptual process and its supertype activity are these goals. The actions of the conceptual process are purposeful, whereas the actions of the activity are not necessarily purposeful. A conceptual process embodies the mechanisms that cause the ordered set of actions. The action mechanisms of the conceptual process bring about change, which in turn, like the conceptual activity, results in an ordered set of scenes that take place over time.

Modelers use the conceptual process to describe processes of all types including both the type that occurs in nature as well as the process artifacts purposefully built by humans. Therefore, there are two subtypes of conceptual process of interest to enterprise modeling: the human-built process artifact and the process step. Modelers use the process artifact to describe the purpose-built process that humans design and implement to accomplish their goals. The process step is the atomic action at the foundation of the process artifact. We will make extensive use of these process concepts in enterprise modeling. An enterprise is a deliberate evolving set of scenes caused by processes and their process steps. We will discuss these processes in detail in Chapter 7. For now, we will only summarize them:

- **Process artifact** The *process artifact* is a subtype of the conceptual process. As mentioned earlier, this subtype of process is a human artifact that modelers use to describe purpose-built processes. Since this type of process is the focus of our concern in this book, we will frequently refer to it simply as process. Human designers endow the process artifact with a mechanism which evokes the change. We will call this the *change mechanism*. Modelers decompose process artifacts into lower level processes. The change mechanism at the higher level is the sequence of actions caused by its lower level processes.

As we will see throughout this book, processes can be decomposed into subprocesses. At the lowest level of decomposition of a process, the change mechanism is a human, a computer, or other machine. In the terminology of processes, modelers call the lowest-level processes *process elements*. Process elements, in turn, invoke process steps. The process elements are definitely processes; it's just that they have the distinction of being at the end of the decomposition. The change mechanism of these lowest-level process elements are information-processing nodes with their embedded physical symbol systems as described in Chapter 4. We will discuss all of this in detail in Chapter 7.

- **Process step** The *process step* is a subtype of the conceptual process. In a process decomposition, modelers call the lowest-level process artifact the *process element*. Process elements invoke sequences of process steps. The change mechanism of the process element executes sequences of process steps. In effect, the process step is an indivisible atomic action. Notice that what constitutes an atomic action depends on the perspective of the modeler. We will discuss process steps in Chapter 7.

◆ **Change mechanism**   The *change mechanism* is a subtype of the conceptual process. We can think of the change mechanism as an abstract machine that executes sequences of process steps. All processes have a change mechanism whether they are process elements or upper-level processes. The change mechanism gives the process its dynamics.

We will see in Chapter 7 that a change mechanism of a process is in fact an information-processing node. Recall that an information processing node is a person, an information machine, or a lower-level information-processing network such as a human organization. At the upper levels of process decomposition, the change mechanism is a modeling device used to analyze the dynamics of the process. At these upper levels, the change mechanism would correspond to the information-processing network abstracted as a complex information-processing node. For the lowest-level processes that deal with the physical world, the change mechanism is an atomic information-processing node such as a person or computer, which has at its core a physical symbol system.

Either way, whether upper or lower level, we model the change mechanism of a process as an information-processing node. This means that we can model the change mechanism of any process as the execution of a script. The script can take many forms. The script could be a set of declarative rules that we would use for modeling the upper-level processes. On the other hand, the script could be an actual procedural algorithm executed by an actual physical symbol system of the lowest-level process. We would use this form of the script to model the lowest levels of process decomposition. The point is that the change mechanism is one single concept no matter what level the process. We will discuss the change mechanism in detail in Chapter 7.

Relation
The fourth major subtype of our conceptual type hierarchy (see Figure 6.1) is the *relation*. Relations connect together the various types of concepts listed earlier. Tepfenhart defines *relation* as follows:

> [A *relation* is] an aspect or quality that connects two or more things or parts as being or belonging or working together. . . . Relations are typically directed with a subject and a target of the relationship. That is, the relationship among objects is directed with at least one entity the subject of the relation and at least one entity the target of the relationship. Usually there are restrictions on the types of subjects and targets accepted by the relationship (Tepfenhart, 1992).

Thus a relation is the connector between concepts. The relation consists of the following subtypes, which occur frequently in any modeling domain:

- **Temporal** This is the primary relation between activities (itself a subtype of the situation concept). One activity is related to another activity by time. Examples of basic temporal relations are "before" or "after." In enterprise modeling, processes, which are subtypes of activity, are usually related by the temporal relation.

- **Case (thematic)** Case relations are the primary relation between activities and entities. An activity produces an action with an entity as the target. The case relation is used by modelers as the supertype of all relations between an activity and an entity. Also, modelers use the case relation as the supertype of certain relations between activities. In this case, an activity is the target of an action produced by another activity. Examples of case relations are "agent" (thing doing the acting), "instrument" (means by which an action is performed), "experiencer" (of an action), "recipient" (of an action), or "result." We will use the case relation in enterprise modeling to describe how processes (i.e., activities) are related to business objects (entities). Also, a process can have a case relation with another process, as when one process controls another.

- **Spatial** Spatial relations describe the relations that occur within space. Space can be both physical and logical. Physical space is the familiar physical universe. In everyday experience, we perceive physical entities in physical space. In physical space, the entities must follow the laws of physics. Logical space is analogous to physical space. It means an abstract universe defined in thought. Like physical space, logical space has dimensions. The modeler defines a logical space in terms of dimensions (usually two or three), which are different attributes of the abstract world in question. Abstract entities in abstract space are governed by laws much like physical entities in physical space. In any space, physical or logical, the concept of location, comparison, and movement are basic.

Spatial relations are the primary relation between entities. Modelers use the spatial relation for not only the relations between physical entities found in physical space but for the abstract entities found in logical space. The nonphysical entities include abstract entities as well as information representation entities, which have both a physical and an abstract interpretation. Spatial relations include not only location concepts such as "on" or "above" but the decomposition of entities, such as a "consists of" relation. We will make extensive use of this relation to describe the aggregations of objects that make up the enterprise.

◆ **Associative**   We use the associative relation to declare an entity of the real world to be an example of a concept. Associative relations "link individual instances of concepts to another generic concept" (Dillon and Tan, 1993). Modelers use associative relations to characterize any type of concept. However, the associative relation is especially useful to characterize entities. An example of an associative relation is an employee of an enterprise. Here the collection is the employees of the enterprise and the associative relation is "employee of." In effect, a specific person who is an employee of the enterprise is an instance of the concept of employee. In general, modelers use the associative relation to portray the various forms of the "member of" relation.

As a modeling device, we say that the concept in question has a *collection of entities,* which are instances of the concept. In effect, the concept is realized by the collection of entities. The concept has a set of properties that define it. We attach this set of defining properties to the collection.

The modeler forms an associative relation between the concept instance and the collection considered as a concept. In effect, the concept instance is a member of the extension of the collection concept as described in Chapter 5. Notice that on the surface this resembles the definition of an object class in which we abstract the essential properties of a group of objects and then formally define an object class. However, the associative collection with its corresponding instances is much less formal then a full-fledged object class with its object instances. The object class is a heavy-weight modeling device that has a strong influence on the decomposition of the modeling domain. On the other hand, the associative collection is a lightweight modeling device with more limited influence on how we decompose the modeling domain.

6.4 Adapting the conceptual type hierarchy

The conceptual hierarchy presents a hierarchy of concepts. It says nothing about how we as modelers might use it to build a model of our domain. Also, the conceptual hierarchy is just that, conceptual. To use the conceptual type hierarchy in enterprise modeling, we must drive it down to the pragmatic level of an object-oriented class hierarchy specialized to the enterprise. To do this, we must understand how the concepts themselves are related in the real world. In this section, we will attempt to explain how we can adapt the conceptual type hierarchy to the job of modeling a real-world domain.

In most modeling domains, especially complex systems, the concepts of *activities*, *entities*, and their *relations* completely capture the essence of the target general system being modeled. This is because the real world as perceived by a modeler consists of complex structures of entities that are affected by activities. Thus if we are to model the enterprise using the object-oriented paradigm, we will have to have object-oriented modeling constructs that capture the essence of entities and activities, as well as their relations.

Figure 6.2 is based on the work of Heather Pfeiffer and Roger Hartley and shows how generic activities, entities, and their relations are typically organized in the real world (Pfeiffer and Hartley, 1992).

The three relations shown in Figure 6.2, temporal, case, and spatial, were defined in the preceding section. The following is a summary of how entities and activities are related by these three relations.

Activities to activities: Temporal relations

The temporal relation is the typical relation between activities in the real world. Figure 6.2 shows two activities: The first activity precedes the second activity either due to sequencing or dependency. For example, if two activities are related by sequencing, then temporal relations such as "before" or "after" will be used. If the activities are related by dependency then relations such as "depends on" or "prerequisite" will be used. These examples are primitive and modelers use them as a basis for more sophisticated temporal relations such as: "support," "assist," "give rise to," "control," "coordinate," "perform," or "synchronize." These more sophisticated examples still have the basic temporal relation of sequencing or dependency at their core. Notice that the temporal relations are usually expressed as verbs since they represent the connection between activities.

Activities to entities: Case relations

Figure 6.2 shows activities in relation to entities by the case relation. Recall that the case relation is the relation when an action expressed as a verb is produced by an

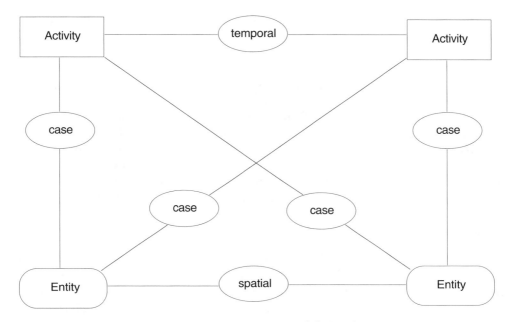

Figure 6.2 *Activities, entities, and their relations.*

activity with an entity as the object. The activity that occurs first (upper left) can be related to either entity below by a case relation as can the activity that occurs later (upper right). Thus an activity will be related to an entity by such relations as "patient," "instrument," or "experiencer." These examples are primitive and serve as the basis for many more sophisticated case relations such as: "make," "affect," "procure," "regulate," or "enhance." These more sophisticated examples of case relations still have the activity-verb-entity format typical of the case relation. Also, notice that case relations are usually expressed as verbs if stated from the standpoint of the activity. However, case relations may also be expressed as nouns if stated from the standpoint of the entity being acted upon.

Entities to entities: Spatial relations
Finally, we see in Figure 6.2 that entities are typically related to each other by spatial relations. Recall that spatial relations not only mean physical space but logical space. Examples of typical spatial relations include "above," "below," "attached," or "interconnect," as well as composition relations such as "part of" or "consists of." Modelers use these primitive relations as a basis for defining more sophisticated spatial relations such as: "correspondence," "association," and "consolidation." These more sophisticated forms of spatial relations still have the essential concept

of logical space at their core. Also notice that spatial relations are often expressed as nouns.

Implications to modeling

These are not the only relations that can occur between activities or entities, but they are typical and occur over and over in the real world. Thus as modelers, we must capture them in our modeling domain. In general, we see from Figure 6.2 that in any system, activities and entities form a duality in which activities cause actions to be visited upon entities. A modeler can use the concepts of activities, entities, and their relations shown in Figure 6.2 to construct a model of any general system. Therefore, our object-oriented class hierarchy must be able to model this primary structure found in the real world and shown in the figure.

6.5 Conclusion

This chapter introduced conceptual modeling and its principal tool, the conceptual type hierarchy. We saw that scholars build conceptual type hierarchies to capture the essence of the structure and functioning of the real world. This chapter introduced the conceptual type hierarchy we will use in this book, which is specialized to the needs of enterprise modeling. We founded our conceptual type hierarchy on the work of many scholars in the field of conceptual modeling. The conceptual hierarchy we have chosen allows us to model a complex real world system of which the enterprise is a prime example. Our conceptual type hierarchy allows us to describe the ideas of existence of objects (entities), complexity of object structures (scenes), the evolving snapshots of that structure (situations), and the connections between concepts (relations). All concepts we encounter in the domain of enterprise modeling must fall into one of these four supertypes. Also, we saw in this chapter that there are four supertype relations between these concepts, which we can identify and use in enterprise modeling.

By using a conceptual type hierarchy as the starting point for our object-oriented enterprise class hierarchy, we are assured that we are capturing and modeling the reality of the world of which the enterprise is an example. Our conceptual type hierarchy will serve as the intellectual grounding for defining an object-oriented class hierarchy for enterprise modeling. That is, each node of our conceptual type hierarchy defines an important concept type or subtype that we will use in object-oriented enterprise modeling.

Chapter **7**

The Conceptual Process and Its Subtypes

7.1 Introduction

This chapter describes one of the most important branches of the conceptual type hierarchy, that of the conceptual process and its subtypes. As introduced in Chapter 6, the conceptual process is a subtype of the activity that causes change to be visited on entities. However, the conceptual process has a significant component: goals. The conceptual process has purposefulness in which it accomplishes goals.

The word *process* is used extensively in both business reengineering and computer science. In a later chapter, we will develop a definition of the *business process*. For now, our goal is to build a very strong theoretical foundation for the conceptual process and its various subtypes. In Chapter 8, we will use the ideas developed here to define the process object and its corresponding process class. But in this chapter, we'll discuss the conceptual process and its subtypes without particular concern for their object-oriented properties.

Many authors have presented definitions of the process, and many of the ideas of this chapter are adapted in part from the work of B. Curtis, M. I. Kellner, and J. Over

(Curtis et al, 1992) as well as the work of F. B. Vernadat (Vernadat, 1992), and P. J. Russell (Russell, 1991).

7.2 The conceptual process

Let's review where the conceptual process fits into the conceptual type hierarchy, starting from the top. As we saw in Chapter 6(see Figure 6.1), the *situation* is one of the "big four" of subtypes of our conceptual type hierarchy. The *activity* is one of the subtypes of the situation. An activity relates to change over a period of several clock ticks of the system. Modelers describe the activity by the set of scenes that result in which "each scene is linked to the preceding and following scene by an action" (Tepfenhart, 1992). The scenes themselves are made up of conceptual entities in complex relations. After one or more clock ticks a new scene will emerge. This wouldn't happen on its own—some mechanism has to cause it. The conceptual activity is the mechanism that causes change in the world.

What if the change were deliberate, that is, it were done to pursue goals? In effect, what if the set of scenes that emerged were purposeful? This brings us down to the major subtype of activity we will study in this chapter, the conceptual process and its subtypes the process artifact, process step, and change mechanism. In the first section of this chapter we will discuss the conceptual process, and in later sections we will discuss the process artifact, the process step, and the change mechanism.

Looking inside the conceptual process

The conceptual process is described as a sequence of scenes, each of which is made up of entities in complex relations. As observers, we would see a conceptual process by its results, a changing set of entities and their relations. The set of entities and relations can be viewed as a general system in operation. Thus the conceptual process can be thought of as the driving force of a general system in which a set of entities and their relations undergo dynamic changes that result in the accomplishment of goals. Modelers use the conceptual process to describe all types of processes, including those found in nature as well as the artifacts that are purpose-built by humans. Figure 7.1 shows the essential components of the conceptual process. Each component is summarized in the following sections..

Events

A conceptual process is associated with a set of events, causing it to be activated as well as affect its ordered sequence of actions once activated. Recall that an event is a significant change in the larger environment of the conceptual process,

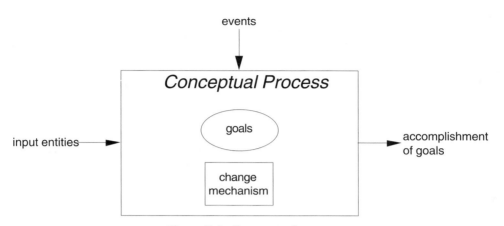

Figure 7.1 *Conceptual process.*

occurring in less than a clock tick. Since it happens in less than a clock tick, the event has no interesting structure that can be analyzed (although if measured using a shorter clock tick it might). Once activated, the conceptual process will operate continuously, causing new scenes to emerge as the clock of the system ticks away. As it operates, it may be influenced by additional events received from the environment. Eventually, the conceptual process may stop because of the receipt of an event.

Goals

Conceptual processes have a set of goals that they will pursue once activated. The accomplishment of goals usually involves changing the state of the entities associated with the process as well as the relations among the entities. The accomplishment of its goals is the reason the conceptual process exists or continues to exist. We can think of goals as being part of the state of the conceptual process. Goals are implied by the internal structure of the conceptual process as well as by the entities of the environment, or they are actually encoded as information and interpreted by the change mechanism of the conceptual process.

The domain of change of a conceptual process is the set of entities and their relations, which undergo change in time. When we focus on the set of entities and their relations, we can describe the conceptual process as a general system. As we learned in the first part of this book, a general system is a set of related entities that work together for the overall objectives of the whole. How do system objectives relate to process goals? Process goals are in fact equivalent to system objectives when considering a conceptual process as the driving force of a general system. We are just using the terminology from two different fields of study. However, the connotation of the objectives of the general system is much more primitive or simple than the connotation of the goals of the process. System objectives can be as simple as the system remaining intact over time. On the other hand, process goals are elevated to the stature of values, as determined by human judgment.

Input entities

Conceptual processes affect input entities that come from the environment. Entities are acted upon by the various actions of the conceptual process to discharge the goals of the conceptual process. In our conceptual type hierarchy, an input entity could be a physical entity, an abstract entity, or an information-representation entity. As an entity is affected, it undergoes a corresponding state change. Typically, conceptual processes receive input entities recently affected by other conceptual processes in their environment. For the conceptual process, we cannot (yet) describe the flow of entities as a flow of products. Rather, a conceptual process simply changes the state of entities in the environment. Once the state of an entity is changed, it becomes eligible as input to other conceptual processes in the environment. However, the deliberate flow of entities considered as products is an important characteristic of the process artifact discussed in the next section.

Decomposing the conceptual process

Any conceptual process can be readily decomposed into more finite conceptual processes as shown in the example in Figure 7.2. This is because actions that are the basis of processes, by their nature can be partitioned into subactions. The principle of process decomposition is that a process is implemented by a set of subprocesses. In effect, the subprocesses provide the sequence of actions of the process.

Decomposition is not done in a vacuum. It is associated with the decomposition of the goals of the conceptual process. A conceptual process is decomposed by decomposing its goal. Actions follow goals: the decomposition of the actions into subactions corresponds to the decomposition of the goals into subgoals. We can describe these subactions as conceptual processes if they meet the definition of conceptual processes: we must be able to describe the subaction as a sequence of actions that results in reaching a set of subgoals. This decomposition capability is extended to all the subtypes of the conceptual process and we will use it extensively in building the process model of the enterprise.

The decomposition of processes into subprocesses (or the reverse composition of subprocesses into processes) is an abstraction tool to simplify the modeling project. As we model a process, we can replace the process with its set of subprocesses and vice versa as shown in Figure 7.2. Decomposition is the work of the modeler—

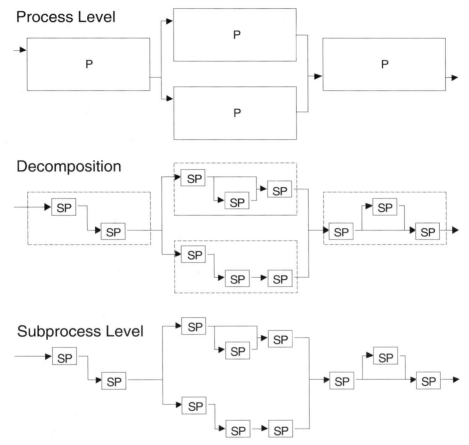

Figure 7.2 *Process decomposition (P = process; SP = subprocess).*

to analyze each of the processes (top of Figure 7.2) and identify their subprocesses (bottom of Figure 7.2). This is our old friend *abstraction* again. In effect, if we are interested in less detail, we will replace a set of complex subprocesses with the simpler process that has the same interfaces with the environment.

We decompose a process by honoring its interfaces with the environment. That is, each input entity or event of a process represents an interface with the environment that the subprocesses must implement. For example, in Figure 7.2, the subprocesses at the bottom of figure implement the interfaces of the process (input, events) at the top of the figure. For each interface at the process level, there must be a corresponding interface to one of its subprocesses. We will return to the subject of process decomposition in the last section of this chapter, but for now we will use these ideas of decomposition and subprocesses in our discussion of the conceptual process and its subtypes.

Change mechanism

In Figure 7.1, we see that the conceptual process has a component called the *change mechanism*. The change mechanism is itself a subtype of the conceptual process, and we will discuss it in its own section below. For now, we want to discuss the change mechanism as a modeling device to account for not only the subprocesses but their coordination by events. That is, we can think of the change mechanism as a black box that contains the subprocesses. Also, we can think of the change mechanism as causing the sequence of actions to accomplish the subgoals of the subprocess. Earlier, we saw that events activate and coordinate subprocesses of the subprocess for carrying out their sequence of actions. Finally, we can think of the change mechanism as the component of the conceptual process that reacts to events delivered from external sources and responds by creating its own sequence of external events. Thus the change mechanism is an abstraction that consolidates the complexity of the conceptual process.

However, for many conceptual processes, the change mechanism is more than an abstraction. There may be an actual physical component that contains the subprocesses and coordinates their interaction. As we will see later in this chapter, this is especially true of the process artifact. Any complex machine such as an automobile engine would have such a physical change mechanism. As a conceptual process, the automobile engine takes in entities of air and fuel and produces the goal of usable force as well as exhaust. The change mechanism of the automobile engine is the static arrangement of its subprocesses (e.g., carburetor, cylinders, transmission, etc.) physically housed inside the engine. In the case of the automobile engine, events are deterministic following the laws of science. However, for other conceptual processes, the change mechanism is just an abstraction to simplify the modeling project. In this book, we will assert that all conceptual processes as well as the various process subtypes have a change mechanism, whether real or abstract.

The change mechanism of a conceptual process is closely related to its decomposition into a set of subprocesses. As we saw earlier, it is the subprocesses that accomplish the goals of the larger process as they, in turn, accomplish their own subgoals. The actions of the subprocesses must be coordinated to accomplish the goals of the larger process. For complex processes (e.g., the business process), this coordination is also complex, requiring purposeful scheduling and rendezvous of results of the subprocesses. For simpler processes (e.g., the automobile engine), the static structure of the flow of the subprocesses accomplishes the coordination.

We can model this coordination, whether complex or simple, as residing in the change mechanism. That is, we can think of any intelligence that a process requires to accomplish the coordination of its subprocess as residing in its change mechanism as a modeling device.

The creation of events by various change mechanisms occurs at each level of process decomposition. That is, each process will have a change mechanism that encompasses the subprocesses and each subprocess will have its own change mechanism. How does the change mechanism of the process relate to the change mechanisms of the subprocesses? We have established a modeling convention that the change mechanism of a process creates and delivers events to the change mechanisms of its decomposed subprocesses. The change mechanisms of the sub-processes, in turn, accomplish their subactions for the larger process by creating and delivering events for their own subprocesses and so on.

The events produced by the change mechanism control and coordinate the actions of the subprocesses. How does a complex process actually implement this control/coordination function in its change mechanism? Later in this chapter, we will see how one or more specialized subprocesses conduct this control/coordination function. Like any other subprocess, we model these specialized subprocesses as being contained in the change mechanism of their process. We will return to this point in a moment. For now, we want to be at the conceptual level of description, so we will define the change mechanism as simply an abstract machine capable of creating an ordered sequence of events over time to control and coordinate its subprocesses.

We can usually decompose processes into subprocesses to many levels of ever increasing detail. When does process decomposition end? This is equivalent to asking when does our target process actually get something done aside from the coordination of the various levels of subprocesses or creation of events to them. The answer is that the decomposition eventually reaches the physical level where the actions and events are physical phenomena that obey scientific laws. It is very important to keep in mind that the physical level is the only structural reality. Above the physical level, the various process composition levels are just modeling abstractions.

Script

We can model the change mechanism of a conceptual process as a script that defines the sequence of actions of its subprocesses. We introduced scripts in Chapter 4. Scripts represent a sequence of physical symbols (i.e., information) which a change mechanism interprets as a sequence of commands. We then model the change mechanism as creating its events as a result of executing its script. That is, we are using the idea of a script to describe the orderly dynamic activity of the change mechanism to create its events over time. Notice we are not saying there is actually a script that is executed (although there may be). Rather, we model the orderly activities of the change mechanism as the execution of a script.

Accomplishment of goals

The output of the conceptual process as shown in Figure 7.1 is the accomplishment of its goals. At the minimum, this will take the form of internal state change of entities in the environment. In its most sophisticated form, the accomplishment of goals will take the form of the creation of products.

7.3 Process artifact

The process artifact is a subtype of the conceptual process and inherits all of its characteristics. However, unlike the conceptual process that can occur in nature, the process artifact is a purpose-built process that humans create to accomplish their goals. It has several internal components that are not present in its conceptual process supertype. In particular, the process artifact deliberately transforms input entities into output entities. Modelers describe these output entities as products that have economic value. To accomplish this, the process artifact consumes resources and operates under the direction of "boss" process artifacts.

Looking inside the process artifact

Figure 7.3 shows the components of the process artifact. Each component is summarized in the following sections.

Goals

Like its conceptual process supertype, the process artifact pursues goals. The major difference is that the conceptual process can be a part of a natural system in which the goals are implicit or exist for no apparent reason other than to account for the continued integrity of the natural process. The goals of the process artifact are based on human values. The creation of the output entities (i.e., products) accomplishes the goals of the process artifact. Goals are part of the state of the process artifact and may be actual information encoded as physical symbol sequences or merely implied by the structure of the process artifact.

Capabilities

Process artifacts have a set of capabilities that are used to select the process artifacts for use in a larger process. This is because processes are resources that may be allocated as subprocesses to other processes. The capabilities of a process artifact are its technical abilities and include its functional abilities, performance abilities, or quality abilities. Capabilities are part of the state of the process and are represented as actual information or merely implied by the structure of the process artifact.

Input-output entities

Modelers describe the process artifacts in terms of a product cycle in which it transforms input entities into output entities representing the product of the process artifact. The process repeats the product cycle continuously during its operation. During each product cycle, the process artifact takes in one or more entities and transforms them into an output entity. These input entities are the output from upstream process artifacts in the environment. The process changes the state of an input entity as it is transformed or incorporated into the output entity. Entities can be physical entities, abstract entities, or information-representation entities. The input-output transformation is the purpose of the process and represents the accomplishment of the human goals for which it was created.

Preconditions

Process artifacts have a set of preconditions which must be satisfied before the process will start another product cycle. Preconditions are part of the state of the

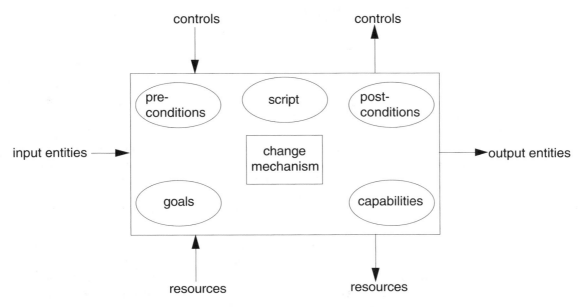

Figure 7.3 *Process artifact.*

process artifact and are represented as actual information or implied by the structure of the process artifact. Modelers identify the preconditions and document them as declarative rules, that is, statements about the current state of the process, the environment, or the event(s) that invoke it.

Postconditions

Process artifacts have a set of postconditions that represent the possible ending states of a product cycle of the process. As with preconditions, modelers identify the postconditions and document them as declarative rules. Once the process artifact completes a product cycle, it will arrive at one of these postconditions. Postconditions are part of the state of the process artifact and are represented as actual information or implied by the structure of the process artifact at that point.

Decomposition of process artifacts

Like its conceptual process supertype, modelers decompose process artifacts into lower-level process artifacts. Later in this chapter we will call the lowest level of process decomposition the *process element*. We use this lowest level to describe the physical level of decomposition in which the change mechanism is an information processing node such as a person, computer, or other machine. However, as we will see, what constitutes the lowest level of a process decomposition model depends on the scope of the modeling project and thus may not necessarily be the physical level.

Control/coordination hierarchy

The human designers usually arrange process artifacts into control/coordination hierarchies. As we learned in Chapter 3, the purpose of a control/coordination hierarchy is the constraint of subsystems in order to accomplish the overall purpose of the larger system. Also, for complex systems, control/coordination is necessary to keep the many subsystems working together. Figure 7.4 shows an example of a set of process artifacts arranged into a typical control/coordination hierarchy. In the figure, the Process P1 controls Processes P2 and P3. Process P3 controls Processes P4 and P5. The product flow is from P2 to P3 to P4 to P5.

It should be noted that the control/coordination hierarchy is not the same as the process decomposition hierarchy that we discussed in the preceding section (see Figure 7.2). The process decomposition hierarchy is an abstraction device that simplifies the modeling project. The control/coordination hierarchy describes the actual structure of process artifacts acting together at the same level of decomposition.

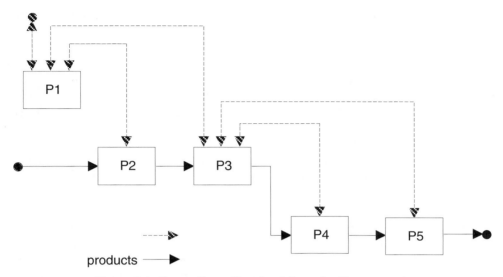

Figure 7.4 *Control/coordination hierarchy (P = process).*

Change mechanism

We can model the change mechanism of the process artifact, like its conceptual process supertype, as an abstract machine. The change mechanism is itself a sub-type of the conceptual process, and we will discuss it in detail in a moment. As we saw earlier with the conceptual process, the change mechanism of the process artifact is closely associated with its decomposition; the change mechanism of the process artifact represents the abstraction of its subprocesses considered as a black box. Similar to the conceptual process, the change mechanism of the process artifact creates events that activate the subprocesses to accomplish the goals of the process artifact; sequences of events cause the subprocesses to be activated to accomplish the goals of the process artifact collectively.

In later chapters of this book, we will define the change mechanism of the process artifact in concrete terms of the information-processing node defined in Chapter 4. But for now, we want to think of the change mechanism of the process artifact as cre-ating a series of events that it delivers to its subprocesses.

Since the process artifact is human-made, the human creators endow the change mechanism with purposefulness to deliberately cause the accomplish-ment of the overall goals of the process artifact. Process artifacts typically imple-ment this purposefulness by a coordination/control hierarchy as described earlier. That is, the change mechanism is the black-box abstraction of the set of sub-processes and the human designer empowers one or more of these subprocesses to perform the actual coordination/control function for directing the other subprocesses at that level of process decomposition.

We can model this deliberate purposefulness of the change mechanism as the execution of a script that defines the sequence of actions of its subprocesses. Similar to the conceptual process, we are using the script as a modeling device. An actual change mechanism does not necessarily have a real script although in many process artifacts, there is in fact a script that is executed by its change mechanism. As mentioned earlier, we usually model the typical change mechanism as a set of subprocesses arranged in a control/coordination hierarchy. In this case, we would model the execution of the script as being the responsibility of the designated control/coordination subprocess.

Controls

We can model the change mechanism of a process artifact as receiving control events that originate in the environment. For the typical process artifact, the change mechanism of the higher-level process artifact (i.e., in the control/coordination hierarchy) creates these control events. Control events may have associated information directing or constraining the change mechanism of the target process artifact. We call a control event with its associated information a *control* and we use the idea of controls to model the transfer and feedback of control and coordination to keep subprocesses working together on the goals of the larger process.

We use controls as a modeling device as follows: the target change mechanism receives and synthesizes the controls resulting in the execution of a customized set of actions. The resulting actions satisfy the implied constraints of the control. During its operation, the target change mechanism will, in turn, create its own output controls, which the change mechanism delivers as information-laden events to its lower-level subprocesses. Subprocesses are obligated to report their status to their higher level process so control channels are bi-directional. To report status, the process artifact creates a control (event plus information), which it delivers to its superior process artifact. The superior process artifact treats the status report like any other control, that is, as an event with corresponding information.

In building a process model, we establish the convention for the protocol of control and coordination as shown in the example of Figure 7.5. In this figure, we see a process labeled 1.0 consisting of two subprocesses labeled 1.1 and 1.2. The process 1.2 consists of two subprocesses, 1.2.1 and 1.2.2. The subprocess 1.1 is the control subprocess for the larger process 1.0. Similarly, the subprocess 1.2.1 is the control subprocess of the process 1.2, itself a subprocess of 1.0. The control subprocess 1.1, acting in behalf of its process 1.0, receives controls and gives feedback to an unspecified process artifact in the environment. Similarly, the

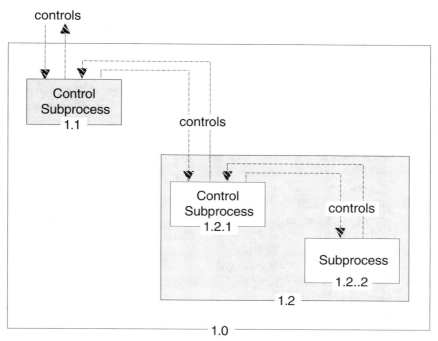

Figure 7.5 *Controls.*

subprocess 1.2.2 receives controls and gives feedback to its control subprocess 1.2.1. The control subprocess 1.2.1 communicates with the control subprocess 1.1. We have established these conventions to simplify the modeling project without constraining it.

Resources

The execution of a process artifact requires the involvement, consumption, or depletion of resources. The human creators of a process artifact, acting under economic motivations, provide it with the required resources.

Resources are either entities or change mechanisms. Resources that are entities are physical, abstract, or information-representation entities from the conceptual type hierarchy. The use of an entity as a resource changes its state. Resources that are change mechanisms are existing groups of subprocesses that already exist as an allocatable unit. Ordinarily, the change mechanism would be allocated when the process artifact is first created.

Obviously, the most important type of resource is the change mechanism and we think of them as abstract machines executing a script to harness their sets of subprocesses. Thus modelers classify resources as to their capabilities as change mechanisms, ranging from the passive to the active. Passive resources that are simply entities have no independent behavior and the process artifact uses or consumes them. An example of a passive resource is a tool or other physical entity. Active resources are change mechanisms with independent behavior and varying degrees of capabilities. An example of an active resource is a numerically controlled drill that serves as the change mechanism for a finite process artifact. The human worker is also a change mechanism and the most important resource for any process artifact.

Specialized process artifacts perform the allocation of resources to other process artifacts. Normally, the control/coordination subprocess (such as subprocess 1.1 or 1.21 in the example of Figure 7.5) performs the task of resource allocation. In this figure, subprocess 1.1 would allocate resources to the subprocesses it controls (e.g., subprocess 1.2 in the figure). Subprocess 1.2.1 which is the control subprocess of 1.2 would then allocate these resources to the various subprocesses it controls (e.g., subprocess 1.2.2). The allocation of resources occurs both when the process artifact is created as well as during its operation. Similarly, resources are released by the process artifact during its operation or when it is dissolved.

Process artifacts create or provide resources to be consumed by other process artifacts. Ordinarily, upstream process artifacts create or provide resources, whether entities or change mechanisms, as their output products. For example, in Figure 7.6, we see a product flow from process 1.0 to process 2.0. Process 3.0 creates or provides a resource for process 2.0. Thus not only is there a sequence dependency to produce or provide the input entities of the current process artifact, there is also the dependency of upstream process artifacts to produce the necessary resources to be used by the current process artifact.

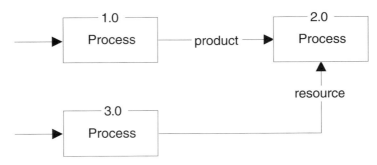

Figure 7.6 *Resources.*

7.4 Process steps

The process step is a subtype of the conceptual process that models the atomic actions in the hierarchy of process decomposition. Thus the process step is both a subtype of the conceptual type hierarchy and the atomic level of process decomposition. Process steps are a modeling construct we use to describe the unit of work of the process element. That is, it is a process element will execute a series of process steps.

In the next section, we will discuss in more detail our nomenclature for process decomposition in which we identify three distinct levels of decomposition: the process, the process element, and the process step. For modeling purposes, we have established the convention that the process step is the atomic level of process decomposition. In our nomenclature, process elements execute process steps. Notice that the process element is also a primitive level of decomposition, just above the process step. A given process element executes a series of process steps.

As modelers, we build our process model by decomposing each process into its various subprocesses (e.g., see Figure 7.2) and continue decomposing until we reach the level of detail that matches the scope of our modeling project. Once we have completed the process decomposition, we have at the bottom level a series of process steps representing the atomic actions, which are executed by process elements. The three levels of process decomposition are relative to each other and in practice seldom represent the ultimate decomposition possible, which is physical reality. Notice that if we weren't down to the process element level, we wouldn't be able to speak of atomic actions, either. Also, once we regard our process decomposition as at the lowest level, we can only speak in terms of the process element level executing the atomic actions of its process steps. The caveat is that a process element may not actually be an elementary physical process but rather a modeling convention because of the scope of the modeling project. Thus process steps are both a modeling device and, in fact, may represent physical reality if we have decomposed our process model to the ultimate physical level.

Looking inside the process step

Because it represents an atomic action, the process step does not have most of the components of the process artifact described previously. Figure 7.7 shows the simple components of the process step, which are explained in the following sections.

Event (input)

An input event invokes the process step. The event has no information content. It is just an unstructured signal which causes the process step to execute one product cycle.

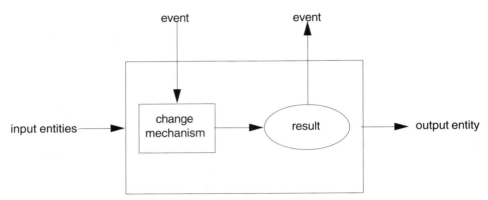

Figure 7.7 *Process step.*

Input entities
The process step takes in one or more input entities, which may be physical entities, abstract entities, or information-representation entities.

Change mechanism
The change mechanism of the process step is a simple atomic action, which transforms one or more input entities into the output entity. The atomic action of the change mechanism is indivisible for modeling purposes and has no interesting structure because it is, by definition, atomic. The atomic action cannot be suspended or stopped once triggered.

Output entity
The atomic action changes the state of the input entities and transforms them into an output entity. If there is more than one input entity, they are combined, integrated, or composed to form a single output entity.

Result
This is a state attribute indicating success or failure of the most recent invocation of the product cycle of the process step. The atomic action of the process step either executes successfully or fails completely. The process step is modeled as maintaining this one piece of state information.

Event (output)
The process step returns its result as an event to the change mechanism of the process element that invoked the process step.

7.5 Change mechanism

In this book, we will account for the dynamic behavior of a process by modeling it as having a change mechanism. The change mechanism is a subtype of the conceptual process. All processes (e.g., conceptual processes, process artifacts, process steps) contain, as one of their integral components, a change mechanism. The change mechanism implements the sequence of actions of the process, or its dynamic behavior. In effect, the change mechanism models the collective action of the subprocesses and can be thought of as containing them as well as coordinating their interactions.

Change mechanisms as information-processing nodes

The change mechanism integrates two important ideas in this book: that of the dynamic behavior of the process and the information-processing node. In Chapter 8, we will identify the change mechanism of the process artifact as being, in fact, an information-processing node. While we will discuss it in detail later, for now we can summarize this important relationship between the change mechanism and the information-processing node.

Recall that the big difference between the information-processing node and the common system is the use of information. The information-processing node receives, stores, uses, and sends information within the information-processing network in which it is embedded. Actually, the use of information by the information-processing node has a much deeper significance according to Allen Newell and Herbert Simon: adaptivity. According to Newell and Simon, the purpose of information is to pursue adaptivity to the environment. In effect, information makes adaptivity possible and adaptivity requires information (Newell and Simon, 1972; Simon, 1981; Newell and Simon, 1987).

Since the change mechanism is an information-processing node, it is embedded in an information-processing network. That is, the change mechanism is a node in an information processing network. This means that the change mechanism is embedded in a communications infrastructure provided by an information-processing network. The change mechanism has the internal components to receive and send information using the basic model of communications as defined by Claude Shannon and Warren Weaver (described in Chapter 4). The information-processing node, acting as the change mechanism of a process, receives messages sent to the process by other nodes in the network. These messages include the events and the various information symbol sequences with which processes communicate with each other.

The expectation of the sending information-processing node (i.e., which is itself a change mechanism for its own process) is that the target process will asynchronously service its message, that is, not act on it immediately. The sending information-processing node acting as a change mechanism is then free to do something else in the meantime until the receiving change mechanism responds to the request and sends a result back. This means that the change mechanism of any process must operate asynchronously from the other parts of the system, including its own sub-processes. This is because the various subprocesses of a process must also carry out their activities independently. This is how the world is, and the change mechanism must model asynchronous activity correctly.

Looking inside the elementary change mechanism

While every process has a change mechanism, the change mechanism of the elementary physical process models reality. This level represents an actual physical component, namely the atomic information-processing node such as a person or computerized machine. It is also the most sophisticated level of the change mechanism.

The elementary change mechanism must be capable of responding to events and messages from the environment. As introduced earlier, the elementary change mechanism must implement two modes of response: asynchronous and synchronous. Figure 7.8 shows the essential components of the elementary change mechanism. Notice that this is a modeling structure to account for asynchronous and synchro-

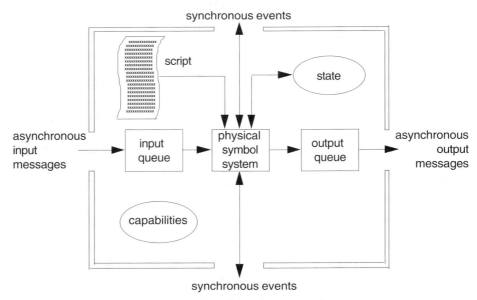

Figure 7.8 *Model of the change mechanism.*

nous activity and that actual physical change mechanisms may differ in the way they implement these basic capabilities.

Change mechanisms of higher-level processes

The change mechanism of a high-level process is difficult to describe since it embodies a set of subprocesses in complex interaction controlled and coordinated by events. In the case of the process artifact, for the highest levels of decomposition, the change mechanism corresponds to a high-level information processing node such as a human organization. At this level, the change mechanism is a collective result as opposed to an identifiable physical component. For example, a high-level process that has a human organization as its change mechanism will create its sequence of actions as the result of the collective subactions of the people in the organization considered as a whole.

While Figure 7.8 models an elementary change mechanism, this figure also models the change mechanism of higher-level processes. One would do this to simplify the abstraction of the high-level change mechanism in question. That is, rather than attempt to describe it as a set of subprocesses in complex interaction, such as a human organization, it is much easier to abstract it in terms of the components shown in Figure 7.8.

Asynchronous input messages

The outside world communicates with the elementary change mechanism by sending it asynchronous messages as shown in Figure 7.8. A message is an event with accompanying information, created by the elementary change mechanism of some other process. The elementary change mechanism has this capability since it is also an information-processing node.

We model the elementary change mechanism as having an input queue. The change mechanism places input messages on the queue as they are received. The input queue allows any number of input messages to be received and guarantees the integrity of each (i.e., that each will be received and safely stored away). Some sort of mechanism like an input queue must be present to allow an elementary change mechanism to operate asynchronously with the messages from the outside world. We have merely consolidated this need into the succinct mechanism of a queue, the simplest form of the capability. Actual elementary change mechanisms may have some equivalent mechanism that provides the same capability. For modeling purposes, the queue works well to describe this capability.

Physical symbol system

The central component of the elementary change mechanism is its physical symbol system, shown at the center of Figure 7.8 and defined in Chapter 4. The physical symbol system executes a script, which generates a sequence of synchronous events (more on this later). The physical symbol system represents the elementary change mechanism's capability to achieve asynchronous operation by conducting its own independent course of action—its thread of control. The thread of control of the physical symbol system will eventually decide that its next operation should be to respond to a message on the input queue. The physical symbol system retrieves the message asynchronously of its receipt. Under the control of its script, the physical symbol system interprets the message using its various elementary operations as discussed in Chapter 4. The interpretation may result in the creation of events delivered to the processes that are external to the change mechanism. We will return to this point shortly in connection with the execution of the change mechanism script.

Script

We model the physical symbol system component of the elementary change mechanism as executing a script. We introduced the term *script* in Chapter 4. Recall that a script represents a sequence of physical symbols (i.e., information) interpreted by the physical symbol system as a sequence of commands. The physical symbol system creates its events as a result of interpreting its script. We use the script to model the specification of the event sequence. The change mechanism delivers the events to its associated processes as either synchronous events or asynchronous messages.

Scripts are useful modeling constructs for any change mechanism, regardless of its level of decomposition. Scripts have different forms depending on the level of the corresponding process in the decomposition of processes. We model the script of higher-level processes simply as an ordered set of declarative rules—the way we would model the script of a human organization. We model the script of high-level processes as declarative rules to capture the idea of an abstract machine creating events to other processes. In this case, declarative rules model the creation of events delivered to other processes.

We state declarative rules in the following form: "if (Subprocess w (Postcondition x), send Event y to Process z)." In this statement, the high-level change mechanism modeled as an abstract machine performs a test of Subprocess w to see if it achieved a Postcondition x. Subprocess w is one of the subprocesses of the process. If so, the high-level change mechanism sends Event y to Process z. Event y may be either an asynchronous message or a synchronous event. Process z may be one of the subprocesses of the process or another process in the environment.

Scripts that consist of such declarative rules, in effect, declare what will happen under all possible conditions of their high-level process. The change mechanism required to execute such a script can be relatively simple and, in fact, may not physically exist (i.e., it is merely a convenient modeling construct to describe complexity). In this case, the declarative rules themselves would force the system to achieve its next scene. The only modeling requirement is that there would be a series of clock ticks to allow an orderly sequence of the scenes to create the necessary postconditions to cause the next scene. In this way, we are just using the script as a modeling device to describe a complex process that may not need a script at all since it is deterministic (e.g., under natural or human laws).

What about the script of the lowest level of process decomposition? Earlier in this chapter, we introduced the term *process element* to model this lowest level. We will discuss the process element in detail later but for now we can say that the process element represents the lowest level of decomposition of a process model and usually models the physical level. It is this physical level that is shown in Figure 7.8 as the elementary change mechanism. The process element performs the atomic actions called *process steps,* which were also introduced earlier in the chapter. We model the script of this lowest level with a specialized type of script. The script of a process element is our traditional view of the script as introduced in Chapter 4. The elementary change mechanism interprets and executes this type of script as a procedural algorithm consisting of the atomic process steps.

Different scripts define different behaviors of the change mechanism. A *role* is a specific script of a change mechanism. When the responsibilities of the change mechanism are to be changed, its script is changed. The role (i.e., script) of a change mechanism may be one of coordination and control. This would be a specialized role rather than the usual production-role of transforming input-entities to output-entities of the process. Coordination and control are necessary because resources such as change mechanisms (i.e., people and machines) are usually not permanently associated with a process element from a structural standpoint. Specialized coordination/control subprocesses perform the role of resource allocation assigning and reassigning resources to different processes over time. For example, people who are typical change mechanisms (i.e., they are resources) are reassigned to various tasks as a process precedes.

Synchronous events

The synchronous mode of communication with the environment is in the form of synchronous events. In Figure 7.8, we see synchronous events entering and leaving the change mechanism. At the top of Figure 7.8, input synchronous events enter the change mechanism. Synchronous events differ from asynchronous messages in the expectation of the sender and receiver. A sender of a synchronous event will stop its operation until the receiver of the event answers, as indicated by the receipt of the response to the event. Thus an input synchronous event preempts the current operation of the change mechanism and it must respond to the event. What happens if the change mechanism receives another synchronous event while it is responding to a previous synchronous event? We will model this situation very simply: the new event will be lost and the response sent back to the sender will indicate this. The sender can always resend the rejected synchronous event later. Also, at the bottom of Figure 7.8, we see synchronous events being generated by the physical symbol system as well as the event responses being received back. These generated events are sent to the change mechanisms of other processes. The sending change mechanism suspends its operation until it receives a response from the receiving change mechanism. The response could be the rejection of the synchronous event.

Asynchronous output messages

We model the change mechanism's asynchronous mode of communication with the environment as output messages as shown in Figure 7.8. The elementary change mechanism may decide to communicate with an external process possibly as a result of recent messages or events it has received. The elementary change mechanism will place its output messages in the output queue shown in Figure 7.8. This output queue is similar to the input queue in that it is a modeling construct that permits the physical symbol system to go about its business without having to worry about actually sending the results back to the original requester. In the case of responses to previously received messages, the output queue is responsible for sending out each of its messages to the corresponding requester who made the original request.

Other threads of control

For completeness, we must make one final point about the thread of control that provides the asynchronous operation of the elementary change mechanism. Earlier, we said that the elementary change mechanism has a centralized thread of control conducted by the physical symbol system as shown in Figure 7.8. There are also two other hidden threads of control, namely the input queue's thread of control and the output queue's thread of control. Three threads of control are necessary to permit these three functions to operate independently and asynchronously. That is, the change mechanism performs the actions of receiving input messages independently of the central thread of control of the change mechanism. Similarly, the change mechanism performs the actions of sending output messages independently of the central thread of control.

Conclusion

As we saw in this section, an elementary change mechanism has a physical symbol system capable of effecting its sequence of actions. If we accept that the change mechanism is an example of an information-processing node, we can conclude that an elementary change mechanism has a physical symbol system as described in Chapter 4. Recall that the physical symbol system is the working component of an information-processing node. We model it as an abstract machine that executes a script to effect a sequence of actions. The control component of the physical symbol system has the basic capability of interpreting the symbol sequences of the script and designating them as surrogates for actions against lower-level processes or entities. The physical symbol system is capable of accomplishing each of the atomic actions of its script, its script consisting of the series of process steps associated with the change mechanism.

In many cases, the change mechanism is not only modeled as having a physical symbol system but, in fact, may have the equivalent of one. For example, a computer processor, a typical change mechanism of many different types of processes, is the quintessential physical symbol system.

7.6 The three generic levels of the process model

Earlier in this chapter, we discussed the four subtypes of the conceptual activity: the conceptual process, the process artifact, process step, and the change mechanism. We also saw how we decompose the process artifact into subactions that implement subgoals. The decomposition of process artifacts into subprocesses and the decomposition of these subprocesses to yet lower-level subprocesses can continue depending on the level of granularity of the modeling project. However, as we stated earlier in this chapter, we distinguish among three modeling levels: the process, the process element, and the process step. The distinction between these levels is largely a convention of the modeling project, although as we'll see below, they may correspond to the actual reality of a system. We will describe and compare them in this section.

Process (P)

The *process* is the first generic level of process decomposition (Figure 7.9). It consists of high-level process artifacts and is an abstraction in the sense that it does not have physical reality per se. This level organizes and brings structure to the lower-level subprocesses. As modelers, we decompose processes into subprocesses, which may also be at this first generic level of process since the subprocesses lack physical reality and are used to organize their own lower levels. We model the

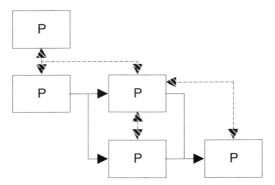

Figure 7.9 *The process generic level (P = process).*

change mechanism of the processes at this generic level as an abstract machine that enforces a set of declarative rules. The declarative rules declare what is possible in the future based on the postconditions of the various subprocesses now. However, such a change mechanism may not actually exist, and we use it as a convenient way to describe the complexity of a deterministic system. In the decomposition of processes into subprocesses, we eventually reach the level of the *process element*.

Process element (PE)

The next generic level of process decomposition (after the process itself) is the *process element* (Figure 7.10). Process elements represent the next to the lowest level of process decomposition just above the process step. As we saw earlier, the upper-level processes are abstractions we use to organize the complex activities of subprocesses. Eventually, through successive decomposition, we reach the level of process elements. Thus complex processes ultimately consist of multiple process elements that do the actual work of the process. Normally process elements are used to describe the physical tasks that cause the actual transformation of input entities to output entities in a sequence of process steps. For example, a milling machine pursuing a task is an example of a physical process element. However, the process element being the next-to-lowest level of process decomposition is also a modeling convention declared when we reach the limitation of the scope of our modeling project.

We model the behavior of the process element as the execution of a script that is a procedural algorithm. Thus the script of the generic process element is different from the script of the generic process described earlier. The process element script is a sequence of commands interpreted by the change mechanism. We call its

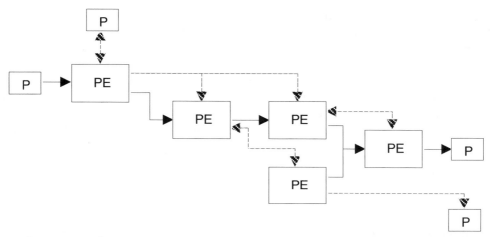

Figure 7.10 *The process element generic level (PE = process element, P = process).*

script a *procedural algorithm* because it explicitly defines the commands that the physical symbol system of its change mechanism will execute. Contrast this to the script of the higher-level process, which is a set of declarative rules of what is possible next. We describe the script of a process element as a transform function *F*:

$$F(\text{input entities, input resources, input controls, input state})$$

$$= (\text{output entity, output resources, output controls, output state})$$

In this function, input entities, input resources, input controls, and input state are combined to produce output entities, output resources, output controls, and output state.

Process step (PS)

The final generic level of process decomposition (after processes and process elements) is the *process step* (Figure 7.11). The process step is both a subtype of the conceptual process and the final generic level of process decomposition. We introduced it earlier (see Figure 7.7) and summarize it here to complete our discussion of the three generic levels.

The process step is the lowest level of decomposition in the process hierarchy; that is, process elements are decomposed into process steps. The process step is an atomic action with its corresponding atomic mechanism, and further decomposition is not necessary from the standpoint of modeling. The script of the process element invokes process steps to execute the next atomic action; the process step is started by an event that originates from its parent process element. The process step has no preconditions of its own. Once it receives its startup event, the process step executes its product cycle unconditionally. The process step either completely takes place or does not take place at all. It maintains a single state attribute indicating the success or failure of its most recent invocation. At the end of each of its product cycles, the process step updates its state attribute with an indication of success or failure and it generates an event as the response to the original input event. Thus we express its postcondition as a simple binary result.

The process step can be modeled as a function F:

F(input-entities) = output-entity

7.7 Conclusion

In this chapter we described one of the most important branches of the conceptual type hierarchy, that of the conceptual process and its subtypes. We defined the conceptual process as a subtype of the conceptual activity. The conceptual activity can be described as a sequence of actions that causes a series of scenes to emerge. Each scene is made up of entities in complex relations. The conceptual process differs from its activity supertype in that its sequence of scenes is purposeful and accomplishes goals. Conceptual processes are abstractions that describe the sequence of scenes of a set of entities and their relations. The only reality is the ever-changing entities and their relations. However, as observers we could describe the set of entities and their relations as a general system. In this case, the conceptual process is the force that drives this general system and causes it to change to accomplish goals. We can thus use the concepts and methodologies of general systems theory in analyzing the conceptual process and its subtypes.

In this chapter, we described the three subtypes of the conceptual process: the

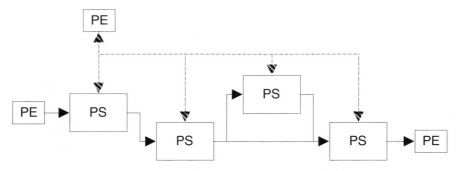

Figure 7.11 *The process step generic level*
(PS = process step, PE = process element).

process artifact, process step, and change mechanism. We saw that the process artifact is purpose-built by humans for accomplishing their goals. The process artifact is the intellectual foundation of the business process we will use to model the enterprise. In Chapter 8, we will use the definition of the process artifact to define the process object and its corresponding process class. We will place the process class near the top of our emerging object-oriented enterprise modeling class hierarchy as an abstract class. Then we will use this abstract process class as the superclass to define the business process classes and their corresponding subclasses in a later chapter.

We also discussed the change mechanism in this chapter. Not only is the change mechanism a subtype of the conceptual process, it is also a component of all processes (i.e., conceptual processes, process artifacts, and process steps). The change mechanism implements the sequence of actions of the process. The change mechanism of a process models the collective actions of its subprocesses. The change mechanism coordinates the actions of the subprocesses and we can model it as a black-box that contains the subprocesses. In Chapter 8, we will make the point that the change mechanism of the process artifact is in fact an information-processing node. This means that the change mechanism of the process artifact is either a person, an information machine (e.g., a computer), or a lower-level information-processing network (e.g., an organization).

Finally, we saw that the conceptual process or any of its subtypes can be decomposed into lower-level subprocesses because activity by its nature can be decomposed into subactivities. Processes are decomposed into subprocesses by decomposing their goals into subgoals. In decomposing a process, three generic levels are distinguished: the process, the process element, and the process step. The process level consists of one or more process artifacts, which may be abstractions for modeling purposes. The process element is the real level that does the actual work. The lowest-level process step models the atomic actions in the hierarchy of process decomposition. Process elements consist of a series of process steps. Process steps are intended to model the physical level of process decomposition, although this lowest level may actually be an arbitrary boundary to limit the scope of our modeling project.

Chapter 8

Object-Oriented Modeling

8.1 Introduction

This chapter discusses how we can use the object-oriented paradigm to build models of complex systems such as the enterprise. This will give us the vocabulary and concepts for discussing the enterprise as a system of objects in the remainder of the book.

In this chapter, we will address the conceptual type hierarchy introduced in Chapters 6 and 7. There we saw that any modeling domain has four general concepts: situations, entities, scenes, and relations. Recall that we had some unfinished business, that of adapting our conceptual type hierarchy to appropriate object-oriented constructs. In particular, one of our overriding and recurring tasks in the remainder of this book is to define an object-oriented class hierarchy suitable for modeling the enterprise. At the end of this chapter, we should have the necessary object-oriented modeling constructs to model a general system. This will be a start on our task of modeling the enterprise, itself a general system, in terms of the object-oriented paradigm. In later chapters, we will use the results developed here and specialize them to the enterprise.

We will begin this task by adapting the four major concepts of our conceptual type hierarchy to object-oriented constructs. Earlier we saw that the conceptual situation has a subtype of the conceptual process, which in turn has a subtype of the process artifact, our main interest in this book. Thus to transform the conceptual type hierarchy to the object-oriented paradigm properly, we must deal with four modeling concepts: process, entity, scene, and relation. Note that we don't have to deal directly with the situation supertype but rather its process artifact subtype.

We will see in this chapter that we can easily express the first two of these concepts, the process and the entity, in terms of object-oriented constructs. First, we will define the abstract entity class that we will use to model the entities of our conceptual type hierarchy. Recall that an abstract class is near the top of the class inheritance hierarchy and is not intended to be used to instantiate (create) objects. Rather abstract classes are used to clarify and organize concepts. The abstract entity class we define can be subclassed to model the various real entities of any general system that may be physical (e.g., a machine), abstract (e.g., a contract) or information-representations (e.g., a personnel record). Next, we will define the abstract process class we will use to model the process artifacts of our conceptual type hierarchy. The abstract process class we define can be subclassed to define the various real processes of a general system. Recall that processes represent systems dynamics (e.g., prepare payroll) and cause a change in the state of other objects, typically entity objects or other process objects. We will place these two, the abstract entity class and the abstract process class, near the top of our object-oriented inheritance hierarchy for modeling a general system.

Once the abstract process and entity classes are defined, we continue with a discussion of the relation and the scene. Recall that a relation is a connection between two entities, two processes, or an entity and a process that belong together, work together, or exist together. Scenes are the structural snapshots of a system at a point in time. Scenes, typically made up of entity objects arranged in complex relations, evolve from snapshot to snapshot under the control and coordination of process objects. Scenes are held together by the relations between their entity objects. In this chapter, we define the various object relations we will need to model the generic scene of a general system. Also, we present an explanation of the class-relations diagram, which will be our tool for documenting the scene as a complex lattice of collaborating entity and process objects.

Notice that we are not speaking (yet) in terms of implementing the enterprise using our enterprise modeling object-oriented class hierarchy. However, this is our hidden agenda. First, we intend to define classes for *modeling* the enterprise using the object-oriented paradigm. At this early stage, we can be optimistic that our enterprise modeling class hierarchy could serve as the starting point for constructing an *implementation* object-oriented class hierarchy to be used, for example, during the software development phase of enterprise implementation. We will return to this topic in Chapter 25.

8.2 Modeling entities: Entity class

The entity is a major subtype among the "big four" of subtypes of our conceptual type hierarchy described in Chapter 6. Recall that entities of our conceptual type hierarchy are physical entities, abstract entities, or information-representation entities. In the general system, we use the entity to model the "things" of the system. In this section, we define the entity class. We will model system entities as entity objects that we would instantiate from our entity class. In enterprise modeling, entity objects represent the corporal part of the enterprise: the realization of its constituent parts both physical as well as non-physical. At our level of abstraction now, we are at the highest levels of our object-oriented class hierarchy. In later chapters, we will use the definition of the abstract entity class we develop here as a starting point for defining subclasses representing the enterprise entity classes.

Figure 8.1 shows the various parts of our entity object. We will use the ideas behind this entity object to define a proper abstract entity class and will then use our abstract entity class to build the various entity subclasses to model the various enterprise entities. Thus, the entity object of Figure 8.1 is at the highest level of abstraction. During enterprise modeling, we can use our subhierarchy of entity classes to instantiate entity objects in our enterprise model.

In many ways, our entity object is the embodiment of the classic object defined in Chapter 5. The entity object is a black box with internal components that consist of services and a state (top part of Figure 8.1). The services surround and protect the state of the entity object. The definition of the state of the entity object is identical to the definition we have been using throughout this book, originally encountered in Chapter 1 and expanded in Chapter 5. The state represents the accumulated past history of the entity object. The state is available to the various services of the entity object to guide and be used in their operation. Only the services of the entity object can change the state.

The bottom part of Figure 8.1 shows the decomposition and meaning of the state of the generic entity object as well as the relations between the entity object and the outside world. These relations will be the message paths that the entity object uses to communicate with the outside world. Obviously, the entity object shown in Figure 8.1 is very generic and would not actually be an object in a real modeling domain. It merely shows the kinds of components that could be present in an actual entity object. We will discuss each of the components of the state of the entity object and its relations in this section.

Services

Figure 8.1 (top) shows a set of services surrounding a state of the entity object. We discussed object services at length in Chapter 5. We account for changes in the state of an entity object by the actions of its services. We describe the service as an abstract mechanism that changes the state of the object. A message from another object in the environment causes the service to be performed. Most real world objects don't actually have services as indicated in Figure 8.1 (i.e., they usually

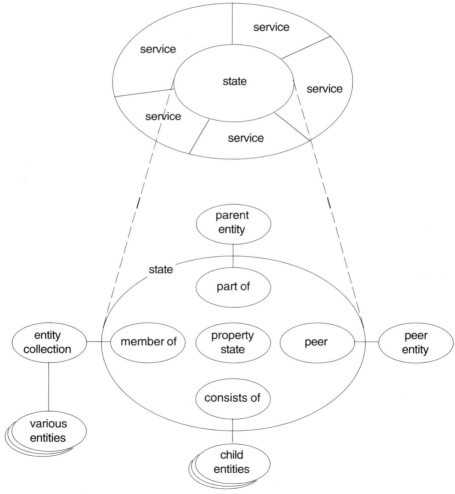

Figure 8.1 *Entity object.*

don't have identifiable mechanisms). Rather, we are using the service to model the behavior of entity objects.

State

The top of Figure 8.1 shows the state of the entity object, which is shown in detail at the bottom of Figure 8.1. At a glance, we see that Figure 8.1 models the state of an entity object as associations with other entity objects. This is a modeling device, and most real world entities don't have an actual state that remembers its associations with other real-world entities. We model entity objects as having three different types of associations shown in Figure 8.1.

First, any entity in the real world consists of other entities down to the limit of our universe of study. We create models of real-world entities by decomposing them into a collection of lower-level entities.

Second, any entity in the real world is part of larger entities up to the limit of our universe of study. We create models of real-world entities by composing them into higher-level entities. The composition and decomposition of entities are examples of the conceptual *spatial* relation we introduced in Chapter 6. Thus, our entity object must be capable of expressing its structural hierarchy.

Third, the entity object does not stand alone; it knows about other entity objects in its environment. In Figure 8.1, we call these *peer entity objects*. The peer relation is an example of the conceptual case relation we introduced in Chapter 6. We can say that much of the state of an entity object is knowing about its peer entity objects.

Parent entity

The parent entity shown at the top of Figure 8.1 represents the larger entity of which our entity is a part. Notice that whether we acknowledge the parent entity object is a modeling decision, related to the scope of our project. However, our abstract entity class must be capable of expressing this relation since any entity in the real world is part of a larger entity. We model the entity object as knowing about its parent by the state information labeled "part of" in Figure 8.1. The line leading from the "parent entity" to the "part of" is an example of the "whole-part" relation. The whole-part relation is the object-oriented construct used to model the conceptual space relation. We will discuss the whole-part relation in more detail later in this chapter.

Child entities

Any entity object is potentially capable of being decomposed into lower-level entity objects. Like the parent entity object, whether we choose to acknowledge the lower-level entity objects in a specific case is a modeling decision relating to the scope of the project. However, our abstract entity class must be capable of expressing this relation. We model the entity object as knowing about its children by the state information labeled "consists of" in Figure 8.1. The line leading from the "child entities" to the "consists of" is an example of the "whole-part" relation we will discuss later in this chapter.

Peer entities

Any entity object will likely have relations with peer entity objects. We model the entity object as knowing about one of its peers by the state information labeled "peer" in Figure 8.1. A typical entity object will have several of these. The line leading from the "peer entity" to "peer" is an example of the "using" relation, which we will discuss later in this chapter. The using relation is the object-oriented implementation of the conceptual case relation.

Entity collection

Any entity object will likely be a member of various collections. For example, in a typical enterprise, a person may be an employee (i.e., a member of the collection of employees of the enterprise), a customer (i.e., a member of the collection of customers of the enterprise), and an owner (i.e., a member of the collection of common stock owners of the enterprise). The state of an entity object contains information about the various collections of which it is a member. In Figure 8.1, these various collection memberships are indicated by "member of." The typical entity object will have one or more of these. The line leading from the "member of" to the "entity collection" is an example of the *associative* relation, which we will discuss later in this chapter.

The "entity collection" is a specialized entity object that manages a collection of other objects. It is a modeling device. We can think of the entity collection as a list of the various member entity objects. Figure 8.1 shows these various entities as part of the entity collection. The underlying entity objects of a collection can be members of many different collections. The act of making an entity object a member of an entity collection is very fundamental to modeling the general system. It is called *classification*. The decision to classify an entity object is usually the responsibility of a process object acting on the entity object or the entity object itself reacting to an event delivered from a process object. Either way, the entity object does not decide on its own to classify itself but responds directly or indirectly to the demands of a process object. The act of classification involves making the connection between the entity object and the entity collection. We model the act of classification as the joint responsibility of the entity object and entity collection object to honor their encapsulation. That is, our model portrays an entity collection object as having a service that puts the entity object being classified on its list (i.e., updates its state). Also, the entity object being classified has a service that makes the connection to the entity collection object (i.e., updates its state).

Property state

Another major responsibility of the entity object is to represent its properties. Recall that when we originally defined the properties of an object in Chapter 5, we distinguished between properties and attributes. We saw that any object has intrinsic properties in the scientific sense whether we choose to acknowledge them or not. By contrast, an attribute is the acknowledgment of a property that represents a noteworthy feature assigned by us, the modelers, to the object.

Thus the properties state of Figure 8.1 is a modeling device that consists of the subset of attributes we as modelers consider noteworthy. Entities in the real world have corporal existence and represent anything we choose to evaluate as a whole and to acknowledge in our model. As such, we know entities by their properties, which define them and isolate them as noteworthy for our consideration. We model the entity object as having a properties state to represent its properties we consider important.

8.3 Modeling processes: Process class

In Chapter 6, we introduced the *situation* as one of the "big four" conceptual subtypes (in addition to *scenes*, *entities*, and *relations*). We saw that the situation has the subtype *activity*, which in turn has the subtype *conceptual process*. We described the conceptual process at length in Chapter 7. There, we learned that the conceptual process is a very special subtype of activity because it, unlike its activity supertype, is purposeful; it pursues goals. Going down the hierarchy, the *process artifact* is a subtype of the conceptual process. The process artifact is purpose-built which humans employ to accomplish their goals. Thus the process artifact is particularly important to enterprise modeling.

Now we need to define an abstract process class to be placed in our enterprise modeling class hierarchy. Figure 8.2 shows a generic process object that we will use in our discussion. A process object is a surrogate for an actual process artifact, and we will use it for modeling the actual process artifact. We have based our process object in part on the work of Peter Wegner (Wegner, 1989), B. Curtis, M. I. Kellner and J. Over (Curtis et al, 1992), F. B. Vernadat (Vernadat, 1992), and P. J. Russell (Russell, 1991).

We see that our generic process object of Figure 8.2 actually consists of an aggregate of other objects, both lower-level process objects as well as various entity

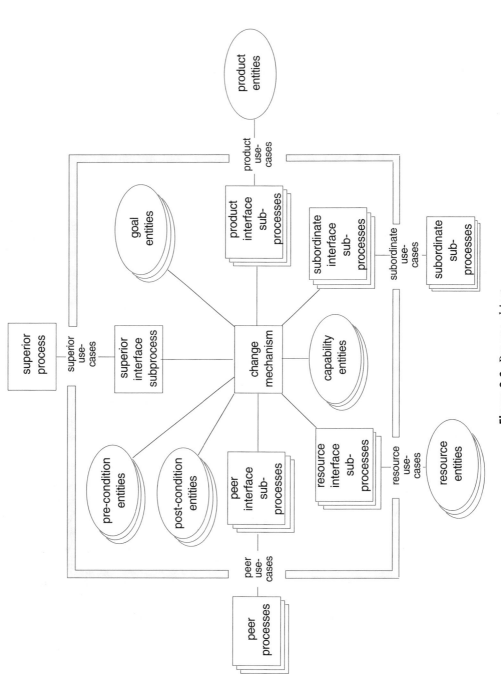

Figure 8.2 *Process object.*

objects. These other objects are also surrogates, and we use them to model the constituent parts of the whole. Figure 8.2 shows the relations between the typical aggregate objects that make up our generic process object as well as the relations of our process object with the outside world. These relations are the message paths that will exist between them. Our process object as shown is fully loaded with a complete set of components. In practice, a process object may not have all of these components.

Subprocesses

Figure 8.2 shows the various subprocesses of the process object as rectangles. These are process artifacts in their own right, and we would also implement them as process objects. Thus our process object is recursive in the sense that its sub-processes use an identical concept as the whole. This recursive definition of processes will greatly simplify the modeling of the enterprise, making it possible to define business processes and subprocesses using one construct. Then the process objects of the enterprise can be instantiated from the process class or its sub-classes. Thus we will be able to capture, in a few simple concepts, the entire activity of an enterprise.

Entities

The process object will have a complement of entity objects. The entity objects are shown as ovals in Figure 8.2. Entity objects will have the basic structure and function described in the preceding section. Like the process object, we will be able to define a series of entity classes in our object-oriented class inheritance hierarchy. Thus we will be able to capture the essence of the enterprise's products and resources in a few concepts.

Use-cases

Our process object has various ports that permit exchanges with the external environment, shown as openings in the enclosure of the process object in Figure 8.2. We call these exchanges use-cases. A use-case is a modeling construct developed by Ivar Jacobson and described in (Jacobson, 1992). We will discuss use-cases at length in Chapter 14. For now, we will give a short definition of the use-case. A *use-case* defines and models the exchange scenario between two subsystems of a larger system that occurs over an extended period (i.e., several individual exchanges). We describe the use-case in terms of an actor that is external to the process object in question. The actor, which is itself a process object, either needs the services or products of the target process object or vice versa, the process object needs its services or products. The use-case dialogs occur over the message channels shown in Figure 8.2. The use-case consists of object messages an object sends to another object as described in Chapter 5. The message invokes an object service in the receiving object that may, in turn, respond with its own object message to advance the use-case between the two objects.

Change mechanism

The change mechanism at the center of Figure 8.2 is a special controlling sub-process. The change mechanism, which was described in Chapter 7, was defined as implementing the sequence of actions of the process, its dynamic behavior. In effect, the change mechanism of the conceptual process models the collective action of the subprocesses and can be thought of as containing them as well as coordinating their interactions. In our process object, we must endow the change mechanism with a more concrete role than the one described for the conceptual process. In our process object, the change mechanism represents the primitive capability of the thread of control of the process object, that is, its continuous and unending operation.

The change mechanism of the process object is the master subprocess that controls and coordinates the other subprocesses of the process object. Figure 8.3 shows the internal components of the change mechanism of the process object. The various subprocess objects of the larger process object, including the change mechanism itself, operate asynchronously. The change mechanism performs the coordination and synchronization of the various subprocesses. The change mechanism has the capability of controlling parallelism and rendezvous among the various subprocesses it controls.

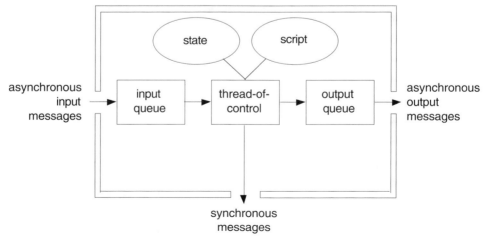

Figure 8.3 *Change mechanism.*

In our description of the conceptual process (see Chapter 7), we described the change mechanism of the process artifact and concluded that it is an information-processing node. Examples of information-processing nodes are people, computers, and human organizations. In Chapter 7, we saw that the change mechanism of the lowest-level physical process element (e.g., person, computer) has a physical symbol system as an integral part of its change mechanism. The physical symbol system was first introduced and defined in Chapter 4. Recall that we model the physical symbol system as a continuously running script interpreted by the controller of the physical symbol system.

The change mechanism of our process object must model the change mechanism of the process artifact, which in its most sophisticated form is a person or computer. In Figure 8.3, we see the components that will be necessary to accomplish this. First, the change mechanism of a process object is a continuously running thread of control. Notice that we don't need to actually define the physical mechanism to model the thread of control. Rather, all we have to do for modeling is describe its external behavior. The change mechanism maintains its own state(as shown in Figure 8.3) that controls the thread of control, allowing it to operate asynchronously. Two other threads of control are needed: the input queue and the output queue. We mention them only for completeness. They can be thought of as specialized scripts with their corresponding states that provide the message input and output services for the main thread of control of the change mechanism.

As modelers, we can think of the change mechanism of the process object as executing a script. This means we can define the actions of the change mechanism of the process object by its script. The thread of control is the operational manifestation of its script. The script specifies sequences of commands that designate actions against other process objects or entity objects. Scripts are a very versatile modeling device because they can easily show not only sequential but conditional operation in which the change mechanism selects its next command based on the state of the process object.

The actual process artifact, which the process object models, may be at any level of the decomposition hierarchy of process artifacts as described in Chapter 6. There we learned that we decompose process artifacts into lower-level process artifacts. The upper layer process artifacts are abstractions that organize the various lower layers of subprocesses. The lowest level process artifacts are called *process elements*. Recall that in the hierarchy of process artifacts, the process element is intended to represent physical reality and implements the actual change mechanism, transforming physical input into physical output. The change mechanism of our process object must be capable of modeling each of these levels from the highest-level abstract process artifact to the lowest-level real process element.

The commands of the script of a process object invoke a process step representing the lowest layer in the process decomposition hierarchy. The process step, described in Chapter 7, is the atomic action in the hierarchy and further decomposition is not applicable. We model the process step as an object service, invoked by object messages as shown in Figure 8.3. Some of these object messages sent to the various object services are synchronous and the thread of control is then transferred to the receiving object service. This is the case of entity object services. Other object messages are sent asynchronously with no expectation of return. This is usually the case of process object services.

Messages sent from other process objects arrive at the port of the change mechanism asynchronously, that is, independently and without expectation of synchronous response. The input queue, operating independently, stores these asynchronous input messages, as shown in Figure 8.3. The central thread of control will eventually decide to react to an input message. In its execution, the thread of control will send synchronous messages to entity objects as shown in the figure. These synchronous messages are part of the continuous running central thread of control and differ from the asynchronous input messages in that they have an expectation of response before the thread of control will resume. Eventually, the central thread of control will send a message to other process objects. These asynchronous output messages are first placed in the output queue, which operates independently from the central thread of control as shown in Figure 8.3. In this way, the change mechanism of the process object implements the asynchronous operation of the process object.

Superior process

The process object (Figure 8.2) has a superior process object commanding it, reflecting the command and control hierarchy described in Chapter 3. The superior process object may have instantiated (created) the process object in the first place. The superior process object may from time to time conduct use-cases with the process object, itself having one or more specialized subprocesses (indicated by the superior interface subprocesses in Figure 8.2). These specialized subprocesses are under the command of the change mechanism and will conduct the use-cases with the superior process on behalf of the process object. The superior interface subprocesses operates asynchronously from the change mechanism but communicates with it as needed, using the facilities described earlier in "Change Mechanism."

Subordinate subprocesses

The process object (Figure 8.2) may have one or more subprocesses, which it commands. This is also an example of the command and control hierarchy described in Chapter 3. The subordinate subprocesses are also process objects that communicate via use-cases with their master process object. The process object has one or more specialized subprocesses shown as the subordinate interface subprocesses in Figure 8.2. These subordinate subprocesses operate asynchronously from the change mechanism and communicate with it via object message passing, using the facilities described in "Change Mechanism."

Peer processes

The process object (Figure 8.2) may have one or more peer processes, which are themselves process objects. The process object and its peer process objects communicate via use-cases. These use-cases are conducted by specialized peer interface subprocesses that operate asynchronously from the change mechanism process but communicate with it as needed. We will see in the case of the business process object that these peer objects are typically customers or suppliers, which conduct frequent use-cases with the business process object.

Resource entities

The process object (Figure 8.2) requires resources to conduct its change activities. The resources are represented by entity objects that are consumed or used during the activities of the process object. The process object will have specialized resource interface subprocesses to conduct asynchronous use-cases with the resource entity objects. These use-cases will coordinate or direct the resource entity objects in the sequence of activities of the process object.

Product entities

The process object will create or enhance products that represent the discharging of the goals of the process object. The process object will model the products as product entity objects as shown in Figure 8.2. The process object will have one or more specialized product interface subprocesses that conduct asynchronous use-cases with the product entity objects. These use-cases cause the product object to be created or enhanced. This is much more fundamental than the other use-cases of the process object. Here, the process object is operating as the metalevel of the lower-level product entity objects as explained in Chapter 3. The use-cases of process object control and monitor the product entity objects and change them, resulting in the completed or enhanced product.

Precondition entities

The process object (Figure 8.2) has a collection of precondition entity objects. François Vernadat defines preconditions as a combination of objectives and constraints that model the system rules imposed on the process artifacts. In the enterprise, modelers call these one form of business rules. Business rules are the management rules, regulations, and internal policies of the enterprise (Vernadat, 1992). The preconditions of a process object are the rules under which it will operate. The preconditions also define the conditions under which it will start operation, continue operations, and end operations.

Postcondition entities

The process object (Figure 8.2) has a collection of post-condition entity objects. These entities define the possible ending states of the process object when it terminates a product cycle. The actual ending status of the product cycle will be one or more of these postconditions.

Capability entities

The process object (Figure 8.2) has a set of capability entity objects. The capability entity objects define the technical capabilities of the process object. The capability entities describe its functional abilities, performance abilities, or quality abilities. A process object will be instantiated with a certain set of capabilities that define how the process object can be used. In many real-world systems, process objects use negotiation and brokerage use-cases to select and assign the tasks of the system. The negotiation and brokerage use-cases refer to the capabilities of process objects to qualify and select them.

Goal entities

The process object (Figure 8.2) has a set of goal entities. The goal-entity objects define the goals of the process object. A process object is instantiated with a certain set of goals. A goal is a proposed future state of the process object.

Comparing the process object and the entity object

It is instructive to compare the process object and the entity object. Obviously, the big difference between them is in their dynamic behavior. The entity object is essentially inert and sits there until disturbed by a requested service. Once the entity object receives a request, it goes into action and produces its output and updates its state as necessary. Then the entity object goes back to sleep and awaits the next request. We would say the entity object is passive, responding when asked but not having any independence whatsoever.

The process object, on the other hand, has its own independence. We model the process object as being a continuous, independent activity. We refer to this as its *thread of control.* It is a model of the basic capability provided by the physical symbol system that makes up the elementary change mechanism of the process artifact being modeled. The independent thread of control determines the sequence of operations of our process object. The thread of control of a process object is an unending object service that makes use of the services of the lower-level entity objects under its control.

8.4 Modeling relations

Relations are another of the "big four" of concepts from our conceptual type hierarchy (i.e., the others being the entity, situation, and scene). Conceptual relations become object relations in the object-oriented paradigm. We have seen from the discussion of our conceptual type hierarchy that there are several relations we must portray: the case relation, the spatial relation, the associative relation, and the temporal relation. In this section we will discuss the object-oriented interpretation of these conceptual relations.

Definition: Object relation
A relation is a connection between objects. Why would two objects want to be connected? Objects by themselves can't do much. They depend on each other for services and structure. Grady Booch defines a relation between two objects as "the assumptions that each makes about the other, including what operations can be performed and what behavior results" (Booch, 1991).

Class relations versus instance relations
We saw in Chapter 5 that an object is instantiated (or created) from its class. In defining relations, we must make a distinction between the relations between two classes and the corresponding relations between two objects that are instantiated from those two classes. On one hand, a class relation between two classes defines a fundamental connection between them. Every object instantiated from the two classes will have that relation. Such a relation is really a statement that is part of the definition of the concept of the class. Recall that we define the concept behind a class as its *intension*. In enterprise modeling, the class relation is the one we will use the most because we are interested in generic properties.

On the other hand, once objects are instantiated from their respective classes, they will implement these class relations. This is called an *instance relation*. These instance relations become important when the owners and engineers of the enterprise actually build or reengineer it. For an enterprise, instance relations represent its reality, how it is actually constructed.

Implementing the conceptual spatial relation: The whole/part relation

We use entity objects to model the physical entities, abstract entities, or information-representation entities introduced in our conceptual type hierarchy. Entity objects represent the corporal part of a system, its body or mass. A given entity object from the real world can always be decomposed into other entity objects. For example:

- Physical entities can be readily decomposed and could eventually be decomposed to the level of atoms and beyond.

- Abstract entities can be decomposed into lower-level abstractions that, after successive decomposition, become language-independent primitive concepts from conceptual modeling as well as formation rules such as semantic principles, grammar, or the laws of logic.

- Information objects can be decomposed eventually to the binary digits that make up their symbol sequences. From there, we could decompose them as physical entities that encode the symbols of their symbol sequences.

In our conceptual type hierarchy, we introduced the spatial relationship. Composition and decomposition is a spatial relation in our conceptual type hierarchy and we must drive it down to an appropriate relation in the object-oriented paradigm. In the object-oriented paradigm, the whole/part relation implements this conceptual spatial relation of composition and decomposition. We use the whole/part relation both to decompose entities into simpler entities and to compose complex entities from simpler entities. We also use the whole/part relation to decompose processes into subprocesses and to compose processes from subprocesses.

Implementing the conceptual case relation: The using relation

In our conceptual type hierarchy, we introduced the case relation. Recall that the case relation in the conceptual type hierarchy expresses the concept of interaction between concepts. We saw that the case relation is the primary relation between activities and entities. In a case relation, an activity produces an action with an entity as the target. Another use of the case relation is between activities: an activity produces an action on another activity. As with the other relations, we need to drive the concept of the case relation down to the pragmatic level of the object-oriented paradigm. We will implement the case relation of the conceptual type hierarchy as the using relation in the object-oriented paradigm.

We saw in Chapter 5 that objects spend much of their existence interacting with one another. The primary reason for the using relation between objects is that one object needs to have another object do something, in other words, perform a service. The services of an object are the conceptual activities that have case relations with other objects. The using relation will be our way of modeling these case relations. In effect, the using relation is how the potential dynamics of a system becomes reality—by the interaction of its objects.

We model the interaction of objects using the idea of message passing: one object passes a message to another object to cause the interaction. We acknowledge that message passing between real world objects is a modeling device. Among real world objects, message passing may not really exist, but we are using it to express the interaction between objects in a succinct and efficient way for the purpose of modeling. Thus the using relation between two objects expresses the potential that one object will some time have another object do something that we model as the first object passing a message to the other object to request the performance of a service.

Implementing the conceptual associative relation:
The associative relation

In our conceptual type hierarchy, we introduced the associative relation. Recall that we use the associative relation to declare an entity of the real world to be an example of a concept. As a modeling device, we say that the concept in question has a collection of entities that are examples of the concept. In effect, the concept is realized in the real world by the collection of entities. The concept has a set of properties which define it. We would say that the "intension" of the concept is defined by its set of properties. As a modeling device, we attach this set of defining properties to the collection. If an instance of a concept is a member of the collection then we would say that it is part of the *extension* of the concept.

We can implement the conceptual associative relation directly in the object-oriented paradigm as the associative relation. The object-oriented version of the associative relation is between the entity object in question and the collection object. Associative relations are particularly useful for categorizing an entity object. In effect, by making an entity object a member of a collection, we are endowing it with the properties that define the collection.

Implementing the conceptual temporal relation:
Process dependency relation

To complete our discussion of the implementation of the conceptual relations in the object-oriented paradigm, we must consider the conceptual temporal relation. Recall that we use the conceptual temporal relation between activities in which one activity is related to another activity by time. Examples of basic temporal relations are "before" or "after." The implication of the conceptual temporal relation is one of dependency or prerequisite activity.

We will implement the conceptual temporal relation as the process dependency relation. For example, consider two processes, Process 1 and Process 2. We would say that Process 2 has the process dependency relation with Process 1 if Process 2 cannot take place, for whatever reason, until Process 1 is completed. We will make extensive use of the process dependency relation in future chapters that discuss the flow of business processes in the enterprise. Notice that we don't actually specify why Process 2 cannot take place until Process 1 is completed in the temporal relation.

Entity constraints

The three relations—whole-part, using, and associative—implement the structure of entity objects and the behavior between entity objects. These entity relations imply potential integrity problems. Individual entity objects protect their integrity as well as the overall system by restricting these relations. We call these restrictions placed on entity relations *constraints*. In the words of Subodh Bapat, "a constraint is a mechanism which places limits on an object's structure and behavior. A constraint compels an object to confine itself within the bounds it specifies" (Bapat, 1994).

Thus constraints are the limitations that an entity object enforces on its behavior, its structure, and its relations. The internal services of the entity object actually implement these constraints. We model these internal services as rules stated as propositions of the form "if *x*, then *y*." In enterprise modeling, constraints are one form of business rule, which we will discuss in Chapter 13. Constraints apply both to the structure and behavior of an object. We will consider each type of constraint in the following:

- ◆ **Structural constraints** Structural constraints apply to the systems corporal structure as manifested by its entities and their relations. In particular, structural constraints apply to the whole/part relation and the associative relation which must be limited or controlled. Structural constraints express whether two objects have a mandatory relation or merely an optional one. For example, some entity objects exist only because another entity object exists. An example is the purchase order object, which has a whole-part relation with its various line item objects. A line-item object defines the details of a specific product being purchased by the purchase order. The purchase order's line-item object exists only because the purchase order exists. However, the existence of the purchase order does not depend on the existence of a specific line item object.

Figure 8.4 *One-to-one relation.*

Figure 8.5 *One-to-many relation.*

We define structural constraints by the number of objects that are mandatory and/or optional for the relation to exist in the first place. For example, we might have a mandatory constraint that a purchase order object must have at least one line-item object (this is actually an example of a business rule to be discussed in a future chapter). Also, for a line item object to exist it must be linked to exactly one purchase order object. We can express these types of constraints using the idea of the cardinality of the relation. Cardinalities are the number of objects that participate in each side of the relation. We use cardinalities to express both numbers of objects required in the relation and the mandatory/optional nature of the relation. We indicate the number and optionality of the relation by labeling the relation with either a number or a span of numbers. The following cardinalities of relations are important to enterprise modeling:

One-to-one   There is one of each of the objects (Figure 8.4). For example, a company has one headquarters building. We can express this as a mandatory constraint by saying that there must be one of each of the objects. Another way of thinking of it is that if there is one of the first object (company), there must be one of the second object (headquarters building). In Figure 8.4, the relation is mandatory and one-to-one.

One-to-many   For a given object, there are many of the other objects (Figure 8.5). This is the basic form of the associative relation. One entity object is a member of a collection of entity objects. Stated as a mandatory constraint, this relation is that for the one object there must be at

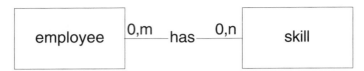

Figure 8.6 *Many-to-many relation.*

least one of the other object. For example, a company has a collection of many employees but a it must have at least one employee; in other words, the collection of employees of a company cannot ever be empty. In Figure 8.5, the relation expresses a mandatory one-to-many relation in which there is at least one employee and exactly one company.

Many-to-Many   For a given object there are many of the other objects (Figure 8.6). Also, when considering one of these other objects, many of the first objects are related to it, too. This is really a compound relation consisting of two of the one-to-many relations. For example, an employee has many skills and for each skill, there are many employees who also have it. In Figure 8.6, the relation expresses a many-to-many relation in which there can be from 0 to n skills per employee and for each skill, there can be from 0 to m employees who have that skill.

◆ **Behavioral constraints**   The other major type of constraint (besides the structural constraint) is the behavioral constraint. Behavioral constraints limit and control the using relation, that is, the invocation of services that one object requests of another. In particular, behavioral constraints control or limit the state of the object expressed by its attributes. We express behavioral constraints as preconditions and postconditions that exist before and after the invocation of an object's service:

Preconditions   The set of precondition constraints defines the environment that must exist before the object will perform the requested service. Precondition constraints express the requirements of the state of the object before it can invoke the service. For example, the object must be in a certain state to invoke the service.

Postconditions   The set of postcondition constraints defines the environment that will exist after the invocation of the service. Postcondition constraints express the limits on the state of the object after the invocation of the service. For example, the state properties have certain values or ranges of values as a postcondition.

8.5 Modeling scenes: The class-relations diagram

Scenes are the final concept of the "big four" that we must be able to model in terms of the object-oriented paradigm. In the previous section we discussed the generic relations that objects have with each other. These relations will be especially useful for modeling a complex hierarchical-multilayer system introduced in Chapter 3. The objects that make up a system form complex relations with each other, defining the structure of the system at a point in time. In our conceptual type hierarchy (defined in Chapter 6), the scene is the major subtype used to portray entities and their complex relations. The scene is a snapshot of the system that models the structure of the system at a point in time. In this section, we will introduce the class-relations diagram as a tool for diagramming the complex lattices of entity objects that exist in the typical hierarchical-multilayer system. We will be using the concept of the scene from our conceptual type hierarchy as a jumping off point to define the class-relations diagram.

The entity-relation diagram revisited

The class-relations diagram is a special case of the entity-relation diagram introduced in Chapter 2. Recall that we use the entity-relation diagram to model the structure of a system. In the entity-relation diagram, we call the nodes *entities* and use them to represent the components of the system. The links are the relations between the entities of the system. We will use an analogous definition for the class-relations diagram: the nodes are classes and the links are relations between classes.

Contents of the class-relations diagram

The class-relations diagram is ideal for showing a global view of a general system. An example of a class-relations diagram is shown in Figure 8.7. The figure shows the major entity product-customer classes of the typical infrastructure-based enterprise such as a telephone company.

This example demonstrates the various components we need to model during enterprise modeling:

- ♦ **Entity classes** The class-relations diagram shows the major entity classes (shown as ovals). Entity objects are instantiated from these entity classes. In the working enterprise, process objects (not shown in Figure 8.7) will produce or change these entity objects. In the figure, the entity classes are linked to each other via various entity relations, discussed previously.

- ♦ **Cardinality** Since this is a high-level class-relations diagram, we show the cardinality of relations with simple arrows in which the arrow indicates the

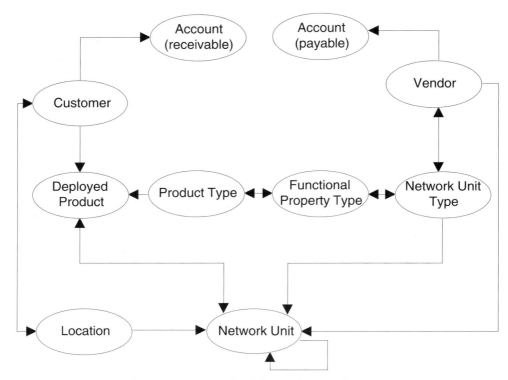

Figure 8.7 *Example of class-relations diagram.*

"many" side of the relation and no arrow indicates the "one" side. An example of a one-to-many is a customer with many account (receivable) objects. An example of a many-to-many is a location with many customers and a customer with many locations.

- **Whole/part relations** The class-relations diagram shows the important whole-part relations. For example, in Figure 8.7, a customer (the whole) can have many deployed products (the parts). A recursive whole/part relation is shown in the figure in which a network unit consists of many lower-level network units.

- **Associative relations** The class-relations diagram shows the important associative relations. For example, in Figure 8.7 a deployed product is classified as a certain product type. In the working enterprise, a product type would have a collection of its deployed products.

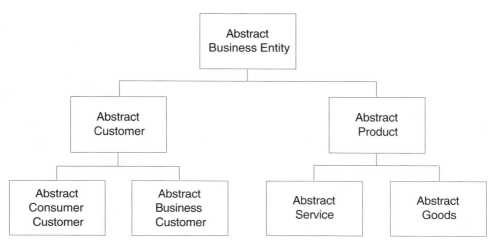

Figure 8.8 *Modeling by abstraction in the class hierarchy.*

Scope of the class-relations diagram

The class-relations diagram contains the entity classes and their relations at a particular level of decomposition and for a particular subsystem of the overall system. Thus we would select the overall system or one of its subsystems and construct a class-relations diagram for it.

We saw in Chapter 1 that modeling is a form of abstraction. To construct a model of a complex system, we draw out its essence into a second simpler system, one with limited scope. This simpler system we call the *model*. We select the capabilities and properties of the model because they not only reflect the essence of the target system but they are also the capabilities and properties that we can, in fact, understand. We are able to reason about the complex target system by reasoning about the model.

The question in modeling a system using the class-relations diagram is, what level of abstraction is appropriate and necessary? Object-oriented systems can be modeled using a natural and simple technique of using the abstract classes of the class hierarchy. Any object-oriented system will have an associated class hierarchy. Recall that the class hierarchy arranges the classes of the system into a hierarchy from the most general to the most specialized. At any level, the class hierarchy is an abstraction of the concepts of the system at a certain level of generalization.

Recall that classes at the higher levels of the class hierarchy are called abstract classes. These higher level classes are not intended to be used to instantiate objects but rather to organize and define the concepts of the classes. The important point is that a class at the higher levels of the class hierarchy defines the essence of the class. The lower-level classes specify the details of specializations of these essential capabilities and properties. The point is that these essential capabilities and properties are a very useful level of abstraction which we can use in modeling. In this book, we will recommend that the modeler be guided by the abstraction levels of the class hierarchy and that the level of abstraction of the class hierarchy be used as a guide to deciding on the scope of abstraction of the class-relations diagram.

For example, the class hierarchy of any enterprise will contain classes representing the two concepts of customer and product. At the lower levels of the class hierarchy, these two will be relatively specialized. Figure 8.8 shows an example of the upper levels of a class hierarchy. In this figure, the third level of the hierarchy has Abstract Consumer Customer and Abstract Business Customer as specializations of the Abstract Customer. Similarly, the third level has Abstract Service and Abstract Goods as specializations of Abstract Product. This level defines a set of concepts that are more specialized than their superclasses. Modeling the enterprise using the third level would produce a much more detailed model than by using the second level.

On the other hand, we could model the enterprise at the second level of the Abstract Customer and Abstract Product. At this level, the abstract classes Customer and Product have enduring relations and services that go to the heart of what they are. For example, a Customer class at this level will define the basic concept of the customer as an external party that buys a product from our enterprise. If we are constructing a high-level model, this is all we want to know about a customer. Thus the class hierarchy is a good way to abstract the underlying essential concepts of the modeling domain and to choose the correct level of abstraction.

One problem with this approach is that we need a class hierarchy in the first place to construct our model. However, the construction of the class hierarchy is the point of our work. We have a chicken-egg dilemma, which we can solve with an iterative developmental process. To illustrate, in the example of the enterprise, we would start at the highest level of generalization and work with the classes such as Abstract Customer and Abstract Product among others. Once we had defined this high level of generalization and the corresponding system at that level of abstraction, we would move down to a lower level. As we define the more specialized classes, we may discover additional capabilities or properties needed in the upper layer. Alternatively, we may modify capabilities and properties of the upper-layer classes. The point of revisiting the upper layer as we define the layer below is to push the generalization of capabilities and properties up to the highest level possible.

8.6 Conclusion

In this chapter, we described how the object-oriented paradigm can be used to build models of complex general systems such as the enterprise. We specifically addressed how to model the four major subtypes of our conceptual type hierarchy: entities, situations, relations, and scenes. We took each major subtype and described how that concept would be modeled in terms of object-oriented constructs.

The first major subtype of our conceptual type hierarchy is the conceptual entity, which expresses object existence. We opened this chapter by defining an abstract entity class. The entity class and its corresponding entity object should find wide use in enterprise modeling: with the abstract entity class, we have a consistent, easily understood modeling device to describe the business entities of the enterprise. We will use entity objects to model physical entities, abstract entities, and information representation entities. The entity objects represent the assets of the enterprise. The various entity objects of the enterprise each have a complex state representing the results of past operations or experience. Our entity class presents a useful model of these business assets and provides us with a coherent way to model the distributed state of the enterprise.

The second major subtype of our conceptual type hierarchy is the conceptual situation, which expresses the evolving snapshots of structure. As we move down the subtypes of the conceptual situation, we come to the conceptual process, which has a subtype of the process artifact. It is the process artifact that we are most concerned with in this book. We described in this chapter how the process artifact can be readily translated into an abstract process class. Our abstract process class can be subclassed to define the specialized process classes of the enterprise. We will see in future chapters of this book that our workhorse technique in enterprise modeling is to decompose the enterprise into business processes. A business process receives input from upstream business processes in the form of materials, information, and energy. It has an internal state that it maintains as it produces its output products and information to the downstream business processes. The business process is a concrete example of a process object that would be based on the process class we defined in this chapter.

The third major subtype of our conceptual type hierarchy is the conceptual relation, which expresses the connection between concepts. In this chapter, we described how the conceptual relation can be expressed in terms of object-oriented constructs. We defined several object relations, including whole/part, using, associative, and process dependency. We discussed entity constraints that control the relations that an entity object can have. Entity constraints are one form of business rules that we will discuss later in Chapter 13.

We closed this chapter with a description of the class-relations diagram. The class-relations diagram is the object-oriented construct to document the fourth of our major subtypes, the conceptual scene that expresses a snapshot of entities in complex relations. The class-relations diagram portrays the structure of a system and documents the entity classes and their enduring relations with each other. We will make extensive use of the class-relations diagram to document the structure of the enterprise.

Chapter 9

Putting it all Together

9.1 Introduction

In Part 1 of this book, we defined the general system and presented the theoretical foundations of the enterprise. We discussed the specialized organization, the hierarchical-multilayer system, found in many complex general systems such as the enterprise. We presented a very specialized general system, the information-processing network, along with its component subsystems, the information-processing nodes. We saw how the enterprise is an example of an information-processing network. This first part of the book presented the domain that we must model.

In Part 2, we presented the modeling tools that we will use to construct an enterprise model and defined the object-oriented paradigm that will serve as our modeling framework. We summarized the academic field of conceptual modeling and defined a conceptual type hierarchy for use in enterprise modeling. We translated the "big four" concepts—the entity, the situation (i.e., the process), the scene, and the relation—into object-oriented modeling constructs.

In this chapter, we will integrate these theoretical underpinnings into a coherent whole. We will present a survey of the requirements of the modeling domain and summarize how our modeling tools will deal with each requirement. Throughout this chapter, we will also comment on the implications to enterprise modeling in general.

9.2 Requirement: Modeling the general system

We have stated many times that the enterprise is a general system. Thus the first requirement of our object-oriented enterprise modeling capability is that it must provide object-oriented constructs suitable for modeling the enterprise as a general system.

Summary: The general system
The general system was introduced in Chapter 1 and was described in detail in Chapter 2. We defined the general system as a set of interrelated objects that together pursue common objectives. The general system receives inputs from the environment and produces output to the environment. This output represents the realization of the objectives of the system, its reason for existence. From this brief introduction, we can see how the enterprise is an example of a general system.

Throughout this book, we have seen how a general system is decomposed into its subsystems that are, in turn, decomposed into lower-level subsystems. At any particular level of decomposition, the subsystems work together to accomplish the overall goals of the larger system, which is itself a subsystem. Our conclusion is that the real world is made up of systems and that every system is a subsystem of a larger system. We saw how this presents a dilemma to the modeler, who must decide the boundary of the system being modeled.

Modeling the general system
In Chapter 6, we saw how a conceptual type hierarchy captures the way the world really is. The conceptual type hierarchy we have adapted in this book has four major subtypes: entities, which model object existence; scenes, which model complexity and structure much like a scene from a movie; situations, which model change or the flow of scenes much like a running movie; and relations, which model the connections between the various concepts. We model the real world by using the subtypes of these four.

Since the general system is a typical feature of the real world, we can conclude that the conceptual type hierarchy captures the essence of how a general system and thus the enterprise really is. This means that we can use our conceptual type hierarchy as a starting point to define our object class inheritance hierarchy. In this way, we can capture the essence of the general system, especially the enterprise. We can be very optimistic that the enterprise, being a general system, should map very well to our conceptual type hierarchy as well as our object class inheritance hierarchy which we derive from it.

Implications to enterprise modeling

Once decomposed, a general system is revealed as being made up of subsystems. One question then is how and when do we hop over to the object-oriented paradigm to analyze the system? We will find that it is most effective to start out by analyzing a system such as the enterprise first as a set of subsystems and then as a set of collaborating objects. That is, at the global level of the whole system, it is useful to analyze the accomplishment of the overall goals of the whole system. This is especially true of the enterprise where stressing wholeness and avoiding suboptimization are well-known prescriptions to business process reengineering. We will discuss this further in Chapter 13.

Once we understand the system and its subsystems as a whole, we can then analyze it in terms of the object-oriented paradigm; that is, we can proceed to model the subsystems as complex arrangements of objects that exchange messages to accomplish the behavior of the system. In Chapter 16, we will discuss this further. Notice that these are not hard and fast rules since any system is a subsystem of a larger system. What we are attempting to define in this book is a modeling methodology that is capable of modeling the various aspects of a general system. We model the general system by sometimes considering it as a decomposition of subsystems in which functionality is important and sometimes by considering as a complex arrangement of objects in which behavior is important. Either way, we have the necessary modeling constructs.

9.3 Requirement: Modeling hierarchical-multilayer systems

How are the subsystems or lattices of objects typically organized to accomplish the overall goals of the system? In Chapter 3, we defined the most typical form of organization of a complex general system, that of a multilayered hierarchy. The enterprise is an example of a general system that uses the hierarchical-multilayer organizational structure. Therefore, a requirement of object-oriented enterprise modeling is that it must provide object-oriented constructs suitable for modeling the enterprise as a hierarchical-multilayer system.

Summary: Hierarchical-multilayer organization

There are actually two major concepts of systems organization here: hierarchy and multiple layers. The hierarchy emphasizes goal-setting, decision-making, and control. In this form of system organization, lower layers make decisions on their own to perform actions. However, the upper layers review these actions after the fact. On the other hand, the multilayered organization is a set of layers each of which implements a functional layer of the overall system. Each layer is an abstraction of functionality with its own principles, concepts, and methodology. Upper layers depend on lower layers to perform their specific functions. We combine the two organizational concepts into a hybrid systems organization, which we call the *hierarchical-multilayer system*. In the hierarchical-multilayer organization, we define the authority echelons that make up the hierarchy in terms of abstraction layers. Thus the hierarchical-multilayer system has an authority aspect and an abstraction aspect.

Modeling hierarchical-multilayer systems

We saw in Chapter 3 that the hierarchical-multilayer system actually consists of a repetition of two generic layers: an operations-layer and its corresponding meta-layer. Let's review each briefly.

An operations-layer provides the operations mechanisms and operations processes—the bread-and-butter production that justifies the system at that level of decomposition. Its meta-layer contains the goals of the system at that level of decomposition and continually monitors and adjusts its operations-layer to make sure the goals are being meant. Going down the hierarchy, an operations-layer is the meta-layer for the next-lower operations-layer. Therefore, any layer of a hierarchical-multilayer system has two roles: as the meta-layer for the next lower level and as the operations-layer for the preceding upper layer. These two atomic layers are repeatedly combined in hierarchical-multilayer systems. This identifies another of the requirements of the object-oriented constructs we will need to model a complex system such as the enterprise.

To properly portray a hierarchical-multilayer system as an object-oriented structure, we need to define these two layers and their generic parts in object-oriented terms. We actually have several things we need to model as follows:

- ◆ **Operations-layer**   Using the terminology of our conceptual type hierarchy, the operations-layer is a scene. That is, it consists of entities that are connected to other entities in complex relations at a snapshot in time. We will use the entity class as our way of modeling these conceptual entities. The entity class was described in detail in Chapter 8. Also, we will use the class-relations diagram to model scenes portraying the entity objects and their complex relations. The class-relations diagram was also described in detail in Chapter 8.

The overall dynamics of the operations-layer is provided by one or more process objects. The process object and its corresponding process class was described in detail in the Chapter 8. The process object allows us to divide the actions of the operations-layer into several threads of control in which each thread operates asynchronously. The process objects drive the entity objects of the operations-layer. The scope of the activities of the entity objects are very limited and local to them. We saw in Chapter 8 how we can use object services to model these local activities.

◆ **Meta-layer**   For the meta-layer, we need to model the goal-activities and goal-state. The goal-activities are actually control mechanisms. The meta-layer continuously executes one or more threads of control to monitor and adjust the operations-layer. Like the operations-layer, the overall dynamics of the meta-layer is implemented by one or more process objects executing asynchronously. We model the goal-state as abstract entity objects and information-representation objects. These are subclasses of the abstract entity class.

We can conclude that we need two types of objects to model a complex hierarchical-multilayer system such as the enterprise: the entity object and the process object. These objects must be capable of expressing a rich repertoire of relations, especially the temporal relation between process objects, the case relation between process objects ,and entity objects, and the spatial relations between entity objects. We can conclude that we can successfully model the hierarchical-multilayer system in terms of the object-oriented constructs we have identified which include our entity class and process class.

Implications to enterprise modeling

We will see in future chapters how these two ideas of the hierarchical-multilayer system, that of coordination/control and abstraction, are very applicable to the enterprise considered as a system. We will see that hierarchies of business processes in the enterprise implement the functions of coordination/control. The business processes themselves are arranged in abstraction layers. Coordination/control implies systems overhead, that is, the system must spend some of its energy and materials to integrate itself. In enterprise modeling, we recognize this as the idea of cost-centers associated with business processes. We will use the measurement of systems overhead to guide the design of the enterprise and its reengineering.

9.4 Requirement: Modeling the information-processing network

The information-processing network described in Chapter 4 provides us with a view of one aspect of the enterprise. The enterprise consists of a vast number of information-processing nodes representing the workers, machines, and organizations of the enterprise. Looking at the enterprise in this way is like looking through a microscope at a living organism. In each case, we see lattices of cells. In the case of the enterprise, the cells are information-processing nodes. Thus our object-oriented modeling constructs must provide the ability to model information-processing networks consisting of information-processing nodes.

Summary: Information-processing network

The information-processing network consists of information-processing nodes interconnected by communication channels. The information-processing nodes are people, information machines (e.g., computers), and lower-level information-processing networks. The information-processing nodes communicate by sending each other physical symbol sequences representing information. The receiver will generally respond to a symbol sequence by doing something noticeable such as altering its internal state and possibly sending its own physical symbol sequences to other information-processing nodes connected to the network. The information-processing nodes exchange symbol sequences along channels governed by the Shannon theory of information. We measure the information content of these symbol sequences in terms of both their novelty and the amount of uncertainty that a symbol sequence removes from the receiver.

Modeling the information-processing network

We saw in Chapter 5 that object-oriented systems consist of lattices of objects that offer services to each other and communicate by passing each other messages. The information-processing network with its interlocking lattices of information-processing nodes is conceptually identical to the object-oriented system consisting of lattices of objects. Both information-processing nodes and objects exchange messages to discharge the duties of the larger system. Thus we can be very optimistically that the information-processing network should map straight-across to the object-oriented paradigm.

Implications to enterprise modeling

A very important aspect of the information-processing network of an enterprise is that it extends far beyond the legal boundary of the enterprise. While the enterprise will have a boundary defined in legal terms (e.g., a corporation is defined by its articles of incorporation, a government agency is limited by statute) we are interested here in its system boundary. The enterprise is part of a larger information-processing network. In this view, the enterprise is a subsystem to a larger system consisting of the business channel, the general business community, government agencies, and the general population. We can accomplish much of the optimization of the enterprise by considering this larger infrastructure, especially the network of customers and suppliers of the enterprise.

The communication channels of the enterprise can take many different forms. We normally think of communication channels as physical "wires" connecting communicating agents (e.g., telephone loops, computer cable, etc.). However, our concept of communications channels is much more general than that. For example, members of a team working in a skunk works would be an example of an infrastructure of communication channels. The location of the team members in a single room provides the communication channel infrastructure. Another example is an infrastructure of communication channels among employees and executive management in which employees are always aware of the larger mission of the enterprise. We will see in Chapter 23 that providing all of these communications channels is a critical part in building a successful enterprise.

9.5 Requirement: Modeling the physical symbol system

In Chapter 4, we introduced Newell and Simon's physical symbol system. The physical symbol system is an abstract machine that is at the core of a physical information-processing node and the component that gives it its information-processing capabilities. A physical symbol system is a modeling device, which we use to model the information processing capability of a person or an information machine such a computer. We model the physical symbol system as executing a script. The physical symbol system is very important to enterprise modeling because it provides a succinct way to model the behavior of the physical information-processing nodes that make up the enterprise's information-processing network, or its infrastructure. Thus our object-oriented modeling constructs must provide the ability to model the physical symbol system.

Summary: Physical symbol system
The physical symbol system purposefully takes advantage of information. The physical symbol system contains state information representing both information that models its environment as well as its scripts. The scripts, which are sequences of action, are stored as symbol structures, along with other symbol structures, in the state-memory. The script is executed by the very-specialized control component of

the physical symbol system. The control component is capable of interpreting a physical symbol sequence and designating the symbols as surrogates for lower-level processes or entities. The control component of the machine interprets the scripts to cause the production of information or materials to the environment. In the process, the physical symbol system undergoes a state transition that results in a change to its state information. We define a thread of control as the continuous operation of the control component of the physical symbol system to interpret its script. In effect, a script defines the behavior of the physical symbol system and hence, the behavior of the information-processing node.

While the physical symbol system is a modeling device, many types of information-processing nodes actually consist of physical symbol systems. For example, the computer processor is, in fact, a physical symbol system. In this case, the script is a computer program. On the other hand, while we can't reduce the massively complex human mind to a simple physical symbol system, we can at least model the role of the worker as a physical symbol system executing the script of the role.

Modeling the physical symbol system

We can see that the workings of a physical symbol system are an example of a conceptual activity defined in our conceptual type hierarchy. The physical symbol system causes change to be visited on entities. In effect, the dynamic mechanism of the information-processing node is a real-world example of a conceptual activity. We saw in Chapter 5 that objects are defined, in part, by their services and that services can be modeled using scripts. We can model the operation of the control component of a physical symbol system as the execution of the services of a corresponding object designed to model the physical symbol system (or its information-processing node). Thus we can be optimistic that the physical symbol system will map well to the object-oriented paradigm.

While we are optimistic that we could model the physical symbol system as an object, a more fundamental question concerns the conceptual activity. Recall that the conceptual activity is a subtype of the conceptual situation. The conceptual activity is especially important to modeling the general system because it represents the actual change mechanism, the dynamic property of a general system. So far, we have regarded the conceptual activity as an unspecified mechanism that causes change in entities.

Can we make a connection between the conceptual activity and the services of an object to properly model the conceptual activity? The answer is yes. We can model the conceptual activity as the services of an object. For the entity object, the services represent activities that are invoked individually. In the case of the process object, a continuously running service represents the thread of control. This means that in any real-world modeling domain such as the enterprise, all system dynamics can be interpreted as the execution of object services. While we have a right to be optimistic that we can map the conceptual activity to the object service for modeling purposes, whether the world is really this way is another question and is a sticky philosophical question beyond the scope of this book.

Implications for enterprise modeling

Earlier, we reviewed how a script is used by the controller of a physical symbol system for defining and controlling the state changes of a process. This leads to the important idea of using the scripting concept to define business processes in the enterprise. This would occur at the lowest level of decomposition in which we use scripts to describe the sequence of operations of the process elements. We can think of these scripts as analogous to computer programs, which are able to make use of reusable functions as appropriate.

In particular, the technique for constructing scripts with reusable functions consisting of sequences of elementary information processes or lower level functions, should find wide use in enterprise modeling. The enterprise consists of thousands of value-adding transformations that follow the paradigm of the abstract function. With the function, we have a consistent, easily understood modeling device to describe the reusable transformations of the enterprise at the lower levels.

We saw in Chapter 4 that the use of information by the information-processing node has a much deeper significance, that of adaptivity. According to Allen Newell and Herbert Simon, the purpose of information is to pursue adaptivity to the environment. In effect, information makes adaptivity possible and adaptivity requires information. We can conclude that all information-processing nodes, whether they are a human being, a real-time factory-control system or a data-processing payroll system, are actually goal-seeking, adaptive systems. This means that as we design our information-processing nodes of the enterprise, the paradigm underlying their architecture will be characterized as goal-seeking and adaptive. In particular, we should be able to trace all the properties of any information-processing node as supporting goal-seeking and/or adaptation either directly or indirectly.

Part 3

Business Foundations of Object-Oriented Enterprise Modeling

Introduction to Part 3

IN THIS SECTION OF THE BOOK, we focus on the business or enterprise foundations upon which we have based object-oriented enterprise modeling. The intent of this section is to identify essential general business principles and to relate them to the academic constructs of general systems and object-oriented theory identified in the first portions of the book. Synergy among these principles and constructs leads to fundamental conclusions that, in turn, provide the basis for our approach to defining and modeling the enterprise.

We will synthesize these fundamental conclusions in the form of seven primary postulates upon which this methodology is based. The following chapters comprise Part 3:

- ◆ Chapter 10 introduces some general business theory as background and introduces the notion of fractals.

- ◆ Chapter 11 provides an introduction to the concepts of enterprises and industries as systems; enterprises as information-processing systems, specifically, the common enterprise infrastructure; the functional business process abstraction; and business process abstractions as fractals.

♦ Chapter 12 presents our conclusions regarding a fundamental framework for enterprises derived from the synthesis of principals and ideas presented in the preceding chapters. Included here are the development of concepts of two related ideas: the theory that enterprises are value based systems and the theory that industry imperatives and strategic mandates are approaches to creating a strategic framework providing vision, strategy and operating management direction to the enterprise.

Chapter 10

General Business Foundations

10.1 Introduction

The general business foundations presented in this chapter reflect some significant thinking from outside the systems and information management arenas. These business foundations have influenced our views of the purpose and content of enterprise modeling. We by no means intend for this to serve as a primer for the concepts and theory presented. It is simply necessary to establish a minimal background and context for the logical constructs supporting our view of object-oriented enterprise modeling. We recommend that the interested reader pursue the published work of the originators of these concepts and the explanatory works of other authors.

The first two sections of the chapter deal with some high-impact business constructs: Porter's value chain and Tregoe's strategic framework. The last section provides a very brief introduction to fractals, a field in the emerging science of chaos.

These constructs, along with those presented in Part 1, have combined with our real-world experiences to become the basis for our view of enterprise modeling. Chapters 11 and 12 discuss the synergy and leverage between these disparate conceptual areas that result in the logic for the content and approach to the object-oriented enterprise modeling process.

10.2 Value chains and value systems—Michael Porter

Perhaps the single largest influence upon the way we think about enterprises, particularly business enterprises, has been Professor Michael Porter's work. While at Harvard Business School, Porter developed a very highly regarded Masters of Business Administration course on industry and competitive analysis. He has written three books particularly relevant to this work: _Competitive Advantage_ (1980), _Competitive Strategy_ (1985), and _The Competitive Advantage of Nations_ (1990). In addition, Porter supports a business consultancy practice, leveraging his concepts and expertise to some of the largest enterprises in the world.

Specifically, Porter's concepts of value creation as a core for understanding markets, businesses, and competition is continually reflected in these pages. Similarly, Porter's structure and approach to market, industry, and competitor analyses are broadly and liberally leveraged.

While Chapter 14 deals extensively with the value chain construct as one structural "view" of an enterprise and what that means to object-oriented enterprise modeling, it is introduced here in the context of enterprise fundamentals and theory. In his value chain approach, Porter proposes that the basis for every enterprise is the process of taking some source material(s) and manipulating them such that value is added to those materials. The overall process consists of a series, or chain, of smaller value adding steps; hence the _value chain_. _Value_ has two significant attributes in this context. A product's value is always determined by those who consume or use the product. The measure of value is determined by what these consumers will exchange (money typically) in order to derive benefit from the product.

In fact, many enterprises participate in the generation of value in goods and services consumed by every market. This extended chain of value adding steps or processes represents the operational steps or processes of many individual businesses. In addition, there are goods and services, which, although not specifically designed or intended for a specific market, can be used as alternatives to products that were so designed and targeted. Moreover, Porter states that the competitiveness of any business is determined by that business' position in the overall value chain of an industry, or in our terms, the _value system_ that is made up of all suppliers, direct competitive product providers, substitution product providers, and consumers (Porter, 1985).

In addition to a significant degree of insight regarding the dynamics of markets and businesses, Porter also presents a picture of business that is very different from the one that "Western" business managers might recognize. That picture is that almost everything that matters to a business is external to the enterprise itself. Starting with the markets, which must ultimately determine and define any enterprise, all the way through to the concept of the value system, all of Porter's discussions of competitive opportunity and advantage are within the context of the external environment within which businesses operate. While there is no denying the importance of what an enterprise actually does, clearly the majority of management factors in the Porter view of the world are those that are in the "external environment." Therefore, the most important relationships an enterprise model must reflect and represent are those between the enterprise (and/or its components) and external entities (customers, suppliers, regulators, and competitors).

Quite aside from the value chain construct, we have gained (and continue to learn) a great deal from Porter's 1980 work, *Competitive Strategy: Techniques for Analyzing Industries and Competitors*. It can be argued that this volume is the primer on how to understand an enterprise's position in the world. As can be seen in the methodology, the approaches put down by Porter in that work can be relied upon to collect, analyze, and evaluate the relationship values of the environment within which the enterprise must exist.

Similarly, his 1985 work, *Competitive Advantage: Creating and Sustaining Superior Performance*, provides much guidance on how to synthesize strategic positioning for competitive success within industries. These factors are exceedingly important in establishing the external and internal values with which every enterprise functions. These values will be the bases for rational and effective enterprise structure and operations. It is the system of values that is used to derive, validate, and then sustain each and every tangible interrelationship that make up the enterprise model.

10.3 Driving force and strategic framework— Benjamin Tregoe and John Zimmerman

The concepts of Benjamin Tregoe and John Zimmerman regarding a "driving force" in business planning and management are fundamental to the constructs of Object-Oriented Enterprise Modeling. Their concept of driving force is used to clarify and communicate strategic options. It is an impartial method for putting competing points of view on the table and ultimately for deriving an organization's future strategy. According to Tregoe and Zimmerman, strategy is "vision directed at what the organization should be, and not how the organization will get there. (Strategy is) the framework which guides those choices that determine the nature and direction of an organization. (Tregoe and Zimmerman, 1980)

Table 10.1 Categories of strategic areas

Category	Strategic area
Products/Markets	Products Offered
	Market Needs
Capabilities	Technology
	Production Capability
	Method of Sale
	Method of Distribution
	Natural Resources
Results	Size/Growth
	Return/Profit

Driving force

Tregoe and Zimmerman propose that there are only nine fundamental strategic areas with which enterprise management are concerned and that, of these, one that is of paramount importance to any given business. This strategic area is so important that whenever there are conflicting business choices, the option that most benefits or supports the overriding strategic area is always chosen. This strategic area, then, becomes the driving force for that enterprise. The nine strategic areas are grouped into three categories as shown in Table 10.1.

The strategic area of "products offered" relates to the products and ongoing support or maintenance services an enterprise offers. These are defined in terms of common characteristics such as needs met, functions performed, scale and durability, and so on. An organization that holds this as its driving force believes these products are the key to its long-term success. The idea is that these products can be leveraged into new geographic and/or need-based markets. It constantly focuses on improving and extending these products. All other strategic areas of the business will be directed toward supporting the effective development, production, promotion, sale, delivery, and servicing of these specific products. When one market for their products begins to "dry up," these businesses will put a priority on finding alternative markets rather than changing the product to meet the changing market need. General Motors might be considered an example of this kind of business, the focus being the automobile product.

The "market needs" strategic area is focused upon those markets served by the organization. Zimmerman and Tregoe define a *market* as "a group of current or potential buyers or end users who share common needs" (Tregoe and Zimmerman,

1980). These groups may be limited by geography. The market-need–focused enterprise will attempt to provide whatever products are necessary to satisfy the given market(s). In essence, these businesses believe that their future strength lies in their superior knowledge of the market. The test of a true market-based enterprise is whether the products offered really change based upon the changing needs of the given markets. Playboy Enterprises has exhibited a market-needs based behavior over its history.

"Technology" is considered another strategic area by Tregoe and Zimmerman. Technology is a field of knowledge and/or expertise associated with a specific discipline and includes the skills and knowledge of those working within the discipline as well as the mechanical tools, equipment, and facilities that support it. This strategic area often becomes the driving force for enterprises that establish a proprietary advantage in a technical field. This historically has been from ownership of patents. Today, proprietary aspects are maintained on the basis of secrecy and complexity that limits the risk of reproduction during the life span of the technology involved (a continuously decreasing time frame). Pharmaceutical firms such as Merck are examples of businesses with a technologic driving force.

The strategic area of "production capability" encompasses production methods and procedures and physical infrastructure (factory) capacity. An organization with this as its driving force will offer only products and services that can be produced with its existing capability. Both assembly-line and job-shop types of businesses frequently have this driving force. A steel fabricator such as US Steel is an example.

The strategic areas of "method of sale" and "method of distribution" are both very similar in concept to production capability. Instead of the methods and procedures and physical infrastructure capacity of production, these areas address sales and distribution, respectively. The method of sales is the primary way in which the enterprise convinces consumers to buy its products. Sharper Image and Home Shopping Network are examples of enterprises based upon methods of sale. The method of distribution is the way in which product reaches customers. McDonald's exhibits characteristic behavior of a distribution-based business.

The strategic area of "natural resources" encompasses the ownership and access to natural resources critical to an enterprise's success. Enterprises with this focus mobilize around the ability to maximize the use of natural resources under their control. They are constantly looking for new markets, products, extraction (i.e., production) techniques—anything that will extend the consumption of the natural resources within their control. Exxon is an easy example.

The strategic areas of "size/growth" and "return/profit" are similar in that they represent a focus of advantages to an enterprise's ownership. Environments where either of these are of primary importance will do anything to either extend the equity value of the enterprise or generate profit, respectively. Multinational conglomerates are examples of size/growth-based enterprises. Boise Cascade operated this way during the 1960s. Return/profit seemed to be favored increasingly during the 1980s when the only thing that mattered to most US companies was the quarterly return. ITT has historically behaved as a profit-centered business.

The ability to identify meaningful strategic areas that affect industries and to establish a useful driving force for individual enterprises is an extremely powerful part of our business-modeling environment.

The strategic framework

Similarly, the idea of a definable framework of strategies leading an enterprise's progress across a specific time frame has directly contributed to our business modeling practices. According to Tregoe and Zimmerman, such a framework "will direct choices about the kinds of products the organization will and will not consider, the geographic markets and market segments or customer groups it will and will not serve, the key capabilities or resources necessary to support those products and markets, the growth and return required, and the allocation or resources (Tregoe and Zimmerman, 1980). Tregoe and Zimmerman call such a structure of strategies the *strategic framework*.

Tregoe and Zimmerman derive the strategic framework from the driving force as represented in Figure 10.1.

With the driving force as the unifying concept, the strategic framework is the best definition of what the enterprise really is, and it is usually the best and most consistent means of communicating this definition within and without the business:

◆ It becomes possible to identify guiding factors that will predetermine the actions and outcome of a specific enterprise as it faces operating decision points.

◆ The driving force concept establishes a basis or platform for a strategy framework with which to plan and operate an enterprise.

◆ Driving forces can be leveraged as the "glue" that keeps disparate resources centered on delivering common value to customers.

◆ Having identified such factors, it is possible to use them as one litmus test for inclusion or outsourcing decisions about specific functional business processes.

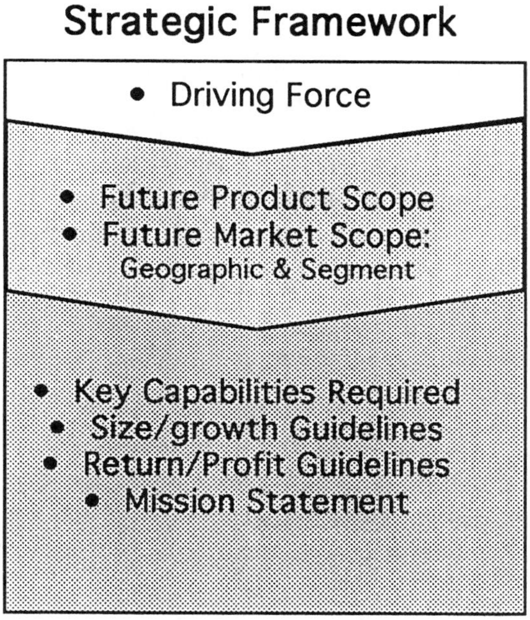

Strategic Framework

Figure 10.1 *Tregoe and Zimmerman's strategic framework.*

10.4 Chaos and fractals—Benoit Mendelbrot

In recent years, physicists, astronomers, economists, and biologists, among others, have been developing alternatives for understanding the vast complexities that exist in the natural world. These alternatives are evolving into the science of "chaos." The science of chaos is said to provide order and pattern where formerly only the random, erratic, and unpredictable have been seen. Though not representative of mainstream business fundamentals, this new science clearly seems appropriate for the environments in which most enterprises and organizations operate. In the prologue to his book *Chaos: Making a New Science,* James Gleick characterizes the pioneers of chaos theory in the following manner:

> They had an eye for pattern, especially pattern that appeared on different scales at the same time. They had a taste for randomness and complexity, for jagged edges and sudden leaps. . . . They feel that they are turning back a trend in science toward reductionism, the analysis of systems in terms of their constituent parts: quarks,

> chromosomes, or neurons. They believe that they are looking for the whole. (Gleick, 1987)

In our experience, this is precisely appropriate to business enterprise today and captures the essence of what enterprise modeling must accommodate and communicate. In one sense, it runs counter to much of the abstraction and system decomposition we discussed in Part 1, but, in another sense, this approach of turning back reductionism and looking for the whole is exactly what is required in today's enterprise management environments and is the essence of the optimization process within the context of the general system.

While all fields in this chaos science will probably result in great benefits for understanding, planning, and managing enterprises of the future, one field of the new science has caught our imagination as particularly apt for enterprise modeling today—the field of fractals.

While with IBM's Thomas J. Watson Research Center, Benoit Mendelbrot developed the concept of fractal geometry, or fractional dimensions. Developed from initial work analyzing fluctuations in cotton prices over a hundred year period, Mendelbrot's fractal theory is a way to measure things that have no precise definition, things such as the degree of roughness of an object or the extent of jaggedness of broken glass.

Mendelbrot's claim is that the degree of irregularity of any given subject remains constant over scale. Among other things, the ability to measure irregularity allows one to observe patterns in the irregularity, making the irregular regular! It is this aspect of fractals which is of most immediate interest: that we can observe (and create) patterns of process and relationships that will remain constant at random scale and in any of the relation dimensions (e.g., time, space, cause, values). Mendelbrot's approach is to observe phenomena, abstract patterns of interaction, and extrapolate and/or interpolate these patterns at varying scale and scope.

One significant difference between Mendelbrot's abstraction approach and that described in Chapter 1 of this book is that both Hoare (1972) and Work and Balmforth (1993) characterize abstraction in terms of ignoring differences or dispensable qualities of things. In essence, their abstractions are based upon elimination of the randomness in which Mendelbrot finds pattern. These constructs are not, however, inconsistent. *The Oxford Dictionary of Computing* defines *abstraction* as "the principle of ignoring those aspects of a subject that are not relevant to the current purpose in order to concentrate more fully on those that are." Mendelbrot's approach simply ignores the obvious similarities to focus on random, seemingly accidental associations. If one can exercise Mendelbrot's abstraction approach, the scope of objects subject to systems theory is expanded dramatically. By definition, those types of patterns captured as fractals are random and beyond the control of any "system." Therefore, they are said to be outside the system but within the domain of the system's environment. As every business leader knows too well, finding a way for manageable systems to subsume significant portions of the unpredictable environment would produce unimaginable benefits.

It occurs to us that this is precisely what is being attempted in several disparate disciplines. Entrepreneurs have built wildly successful enterprises upon one abstract business paradigm that is leverageable at multiple scales (this is frequently demonstrated with successful sales techniques, although Fred Smith's "hub and spoke" distribution model at Federal Express is probably a more concrete example). Good software engineers have been attempting to achieve it with software reuse for years. Indeed, the object-oriented paradigm itself is an abstracted, repeatable, patterned approach—arguably, a fractal!

With so many disparate examples occurring all of the time and all around us, fractals seem particularly apropos to the problem of modeling enterprise processes. (Besides, the concept seems to match the crazy way in which we have always viewed the world!)

10.5 Conclusion

In addition to the systems-based theory presented in Part 1, we see at least five themes that have significant impact upon the constructs of visualizing and managing enterprise operations. While there are certainly many other equally significant bodies of thought, these five have had the greatest academic influence upon the function and process of enterprise modeling as it is presented here. The five constructs as we have interpreted them are summarized as follows:

- ◆ The essence of the enterprise process can be thought of as a chain of activities, each adding value successively to some resource to provide product to a marketplace.

- ◆ Most of an enterprise's relationships, interactions, and processes involve components outside the domain of the enterprise itself.

- ◆ A finite number of unique but identifiable and manageable strategic forces drive any enterprise.

- ◆ A simple and cogent strategic framework based upon identified strategic forces is imperative for effective enterprise leadership and effectiveness.

- ◆ It is possible to establish abstract patterns that maintain integrity independent of the scale, scope, and process content to which they are applied.

It is easy to see or imagine significant applications for and subsequent benefit from any one of these constructs. In some cases individual constructs may be leveraged independent from any others (in this chapter or from Part 1). However, our next step is to discuss the synergies within the foundation theory and to relate the concepts that we synthesized from them.

Chapter **11**)

Five Constructs for the Enterprise System

11.1 Introduction

So far, we've presented a great deal of background to the logic and thinking that has guided our development of the object-oriented enterprise modeling process. As we have interrelated this background logic and combined it with our experiences in the real world, we have developed some useful logical constructs. This chapter presents five of these constructs:

- ◆ The enterprise as a general system

- ◆ Enterprises as information-processing systems

- ◆ The unified enterprise infrastructure

- ◆ Functional abstractions of enterprise processes

- ◆ Enterprise fractals: a new basis for business

Together, they are leveraged repeatedly in the process of creating effective enterprise objectives and efficient enterprise process designs.

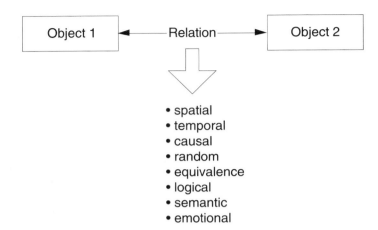

Figure 11.1 *Relation.*

11.2 The enterprise as a general system

We embrace the notion that every enterprise is, in fact, a general system. With every description of *system* we have come across, there is a consistent and persistent match with what we know enterprises to be. The general system was defined to be "a set of interrelated objects which together pursue common objectives." Remembering that objects are the "things" in a system, this is equally as good a definition of an enterprise as it is a system. The traditional definition of business is "an organization that exists for the purpose of making profits." Although there is much debate as to whether the profit motive is the common objective of business, we believe it to be valid to assume that all enterprises, including businesses, are groups of entities organized to pursue a common objective.

All of the descriptions and definitions of the various perspectives and approaches to systems are equally translatable to enterprise organizations. To illustrate the point, consider one of the concepts represented in Figure 11.1. Remember that the "relation" expresses the dependence of one object on another —or, in the context of an enterprise, between "things." These might be a tool and an employee, a product and a customer, or a tool and a product. You get the idea. The point is that every enterprise is affected by the "relations" between those objects within which it interrelates directly.

The types of relations provided in the figure are completely applicable to the enterprise. If we flip back through Part 1 of the book and take any of the system concepts presented there, we can readily fit them into a business abstraction. Table 11.1

Table 11.1 System concepts

Modeling	Hierarchical-multilayer systems	System decomposition
Closed Systems	State - Process Dichotomies	Homeostasis
Meta-Layer	Object Relations	Message Pragmatics
Semantic Memory	Information-Processing Nodes	Encapsulation

is a random list of some concepts from Part 1. Take a minute to consider them and see if you can't easily fit them to your experiences with enterprise organizations.

This applicability of systems theory to organizational enterprises is extremely significant. It provides us with the opportunity to take the disciplines and tools associated with general systems and apply them to the enterprise. This, in turn, has impacted the way we approach the issues involved with planning and operating a business.

We are clearly not the first to make the connection between business and systems. McKinsey and Company first developed the business system concept. McKinsey offered the idea that a firm is a series of functions and that analyzing how each function is performed relative to competitors (more commonly known today as "benchmarking") can provide useful insights. McKinsey also emphasized the power of redefining the business system to gain competitive advantage, an important idea. Their business system concept, however, speaks only to broad functions rather than processes. Such an approach does not distinguish between types of activities or uses of processes, and it does not show how they are related. The concept is also limited to the internal functions of an enterprise and doesn't accommodate the full scope of the value chain and the enterprise's environment. The most complete descriptions of McKinsey's business system concept are Gluck (1980), and Bauron (1981).

The McKinsey business system concept is fairly limited and we are extending the systems–business analogy to its logical limits in this work. We argue that every enterprise is a system in every sense of the term. Similarly, we would argue that each enterprise is a subsystem in many other larger-scale systems such as industries, economies, and societies.

An industry can be described as a group of firms contributing value toward creation of products that are close substitutes for one another (Porter, 1980). Many businesses participate in multiple industries. We define an economy in this context as the procurement, production, distribution, and consumption of goods and services within a given domain. This description is almost identical to the functional structure of most industries. Therefore, businesses are clearly component elements of economies (in many cases, enterprises and economies can even be the same thing). Societies are enduring and cooperative social groups with organized patterns of relationships. Since all systems exhibit organizational and functional relationships among their entities, by our definition all enterprises are societies. Clearly, they also intersect with and contribute to other societal systems.

The extent to which such broader-scale structures as industries, economies, and societies can be considered true "systems" is limited only by the degree and extent to which control can be exerted over them (remember that entities that affect a system and are, or can be, under the control or direct influence of a system are, by definition, part of that system. Involved entities that are not controllable by the system are considered to be part of the system's environment). Admittedly, since much of what is involved in such broad realms as economies is environmental, the systems analog applies currently to a limited subset of these broader scale structures. However, it is clear that capabilities to strongly influence (and even directly manage) traditional environmental elements of structures like economies or industries are increasing rapidly.

It seems obvious to us that enterprises are general systems. Most of us would agree that it is equally obvious that the disciplines of systems are not consistently applied to most enterprises (business and government enterprises in particular). Similarly, we do not often see business disciplines reflecting leadership (purpose, values, and strategy) being leveraged into systems theory. Synergizing the strengths of these fundamentals in an integrated modeling process should provide significant advantage to the understanding, positioning, and management of enterprise systems.

11.3 Enterprises as information-processing networks

Merging the theoretical constructs of hierarchical-multilayer systems, information-processing networks, and physical symbol systems we conclude that enterprises operate as information-processing systems in their own right. The function and process of the hierarchical-multilayer system requires the ability to contain and communicate a rich repertoire of relations between and among entity and process objects of the system. Such an environment requires the existence of interconnected information processing capabilities distributed throughout the infrastructure.

Knowledge of this rich repertoire, the existence of the various system processing objects, and the ability to communicate between them establishes the existence of an information-processing network within every enterprise. Accordingly, the process and entity objects of the hierarchical-multilayer system must also be viewed as information processing nodes in the information-processing network system. Note that, using Newell and Simon's physical symbol system, these nodes can be anything that processes information: humans, computers, calculators, etc. Further, we can say that the repertoire of relations between and among entities will be communicated in physical symbol sequences (Newell and Simon) over channels governed by the Shannon theory of information. The physical symbol scripts define and communicate the behavior of each information processing node, hence following hierarchical-multilayer systems theory, monitoring all scripts of the enterprise provides a picture of the behavior of the enterprise processes.

We can also see that a complete and accurate view of the information-processing network (in all of its forms) provides an opportunity to view and understand the logical operating topology of the enterprise. This is the next best thing to having a physically operating artifact—a process model—reflecting all of the interactions between the entities and objects of the enterprise. Note that you still won't know logical content, although you do when this model is augmented by the operations-layer and meta-layer models, the physical symbol script content, and the ability to interpret them.

Accordingly, the scope (and scale) of the information-processing network of which every enterprise is a part extends well beyond the physical boundaries of the enterprise itself. As discussed earlier in this chapter, the information—the knowledge of the repertoire of relations—must include the larger-scale systems of industries, economies, and societies. The ability to optimize an enterprise's contribution to an overall value system depends increasingly upon integration into the broader scale information-processing networks. Many implementations of just-in-time inventorying, customer-controlled manufacturing, and non-invoiced payment contracts are examples of improving an enterprise's value generation efficiency by extending into a larger-scoped information-processing system.

Taking an information processing network view of the enterprise system can result in extending the scope of the enterprise domain allowing significant improvement in value generation and delivery. Further, the information processing network view can be used to originate an operational model of the logical hierarchical relationships of process objects and entity objects of an enterprise system. Further, this can provide the basis for a model depicting the behavior of the enterprise system.

11.4 The unified enterprise infrastructure

We have inferred from these theoretical constructs that the physical infrastructure of an enterprise tends to operate as a single integrated whole. This is our observation as well as our experience in actual business environments. Again, our generic definition of a general system is "a set of interrelated objects that together pursue common objectives." We believe this to apply equally well to physical infrastructures and to other described systems.

In the context of this work, we consider the physical infrastructure of an enterprise to be the underlying foundation of capital goods and facilities necessary for the enterprise to actually operate. These goods and facilities may or may not be owned directly by the enterprise itself. For our purposes, it is only necessary that the enterprise have control over their use. Examples of infrastructure elements would include: buildings, computers, communications facilities, tools, factories, vehicles, almost anything that isn't consumable.

Like any other system, infrastructure tends to be less effective and efficient when it is engineered, deployed, and operated in autonomous pieces. For example, buildings obtained without knowledge of operating business requirements have little chance of nearing optimal performance in any relation with other business objects. Table 11.2 amplifies this example.

While this may seem to be a trivial example that no reasonable individual would pursue, infrastructure resources are procured every day by autonomous enterprise sub-groups without sufficient consideration of the enterprise system they are to support. It would be surprising if the reader can't quickly think of several examples from their own experience.

In contrast, we see several references in the theoretical system constructs that indicate the necessity (or at least advantages) of taking a systemic view of infrastructure. The following are three examples from the earlier foundations material:

> **1.** From Chapter 10, Porter's view is that almost everything that matters to a business is external to the enterprise itself. If the most important relation-

Table 11.2 Example suboptimization of infrastructure relations

Relation	Optimization issue
Spatial	Is it geographically where it needs to be? Is it the optimal size?
Temporal	Can the building be accessed when it is needed?
Causal	Does its use cause or require extra supporting objects or processes?
Equivalence	Is there another, redundant facility that will serve as well?

ships an enterprise model must reflect and represent are those between the enterprise components and external entities (customers, suppliers, regulators, and competitors), it should follow that the development of the infrastructure supporting that model should adequately address the relations between itself (the infrastructure system entities) and impacts upon those external entities.

2. Simon tells us that process models "provide the means for producing or generating objects having the desired characteristics" (Simon, 1984). This implies that some determination of physical infrastructure is made during development of process models. Accordingly, enterprise process modeling implies an enterprise-wide view of infrastructure.

3. The infrastructure system view is a differentiated subsystem that is specialized to one purpose, in this case, the physical capacity to perform the functions of the enterprise. Thomas Athey has told us that "a distinguishing characteristic of systems thinking is the realization that (*a*) the whole is more than the sum of the parts (subsystems), and (*b*) what is best for the subsystems (components) is not necessarily what is best for the overall system and vice versa" (Athey, 1982).

The physical infrastructure of an enterprise can be considered a subsystem of the overall enterprise system. Accordingly, there are significant and compelling reasons to ensure that the infrastructure is managed and controlled in a systemic enterprise-wide manner. A common practice in U.S. enterprise is for specialized infrastructure domains to evolve, which often lose sight of the common objectives of the enterprise system. Example domains might evolve around such physical objects as computing system platforms; telecommunications facilities; land, buildings, structures, and rights-of-way; clerical support tools and facilities; or motor vehicles.

11.5 Functional abstractions of enterprise processes

The use of abstractions to "make sense of something we don't understand in terms of something we do understand" (Work and Balmworth, 1993) is an important principle from Part 1. Most of us have used abstractions all of our lives by creating analogies that help others (or ourselves) understand concepts or ideas. However, combining the concept of abstraction with other system theory can add discipline and process to the idea. In addition, the combination can provide focus for knowing when and how to use abstractions. This principle is also critical to our understanding of what models (abstractions all) are not!

Several definitions of *abstraction* were provided in Chapter 1. The two most germane to the discussion here are:

> In the development of the understanding of *complex* phenomena, the most powerful *tool* available to the human intellect is abstraction. Abstraction rises from the recognition of similarities between certain objects, situations, or processes in the real (comprehended) world and the decision to concentrate on these similarities, and to ignore, for the time being, their differences (emphasis added). (Hoare, 1972)

and

> Abstraction is a mental act which separates that which is characteristic of a thing from its accidental associations. (Work and Balmforth, 1993)

Abstraction is so very critical to us in this process of designing enterprises for several reasons:

- ◆ Enterprise systems are extremely complex and the systems with which they interact are generally more complex still.

- ◆ The scope and scale of most enterprises is so broad and vast that understanding effects from changes (within the enterprise system or without) is difficult or impossible without use of abstract modeling.

- ◆ Similarly, abstractions allow for the rational selection of options for change to or creation of an enterprise system.

- ◆ As described earlier, enterprise systems have multiple perspective views of the entities, processes, and their relationships. Abstraction facilitates the conceptualization, communication, and management of these views.

- ◆ Abstraction encourages the communication of the essence of corporate enterprise values, purpose, and direction.

There are literally hundreds of abstractions being used in this book. Indeed, it would be impossible for us to formulate and communicate the concept of object-oriented enterprise modeling without the abstraction tool. Similarly, it is impossible to design, implement, and operate today's enterprises without the ability to abstract the multiple entities and relationships of which they consist.

By applying the object-oriented paradigm, we are immediately provided some limits and boundaries within which our abstractions must always fit. Specifically, abstractions must have two characteristics: they must be consistent with and fit the nature of other abstractions with which they interrelate, and they must encompass both the physical and intellectual aspects of the subject abstracted. Each of these constraints is discussed in more detail shortly.

The object-oriented model suggests that everything—that is, every definable entity—must have definable characteristics that represent each entity's relationship(s) with all other entities. This implies a requirement for consistency in semantics describing all objects within any global object space. Abstractions are encouraged to recognize and use objects that can be defined and interrelated with other abstractions and models. In this way, we are able to develop one or more abstracted pictures of one or more global systemic worlds, and we can do so in such a way that every picture has consistency of form, semantics, and style, which can then be rationally compared and interrelated.

Equally important is the object-oriented construct of inheritance: that an object is a member of a class that inherits properties from a superclass. This is especially important in the business environment as leaders attempt to generate abstract concepts that translate equally and consistently to the differing functional elements of the enterprise structure. The ability to capture the physical and process characteristics of objects as well as the values, concepts, and intellectual constructs that are associated with those same physical objects is essential to achieving consistency of purpose throughout the physical and political domains of an enterprise. As we will see, this enables and supports a correlation between the logical rationale—the value system—for the existence of entities, scenes, situations, and the relations between them. Therefore, when we add, subtract, or change any of these aspects, we have the opportunity via inheritance to project or anticipate (and therefore control) the impacts of change upon the logical values of the enterprise.

In summary, abstraction is an extremely useful tool for the comprehension and communication of complex systems like the enterprise. Further, guiding abstractions to fit within object-oriented, information-processing, and information-network theory encourages the extensible accumulation of interrelated abstractions. They also provide the potential for capturing and correlating semantic memory attributes with objects on the same basis as episodic memory attributes. This permits the values of a global enterprise to be associated continuously with its various abstracted subentities. Finally, the abstraction construct allows us to make artifacts of fundamental, building-block business processes that apply up and down the hierarchical-multilayer continuum of the enterprise. We call these *abstract business processes* (APBs). They are discussed in detail in Chapter 18.

11.6 Enterprise fractals: A new basis for business?

Fractal geometry has very exciting potential for the understanding and management of complex enterprise systems. We are just beginning to comprehend and appreciate the capabilities this new field offers to enterprise management.

The obvious opportunities involve the identification of new abstractions regarding patterns in market demand, economics, social value, geopolitics, and so on—all areas that have historically been part of the environment and beyond the control of the enterprise system. These abstract patterns occur independent of the scale of time, space, logic, or any of the other categories of relation between objects in all aspects of the historic domain of environment (including the physical one).

Theoretically, one or more process relationship abstractions, or generic process model(s), should be identifiable that work for the enterprise as a whole as well as at multiple hierarchical levels within the enterprise. Chapter 18 presents a sample ABP that is an abstraction of a commercial business process (an extension of Porter's generic value chain (Porter, 1985)). This ABP abstraction demonstrates properties of scale independence described in Chapter 10's brief discussion of fractal theory.

A less obvious opportunity for fractal geometry is in helping to define the individual business enterprise. We can begin to see this opportunity within the context of Tregoe and Zimmerman's strategic framework described in Chapter 10. (Tregoe and Zimmerman, 1980) Tregoe and Zimmerman use nine strategic areas to identify one driving force that is the basis for an enterprise's positioning and operational strategies. Of the nine strategic areas, at least five have high potential for being uniquely extended with fractal geometry: market needs, production process, sales process, distribution process, and natural resources.

Of this group of strategic areas, fractal abstractions can generate new and unique market definitions by identifying previously overlooked relationships driving the causes and effects of market needs. Similarly, natural resource deposits are already being located using fractal relationships between geophysical characteristics never considered previously. For enterprises whose driving force is a specific market or a natural resource and that can generate or control such fractals as intellectual property, the fractals themselves can become their business' defining elements.

Fractal abstractions can be equally powerful tools for helping process-based businesses to understand the opportunity of process leverage. For example, an express courier business (such as Federal Express) may today operate as if the distribution-processing capability (infrastructure and method) were its "driving force." The resulting strategic positioning and enterprise result may be extremely effective and respectable in today's terms. But what if a fractal abstraction is developed demonstrating the power to leverage the same process model (hub and spoke distribution) throughout the multilayer hierarchy of the enterprise itself or, even better, extend it with propriety across the whole global express courier industry? Better yet, what if it could leverage it across every market dealing with distributed anything?

This is the kind of potential that can be offered by abstractions that have no limits in scope and scale. Fractals will have a great deal to do with how we define and implement enterprises in the future. They will expand the domains of the enterprise systems in two ways. Fractals allow such systems to subsume aspects of the unpredictable environments around them, and they can extend the applicability of some present enterprise systems to envelope other existing systems or totally new ones. One very welcome benefit of embracing fractals specifically (and the science of chaos in general) is that they broaden our horizons of thought and help us to avoid suboptimization, which can be caused by too much decomposition. This can be a wonderful stimulus to innovation all by itself.

11.7 Conclusion

It seems obvious to us that enterprises are general systems. It is also obvious that many of the disciplines of systems are not consistently applied to enterprises (business and government enterprises in particular). It is equally apparent that current disciplines from business are not being leveraged into systems theory. Synergizing the strengths of these fundamentals in an integrated modeling process should provide significant advantage to the understanding, positioning, and management of enterprise systems.

Taking an information-processing network view of the enterprise system can result in extending the scope of the enterprise domain allowing significant improvement in value generation and delivery. Further, the information processing network view can be used to originate an operational model of the logical hierarchical relationships of process objects and entity objects of an enterprise system. Further, this can provide the basis for a model depicting the behavior of the enterprise system.

The physical infrastructure of an enterprise can be considered a subsystem of the overall enterprise system. Accordingly, there are significant and compelling reasons to ensure that the infrastructure is managed and controlled in a systemic enterprise-wide manner. Both common experience and theoretical principles indicate that physical infrastructure needs to be managed as an integrated subsystem of the enterprise.

Abstraction is an extremely useful tool for the comprehension and communication of complex systems such as the enterprise. Further, guiding abstractions to fit within object-oriented, information-processing, and information-network theory encourages the extensible accumulation of interrelated abstractions. This also provides the potential for capturing and correlating semantic memory attributes with objects on the same basis as episodic memory attributes. This permits the values of an enterprise to be associated continuously with the various abstracted entities of that enterprise. Finally, the abstraction construct allows us to make artifacts of fundamental, building block business processes, or abstract business processes, which apply up and down the hierarchical-multilayer continuum of the enterprise.

Fractals will have a great deal to do with how we define and implement enterprises in the future. They will expand the domains of the enterprise systems in two ways. Fractals allow such systems to subsume aspects of the unpredictable environments around them, and they can extend the applicability of some present enterprise systems to envelope other existing systems or totally new ones.

Finally, we conclude that the theoretical disciplines necessary to abstract and model our complex enterprise environments do exist. We believe that today's technologies, methods and procedures, and intellectual tools are sufficient to deal with enterprises as systems. We can proceed with confidence toward a methodology for modeling new and existing enterprises.

Chapter 12

Two Pivotal Constructs

12.1 Introduction

We have leveraged the five principle constructs presented in Chapter 11 throughout our development of the object-oriented enterprise modeling process. As we have interrelated these systemic principles with the background business logic and combined it all with our experiences in the real world, we have come to some useful conclusions. This chapter presents these conclusions in the form of two additional principle constructs: the value system and the strategic framework. Together, they establish a fulcrum from which to leverage effective enterprise objectives and efficient enterprise process designs.

Both of these constructs and the five presented in Chapter 11 are necessary but not sufficient by themselves to support the object-oriented enterprise modeling approach to establishing superior models of enterprise. Using the analogy of the fulcrum and lever, the two constructs presented in this chapter can be thought of as the intellectual base, the fulcrum, upon which the intellectual integrity of the exercise pivots. The general system constructs presented in Chapter 11 can be considered as the lever.

12.2 The value system construct

In this section, we put forth the notion that every enterprise system is a part of a global system of values—a system of semantics, if you will. Our experience is that the global value system is so vast in scope that we haven't currently the skills or resources to grapple with it all at once. Therefore, we address three distinct value systems as we try to understand the enterprise environment (a total of four when we include values associated with the workforce). These value systems are the market system, the industry system, and the sociopolitical system (a societal system is also included in some cases). Five separate theoretical constructs have lead us to synthesize the overall enterprise value system from these value processes. These include:

◆ Porter's assertions regarding the value systems of industries

◆ The observation that virtually all strategic relationships are external to the enterprise

◆ The theoretical existence of systems within environments

◆ Practical experience with preliminary fractal theory

◆ Personal experience with business enterprise

Some exposure to the less esoteric of these observations is provided next.

Industries and value systems

Porter states that the competitiveness of any business is determined by its position in the overall value chain, or in our terms, the *value system* (Porter, 1985). From this, we infer the existence of broader systems than enterprise systems. We recognize that the chain of value in this context is limited to the value of the end product as determined by the consumer. However, implied in the model is that knowledge exists within the overall industry to recognize and produce this value. Further, this knowledge must exist at more points than just at the final industry-to-consumer delivery point. We therefore assume this to be an integrated system of information regarding the industry and the particular marketplace. Our working definition of an *industry* is the "value system" that is made up of all suppliers, direct competitive product providers, substitution product providers, and consumers.

Focusing strategy outside the enterprise

The observation that all major strategic competitive relationships that enterprises accommodate are external to the enterprise system also started us thinking along the lines of some greater industry value system. The construct here is that every business has to establish positions from which it hopes to achieve competitive advantage. These positions (sometimes logically perceived, sometimes spatial) are always relative to entities that are external to the enterprise itself. Porter establishes the competitive forces to be (Porter, 1980):

◆ The market

◆ Suppliers

◆ Products

◆ New and potential competitive entrants

◆ Segment competitors

Enterprise success or failure is determined by many factors, but the choices made in these areas are critical according to Porter. In this context, Porter believes that "a useful working industry definition should encompass all segments for which segment interrelationships are very strong" (Porter, 1985).

This implies that a universal set of values applies to all participants within a given market segment. In most situations, all participants do not understand the values in the same manner, but in certain circumstances, *de facto* or *de jure* standards exist across some domain of common value that all players share.

Focus on three separate value systems

This methodology always considers three fundamental value systems: market values; industry values; and sociopolitical values.

Market values relate to quantitative and qualitative components of product worth. This includes a product's innate worth, value associated with temporal considerations, transaction considerations and costs affecting value, etc., and value associated with purely perceptual image.

Industry values identify current and future potential opportunity associated with an enterprise's actions and positioning. Such industry values deal with a business' geographic, resource control, market segment, qualitative and quantitative product positions relative to other participants of the industry.

Socio-political values deal with those constraints and expectations which are determined within organized society and its institutions (typically, executive, legislative, and judicial). These values constitute the political mores under which those institutions operate and function and the social mores governing people's actions, relationships, and reactions.

These values can range from being "green" (ecologically responsible), to supporting community affairs, to creating monopoly control of some markets. Such values can be extremely broad or very narrow and specific. In general, the synthesis and integration of these various external values is what enables successful enterprises to achieve effective and successful internal value systems. This methodology establishes a structure wherein these external values can be assessed and integrated with the values internal to the enterprise. Most important, it provides the opportunity to maintain a relationship between these values and all activities of the enterprise.

Ramifications of an external value focus

The most important relationships an enterprise model must represent are those between the enterprise (and/or its component entities) and external entities (customers, suppliers, regulators, and competitors). It is critical to capture and evaluate the perceptions of these communities to retain an effective grasp of the environmental values that affect the enterprise.

This approach of assessing enterprise impacts upon an overall value system leads us to make a minor exception to Porter's work on competitive advantage. Porter posits that value adding organizations within large competitive enterprises can effectively relate to consuming organizations within the same enterprise as "customers." We, in fact, have found this to significantly limit the competitive ability of an enterprise. The suboptimal aspects of such an arrangement relate to diseconomies of protected or monopoly markets. In the internal customer scenario, the internal organizations should be as efficient at adding value to the consuming market as openly competitive businesses are or would be. If such organizations can't do this, it won't make business sense for an enterprise to create and maintain such internal protected markets.

Accordingly, we propose to test the significance of internal or external procurement and operation of every process or function within an enterprise's value chain. In essence, enterprise planning must endeavor not only to understand the entire value system within which the business plays but to make reasoned decisions regarding positioning within the value system. In general, however, we have consistently found that the only viable "customers" for enterprise value-adding are external to the enterprise and that they pay in the hard currency critical to that enterprise. In other words, they provide cash flow.

Other thoughts on value systems

One of the exciting things about the object-oriented technology is the capability to associate such esoteric attributes as "value" with objects. There are many significant aspects of this, but the one we will focus on here has to do with establishing, propagating, and maintaining the "character" of an enterprise. We use the term *character* to mean the complex of logical values and ethical traits that are the basis of decisions, which in turn are the genesis for behavior. We posit that by capturing these things about an enterprise and about the environment within which it operates we will be able to rationally and consistently apply them. This will result in consistent behavior. Strategies will identify what directions organizations *should* take. Values will determine the directions that organizations *do* take.

Finally, values have been traditionally relegated as inherent to "culture." Believing that cultures don't change very rapidly (the commonly used figure is 20 years for a substantive value change), most U.S. businesses do not attempt to manage even the internal values of their organizations. Many believe that values management isn't possible. Many others don't think it is necessary. We believe this to be unfortunate, untrue, and ironic. It is possible to educate the organization by capturing the desired enterprise values and the rationale behind them and then instantiating them with case examples.

Peter Drucker likes to relate the "tradition of labor," which is analogous to this "tradition of culture." The concept of the tradition of labor was developed by Adam Smith 200 years ago. Smith believed that the people of what is now central Germany learned to be woodworkers and to make clocks and violins because of their heavy winters and subsequent time on their hands. With importations by immigrants and refugees, Smith said, it takes 200 years to build such a tradition. Drucker adds that this was the case until the 1900s when the Germans invented apprenticeship and condensed the 200 years into 5. Drucker goes on to point out that the advent of training (a U.S. invention during World War I) collapsed the 5 years into 6 months and in some cases to as little as 90 days (Drucker, 1992). We believe that, sociologically, corporate culture has been treated as if it were a thing of tradition and tradition alone.

Conclusions on values and value systems

The overall value system for an industry consists of the values driving its markets, the values governing the relationships of industry participants (cooperatively and competitively), and the sociopolitical values of society. The overall value system will dictate the environment within which an enterprise exists while the value system within an enterprise will define the character of that enterprise.

It is very significant that all of the industry value structures are external to the enterprise itself—they are very different from the ego-centric focus of most enterprises today! Every source of competitive advantage for a business can only be perceived and measured in the context of the business' contribution to these external values. Therefore, within an enterprise, the effectiveness of all functions and processes must be evaluated only by their ability to satisfy the external values—

there can be no customers, suppliers, or competitors internal to the enterprise.

The use of object-oriented technology to maintain associations between attributes of value and other enterprise objects will provide dramatic improvement in enterprise management and effectiveness. Changes—observed and anticipated—can be understood in the context of impacts upon value perceptions in the market, by suppliers, among employees, even of competitors.

Finally, managing the value system will greatly influence enterprise culture. With concerns that intransigent corporate cultures are holding back progress, this represents a real opportunity for changing those traditions of value which are in the way.

12.3 The business definition: A strategic framework

For us, the notion of a driving force that compels business organizations to behave in specific ways has many implications. Understanding the driving issues for one's own enterprise, for the industry value system within which the enterprise participates, and for the marketplace is an extremely important leadership opportunity. With the understanding of these determining values, it becomes realistic to anticipate the requirements and subsequent actions of owners, employees, suppliers, competitors, and market customers. These are the logical origins of a definition of an enterprise:

> Business enterprise . . . requires that the theory of the business be thought through and spelled out. It demands a clear definition of business purpose and business mission. It demands asking, "What is our business and what should it be?" . . . Only a clear definition of purpose of the business makes possible clear and realistic business objectives. It is the foundation for priorities, strategies, plans, and work assignments. It is the starting point for the design of managerial jobs and, above all, for the design of managerial structures. Structure follows strategy. Strategy determines what the key activities are within a given business. Strategy requires knowing "what our business is and what it should be." (Drucker, 1973)

Business or enterprise definition is the essence of any strategic framework. When you get definition, you get strategy and vice versa. However, according to Peter Drucker, "What is our business? is almost always a difficult question. And the answer is usually anything but obvious." (Drucker, 1973) Few managers ever ask the question. Fewer still answer it. We believe that answering that question is the source of significant advantage for all enterprises—competitive or otherwise. The defined business *and* the rationale that produced the definition represent the crux of the value system within the enterprise. Acknowledging this and making it available to the enterprise organization can open the floodgates to innovation and productivity focused directly upon the objectives of the enterprise.

Environmental research

The first step in defining an enterprise is to understand the environments within which the enterprise must function. A research and analysis process identifies the various conditions and environmental elements which, in turn, establish the available business options. This process establishes the state of those elements today and identifies any trends established in the recent (or relevant) past. Issues that cannot be ignored without significant impact on one or more of the various value systems involved are highlighted as our *strategic business imperatives*.

These strategic imperatives represent a broad agenda for achieving successful entry and long-term viability in the market (a typical business definition will have 30 or 40 imperatives). These imperatives simply reflect the things that are fundamental to competitive success. Every competitive business must be able to deal with their imperatives if they are to succeed within their industry. The things that matter include both positive opportunities to pursue as well as pitfalls to be avoided.

Strategic business imperatives are imposed upon an enterprise by its owners, the marketplace, competitors, and society. Owners will dictate such things as the necessary return on investment in terms of both profit and equity, minimum growth rates, etc. The market will define the fundamental opportunity for commerce: the functional needs, the value of products or services satisfying those needs, and the attributes of successful products and service. Competitors determine the benchmark cost structures and product/service quality levels with which the enterprise must deal. Society influences, and sometimes dictates through government, the competitive role and scope, price structures, and the ability to access specific technologies of infrastructure businesses.

Mandates for success

Virtually all competitors attempt to leverage similar analysis and planning processes to their strategic advantage. However, most enterprises experience difficulty applying the identified imperative issues in meaningful ways to their businesses. A solution is the synthesis of strategic industry mandates as described in Chapter 10. In this process, strategic imperatives are synthesized into a manageable set of "business tenets," that is, the business mandates. These mandates are used to lead every aspect of the enterprise process.

The 30 or 40 strategic imperatives typically overlap and synergize with one another to a great extent. Sometimes these synergisms will be positive and sometimes they will be negative. The analysis process is typically performed by a single strategist, who categorizes and weighs the functional business contribution of every imperative to each category. Having established and assessed the interrelationships, they are distilled down to the essence of what is necessary for success in the industry—strategic mandates. Typical industries will have 6 to 10 of these.

Strategic mandates are the critically important issues to the business. They are used throughout the planning methodology and later in daily management. The relationship of any object within the enterprise system to these mandates can now be established and maintained—this is an intensely powerful tool.

Finding the driving force

According to Tregoe and Zimmerman, strategic areas are those things that can "decisively affect and influence the nature and direction of any organization" (Tregoe and Zimmerman, 1980). As discussed in Chapter 10, they are grouped into three categories, which are outlined in Table 12.1.

As established in Chapter 10, Tregoe and Zimmerman believe that one of these strategic areas is always of primary importance to every enterprise (Tregoe and Zimmerman, 1980). We have observed this phenomena in the real world as well. We have also observed that enterprise leadership frequently has no idea of what their driving force is and more often still, that the rest of the organization has no idea either. We have also observed that the professed (read "politically correct") driving force is not the real driving force that affects the business. For existing business operations, the following is the easiest way to determine the driving force:

- ◆ Review the major operational business decisions of the past few years

- ◆ Identify strategic actions taken when strategic areas conflicted

- ◆ The strategic area that dictated these actions is the driving force

This tells us what the actual driving force of an enterprise is, but it does not tell us if it is an appropriate choice. Understanding appropriateness requires additional research.

A choice of words

While the strategic areas are extremely powerful, especially within the context of business in the industrial age, it appears to us that they might benefit from some expansion of semantics relative to the emerging services led economy. This is caused by pressures from two different directions.

Table 12.1 Categories of strategic areas

Category	Strategic area
Products / Markets	Products offered
	Market needs
Capabilities	Technology
	Production capability
	Sales channel
	Distribution channel
	People/human resources
Results	Size/growth
	Return/profit

First, when presenting novel concepts (or any new theory at all) in the real world of business, the semantics don't match well. The words mean something different within the context of the management of specific businesses than is intended— even as defined in a standard English dictionary. Even the term *driving force* itself is used differently by Porter than it is by Tregoe and Zimmerman. Still, the framework and the concepts are extremely valuable in understanding the dynamics of decision-making and control in enterprise organizations.

The second direction of pressure to expand semantics is due to the changing nature of industry and enterprise. The significance of process (how an entity does what it does) on competitive success is growing. The importance of access to natural resources and even technology is decreasing (this is not to say that their roles in value systems are diminished in any way, only that their availability is or will be nearly ubiquitous across the globe; i.e., they are less significant to strategic differentiation between firms). Accordingly, resource or infrastructure areas such as human resources (traditionally included in the production capability strategic area) are increasing in strategic significance.

It is inevitably necessary to settle on strategic areas (and subsequently a driving force) that are somehow unique to the specific business. We have learned to anticipate this reality and use these defined categories to structure an approach for isolating critical imperatives to which the enterprise must respond.

Products and markets

The products and markets category of strategic areas will always be required in the development of any business definition. This will be where a pre-established product or product-set will be defined. Pre-established products are those which the leadership has determined to be part or all of the business' market solution—the value derived from the enterprise. In this analysis, historical data regarding sales revenue, market-share, value chain costs and benchmark comparisons, etc. are accumulated and assessed in comparison to current and future competitive alternatives. The market-needs strategic area was covered earlier in the evaluation of the market value system.

Capabilities

In contrast, the capabilities category may contain strategic areas that are not deemed to be of fundamental strategic significance to the enterprise, depending upon the industry involved. Examples may include the distribution or sales channels, or possibly production capability (businesses that are primarily channels or integrators that subcontract all manufacturing, including final assembly). Increasingly, viable enterprises are being created that succeed because they bypass or in some way obviate one or more of these traditional process components of the industry value chain (but not the value component itself). Conversely, the industry position established for a business may minimize the strategic significance of any given capability strategic area.

An example of the varying strategic importance of a strategic area can be seen with technology, which affects business ubiquitously, yet it is not significant universally. For many businesses, so many technology options are of comparable cost and efficiency and are available on a commodity basis that specific strategic technology concerns are nonexistent. Conversely, businesses that require a large investment in technology infrastructure (e.g., utilities) find technology extremely strategic. For those businesses with large infrastructure expenditures, understanding the trends in pricing, capabilities, and availability of future technology should be a major factor that affects industry positioning, product planning, infrastructure architecture, and operating approach.

One strategic area in this group that we are finding to be increasingly significant is the people and human resources area—so much so that we now believe that this strategic area must always be assessed and considered. "In the 21st century, the skills and education of the workforce will be the dominant competitive weapon" (Thurow, 1993).

In one sense, the types of information to be gathered regarding the potential workforce necessary to operate the subject enterprise are like any other resource. That is, what are the:

- ◆ Costs—procurement and ongoing
- ◆ Functional capabilities

- ◆ Durability

- ◆ Availability

- ◆ Competitor positions

In addition to these types of issues, there is the need to understand various societal and cultural impacts on the available workforce. These include such issues as competing loyalties, desires for mobility, expectations relative to autonomy, educational and training limits, etc. Obviously, this can be a very complex area, but increasingly, it can encompass the single factor that will make or break an enterprise.

An example might be the ability of the currently available pool of computer programming talent to support the systems technology of the business. This would be a concern both in terms of current education and training, and of the ability to learn and then perform in the new or desired technology environment. (This example exists in the instance of the shift from hierarchical procedural programming languages to less structured object-oriented technologies. As occurred during the shift from the second to third generation programming, fewer than half of the current procedure-based programmers will be able to make the shift to the new object-oriented environments—and only a portion of them will want to continue programming in the new environment).

Results

The results category of strategic areas most frequently reflects the desires of the ownership regarding the business performance of the enterprise. This most often relates to the two strategic areas identified: size and growth and return/profit. These two areas frequently have explicit owner-imposed objectives that must be accommodated by the business. Alternatively, they reflect implicit objectives derived from the behavior of the investment and money markets. To pay competitive rates for short- and long-term borrowings or to attract the highest possible price per share, the business' performance must meet certain expectations.

This portion of the knowledge-gathering process is most straightforward. It entails identifying the competitive market-ranking criterion for different types of financing. In addition to the bond-rating scenario, this includes a competitive analysis of alternative stocks with which the enterprise will likely be grouped (and with which it must therefore compete for investment funds). It also identifies the required competitive performance levels (rate of return on investment (ROI), price-to-earnings ratio (PE), rate of return on equity (ROE), etc.). Having determined these levels of performance, it is then necessary to review them with enterprise leadership (and/or ownership) to validate actual owner and leader expectations. The results of that dialogue establishes the objective performance required in these areas and identifies the relative priority that these metrics have within the enterprise's internal value system. For the enterprise in question, these levels of performance become strategic imperatives and, most often, one of the mandates by which the business is managed.

Having established the imperatives with which the enterprise must deal, the strategic framework can begin to take form with the synthesis of the strategic mandates as described earlier. The mandates will reflect the value system as it has emerged from the research as well as identify critical issues and opportunities. The competitive positioning and strategy of the enterprise is developed in direct response to these strategic mandates and the value system itself. It is with this domain that we now have the ability to complete a strategic framework, the business definition itself. Using Tregoe and Zimmerman's framework model as a contextual reference, our business definition structure will contain the elements shown in Figure 12.1.

Framework summary

Every enterprise needs a logical set of parameters that defines itself. Definition is the essence of strategy. This entails the creation of a strategic framework to guide business decisions and actions. This framework should define the values, character, nature, and generic objectives of the enterprise. Identifying these things requires an understanding of the driving forces of the organization, its markets, and the industry. Providing a clear enterprise definition and the thinking behind it is the best way to empower participants to satisfy the goals of the enterprise creatively and effectively.

Appropriate knowledge of the environments within which the enterprise functions can be achieved with a systematic research and analysis method. This approach is designed to capture and isolate issues that cannot be ignored if one is to achieve industry success—that is, the strategic business imperatives. Typically, 30 to 40 imperatives are imposed upon an enterprise by its owners, the marketplace, competitors, suppliers, etc. These imperative issues are then synthesized into a handful (6 to 10) of business mandates that can be used as operating tenets to lead every aspect of enterprise operations. These strategic mandates are the critically important issues to an enterprise.

In every enterprise, one strategic mandate will overshadow all others. That mandate is the driving force of the enterprise and it will always decide those issues that have conflicting impacts among the strategic mandates. As basic as this may seem, most enterprises today do not have consistent awareness of their driving-force mandate within the leadership.

We have found that mapping strategic mandates to the Tregoe and Zimmerman strategic framework model is helpful in achieving understanding

Business Definition

- Strategic Mandates

- Fundamental Strategy
- Future Market Scope:
  Geographic & Segment
- Future Product Scope

- Key Capabilities Required
- Size/growth Guidelines
- Return/Profit Guidelines
- Mission Statement

Figure 12.1 *future strategy business planning® strategic framework.*

and acceptance of the driving force concept and agreement as to driving force definition. The Tregoe/Zimmerman strategic-framework approach involves evaluating the strategic mandates from the perspective of nine strategic areas that are grouped into three categories: products and markets, capabilities, and results. The subsequent results are organized into the business definition identifying the strategic mandates, fundamental market and industry positioning strategies, and mission statement, objectives, and resource requirements (see Figure 12.1).

12.4 Conclusion

We believe that the enterprise definition and strategic framework provide a very necessary logical structure with which to support and manage an operating enterprise, but we also know that this highly concrete, objective-based set of logical guidance is insufficient to achieve consistent and effective results. Without a defining moral corporate character, logical decisions will be based upon the value judgments of individuals. Identifying the value systems of the enterprise and its environment provides the other half of what is required to establish and maintain effective leadership guidelines. These two elements, structure and character, are integrated in the synthesis of the strategic mandates and the construction of the strategic framework.

Identifying and capturing the relationships between components of the strategic framework—the strategic mandates—and elements of the actual enterprise (physical and logical) enables management of enterprise-element change impacts upon enterprise values. And doing so with object oriented technology allows this change management to be effective independent of the scope and/or scale of the change-element or the impact.

Merging enterprise structure and character also assures that the enterprise will remain focused upon the external value systems that will determine its opportunities. This means that the definition of what the enterprise is can be tied to these external value needs rather than being limited to what the enterprise does now and/or how it does what it does. Such an external focus is essential for continuous enterprise reinvention to occur successfully.

Articulating a business definition that integrates logical strategic structure and enterprise values is the key to achieving consistency between vision, competitive strategy, and tactical operations.

Part **4**

Enterprise Architectural Views

Introduction to Part 4

THE ENTERPRISE IS A GENERAL SYSTEM. In Chapter 2 we learned that any general system can be analyzed from three perspectives:

- ◆ The functional perspective analyzes the overall purpose of the system as manifested by its transformations of energy, materials, or information.

- ◆ The structural perspective analyzes the configuration of its component parts and their relations with each other.

- ◆ The behavioral perspective analyzes the state changes of each component of the system over time.

These three perspectives are the foundation of system analysis and form the basis for our enterprise modeling methodology. In this part of the book, we use these three perspectives of systems analysis to define three views of the enterprise. We will use the term *view* to mean the definition of the properties and the corresponding discussion of one of these three perspectives of analysis. These three views are collectively called the enterprise architecture.

The main result of defining one of the views is the documentation of the set of architectural properties of the view. We use the term *architectural properties* because of their stature in defining the whole enterprise. As it turns out, most business enterprises have similar architectural properties and one can define several generic architectural properties to be used as building blocks. We will use our three views when we present our object-oriented enterprise modeling methodology in Part 5 of the book. We will define the views in sufficient detail here so that the reader is educated on the various views when we make use of them in explaining our methodology in Part 5. Along with these views, we also present in this part of the book a set of useful enterprise modeling tools to define and analyze them.

This part of the book consists of four chapters:

- Chapter 13 introduces the functional view of the enterprise. The principal tool here is function modeling. We will see how the enterprise is decomposed into a set of nonoverlapping functions. The enterprise functions combine to realize the purpose of the enterprise. The chapter describes and defines the Porter value chain. We use the Porter value chain as our strawboss functional decomposition of the enterprise. This chapter defines and discusses business process modeling. A business process is an ongoing series of activities that has identifiable inputs/outputs and beginning/end points. The business functions of the enterprise are decomposed into business processes. The business process is one of the central constructs of enterprise modeling.

- Chapter 14 continues with the functional view of the enterprise and focuses on the special topic of the abstract business process (ABP). The ABP, based on the Porter value chain, is a generalization of the business process introduced in Chapter 13. We will see that an enterprise is recursively defined by the ABP and its decomposition into lower-level ABPs. This chapter concludes by presenting the technique we will use to define ABPs. We will adapt the ideas of Ivar Jacobson's use-case technique, which defines an ABP in terms of its interactions with other ABPs. In short, an ABP is the sum of its use-cases. In its most general incarnation, a use-case defines the interaction between information-processing nodes (described in Chapter 4).

- Chapter 15 presents the structural view of the enterprise. The principal modeling construct here is the hierarchical-multilayer organization of the enterprise, that is, its coordination/control structure coupled with its abstraction layering. Hierarchical-multilayer systems were introduced in the first part of the book (see Chapter 3). Now we will use these ideas to define the structure of the enterprise. We will see that several enterprise hierarchical layers coexist and provide various structures to the same set of enterprise objects.

◆ Chapter 16 presents the behavioral view of the enterprise. The principal abstraction in this chapter is the global object space (GOS). The GOS is the representation of the enterprise as a total object-oriented environment. That is, during enterprise modeling, the objects used to model the enterprise can be thought of as residing in a logical space we call the GOS. Later during implementation, the physical, abstract, and software objects that implement the enterprise will reside in the distributed space of the GOS. We will see that the GOS incorporates many of the theoretical concepts introduced in previous chapters: the hierarchical-multilayer system, the information-processing network, the entity object, the process object, and, of course, the object-oriented paradigm.

Chapter 13

The Functional View of the Enterprise

13.1 Introduction

This chapter defines the functional view of the enterprise. The functional view is one of the three perspectives of a general system (the other two perspectives are the structural and the behavioral, which we will discuss in later chapters). The functional view is concerned with the accomplishment of the objectives of the enterprise, that is, the transformation of input to output to accomplish its objectives. The functional view is implemented by the combined efforts of the business processes of the enterprise. This view is the "what" of the enterprise.

This chapter begins by introducing functional modeling. We will see how the enterprise is decomposed into a set of nonoverlapping functions that combine to realize the purpose of the enterprise. As a modeling convenience, business functions are grouped into functional areas. In the chapter, we will see how the business functions are further decomposed into business processes.

Next in this chapter, we will show how the Porter value chain can be used as a first-cut, strawboss decomposition of the enterprise into functional areas. The work of Michael Porter was introduced in Chapter 10, where we noted that Porter's writings on competitive advantage (Porter, 1980), (Porter, 1985) have been one of the major influences upon the way we think about enterprises. Porter has developed his theories to include tools and techniques for analyzing competitive advantage. This chapter describes and defines his principle tool: the Porter value chain. We will see how the Porter value chain is used to analyze the activities that an enterprise performs and how they interact. Porter puts it this way: "The value chain disaggregates a firm into its strategically relevant activities in order to understand the behavior of costs and the existing and potential sources of differentiation" (Porter, 1985).

Next, this chapter defines and discusses business process modeling. The business process is one of the central ideas of enterprise modeling. Business processes are constructs used to decompose the business function. Functions and processes differ in the sense that a function is ongoing whereas a process could be done only once. Also, functions are not executable but processes are. For example, processes could be represented by a script executed by an information processing node. The business processes accomplish the behavior of the enterprise to realize its objectives. Business processes are arranged into process dependency flows. The business process dependencies are actually value chains as proposed by Porter. The value chains are activated by business events. The business processes operate under business rules.

This chapter closes by defining business rules. Business rules are the collective business knowledge of the enterprise stated in a succinct rule-oriented format. Business rules fall into one of three categories: functional business rules representing the big picture of laws and policies; structural business rules representing the constraints placed on business entities; and behavioral business rules, which control the ordered set of state changes executed by the enterprise's business processes it traverses over time.

13.2 Business function

The enterprise consists of a set of nonoverlapping business functions. The starting point for defining or analyzing the enterprise is the identification of its set of business functions. In this section, we will define and discuss the business function. Many of the ideas in this section are taken from the work of James Martin (Martin, 1992) and Michael Porter (Porter, 1985).

Definition: Business function

James Martin defines a business function as "a group of activities which together support one aspect of furthering the mission of the enterprise" (Martin, 1992). The characteristics of a business function are as follows:

◆ Business functions are mutually exclusive and do not overlap. The sum of the business functions is equivalent to the enterprise. However, business functions may overlap chronologically.

◆ Business functions have different skill, knowledge, and experience requirements and are governed by different policies and procedures.

◆ Business functions do not represent sequence or flow (that's the job of business processes, which we will discuss later in this chapter).

◆ Business functions do not change except when the enterprise is reengineered. The enterprise must generally carry out the same set of business functions no matter how it is organized or what technology it uses.

◆ Two enterprises in the same line of business will tend to have commonalty in their business functions.

◆ Business functions are named with nouns or gerunds (words ending in *-ing*). Examples of business functions are *machine operations* (noun), *machining* (gerund), *budget management* (noun), *managing the budget* (gerund), *materials purchases* (noun), or *purchasing materials* (gerund).

◆ The decomposition of the enterprise into business functions can be represented by a function chart. This is not the same as the enterprise's organization chart. The function chart of the enterprise will remain relatively stable while the organization chart may change. We will define the function chart in a moment.

Functional areas

As a practical matter, business functions are grouped into functional areas. A functional area is the first-level decomposition of the enterprise into major activity areas. Figure 13.1 shows the decomposition of the enterprise into functional areas. Decomposing the enterprise into functional areas is done by both a top-down and bottom-up approach; however, functional areas are usually defined from the bottom up starting with the set the business functions. Functional areas help to organize the functional model into understandable categories.

13.3 The Porter value chain

Michael Porter has developed his theories to include tools and techniques for analyzing competitive advantage. In this section, we will describe Porter's principal tool for value analysis: the Porter value chain. In effect, the Porter value chain decomposes the generic enterprise into a set of generic functional areas. Any

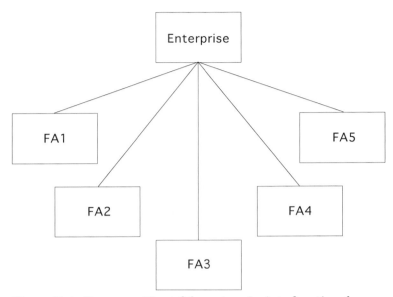

Figure 13.1 *Decomposition of the enterprise into functional areas.*

enterprise will more or less have this set of functional areas. Porter describes achieving competitive advantage as follows: "Competitive advantage cannot be understood by looking at a firm as a whole. It stems from the many discrete activities a firm performs" (Porter, 1985). We can use the Porter value chain as a first-cut, strawboss for defining the functional areas of the enterprise. In this section we will define the value chain as originally proposed by Porter. In later chapters, we will propose some modifications to it that make it more compatible with recent developments in business planning.

Definition: Porter value chain
The value chain is the basic tool proposed by Porter to analyze the activities that a firm performs and their interactions. The Porter value chain is shown in Figure 13.2. Porter describes his value chain as follows:

> Every firm is a collection of activities that are performed to design, produce, market, deliver, and support its product. All of these activities can be represented using a value chain. . . . A firm's value chain and the way it performs individual activities are a reflection of its history, its strategy, its approach to implementing its strategy, and the underlying economics of the activities themselves. (Porter, 1985)

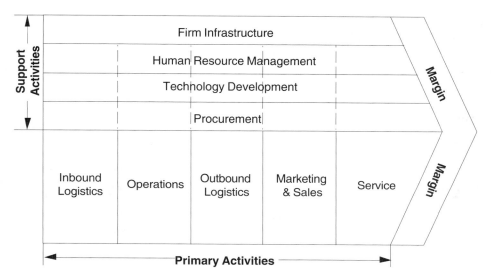

Figure 13.2 *Porter value chain.*

What does Porter mean by the word *value?* "In competitive terms, value is the amount buyers are willing to pay for what a firm provides" (Porter, 1985). Value can be measured very simply: it is the total revenue that the enterprise takes in. The revenue is based on the price the enterprise's products command in a competitive market. The creation of value is at the heart of any business strategy. An enterprise is profitable and can continue to exist if the value it commands exceeds the costs involved in creating the products of the enterprise. The difference between the total revenue and the total cost is called *margin*. Thus in Figure 13.2, the total revenue is represented by the outside boundary and the total cost is measured by the inside boundary. The difference is shown as the margin. It is the size of this margin that is the pragmatic issue of any business strategy. On one hand, we have the costs, which are certain, and on the other, we have the value, which is very uncertain. The reward for balancing the certainty of costs against the uncertainty of value is the margin.

As we see in Figure 13.2, the Porter value chain consists of the division of the enterprise into very broad functional areas (e.g., inbound logistics, firm infrastructure). Notice that there are two types of functional areas: primary and support. We will discuss each component of the Porter value chain in the following sections. In particular, it should be noted that any of these broad functional areas such as inbound logistics is further decomposed into a series of value activities, which we will discuss next.

Definition: Value activity

The value chain is made up of value activities. Value activities "are the physically and technologically distinct activities a firm performs. These are the building blocks by which a firm creates a product valuable to its buyers" (Porter, 1985). This fundamental building block to the value chain can be thought of as an abstract "factory," which has its own economic purpose (see Figure 13.3).

The value activity as defined by Porter has the following characteristics:

- ◆ It purchases inputs.

- ◆ It produces a product, which takes the form of either an asset or a liability.

- ◆ It usually makes use of people resources (both labor and management).

- ◆ It usually makes use of technology (human artifacts), which includes machines, procedures, know-how, and product technology (i.e., the product itself).

- ◆ It makes use of information (both stored and derived from the environment) and produces and stores information as a byproduct.

- ◆ It consists of internal activities that make up the larger value activity. The internal activities directly or indirectly participate in the production of the product or assure quality of current or previously produced products of the value activity. Porter calls these *direct, indirect,* and *quality assurance* activities.

    - • **Direct activities** These are activities directly involved in the product of the value activity. Examples include assembly, parts machining, sales force operation, advertising, product design, and recruiting.

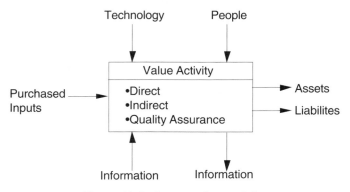

Figure 13.3 *Porter value activity.*

- **Indirect activities** Indirect activities make it possible to perform the direct activities of the larger value activity on a continuing basis. Examples include maintenance, scheduling, operation of facilities, sales force administration, research administration, and vendor record keeping.

- **Quality assurance activities** These activities ensure the quality of other activities of the larger value activity such as monitoring, inspecting, testing, reviewing, checking, adjusting, and reworking.

The design of a value activity according to Porter is to properly balance the direct, indirect, and quality assurance activities of the broader value activity. There is often a trade-off in the sense that improving an indirect activity or quality assurance activity often leverages a direct activity.

Thus Porter's value activity is similar to our definition of *process,* which we introduced in the Chapters 6 and 7 and discussed as the process object in Chapter 8. Later in this chapter, we will equate Porter's value activity with the *business process,* but for now we will stick with his terminology and definitions to get a complete understanding of his theory.

Primary activities

Primary activities are activities directly involved in creating value for the customer of the enterprise. Primary activities participate in the direct flow of production and consist of the following as shown in Figure 13.2:

- ◆ **Inbound logistics** This is primary activity, which serves as the interface to the upstream supplier value chain.

  Its internal activities are abstracted as:
  - Receive raw materials
  - Store raw materials (warehousing)
  - Disseminate raw materials

  Examples:
  - Receiving
  - Material handling
  - Warehousing (storage)
  - Inventory control
  - Quality control
  - Return to suppliers

◆ **Operations**   This primary activity is the production process that transforms inputs into the final product form.

Its internal activities are abstracted as:

- Receive raw materials (from inbound logistics)
- Transform them into products
- Make products available (to outbound logistics)

Examples:

- Creation of products by manufacturing, assembly, etc.
- Production planning and scheduling
- Materials control
- Product cost control
- Testing and quality control
- Facilities operations and maintenance

◆ **Outbound logistics**   This primary activity serves as the interface to the
downstream value chains (channel, buyer).

Its internal activities can be abstracted into:

- Collect the final product (from operations)
- Store (warehouse) the final product
- Physically distribute the final product to the customer

Examples:

- Collecting outputs from operations
- Storing (warehousing)
- Inventory control
- Order processing
- Scheduling
- Packing
- Shipping
- Delivery
- Fleet operations

◆ **Marketing and sales**   This primary activity provides the means by which
customers can purchase the products of the enterprise. In our version of
the value chain discussed later, we will modify this activity into a distinct

marketing activity that is separate from a sales and service activity. For now, we will stick to Porter's definition.

Its internal activities can be abstracted into:

- Design a set of products and services
- Induce customers to purchase the products and services
- Sell the products and services to the customer

Examples:

- Product design
- Product pricing
- Advertising/promotion
- Quoting
- Selling/contracting
- Order entry
- Sales administration
- Channel relations
- Territory management
- Sales forecasting
- Sales analysis

- **Service** This primary activity provides service to enhance or maintain the value of the product or service. In our version of the value chain, we will combine this with sales to form a sales and service primary activity, but for now, we will use Porter's definition of it.

Its internal activities can be abstracted into:

- Proactively enhance or maintain the value of the product or service
- Reactively enhance or maintain the value of the product or service

Examples:

- Customer relations
- Installation
- Repair
- Training
- Parts supply
- Product adjustment

Support activities

Support activities support the primary activities and each other and consist of the following as shown in Figure 13.2.

◆ **Firm infrastructure**   This support activity provides management and control of the firm. It coordinates the various value activities of the entire value chain and provides general support. We recognize this as the classic meta-layer of a hierarchical-multilayered enterprise introduced in Chapter 3. Also included are general activities that support the entire value chain.

Its internal activities can be abstracted into:

- Define the goals and objectives of the enterprise
- Change the operation of the enterprise's value activities to accomplish the goals and objectives
- Monitor the value chain or parts of it for the accomplishment of the enterprise's goals and objectives
- Conduct general value activities which support all of the enterprise's value activities

Examples:

- General management
- Business planning
- Finance and financial planning
- Accounting
- Legal
- Government affairs
- Quality management

◆ **Human resource management**   This support activity obtains human resources and performs the specialized activities of maintaining this critical resource. This is a function that may be centralized or decentralized in the actual firm since most value activities use human resources.

Its internal activities can be abstracted into:

- Define the current and future human resource requirements
- Formulate and maintain personnel policies
- Obtain the needed human resources
- Maintain the human resource pool as a skills inventory (development, maintenance, allocation)
- Compensate the human resources

Examples:

- Personnel planning
- Recruiting
- Hiring
- Training
- Personnel development
- Compensation policy
- Labor and personnel relations

◆ **Technology development** Every value activity uses technology. In this sense, technology includes any human artifact (including processes and entities) that are used in the value activity. Thus the purpose of technology development is to improve the product or the direct, indirect, or quality assurance activities of producing the product.

Its internal activities can be abstracted into:

- Conduct research on technology
- Design and maintain the design of products, processes, procedures, production machines, etc.

Examples:

- Product research
- Product design
- Technology research
- Engineering development
- Product specification maintenance
- Process and equipment design
- Servicing procedures design

◆ **Procurement** This support activity purchases inputs used in the firm's value chain. This function may be centralized or decentralized in the actual firm since most value activities have a purchasing function themselves. Purchased inputs drive the primary activities but are also important to support activities.

Its internal activities can be abstracted into:

- Define requirements for purchasing
- Conduct purchasing

Figure 13.4 *Porter value system.*

Examples:

- Materials requirements
- Purchasing

Value system

The value chain (i.e., Figure 13.2) is part of an environment as shown in Figure 13.4. Porter calls this the *value system*. Porter puts its this way: "Gaining and sustaining competitive advantage depends on understanding not only a firm's value chain but how the firm fits into the overall value system." (Porter, 1985). The value system is important because suppliers have their own value chains that influence the performance of the enterprise's value chain. Also, Porter points out that "many products pass through the value chains of channels (*channel value*) on their way to the buyer. Channels perform additional activities that affect the buyer, as well as influence the firm's own activities. A firm's product eventually becomes part of the *buyer's value chain*." (Porter, 1985)

We recognize the larger value system as the environment of the enterprise considered as a general system. We described the environment of the general system in Chapter 2. There we defined several different profiles of the environment in which a general system exists including: institutionalized (e.g., government agency), symbiotic (e.g., departments of a company), competitive (e.g., a business enterprise), or emergent (e.g., a personal computer manufacturer).

The environment of the typical enterprise is either competitive or emergent. However, Porter's point is that enterprises would do well to consider themselves in a symbiotic environment with their suppliers, channels, and customers.

Linkages of value activities

The Porter value chain is a system of interdependent activities. Value activities are related by linkages. Linkages determine how value activities affect each other in terms of cost or performance. Linkages can be classified as either optimization or coordination focused. An important type is the vertical linkage in which the linkages with suppliers or channels are analyzed. Vertical linkages provide opportunities for a symbiotic environment to optimize operations between separate value chains. This implies that relationships with suppliers and the channels are not zero-sum, in which one gains at the expense of the other. Linkages imply information:

- Exploiting linkages requires information or information flows that allow optimization or coordination to take place.

- Information systems are vital to gaining competitive advantage from linkages.

The analysis of linkages uses techniques of value engineering to prevent or identify harmful suboptimization in which an activity makes itself efficient without regard to the effect on the entire value chain. We introduced the topic of value engineering in Chapter 2. Porter suggests many techniques of value engineering including:

- Identifying how a function can be performed in different ways

- Analyzing the relationship of indirect activities to direct activities (often, the cost/performance of direct activities is improved by changes in the indirect activities)

- Analyzing the effects of quality assurance and how it can be performed

Adapting the Porter value chain
The Porter value chain is a generic enterprise decomposed into generic categories of activities. We can use the Porter value chain as a first cut at the decomposition of any enterprise into functional areas. Earlier, we defined a functional area as a grouping of business functions for practical reasons of modeling and understanding. Each major category of the Porter value chain (see Figure 13.2) is a functional area of a generic enterprise. In effect, an enterprise consists of a collection of functional areas representing the first-level decomposition of the enterprise into major activity areas.

13.4 Business process

In this section, we will define and discuss the business process. The business process defined in this section is equivalent to the Porter value activity described earlier. A business process collects together enterprise resources to accomplish its purpose. Business processes may be further decomposed into lower-level business processes and eventually into elementary processes depending on the scope of the modeling project. Business processes depend on each other and are arranged into dependency chains that represent primitive value chains.

The business process is the enterprise implementation of the process artifact described in Chapter 7. Recall that the process artifact is the purpose-built process we humans create to accomplish our goals. The process artifact has the business process as a subtype. The business process has all the properties of its supertypes above it in the conceptual type hierarchy, but it introduces the pragmatic properties of an enterprise activity.

Definition: Business process

A business process is a specified activity in an enterprise that is executed repeatedly. Business processes have the following characteristics (Martin, 1990):

- ◆ Business processes have definable beginning and end points.

- ◆ Business processes have inputs of products consisting of energy, materials, or information, which they transform into output products consisting of energy, materials, or information (shortly, we will see that the input and output products of a business process are part of a process dependency flow in which the input products come from upstream business processes and the output products go to downstream business processes).

- ◆ Business processes are created by higher level business processes which monitor and control their operation.

- ◆ Business processes consume resources that are allocated to them by their higher level controlling business process.

- ◆ Business processes report their status to their higher-level controlling business process.

- ◆ Business processes are named with action verbs. Examples of business processes are "create purchase order" or "update inventory."

Decomposition of functions to processes

A business function is decomposed into business processes. Recall that functions are themselves grouped into functional areas as described previously. Figure 13.5 shows a functional area consisting of three functions which are, in turn, decomposed into business processes.

Decomposition of processes to subprocesses

Not shown in Figure 13.5 is that each business process could be further decomposed into lower-level business processes. This is because processes are subtypes of the conceptual activity as described in Chapter 6. Conceptual activities cause change over a period of several clock ticks of the system. At each clock tick the system is made up of a set of entities arranged in a specific configuration. After one or more clock ticks, a different configuration of entities may emerge. The conceptual

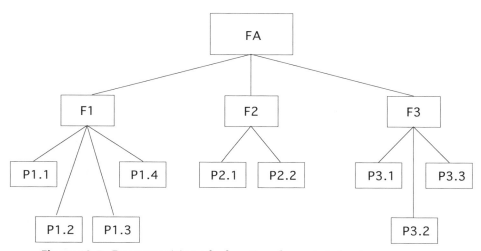

Figure 13.5 *Decomposition of a functional area into business processes.*

activity that causes the next scene to emerge can be regarded as acting on subsets of entities and causing these subsets to assume their new configuration. Thus an activity can be decomposed into subactivities against subsets of entities. In this way, any conceptual process being a subtype of the conceptual activity can be decomposed into lower-level processes.

Processes are decomposed into subprocesses, which are themselves decomposed. Eventually elementary processes are reached, but they are not decomposed further because either we have reached the physical level or it would not be meaningful to do so considering the scope of the modeling project. Figure 13.6 shows the decomposition of a process P1 into its two subprocesses SP1.1 and SP1.2. The subprocess SP1.1 is decomposed into two subprocesses, an elementary process SP1.1.1 and a subprocess SP1.1.2 which is further decomposed into elementary processes SP1.1.2.1 and SP1.1.2.2. Similarly, the subprocess SP1.2 is decomposed into two elementary subprocesses SP1.2.1 and SP1.2.2.

The decomposition of the business process is done independently of how the enterprise is organized into departments. Even if the enterprise is reorganized, the same processes must be carried out somewhere in the enterprise. Note that changing the processes themselves is called *business process reengineering* and is a much more fundamental change to the enterprise than changing its organization chart.

Process dependency

A given business process depends on other business processes. The process dependency model shows how business processes relate to each other and how

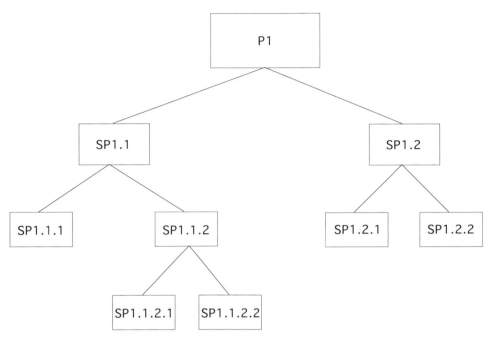

Figure 13.6 *Decomposition of the process (P) into subprocesses (SP).*

they are dependent on each other. A given process is dependent on another process in the sense that the process in question cannot take place until the other process has completed for whatever reason.

Figure 13.7 shows the processes from Figure 13.5 arranged into dependency sequences. We see several forms of dependency:

- ◆ **Straight-line** One process precedes another in a straight line flow as in P3.1 and P3.2 or P1.3 and P1.4.

- ◆ **Many-into-one** Several processes (two or more) precede the invocation of one process as in P1.1 and P1.2 preceding P1.3.

- ◆ **One-into-many** One process precedes the invocation of several (two or more) as in P3.2 preceding P2.1 and P3.3.

In each of these three cases, a dependency exists between the preceding and following processes. We will see in the next section that the invocation of a business process is controlled by business rules.

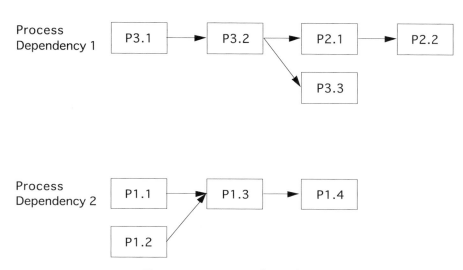

Figure 13.7 *Process dependency.*

13.5 Business rules

The enterprise has a set of business rules representing the conditions, constraints, and policies that control its operation. Business rules are a shorthand language for expressing business knowledge. Carried to its logical extreme, the set of business rules of an enterprise act as the declarative script of the enterprise: no matter what happens, one or more business rules would control what happens after that. We aren't recommending this extreme case but merely use it to clarify the meaning of business rules.

We have stated that the enterprise is an example of a general system. We saw in Chapter 1 that any general system can be analyzed in terms of three perspectives: a structural perspective (documented as an entity-relation diagram), a functional perspective (documented as a transformation-flow diagram), and a behavior perspective (documented as a state-transition diagram). Business rules apply to these three perspectives of the enterprise, and it is useful to categorize business rules in terms of these three perspectives. This is done only for convenience and as a mental jogger to stimulate the definition of the business rules. Thus a given business rule may rightly be classified in more than one of the three perspectives.

In our description of object-oriented modeling, we discussed the topic of object relations and in particular the topic of constraints placed on the relations between objects (see Chapter 8). There we noted that objects enforce constraints by their services. Therefore, the implementation of business rules would be accomplished by the object services of the business objects that implement the enterprise.

Functional business rules

These are the business rules that control the broad transformations of the enterprise—its "what" and "why" rules. Recall that the functional perspective of systems analysis (i.e., as described in Chapter 2) relates to the collective purposefulness of the entities of the system to accomplish the system's overall objectives. Purposefulness is described in terms of the desirability and effects of transforming materials, energy, or information as input to output at a certain level of decomposition of the system.

Functional business rules have the stature of axioms, principles, or laws and are generally much more global in scope than the other business rules. At the higher levels of the decomposition of the enterprise, functional business rules are stated as strategic imperatives. As the enterprise is decomposed into subprocesses the lower-level transformations are controlled by lower-level business rules. The lower-level business rules relate to the more finite decisions and policies that govern the subsystems of the enterprise to make their transformations. At the lowest level of transformation, the functional business rules could be restated as behavioral business rules (described shortly).

In Figure 13.8 we see two levels of decomposition of the enterprise and the functional business rules that govern them. The first-level, labeled Transformation 1, is governed by the set of principles, policies, or laws shown as Functional Business

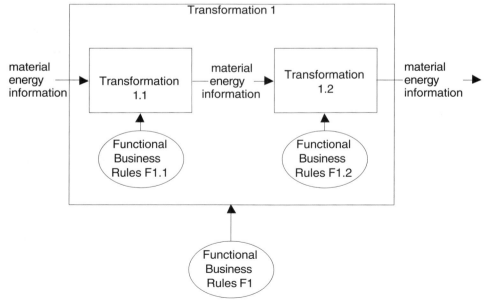

Figure 13.8 *Functional business rules.*

Rules F1. At the next level of decomposition, Transformation 1.1 is governed by Functional Business Rules F1.1 and Transformation 1.2 is governed by Functional Business Rules F1.2. Here are some examples of functional business rules:

- The enterprise will introduce five new products each year.

- The management of human resources is the responsibility of the managers throughout the company as opposed to being established as a separate organization.

- Technical expertise will be contracted to avoid maintaining a costly skill base on fast moving technologies.

- Customer Service will have authority to take any strong action to keep the customer happy and profitable, such as the authority to change the customer's bill when it is wrong.

Structural business rules

These are the business rules that relate to the structure of the enterprise. The structure of the enterprise is its set of entities and their relations at a point in time. The entities of the enterprise may be physical, abstract, or information representations. Structural business rules are usually stated as integrity rules that the entities of the enterprise must obey as they assume new configurations or are changed internally. Thus structural business rules control the relations that entities may form with each other as well as the values of the attributes of the entities. Structural rules are stated as declaratives (e.g., "It must always be true that xxxx") or as derivations (e.g., the formula or logical rule).

In Figure 13.9 we see the two types of structural business rules controlling entity attributes and entity relations, respectively. In Figure 13.9, the attributes of Entity 1 must always correspond to the set of Structural Business Rules E1 and the attributes of Entity 2 must always correspond to the set of Structural Business Rules E2. The relation between Entity 1 and Entity 2 must always correspond to the set of Structural Business Rules R1. Here are some examples of structural business rules:

- A supervisor must have at least 10 employees. (composition relation)

- A vendor list will be maintained in which vendors qualify themselves. (relation of vendor to vendor list)

- Profit = Revenue − Expenses (calculation of profit attribute)

- No employee may earn more than his or her supervisor. (comparison of salary attributes between the employee and the supervisor)

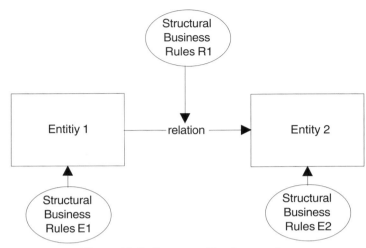

Figure 13.9 *Structural business rules.*

Behavioral business rules

Behavioral business rules are used to control the preconditions and postconditions of system change. Behavioral business rules boil down to the form of when event, if condition then change. System change can be described in terms of state changes as well as processes. Let's consider each in turn.

First, behavioral business rules control the ordered set of state changes that the enterprise or its subsystems traverse over time. Recall that any deterministic system has a state space that defines the states it may assume over time. Each point in the state space defines a legal state of the system and is defined as the combined states of each of its entities at a point in time. The state of an individual entity is defined by its collection of attributes at a point in time. The history of the deterministic system is defined by the path of points it traverses in the state space. Since the enterprise is a deterministic system, we can define a state space for it and describe its behavior in terms of it traversing its state space. The traversals from one point in the state space to another point is controlled by behavioral business rules. In this case, behavioral business rules are attached to the state changes that the system or its subsystems undergo as well as the processes that the system executes. The behavioral business rules attached to state changes are the preconditions and postconditions that must be true before and after the state change.

Second, behavioral business rules control the flow of processes. In this case, we attach behavioral business rules to processes representing the preconditions or postconditions that must be true before and after a process takes place.

state transition

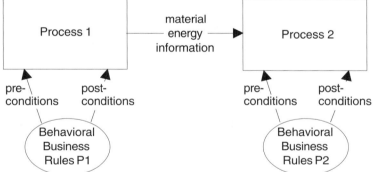

process flow

Figure 13.10 *Behavioral business rules.*

In Figure 13.10, we see the two types of behavioral business rules controlling state transitions and process flows respectively. In the top part of Figure 13.10, we see that State 1 is controlled by the preconditions and postconditions of the set of Behavioral Business Rules S1 and similarly for State 2 with its set of preconditions and postconditions of Behavioral Rules S2. In the bottom part of Figure 13.10 we see that Process 1 is controlled by the preconditions and postconditions of Behavioral Rules P1 and that Process 2 by Behavioral Rules P2. Examples of behavioral business rules:

◆ Customers must set up an account in advance. (precondition to purchase process)

◆ A customer whose account is more than 90 days overdue cannot place a credit purchase order. (precondition to purchase process).

◆ If a customer has purchased more than $1000 in one year, then the customer will be classified as a most-valued customer. (postcondition to customer state transition)

13.6 Conclusion

In this chapter, we discussed the functional view of the enterprise—the what of the enterprise. The functional view starts by defining the business functions of the enterprise—groups of activities that together accomplish one aspect of the mission of the enterprise. We also discussed how the Porter value chain is a very useful modeling device that is actually a first cut at defining the generic functional areas of a generic enterprise. Once stated, the categories of the Porter value chain can be fine-tuned to the specific functional areas of the enterprise in question. The point is that every enterprise will, more or less, have the categories of the Porter value chain as functional areas.

Appendix C presents a description of the Martin-Odell technique of object-flow diagramming. This diagramming technique is an implementation of the Porter value chain as a process model. Each of Porter's value activities are represented as business processes in object-flow diagramming. The technique of object-flow diagramming should prove very useful for understanding and modeling the Porter value chain.

This chapter also defined and discussed process modeling. We saw that business functions are decomposed into business processes. Business processes accomplish the transformations of the enterprise to realize its objectives. Business processes can be decomposed into lower-level business processes as well as arranged into process dependency flows. The business process is the central construct of enterprise modeling and we will refer to it frequently in the remainder of this book.

This chapter closed with a discussion of business rules. A business rule is a declarative statement and thus represents a succinct statement of business knowledge. We saw that there are three major types of business rules: functional, structural, and behavioral.

In the next chapter, we will continue our discussion of the functional view of the enterprise by defining the abstract business process.

Chapter 14

The Abstract Business Process

14.1 Introduction

This chapter is a continuation of the functional view of the enterprise started in Chapter 13 and presents a very important topic of the functional view: the abstract business process (ABP). The ABP is specialization of the business process introduced in Chapter 13.

We will see that the ABP is a recursive modeling structure that is based on the Porter value chain. Recall that the Porter value chain described a generic enterprise as a set of generic functional areas (e.g., inbound logistics, operations, etc.) that any enterprise must have—some more, some less. The point we will make in this chapter is that the Porter value chain is an abstraction of a business process because an enterprise is a business process. The internal activities of the Porter value chain represent the activities that any business process would have to perform. Thus to define what a business process does, one starts by considering it as an example of the Porter value chain, although reduced in scope from the full-blown enterprise. We will see that each ABP is decomposed into lower-level ABPs and that the enterprise is recursively defined by the single, unifying ABP concept.

The design of the enterprise is accomplished by designing and configuring its ABPs. In this chapter, we describe a technique for defining ABPs known as *use cases*. The use-case technique, originated by Ivar Jacobson, models the interactions between ABPs. Stated as a generalization, a use case defines the interaction between information-processing nodes outside of the system and the system itself. In this chapter, we describe the generic use cases that all ABPs have.

14.2 Abstract business process

In the object-oriented enterprise modeling methodology proposed in this book, the business process introduced in Chapter 13 is generalized into what we call the *abstract business process* (ABP). The ABP will lead to the definition of the business process as an object. Recall that we defined the process object in Chapter 8 and generalized it into a process class. In this chapter, we will start with that definition of the process class and define the ABP as a subclass. We will give our new ABP class the attributes and behavior of the business process. Being a subclass, the ABP class will inherit the attributes and behavior of the process class. The ABP class will represent a new abstract class in our growing enterprise modeling class library. We will use the ABP class as the starting point for defining all of the individual business process subclasses of the enterprise. In this section, we will define the internal attributes and behavior of the ABP.

Definition: ABP
The ABP is a generalization of the Porter value chain and is shown in Figure 14.1. In our definition of the ABP, we are asserting that a business process will have the behavior and attributes of the generic enterprise. This generalization should not be surprising since the enterprise is a single, large-scale process that transforms energy, materials, and information. Therefore, we can use the Porter value chain as a generalization to create our business process object class, which we call the ABP. This means that each internal activity category of the Porter value chain represents an abstract activity that a business process would, more or less, have to perform. As shown in Figure 14.1, the ABP has a number of ports, which are used to make exchanges with various components of the environment. The definition of the ABP is recursive: an ABP is made up of lower-level ABPs. In effect, the enterprise can be regarded as a business process defined by the Porter value chain, which is decomposed into business processes, each of which is also defined by the Porter value chain. However, we will deviate somewhat from the Porter value chain in defining the internal structure of our ABP. Figure 14.1 can be used as a reference to the following text.

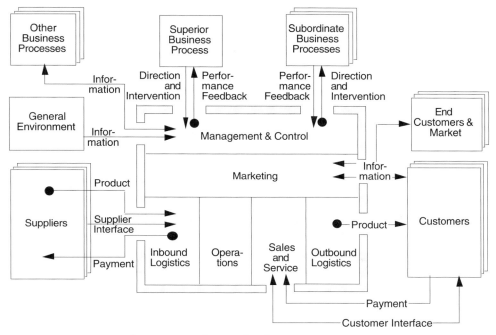

Figure 14.1 *Abstract business process (ABP).*

Decomposition of the ABP

The ABP is a collection of subprocesses arranged in a hierarchical-multilayer structure. Figure 14.2 shows the hierarchical organization of the ABP. We see that the ABP is itself decomposed into a set of six more specialized ABPs showing the recursive nature of its definition. This first level of specialization will be reflected in our enterprise class library as the next lower layer of classes specialized from the ABP class. We will discuss this point later in this chapter.

Figure 14.2 shows that the management and control ABP is at the top of the hierarchy and that the marketing ABP is just below it and controlled by it. These two control the bottom four ABPs. In the following sections, we will describe each of the ABP's subprocesses.

Management and control ABP

The management and control ABP is the superior process to the other sub-processes of the ABP. It serves as the meta-layer in the hierarchical-multilayered

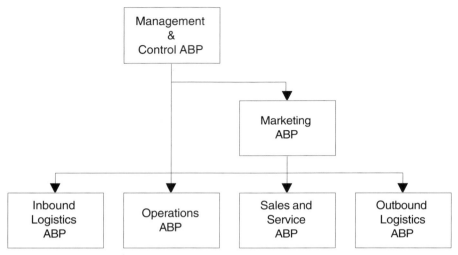

Figure 14.2 _Hierarchical organization of the ABP._

organization of the ABP. It is responsible for servicing three of the ports of the larger ABP:

- ◆ **Input**   As seen in Figure 14.1, the input to the management and control ABP is information. The information is received through an input port of the larger ABP and comes from other business processes (i.e., within or outside of the enterprise) or from the general environment (e.g., observations, research).

- ◆ **Operations**   The principal activity of the management and control ABP is to create the goals of the larger ABP as well as plans for their implementation. The creation of the local goals requires direction and intervention from the superior ABP of the ABP in question. Thus another operational duty of the management and control ABP is to service the port to its superior ABP. Once the goals and plans are created, they must be communicated to the lower-level ABPs. Thus another operational duty of the management and control ABP is to service the port of its subordinate ABPs.

- ◆ **Output**   The outputs from the management and control ABP are the goals of the larger ABP as well as plans for their implementation as explained earlier.

Marketing ABP

The marketing ABP is also a controlling subprocess to the other subprocesses of the larger ABP. It also serves as the meta-layer in the hierarchical-multilayered organization of the ABP. The marketing ABP represents a simplification of the original Porter value chain. The marketing ABP combines the marketing and technology development categories of the Porter value chain. The marketing ABP services one of the ports of the larger ABP, which it uses to monitor the customers of the larger ABP to adjust the operation of the subprocesses for optimizing the overall product:

- ◆ **Input** The information input to the marketing ABP arrives through a port in the larger ABP. Two types of information are received: information from the ultimate end customer of the enterprise and from the downstream customer to the larger ABP of which the marketing ABP is a subprocess.

- ◆ **Operations** The operation of the marketing ABP is to service the input port and collect the customer information. The information is synthesized to produce a redesign of the four operational ABPs below the marketing ABP. This redesign could take the form of new or modified products as well as new or modified activities and technology to produce the products or support their production.

- ◆ **Output** The outputs of the marketing ABP are the directions to the four operational ABPs to change themselves or their products.

Inbound logistics ABP

The inbound logistics ABP, like its counterpart in the Porter value chain, is the interface to upstream ABPs, which create products (raw materials) for the ABP. The inbound logistics ABP services one of the ports of the larger ABP:

- ◆ **Input** The input to the inbound logistics ABP is the products from upstream suppliers.

- ◆ **Operations** The inbound logistics ABP receives and stores the products and pays the respective supplier for them. Also, the inbound logistics ABP provides the general interface to the suppliers which takes the form of miscellaneous information exchanges concerning the products such as schedules, adjustments, etc.

- ◆ **Output** The outputs of the inbound logistics ABP are the products distributed to the various recipients within the larger ABP.

Operations ABP

The operations ABP is similar to its counterpart in the Porter value chain. It is the bread-and-butter of the larger ABP, transforming raw material, information, and energy into the final products of the larger ABP. The operations ABP is completely internal and does not have links to the outside of the larger ABP:

- **Input**   The input to the operations ABP are raw materials, information and energy that are products of upstream ABPs and received via the inbound logistics ABP.

- **Operations**   The operation of the operations ABP is to transform the input raw materials, information, and energy into finished products. This requires receiving the inputs as well as making the finished products available for distribution.

- **Output**   The outputs of the operations ABP are the finished products that are delivered to the outbound logistics ABP (discussed below).

Sales and service ABP

The sales and service ABP is the interface to the customer providing the activities for the customer to obtain the products of the larger ABP as well as the enhancement and maintenance of the product (i.e., its value) to the customer. The sales and service ABP represents a deviation from the Porter value chain. Recall that in Chapter 13 we saw that Porter combined marketing and sales and we commented that that was seldom done in the modern enterprise. Rather, marketing stands alone as a meta-level controlling process (as we have defined it here), and then sales and service are combined into a single customer interface. The sales and service ABP services one of the ports of the larger ABP:

- **Input**   The input to the sales and service ABP is information from the customer of the larger ABP.

- **Operations**   The operation of the sales and service ABP is to provide the interface to the customer. This involves selling products to the customer and receiving payment. Once sold, the sales and service ABP enhances and maintains the value of the product (e.g., repair and maintenance). The sales and service ABP is the general interface to the customer (e.g., scheduling, changes, discrepancies etc.).

- **Output**   The outputs of the sales and service ABP are instructions to the outbound logistics ABP (discussed next) to deliver products to the customer as well as satisfy the customer, who is considered as a resource.

Outbound logistics ABP

The outbound logistics ABP is the physical interface to the customer. It is similar to its counterpart in the Porter value chain. It services one of the ports of the larger ABP of which it is part:

- ◆ **Input**   The input to the outbound logistics ABP is the final product created by the operations ABP described earlier.

- ◆ **Operations**   The operations of the outbound logistics ABP is to collect and store the final products. Then orders are received from the Sales and Service ABP to physically distribute the final products to customers (i.e., downstream ABPs).

- ◆ **Output**   The output of the outbound logistics ABP are the physical products delivered to customers.

14.3 Modeling interaction: Use cases

In the preceding discussion of the abstract business process (ABP), we saw that the ABP has a number of ports through which exchanges with the outside environment take place. The ports are themselves abstractions required to support the encapsulation of the internals of the ABP. We now turn our attention to these exchanges.

An ABP makes exchanges with other ABPs in its environment. These exchanges can be modeled using a technique called *use cases*. Use cases are an analysis and modeling technique originated by Ivar Jacobson (Jacobson, 1992). Jacobson defined *use cases* as a systems analysis technique to describe the scenario of information exchanges between two systems. Jacobson defined a use case as a specific dialog between two systems in which information is sent and received over an extended period of time (i.e., several information exchanges).

According to Jacobson, the use-case technique is a way to discover the requirements of the functionality of a system. Use cases implement a philosophical stance that holds that a system provides a certain value, which is completely defined by its interface with the outside world. This philosophical stance is nearly identical to Porter's concepts of value introduced in the previous chapter. In effect, a system is the sum of its use cases.

In this book, we will employ use cases as a way of modeling all exchanges between abstract business processes. Thus we will employ use cases to model not only information exchanges but also exchanges of materials or energy between abstract business processes. We will find the use-case technique very powerful as an enterprise modeling tool.

In the previous section, we saw that the ABP consisted of six subprocesses, themselves ABPs (i.e., management/control, marketing, inbound logistics, operations, sales/service, and outbound logistics). We also saw that the larger ABP has seven ports through which exchanges with the outside world are conducted. Finally, we observed that the various subprocesses of the ABP are actually responsible for conducting the exchanges through the ports; that is they are responsible for servicing the ports. It is these exchanges conducted through the ports that we will define with the use-case technique.

Processes and information-processing nodes

The interaction through the ports of the ABP represents dynamic behavior. In Chapter 4, we learned that the information-processing node is the basic mechanism that accounts for this dynamic behavior of a process. We called this the process *change mechanism.*

Let's review how the information-processing node provides the actual dynamic behavior of the process. The information-processing nodes have at their core a physical symbol system described by Newell and Simon. An information-processing node receives, stores, uses, and sends information within the information-processing network in which it is embedded. The information-processing node at the lowest level of decomposition is a person or information machine such as a computer. Above this lowest level, information-processing nodes are arranged into information processing networks such as organizations of people. At these higher levels, the information-processing network can be abstracted into a single, unified information-processing node for modeling purposes (e.g., if we are not interested in the lower-level details). Thus we say that an information-processing node is either a person, an information machine, or a lower-level information-processing network.

The dynamic behavior of a process comes from the information-processing nodes embedded in it, including people, computers, or lower-level information-processing networks. Taking it down a step, the dynamic behavior of the information-processing node ultimately rests with the physical symbol system that is at its core. We will use information-processing nodes in our definition of use cases.

Actors

The use-case technique starts by isolating an ABP to be analyzed from its environment and then defining its *actors.* In the broadest definition, actors exchange information, materials, or energy with the ABP in question. Actors are external to the ABP in question and can be thought of as unspecified systems in the environment (using the terminology of Chapter 2). At the enterprise level of modeling, the use-case technique can be used to analyze all the exchanges of materials, energy, and information that an actor and the target ABP have. However, all exchanges will inevitably involve the exchange of information, so information will be a major part of the use cases between the ABP and the various actors.

In isolating the actors of an ABP, we consider only the systems outside the boundary of the ABP. The lower-level subprocesses inside the ABP boundary are not considered actors to it even though they are active among themselves. ABPs are made up of people and computers that interact in complex ways as part of the larger ABP. The people or computers within the boundary of the ABP are not actors to it. They are, in fact, part of the subprocesses of the ABP in question. However, they will be actors to each other. Thus as our analysis proceeds down to that level of decomposition, we will isolate one of these ABPs and then regard the other ABPs around it as its potential actors.

An actor is an information-processing node embedded in its own ABP out of view to us. For the most part, human actors tend to have much more complex interchanges and are usually the focus of this analysis. Also, we will often personify the actors and think of them as people to better conceptualize their activities. However, any information-processing node such as a computer or a lower-level information-processing network embedded in the external ABP can also be a bona fide actor to the ABP in question. Figure 14.3 shows the relation of a target ABP and its actors.

In Figure 14.3, our focus is the ABP labeled B, which consists of two information-processing nodes B1 and B2. Assume B1 is a person. The ABP labeled A is external in the environment of our target ABP B and is invisible to us except for its information processing node labeled A1. The two (i.e., information-processing node A1 and our ABP B) must make exchanges. Then, A1 would be considered an actor of B since we are concerned with B (i.e., in our current modeling work). Now assume the node B2 becomes our focus. Then node B1, which in our case happens to be a person, would be considered an actor to B2, but B1, even though it is a person, is not an actor to its larger ABP B.

While actors are information-processing nodes, we do not need to know anything about their internal behavior since they are outside of the scope of our modeling domain (i.e., at that particular moment; as a separate effort, we may focus on them later). From a modeling standpoint, their only important capability is that they send and receive the materials, energy, or information with our focus ABP. We must define in our ABP what will happen when these exchanges occur. Actors are considered to exist already. They exhibit a certain external behavior, which is manifested to our target ABP as these exchanges.

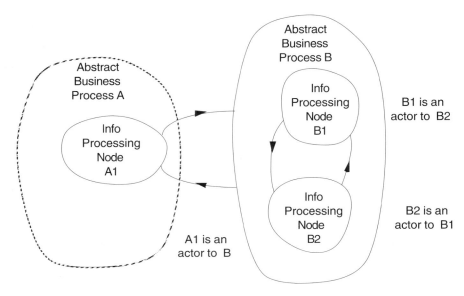

Figure 14.3 *Actors.*

Conducting the exchange through the port

The information-processing nodes will conduct exchanges through the ports of the ABP, acting on behalf of their larger ABP subprocess. For example, in the Inbound Logistics ABP (i.e., a subprocess of the larger ABP), the exchange that receives products from upstream suppliers will be conducted by information-processing nodes, which may be decomposed into lower-level information-processing networks, which are decomposed eventually to humans or information machines. The information-processing nodes are organized into subprocesses to discharge the functions of the Inbound Logistics ABP (e.g., see Figure 14.1). The subprocesses will be organized into larger subprocesses that may, in turn, be part of yet larger subprocesses until we reach the level of the inbound logistics ABP itself. The point is that an exchange through a port is conducted by an information-processing node ultimately made up of humans or information machines as shown in Figure 14.4

Use cases

The exchange of materials, energy, or information between an actor and the information-processing node of the ABP in question occurs in a well-defined scenario. These scenarios are called *use cases*. A use case is a dialog between an actor and the

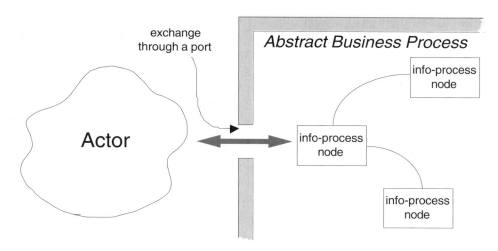

Figure 14.4 *Exchanges between an ABP and an actor.*

ABP in question. It is often initiated by the actor when the actor wants to make an exchange with the ABP, but it can be initiated by the ABP when it must obtain an exchange from the actor.

Elementary information-processing nodes play different roles in an enterprise. For example, a person can be an employee of an enterprise as well as a customer of the enterprise. This same person can simultaneously be a machinist, a union steward, and the coordinator of the annual company picnic. In each of these, a single information-processing node is playing several different roles. Roles are defined as a specific responsibility that the information-processing node must fulfill. As we saw in Chapter 4, these different roles are modeled as different scripts executed by the elementary information-processing node. Recall that an elementary information-processing node and, in particular, its physical symbol system is capable of performing a script of commands, which it interprets and executes by sending its own commands to lower-level components.

Thus we analyze and describe use cases as software abstractions. We are using the term *software* in its most general sense as a symbol sequence executed by a physical symbol system. The deliverable of use-case modeling is the information processing node's script, which defines the primary course of interaction as well as variants of the primary course, especially error sequences. Since we are not modeling the actor (i.e., at this point in time), its script will be just a naive description of its external behavior with no consideration of what its real internal behavior is. At a different time, the actor may be the focus of the modeling effort, in which case its script would be defined in detail.

We have been speaking of use cases as a tool for modeling a system. A very important use of modeling is in the design of a system where use cases really shine. According to Jacobson, use cases become the basis for defining what a system does. In this view, most of the functionality of a proposed system is determined by the needs of the actors as manifested by the use cases they use. Use cases are identified in the design of a system by looking at each actor and analyzing why the actor must make exchanges with the system being designed. Another important characteristic of use cases that makes them ideal in systems design is that they partition the work of designing a large complex system. A given use case is independent from all other use cases. This means that use cases can be defined by separate analysis efforts by separate teams working concurrently.

A very productive technique for defining use cases is prototyping. That is, the interactive-conversation can be simulated and perfected very quickly by prototyping the conversation between actor and system. At the very least, a system and its actors can be simulated by people playing roles as directed by handwritten scripts that are perfected as the role playing scenario unfolds. This is a technique called *responsibility-driven design* (Wirfs-Brock et al, 1990). Also, if the target system and the use case represent a human-computer interaction, the user-interface can be prototyped using tools from that domain.

Interaction diagrams

The principal tool for defining and analyzing use cases is the interaction diagram described in (Jacobson, 1992). Interaction diagrams model how the various components of a system interact with each other during a given use case. A system consists of a large set of interacting objects. It is the definition of these interactions that the interaction diagram captures. Jacobson describes the interaction diagram as "a type of diagram used for a long time in the world of communications. There it has the same function as we are striving for, namely to describe the communication between different blocks (system components)." (Jacobson, 1992)

Interaction diagrams describe the internal interactions of the components of the system in response to an external scenario of interaction with an actor. Therefore, as Jacobson stresses, an interaction diagram should be prepared for each use case. In the words of Jacobson: "The interaction diagram describes how each use case is offered by communicating objects. The diagram shows how the participating objects realize the use case through their interaction." (Jacobson, 1992)

We will adapt Jacobson's interaction diagramming technique for enterprise modeling. While interaction diagramming was originally conceived as a technique for software design, we can easily adapt it to enterprise design. We will use interaction diagrams to model the exchanges made between an actor and an ABP. As we will see shortly, an interaction diagram reveals the next lower-level of use cases between the subprocesses that make up the ABP in question. Thus interaction diagrams represent a modeling tool that methodically decomposes the ABP. The level of detail we go to depends on the scope of our modeling project.

Figure 14.5 shows the components of a typical interaction diagram. In this diagram, an actor label "Actor m" conducts the use case labeled "xxxxxx" with the ABP labeled "ABP n."

Figure 14.5 shows the various conventions we will adopt in our version of Jacobson's interaction diagrams. Specifically:

- ◆ An interaction diagram is prepared for each actor–ABP–use case combination. For example, the interaction diagram of Figure 14.5 is for the following combination:

  Actor: actor m

  ABP: ABP n

  Use case: xxxxxx

- ◆ The use case is decomposed into a series of exchanges shown as "exchange 1," "exchange 2," and "exchange 3" in Figure 14.5. The exchanges occurs over time and are arranged downward as time advances. An exchange represents the flow of materials, energy, or information between the actor and the ABP. The sequence of exchanges is documented as a script.

- ◆ An exchange is made through the specific port of the ABP that connects the actor and the ABP. The interaction diagram of Figure 14.5 calls attention to this by showing "exchange 1," "exchange 2," and "exchange 3" occurring through a port (i.e., the actual interaction diagram does not need to show this).

- ◆ The subprocesses of the ABP are listed along the top of the diagram as shown in Figure 14.5. The subprocesses are themselves ABPs and represent the decomposition of the ABP being analyzed. For example, in Figure 14.5, "ABP n" is decomposed into "ABP n.1," "ABP n.2," "ABP n.3," and "ABP n.4."

- ◆ Arrows are used to show the exchanges between the subprocess ABPs as a result of an exchange with the actor. These exchanges between the subprocess ABPs are also use cases. In Figure 14.5, we have labeled them "use case a" through "use case g." They are not decompositions of the broader use case but rather independent use cases triggered as a result of one of the various exchanges between the actor and the ABP of the larger use case. They will have their own interaction diagram when the time comes to define them in detail.

◆ The initial exchange between the actor and the ABP will actually be with one of the subprocess ABP's. For example, in Figure 14.5, "exchange 1" is made with "ABP n.1" and "exchange 2" is made with "ABP n.3."

14.4 Generic use cases of the ABP

The abstract business process (ABP) can be modeled with a generic set of use cases. The generic use cases correspond to the various exchanges that the ABP makes with its actors through its various ports. Figure 14.6 shows the generic use cases of the ABP.

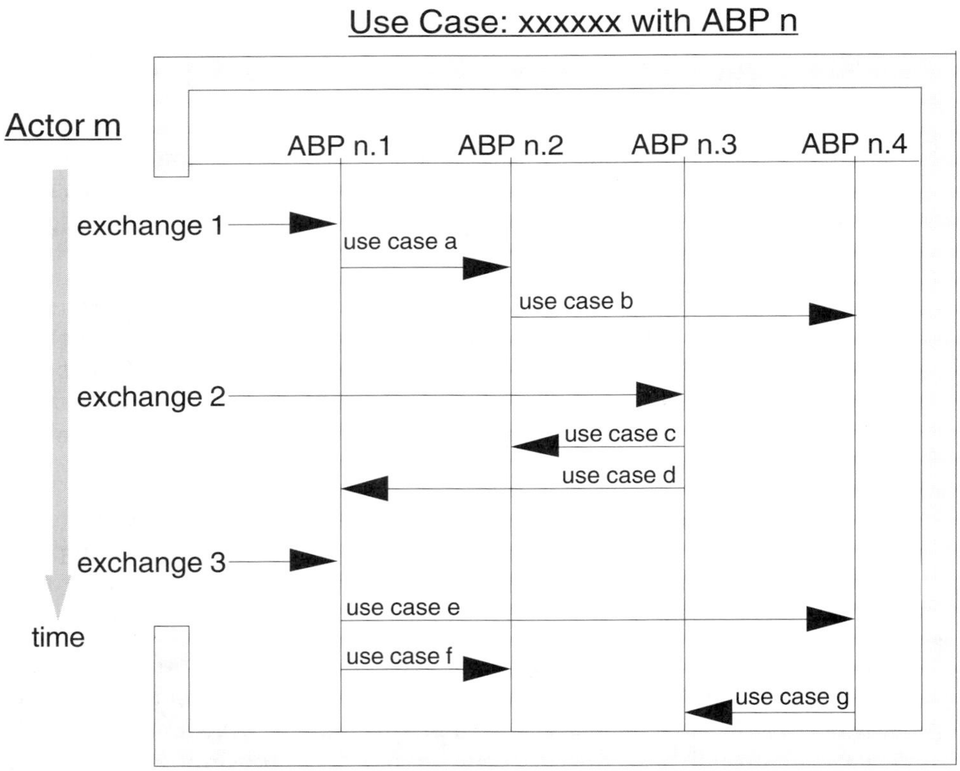

Figure 14.5 *Interaction diagram.*

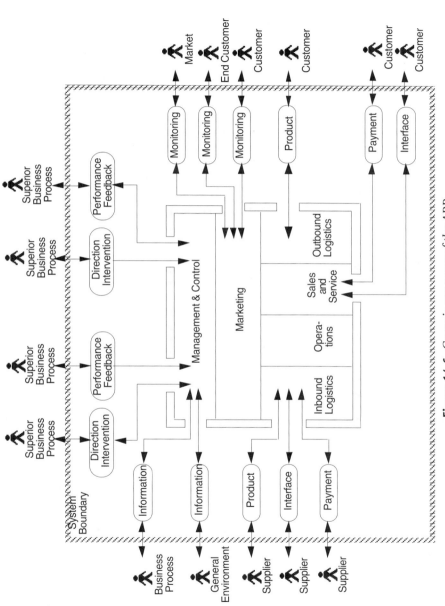

Figure 14.6 *Generic use cases of the ABP.*

The generic use cases shown in Figure 14.6 represent the scenarios that any ABP would, more or less, have to perform. In the figure, the generic use cases are shown with actors as people. This corresponds to our tendency to personify the actor to better capture the full scope and sophistication of the exchange. However, as pointed out earlier, the actor is an information-processing node embedded in its own ABP, which is not visible to us. Thus the actor could be an information machine, such as a computer, or a lower-level information-processing network, such as an organization of people. This section presents a brief description of the generic use cases of the ABP shown in Figure 14.6. Each use case is described with the purpose of the use case, the responsible subprocess ABP, which must carry out the use case, the actor subprocess ABP and a summary of the materials, energy, or information exchanged. The information presented in this section is based, in part, on the work of Allan Scherr (Scherr, 1993).

Supplier use cases

On the left hand side of Figure 14.6 are the use cases for the exchanges between the ABP and its suppliers. The figure summarizes the use cases that actually consist of the following six individual use cases:

- **Supplier Interface (opening)**

  Purpose: Opening communication with the supplier

  Responsibility: Inbound logistics ABP

  Actor: Supplier sales and service ABP

  Exchange: Offer from the supplier to sell a product or request from the ABP to purchase a product

- **Supplier Interface (negotiation)**

  Purpose: Negotiation with the supplier on the product specifications, product price, delivery schedule, payment schedule, etc.

  Responsibility: Inbound logistics ABP

  Actor: Supplier sales and service ABP

  Exchange: Repeated information exchanges between the ABP and the supplier on the conditions of satisfaction. Agreement is reached when the supplier accepts the ABP's request or the ABP accepts the supplier's offer.

- **Supplier Product Transfer**

  Purpose: Transfer of the negotiated product from the supplier to the ABP

Responsibility: Inbound logistics ABP

Actor: Supplier outbound logistics ABP

Exchange: New products or servicing of previously delivered products from the supplier to the ABP.

◆ **Supplier Assessment**

Purpose: Assessment of the delivered product or servicing and comparison with the conditions of satisfaction

Responsibility: Inbound logistics ABP

Actor: Supplier sales and service ABP

Exchange: Acceptance or rejection by the ABP of the product or servicing. If rejection, then either the ABP withdraws (i.e., without taking delivery) or a retry is negotiated with the supplier.

◆ **Supplier Payment**

Purpose: Payment for the product

Responsibility: Inbound logistics ABP

Actor: Supplier sales and service ABP

Exchange: Transfer of money or other legal tender from the ABP to the supplier and notification of its receipt.

◆ **Supplier Interface (service)**

Purpose: Obtain servicing of the product from the supplier such as repair, installation, parts, product adjustment, etc.

Responsibility: Inbound logistics ABP

Actor: Supplier sales and service ABP

Exchange: Negotiation of the requirements for servicing between the ABP and the supplier (the actual servicing will be delivered by the supplier product transfer use case described earlier).

Customer use cases

On the right-hand side of Figure 14.6 are the use cases for the exchanges between the ABP and its customers. These use cases are similar to the corresponding use cases on the supplier side listed earlier. The figure summarizes the supplier use cases, which actually consist of the following six individual use cases:

◆ **Customer Interface (opening)**

Purpose: Opening communication with the customer

Responsibility: Sales and service ABP

Actor: Supplier Inbound logistics ABP

Exchange: An offer from the ABP to sell a product or a request from the customer to purchase a product

◆ **Customer Interface (negotiation)**

Purpose: Negotiation with the customer on the product specifications, product price, delivery schedule, payment schedule, etc.

Responsibility: Sales and service ABP

Actor: Supplier Inbound logistics ABP

Exchange: Repeated information exchanges between the ABP and the customer on the conditions of satisfaction. Agreement is reached when the customer accepts the ABP's offer or the ABP accepts the customer's request.

◆ **Customer Product Transfer**

Purpose: Transfer of the negotiated product from the ABP to the customer.

Responsibility: Outbound logistics ABP

Actor: Customer Inbound logistics ABP

Exchange: New products or servicing of previously delivered products from the ABP to the customer

◆ **Customer Assessment**

Purpose: Customer's assessment of the delivered product and comparison with the conditions of satisfaction

Responsibility: Sales and service ABP

Actor: Supplier inbound logistics ABP

Exchange: Acceptance or rejection by the customer of the product. If rejection, then either the customer withdraws (i.e., without taking delivery) or a retry is negotiated.

◆ **Customer Payment**

Purpose: Payment for products.

Responsibility: Sales and service ABP

Actor: Supplier inbound logistics ABP

Exchange: Transfer of money or other legal tender from the customer to the ABP and notification of its receipt.

◆ **Customer interface (service)**

Purpose: Provide servicing of the product to the customer such as repair, installation, parts, product adjustment, etc.

Responsibility: Sales and service ABP

Actor: Supplier inbound logistics ABP

Exchange: Negotiation of the requirements for servicing between the customer and the ABP (the actual servicing will be delivered by the customer product transfer use case described earlier)

Control-coordination use cases

On the top of Figure 14.6 are the use cases for the exchanges between the ABP and its superior ABP or its subordinate ABPs consisting of the following individual use cases:

◆ **Direction Intervention (superior)**

Purpose: Receipt of intervention from the superior ABP

Responsibility: Management and control ABP

Actor: Superior management and control ABP

Exchange: Information representing commands from the superior ABP to change the operation or products of the ABP

◆ **Performance Feedback (superior)**

Purpose: Reports performance or other feedback to the superior ABP

Responsibility: Management and control ABP

Actor: Superior management and control ABP

Exchange: Information representing the performance or other feedback of the ABP for its superior ABP.

◆ **Direction Intervention (subordinate)**

Purpose: Delivery of intervention to a subordinate ABP of the ABP

Responsibility: Management and control ABP

Actor: Subordinate management and control ABP

Exchange: Information representing commands from the ABP to change the operation or products of the subordinate ABP

◆ **Performance Feedback (subordinate)**

Purpose: Receipt of the performance or other feedback from a subordinate ABP

Responsibility: Management and control ABP

Actor: Subordinate management and control ABP

Exchange: Information representing the performance or other feedback of the subordinate ABP

◆ **Information**

Purpose: Obtain information important to the welfare or operation of the ABP from the environment

Responsibility: Management and control ABP

Actor: Various actors in the general environment

Exchange: Information about the environment of the ABP including industry, channel, competitor, market, technology, or legal/regulatory/policy information.

Marketing use cases

In the middle of Figure 14.6 are the use cases for the exchanges between the Marketing ABP and the environment consisting of the following individual use cases:

◆ **Monitoring (market)**

Purpose: Obtain information about the market of the ABP

Responsibility: Marketing ABP

Actor: Various actors in the general environment that have information about the general market of the ABP

Exchange: Information about the market of the ABP including industry, channel, competitor, etc. information

◆ **Monitoring (end customer)**

Purpose: Obtain information about the actual end customer of the enterprise

Responsibility: Marketing ABP

Actor: The end customer enterprise

Exchange: Information about the end-customer enterprise, especially its needs, which provide an opportunity to satisfy those needs.

◆ **Monitoring (customer)**

Purpose: Obtain information about the downstream customer of the ABP

Responsibility: Marketing ABP

Actor: The downstream customer ABP which purchases the products of the ABP

Exchange: Information about the customer

14.5 Conclusion

In this chapter, we discussed in detail the abstract business process (ABP). We saw that the ABP is a specialization of the business process introduced in Chapter 13. We discussed in Chapter 8 the process object and its corresponding process class. Our ABP will be a subclass of the process class we defined there.

The ABP is based on the Porter value chain and consists of a set of subprocesses. The value activities of the Porter value chain correspond to the subprocesses of the ABP. In other words, the value activities define the attributes and behavior of the ABP. The subprocesses of an ABP are also ABPs, and thus the ABP is recursively defined. This means that the enterprise, at any level of decomposition, is modeled using a single, unifying construct of the ABP.

ABPs have ports through which they make exchanges with their environment. These exchanges can be modeled using a technique originated by Ivar Jacobson called *use cases.* A use case is a dialog between the system and an actor. The important thing about use cases is that they define the functionality of a system. In effect, the functionality of a system is the sum of its use cases. Jacobson comments that "use cases support the fundamental principle of human-interface design: to maintain consistency between the users conceptual picture of the system and the systems actual behavior" (Jacobson, 1991). Use cases are documented by interaction diagrams. In enterprise modeling an interaction diagram shows how the subprocess ABPs of the ABP in question conduct internal interactions in response to the external interaction between the ABP and an actor.

In this chapter, we presented a set of generic use cases. The generic use cases represent the exchange scenarios any ABP would have to make through its ports. When designing a business process, we can use these generic use cases as a starting point or straw boss for the actual use cases of the business process.

Chapter **15**

The Structural View
of the Enterprise

15.1 Introduction

In this chapter, we focus on the structure of the enterprise, that is, the configuration of its physical and abstract components. The structural view of the enterprise actually consists of a physical aspect and a logical aspect. We have already encountered the physical aspect of the structural view. It consists of the information-processing networks introduced in Chapter 4. Information-processing networks are made up of information-processing nodes connected in an infrastructure of communications channels. Therefore, to present a complete picture of the structural view, this chapter starts out with a brief review of the information-processing network and discusses how the infrastructure of the enterprise is related to the functional view of the enterprise discussed in Chapters 13 and 14.

The logical aspect of the structural view of the enterprise is concerned with the configuration of its business processes. In Chapter 14, we generalized the business process into the abstract business process (ABP). We will see in this chapter that the logical structure of the enterprise is determined by the configuration and relations of its ABPs. We will present several decompositions of the ABP, which reveal its characteristics. We will see that the enterprise is structured around the hierarchical-multilayer structure. We introduced the hierarchical-multilayered organization of a system in Chapter 3.

We will see that the enterprise is a control/coordination hierarchy of ABPs. We usually refer to this as its organization chart. Every enterprise has an authority hierarchy in which strategic objectives are decomposed into tactical decisions required to implement the strategic objectives. The organization chart defines the capability to start, stop, and control processes; it is largely a question of resource allocation and deallocation.

Another aspect of the hierarchical-multilayered organization of the enterprise is the abstraction layering of its ABPs. The hierarchical-multilayered organization divides the enterprise into several layers, each consisting of one or more ABPs, which interact with each other to form an abstraction strata. An enterprise has various layers that represent abstractions of functionality or specialization. In fact, this is probably the most visible aspect of the logical structure of the enterprise. We will see that several enterprise-layering patterns coexist and provide various logical structures to the same set ABPs.

15.2 Physical structure: Enterprise infrastructure

Let's start with a discussion of the physical aspect of the structure of the enterprise. The physical structure of the enterprise is sometimes called its *infrastructure,* and we will use these two terms interchangeably. The problem faced by the enterprise modeler is integrating the infrastructure view of the enterprise with its functional view. In part, the problem is to define exactly how the infrastructure view and the functional view are related to each other. In this section, we will attempt to advance the cause of the integration of these two a little more.

Comparing the functional view and the infrastructure view

Let's compare the functional view and the infrastructure view of the enterprise. First, the functional view is based on the concepts of function, functional area, and process defined in Chapter 13. The functional view describes the "what" of the enterprise. The functional view is constructed by first identifying the goals of the enterprise and then decomposing the goals so that they may be accomplished by the collective purposefulness of the components of the enterprise. The functional view is described in terms of transformations of energy, materials, or information that represent the reason for the enterprise. The mechanism of these transformations is the process. Processes are carefully designed and instantiated to accomplish the goals efficiently by various transformations. The transformations result in products that have value to customers. In the functional view, the focus of the enterprise becomes one of value and, as we saw in Chapter 13, the Porter value chain is an ideal tool for describing it.

Second, the infrastructure view of the enterprise is based on the information-processing network and the information-processing node defined in Chapter 4. In that chapter, we saw that the physical structure of the enterprise is an information-processing network consisting of vast networks of information-processing nodes. This gives us the physical implementation of the enterprise, its lattice of active information-processing nodes connected by physical communications channels. Not only does the infrastructure of an enterprise include the physical communications channels, it also includes all of the physical assets to support the communications channels. Thus the infrastructure also includes the buildings, real estate, furniture, or environmental systems, all of which support the network of communications channels. For example, an office building provides the physical environment for the communications channels between people.

A quick review of information-processing nodes

The point where the functional view and the infrastructure view are actually integrated is in the process and its corresponding information-processing nodes. In Chapter 7, we observed that every process has a change mechanism that is an information-processing node. An information-processing node receives, stores, uses, and sends information within the information-processing network in which it is embedded. Let's review briefly how the information-processing node relates to the process.

Information-processing nodes can be organized into higher-level information processing nodes. The information-processing node at the lowest level of decomposition is a person or information machine such as a computer or numerically controlled milling machine. We call these *elementary information processing nodes*. An elementary information-processing node has at its core a physical symbol system described by Newell and Simon as explained in Chapter 4. Above this lowest level, information-processing nodes are arranged into information processing networks such as organizations of people. At these higher levels, the information-processing network can be abstracted into a single, unified information-processing node for modeling purposes (e.g., if we are not interested in the lower-level details). Thus we say that an information-processing node is either a person, an information machine, or a lower-level information-processing network.

The capabilities of the upper level information-processing nodes such as an organization are still the same as any other information processing node: to receive, store, use, and send information within the information-processing network. Like the elementary information-processing node, the upper-level information process-ing node can be modeled as the execution of a script. One big difference is in the physical symbol system of the elementary information-processing node, which is not an identifiable component of the upper-level information-processing node at that layer of decomposition. Rather, the upper-level information processing node, such as an organization, achieves its dynamics by the collective dynamics of its component information-processing nodes, which can ultimately be decomposed to elementary-information processing nodes.

A quick review of the process artifact

In Chapter 7, we introduced the *process artifact*, which is defined as a purpose-built process (i.e., a human construction, hence the use of the term *artifact*). The process artifact is endowed with a change mechanism by its human creators, which provides its dynamic activity.

Process artifacts can be decomposed into lower-level process artifacts for implementing a portion of the activity of the larger process. The lowest level of decomposition is called the *process element*. This level is intended to describe the physical level of decomposition. However, the definition of the lowest level may be a modeling convention based on the scope of the project. Process elements exe-cute sequences of process steps, the atomic actions that actually do the work. While the process elements and hence the process steps may be modeling conven-tions, for physical process elements, the change mechanism is a human or machine capable of performing a sequence of physical process steps.

The change mechanism of the higher-level processes is the sequence and con-trol of the actions of the lower-level processes. The change mechanism of the higher-level processes is an abstraction caused by the collective actions of its lower-level processes, which ultimately consist of humans or machines (even though our modeling project may not reveal them as process elements due to our limited scope). The change mechanism of the higher levels can be described as a set of business rules that the process always honors and, hence, are always true. The business rules are declarative rules that relate the post-conditions of sub-processes and the invocation of subprocesses through time. Thus the dynamic activity of the higher levels is caused by the ever-changing post-conditions of the lower levels as controlled by business rules.

Correlating the functional view and the infrastructure view

The change mechanism of the process artifact is identical to the information pro-cessing node. This is a very important point, which we introduced in Chapter 7 and reinforced in Chapter 8. In particular, we are able to make the correspondence between the lowest-level information-processing node (a person, an information machine such as a computer) and the physical change mechanism of the process (also a person, a computer).

This correlation between information-processing node and physical change mechanism integrates the two major views of the enterprise: the structural view and the functional view. On one hand, we have the structural view consisting of an infrastructure of information-processing nodes connected by lattices of communication channels. On the other, we have the functional view consisting of processes in hierarchical and dependency relations. Figure 15.1 shows an example of the relation between processes and information-processing nodes.

In the example of Figure 15.1, we see in the background the infrastructure view of an enterprise as a complex information-processing network in which information-

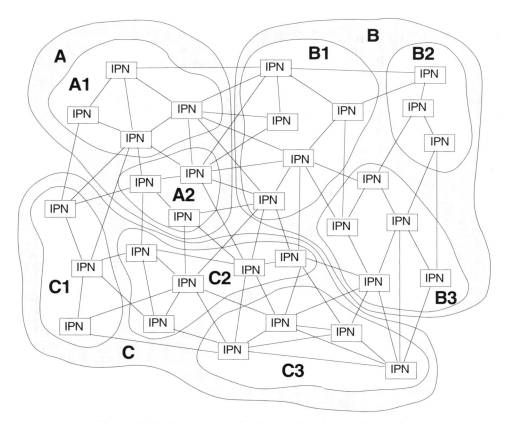

Figure 15.1 *Processes and information-processing nodes.*

processing nodes (labeled IPN in the figure) are connected in a lattice of communication channels. The IPNs are people, information machines, or lower-level information-processing nodes. Superimposed over the information-processing network in Figure 15.1 is the functional view of the enterprise. We see three major processes labeled A, B, and C, which are, in turn, made up of subprocesses. For example, process A is made up of subprocesses A1 and A2, and so on.

As we design the business processes of the enterprise, we are specifying requirements for the design of the enterprise infrastructure. The infrastructure of the enterprise implements the information-processing network. The information-processing network connects its information-processing nodes, which in turn are organized into processes. Figure 15.1 shows how the infrastructure view is more permanent than the functional view. Processes are more temporary than the infrastructure of the enterprise but neither is permanent.

15.3 Logical structure: Configuration of the abstract business processes

In the preceding section, we discussed the physical side of the structural view of the enterprise. Now we will turn our attention to the logical side of the structural view of the enterprise. In discussing the logical structure, we make use of the abstract business process (ABP). We are concerned here with the configuration of the ABPs and their various relations.

The decomposition of the abstract business process (ABP)
As we learned in Chapter 14, the ABP is decomposed into lower-level ABPs. Figure 15.2 shows the decomposition of an abstract business process into its subprocesses, which are themselves ABPs.

Notice that we have produced a lower level of ABPs, each of which is externally identical to its parent ABP (or any other ABP). One question that we will attempt to answer in this section is how far should we go in the decomposition of the ABP. A quick answer is that it depends on the scope of the modeling project. Also, there is a limit to the decomposition because we will eventually reach the elementary level consisting of physical process elements with their physical change mechanisms (i.e., people, computers) and further decomposition is not productive.

Product flows of the ABP
Another way to view the decomposed ABP is in terms of its product flows. That is, each subprocess ABP takes in input and transforms it to output products. The flow of these products can be shown in a diagram such as Figure 15.3:

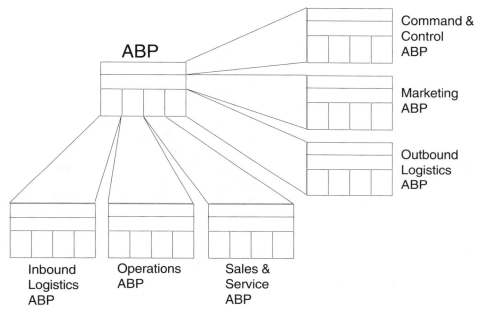

Figure 15.2 *Decomposition of the ABP into ABPs.*

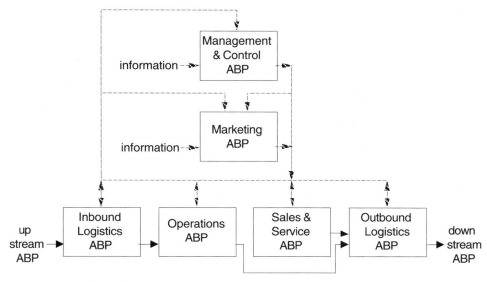

Figure 15.3 *Product flows of the ABP.*

In Figure 15.3, we see the mainline flow of products along the subprocesses at the bottom of the figure indicated by dark lines and arrows. Thus products enter our ABP on the far left from upstream ABPs. The products enter our ABP through its inbound logistics ABP subprocess. At this point, the products are considered raw materials and flow to the operations ABP subprocess. The operations ABP creates the finished products (i.e., relative to our ABP) and makes them available to the outbound logistics ABP subprocess on the far right. In the meantime, the sales and service ABP subprocess sells the finished products to downstream ABPs that are then delivered by the outbound logistics ABP subprocess.

Figure 15.3 also shows the flow of a different type of product, that of information in the form of environmental information, direction, and performance feedback shown as dotted lines and arrows. Thus at the top is the management and control ABP subprocess which takes in information from the environment as its raw material. The products of the management and control ABP subprocess are the economics and goals of the larger ABP, which it translates into directions to the other ABPs subprocesses, receiving performance feedback from them. Similarly, the marketing ABP subprocess takes in information and produces its directions to the mainline flow concerning the design or redesign of products, processes, and technology. The ABP subprocesses of the mainline flow produce performance feedback information, which is delivered as information products to both the management and control subprocess and the marketing subprocess.

Decomposition of the product flow of the ABP

Since an ABP can be decomposed into yet lower-level ABPs, we can decompose the product flow shown in Figure 15.3 into the next lower level. Figure 15.4 shows the original ABP of Figure 15.3 decomposed into the next lower layer of ABPs.

Figure 15.4 shows more accurately the logistics of the product flows. Thus the product flow (dark line) enters via the IL (inbound logistics) and leaves via the OL (outbound logistics). Also, the information products of the M&C (management and control) and the M (marketing) ABP subprocesses are directions to the other ABPs. The direction products enter the top of each of the target ABPs via their own individual M&Cs. The target ABPs deliver their performance feedback from their own M&Cs at their respective tops. The performance feedback enters the M&C or M ABPs through their respective M&Cs.

Second-level decomposition of the product flows of the ABP

Another useful way of looking at the decomposition of the ABP is as a second-level decomposition of the product flows. To form this decomposition, we start with Figure 15.4 and decompose each of the subprocess ABPs into their subprocesses

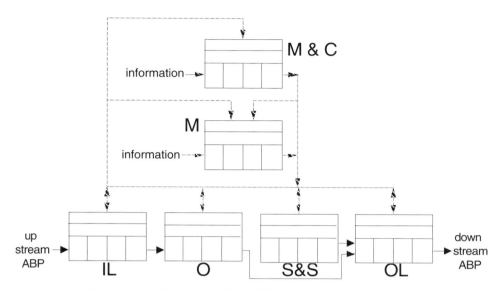

Figure 15.4 *Decomposition of the product flow of the ABP.*

(i.e., we are now at the level of sub-subprocess) and show the details of the product flows between these sub-subprocesses. The result is Figure 15.5.

Figure 15.5 shows the relationship between the process, its subprocesses, and its sub-subprocesses. As pointed out earlier, the product of the Management and Control ABP is directions delivered to its ABPs in the form of information. In Figure 15.5, we see several levels of Management and Control ABPs as well as how they are interconnected. At the subprocess level (i.e., the largest rectangles of Figure 15.5), the management and control ABP (labeled M&C in the figure) provides direction to the other subprocess-level ABPs (labeled M, IL, O, S&S, and OL). Each of these subprocess-level ABPs also have their own Management and Control subprocess ABP, which we would describe as sub-subprocesses relative to Figure 15.5. Each of these sub-subprocess Management and Control ABPs provide direction to the their respective internal ABPs.

The point is that at any level of decomposition, any ABP is only under the direction and control of its M&C ABP at that level of decomposition. M&C ABPs at higher levels of decomposition don't provide direct management and control of the various ABPs of the lower-level decomposition. Rather, the upper M&C ABP provides management and control of the lower M&C ABP, which, in turn, provides its own management and control of its ABPs at its level of decomposition.

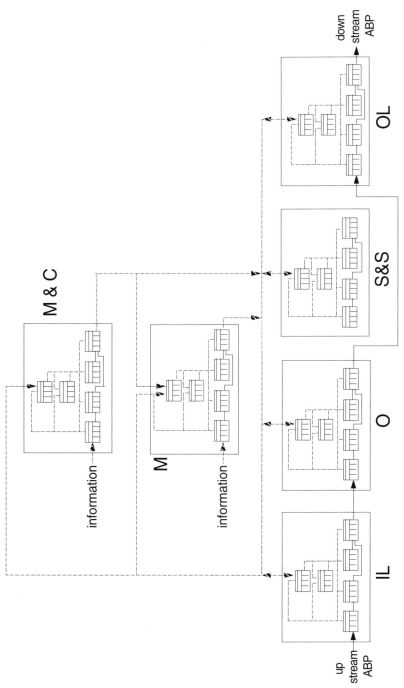

Figure 15.5 *Second-level decomposition of the product flows of the ABP.*

Similarly, for any ABP, the performance feedback flows up to the M&C ABP at that level of decomposition. From there, it flows up to the next higher level of decomposition. Thus, an ABP gives performance feedback only to its own M&C ABP and never directly to the upper ABP.

15.4 How much decomposition?

How much decomposition is necessary to create a meaningful model or give us the necessary visibility for designing the ABP? To answer this question, let's return once more to the process branch of the conceptual type hierarchy described in Chapter 6 and refined in Chapter 7. We saw in those chapters that a process artifact (i.e., the human-engineered process) consists ultimately of process elements, which themselves consist of process steps.

Modeling scope vs. decomposition

In the conceptual-type hierarchy, process elements represent, by definition, the lowest-level process for purposes of modeling. Process elements hold the lowest-level position because they are the last level of processes revealed in the decomposition. The modeler has defined the scope of the modeling project and has defined this level of decomposition because it would gain nothing to further decompose a given process element. Thus even though the modeler knows that a process element could be further decomposed, he or she regards it as the lowest level in the model.

Process elements consist of a series of process steps. Process steps implement the atomic transformations of the process element. A process step takes in input and transforms it into output. Again, this is considered atomic for purposes of modeling. That is, once we arrive at the process element, we decompose it into atomic process steps that we do not further decompose because of the scope of the modeling project. Process steps can be strung together by their process element to form a complex sequence of transformations. The combined results of the various process steps is the output of the process element. Process steps can be modeled using a procedural script executed by the process element in which each process step is a command in the script.

Decomposing ABPs into process elements

Process elements are not ABPs by definition. The lowest level of ABP we reach in our decomposition is, by definition, decomposed into the process-element level. The point is that process elements do not have the complete set of the six sub-processes (i.e., M&C, M, IL, O, S&S, and OL). Once we reach an appropriate level of decomposition of ABPs, we decompose this last level of ABP into process elements. Like the other decompositions, this, too, is a modeling convention. We describe our lowest level of ABP as consisting of process elements, which, in turn, execute process steps. The decomposition of the ABP into process elements defines the internal details of the transformations of that ABP.

Decomposing process elements into process elements

As a practical matter, any process modeling methodology must permit process elements to be decomposed into lower-level process elements. These lower-level process elements reveal yet more details of the transformations and simplify the design of the physical processes.

For example, the process model of a paper mill might identify finishing as an elementary process. However, this elementary process can be decomposed into cutting, trimming, etc. The difference between an upper-level process element (e.g., finishing) and its lower-level process elements (e.g., cutting, trimming) is their assumed primitive level. The lower-level process elements have no global perspective as they pursue their finite activities under their restricted goals.

On the other hand, the so-called upper-level process elements such as finishing are part of the functional view of the enterprise, which is part of the global perspective of goals being accomplished. The lower levels of process elements are used to design physical transformations, while the upper level of the process elements is a modeling concept representing the lowest logical level used to design the enterprise to accomplish its goals under the restricted scope of the modeling project.

So . . . how much decomposition?

For many ABPs, the question of how much decomposition is a moot point because as we decompose, we quickly reach the level of physical process elements with their physical information-processing nodes (people, computers). This is especially true of all of the ABPs except the operations ABP. Therefore, we can divide the question of how much decomposition into two parts: decomposition of the operations ABP and decomposition of the non-operations ABP (i.e., the other five ABPs). We'll start with the decomposition of the non-operations ABP:

- ◆ **Decomposition of the non-operations ABPs** The five ABPs (M&C, M, IL, S&S, and OL) usually have very shallow decompositions before the physical level is reached. For example, at the lower left of Figure 15.5, we have the inbound logistics subprocess ABP, labeled IL. The inbound logistics ABP serves as the interface to the upstream suppliers. In Figure 15.5, the IL subprocess ABP is decomposed into its own standard set of six subprocess

ABPs (in this case, sub-subprocesses). Of the six, one of them is the lower-level inbound logistics ABP.

What is the relation between this sub-subprocess inbound logistics ABP and the subprocess inbound logistics ABP at the upper level of decomposition? The answer is that only one physical inbound logistics process element actually takes physical input from the upstream suppliers. As soon as this physical level is reached in the decomposition of the inbound logistics ABP, we don't need to go any further—we couldn't anyway. As a rule of thumb, the five non-operations ABPs tend to have shallow, one- or two- (occasionally three-) level decompositions. For the inbound logistics sub-process of large enterprises, the decompositions of these five are "wide and thin." This also applies to the other five subprocesses as well. While the five in a large enterprise have shallow decompositions, they nevertheless may have larger numbers of information-processing nodes performing parallel process elements, each with similar duties.

◆ **Decomposition of the operations ABPs**   The operations ABP usually has a much deeper decomposition before the level of physical process elements with their physical information-processing nodes is reached. Also, once the physical process element level is reached, it will have its own hierarchy of process element decomposition as process elements are decomposed into lower-level process elements. The operations ABP is the bread-and-butter subprocess that produces the end products of the larger ABP. It is like a little enterprise in its own right, with a full complement of the six ABPs. For example, the operations ABP in Figure 15.5, labeled O, takes in input products and creates output products using its six internal sub-processes.

What is the relationship between this lower-level operations ABP and the upper-level operations ABP? The lower-level is itself like a little enterprise with a full-complement of its own six ABPs and, in particular, its own operations ABP. There is only one physical transformation at the lowest level, which consists of a series of process steps that produce the physical product. This lowest-level physical transformation may be complex, involving many physical transformations (e.g., a factory assembly line), but it still results in a single product instance for each of its cycles.

These physical transformations are not ABPs. Rather, they are process steps executed by process elements. Thus in our decomposition of the operations ABP, we eventually reach the level of the process element where the actual physical transformations take place. However, as we progress through lower and lower decompositions of the ABPs, we can choose to stop at any level. At that point we would have a view of process elements (i.e., from a modeling standpoint), which by definition consist of process steps.

15.5 Organizations: Authority

Another concept of the structure of the enterprise is the organizational structure. The organization chart is a familiar part of every organization and is often the focus of attention by the members of an organization. In this book, we will adapt a nonpsychological definition of the organization and will define it as a specialized information-processing network. Many of the concepts of the organization presented below are derived from the work of Carl Hewitt and Jeff Inman (Hewitt and Inman, 1991). We will extend Hewitt and Inman's definition to include our concepts of information-processing networks, information-processing nodes and ABPs.

Definition: Organization

An organization is an information-processing network that is responsible for one or more business processes. The information-processing nodes that make up the organization are purposely put together to serve as the change mechanisms of the business processes assigned to the organization. The organization's business processes could include full-fledged ABPs or merely processes elements (i.e., depending on the level of decomposition of the organization; we will discuss this in a moment). An information-processing node can be a member of more than one organization.

The grouping of information-processing nodes into organizations is semi-permanent in the sense that they are assigned for a relatively long period of time (e.g. many product cycles). Information-processing nodes include both people and computers and their permanent assignment (relatively speaking) to an organization is primarily for efficiency reasons. That is, both humans and computers tend to be more efficient in their work when they are in a stable, permanent position. However, stability is primarily a human need. Organizations are designed to provide this stability. Thus an organization allows information-processing nodes to be (semi) permanently allocated as the change mechanisms of business processes.

Boundary of the organization

Ideally, the boundary of the organization is equivalent to the boundary of the single business process assigned to it. That is, one organization is directly mapped to one business process and vice versa. However, in practice, an organization could be assigned more than one business process. In this case, the multiple business processes must be connected in a dependency value chain. We discussed dependency value chains in Chapter 13 but in summary this means the business processes are arranged in sequences in which products flow from business process to business process. The point of the dependency value chain is that the customer value of the products is increased as they pass from business process to business process within the sequence. It should be noted that it is incorrect to assign independent business processes to an organization. That is, if two business processes are not integral parts of a dependency value chain, they should not be assigned to the same organization.

The information-processing nodes that are members of an organization serve as change mechanisms to the process elements of the decomposed business processes assigned to the organization. A given information-processing node can be a member of more than one organization. In this case, the information-processing node must divide its time among the organizations in which it is a member. Multiple memberships in organizations is possible because an information-processing node is connected by communication channels that are not restricted to one organization.

Global functions of the organization

To execute its assigned business processes, the organization must accomplish global functions on behalf of its various member information-processing nodes. These global functions are performed by specialized business processes of the organization and are in addition to the various functions of the assigned business processes. That is, the specialized organizational business processes operate at the global level of the organization and are not to be confused with the business processes assigned to the organization. Carl Hewitt and Jeff Inman identify the following global functions of the organization (Hewitt and Inman, 1991) which we have adapted to our concepts of information-processing networks:

◆ **Allocation function: provides resources for business processes**　The business processes of the organization consume resources. Therefore, the first global function of an organization is to allocate resources; the organization has specialized business processes that accomplish this. Resources include any materials, energy, and information required to execute the assigned business processes. Resources by definition are expensive or limited in availability. The most expensive and limited resources are the information-processing nodes themselves.

Information is a special resource that will be required by any business process. No matter what type of organization it is, every information-processing node will be involved in the exchange of information with other information-processing nodes in the organization. These information exchanges are conducted using the infrastructure of the information-processing network. Therefore, every business process assigned to the organization will imply the consumption of information resources including processing, storage, and communications. The specialized allocation functions must manage the limited information resources as necessary to permit the information-processing nodes to complete their assigned business processes. Notice that information processing resources include not only the physical resources (e.g., processing, storage and communications) but the use of the information channels. For example, the latter might take the form of scheduling meetings between people for concentrating communication.

◆ **Membership function: keeps track of membership in the organization** Organizations consists of information-processing nodes (we will discuss this shortly). The membership function creates new memberships and terminates existing memberships as the organization evolves. Also, the membership function includes paying the human information-processing nodes for their services.

◆ **Reporting function: provides organizational information to other organizations** Information must be transmitted from the organization to other organizations concerning the status of the organization (e.g., what business processes are assigned to the organization, which information-processing nodes are in the organization, which resources are assigned to the organization and their status, the accounting for money assigned to the organization, etc.). Notice that this reporting is specialized to organizational business to coordinate the activities between organizations and is not to be confused with the feedback loops in which the business processes report their status to their superior business processes. That is, organizational reporting is largely a housekeeping function to optimize the intra-organizational relations or to maintain the organization as an enterprise structural component.

◆ **Boundary function: controls the organization's boundary** This global function controls the boundary of the organization. The organizational boundary defines its limits of responsibility and is defined in terms of the business processes assigned to the organization. That is, any change to the boundary of an organization is made in terms of the inclusion or exclusion of whole business processes. Organizational boundaries separate the resources used by different organizations helping them account for their own responsibilities without interference from others.

◆ **Management function: controls the integrity of the organization**   This global organizational function sets policies that the member information-processing nodes must follow. Information-processing nodes may be capable of volition (e.g., as in the case of humans) and policies must be set and enforced. These policies generally protect or maintain the global perspective of the organization at the expense of the individuality of the members.

The organization as a group of information-processing nodes

We stated earlier that an organization consists of information-processing nodes. As we have stated many times in this book, information-processing nodes are the change mechanisms of business processes. Also, we have stated many times that information-processing nodes are not necessarily atomic and may be an abstraction for an underlying information-processing network consisting of multiple information-processing nodes connected together in a lattice of communications channels.

An organization can be identified at any level of decomposition. At the lowest level, people or information machines form the organization. At higher levels, information-processing networks abstracted as information-processing nodes form the organization. We could look inside of these abstracted information-processing nodes and see an information-processing network.

Higher-level organizations are assigned higher-level ABPs, which are decomposed and ultimately implemented by the physical information-processing nodes of the process elements at the lowest level of decomposition. Each ABP, no matter at what level, has a change mechanism implemented by an information-processing node. For the higher-level ABPs, the information-processing nodes will likewise be at a correspondingly higher level; that is, they will actually be information-processing networks if we look inside their black boxes of abstraction.

Creating organizations

The creation of an organization in an enterprise is done by the management and control ABP and specifically a business operations planning subprocess (i.e., itself an ABP). Since organizations tend to be permanent, their creation is a relatively rare event compared to the creation or changes to business processes. That is, the definition of the business processes changes faster than the organizations of a typical enterprise (but neither changes very quickly). The creation of an organization means allocating its collection of information-processing nodes and other resources to it. Also, one or more business processes is assigned to the organization when it is created. The business operations planning ABP that creates an organization is a typical meta-level business process (i.e., in the terminology of hierarchical multilayer systems). During its lifetime, an organization may be assigned additional resources or have some of its resources taken away by a meta-level business operations planning process. We will discuss business operations planning in Chapter 22.

Creating business processes

In a typical enterprise, the higher-level ABPs are created by the same business operations planning ABP (i.e., as a subprocess of the management and control ABP) that creates organizations as described earlier. Higher-level ABPs tend to be permanent and their creation is a rare event. However, the creation of lower-level business processes (i.e., lower-level ABPs or process elements) is less rare. The lower-level business processes are created by the organization itself as it discharges its duties. Thus the allocation process of an organization is to continually allocate and reallocate resources, especially information-processing nodes to its business processes. Notice that this is a meta-level function relative to the business processes.

Allocating organizational resources

The assignment of resources is the point where the concept of _authority_ enters the discussion of organizations. The primary resources that must be assigned are the information-processing nodes of the organization, which includes both people and computers. A given information-processing node may be assigned to one or more business processes. Thus a given information-processing node may serve as a change mechanism for more than one business process sharing its time between them.

The assignment of resources to business processes is accomplished by the organizational allocation business process and is one of the global functions of the organization as explained above. Once a resource is assigned to a business process by the organization (i.e., the global organizational business process), then the resource is under the control of that business process. During the life cycle of the business process, a resource may be assigned and reassigned internally within the auspices of the business process.

Thus there is a three-tier allocation of resources in the enterprise: the first tier is at the business operations planning meta-level where resources are assigned (or reassigned) to an organization as the organization is created or during its lifetime; the second tier is at the organizational level where resources owned by the organization are assigned or reassigned to its business processes; the third tier is internal to the business process itself where business process controlled resources are assigned and reassigned as needed. Figure 15.6 shows the three tiers of resource allocation in an enterprise.

Figure 15.6 shows a meta-level ABP, a management and control process, creating an organization and assigning resources to it (tier 1). Also, throughout its lifetime, the organization will be reassigned resources by meta-level ABPs. Once created, the organization will manage its resources and continually assign or reassign its resources to its ABPs (tier 2). For its part, an ABP will continually assign or reassign its resources to its own subprocesses as it discharges its duties. Notice no time frequency is implied by the figure. Thus some business processes could be

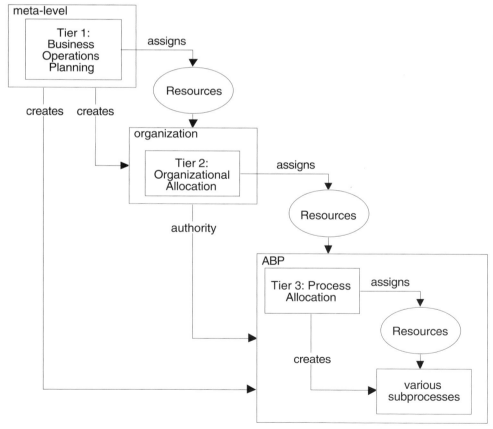

Figure 15.6 *Three tiers of resource allocation.*

created and eliminated very frequently as the activities of the enterprise change, while other business processes—especially the high-level ABPs— could be permanent and created when the enterprise is created and never eliminated.

While the most important resources in Figure 15.6 are the information-processing nodes, other resources are assigned including information infrastructure or other capital items such as floor space. The information infrastructure is especially important because it implements or supports the channels of the information-processing network to which the information-processing nodes are connected.

15.6 Abstraction layers of the enterprise

The previous sections discussed the configuration of the ABPs of the enterprise. In those sections, the emphasis was on the various transformations of inputs to products and the corresponding structure and organization of the enterprise to accomplish these transformations. Now we will describe another aspect of the structure of the enterprise, that of its hierarchical-multilayer organization.

A quick review of hierarchical-multilayer systems organization

We presented a detailed definition of hierarchical-multilayer systems in Chapter 3. In that chapter, we learned that the subsystems of a general system are often arranged in hierarchical layers (i.e., strata) with the following characteristics:

- **Specialization of the layers** Any particular layer tends to be specialized around a set of competencies or skills and has its own discipline or body of knowledge.

- **Vertical arrangement** The layers are stacked one on top of another in which the layers use the layers below to perform services or create products for them.

- **Asymmetrical interdependence** The upper layers depend on lower layers to help discharge their duties, but the lower layers do not depend on upper layers and often don't even know about them.

- **Reduction in information** Upper layers have a deeper understanding of the world but have less detailed information about it. The information at the higher levels is synthesized and abstracted. Lower layers have a superficial understanding of the world but a relative abundance of detailed information.

- **Right of intervention** The lower layers are constrained by the upper layers so that the goals of the upper layers are realized.

- **Autonomy of lower layers**   The subsystems of the lower layers do have freedom to act independently within the constraints of the upper layers. This is because of the limits of time that the lower level has to respond to events.

Definition: Structural patterns

An enterprise will have many different hierarchical-multilayered structures. The various hierarchical-multilayered structures of the enterprise can be generalized into a series of structural patterns. A structural pattern is a broad-based paradigm, model, or example of a useful principle that can be used to organize the business processes of the enterprise. These structural patterns can be used and reused to guide the design of the enterprise (or its subsets). The various structural patterns are identified and distinguished by the flows of entities (i.e., physical, abstract, information representation) among the various ABPs of the enterprise.

Structural pattern: The ABP layers

We have already encountered a structural pattern in our discussion of the ABP in the previous sections of this chapter. The ABP itself has a hierarchical-multilayer structure consisting of three layers as shown in Figure 15.7.

The ABP layers structural pattern of Figure 15.7 is one of many used by the enterprise modeler to define and design ABPs. As shown in the figure, the three layers of the ABP are abstraction strata that relate to the flow of entities to and from the various ABP subprocesses as follows:

- **Economics and goals**   This is the abstraction layer that transforms input information into economic knowledge and produces the goals of the ABP.

- **Market information processing and control**   This is the layer that buys and transforms environmental marketing information into the definition of products as well as the definition of the technology and processes to produce the products.

- **Production**   This is the layer that buys and transforms input products from suppliers to final products, which are sold to customers. This layer also services the products once they are sold to customers.

Structural patterns starter set

This definition of the three layers of the ABP is an example of a structural pattern. It can be used to design ABPs and is thus reusable. In Appendix A, we will present a starter set of structural patterns that can be reused to design the enterprise or parts of it.

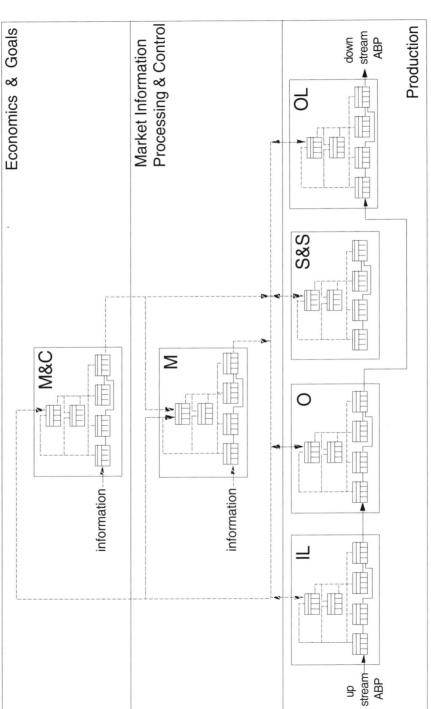

Figure 15.7 *Structural pattern: abstraction layers of the ABP.*

15.7 Conclusion

In this chapter, we discussed the structural view of the enterprise, one of the three views used for analyzing a general system, the other two being the functional view and the behavioral view. In Chapter 14, we discussed the functional view, and in Chapter 16, we will discuss the behavioral view.

The structural view of the enterprise, with both a physical aspect and a logical aspect, describes the configuration of the parts of the enterprise. The physical aspect focuses on the communications infrastructure of the enterprise consisting of information-processing networks in which information-processing nodes are connected in lattices of communications channels. Information-processing nodes are the change mechanisms of the business processes, the principal construct of the functional view of the enterprise. Thus in this chapter we saw how the functional view and the structural view are related through the information-processing node.

The logical aspect of the structural view is concerned with the configuration of ABPs and their relations. The ABP is decomposed into six subprocesses, which are themselves ABPs. The six subprocess ABPs are joined by product flows as well as control/coordination relations that make up the logical aspect of the enterprise structure. The decomposition of ABPs will eventually reach the level of process elements where the real physical transformations take place defining the lowest level of logical structure.

In this chapter, we also defined the organization as a specialized information-processing network of semi-permanent information-processing nodes put together in an authority relation. The organization has responsibility for the execution of one or more business processes. The organization executes several specialized business processes to accomplish its global functions of allocation, reporting, membership, liaison, and management.

We closed this chapter with an introduction to the structural patterns of the enterprise. We learned that a structural pattern is a broad-based, reusable pattern to organize business processes. A starter set of structural patterns is presented in Appendix A.

Chapter 16

The Behavioral View of the Enterprise

16.1 Introduction

This chapter is the culmination of part 4 of the book and describes the behavioral view of the enterprise. The behavior of any general system relates to its dynamics, or its internal change over time. The behavioral view is one of the three views in which a general system is analyzed and modeled (the other two are the functional view and the structural view). The behavioral view is formed by opening up the black box of the system and looking inside. There we will see its internal components. Some of the components may be very active and change frequently; others may lie dormant and change only occasionally, if at all. As unbiased observers, we know this because we are able to record the state of each component from one moment to the next and determine objectively whether a change has occurred or not. Thus the behavioral view describes the state of each component of a general system and the conditions that cause each of their states to change.

The structural view reveals the component objects of the enterprise. That is, the working enterprise consists of a vast collection of interacting components from the physical and logical structure, which we model as objects using the object-oriented paradigm. In Chapter 8, we introduced the two principal classes of enterprise objects: the entity class and the process class. Objects readily lend themselves to behavioral analysis using the technique of state-transition diagramming. However, we will see that state-transition diagramming is intended for the finite, low-level components of the enterprise and does not lend itself particularly well to the global, higher-level components, which we encounter in enterprise modeling.

Thus we must supplement the modeling formalism of state-transition diagramming with the more primitive approach of describing the general behavior of the enterprise using text. In this regard, we will present a generic description of the behavior of the enterprise. Our description will focus on the behavior of the objects that make up the generic enterprise. To do this, we must leave the discipline of enterprise modeling and describe the operation of the working enterprise after it has been built. To produce this description of the behavior of the operating enterprise, we ask the following question: while our work in enterprise modeling is to construct a model of our enterprise using the object-oriented paradigm, what would our enterprise look like if it where implemented using the object-oriented modeling constructs we have used in our model of it?

In answering this question, we would find that the enterprise will be implemented as a vast network of interacting objects. In this book, we call this network of objects the *global object space* (GOS). In this chapter, we will describe a generic GOS that represents the behavior of the generic enterprise if implemented as a total object-oriented environment. All the objects of the enterprise would reside in the GOS or have surrogates in it. With a fully implemented GOS, much of the operation of the enterprise would be automated (never touched by humans). Routine tasks such as routing work or monitoring equipment would be handled automatically in the GOS. People would be the integral part of the enterprise, managing it on an exception basis. We will see that the GOS incorporates many of the theoretical concepts introduced in previous chapters: the hierarchical-multilayer system, the information-processing network, the entity object, the process object—all integrated under the umbrella of the object-oriented paradigm. It is the GOS that will account for the behavior of the enterprise so its description is important to the current chapter describing the behavioral view of the enterprise.

16.2 The meaning of enterprise behavior

The behavior view of the enterprise is created by analyzing its various components. What are these components? We have seen in Chapter 15 that the components of the enterprise consist of two different types of structures. First, there is the physical structure of the enterprise consisting of its infrastructure of information-processing nodes arranged into information-processing networks. Second, there is a logical structure consisting of its configuration of business processes causing the transformations of materials, energy, or information to achieve the goals of the enterprise. These two structures, the physical and the logical, are the components that are analyzed in the behavioral view of the enterprise.

A quick review of the state-transition diagram

The state-transition diagram is the principal tool used to analyze and document the behavior of a general system. It was introduced in Chapter 2 and describes the states that a component assumes over time and the events that cause the transitions to new states. The state of a component is the values of its attributes at a point in time. Recall that an attribute is a feature assigned by us humans to describe a component unambiguously. The values of the collection of attributes of a component at a point in time is defined as its state. We can say that a component could achieve a future state only if there is a valid transition to that future state. However, even then the component might not be eligible to make the state transition. Therefore, whether or not a component will actually make a given state-transition is another aspect of behavioral modeling. Let's look at this in more detail.

First, to make a state transition, a specific event must occur, which by its nature is capable of causing the state transition. Second, before making a state transition, the necessary environment must be present in advance before the component would actually make the state transition. This environment is called the *precondition* of the state-transition as we described in Chapter 13. Both events and preconditions are defined as if the system were completely deterministic. That is, if the component is in the necessary initial state and if the preconditions are all satisfied and if the necessary trigger event occurs, then the component will progress to the new state.

So far, we have been describing the analysis of the behavior of an existing system. However, the other use of the behavioral view is in the design of a system. The state-transition diagram of each major component of a proposed system is part of the documentation that would be produced in the design of the system.

Analyzing the behavior of the enterprise

To analyze a general system completely, a state-transition diagram would be constructed for each of its components. As a practical matter, state-transition diagrams are constructed for only the most important or interesting components of the system. The procedures for constructing a state-transition diagram are as follows:

♦ Both processes and entities have state, and a state-transition diagram can be constructed for either.

- ◆ A component cannot be in two states simultaneously. To honor this, in the case of processes, the state-transition diagram must take into account the asynchronous operation of the subprocesses of the process, which have their own state.

- ◆ A component will have many states throughout its life. At any point in time, a component will be in only one of its predefined states.

- ◆ A component moves to a new state only if there is a valid state transition to that new state from its current state.

- ◆ A component moves to a new state only if the preconditions of that new state are met.

- ◆ A component moves to a new state only if the trigger event of that state transition occurs.

Entity state-transition diagramming

Entities can readily be analyzed by a state-transition diagram. For example, in Figure 16.1 we see the various states of a customer order.

In Figure 16.1, we see that a customer order starts in the "received" state. Once received it enters the "acknowledged" state, meaning the customer has been informed that the order has been received. From there it enters one of three states: "canceled," if the customer cancels the order; "back ordered," if the enterprise

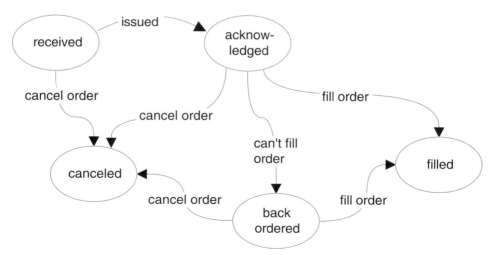

Figure 16.1 *State-transition diagram of a customer order.*

doesn't have the necessary stock to fill the order; or "filled," if it does. Once it is back-ordered, the order will progress to either the "filled" state or the "canceled" state if the customer cancels the order in the meantime.

Process state-transition diagramming

Processes can also be analyzed by a state-transition diagram. For example, in Figure 16.2 we see the various states of a generic process.

In Figure 16.2, a generic process is triggered and immediately enters the state of "starting." From there it waits for input in the "waiting" state. When it is waiting, it can go to one of three other states: "operating," when input arrives; "ending," if a shut down event is received; or "maintaining," if maintenance work on itself is needed. Notice that the process can only do one thing at a time and be in only one state at a time.

Since a process can only be in one state at a time, its subprocesses (which are asynchronous) cannot be considered part of the state of the process. This means that events must be decomposed to subevents for the subprocesses. Figure 16.3 shows the decomposition of a process event to subprocess events for the inbound logistics process (i.e., one of the subprocesses of the abstract business process).

In Figure 16.3, we see the inbound logistics ABP at the top with possible states similar to those of the generic process shown in Figure 16.2. The inbound logistics ABP has subprocesses shown at the bottom. These subprocesses represent

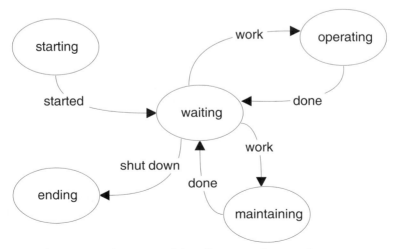

Figure 16.2 *State-transition diagram of a generic process.*

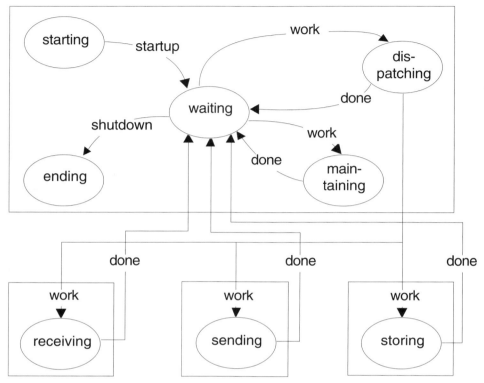

Figure 16.3 *State transition of inbound logistics process.*

the decomposition of the inbound logistics process and they must each operate asynchronously. This means that the states of the subprocesses must be independent from each other in the sense that a state transition in one subprocess is completely independent from a state transition in another subprocess. Nevertheless, the ABP process itself must be modeled by a proper state-transition diagram. We model the state of the ABP process by asserting that when the inbound logistics ABP receives work, it enters the state of "dispatching" and sends one of its four subprocesses a "work" event. When complete, the subprocess creates an event of "done." In this way, the subprocesses will have their own state-transition diagrams, which are independent of the ABP state-transition diagram except for the events of "work" and "done." Also, the ABP process maintains a summary state attribute for each of its subprocesses. For example, an active receiving subprocess is in a state of "receiving."

Conclusion

We see that the behavioral view deals with the finite structure of the enterprise and may be less applicable to the upper levels of decomposition with which we work in enterprise modeling. For this reason, we must supplement the few meaningful state-transition diagrams that we can construct with a text description of the behavior of the enterprise. Such a description will serve as a requirements description for the engineers who eventually build the enterprise. In the next section, we will offer a text description of the behavior of a fully object-oriented generic enterprise.

16.3 The global object space

The global object space (GOS) is a logical construct used to describe the fully object-oriented enterprise. The GOS would be the result of implementing the enterprise using the methodologies outlined in this book. In speculating about the GOS, we are deviating from the basic purpose of this book of describing enterprise modeling. We are going to allow ourselves a brief moment to imagine what could actually be built using the most sophisticated approach possible to round out our behavioral view. The GOS would be the result of designing then constructing an enterprise from our enterprise model. However, the various engineering projects to actually design and construct the enterprise are beyond the scope of this book. While we do not present details of the engineering disciplines, we can at least look at the concept of the GOS. This will help to clarify our efforts in enterprise modeling. It is the opinion of the authors that the GOS is the prize of object-oriented enterprise modeling.

Concept of the GOS

The GOS is a fully object-oriented enterprise. In effect, the enterprise is made of a large number of interacting software and physical objects that operate as an integrated whole, hence the use of the term *global object space*. It is implemented using distributed computer technology as well as intelligent network technology and represents the principal, dominating architectural feature of our proposed generic enterprise. We can speak of the enterprise as a very sophisticated human-machine collaboration.

Figure 16.4 is a very simplified view of the vast network of objects that would be part of the GOS of a typical enterprise. However, Figure 16.4 does show the major components of the GOS:

We will explain the operation and components of the GOS in considerable detail shortly. However, it is important to note the overall structure and components of the GOS as shown in Figure 16.4:

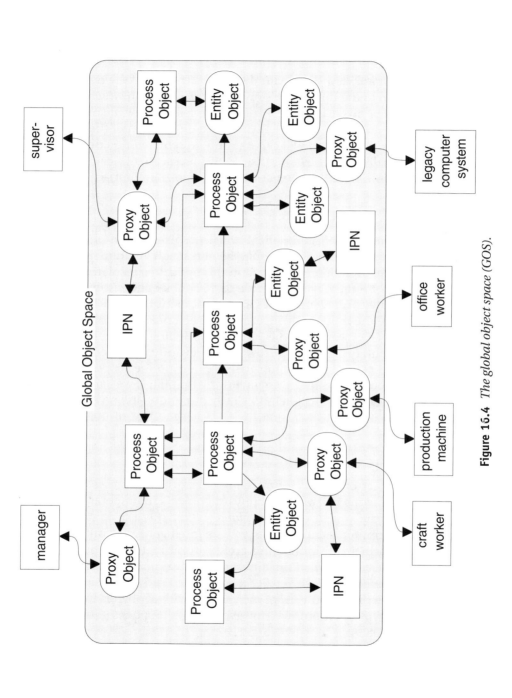

Figure 16.4 *The global object space (GOS).*

◆ **Inside vs. outside the GOS**   In the figure, we see that there are a number of objects within the boundary of the GOS as well as a number of components outside of the GOS including humans (manager, supervisor, craft worker, office worker) or various machines (production machine, legacy computer system). This distinction of being inside the GOS or outside the GOS is important and we will discuss it at length later.

◆ **Objects**   We see various objects inside the enclosure of the GOS. Three basic types of objects are shown in the figure: process objects, entity objects, and proxy objects. We will describe these in more detail later.

◆ **Communications infrastructure**   The figure shows the various components of the GOS connected by lines and arrows. The lines represent object message paths, which are transported on a communications infrastructure. The infrastructure is like an open-bus, everywhere available in the GOS. The objects communicate using a universal protocol that is honored by all of the objects in the GOS. In fact, the basic criteria for being inside vs. outside of the GOS is the capability to support this protocol. The protocol not only communicates information messages but supports management functions of the infrastructure to monitor and control it.

◆ **Process objects**   The figure shows various process objects representing the activity of the enterprise. The process objects are connected by command/ control hierarchies as well as dependency flows.

◆ **Entity objects**   The entity objects in the figure are connected to various process objects as well as to each other. Entity objects represent the "things" of the enterprise.

◆ **Proxy objects**   Proxy objects are surrogates for external objects outside of the GOS. An external object is outside of the GOS because it cannot meet the standards of the GOS such as the ability to support the messaging protocol.

◆ **Information processing nodes (IPNs)**   In Figure 16.4, IPNs are the machine information-processing nodes (e.g., computers) that are capable of meeting the standards of the GOS. We will discuss them in greater detail shortly.

◆ **People (manager, supervisor, craft worker, office worker)**   In this book, we have continually stated that people are an example of information-processing nodes. However, for purposes of modeling the GOS, we regard people as outside of the GOS. People are one of the external objects not in the GOS but represented by proxy objects in the GOS.

◆ **Legacy computer systems, production machines**   Figure 16.4 shows various other components outside of the GOS, including legacy computer systems and miscellaneous production machines. They are external to the GOS because they cannot meet its standards and thus are represented by proxy objects.

Software objects vs. real world objects

Most of the objects of the enterprise will live inside the GOS. An object is inside the GOS because it is capable of meeting the standards of the GOS, especially the communications protocol. That is, an object inside the GOS is capable of being sent object messages as well as GOS management messages and in turn sending object messages or responding to the GOS management messages. The objects in the GOS include not only the software objects but the machine information processing nodes (i.e., production machines, computers, information machines) capable of supporting the communications protocol of the object space. Some machines will have to be outside of the GOS because they can't do this (i.e., they will be represented by proxy objects). Notice that we do not consider humans as being within the boundary of the GOS. Rather, humans are represented by proxy objects. The reason is that humans are the most expensive resource and one of the points of the GOS is to automate their duties as much as possible. Thus, a person who is the change mechanism of a process element will be represented to the corresponding process object as a proxy object. Later in this chapter we will define a subclass of the process object called the personal assistant object, which is specialized to serve as a human surrogate.

Let's briefly describe the two types of objects in the GOS: software objects and physical objects:

◆ **Software objects**   The software objects exist as constructs of object-oriented computer technology. Their object services are implemented by computer programming and their state is represented by computer data. Software objects are created and maintained within a distributed computer environment. The software objects will be physically distributed across the various processors of the distributed computer network. Where a software object actually resides will be largely a systems management decision. Software objects are instantiated from the various object classes in the object-oriented class library of the software development environment. Software objects include the various process objects, entity objects, and proxy objects shown in Figure 16.4.

◆ **Physical objects**   Physical objects will be the machine information-processing nodes labeled IPN in Figure 16.4. Recall that at the lowest level of decomposition, an information processing node has a physical symbol system. A physical symbol system is a general system whose state is implemented as physical information symbols. The information processing node is capable of sending and receiving physical symbol sequences (e.g., to other software and physical objects in the GOS) using the physical channels of the information processing network. We recognize these physical symbol sequences as messages. Once a message is received, the information processing node changes its state, using the message as a signal to invoke the internal processing of its physical symbol system. A side effect is that the state of the information processing node may be changed.

Notice that there is a big difference between the computers that provide residency for software objects and the information-processing nodes discussed here. While we have pointed out many times that the computer is an information-processing node, in the case of software objects, the resident computer is transparent to the definition of a software object.

16.4 Characteristics of the GOS

The global object space will be implemented by the various software and physical objects summarized earlier. The meaning of *object orientation* as we learned in Chapter 5 is that each object keeps track of its own state instead of having a master system function keeping track of the global system state. An important aspect of the GOS is that no object in the GOS has total information. In the vast scale contemplated, it would be impossible to have a central database of information. Rather, the global object space will operate as a society of objects. If an object wants to find out something, it will have to send messages to other objects. This section discusses the characteristics of the GOS.

Hierarchical-multilayered organization
The global object space will have a hierarchical-multilayered organization. The layers of the global object space will use the various structural patterns described in Appendix A. This shouldn't be surprising since the structural patterns presented in Appendix A are intended for the design of the enterprise and the GOS is its most dominant feature and thus would be subject to the structural patterns.

The GOS will contain process objects that implement the business processes of the enterprise, so the most conspicuous hierarchical layering of the GOS will be the process objects. As we've seen in earlier chapters, process objects are formed into hierarchies in which "boss" processes command lower-level objects and get feedback on their status. The process objects will operate automatically, exchanging messages with each other as they do their work. Occasionally, they will need input or decisions from outside of the global object space, especially from their human overseers. Then the corresponding proxy object will be used to communicate with the external object. We will discuss this in much greater detail later.

GOS dynamics

To send a message to another object, an object needs to know only the identity of the other object. It is not necessary to know where the target object is physically as the infrastructure of the GOS will know how to get the message to the target object. While any object in the global object space can, in principal, communicate with any other object, only a few communications patterns will actually be used. The principal pattern of communication will be in behalf of the control/coordination hierarchy of the process objects. Sally Shlaer and Stephen Mellor describe the communications patterns of an object space such as the GOS (Shlaer and Mellor, 1992). Shlaer and Mellor propose that an object space is arranged into echelons from the most intelligent objects in the top echelons to the least intelligent objects in the bottom echelons. The objects in the top echelons have qualities of knowledge, context, and purpose. By contrast, the objects in the lower echelons have an obedient character, compatible with their limited awareness of the environment as a whole. The top-echelon objects delegate work to the less intelligent lower-echelon objects and coordinate their life cycles as the work is carried out.

Shlaer and Mellor describe the patterns of communications as top-driven or bottom-driven (Shlaer and Mellor, 1992). In the top-driven case, an event is received by a top-echelon object of the global object space from the external world, such as a human operator. The top-echelon object has sufficient knowledge and context to direct the actions of lower-echelon objects to respond to the event. For example, a top-echelon object may be a process object that delegates work downwards by means of internal object messages to lower-echelon process objects.

In the case of bottom-driven communications, a lower-echelon object in the global object space is the target of the event. The lower-echelon object is typically a proxy object representing an external object outside of the GOS. These events directed at lower-echelon objects will be unsolicited, such as an alert from a production machine needing to communicate a significant change in its state. The lower-echelon object does not have the necessary knowledge or context to respond so it sends internal messages to higher-echelon objects. Eventually, an object with sufficient global knowledge and context is reached where a global-level response to the event may be formulated. The top-echelon object then delegates the response back downward to lower-echelon objects.

Heterarchical organization of the GOS

The patterns of messages presented in the previous subsection describe a hierarchical relationship in which the objects are related by control/coordination. However, this is not the only major way objects will know and communicate with each other in the GOS. The objects of the GOS will also have an aspect of autonomy. While there will be hierarchies of objects in the GOS, the GOS is not completely a hierarchy. Rather, it consists of some hierarchical objects as well as loosely coupled, autonomous objects. In this regard, we will use the ideas of D. Veeramani, B. Bhargava, and M. Barash in their work (Veeramani, et al., 1993). Their ideas are embodied in what they term the heterarchical organization. According to them, the heterarchical-controlled system consists of autonomous objects that use a distributed control approach rather than the centralized control approach of the hierarchical system. The heterogeneous agents achieve distributed control by exchanging information and negotiating with each other. Veeramani et al. give an example of a manufacturing enterprise in which "distributed control is achieved through an auction-based scheme in which machines place bids on work pieces awaiting processing, and negotiate with system entities to obtain cutting tools and transport vehicles" (Veeramani, et al., 1993).

Figures 16.5 compares the hierarchical and the heterarchical forms of organization. In Figure 16.5 we see several very important distinctions between the hierarchical and heterarchical form of organization:

- Control in a hierarchy is top-down. A component cannot act without proper authorization. The heterarchical approach is more robust from failures in the system than the hierarchical control paradigm.

- The heterarchical control approach requires a high level of intelligence among system entities to permit autonomous decision making.

Feature	Hierarchy	Heterarchy
control	centralized	decentralized
work allocation	command/control	auction-based
control	supervisory	autonomy
structure	pyramidal, rigid	flat, flexible
information	global (at highest level)	local (no global info)

Figure 16.5 *Hierarchical vs. heterarchical (Veeramani et al., 1993).*

♦ In a heterarchy, the allocation and scheduling of work will be opportunistic and will use a bidding procedure involving work pieces, machines, etc.

♦ The components of a heterarchy must possess abilities for information broadcasting/receiving and autonomous decision making. These abilities are fundamental for operation in a distributed-control environment because there is no object that has knowledge of the state of the entire system. The heterarchical control approach requires a much more extensive communications network.

♦ In a heterarchy there is no global information nor are there information hierarchies. Thus the heterarchy is more accommodating to system reconfiguration.

Applications in the GOS

Is there a concept of the application in the GOS? We can say yes, that an application would be represented by an application object. What, then, is the relationship between a process object and an application object? A process object is the embodiment of the dynamics of the enterprise to pursue its goals. On the other hand, an application object is a window onto the lattice of objects which make up the GOS. An application could be thought of as the window on a glass bottom boat in which a tourist on the boat could peer down to the sea life below the surface. In our case, the application provides the window in which an observer can peer down to the complex world of the objects residing below the surface of the GOS.

Besides being a window, applications are editing tools that change, create, or destroy the objects of the GOS. As an editing tool, an application is used to disturb the natural state of the objects in the GOS by either changing their attributes or changing their structural relations. Application objects are the least valuable of the objects within the GOS. They are quickly constructed, often for special purposes. Since their basic purpose is to alter the normal automatic behavior of the GOS, they are often constructed to provide such temporary processing for new products or special projects of the enterprise.

16.5 Proxy objects

As mentioned several times earlier, a major part of the GOS is its proxy objects. Proxy objects are software objects that represent objects outside of the GOS. For example, an external object may be outside the GOS because of nonconformity with the communications and processing standards and protocols of the GOS. The external object is nevertheless an integral part of the enterprise considered as an

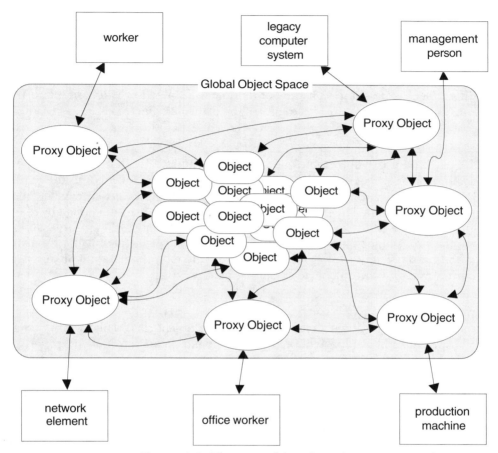

Figure 16.6 *The proxy objects in action.*

integrated system. The proxy object stands in for the external object as if the external object were part of the GOS. Figure 16.4 shows several external objects represented by proxy object including production machines, people, legacy systems, or data stores.

Figure 16.6 shows the proxy objects of the GOS in action. Notice that a proxy object can be thought of as residing near the border of the GOS, in close proximity to its external object. The mass of objects in the center represents the various internal objects (i.e., process, entity, physical objects, or other proxy objects) of the GOS. They communicate with the external object by communicating with the corresponding proxy object.

Accessing a proxy object

The proxy object is accessible using the standard message-passing facility of the GOS. The other objects of the GOS regard the proxy object as actually representing the external object. Whenever an object of the GOS sends a message to the external object, it does so by sending the message to the corresponding proxy object. The sending object is unaware that the actual object in question is external and that the message is being sent to a surrogate of the external object.

Accessing the external object

For its part, the proxy object knows how to communicate with its external object. For example, the proxy object knows how to drive the low-level communications protocols, which are usually required to access the remote external object such as a production machine. The proxy object will represent the external object by maintaining a shadow state corresponding to the external object. When a message is sent to the proxy object, it will respond on behalf of the external object, mimicking its operation. This may require that it communicate with the external object using the communications protocols to update its shadow state.

Wrapper objects

A subclass of the proxy object class is the wrapper object class. The wrapper object class is specialized to the task of being the surrogate to an external computer system. A wrapper object is a way of hiding complexity, in our case external computer systems, which are by definition not object-oriented. In particular, the legacy system wrapper object can be used to represent a legacy system to the other objects of the GOS. The wrapper object abstracts the traditional, transaction-based computer application and represents it to the objects in the GOS as a set of object services. The wrapper object can also be used to represent specialized, nontraditional computer systems such as telecommunications network elements. The wrapper object is an ideal conversion mechanism that gradually incorporates external systems into the GOS. Figure 16.7 shows the generic wrapper object in action:

In Figure 16.7, an external system is incorporated into the GOS using a wrapper object. The wrapper object provides the services of the external object to the other objects in the GOS. These services are defined in terms of the needs of the objects in the GOS and indirectly reflect the specific functionality of the underlying external system. The wrapper object in turn communicates with the underlying external system using the physical communications network of the external system. The sophistication of this communication can be as simple as terminal (keyboard) input coupled with screen output delivered to the wrapper object from the communications substrate. The communications could be as sophisticated as a peer-to-peer relation in which the wrapper object and the target legacy system exchange messages using a defined protocol.

Ivar Jacobson has pointed out that his use-case technique defined in Chapter 14 can be used to realign legacy system functionality (Jacobson, 1994). The analysis of the legacy systems would include building of a complete use-case model representing the requirements of the enterprise stated in today's terms. These requirements will be more or less provided by the legacy systems. That is, there probably won't be a one-to-one correspondence between today's requirements and the functionality of the legacy system. In this case, the modern requirements of the enterprise can be satisfied by using wrapper objects to implement today's use cases.

Personal assistants

Another subclass of the proxy object class is the personal assistant object class. The personal assistant allows humans to be completely integrated into the GOS, for example to serve as change mechanisms of process objects. The personal assistant object class specializes the proxy object as the surrogate of a person. Many of the ideas of personal assistants presented below have been adopted from the work of Jeff Pan and Jay Tenenbaum (Pan and Tenenbaum, 1991).

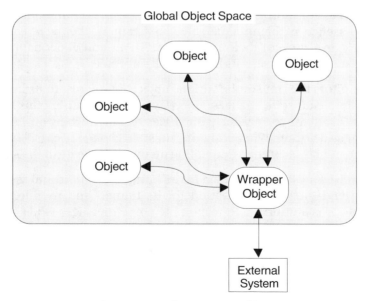

Figure 16.7 *The wrapper object.*

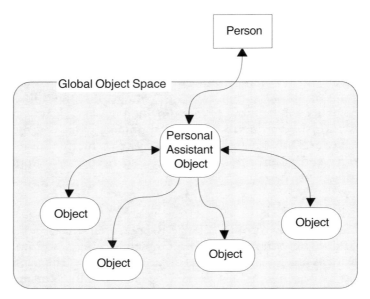

Figure 16.8 *The personal assistant object.*

In Figure 16.8, a person is incorporated into the GOS with a personal assistant object. The essence of being a personal assistant is "being *alive*—responding *autonomously* and *proactively* to perceptions" (Pan and Tenenbaum, 1991). The personal assistant object keeps its human well informed:

- ◆ It monitors the state of the various objects of interest to its human looking for significant state changes. One way of accomplishing this is for the personal assistant to register with target objects to be notified when state changes do occur. When a significant state change occurs it either handles it or contacts its human depending on the complexity of the situation.

- ◆ It receives messages intended for its human. The personal assistant is programmed to filter information for its human and monitor for unusual events. It is authorized to respond to some messages while others it must contact its human.

- ◆ Personal assistants always know whom to tell about significant events or state changes. They can escalate problems to their human if necessary or to other objects in the GOS. They typically contact their human using various communication techniques such as desktop applications, E-mail, beeper, fax, telephone, etc.

All interaction from the human to the GOS is through the personal assistant. Thus the automatic mode of response of the personal assistant is preempted when its human decides to take over.

The personal assistant maintains the following state information:

- ◆ Where its human is

- ◆ How its human can be reached.

- ◆ A list of its capabilities

- ◆ A list of tasks that it is qualified to perform

- ◆ A list of its responsibilities (a list of tasks currently assigned)

- ◆ Activity definition (e.g., scripts) for tasks

16.6 Converging standards—making the GOS possible

The lack of standards could be the single most significant roadblock to adapting a major technology undertaking like the GOS. No enterprise will ever attempt a GOS implementation without the certainty of a common industry approach to the underlying technologies. The classic problem of portability of development investment is at the heart of the issue. Can the investment in a sophisticated solution using today's technology be leveraged into tomorrow's technology? Also of concern to technology strategists is that most hybrid object technology products are from small companies that may not be around in a couple of years.

There are major efforts underway to develop standards that will make the GOS possible. These standards actually represent the convergence of three different technology families: distributed computing, network management, and object-orientation. Figure 16.9 depicts the major technology standards that are rapidly converging. These converging technologies and standards will make possible the GOS as an implementation architecture of the enterprise. The converging standards are discussed in the following sections.

ISO—open distributed processing

The hardware technology substrate of the GOS will be an open-distributed computer system. Open Distributed Processing (ODP) is an international standard for distributed systems sponsored by ISO (International Standards Organization). ODP defines the standards to which a distributed system must conform from an application perspective (i.e., ODP does not focus on the communication architec-

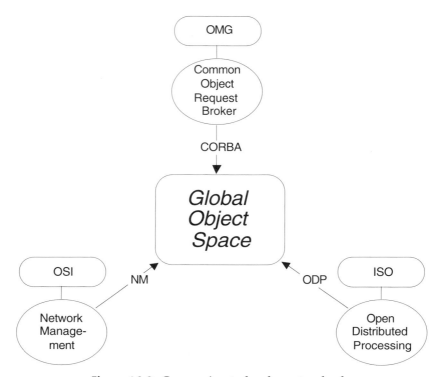

Figure 16.9 *Converging technology standards.*

ture). The ODP is a complete standard that controls the distributed technology substrate from several viewpoints:

- ◆ **Enterprise viewpoint** ODP begins by considering business requirements and describes applications from the standpoint of value delivered to the enterprise.

- ◆ **Information viewpoint** ODP provides a high-level viewpoint of the information model, which is expressed in object-oriented concepts.

- ◆ **Computation viewpoint** ODP describes the computations of the system in terms of software components, their interfaces, and the messages they exchange.

- ◆ **Engineering viewpoint** ODP describes the physical substrate of the distributed system including its configuration, location of components, and performance.

- **Technology viewpoint** ODP provides a view of the actual hardware and software of the distributed system.

At any given point in time, the GOS will have different types of equipment supplied by multiple vendors, which have varying degrees of communication and information processing capabilities. Having an international standard controlling open-distributed processing is mandatory before an enterprise will ever make a commitment to the GOS concept. In this way, a standardized technology substrate will be available in which new equipment can be plugged in to the GOS.

OSI—network management

Telecommunications network management has already implemented many of the features of the GOS as well as providing an example of how a complex standard can be realized internationally. The purpose of network management is to control and administer a telecommunications network. This includes monitoring the operation of the network (performance, faults) and reacting to various conditions (reconfiguration, diagnostics). Also, security management and accounting are important functions of network management. Physically, a network management system is a distributed-computer application that uses the telecommunications network to do its work. There are two major network management standards: OSI (Open Systems Interconnection) CMIP and Internet SNMP. OSI is a much larger and more comprehensive international standard and will be used in this book as a building block for the GOS, although we do acknowledge and admire the pragmatic approach of the SNMP. Network management includes:

- **The physical network** The telecommunications network consists of four types of hardware: terminals, transmission devices, communication links, and processors. These can be abstracted as nodes and links. The links (e.g., telephone lines) have varying transmission capabilities and the nodes (e.g. switches, cross connects, network elements) have varying information processing capabilities (send, receive, process, store). The modern network is completely heterogeneous in which the physical devices are from different vendors and different technology generations. The integral components of the network hardware are off-the-shelf computer processors and components, which are provided by various computer technology vendors on an OEM (other equipment manufactured) basis. The modern physical network is in reality a distributed-computing system. It has the necessary standards to allow the plugging-in of new or different hardware components anywhere anytime.

◆ **Network management protocol** The network management system uses a special network management protocol to perform its functions. That is, it sends and receives network management messages using a formal language. The various components of the network (i.e., the nodes) are programmed to understand this formal language and respond as appropriate to network management protocol messages. This means that all of the nodes of the network must support a common standard. There are two major network management protocols representing the two major standards: SNMP (Simple Network Management Protocol sponsored by the Internet) and CMIP (Common Management Information Protocol sponsored by OSI). Thus network vendors support one or both of these protocol standards in their products.

◆ **Network management database** Network management is able to perform its sophisticated functions because it contains detailed information about the network. The information is distributed and physically stored throughout the network using standardized formats and semantics. A major component of the information is the representation of a managed object, which is anything in the network that needs to be managed. Managed objects are represented using object-oriented concepts. A managed object includes information on the kinds of operations it can perform, the kinds of information it can send or receive, and its place in the network configuration.

Network management has solved many of the problems that our proposed global object space would also have to solve, including:

◆ **Heterogeneous domain** A network management application successfully operates in a completely heterogeneous domain consisting of multiple vendors, multiple technologies, and multiple generations of technology.

◆ **Standards** Network management is controlled by international standards bodies.

◆ **Object-orientation** Network management is evolving an object-oriented definition of the network.

The GOS will require management similar to network management. The management of the GOS will be required to not only control and administer the physical substrate but also its logical structure. The concepts of OSI network management can be used as a starting point for designing the GOS management.

OMG—common object request broker (CORBA)

Any global object space for even a small enterprise will be a large and complex object-oriented system. It cannot be done without multiple object vendors representing multiple disciplines and expertises. This points out the need for object-oriented industry standards to be in place before an enterprise could prudently embark on the road to the GOS. The need for standards to govern such huge object-oriented systems is recognized in the technology industry and has resulted in the formation of the Object Management Group (OMG). The OMG is an international trade association incorporated as nonprofit in the United States. The OMG receives funding on a yearly dues basis from its diverse membership of over 500 (as of 1995) information systems corporations (OMG, 1990).

The current work of the OMG standardization process is the Object Management Architecture (OMA). The OMA defines the mechanism that allows client objects to issue requests to conforming server objects to receive responses. In addition, the OMA identifies operations that all conforming objects must support and optional facilities (common classes) that are useful to a wide range of applications. The four major parts of the OMA are:

- ◆ **Common object request broker architecture** The Common Object Request Broker Architecture (CORBA) provides a standardized mechanism called an object request broker (ORB). An ORB conforming to CORBA allows conforming objects to make and receive requests and responses transparently. In so doing, the ORB provides interoperability between applications on different machines in heterogeneous distributed environments and seamlessly interconnects multiple object systems (OMG, 1990), (OMG, 1991).

- ◆ **Object services** The Object Services component standardizes the lifecycle management of objects. Services are provided to create objects, to control access to objects, to keep track of relocated objects and to control the relationships between objects (class management) (OMG, 1990).

- ◆ **Common facilities** The Common Facilities component includes facilities that are useful in many applications domains and which are made available through OMA-compliant object interfaces. For developers, Common Facilities reduces the effort needed to build OMA-compliant applications. A service can be classified as a Common Facility when it communicates using the ORB and has an OMA-compliant object interface (OMG, 1990).

- ◆ **Applications objects** The Applications Objects part of the architecture represents those application objects performing specific tasks for users. An application is typically built from a large number of basic object classes, partly specific for the application, partly from the set of common facilities (OMG, 1990).

The Object Management Architecture (OMA) is the emerging standard for distributed-object management systems such as the GOS. New systems development efforts that propose the use of object-oriented technology such as the GOS proposed here will now have the advantage of this standard. In the future, large, complex systems can be built from object components, both purchased in the industry and developed in-house. The glue that will hold these diverse components together is the OMA standard.

16.7 Conclusion

In this chapter, we discussed the behavioral view of the enterprise, which like any general system, is a detailed, microscopic look at how each of its components acts over time. The behavioral view of an existing general system is formed by opening up its black box and looking inside at its various components as the system operates. Since we are mere observers looking inside the black box of a system, we use tools that allow us to record and analyze the life cycle of each of the individual components of the system. In particular, we use tools that allow us to describe the changes of a given component over time. Our foremost tool to describe the behavior of a general system is the state-transition diagram.

Since enterprise modeling focuses on the macroscopic rather than microscopic aspects, state-transition modeling is not appropriate for expressing the behavior of the enterprise. Therefore, we rely on text descriptions of the enterprise's behavior. We describe in general terms how the enterprise will behave once implemented. Our description of enterprise behavior regards the enterprise as being implemented using the object-oriented paradigm. In this chapter, we introduced a new term, the global object space (GOS) to describe the object-oriented implementation of the enterprise.

The GOS is made up of vast numbers of business objects that interact by sending each other messages. Objects that are internal to the GOS include process objects, entity objects and proxy objects. Proxy objects are the internal representation of external objects that cannot meet the standards of the GOS. The GOS has the necessary communications infrastructure to support the communications of its objects.

The GOS is a hierarchical-multilayered structure in which the objects have autonomy. No single object is aware of the global state of the GOS—there is no centralized database approach. We concluded that the GOS must exhibit properties of a heterarchical organization of autonomous agents that negotiate and barter with each other to accomplish the goals of the enterprise.

The GOS represents a very promising but massive commitment to leading-edge technology. No enterprise will undertake a GOS implementation without the certainty of industry standards. Three industry standards are important to the GOS concept: First, the ISO standard of Open Distributed Processing (ODP) defines the standards of the technology substrate of distributed computer systems which will be required to implement the GOS; second, the OSI standard of network management provides an architecture for the administration and management functions which the GOS will require; and third, the OMG standard of the Common Object Request Broker (CORBA) defines the standards of object-oriented technology required by the GOS. Thus, we can be optimistic that the necessary industry standards are being developed and adapted.

Part 5

future
strategy
business
planning®
Methodology

Introduction to Part 5

THIS SECTION PRESENTS THE OBJECT–ORIENTED enterprise modeling methodology developed by the authors which is called Future Strategy Business Planning® (fsbp®). We present the methodology in two ways.

The first, presented in Chapter 17, is an overview of the entire methodology. This chapter describes each of the seven stages of the approach. It demonstrates the relationships between each stage and the background theory supporting that stage. This chapter also illustrates the flow and dependencies that exist among-tages of the method. Chapter 17 is intended to provide an understanding of the overall structure, value, and logic of the object-oriented enterprise modeling methodology.

The methodology is presented stage by stage in Chapters 18–25 with sufficient detail to provide guidance for the actual conduct and implementation of the method within the context of a real business opportunity. Chapters 18–25 provide specific output requirements, process and method activities that will facilitate creating those outputs, and some illustrative examples. These chapters are focused on the actual implementation or operation of the object-oriented enterprise modeling methodology.

Chapter 17

An Object-Oriented Enterprise Modeling Methodology

17.1 Introduction

The object-oriented enterprise modeling methodology that the authors call *future strategy business planning* (fsbp®) was developed with a holistic approach to the fundamentals of competitive business. Borrowing from, integrating, and synergizing the theories and work of others, we have created and applied an extremely powerful business planning process. The process extends from the most strategic and conceptual—competitive industry and market analysis—to the most discrete levels of business operations—process use cases.

While addressing this broad scope of planning, we realized the need to retain and reflect higher-level drivers and strategies for later application to the increasingly discrete and tactical planning levels. Again, overlapping but previously unrelated theory and methodology provided the answer. The solution is a model that allows abstraction of any aspect of the business environment as a whole, in parts, and at its most basic elements. These basic elements include the functional and structural aspects of business that are considered traditionally, but they also encompass the motivating values of the enterprise environment. By abstracting an enterprise process and classifying its elements uniformly, we can identify the values that govern the process as well as structure and interrelate its use with other processes. These descriptions of abstracted processes provide quantitative continuity across the spectrum of the methodology.

The result is the object-oriented enterprise model. This artifact is an object-based description and picture of the functions, processes, uses, structure, and values. The relationships among the elements in the picture can always be viewed from every one of these perspectives.

Future strategy business planning (fsbp®) goes through seven stages in addressing enterprise-wide process design and enterprise reinvention that will result in the enterprise model. The product of each stage is a book providing the comprehensive details regarding source information, the assessment processes used, the resulting strategies, a desired design model, and an approach for actualizing the desired model.

Figure 17.1 illustrates the applicability of the seven process stages toward three echelons of process reengineering. The more darkly shaded area represents gen-

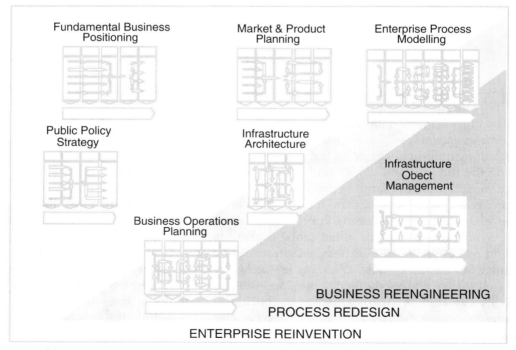

Figure 17.1 *The methodology scope versus scope of enterprise reengineering.*

eral business reengineering (the first echelon), the lighter-shaded area (the second echelon, it encompasses the first echelon as well) reflects the domain of process redesign, and all aspects of the business environment are included in business reinvention (the third echelon).

Figure 17.2 illustrates the content of these products. Meeting these deliverable requirements provides structure and discipline to the process. The total product represented by these books is much more than an operating and implementation plan for the business. It is a repository of the insight behind the enterprise. As such, these books become effective tools for communicating the vision, strategies, and values of the enterprise and are arguably the most effective tools in overcoming cultural intransigence within the enterprise's organization.

17.2 Process map

Figure 17.3 is a process map of the seven stages of the methodology. Each stage is given its own number for identification purposes (e.g., public policy strategy is assigned stage 3). We will summarize each stage here and define them in more detail in the remaining sections of this document:

- ◆ The business definition (stage 1) defines the business—its scope, its business position, its key policies, and its implementation strategy.

- ◆ The market and product plan (stage 2) defines the market, the product set, and the sales plan.

- ◆ The public policy strategy (stage 3) defines the position and image that the enterprise presents on public issues (national, regulatory, industry, market).

- ◆ The enterprise model (stage 4) defines the functions and business process (current and future) of the enterprise and their relationships.

- ◆ The business operations plan (stage 5) defines the functional and organizational structure, the business resource, the business systems (management, people, methods, tools), and transition and growth plans.

- ◆ The infrastructure architecture (stage 6) defines the logical view of the distributed enterprise as well as the physical view of the distributed enterprise.

- ◆ The infrastructure objects (stage 7) defines the architecture of the global object space, summarizes the contents of the object class library, and summarizes the entity objects and their relations.

The Enterprise Modeling Process

Book I	Business Definition	Research & Analysis Matrices Competitive Imperatives & Strategic Mandates Competitive Strategy Definition Operating Strategies & Definitions
Book II	Market & Product Plan	Market Analysis Positioning Analysis Market Objectives Market & Product Strategy
Book III	Public Policy Strategy	Strategic Policy Issues Policy Positioning Strategies Statements of Key Policy Tactical Approaches to Policy
Book IV	Enterprise Model	Analysis & Structure of Enterprise Functions Business Process Definitions Business Process Flow Models

Book V	Business Operations Plan	Start-Up Plan & On-Going Plan
		    Organizational Structure
		    Resources and prioritization
		    Business Systems Definition
		    Transition or Growth Tactical Plans

Book VI	Technology Infrastructure Architecture	Common Technology Architecture Logical Structure & Framework Physical Technology Architecture
Book VII	Infrastructure Objects	Infrastructure Object Logical Summary Overview of Object Relationships High Level Enterprise Object Definition
Back Matter	Appendices Research	Planning Theory & Methodology Summaries Glossary Bibliography

Figure 17.2 *Future strategy business planning document suite.*

Having presented the methodology in these hierarchical steps, we must say that it is not intended to be a step-wise process. Instead, the approach is iterative, particularly as the effort progresses from the highly strategic to the tactical implementations. The most significant factor to keep in mind is the sequence and interdependence of the information that is gathered, assessed, and generated.

♦ An enterprise must first have a strategic foundation as a basis for its being, a vision of itself.

♦ Given that vision, advantageous and efficient product/service solutions must be identified.

♦ Given those product/service plans, competitive approaches to the process of their creation and delivery must be identified.

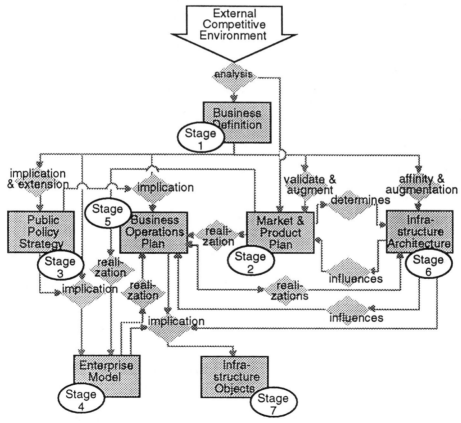

Figure 17.3 *Overview of the methodology.*

◆ Knowing the products and how they will be produced, it is only now time to create the most efficient approach to the management of the business processes—how you will organize. It is also time to consider the infrastructure necessary to support the enterprise's customers and its business processes; the technology architecture goes here.

Throughout all of this, it is vital to accumulate, track, and have accessible all information regarding the enterprise: from its vision, to its market and customers, to the physical equipment that it uses to make it all happen.

Many tools are available to support these individual activities. Our approach doesn't replace or compete with any of them. Rather, it is a methodology for structuring and interrelating the use of such tools so that they leverage appropriate information regarding the value systems within which the enterprise must function. Our approach encourages clear and compelling leadership and communication within an enterprise. It does not, in itself, create such things as positioning strategy, market strategy, or class libraries.

17.3 Business definition (Stage 1)

The components of the business definition are as follows:

◆ Clearly defines the business's

- Scope

- Position

- Key policies

◆ Explains the rationale for the recommended core business

◆ Points out the implications of not adhering to the proposed business definition

◆ Clearly identifies transition and implementation strategies for achieving the defined enterprise

◆ Clearly identifies transition and implementation strategies for achieving the defined enterprise

The methodology begins with the business definition, which is the basis for all other phases of enterprise modeling. The purpose of the business definition is to clearly define the recommended business, including its scope, business positions, and key policies. The business definition also explains the rationale for the recommended core business and points out the business implications of not adhering to the proposed business definition. The business definition is delivered in the form of a comprehensive document. The content and the development process associated with the business definition phase are graphically represented in Figure 17.4.

Creating the business definition document begins with in-depth research and analysis of the target industry. The research and analysis focuses on five areas: industry analysis, competitor analysis, market analysis, technology analysis, and legal, regulatory, and policy analysis. This phase generally uses secondary research to develop a fundamental understanding of these areas. Within each research area, information is evaluated and correlated into categories based on proven criteria.

This data is then loaded into matrices (as in the example of Figure 17.5), which provides a graphic view of the subject area. The existence of competitive business

future strategy business plan ®
Stage I — "Business Definition"
Development Process

Research & Analysis	Strategic Opportunities & Threats	Things that Matter	Fundamental Strategy	Enterprise Definitions
Industry	Imperatives			Target Market
Competitors	Imperatives			Operating Structure
Market	Imperatives	Strategic Mandates	Develop Fundamental Strategy	Infrstructure Architecture
Technology	Imperatives			
Legal, Regulatory, & Policy	Imperatives			Industry Position
Research, Analyses, & Matrices	Strategic Imperative Development	Mandate Synthesis	Competitive Strategy	Operating Strategies Defined

fsbp
Book I

The Business Definition

Figure 17.4 *Business definition content and development process.*

Information Content of Large Industry Markets

Industry / Information Content	Manufacturing	Utilities	Information Provider	Communications Provider	Natural Resources	Education	Government	Transportation & Travel	Health Services	Management Services	Sales & Distribution	Entertainment Programming	Distribution	Finance	Consumer Services	Agri-Business	
Procurement																	36
Process																	42
Distribution																	31
Size in $$																	32
# of Players																	19
	10	10	10	10	10	12	11	10	12	7	11	10	7	13	8	10	

1	Low Information Content	2	Moderate Information Content	3	High Information Content

Figure 17.5 *Sample matrix from the business definition.*

imperatives within each subject domain are then diagnosed. These strategic imperatives represent a broad agenda for achieving successful entry and/or long-term viability in the market (a typical business definition will have 30 or 40 imperatives). As described in Chapter 12, these imperatives simply reflect the things that are fundamental to competitive success that any business must be able to deal with to succeed within the industry. The things that matter include both positive opportunities to pursue as well as pitfalls to be avoided.

Next, the strategic imperatives are synthesized into a small set of strategic mandates. The 30 or 40 strategic imperatives typically overlap and synergize with one another. Sometimes these synergies will be positive and sometimes they will be negative. The interrelationships are established and assessed and then distilled down to the essence of what is necessary for success in the industry that of the strategic mandates. A typical industry will have 6 to 10 strategic mandates, which are the critically important issues to the business. As Chapter 12 indicates, they are used throughout the methodology and ultimately in daily management. These mandates are the motivating logic and values behind every business decision of the enterprise.

Once the strategic imperatives and mandates are defined, the methodology develops a fundamental business strategy for the enterprise. This strategy defines the fundamentals of the business: the target industry and the business' desired strategic position within it, the target market and how to approach it both from the perspective of the customers' needs and values as well as competitor position, the general product strategy, and the generic operating strategy. In particular, the fundamental strategy identifies exactly how the business will satisfy the strategic mandates defined previously.

The process of establishing the enterprise's fundamental strategies begins with a fairly traditional strengths, weaknesses, opportunity, and threat (SWOT) analysis. This requires filling in some additional information regarding the competitive environment in which the customer wishes to participate. Specifically, additional data is required regarding the resources and capabilities of the business enterprise. This is the same type of data and assessment as was used in the competitor analysis. Strengths and weaknesses of all players are then mapped against the opportunities and threats that define the competitive environment. Various alternative strategies are then established and evaluated for effectiveness against the strategic mandates, again using the matrix process.

The business definition next defines the enterprise's operating structure. This definition is a blueprint for establishing the operation of an enterprise value-adding system that will accommodate the other fundamental strategies. This structural operating approach is also used to derive the enterprise model that will be produced in the enterprise model stage (stage 4) of the methodology. The enterprise definition interrelates competitive strategies in four areas: industry position, the target market, operating structure, and infrastructure architecture.

The business definition ends with a strategy for deployment or transition into the desired business position and state. This is the framework that provides a sequence and priority for activities needed to implement the defined enterprise efficiently.

17.4 Market and product planning (Stage 2)

The components of market and product planning are as follows:

- ◆ Identifies the market that offers the most opportunity

- ◆ Identifies the set of generic products

The market and product planning stage produces a comprehensive document that represents the results of a market study conducted by the enterprise engineering team. The objectives of this phase are three-fold:

- Identify the market that offers the most opportunity for the enterprise according to its selected fundamental strategies and the strategic mandates.

- Develop the set of generic products the enterprise should provide to that market in terms of customer value, cost constraints, price structure, quality, etc.

- Establish how to take these products to market.

The considerable knowledge gained in completing the business definition is used as a jumping off point to focus on these marketing specifics. The content and the development process associated with the marketing and product plan stage are shown in Figure 17.6.

The market and product plan starts with in-depth research and analysis of the target market environment and focuses on collecting information in five areas:

- Industry analysis

- Competitor analysis

- Market analysis

- Technology analysis

- Legal, regulatory and policy analysis

The purpose of this work is to synthesize and understand the target market environment. Subtleties such as the following are identified during this effort:

- Customer segmentation

- Current products and potential substitute products

- Current competitive participation and potential new competition

- Economic dynamics specific to the market

- Buying behavior of the target industry (who the buyers are, when they buy, and why they buy)

To perform this analysis, the market is divided into segments that represent historical or natural groupings of customers. We analyze the existing elements of the

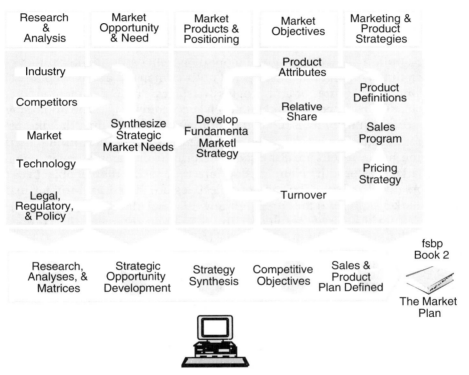

future strategy business plan ®
Stage 2 — "Market & Product Planning"
Development Process

Figure 17.6 *Market and product plan (stage 2) content and development process.*

target industry including current providers and paying particular attention to potential competitors. Economic trends are documented and evaluated in terms of how they may affect the target industry. This information is used to generate a preliminary market survey. This primary research provides additional information regarding the needs in the market and how customers perceive that their needs are being or should be met. The survey is crafted to determine the subtleties of the market's buying behavior.

This information is now synthesized to develop specific market objectives relative to the specific market attributes identified. The target market opportunity is discretely defined based upon functional need, buyer characteristics, quality metrics, and price. These consumer-oriented objectives are then supplemented with the enterprise's strategic objectives relative to margins, position, infrastructure leverage, and growth. Intelligence regarding competitor activity and response is then added to the equation. This process results in a discrete definition of product requirements.

From these product requirements, various product solutions are developed and evaluated generating a preliminary product profile. These products are then tested for market applicability with another, more comprehensive, market survey. This survey is careful to differentiate buying and utilization needs and perceptions. The survey is conducted in three or four progressive stages. Product refinement reflecting survey feedback is incorporated into each succeeding stage. The initial stage is limited in scale to a few representative customers. As the product definitions are refined, more customers are included in the survey. In addition to defining the products, the survey results are also used to determine the sales strategy.

Next, market and product planning develops the specific market objectives that the enterprise will pursue. The market objectives are stated in terms of market position, market share, and the corresponding financial objectives. These goals are established from the survey results for the developed products, the competitor analysis results, and the enterprise's internal requirements.

Market and product planning concludes by defining the market and product strategy. The market and product strategy identifies specific market segments to pursue, strategic positioning within those segments, product strategies relative to functionality, delivery, and quality, sales strategies, and price positioning.

17.5 Public policy strategy (Stage 3)

The components of public policy strategy are as follows:

◆ Defines the position and image that the enterprise presents on public issues; determines the enterprise's intended position and role as a "corporate citizen"

◆ Public issues are governmental, regulatory, industry, and market conditions that are used to judge or determine the societal character of the enterprise

Once the market and product plan is completed, the methodology begins to focus on the details of the emerging enterprise. One aspect that is especially important to all enterprises is public policy. Public policy involves the position and image that the enterprise will present to the community in general. This includes the enterprise's business position and its intended contribution to relevant national policies. It also entails positions with regulators and lawmakers, postures with investors, and general public image. The methodology develops a public policy strategy that defines the business position on and approach to public issues in which the enterprise must participate to accomplish its goals. Figure 17.7 shows the content and the development process associated with the public policy strategy stage.

The public policy strategy definition begins by identifying and documenting the issues themselves. The results from the legal and regulatory trends analysis in the business definition (stage 1) are leveraged here. The issues are categorized into the following levels: national, regulatory, industry, and market. For example, in a

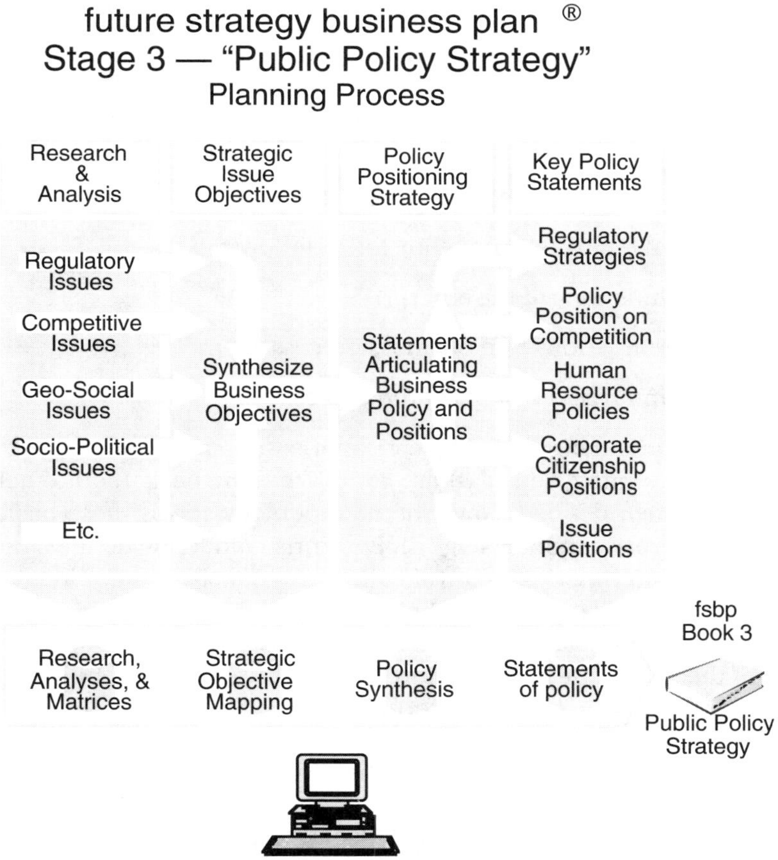

future strategy business plan ®
Stage 3 — "Public Policy Strategy"
Planning Process

Research & Analysis	Strategic Issue Objectives	Policy Positioning Strategy	Key Policy Statements
Regulatory Issues			Regulatory Strategies
Competitive Issues			Policy Position on Competition
Geo-Social Issues	Synthesize Business Objectives	Statements Articulating Business Policy and Positions	Human Resource Policies
Socio-Political Issues			Corporate Citizenship Positions
Etc.			Issue Positions

fsbp
Book 3

Research, Analyses, & Matrices	Strategic Objective Mapping	Policy Synthesis	Statements of policy

Public Policy Strategy

Figure 17.7 *Public policy strategy (stage 3) content and development process.*

telecommunications-carrier enterprise, the public policy issues could include issues such as universal service, competition, number plans, forms of regulation, and so on. The public policy strategy continues by developing the general direction to take on each of the issues identified earlier. Once again, specific strategies are selected based upon their potential to satisfy the strategic mandates and imperatives.

The public policy strategy then defines in detail the key policies of the enterprise, their interrelationships, and the rationale behind them. This includes the enterprise's statement of its position on each key issue.

If appropriate, the public policy strategy concludes with a tactical plan of what should be done in the short term with regard to policy. These activities are necessary to develop the content of some policy proposals. For example, a telecommunications-carrier enterprise might have determined in its public policy strategy that it must support the establishment of an independent administration of the North American Numbering Plan. In the absence of a viable proposal for independent administration, it is then necessary to develop and introduce such a proposal.

17.6 Enterprise modeling (Stage 4)

The components of enterprise modeling are as follows:

◆ Defines the functions of the enterprise

◆ Decomposes functions into business processes

◆ Defines the interrelationships of the processes

Once the business definition (stage 1), marketing and product plan (stage 2), and public policy strategy (stage 3) are completed, the basic requirements of the enterprise have been defined. Now, the methodology solves these basic requirements by the enterprise model (stage 4). Enterprise modeling defines the business processes of the enterprise, which will collectively satisfy the requirements established and documented in the preceding stages.

Not an organization chart, this structure addresses the operating processes and functions of the enterprise and their interrelationships. Getting this right is critical to the competitive success of the enterprise. The structure that is established will bear directly on the efficiency and quality of service, the extent of flexibility to change any aspect of the business, and, therefore, the business's overall ability to compete. These processes are defined in terms of the value added to consumers of the enterprise's products and services. Once again, proposed solutions are measured against their ability to satisfy the strategic mandates and imperatives established in the business definition (stage 1).

future strategy business plan ®
Stage 4 — "Enterprise Modeling"
Development Process

Synthisize Strategies & Constraints	Model Business Functions	Function Abstraction & Integration	Map Process Dependencies	Process Value Flow Definitions	Generate Enterprise Structure
Business Definition					Usage Layers
Mandates & Imperatives					
Market Strategy Corp. Rules	Value Adding Function Definition	Abstraction, Synthesis, & Integration	Process Relationship Mapping	Process Flow Definition	Usage Layers
Product Plan					
Public Policy					Usage Layers

Business Rules	Functional Business Model	Abstract Business Processes	Process Dependency Model	Business Process Flows	Hierarchical Multilayer Structure

fsbp
Book 4

The Enterprise Process Model

Figure 17.8 *Enterprise modeling (stage 4) content and development process.*

Basic value engineering is applied to organize the business processes into value chains as well as coordination hierarchies. The enterprise model is delivered as a comprehensive document containing text descriptions and diagrams of the proposed enterprise model. The content and the development process associated with the enterprise modeling stage are shown in Figure 17.8.

Construction of the enterprise model begins with the functional business model. The functional business model defines what the enterprise does by decomposing it into functions and decomposing each function into processes. Next, the budding enterprise model is expanded to the level of the process dependency model. The process dependency model shows how each process (derived earlier in the functional business model) relates to the others and how they are interdependent.

Once the functional business model and process dependency model are well understood, the abstract business processes are defined. The abstract business processes implement the dynamic behavior of the enterprise. The concept of abstract business processes is a unique feature of this process (see Chapter 16) and leads to the object-oriented process definition of the enterprise described later in this chapter in the section on infrastructure objects (stage 7). This work includes arranging the abstract business processes into hierarchies for coordination and control and applying general value engineering to the processes. Value engineering includes designing and arranging the business processes considering cost, quality, speed, and efficiency. The enterprise model is closely related to later steps in the methodology, specifically the business operations plan (stage 5) and the infrastructure architecture (stage 6)

Once the abstract business processes are arranged in flows and hierarchies, the behavior of the processes themselves is defined. Each abstract business process is considered in turn and its major interfaces to its environment are defined in terms of use cases. A use case is an exchange between an actor (e.g., a person or system) and a business process. It is a sequence of transactions that defines the basic behavior of the business process. That is, the behavior of the business process is the collective behavior of its various use cases. This information will be used to define the object behavior of the abstract business process objects in the infrastructure objects stage of the process (stage 7).

17.7 Business operations planning (Stage 5)

The components of business operations planning are as follows:

- ◆ Defines the functional and organizational structure

- ◆ Defines the business resources from a functional standpoint

- ◆ Defines the business support systems (management, people, methods, tools)

- ◆ Defines the business transition and growth strategies

We next proceed to the business operations plan (stage 5). This stage depends on the previous results of the business definition (stage 1) and public policy strategy (stage 2). In particular, the business operations plan (stage 5) is the realization of the enterprise model (stage 4). That is, the market and product plan (stage 2) proposes a line of business that is realized by the enterprise model (stage 4). The enterprise model (stage 4) is, in turn, realized by the business operations plan (stage 5). The output of these stages is of sufficient detail to support requests for proposal (RFPs) for contracts to engineer, furnish, and install the necessary infrastructure to operate the enterprise. This output must also be able to support the implementation of the subsequently awarded projects.

Business operations planning is conducted in terms of two states of operation: the ongoing or steady-state operations that you want to achieve as an ideal and the operating conditions of initial start-up (a new business) or transition (an existing business) necessary to get from where the business is to that ideal. The business operations plan is the product of this planning phase and presents the following from the perspectives of initial start-up and ongoing activities:

◆ Functional and organizational structure

◆ Defined and prioritized resource requirements

◆ Business support processes and systems and their inter-relationships

◆ Transition and growth strategies

The business operations plan is delivered as a document that can be used by managers responsible for actualizing the enterprise engineering plan. The content and the development process associated with the business operations planning stage are shown in Figure 17.9.

Business operations planning begins with the functional operating structure of the enterprise defined during enterprise modeling (enterprise model stage 4) and the functional operating strategies established in the business definition process (business definition stage 1). An organization structure is designed around these functional processes and operating strategies as if the business were in a steady-state operating mode.

The business operations plan proceeds to the definition of the business systems including management, people, methods, and tools. High-level job descriptions and skill requirements are developed for all positions. The availability and costs of these human resources is determined and a compensation structure is established. The outlines of nontechnical management methods are developed, which will maximize the effectiveness of the functional enterprise model developed earlier in the enterprise model stage (stage 4).

Next, the major business resources are defined followed by the definition of specific physical assets, which are a special case of the business resource definition. Physical resources include buildings, office space, and special structures to house technology infrastructure such as transmission equipment or computer centers.

These assets are defined in terms of capacity, siting, and unique functional requirements. Availability and cost are determined and a procurement strategy established. The information about physical assets will also be used to design the infrastructure of the enterprise in the infrastructure architecture stage (stage 6).

The business operations plan concludes with the start-up operating structure of the enterprise and a plan to transition to steady-state operations (this includes all of the elements provided with the steady-state operating plan). The transition or implementation plan consists of as many manageable and achievable programs

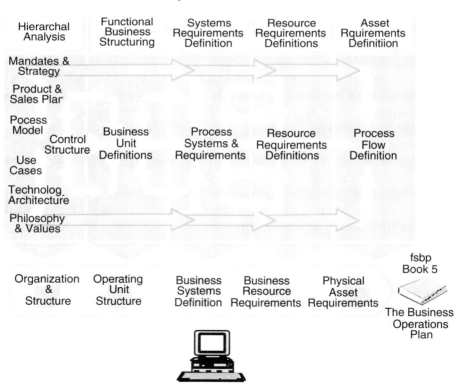

Figure 17.9 *Business operations plan (stage 5) content and development process.*

and projects as are necessary for the defined business. Typically, no program or project will exceed a six-month development and implementation time frame. A general time line of these activities and their associated resource requirements is developed and included in the business operations plan.

17.8 Infrastructure architecture (Stage 6)

The components of infrastructure architecture are as follows:

- ◆ Defines the design principles of the enterprise infrastructure

- ◆ Defines the logical view of the distributed enterprise

- ◆ Defines the general physical view of the distributed enterprise

The infrastructure architecture stage defines the technology architecture of the enterprise including its logical and physical views. The infrastructure architecture is determined, in part, by the market and product plan (stage 2) and, in turn, also influences the market and product plan especially in an infrastructure based enterprise. That is, an infrastructure based enterprise such as an electric power distribution company depends on its infrastructure to provide its products and services. The infrastructure architecture is delivered as a comprehensive document. The content and the development process associated with the infrastructure architecture stage are shown in Figure 17.10.

The infrastructure architecture begins with a definition of the design principles of the enterprise infrastructure. We have found that the most successful design principle of the enterprise infrastructure will be one that stresses a single, unified, infrastructure that is organizationally, logically, and physically integrated. This philosophy will be very useful when considering the enterprise as a global object space, a topic of the infrastructure objects (stage 7) stage.

Once this philosophical stance is clarified, the infrastructure architecture analysis proceeds to the definition of the logical structure (not physical or technical, yet) and framework of the infrastructure of the distributed enterprise. In this view, the distributed enterprise consists of business units spread over geographical areas which may be large (e.g., national, international), or small (e.g., campus, a single building). Therefore, the logical structure and framework of the enterprise must account for the complexity of the infrastructure interconnections, paths, and nodes.

The infrastructure architecture concludes with a physical technology view. This view will define the capabilities, technology families, and location of major components of the physical infrastructure. This work will be suitable for inclusion in

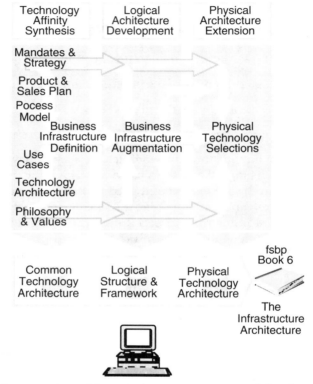

future strategy business plan ®
Stage 6 — "Infrastructure Architecture"
Development Process

Figure 17.10 *Infrastructure architecture (stage 6) content and development process.*

RFPs that request bids on the infrastructure. A significant component of the physical technology architecture is an evaluation of its future evolution and a definition of its changing capabilities.

17.9 Infrastructure objects (Stage 7)

The components of infrastructure objects are as follows:

◆ Defines the architecture of the global object space

◆ Summarizes the contents of the enterprise modeling class hierarchy

◆ Summarizes the entity objects and their relations

◆ Completes the abstract business process hierarchy

◆ Defines the applications list

◆ Defines the procured technology components

Once the enterprise model (stage 4), business operations plan (stage 5), and infrastructure architecture (stage 6) are developed, the methodology enters its last phase, that of defining the infrastructure objects (stage 7). The objects of the enterprise will exist in a global object space which is defined in this stage of the work. The global object space is a representation of the enterprise as an object-oriented environment. That is, the entire enterprise including all of its functions, behavior, and entities are modeled as objects.

Notice that at this point, we are using the global object space as a conceptual structure for object-oriented enterprise modeling. Later, during implementation, it will evolve to the software implementation of the enterprise. Carried to its logical conclusion, the global object space accounts for the entire enterprise and all of its dynamic behavior. In the most sophisticated implementation of this concept we could speak of the "bootable enterprise," which is "initially loaded" and subsequently operated analogous to the booting and operation of a computer.

The global object space consists of three components: an enterprise object class library, enterprise objects themselves, and relations among the enterprise objects. In effect, the global object space accounts for the object orientation of the enterprise: the enterprise object class library provides the mechanism for generating the enterprise objects, which through time will form, dissolve, and reform relations with each other. At this point, the global object space takes shape as a general model of these three types of components. In subsequent phases of systemic implementation, the global object space will become more and more defined.

The infrastructure objects (stage 7) presents the object-oriented architecture of the emerging enterprise as a document summarizing the object environment. The content and the development process associated with the infrastructure object definition stage are shown in Figure 17.11.

The infrastructure objects definition begins with a definition of the object architecture. The global object space will be defined as a hierarchical multilayer system. There are actually two organizational concepts here: that of hierarchical organization and that of multilayer organization. The hierarchical aspect means that the various objects of the global object space will be arranged in hierarchies in which a coordination/control function is part of the larger system. The multilayer aspect means the division of the enterprise into functional abstraction layers. An important part of the definition of the layering is the hierarchical organization of the abstract business processes initially defined in the enterprise model (stage 4) and enhanced in the business operations plan (stage 5). Recall that the abstract business processes implement the value chains of the enterprise.

Once the object architecture of the global object is defined, then the enterprise modeling class library can be described. The enterprise modeling class library is an important component of the global object space and defines the inheritance hierarchies of objects found in the enterprise. Inheritance is very important because it allows reusability not only of software itself but of concepts. The process represents a conceptual view of the enterprise which must later be designed and constructed (e.g., by letting RFPs or commissioning projects within the enterprise). However, at this early stage, we can start defining the infrastructure objects and

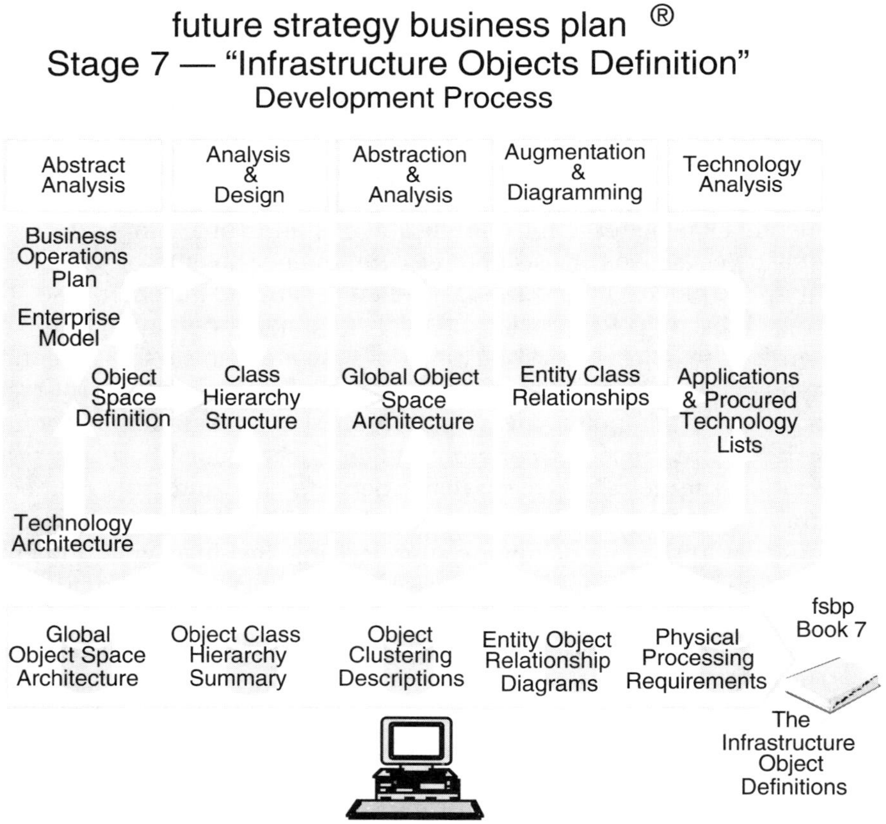

future strategy business plan ®
Stage 7 — "Infrastructure Objects Definition"
Development Process

| Abstract Analysis | Analysis & Design | Abstraction & Analysis | Augmentation & Diagramming | Technology Analysis |

Business Operations Plan

Enterprise Model

| Object Space Definition | Class Hierarchy Structure | Global Object Space Architecture | Entity Class Relationships | Applications & Procured Technology Lists |

Technology Architecture

| Global Object Space Architecture | Object Class Hierarchy Summary | Object Clustering Descriptions | Entity Object Relationship Diagrams | Physical Processing Requirements |

fsbp Book 7

The Infrastructure Object Definitions

Figure 17.11 *Infrastructure objects definition (stage 7) content and development process.*

their inheritance hierarchies. This will organize and clarify the future work that is needed to actually build the enterprise and its systems.

The inheritance hierarchy of the enterprise object class library will be built using the concepts of John Sowa. Using Sowa's type hierarchies, we will see that there are two types of objects in the enterprise: the entities and the situations. Entities are the real-world objects that may be physical (e.g., a machine) or abstractions (e.g., a contract). Situation objects are dynamic and are defined by causing a change in the state of other objects. Situation objects include primarily processes (e.g., payroll preparation) and actions (e.g., cut a payroll check). When the software objects are later implemented (i.e., during software analysis, design, and construction), they can take advantage of the inheritance hierarchies established here to leverage reusability. These inheritance hierarchies are identified at this early stage and are summarized in this part of the work.

The situation objects we will define center around the abstract business processes of the enterprise. Recall that the methodology generalizes the business process into a generic structure which we call the abstract business process. The abstract business processes will become process objects and are one of the building blocks of the global object space of the enterprise mentioned earlier. These objects implement the dynamic behavior of the enterprise. They are recursively defined in the sense that a given abstract business process will consist of lower-level abstract business processes. the same construct is used at each level. At any given level of definition, the analyst is working with a single, unifying concept. The abstract business processes are organized into object class inheritance hierarchies to take advantage of reusability. These inheritance hierarchies of the abstract business process objects are identified and summarized in the output of this stage.

Also, the functionality of the major applications is summarized at this point (procurement or development and implementation plans for these applications are summarized at this point as well). Applications are transient artifacts that have a limited life span and are considered the least valuable objects in the global object space. The most valuable objects of the global object space are the entity objects followed by the abstract business process objects. Applications, for the most part implement the use cases of the abstract business processes. Recall that a use case is an exchange scenario between a process and a person or a system. Applications provide views into the objects of the global object space much like a glass-bottom boat provides a view of the undersea world. Applications allow navigation and updating of the enterprise objects within the discipline of business constraints.

The entity objects we will define in the enterprise model include the real-world objects that correspond to the physical and abstract entities of the enterprise. They are the machines, people, materials, and information that combine to accomplish the mandates and imperatives of the enterprise. These objects start to reveal themselves in the earlier stages and are formally defined at this stage. As mentioned earlier, these are the really valuable objects in the global object space.

An important part of the definition of the entity objects will be the entity class-relations diagram. This diagram will in effect be a conceptual data model of the enterprise and shows the major classes of entity objects and their relations. The entity objects can take advantage of inheritance hierarchies, which will be identified and summarized in this part of the work.

Another important component of the global object space will procured technology. For example, all of the infrastructure object definitions can take advantage of industry foundation classes. These object classes (objects in their own right) represent the utilitarian or common components of any enterprise. They originate as purchased libraries or are designed and constructed by the enterprise itself with the intention of building reusable assets. In the infrastructure objects document, we will define and summarize the foundation classes.

The final component of the infrastructure object environment that must be defined are the technical capabilities of the distributed object environment. For many enterprises, the distributed object environment will be implemented using an object-oriented data base environment as an integral component. We therefore define the general capabilities of the distributed object environment and its object-oriented database. This will be part of the procured technology of the global object space.

Chapter 18

Business Definition (Stage 1)

18.1 Introduction

The content and development process of the business definition are graphically represented in Figure 18.1 from the fsbp®.

The purpose of the business definition is to clearly identify the subject enterprise such that all future decisions regarding its structure, direction, and management can be derived from an established and complete rationale. The business definition, then, is the representation of a "strategic framework" as called for by Tregoe and Zimmerman (described in Chapter 12). As a strategic framework, the business definition provides the touchstones for planning, management, and operation of the enterprise.

18.2 Business definition methodology summary

Beginning with the objectives of the business' owners, the business definition process isolates the aspects of the environment that are imperative for success. These imperatives, in turn, are synthesized into a handful of strategic mandates.

future strategy business plan ®
Stage I — "Business Definition"
Development Process

Research & Analysis	Strategic Opportunities & Threats	Things that Matter	Fundamental Strategy	Enterprise Definitions
Industry	Imperatives			Target Market
Competitors	Imperatives			Operating Structure
Market	Imperatives	Strategic Mandates	Develop Fundamental Strategy	Infrstructure Architecture
Technology	Imperatives			
Legal, Regulatory, & Policy	Imperatives			Industry Position

fsbp
Book I

Research, Analyses, & Matrices	Strategic Imperative Development	Mandate Synthesis	Competitive Strategy	Operating Strategies Defined

The Business Definition

Figure 18.1 *Business definition, stage 1.*

Recall from Chapter 12 that this brief list of *things that really matter* are then used throughout the planning process and ultimately in daily business management. The industry fundamentals addressed in the business definition include:

◆ Market need and opportunity by segment

◆ Industry competitiveness and structure

◆ Competitive abilities of current participants

◆ Legal, regulatory, and public policy trends, limitations, and opportunities (socio-political trends)

◆ Strategic areas (Tregoe and Zimmerman, 1980) that are particularly germane to the subject enterprise

Using knowledge of these fundamentals, the business definition establishes the scope of enterprise within the context of products and markets; the positioning of the business relative to the various value systems within which it operates; and the key values and policies which determine such diverse needs as size and growth, profit and return, and mission and success. The business definition provides these things both quantitatively—what are the objective numbers (market share, rate of return, etc.)—and qualitatively, providing the rationale behind options, choices, and the entire cohesive entity that is the enterprise. Figure 18.2 provides a summary of steps and process relationships needed to complete stage 1 of the methodology, the business definition.

18.3 Business definition interfaces

Figure 18.2 clearly shows that the business definition directly drives every other stage of the methodology except the infrastructure objects process (Stage 7). Simply put, the business definition is the basis upon which the enterprise will be (re)created. As such, it must provide sufficient structure and direction to enable (if not assure) success. To accomplish this, the practitioner of the process must provide a complete list of the issues that will matter to the enterprise as well as some vision regarding how the enterprise will relate to those issues. If effectively established, these critical things will provide vital assistance and direction to all of the subsequent stages of the process. Perhaps more significant though, is the potential for ongoing influence and direction that a well-conceived business definition will provide for any enterprise.

18.4 Research and analysis

This definition process begins by establishing options and choices for positioning the business or enterprise within the value systems associated with the particular business in question. This methodology always considers three fundamental value systems: the market system, the industry system, and the sociopolitical system. In addition, there are impacts and considerations associated with specific strategic areas (Tregoe and Zimmerman, 1980) that may or may not be particularly germane to the enterprise under consideration. Our approach is to identify things that every enterprise must deal with to maximize success within the targeted value systems. These industry- and market-wide requirements are the strategic business imperatives.

Remember from Chapter 12 that strategic business imperatives are imposed upon an enterprise by its owners, the marketplace, competitors, and society. The research and analysis process identifies the issues that cannot be ignored without significant impact on one or more of the various value systems involved. The

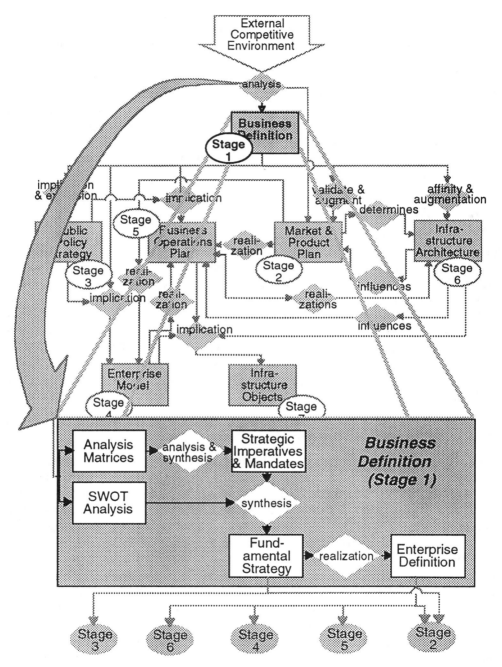

Figure 18.2 *Business definition methodology (stage 1).*

approach used by the authors in researching and analyzing the interrelated value systems is largely that presented and explained by Michael Porter in his 1980 work *Competitive Strategy: Techniques for Analyzing Industries and Competitors* (Porter, 1980). However, any of several well-established and widely used environmental scanning methods may be employed to good effect. Our approach is to first analyze the value system of the overall industry and then assess the values at work in the marketplace. Next, we consider the strategic areas (Tregoe and Zimmerman, 1980) and, finally, try to understand the societal impacts upon all of these value systems (these two steps aren't specifically addressed by Porter's work). We then evaluate the alternative positions, capabilities, and intentions of competitors relative to these value systems.

Information and knowledge accumulation

It is not our intent in this work to provide instruction on how to achieve or perform the information gathering activity. Indeed, information and knowledge accumulation is often contracted from professional information gatherers and analysts. It is, however, critical to identify the appropriate information requirements for the process. Porter's framework for competitive analysis is an excellent source for guidance in this regard. Also, since there are significant interrelationships and cross dependencies among all of the associated value systems, information gathering for them is normally conducted concurrently, often by the same researchers.

There are several reasons for considering the help of professional researchers in this phase. Professional researchers will be able to help you understand how much of the required information is probably available in existing research (secondary research) and how much will have to be accumulated and established specifically for the definition effort (primary research). They will be able to help establish an efficient approach to secondary research. When appropriate, they will also provide excellent expertise in developing effective and efficient approaches to conducting primary research.

An appropriate starting point for knowledge accumulation is the assessment of the environment in which the enterprise will operate. This entails establishing the industry's state, the competitive industry structure, and its scope. Using Porter's approach, this involves finding the "structural determinants of the intensity of competition . . . among a group of firms producing products that are close substitutes for each other" (Porter, 1980). The five information areas, or groups of determinants, that the Porter approach pursues are:

- ◆ Threat of competitive entry

- ◆ Leverage and bargaining power of suppliers

- Threat of product/service substitution

- Leverage and bargaining power of buyers

- Rivalry between existing competitors

The last area is specifically addressed using the Porter framework-for-competitor-analysis" approach (Porter, 1980).

Anticipation of future states and activities within the system

The information accumulated must be evaluated to determine the significance and permanence that this data will have on the future value systems within which the enterprise must operate, that is, the scope, scale, and duration of impact within the industry. These evaluations are most effective when done from three perspectives:

- What are the environmental trends that exist and which are likely to continue?

- What are probable competitor actions and reactions to potential changes in the value system?

- What are the societal trends and directions—actions and reactions as they affect values?

In assessing the impact of the strategic areas upon the business, those most critical to the enterprise will become apparent. It is important that these significant strategic areas are included in this process of anticipating the future. Use of matrices is extremely helpful in both the process of determining the relevance of the strategic areas and in establishing their current and potential states and influence upon the involved value systems (refer to Appendix D on matrix analysis).

18.5 Evaluating the industry's value systems

Deciding where to position and how to operate a competitive business enterprise is based upon a wide range of factors which reflect the value systems of the industry. These include current status and trends of the relationships between competitors, suppliers, markets, technology application, business practice, human factors, and government regulation and policy. By assessing and then interrelating these factors, we can determine probable views of the future industry structure and position the enterprise to leverage these changes. Again, these factors and values are articulated within the strategic business imperatives, industry mandates, and fundamental enterprise strategies, the strategic foundation described in Chapter 12.

Research and analysis of this business environment are required to establish the status and trends. The following analyses will present distinct strategic requirements and opportunities relevant to the subject business as derived by the authors' research and experience in several different areas. Each analysis represents a "section" within the environmental analysis "chapter" of the business definition. A sample set of analyses is presented here:

Industry environment	(Section 1.1)
Market need and opportunity	(Section 1.2)
Competitive opportunity and threat	(Section 1.3)
People and human resources	(Section 1.4)
Technology trends	(Section 1.5)
Legal, regulatory, and policy constraints	(Section 1.6)
Competitive enterprise values and attributes	(Section 1.7)

Synopses of the research, analysis, and recognized trends in each of these areas are retained and placed in the backmatter documentation as Appendices to the future strategy business plan.

The starting point for evaluating the environment in which the new enterprise will operate is with the industry itself. Three areas are of special importance for establishing or maintaining an effective strategy: the evolutionary state of the industry; its structure based upon the participants' strategies; and the industry's functional scope and the degree and structure of integration among competitor teams. We address each in turn.

The industry's evolutionary state

> Structural analysis (of an industry) gives us a framework for understanding the competitive forces operating in (that) industry that are crucial to developing competitive strategy. It is clear, however, that industries' structures change, often in fundamental ways. . . . Industry evolution takes on critical importance for formulation of strategy. It can increase or decrease the basic attractiveness of an industry as an investment opportunity, and it often requires the firm to make strategic adjustments (Porter, 1980).

The evolutionary state of an industry can be said to be its current generic competitive condition. In this context, we generally classify industries into one of many generic environments identified along three key dimensions:

- Competitive concentration

- Industry maturity

- Global competition

Competitive concentration can be viewed in the context of two extremes: monopolistic power and fragmented power. When all competitive power and forces are under the control of one player, there is ultimate concentration or monopolistic power. Fragmentation is any condition in which there are no market leaders with the power to shape industry events, that is, there is no concentration of competitive power. Industry maturity is stated in terms of emerging, mature, or declining stages. Industries positioned strategically in local or national markets that can be affected fundamentally by foreign players' coordinated worldwide strategies face global competition.

So, in this stage, we are looking to determine that a industry is concentrated, emerging, and domestic—or perhaps it might be fragmented, declining, and global. The industry state can be any of 12 potential combinations of the seven elements in the three dimensions considered.

Porter's *Techniques for Analyzing Industries and Competitors* (Porter, 1980) is the definitive source for procedures identifying these industry conditions and their strategic implications.

The structure of the industry

> The essence of formulating competitive strategy is relating a company to its environment. Although the relevant environment is very broad, encompassing social as well as economic forces, the key aspect of the firm's environment is the industry or industries in which it competes. Industry structure has a strong influence in determining the competitive rules of the game as well as the strategies potentially available to the firm (Porter, 1980).

Recall that our working definition of an industry is a group of firms contributing value to create products that are close substitutes for one another. As indicated in Chapter 12, this implies a value system of many enterprises in several competing groups (usually working sequentially, adding increasing value to a product(s) to be consumed in a specific marketplace).

Within this value system, we generically group comparable competitors and/or competitor partnerships together and then demonstrate or position their fundamental strategies relative to Porter's three generic strategies discussed earlier (Porter, 1980). Figure 18.3 is a graphic example of an output from this stage which articulates the two factors of strategic grouping and generic strategy positioning. The circles represent groups of participants and the positioning of the circles on the generic strategy continuum reflects the group's generic strategy. Note that there isn't a good or a bad generic strategy per se. In general, an enterprise or team of firms doesn't want to be stuck between two or more strategies.

Industry scope and integration

Industry scope is the subjective description of the demarcation between industry participants and their suppliers, customers, potential direct competitors and substitutes for industry product (Porter's "driving forces" (Porter, 1980)). Industry integration is the subjective description of the amount of symbiosis which exists between and among the participants of Porter's five different driving forces, the structural determinants of the intensity of competition listed a few pages back.

Figure 18.4 shows the telecommunications carrier industry's changing scope and the relative vertical integration of strategic groups. A simple demonstration of change in industry scope was the deregulation of customer premises equipment (CPE) in the industry. While some of the local exchange carriers (LEC) continue to offer house wiring and maintenance, most of these functions have moved into the

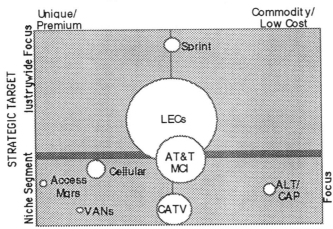

Figure 18.3 *1992 North American telecom carriers.*

electrical services industry. Similarly, customer telephone equipment, although sometimes packaged by LEC affiliates, is rapidly moving into the office services or home electronics industries. Strategically, these services and products are outside the scope of today's carrier industry.

A larger and more significant shift is currently underway. Access management is rapidly moving out of the telecommunications carrier environment. This is occurring as CPE, now beyond the carrier industry's control, develops substitute capabilities for these functions. Similarly, many features and enhanced services traditionally imbedded in the public network are now offered competitively either by CPE or by information service providers.

An analysis of the trends associated with the dynamics of this industry's structure in 1991 results in concluding that the highest risk from substitution is at both ends of the functional continuum.

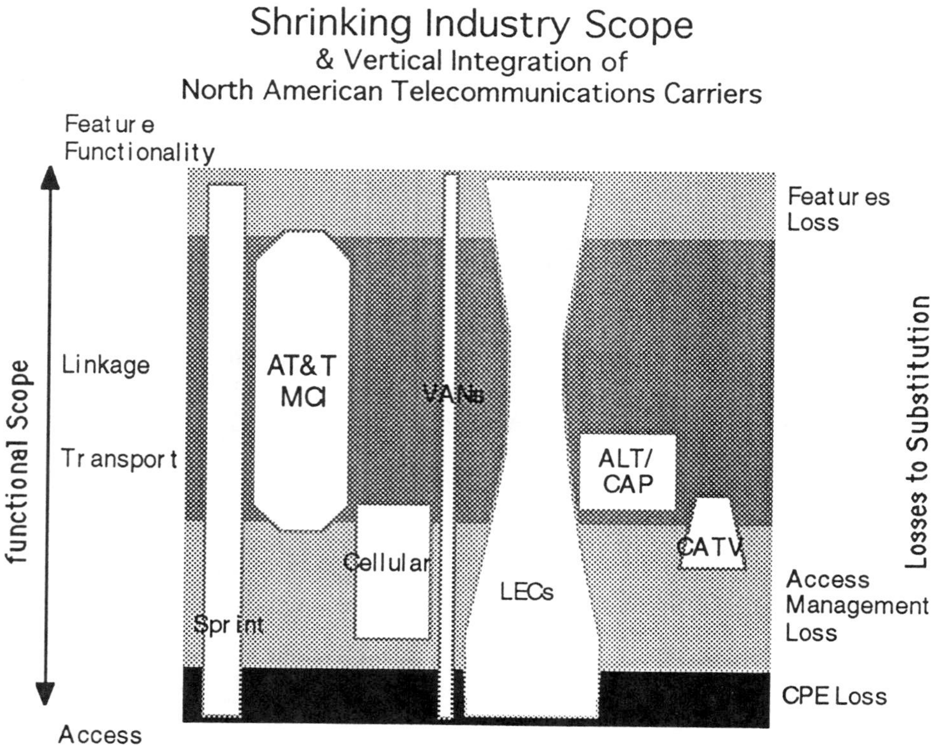

Figure 18.4 *Relative vertical integration of telecom carriers (1991).*

18.6 Evaluating the market value system

The market an enterprise serves is perhaps the most definitive element in the character of any business. It is, after all, the market's determination of value that will establish the viability of a given enterprise's product(s) and therefore of the enterprise itself. An appropriate market and an effective description of it is vital to the creation of a viable business definition.

Defining the marketplace during this phase of business definition is a function of identifying existing or potential purchasers of the value-added products generated by an existing enterprise's functional processes. Or, in a start-up enterprise, market definition entails specifying the purchasers based upon the primary opportunities that motivate the new business. In the new-business scenario (as well as in the situation where a business is open to completely new business directions), this involves identification and acceptance of the factors motivating the leadership (those three of four managers who ultimately have responsibility and accountability for the enterprise as a whole and who in fact control the business) to undertake the discovery process. These could be any number of factors but usually are associated with one or more of the strategic areas as discussed in the business foundations chapter (Chapter 12). In existing enterprises, this is much easier as a market typically exists.

In either case (existing and new), the understanding of the market must be defined and/or validated concretely. This process must provide adequate detail to allow a specific enterprise market positioning strategy to be established. This section will present the key issues to consider when defining the marketplace.

Defining the market

For our purposes, we have described a *marketplace* as an area of economic force within which value is perceived, priced based upon supply and demand, and subsequently traded or sold. The process of establishing an initial market definition adequate to the purpose of business positioning includes four fundamental steps:

◆ A general overview of the business and economic climate within the geographic domain of the intended market

◆ A specific description of purchaser needs to be fulfilled by the proposed business definition

◆ A specific overview of the economics of the described market

◆ A specific review of purchasing behavior within the market

The first subject—the general economic overview—is usually supported completely from secondary research. This contains just what is implied by a general overview of the economic climate of the generic market domain being considered. The overview includes such things as the numbers and types of businesses, households, individuals, retail outlets, media providers, etc. in the geographic area—whatever is relevant to the market being considered.

The description of purchaser needs must be as concise and discrete as possible. This is often the most challenging task in the entire business-definition process. It requires that the team articulate the needs as established and recognized in the market-value system the business intends to address and leverage. This description cannot be made in terms of the product or service intended to be offered. That is, it cannot say that the need is for "athletic shoes" but for a consumer product providing "adequate traction, support, and protection of the feet while providing or conveying personal, sport, or team identity."

The specific overview of economics in the marketplace relates the projected number of dollars available to be spent on solutions to the described needs. If identifiable, this will include the high-level elasticities that play in the market. The total number of purchasers, potential and actual, are also included here.

The purchasing behavior of the marketplace includes identifying such things as:

- Purchase "decider"

- Purchasing frequency

- Purchasing channel(s)

- Purchase timing considerations

- Purchase reasons

The last three steps require both primary and secondary research efforts. The degree of primary research—direct contact with and observation of the market and its participants—is determined by the degree of risk associated with the accuracy of the findings. At this stage of the process, most of the information collected and knowledge synthesized from secondary research is accurate enough for the purpose. However, a brief poll or survey to validate the final market description is usually a good idea. Detailed validation will occur in subsequent phases of the business-planning approach.

Segmenting the market

While generic statements of need and buying behavior across an entire market were established earlier, positioning the enterprise within the market and industry value systems requires segmentation. Market segmentation focuses the marketing and sales activities within an enterprise's value chain. According to Porter, "market segmentation is concerned with identifying differences in buyer needs and purchasing behavior, allowing a firm to serve segments that match its capabilities with distinct marketing programs" (Porter, 1985).

Market segments can be identified by unique combinations of market characteristics. An example defining one market segment's needs might be for: a consumer product providing "adequate traction, support, and protection of the feet while providing or supporting personal, sport, or team identity while playing basketball." This can be further isolated as a segment if we include a price range, repurchase cycle, etc. The types of information that segmentation analysis should provide include such things as:

- Reasons to integrate with another segment's product (original equipment manufacturer, or OEM; e.g., I sell my shoe laces to the basketball shoe manufacturer) or to be an integrator of others' products

- Who (what) is the market's preferred channel medium

- Benefits and disadvantages of being or using sales agents

- The degree of substitution risk associated with alternative segments

- Segment impacts upon the value chains of suppliers, buyers, and the proposed business

- Demand elasticities within and between segments

As many segments as possible should be identified and a matrix developed representing spatially the relationships between segments; establishing and quantifying the pros and cons associated with each (see Appendix D on matrix analysis for more background on this approach).

18.7 Evaluating the competition

> A central aspect of strategy formulation is perceptive competitor analysis. . . . Despite the clear need for sophisticated competitor analysis in strategy formulation, such analysis is sometimes not done explicitly or comprehensively in practice" (Porter, 1980).

At this juncture, an extended analysis and evaluation of current or expected competitors within the subject industry is performed. Five competitive analysis matrices are used to represent and structure these evaluations. Competitors are first evaluated in four areas: goals and objectives; assumptions and internal beliefs; capabilities; and their strategies. Each competitor is assessed by category from the perspective of a new competitive business. Given the results of these four analyses, we then provide an overall competitive analysis matrix, which will demonstrate the degree of competitiveness within the subject industry.

It might be helpful to refer to Appendix D on matrix analyses while considering this section as the example of multiple "nested" matrix analysis used there is from competitor analysis.

The first of these matrices evaluates and ranks competitors' goals and objectives in 10 areas. Table D.1 in Appendix D on matrices provides definitions for each area and the rating criteria applied. One category column that isn't on the tables (because it can only be assessed after all the evaluation tables are completed) is consistency. This is used in the same manner for all of the competitive assessments. Consistency is the degree to which a competitor's position in all matrix categories are consistent and leverage together to achieve the stated mission.

Among other things, this competitor analysis demonstrates which enterprise is most closely focused upon the same target market(s) as the subject enterprise. It also gives a feel for the degree or intensity of that focus. Remember to keep these results in context with those of the three remaining competitive analyses as they are described later in this chapter.

In the second analysis, the strategies of the competitors are evaluated based upon their apparent viability relative to the current environment, the current state of their business, and emerging trends. The categories assessed are fairly straightforward and the ratings are similar to those in the goal analysis. From the assessments in this matrix, we can see such things as which competitors' strategic approaches are especially appropriate to achieving their own goals, which meet emerging industry trends, and how existing competitors stack up to the projected industry conditions and the subject enterprises' strategies for capitalizing on those conditions.

The third competitor analysis component deals with competitors' views and beliefs about themselves and the industry environment. In this analysis, some of the same categories are addressed as in the other three competitor assessments. However, this evaluation looks at the categories from the perspective of competitors' subjective beliefs about each category. At least one thing that will stand out when considering the results of this matrix is which competitors have a fairly realistic grasp of the world.

The final component analysis deals with competitors' capabilities to initiate and react to events. The first three diagnoses dealt with competitors' likely competitive activity, the nature of that activity, and its probable intensity. The categories addressed in the capability assessment deal with operational resources, skills associated with their management and use, and the degree to which they complement each other. This area deals with competitors' abilities to exert their individual wills upon the industry, including the subject company.

The fourth and final step in the competitor analysis process is to accumulate the results of the individual assessments in the four areas just discussed into one overall matrix. Consistency and leverage between results from the four phases are evaluated for each competitor. By multiplying the total ratings from goals, assumptions, strategy, and capability by the consistency rating, we derive an overall competitiveness value for each player.

Collectively, these matrices demonstrate areas of industry weakness and or strength. For example, low or high total valuations of strategies and capabilities around any given subject area represent competitive weaknesses or strengths. Successful industry participants take advantage of such knowledge.

18.8 Assessing relevant strategic areas

Recall that according to Tregoe and Zimmerman, strategic areas are things that can "decisively affect and influence the nature and direction of any organization," (Tregoe and Zimmerman, 1980). As discussed in Chapter 10, these are grouped into three categories, as shown in the table below.

The products and markets category of strategic areas will always be required in the development of any business definition. This will be where a pre-established product or product set will be defined. Pre-established products are those which

Categories of strategic areas

Category	*Strategic area*
Products and markets:	Products offered: Market needs
Strategic Capabilities:	Technology Production capability Sales channel Distribution channel People/human resources
Results:	Size/growth Return/profit

the leadership has determined to be part or all of the business' market solution—the value derived from the enterprise. In this analysis, historical data regarding sales revenue, market share, value-chain costs, benchmark comparisons, etc. are accumulated and assessed in comparison to current and future competitive alternatives. The market needs strategic area has been adequately covered earlier in the evaluation of the market value system.

Strategic capability is assessed to determine the industry environment (strengths, weakness, threats, and/or opportunities) and any associated strategic imperatives uncovered and articulated. The appropriateness of considering each capability as a strategic area is evaluated in the context of the accumulated market and industry knowledge. Every strategic area is not of equal importance to every industry.

The people and human resources area, however, must always be assessed and considered as strategic until convincingly determined otherwise. The types of information to be gathered regarding the necessary workforce are, in one sense, like any other resource. That is, what are the

- Costs, both of procurement and ongoing

- Functional capabilities

- Durability

- Availability

- Competitor positions

While the discrete detail on these and other resources is established in Stage 5 operations planning, we must understand various societal and cultural ramifications regarding the available workforce on our subject enterprise. We must assess such issues as competing loyalties, desires for mobility, expectations relative to autonomy, educational and training limits, etc. This is a complex area, but increasingly, it can encompass the single biggest factor that will make or break an enterprise. Again, this is an area where it may be appropriate to supplement the project team with professional expertise. As in the other strategic areas, the task is to identify strategic imperatives based on the subject environment.

The last category of strategic areas to assess is results. This typically reflects the ownership's requirements (desires) relative to: size and growth; and return or profit. This portion of the knowledge-gathering process is most straightforward for privately held enterprises—ask the owners.

For publicly or widely held businesses, the determination of results entails identifying the competitive-market ranking criteria for different types of financing. In addition to the bond rating scenario, this includes a competitive analysis of alternative stocks with which the enterprise will likely be grouped and what the competitive performance levels are (ROI, PE, ROE, etc.). Having determined these expected levels of performance, it is then necessary to review them with enterprise leadership (and/or ownership) to validate actual owner and leadership expectations. The results of that dialog establish the objective performance required in these areas and establishes the relative priority that these metrics have within the enterprise's internal value system. For the business in question, these levels of performance become strategic imperatives and, most often, one of the mandates with which the business is managed.

18.9 Identifying sociopolitical value systems and issues

This is an area that varies in perceived importance among industries. It encompasses such social intents as are codified in law and regulation but also includes less tangible standards of behavior as current business ethics, norms, and mores as practiced within the subject industry. Most specifically, this subject area includes the human values that will be specific to the enterprise under consideration. These are the integration of human, social, and business goals into enterprise policy.

In many ways, this subject is the most esoteric of those addressed in the knowledge accumulation process. For this reason, it is even more important that it be effectively and consistently defined and communicated throughout the enterprise organization. It is with policy that organizational entities attempt to establish common internal values and with which they try to influence external perceptions of themselves. Therefore, this section will have a great deal to do with creating a common enterprise value system; something that has become a competitive necessity.

This category is also of strategic importance since society has the ability (and increasingly, the will) to limit, direct, or otherwise encumber the conduct of the commerce occurring within its midst. It is, therefore, necessary for every enterprise to understand and position to advantage such issues as license and regulatory control over market entry, taxation, infrastructure subsidization, foreign duties, and trade policies to name a few. These governmental, legal, and regulatory issues are identifiable via secondary research. The scope of this information accumulation effort goes beyond the positions being taken by government or its various constituencies. Specifically, this process needs to include the positioning and participation, if any, of potential competitors, suppliers, customers, and partners.

Given this intelligence, it is then necessary to present the leadership of the subject enterprise with a summation of the positioning of other enterprises and organizations. The purpose of this is to solicit their reactions and preferences relative to the enterprise's own values and positions on the same issues. This feedback

Information Content of Large Industry Markets

Industry / Information Content	Manufacturing	Utilities	Information Provider	Communications Provider	Natural Resources	Education	Government	Transportation & Travel	Health Services	Management Services	Sales & Distribution	Entertainment Programming	Distribution	Finance	Consumer Services	Agri-Business	
Procurement																	36
Process																	42
Distribution																	31
Size in $$																	32
# of Players																	19
	10	10	10	10	10	12	11	10	12	7	11	10	7	13	8	10	

1	Low Information Content	2	Moderate Information Content	3	High Information Content

Figure 18.5 *Sample matrix of the business definition.*

is critical and the answers cannot be assumed. The results of this interaction will generate the real human-value statements the enterprise will present to the outside world as well as throughout its own organization. These values can be directly stated as strategic imperatives for the purposes of the immediate exercise.

18.10 Synthesizing strategic mandates

The data from the preceding information accumulation steps is loaded into matrices such as the one in Figure 18.5. These matrices provide a graphic view of the subject area. The existence of competitive business imperatives within each subject domain are then diagnosed (recall that a typical business definition will have 30 or 40 imperatives).

Usually, the 30 or 40 strategic imperatives overlap and synergize with one another to a great extent. Sometimes these synergies will be positive and sometimes they will be negative. Two things typically become obvious at this point: there is a great deal of extremely interesting and powerful information represented in the matrix, and there is too much information with too many interrelationships to be easily usable. Again, our solution is to boil these imperatives into a manageable set of business tenants, the strategic mandates described in Chapter 12. These mandates are used to lead every aspect of the enterprise process.

The analysis process is typically performed by a single strategist, who categorizes and weights the functional business contribution of each imperative to each category. Having established and assessed the interrelationships, they are distilled to the essence of what is necessary for success in the industry, or what we call *strategic mandates*. A typical industry will have 6 to 10 of these (note that having 6 mandates is significantly better than having 10).

The synthesis process results in three things:

◆ A definition of each mandate

◆ A list of the imperatives that were leveraged to generate each mandate

◆ A demonstration of the degree of synergy and symbiosis that exists with each of the other mandates

The degree of "tightness" in this product will be a strong indicator of the effectiveness of the definitions. The business definition output from this process consists of the mandate definitions and a discussion of the synergies between the involved imperatives. This is followed by a discussion of the interdependence and leverage between the mandates.

18.11 Strategy and positioning evaluation

We have now come to the essence of business definition. The choice of market value system, industry system, and the relative competitive positions within them make up at least two-thirds of the real description of any enterprise. The remaining third of the definition consists of the internal value system that is established within the business entity.

The competitive strategy and positioning of the enterprise is developed in direct response to the strategic mandates just identified. Accordingly, a useful place to start is to assess the implied positioning strategies of the existing competition. To do this, the first order of business is to identify, using the competitor analysis data, each player's position relative to Porter's five competitive forces, that is, where or how are they positioned:

- In the market

- Among suppliers

- With product(s)

- Against new entries

- Among segment competitors

Summary presentations of these and the competitor analyses should then be presented to enterprise leadership—those three of four managers who ultimately have responsibility and accountability for the enterprise as a whole and who in fact control the business. This session is arguably the most critical single component of the entire object-oriented enterprise modeling approach. The meeting should entail detailed discussion and debate of the pros and cons both of the subjective elements of evaluation as well as of perceived positioning and strategies. This review of the current strategic landscape will require three to four hours. In this session, no specific effort is made to establish a definitive enterprise position or response. The leadership should take at least a day to let the knowledge and details "sink in" before formulating their own strategy.

The strategy formulation process actually begins as the leadership and the process team mull over the details of the competitive review. Specific potentials and opportunities evolve in the minds of individual players. A subsequent positioning session is convened during which these ideas for positioning are aired and at least three different overall approaches are articulated and accepted for further analysis and evaluation. Frequently, one or more of these overall approaches represent the position(s) of the strongest competitor(s).

These strategic options are then compared and assessed against the efficiency with which they satisfy the business' strategic mandates. The idea of efficiency is important. This matrix doesn't just measure the degree of coverage in each mandate area a strategy offers. It also considers the expense associated with whatever coverage is obtained. Again, the matrix analysis approach is extremely helpful in representing and comparing the results of these analyses. A sample strategy analysis matrix from the telecommunications carrier industry is illustrative of the approach. As can be seen in Figure 18.6, the value of the matrix is directly dependent upon the amount of knowledge known about each strategy and each mandate. Few of either will likely be intuitively obvious without the background from the first phases of the business definition process.

With few exceptions, the superior strategy is immediately apparent (or it is equally apparent that there is no adequately strong position yet identified). If the latter is the case, the process must step back to the formulation stage with empha-

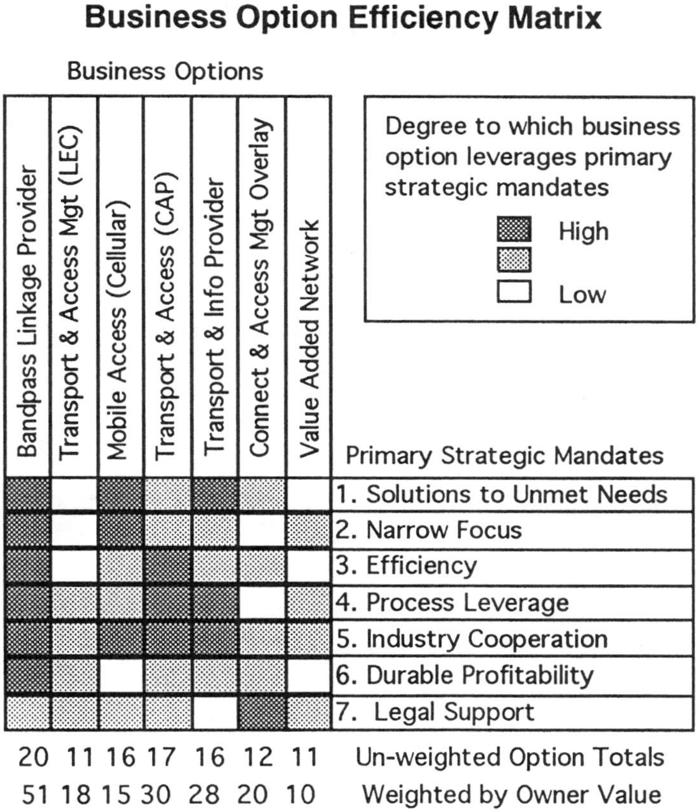

Business Option Efficiency Matrix

Business Options

Business Options							Degree to which business option leverages primary strategic mandates
Bandpass Linkage Provider	Transport & Access Mgt (LEC)	Mobile Access (Cellular)	Transport & Access (CAP)	Transport & Info Provider	Connect & Access Mgt Overlay	Value Added Network	▦ High / ▨ / ☐ Low

Primary Strategic Mandates

1. Solutions to Unmet Needs
2. Narrow Focus
3. Efficiency
4. Process Leverage
5. Industry Cooperation
6. Durable Profitability
7. Legal Support

| 20 | 11 | 16 | 17 | 16 | 12 | 11 | Un-weighted Option Totals |
| 51 | 18 | 15 | 30 | 28 | 20 | 10 | Weighted by Owner Value |

Figure 18.6 *Mandate coverage matrix.*

sis on the areas of weakness, which will have been made obvious by the matrix analysis. Typically, these areas of weakness are identified during the generation and assessment of alternative strategies. When none of the considered strategies stand out as clearly superior, one or more new alternatives are developed and added to the original field of strategies being evaluated. If there is still no clear winning strategy, it is time to reconsider the validity of the opportunity in the subject industry.

It is very important that the leadership be in strong consensus on the selection and articulation of the enterprise's fundamental strategic position targets. When the environmental analyses are conducted appropriately and the enterprise leaders are kept involved and informed, this is not normally a problem. However, there are times when genuine differences make consensus difficult. It is critical that the process not proceed until there is genuine agreement. In our experience, without such agreement and commitment at this stage, the process should stop here.

As mentioned earlier, this is the point upon which the success of the leadership process and enterprise as a whole will pivot. Buy-in here, not just acceptance, assures that there are no surprises in the remainder of the process. All that ensues from this point, including the ultimate daily operation of the enterprise, is determined almost completely by strategic mandates and the business positioning strategy. If you don't have it right, it's not worth trying to kid yourself that you do.

18.12 Tactical implications of strategic positioning

Having selected a fundamental positioning approach, it is still necessary to respond to "weaknesses" in the strategy. It is seldom possible to develop "perfect" approaches to every business condition, so it is necessary to develop and associate a risk analysis with the selected positions.

In articulating the accepted strategic approach, finite and discrete descriptions are established for the following:

- ◆ Target market

- ◆ Generic product profile

- ◆ Market channel(s)

- ◆ Industry segment

- ◆ Supplier scope and positions

With these definitions, it is now possible to establish a value chain through the complete value system within which the enterprise will operate. Only now can an internal high-level value chain and process flow for the business itself be established.

With the work completed thus far (the defined mandates, business positioning strategy, the five definitions, the risk analyses, and the value chain), many critical aspects of the business should be coming into focus. As this occurs, issues will be identified which need to be clarified and pursued. Some of these issues are the obvious implications that positioning strategy has on the various aspects of the enterprise. In this stage of the business definition, we take the opportunity to gather these, evaluate and sort them, and then articulate them for the appropriate planning processes.

As such, this process is capturing the tactical implications of the strategy. Generally, some statement of these implications and/or issues to be pursued are provided for each of the remaining phases in the overall methodology: market and product planning; socio-political strategy and policy; value chain operations planning; enterprise modeling; and infrastructure architecture. In a real sense, this process fleshes out the output requirements for the subsequent phases of the methodology. Examples of these tactical considerations for each area are provided in the following sections.

Market and product positioning

The market definition, product concept, and channel positioning are articulated in this section. The market definition should be extremely tight conceptually (and very specific) at this point, but the others will probably be strong conceptually but with few specifics. Accordingly, the specifics required to validate or strengthen the conceptual statements are identified here.

The aspects of market intelligence that need to be strengthened and/or validated are identified. Also, the desired product definition and product positioning construct is frequently established here. Potential or example channel tactics are identified. The channel and sales approach may include tentative partners or agents for consideration (if appropriate to the strategy).

Sociopolitical strategy and policy

During the research and analysis, areas presently in debate, values, laws, or regulations conflicting with enterprise interests, desirable policy effects, and common internal values are uncovered or encountered. This is the place to identify such items for follow-up or resolution. They might include preparing a position paper establishing the enterprise's recommendation for some legislative issue or general industry need.

A section that represents the values the team has recognized as common, beneficial, and representative of the enterprise should be provided. These values should also be accompanied by a list of values that have been deemed necessary to success relative to the strategic mandates. These will be valuable input to an effort to establish and articulate the desired enterprise values.

Enterprise modeling

An initial value chain and process flow are created and included here.

Value chain operations planning

The initial value chain and process flow are included here as well. The intent is to demonstrate the structural approach to operations which the leadership assumes and to provide a starting point for both the enterprise modeling and operations planning phases. The initial tactical inputs to each of the other phases are integrated here as well. This entails identifying requirements and dependencies implied by these data and pointing out issues requiring early resolution.

18.13 Metamodel: The business definition

The metamodel of the business definition process, Figure 18.7, demonstrates the major products created in this first stage of the methodology. It also demonstrates the formal interrelationships that exist between these outputs and other processes

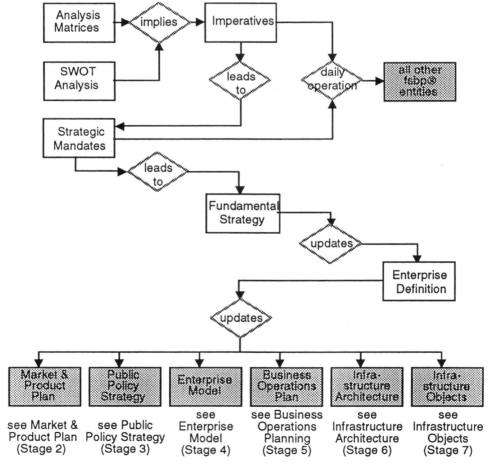

Figure 18.7 *Metamodel of the business definition.*

within the methodology. The gray rectangles represent the other planning processes of this approach.

18.14 Deliverables and conclusion: The business definition

As stated several times before, the business definition is the anchor for managing the business. This process should normally take between two and three months for new and relatively simple (that is to say, "non-complex") businesses. But don't be surprised if six to eight months are required for existing complex businesses or ones in which there is fundamental dissension among the leadership regarding what the business should be. Still, be patient and be certain that these basics are indeed covered appropriately. When we don't deal with these basic issues at this point, we will be building the foundation of our business on shifting sand.

Whether the remaining phases of this methodology are pursued or not, completing the steps outlined here will greatly facilitate the process of establishing and sustaining a prosperous enterprise.

Chapter 19

Market and Product Planning (Stage 2)

19.1 Introduction

Market and product planning make up the second stage in the methodology. Figure 19.1 is a representation of the processes and deliverables associated with the market and product planning stage of the process.

The market and product plan produces a comprehensive document that presents the results of a market study conducted by the enterprise engineering team. The objectives of this stage are three-fold. First, define the market that offers the most opportunity for the enterprise according to its selected fundamental strategies and the strategic mandates. Second, identify the set of generic products the enterprise should provide to that market in terms of customer value, cost constraints, price structure, quality, etc. Third, establish how the enterprise is going to get these products to market. The considerable knowledge and direction gained in completing the business definition (Chapter 19) is used as a jumping-off point to focus on these marketing specifics.

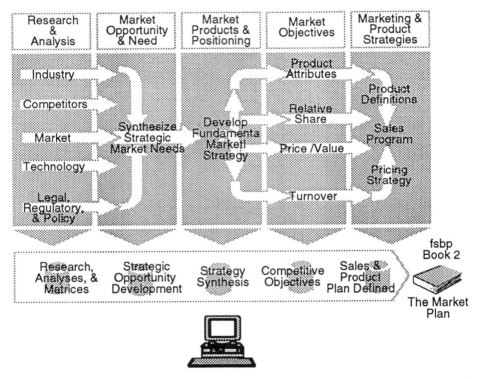

Figure 19.1 _Market and product planning (stage 2)._

19.2 Market and product planning methodology summary

The market and product research and analysis conducted in the business definition stage was necessarily constrained to a fairly high level. In this stage, the market (and subsequently the product) strategies and tactics must be brought to a level of detail sufficient to allow implementation of product marketing, product development, and sales program development. Thus far, only a high-level (although extremely cogent) definition of the enterprise's market place has been developed. It is necessary to focus in on this target market to validate the given direction, develop specific responses to specific opportunities, and to establish finite customer marketplace objectives.

The content and the development processes associated with the marketing and product plan stage of the methodology are illustrated in Figure 19.2.

19.3 Market and product planning interfaces

The most obvious (and primary) driver for this stage is the market definition provided from the business definition. However, the strategic imperatives and strategic mandates are also critical inputs that will be used to validate and guide the creation and synthesis of specific strategies and product plans throughout this stage of the methodology. Also note that there will need to be concurrent and iterative interaction between this stage and public policy planning (stage 3) described in the next chapter. The findings in each will mutually influence the work in the other.

The results of this stage will be directly used in the enterprise model (stage 4) and in the business operations plan (stage 5). The enterprise model will reflect the functions and processes necessary to create the defined value (the product or service) and deliver that value to the intended market place. The business operations plan will establish the required resources as well as the methods and procedures necessary to actualize operation of the enterprise and achieve its objectives in the market place.

In addition, the market and product plan will be used as requirements for the infrastructure architecture (stage 6) process. The defined products, sales channel(s) and processes, and market objectives will greatly influence the design and relational structure of the enterprise's capital infrastructure.

19.4 Market analysis

The market and product plan starts with in-depth research and analysis of the market environment targeted by the business definition. This analysis focuses on detailed information in five areas:

- Industry analysis

- Competitor analysis

- Market analysis

- Technology analysis

- Legal, regulatory, and policy analysis

The purpose of this work is to integrate the available information and knowledge to identify and understand every niche opportunity within the target market environment. Subtle definitions for the following are generated in this part of the work:

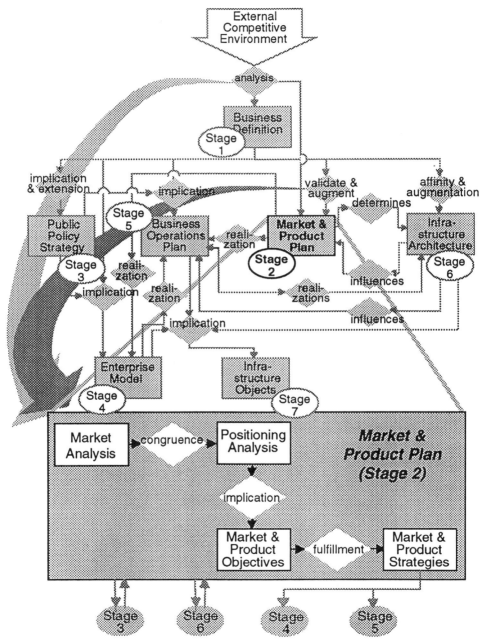

Figure 19.2 *Market and product plan summary (stage 2).*

- ◆ Customer segmentation (what are historical and natural groupings of customers and customer needs)

- ◆ Current products and potential substitute products (what are all of the products being applied—directly and indirectly—to these customer segments)

- ◆ Current competitive participation and potential new competition (who are providing these products currently, who is planning to provide product in each segment, and who has products that might be used as substitutes by consumers in each segment)

- ◆ Economic dynamics specific to the market (what are the economic drivers in each segment and what trends have been identified and can be anticipated to continue)

- ◆ Buying behavior of the target industry (who the buyers are, when they buy, and why they buy)

The analysis information for the segments is used to generate a preliminary market survey. This primary research is designed to provide additional information regarding the needs in the market and how customers perceive that their needs are being or should be met. The survey is crafted to determine the subtleties of the following:

- ◆ Customers' perceptions of their needs

- ◆ Market's buying behavior

- ◆ Demand elasticities of price, substitution, access, etc.

Each market opportunity is clearly defined on the customer bases of functional need, quality, price, propensity to purchase, and ability to purchase. The opportunities are further defined based upon competitors' current share, ability to adapt and penetrate, price (and price flexibility), potential new entry, and substitution. These basic values are established both from customers' own perceptions and from external observations of customer and competitor behavior. Within the given market domain, specific niche opportunities are identified and evaluated against the objectives and needs of the enterprise—the strategic mandates. The discrete definitions of these opportunities along with their opportunity size are provided as input into the next step of this market and product planning stage.

The disciplines and methodologies necessary to complete the various aspects of this section are significant in and of themselves. Fortunately, there are many alternative providers of these services upon whom we can rely to complete the detail work. Accordingly, portions of the detailed market analysis are typically contracted in two or three pieces: the secondary research and subsequent niche analysis associated with the first portion; the development and administration of the primary research (the surveys); and the assessment, synthesis, and definition into discrete opportunities.

19.5 Positioning analysis

The information on niche opportunities is now further analyzed to establish generic market objectives for each discrete market opportunity. These objectives will reflect an intended "position" within each niche relative to both customers and competitors, resulting in an overall strategic market position that the business will attempt to achieve. An additional output from this process is the creation of the objectives for and requirements of the enterprise's products.

As described in stage 1, the business definition, each opportunity is discretely defined and rated by several customer and competitor factors. These factors are then supplemented with opportunity ratings relative to the enterprise's strategic objectives for margins, position, infrastructure leverage, and growth. The end result is a discrete definition of all of the niche opportunities. Again, using the matrix methodology described in Appendix D can be very helpful here. Incorporating all identified niches into an opportunity matrix will simplify the positioning analysis process.

The evaluation of a market opportunity matrix will result in an understanding of the desired position and objectives relative to each of the identified opportunities. Some will present significant immediate opportunity, while others will present no opportunity or risk at all. Some niches will demonstrate only risk. For each opportunity, market planners must establish the specific product capability, pricing, share requirements, etc. that the enterprise should bring to bear to optimize its leverage and exploitation of the overall opportunities that the market provides.

This is an iterative process pitting the strategic mandates, desires for competitive position, and individual market opportunities against one another. This process of establishing the interrelationships between these market factors is the essence of competitive business strategy. It is a far-reaching process that will determine the opportunity for competitive success. The composite results of the objectives for all of the niche opportunities will establish the objectives and requirements for the enterprise's product(s).

19.6 Market and product objectives

From these product requirements, various product solutions are developed and evaluated generating a preliminary product profile. These products are then tested for market applicability with another, more comprehensive, market survey. This survey is careful to differentiate buying and utilization needs and perceptions. The survey is conducted in three or four progressive stages. Product refinement reflecting survey feedback is incorporated into each succeeding stage. The initial stage is limited in scale to a few representative customers. As the product definitions are refined, more customers are included in the survey. In addition to defining the products, the survey results will also be used in generating the sales strategy.

Having achieved an initial view of products and the opportunities to which they are being addressed, market and product planning now develops the specific market objectives the enterprise will pursue. This entails what the enterprise will actually attempt to achieve given specific products in specific markets. These objectives differ from previous generic goals in the sense that they will state specific revenue, transaction, and perceived quality objectives for each product in each market. The market objectives are stated in terms of market position (as determined in the previous section), market share (as indicated by survey results), and the corresponding financial objectives (required by the business mandates).

The process begins by preparing scenario models for each of the products/niches addressed. Scenario models attempt to demonstrate the effects of shifts in such things as customer needs, industry structure, industry evolution, and competitor moves. It is the responsibility of the enterprise engineering team to establish the scope of plausible changes that could affect the environment and to predict probabilities associated with each. These variables are loaded into the models for use by the business engineering team and the enterprise leadership in establishing the finite objectives.

The finite market objectives are metrics used in the management of the business. In addition to traditional revenue targets, these market objectives include quantitative goals for areas such as market share, cost of sales, "units" sold, customer-perceived quality, etc. The finite goals are established based upon results that are necessary, but still viable, to actualize a desired future scenario within the marketplace.

It is important to keep these goals in perspective as they are established and subsequently used to manage the enterprise. They are not an end in themselves, but only reflect a view at one point in time of what is necessary and appropriate performance. In time, that view will become less and less appropriate. Accordingly, this process of establishing specific market goals must be an ongoing, continuous part of business operations.

19.7 Market and product strategy

Market and product planning concludes by defining the strategy and tactics to be used to achieve the market and product objectives. The market and product strategy identifies, for each specific market segment being pursued, the product, sales, and price positioning strategies. Product strategy is developed and articulated in terms of such things as functionality, delivery, and quality.

Articulating this is primarily a function of capturing the results of the opportunity matrix evaluation process described in Section 19.4. The relationships and rationale used to establish the enterprise's desired positions reflects not only market strategy but the logic behind it as well. Each strategic step identified should reflect the probable impact upon the strategic mandates and upon other strategic steps within that market segment as well as between the other segments.

One additional component to be established with the conclusion of this stage is the definition of a product development strategy. The requirements and objectives for the products in each market segment have provided the functional and quality performance characteristics to be provided by the enterprise's products. It is now necessary to establish an approach achieving the creation of those products. This strategy is most often accomplished by experts within the specific market service and product manufacturing arenas. If this expertise is not available within the enterprise engineering team, it must be acquired before this stage can be completed effectively. Again, there are frequently (depending upon the specific industry involved) independent resources available with whom to contract these services as required.

19.8 Metamodel: Market and product planning

Figure 19.3 shows a metamodel of market and product planning, which illustrates the functional planning entities of this stage. These planning entities are pictured as rectangles. This figure also shows the relationships between the functional planning entities and these are shown as diamonds. The practitioner of this stage in the methodology will have executed a process model that approximates that shown in Figure 19.3.

19.9 Deliverables: Market and product planning

The deliverables from this stage are relatively straightforward and are delivered as a comprehensive document. The details of the various studies conducted during this process are provided as appendices to the main text. The document table of contents would typically appear as follows:

- ◆ Research and survey results

- ◆ Niche market opportunity definitions

- ◆ Market opportunity matrix

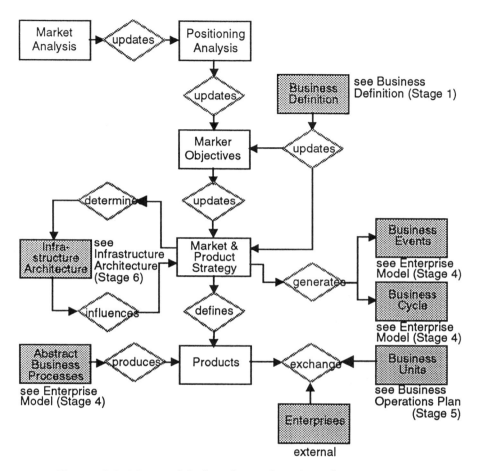

Figure 19.3 *Metamodel of market and product planning (stage 2).*

- ◆ Enterprise objectives for each niche opportunity
- ◆ Product requirements and objectives
- ◆ Product research and survey results
- ◆ Marketing and product strategy
- ◆ Product development strategy
- ◆ Appendices: research and survey details

Chapter **20**

Public Policy Strategy (Stage 3)

20.1 Introduction

Figure 20.1 provides a look at the processes and outputs from the public policy strategy definition process of the methodology.

The public policy strategy definition is delivered as a document outlining both the strategies and the specific policies that will be advocated by the enterprise. These enterprise positions are presented within the context of the enterprise's motivations—the strategic Imperatives and mandates—for taking them. In addition to establishing these definitions, the document is designed to be used as an employee handbook regarding company policy. Unlike many other outputs from the methodology, the public policy strategy outputs are intended to have both internal and external exposure.

20.2 Public policy strategy method summary

Chapter 20 provides structure and insight into the policy development stage of the process. As the market and product plan stage is being completed, the methodology

future strategy business plan ®
Stage 3 — "Public Policy Strategy"
Planning Process

Figure 20.1 *Public policy strategy definition (stage 3).*

begins to focus increasingly on establishing the details of the emerging enterprise. As this occurs, it becomes more important to provide a policy or position basis from which team members can independently, yet consistently, make judgments and decisions regarding the validity of function and process relationships. The public policy strategy process is meant to help fill this need.

On one hand, public policy involves the values and attributes that the organization believes that it has or wants to possess. On another, public policy provides the position and image that the enterprise will present to the community in general. This stage of the methodology develops a public policy strategy that defines the business position on and approach to public issues in which the enterprise must participate to accomplish its goals. As always, this stage of the process will rely upon the strategic mandates and imperatives established in the business definition to validate policy effectiveness relative to these enterprise goals.

In addition to supporting the strategic framework elements of strategic mandates and imperatives, this policy stage is very much focused upon the need to understand and manage the value system within which the enterprise exists. As discussed in Chapter 12, the markets' values placed upon products and services are only the tip of the iceberg within the context of the overall value system. Every enterprise—every organization—must understand the values of its environment, know how and why it intends to meet its objectives within the value structure, and articulate and communicate this to all participants. This is true for every participant in the value system: suppliers, employees, regulators, partners, and customers.

Figure 20.2 shows the steps that make up the public policy strategy definition stage of the methodology.

20.3 Public policy strategy definition interfaces

Policy strategy definition occurs in the context of the overall methodology as demonstrated in Figure 20.2. The initial stage of the methodology, business definition (stage 1), will have established strategic issues to be addressed and the context within which successful strategies for dealing with those issues will need to operate. Concurrent (with this policy stage) development and extension of the market and product planning stage may have some impact upon these preliminarily established issues. The market positioning issues must therefore be validated within the process of these two concurrent stages.

In particular, the business definition will have provided the practitioner(s) of this policy generation stage with the strategic imperatives and mandates against which all such strategies and positioning must demonstrate superior leverage and advantage.

The results of this stage are used directly in developing the enterprise model (stage 4) and the business operations plan (stage 5). The strategies and tactics established here are fundamental guidelines for each of these two processes. In particular, the public policy statements developed in this stage are used as the basis for business rules structuring the enterprise model to be developed in stage 4.

Just as the output of public policy strategy definition is used to establish the very flow and content of the enterprise system, it is also meant to be used on a daily basis in the physical operation of that system. Accordingly, deliverables from this process stage will be published and distributed within the domain of the enterprise system (this implies that the public policy strategy definition process is continuous—even after initiating or reconfiguring enterprise operations).

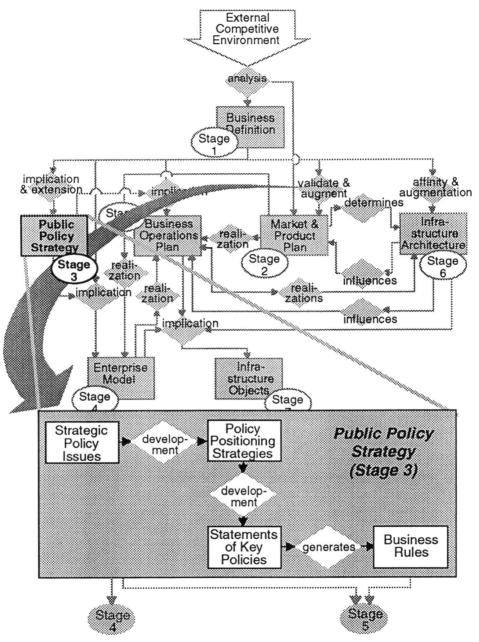

Figure 20.2 *Public policy strategy (stage 3) summary.*

20.4 Strategic issue definition

The public policy strategy definition begins by identifying and documenting the issues themselves. The results from the strategic imperative, strategic mandate, and legal and regulatory trends analysis in the business definition (stage 1) are leveraged here.

Using these results from the business definition stage as a start point, each issue is further assessed and analyzed. Detailed concerns, problems, and/or deficiencies are identified for each issue. The issues are categorized into the following levels: national, regulatory, industry, and market. Within each issue, concerns are characterized regarding their impacts internal and external to the enterprise. The issues are then correlated with the strategic mandates and assessments made as to their potential impact upon the enterprise's ability to satisfy the mandates.

During this procedure, relationships between and among the issues are identified and clearly documented. This descriptive list of issues and their interrelationships are used to begin the next phase of the policy strategy definition stage of the process.

20.5 Policy strategy and positioning

The public policy strategy continues by developing the general direction to take on each of the issues identified earlier. In general, this is necessary for two situations: First, there is tacit understanding and agreement among the leadership regarding the strategic position and response to an issue but the business position needs to be captured, illuminated, integrated with other issue responses and communicated to the enterprise as a whole. Second, there is no agreed or commonly considered position regarding a strategic policy issue. The initial response to each of these situations is quite different from the other.

The process must begin by determining which condition exists for each issue. In this process it usually becomes apparent that while the enterprise leadership believes that many of the issues have commonly held but tacit positions and strategy, very few (if any) actually do. The process of determining this condition is accomplished via leadership education, dialogue, and interviews.

Establishing adequate awareness of the real issues—including lack of tacit understanding and commitment to some strategic positions—is the first step in the process to establish strategies and positioned responses. Depending upon the situation that exists within the target enterprise, you may proceed with various education campaigns to achieve an adequate level of awareness and knowledge within enterprise leadership. Typically, a subteam will be established to organize and direct the strategy process. This team will generally participate in enterprise leadership and will synthesize strategic alternatives and positioning scenarios, weeding out those that are clearly least effective in meeting the business' needs. Once again, specific strategies are selected based upon their potential to satisfy the strategic mandates and imperatives. A short list of strategies and positions is typically brought forward to a leadership quorum for presentation, discussion, and approval.

The results from the leadership quorum session are documented and will be used to identify and scope the detailed position definitions that make up the next step of this stage of the process.

20.6 Statements of key and strategic policy

The public policy strategy stage next defines in detail each of the key policies of the enterprise. This is done by way of individual position papers that are generated individually (though not independently). These papers will provide issue definition, background on the issue, the interrelationships with other issues and/or other strategies, and the rationale behind the associated strategic position taken.

Each position paper begins with a clear, concise description of the business issue and the subsequent enterprise position or strategy relative to that issue. This is perhaps the most important single benefit of the process: a statement of the business issue and the enterprise's desired position relative to that issue that is both understandable and communicable.

The position paper goes on to explain the history and/or background of the issue that it covers. This is done particularly in the light of the markets and industry in which the enterprise participates. This background will reflect the organization's own history, and most importantly, the issue is developed in the context of the values of the subject enterprise.

Next, the strategy and/or position that the organization will take in response to the issue is developed in the same context as the issue was developed and described. This is extremely important and useful as it establishes the rationale and interrelationships between strategies in the context of the enterprise's value system. This value system is defined in terms of the strategic imperatives and strategic mandates developed in stage 1, the business definition. This can become a very powerful tool in the creation, recreation, or reinforcement of an enterprise or corporate value system for the target organization.

20.7 Policy rules and tactics

If appropriate, the public policy strategy concludes with a tactical plan of what should be done in the short term with regard to policy. These are activities which are necessary to develop the content of some policy proposals.

For example, a telecommunications carrier enterprise might have determined in its public policy strategy that it must support the establishment of an independent administration of the North American Numbering Plan. In the absence of a viable proposal for independent administration, it is then necessary to develop and introduce such a proposal.

This tactical plan will establish specific policy detail development, not the general policy positions desired by the enterprise (this is specifically what is to be provided by this stage of methodology). Included in the tactical plan(s) would be the objectives for each effort, specific requirements such as needed delivery times and/or interdependencies with other efforts, and the estimated resources necessary to deliver the desired value to the marketplace. As specific policy details are developed, business rules will begin to emerge. Business rules control the structure and daily operation of an enterprise.

20.8 Metamodel: Public policy strategy definition methodology

The following metamodel encompasses the public policy strategy definition that a practitioner of the methodology will generate from this stage of the process. The metamodel illustrates the relationships between issues, strategies identified and developed, and resulting tactical rules or guidelines. Public policy definitions for a real enterprise should conform to the relationships and entities demonstrated in Figure 20.3.

20.9 Deliverables and conclusions: Public policy strategy definition

The Public policy strategy definition is delivered as a comprehensive policy guide. Meant to be used as both an employee handbook and an education tool for the investment community, the guide will contain the following generic set of deliverables:

1. A definition of strategic issues

2. An overall and specific enterprise strategy encompassing the defined issues

3. Specific descriptions of and rationale behind policies for each issue

4. A presentation of the tactical implications of the combined policies

5. An integrated synopsis and guide to enterprise policies

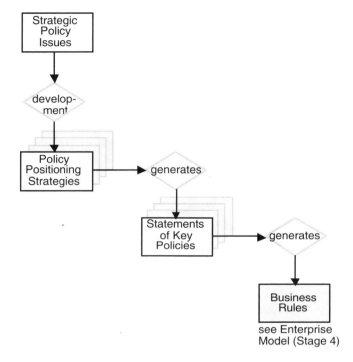

Figure 20.3 *Metamodel of public policy strategy definition.*

As stated previously, the strategic public policy definition process provides the guide book for how to consider and present the enterprise within the context of the external world. This process should take four to six weeks for a new and relatively simple enterprise, but it can take considerably longer if unraveling complex and conflicting policies in some existing environments. Just as with the basics of defining the business in stage 1, giving this adequate effort and thought here will result in significant benefit when the enterprise avoids taking a reactionary course to the events of the public domain.

Chapter 21

Enterprise Model (Stage 4)

21.1 Introduction

This chapter presents the details of the enterprise model stage of our enterprise modeling methodology. Figure 21.1 provides a representation of the processes and outputs of this fourth stage of the methodology.

Once the business definition (stage 1), marketing and product plan (stage 2), and public policy strategy (stage 3) are completed, the basic requirements of the enterprise have been defined. Now, the enterprise modeling methodology solves these basic requirements by the enterprise model. The main work of the enterprise model stage is to define the business processes of the enterprise which will collectively satisfy the requirements established and documented in the preceding three stages. Business strategies are realized by business processes and business processes make business strategies explicit and complete (Scherr, 1993). Once again, proposed solutions are measured against their ability to satisfy the strategic mandates and strategic imperatives established in the business definition stage.

future strategy business plan®
Stage 4 — "Enterprise Modeling"
Development Process

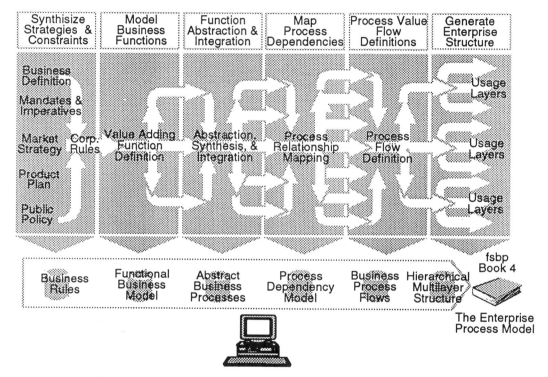

Figure 21.1 *Enterprise model methodology summary (stage 4).*

21.2 Enterprise model methodology summary

The enterprise model is concerned with business processes and their relationships. To define the business processes, we first decompose the enterprise into business functions. Then we decompose the business functions into business processes. The definition of the business processes is our real goal here, and the preliminary step of first defining the business functions will reveal the set of business processes of the enterprise. Once we have defined our business processes, we can analyze and refine their interrelationships including their dependencies and hierarchical relationships. These interrelationships of the business processes will be defined using value engineering principles. Figure 21.2 summarizes the steps to complete the enterprise model and will be used as a reference throughout this chapter:

21.3 Enterprise model interfaces

In Figure 21.2, we see that enterprise model is the culmination of the functional view of the enterprise. The business definition (stage 1) is a major implication of the enterprise model. Also, the enterprise model is the realization of the marketing and product plan (stage 2). We also see in Figure 21.2 that the enterprise model drives the intellectual development of the other stages of the enterprise modeling methodology. Thus the business operations plan (stage 5) is the realization of the enterprise model, which also represents a major implication of the infrastructure objects (stage 7) as well. We will discuss the business operations plan (stage 5) and the infrastructure objects (stage 7) in their own chapters later in this book.

21.4 Business rules

In Figure 21.2, the work flow of constructing the enterprise model (stage 4) begins by starting the list of the business rules of the enterprise. Business rules were described in Chapter 13 and represent the constraints placed on the business. Business rules are the shorthand expression of business knowledge. In effect, the collection of business rules of an enterprise account for the enterprise, its structure, function, and behavior. Business rules are declarative knowledge expressed as a list of statements.

The list of business rules is started early in stage 4 and then is continually updated and revised during the enterprise model stage. Even though most of the business rules will not be revealed to us at this early point, we start the list anyway to make it handy to record them when they are revealed to us. Also, the business rules will be refined and updated as the enterprise modeling methodology progresses through its various other stages. Every time a new business rule is revealed, a quick trip through the work flow of Figure 21.2 should be made to make sure the new business rule is properly reflected within the enterprise model.

The list of business rules can be organized into the following categories corresponding to the three ways a general system is described: functional, structural, and behavioral (this was introduced in Chapter 2). Putting a business rule into one of these three categories is not absolute and a given business rule could fall into more than one category since they often control more than one of the three perspectives. The main purpose of organizing the business rules into these categories is to stimulate the thought process of defining them.

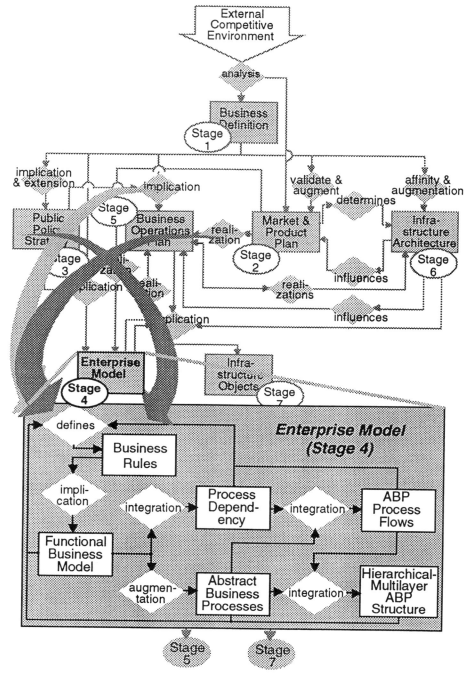

Figure 21.2 *Enterprise model methodology summary (stage 4).*

Functional business rules

As we saw in Chapter 13, the functional business rules have the stature of principles (e.g., deductions from laws) or policies (result of executive decisions) and are thus much more far-reaching in scope than the other business rules. Functional business rules will generally include the following two types:

◆ **Policy business rules**   The functional business rules that are policies (i.e., derived from decisions) can be stated in the form: "It is the policy that _____" (or equivalent).

◆ **Principle/law business rules**   The functional business rules that are principles or laws (i.e., derived from formal knowledge) can be stated in the form: "It is true that _____" (or equivalent).

We already have a good start with our functional business rules because we will include in our list the strategic imperatives and strategic mandates developed in the business definition (stage 1) phase. We will also include the enterprise's public policies developed in the public policy strategy (stage 3). We will decompose each of the imperatives, mandates, and public policies into a series of simpler statements that take the form outlined earlier.

Structural business rules

As we saw in Chapter 13, the structural business rules control the entities of the enterprise and their relations. The entities of the enterprise can be physical entities, abstract entities, or information-representation entities. Initially, few structural business rules will be revealed, but the list will grow as we progress. The collection of structural business rules will be continuously refined and updated as the enterprise model stage progresses. Also, they will be refined and updated as the enterprise modeling methodology progresses through its various other stages. There are two types of structural business rules:

◆ **Entity attribute business rules**   Structural business rules that control the attributes of entities are stated as declaratives of the form: "It must always be true that attribute x of entity y will be z" (or equivalent) or as derivations that state the actual formula or algorithm to derive the attribute in question (e.g., Profit = Revenue – Expenses).

◆ **Relation business rules**   Structural business rules that control the relations between entities are stated as declaratives of the form: "An entity x and an entity y must always be in the relation z" (or equivalent).

Behavioral business rules

As we saw in Chapter 13, the behavioral business rules control the ordered set of state changes that the enterprise or its subsystems traverse over time as effected by the business processes of the enterprise. There are two types of behavioral business rules:

- **State transition business rules**   These behavioral business rules control the state transitions that a component (i.e., process or entity) can undergo. The state transition business rules are declared as preconditions of the state transition in the form: "For component w when event x, if condition y then transition z" or as postconditions of the state transition in the form "For component a after transition b, then it will always be true that c" (or equivalent).

- **Process flow business rules**   These behavioral business rules control the flow of processes. The process flow business rules are declared in the form: "For process w when event x, if condition y then action z" (or equivalent). They are further classified as preconditions (must be true before the product cycle begins, i.e., the production of a unit of product) or postconditions (must be true after the product cycle is complete).

21.5 Functional business model

In Figure 21.2, we see that the next step of the work flow to construct the enterprise model (stage 4) is to develop the functional business model (FBM). The FBM defines what the enterprise does by decomposing it into functions and then decomposing each function into processes.

Definition: Function, process, functional area

We introduced and discussed these terms in detail in Chapter 13. Here is a brief recap of them:

- **Function**   A group of business activities with a significant and well-defined role in furthering the mission of the enterprise (Martin, 1992).

- **Process**   Division of each function into an ongoing series of activities that fulfill part of the function's role. Processes have identifiable inputs/outputs and beginning/end points.

- **Functional area**   The grouping of functions into the major activity areas of the enterprise to simplify the model and enhance understanding.

Defining functional areas

A starting point for defining the functional areas of the enterprise is to start with the Porter value chain as described in Chapter 13. The Porter value chain (Porter, 1985) is a decomposition of a generic enterprise into generic functional areas. Any enterprise will resemble the Porter value chain. Thus the initial decomposition of the enterprise into functional areas will resemble the following functional areas from the Porter value chain:

♦ **Firm infrastructure**   This functional area provides management and control of the enterprise or supports the entire value chain (e.g., general management, business planning, finance, accounting, legal, government affairs, quality management).

♦ **Human resources**   This functional area obtains human resources and performs the specialized activities of their maintenance considered as resources (e.g., recruiting, hiring, training, development, compensation).

♦ **Technology development**   This functional area improves the product or the activities to produce the product (e.g., research, product design, process equipment design, servicing procedures).

♦ **Procurement**   This functional area purchases inputs used in the firm's value chain (e.g., materials requirements, purchasing).

♦ **Inbound logistics**   This functional area is the interface to the upstream supplier value chain and receives, stores, and distributes inputs to the enterprise value chain (e.g., receiving, material handling, warehousing, inventory control, quality control, vehicle scheduling, return to supplier).

♦ **Operations**   This functional area is the primary activity of the enterprise's production process that transforms inputs (considered as raw materials) into the final product form (e.g., fabrication, assembly, production planning and scheduling, manufacturing, materials control, packaging, testing, facilities operations and maintenance).

♦ **Marketing and sales**   This functional area provides the means by which buyers can purchase the enterprise's products and induces them to do so (e.g., advertising, promotion, sales force, selling, order entry, channel relations, pricing).

♦ **Service**   This functional area provides service to enhance or maintain the value of the product (e.g., installation, repair, training, parts, product adjustment, general customer relations).

◆ **Outbound logistics** This functional area serves as the interface to the customer's downstream value chains (e.g., warehousing, order processing, scheduling, delivery, packing, shipping, fleet operation).

Adapting the Porter value chain

Table 21.1 shows an example of the mapping of the typical enterprise into the Porter value chain. On the left, the categories of the Porter value chain are listed and on the right, the corresponding functional areas of a typical enterprise proposed in (Martin, 1992) are listed. The point is that any enterprise can be represented as a Porter value chain. Thus the Porter value chain is an excellent starting point for a model of the functional areas of any enterprise.

Table 21.1 shows how most of the functional areas of a typical enterprise can be mapped one-to-one into the Porter-value-chain categories. Once we portray our enterprise in terms of its generic functional areas from Porter (left column of Table 21.1), we can quickly revise and extend it to its specific functional areas (right column of Table 21.1). Once we have defined the functional areas, we can decompose them into specific functions as shown in the detail points in the right column of Table 21.1. We will discuss the definition of functions in a moment, but first we need to discuss some deviations from the standard Porter value chain. Table 21.1 shows the deviations that a typical enterprise might make with the Porter value chain. In particular:

◆ **Service versus sales versus marketing** Porter proposes that sales and marketing be combined into a single support category called "sales and marketing." However, in the modern enterprise these two are completely different. Sales is usually seen as a customer-service category in the sequence of primary activities while marketing is seen as a management and planning category and would be classified as a support activity. Service is usually seen as allied with sales. Therefore, we will normally separate these functional areas as follows:

  Sales and service functional area

  Marketing functional area

◆ **Operations** The transformation of raw materials into final products of the enterprise is called "operations" in the Porter value chain. In the typical enterprise, this is usually renamed to a term appropriate to the enterprise in question, such as "production," as shown in Table 21.1. Many enterprises separate production into a production-planning functional area and a production (proper) functional area because the production area is so large in scope in many enterprises. This seems like a reasonable approach.

Table 21.1 Adapting the Porter value system

Porter Value Chain	Typical Enterprise (Martin, 1990)
Inbound Logistics	Materials Function Area • Receiving Function • Inventory Control Function • Quality Control Function
Operations	Production Planning Functional Area • Capacity Planning Function • Plant Scheduling Function • Workflow Layout Function
	Production Functional Area • Materials Control Function • Sizing and Cutting Function • Machine Operations Function
Outbound Logistics	Distribution Functional Area • Finished Stock Control Function • Order Serving Function • Packing Function • Shipping Function
Marketing and Sales	Sales Functional Area • Territory Management Function • Selling Function • Sales Administration
Service	Sales Functional Area • Customer Relations
Procurement	Materials Functional Area • Purchasing Function • Materials Requirements Function
Technology Development	Product Planning Functional Area • Product Design Function • Product Specification Maintenance Function • Product Pricing Function
Human Resource Mgmt	Personnel Functional Area • Personnel Planning Function • Recruiting Function • Compensation Policy Function
Firm Infrastructure	Business Planning Functional Area • Market Analysis Function • Product Range Review Function • Sales Forecasting Function
	Finance Functional Area • Financial Planning Function • Capital Acquisition Function • Funds Management Function
	Accounting Functional Area • Creditors and Debtors Function • Cash Flow Function • Payroll Function • Cost Accounting Function • Budget Planning • Profitability Analysis

Remember, we're not trying to make the enterprise into the Porter value chain. Rather, we are using it to understand and describe the first cut of the enterprise's functional areas. Therefore, we will normally separate the operations category into two functional areas:

        Operations planning (e.g., production planning)

        Operations (e.g., production)

♦ **Procurement and human resources**   In many modern enterprises, a philosophical stance against bureaucracy calls for these procurement and human resources to be considered as subfunctions of the primary activities they serve. Thus every functional area of the enterprise will have a procurement function and a human resources function that is integrated into the functional area rather than considered as a separate functional area. We lean in this direction, too.

♦ **Marketing**   Porter proposes that marketing is a primary activity. However, many enterprises consider this a management and control functional area and thus should be categorized as a support activity. This will be our direction, too.

A useful communication tool is to document the decomposition of the enterprise into functional areas using a "composed of" diagram as shown in Figure 13.1.

Defining functions

Once a first cut at the functional areas is complete, the next step in the methodology of the enterprise model (stage 4) is to define the business functions of the enterprise. This is done by considering each functional area in turn. Also, notice that as the functions are being defined, the functional areas will also be changed and perfected. Here are some rules of thumb and pragmatic advice for defining the business functions of the enterprise:

♦ Business functions usually have different skills or kinds of expertise associated with them. A proposed business function that seems to be made up of two completely different disciplines (e.g., different knowledge bases, different training) is probably two different business functions.

♦ In a working enterprise, business functions are usually managed as self-contained concerns. Thus a proposed business function that seems to be made up of two different management responsibilities (e.g., different goals, different time lines, different levels of people, different scopes of responsibility) is probably two different business functions.

- Business functions are governed by their own policies or procedures. Thus a proposed business function that seems to be governed by two different bodies of policies or procedures (e.g., different origins of the procedures, different bodies of law or conventions that imply the policies) is probably two different business functions.

- Business functions should reflect the strategic imperatives and strategic mandates derived in the business definition (stage 1). Thus the enterprise modeler should be able to see how each strategic imperative and mandate is accounted for in the business functions, either directly or by implication.

- Business functions do not overlap, they are mutually exclusive. The sum of the business functions is the enterprise in the sense that the whole is made up of the sum of its parts. Thus all of the activities of the enterprise that further its mission should be covered by the set of business functions.

Business functions are documented in text form. The following should be included in the description of a business functions:

- **Name** Business functions are named with nouns or gerunds (verb form ending in "ing" that acts as a noun).

- **Description** This is a paragraph describing the function. The description should delineate the boundaries of the function. A good technique is to make the description impersonal by starting with "A function which. . . ." At first, the description doesn't have to be complete since it will probably be revisited in the course of completing the enterprise model (stage 4).

A useful way to communicate the decomposition of a functional area into a set of functions is the "composed of" diagram as shown in Figure 13.5 of Chapter 13.

Defining business processes

Once a first cut at the functions of the enterprise is complete, the next step in the methodology of the enterprise model (stage 4) is to decompose each business function into business processes. Each function of the enterprise is considered in turn and is decomposed into its processes. For enterprise modeling, only one or two levels of decomposition is usually sufficient. Thus it is usually not necessary (or even possible) during enterprise modeling to decompose the business functions into physical elementary business processes. The decomposition of business functions into business processes will also cause changes in the definition of the business functions themselves because we will learn more about them. Here are some rules of thumb in defining the business processes of a business function:

- ◆ Typically, a business function will be decomposed into four to eight business processes.

- ◆ Business processes imply flow, in which the various business processes overlap in time (i.e., they can occur at the same time). Also, business processes are coupled, in which the input to a business process is created by one or more upstream business processes. We will discuss process dependency in a moment.

- ◆ It is best to take a business function and make a first cut at all of its business processes before going on to another business function.

- ◆ The business processes of any business function should be comparable to the business processes of the other business functions in scope, importance, significance, complexity, etc.

Business processes are documented using text descriptions. The following should be included in the description of a business process:

- ◆ **Name**   Business processes are named with verb-object pairs. Usually higher-level business processes are named with soft verb forms (ending in -*ing*, -*tion*, -*ment*, -*al*). As one decomposes the business processes into lower-level business processes, the names become more action oriented. The name of a business process reflects "what" and should not reflect "who," "when" or "where."

- ◆ **Description**   The description should be a paragraph that summarizes the activities performed and distinguishes the boundary of the business process. The description should include any product cycles that the business process has. A business process normally performs a product cycle which consists of the activities to produce a standard unit of its products (i.e., one or more in a standardized set using the conventional definition for the industry in question). Business processes that do not have product cycles act once and then go away. We can still say they have a product cycle, namely the activity between their start and end.

- ◆ **Inputs and outputs**   Normally, business processes have many inputs but only one output product. The list of input products will include the business entities (physical, abstract, or information entities) that originate from upstream processes. The output product will be delivered to downstream business processes from the business process in question. The output product is usually the object in the verb-object name of the business process.

- ◆ **Resources**   The list of resources will include people, machines, or other capital items that are used or depleted by the business process.

- ◆ **Preconditions**   The list of preconditions will reference the specific behavioral business rules (i.e., from our growing list of business rules) that control the invocation of a product cycle of the business process. We will discuss this next.

- ◆ **Postconditions**   The list of postconditions will reference the specific behavioral business rules from our list that control the completion of a product cycle of the business process (also discussed in the following section).

21.6 Process dependency

In Figure 21.2, we see that the next step of the work flow to construct the enterprise model (stage 4) is the development of the process dependency model (PDM). In the sequence of the methodology, we have just completed the construction of the functional business model (FBM). The FBM defines what the enterprise does by decomposing it into business functions and decomposing each of those business functions into business processes. Once the business processes are defined, the next step described in this section is to develop the process dependency model (PDM). The PDM shows how the business processes (derived earlier in the FBM) relate to each other and how they are dependent on each other. Several important deliverables are created in this step: the PDM, an update to our growing list of business rules, and the preconditions/ postconditions sections of the business process descriptions began in the FBM.

The meaning of dependency

Process dependency at our high level of modeling (i.e., enterprise modeling) really means prerequisite-postrequisite declarations. Thus business process A is dependent on business process B in the sense that business process B, for whatever reason, cannot take place until business process A has completed a product cycle. Notice that we don't really have to justify the reason for the dependency if we cannot fully articulate it at this early stage. In other words, it is okay at this point to use general business savvy and intuition to define dependencies. Later, the actual dependency can be defined explicitly in terms of the products, resources, or events that the prerequisite business processes create.

Business rules and process dependencies

Process dependencies are stated as business rules. Recall that we started our list of business rules as the first step in the work flow of the enterprise model stage (see Figure 21.2). Now we will focus on the behavioral business rules of our budding list. Behavioral business rules control the flow of processes and are stated as preconditions or postconditions.

We will update our definition of each business process that we began in the FBM step to include its preconditions and postconditions.

◆ **Preconditions** State the names of the business rules that control the invocation of one product cycle of the business process.

◆ **Postconditions** State the names of the business rules that control the completion of one product cycle of the business process.

Business events

A major deliverable for this step of the enterprise model (stage 4) work flow is the list of business events. A business event is an external real-world happening that requires certain action. The event is either solicited or unsolicited (Vernadat, 1992). The proverbial example is the customer order that arrives and must be serviced by the business processes of the enterprise.

Business events are an alternative way that business processes are triggered, the other being another business process acting as the trigger upon the completion of one of its cycles and the flow of its product.

The list of business events is begun at this stage and, like the other deliverables, will be subject to frequent updates as the work of the enterprise model (stage 4) progresses. The description of a business event should include the following:

◆ **Name** This is the name of the business event. The name will take the form of a subject-verb (e.g., "customer arrives") or as an object (e.g., "customer order").

◆ **Description** The description of the business event should include the physical form it will take, its expected frequency, and the basic reason it is created.

◆ **Triggering processes** This is a list of the processes (including external processes) that create the event and for each of the processes, a summary of the actions that would lead the process to create the event.

◆ **Triggered processes** This is a list of business processes that are triggered by this business event.

Object-flow diagramming: Documenting the process dependencies

A useful technique of analyzing and documenting process dependencies is object-flow diagramming explained in Appendix C. This technique was originated by

James Martin and James Odell as a process model based on the concepts of the Porter value chain. The technique is ideal for analyzing dependencies among business processes and tracing value in the value chain.

21.7 Abstract business processes

In Figure 21.2, we see that the next step of the work flow for constructing the enterprise model (stage 4) is to begin defining the abstract business processes. In a previous step, the functional business model (FBM), we defined what the enterprise does by decomposing it into business functions and then decomposing each business function into business processes. This step augments the definition of the business processes and defines the set of Abstract Business Processes (ABPs). We defined and discussed the ABP in detail in Chapter 14. In this step, we are just concerned with defining the set of ABPs. In later steps of the enterprise model stage, we will define the flows and hierarchical organization of the ABPs (which will no doubt cause us to return here again as the definition of ABPs are perfected).

Also concurrent with this step, the work to complete the process dependency model (PDM) described earlier will be underway. This step of defining the ABPs and the step of completing the PDM will be performed iteratively since they interrelate and influence each other. In effect, this formalizes the business processes of the FBM and PDM. The work to complete this step includes documenting and normalizing the ABPs by eliminating redundancies, factoring responsibilities, and performing general value engineering on them. As this work progresses, updates will be made to the growing list of business rules as well as the other parts of the FBM.

Defining use cases

The definition of the ABPs will be accomplished by defining their use cases. We discussed use cases in detail in Chapter 14. There we defined the use case as a sequence of exchanges between an actor and the system being defined. A use case defines a complete scenario that accomplishes an exchange of material, energy or information between the actor and an ABP. A use case is defined in sufficient detail to account for the entire exchange including exceptions and errors carried to their logical conclusion. Use cases focus on the actor and goals of the actor. That is, use cases define the requirements of an ABP from the standpoint of the actors of the ABP. The actors represent customers or users whose use of the ABP justifies the ABP. Before describing how we will define ABPs, we should know how to define and document the use cases of an ABP. Here are some rules of thumb for defining use cases:

◆ Start with the generic use cases identified in Chapter 14 where we described the generic use cases including their actors and the nature of the exchange. The point is that any ABP will have this set of generic use cases although they will be given different names depending on the actual enterprise. Thus any use case we define and refine for our specific ABP will, at its core, really be just one of the generic use cases as follows:

Supplier Use Cases

Supplier Interface (opening)

Supplier Interface (negotiation)

Supplier Product Transfer

Supplier Assessment

Supplier Payment

Supplier Interface (Service)

Customer Use Cases

Customer Interface (opening)

Customer Interface (negotiation)

Customer Product Transfer

Customer Assessment

Customer Payment

Customer Interface (Service)

Control-Coordination Use Cases

Direction Intervention (superior)

Performance Feedback (superior)

Direction Intervention (subordinate)

Performance Feedback (subordinate)

Marketing Use Cases

Monitoring (marketing)

Monitoring (end customer)

Monitoring (customer)

◆ Identify the actors of the ABP. The actors will themselves be ABPs (i.e., which are not being analyzed at the same time we are defining our ABP and thus will be treated as black boxes). The starting point for identifying the actors of an ABP is to consider the actors of the generic use cases listed above. Thus any actor of our ABP (while it may have a different name) will, at its core, really be just one of the generic actors of the generic use cases as follows:

> Customer ABP
>
> Supplier ABP
>
> Superior ABP
>
> Subordinate ABP
>
> Market information provider ABP
>
> Environment information provider ABP

◆ Define the role that will service the use case from the ABP side. Don't forget that ABPs are ultimately made up of information processing nodes (people, machines, lower-level information processing networks). Roles are assigned to information processing nodes and a given information processing node performs many roles. It is a role that actually performs a use case.

◆ Refine the generic use cases into real use cases. To do this, we start with the generic actors and define the set of real actors of the use case in question giving them names and definitions from the domain of the ABP.

◆ Define the specific exchange that the real actor and the ABP will make. Identify the starting event (i.e., reference the list of events) that initiates the use case, preconditions that must be true of the target ABP before the use case can begin (i.e., reference the behavioral business rules of the target ABP), the various endings that the use case could achieve, and the postconditions that will be true of the target ABP for each of the endings (i.e., reference the business rules of the ABP).

◆ Document the use case (described next).

Documenting the use case

Each use case is documented with a standard text description. The following should be included in the description of a use case:

◆ **Name**   Assign a meaningful name or phrase to identify the use case.

◆ **Target ABP**   This will be the name of the ABP that will execute the use case.

◆ **Target role**   This will be the name of the role of the information-processing node that will actually perform the use case (i.e., within the auspices of the ABP).

◆ **Actor**   The name of the actor that executes the use case.

◆ **Description**   The description should be a paragraph that summarizes the exchange that is being made by the use case.

◆ **Preconditions**   The list of preconditions will reference the specific business rules (i.e., from our growing list of business rules) of the target ABP that control the invocation of the use case.

◆ **Postconditions**   The list of postconditions will reference the specific behavioral business rules of the target ABP from our list of business rules that define the ending conditions.

Documenting the roles

Each role is documented with a standard text description. The following should be included in the description of a role:

◆ **Name**   Assign a meaningful name or phrase to identify the role.

◆ **Description**   Describe the role including the type of information-processing node that will perform it.

◆ **Use cases**   List the use cases in which the role is active.

Defining tentative ABPs

Next, we turn our attention to the definition of the ABPs. An ABP consists of subprocesses which are themselves ABPs. As we saw in Chapters 14 and 15, there are six subprocesses of the ABP:

◆ Management and control ABP subprocess

◆ Marketing ABP subprocess

◆ Inbound logistics ABP subprocess

◆ Operations ABP subprocess

◆ Sales and service ABP subprocess

◆ Outbound logistics ABP subprocess

These subprocesses represent the generic activities of any business process. In effect, any business process must be capable of performing them, some more, some less, depending on the actual business process. Of the six, the one that really defines the ABP is its operations ABP subprocess. The other five tend to be generic especially at the upper levels of the ABP process decomposition, which is where we are now. Thus the operations subprocess ABP becomes the focus for defining the broader ABP in question.

The business processes defined in the FBM will now be used as a starting point for defining the set of ABPs:

- ◆ We tentatively categorize each business process of the FBM into the six categories listed above. By doing this, we are asserting that any business process will, at its core, be one of the six. This will result in six lists of business processes.

- ◆ We select business processes from each of the six categories to form tentative ABPs. That is, a set of six business processes that seem to fit together is found by selecting a business process from each of the six lists. The six together form a coherent ABP with all its subprocesses. We start an iteration of matching a set of the six by first finding an operations ABP. Then we match it with its other five ABPs to form a tentative set. Each matching business process is selected because it seems to go with the others. In this way, we combine the business processes to form the full complement of the six subprocesses of a tentative ABP.

- ◆ The heart of each tentative ABP is the operations subprocess. This defines the purpose of the tentative ABP. In actual practice, most of the business processes on the list will correspond to operations ABP subprocesses. Their corresponding other five ABP subprocesses will often be missing or only partially present on the list. In this case, we must return to the functional business model (FBM) step to fill out the list of business processes so that there is a full complement of the six subprocesses for each tentative ABP.

- ◆ We work with our growing list of tentative ABPs until it seems to be complete and we have exhausted the original list of business processes. We can return to this point later if necessary but for now we proceed.

Finalizing the tentative ABPs

The list of tentative ABPs identified earlier will now be finalized. This will result in the list of ABPs, which we can then use in the remaining steps of the enterprise model (stage 4). To finalize an ABP, we focus on its customer and supplier use cases. The identification and documentation of use cases was described earlier in the chapter. For each tentative ABP, we do the following:

◆ For the ABP, we focus on its customers and the products they will receive from it:

We ask: who is the customer of this ABP? The answer must be either another ABP on our growing list of ABPs or the end customer of the enterprise.

We ask: what products will our ABP create for the customer?

◆ Next we define the customer use cases of the ABP:

We ask: what requests will a given customer make of our ABP?

◆ Next we define the supplier use cases:

We ask: what products will be required of our ABP to create its products?

Documenting the ABP

The list of ABPs is begun at this stage and like the other deliverables will be subject to frequent updates as the work of the enterprise model (stage 4) progresses. The description of an ABP should include the following:

◆ **Name**   ABPs, like other business process, are named with verbs. Usually higher-level ABPs are named with soft verb endings (ending in *-ing*, *-tion*, *-ment*, *-al*). The name should reflect "what" and should not reflect "who," "when," or "where."

◆ **Description**   The description should be a paragraph that summarizes the activities performed by the operations ABP subprocess and distinguishes the boundary of the ABP in question.

◆ **Inputs and outputs**   The list of input products will include the business entities (physical, abstract, or information entities) that originate from upstream ABPs.

The output product will be delivered to downstream ABPs.

◆ **Decomposition**   This will be the list of the six business processes that were combined to form this ABP.

◆ **User cases**   We will list the use cases we have identified so far with a summary of their exchanges. This will be a growing list that will be completed in a later step of the enterprise model (stage 4). Each use case is documented as described earlier in the chapter.

21.8 Abstract business process flows

In Figure 21.2, we see that the next step of the work flow to construct the enterprise model (stage 4) is to develop the abstract business process flows. this formalizes the process dependency model (PDM) using the abstract business processes defined in the previous step of the methodology (see section above). This step is performed iteratively with the step defining the hierarchical-multilayer structure of the abstract business processes described in the next section.

The meaning of ABP dependency

At this point, we already know a lot about the dependencies of the business processes of our enterprise since we have already constructed our process dependency model (PDM). Now we expand this model to reflect our set of ABPs, which we defined in the previous step. In the discussion that follows, we will refer to Figure 21.3, which shows a typical flow between two ABPs.

In Figure 21.3, we see two ABPs, ABP 1 and ABP 2, with their subprocess ABPs exposed. ABP 1 receives raw materials from an upstream ABP and, in turn, creates raw materials for ABP 2. We would have already defined ABP 1 and ABP 2 in the previous step of the methodology by collecting together their six subprocess ABPs as shown in Figure 21.3.

Structuring accountability

It is easy to understand the flow that occurs between the ABPs. All we have to do is draw a diagram, such as Figure 21.3, which portrays the products flowing along the primary activities. However, this linear flow is not the point of our current work. It is secondary to the need for defining the accountability of the ABPs to the end cus-

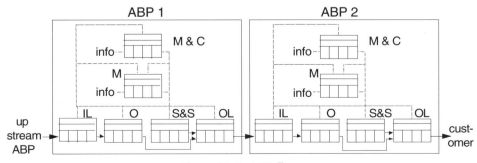

Figure 21.3 *ABP flow.*

tomer. On the right side of Figure 21.3, we see the final products flowing to the end customer. There would be a tendency to focus on this flow as an engineering problem. However, designing the flow of the ABPs is about structuring accountability. We start with the end customer, which is outside the enterprise, and work backwards to the front of the enterprise. The problem is that the numerous subprocesses inside of ABP 1 and ABP 2 must participate in this accountability to the end customer. Here are some rules of thumb to properly structure accountability:

- **Start with the customer-interface negotiation use cases** In the definition of the customer use cases, we defined the customer interface negotiation use cases. In these use cases, the enterprise negotiates with the customer on the terms of the sale. Typical items that are negotiated are product specifications, product price, delivery schedule, payment schedule, etc. In effect, the customer interface negotiation use cases establish the conditions for satisfaction of the customer. These represent the specific responsibilities for which the various ABPs of the enterprise must be responsible. The last ABP in the chain certainly bears the responsibility for meeting all of these conditions. The point is that these responsibilities must be transferred to the upstream ABPs as well.

- **Distribute the end customer accountability to the subprocess use cases** Looking backwards in the value chain, the cascading accountabilities can be observed. Each secondary supplier (i.e., the upstream ABP subprocesses) must be delegated their portion of the customer accountability. The use cases among the various subprocess ABPs must reflect this factoring of the responsibility to the end customer. In particular, each subprocess ABP, acting as a customer to an upstream subprocess ABP, must perform its own version of the customer interface negotiation use case. This is where the actual responsibility to the end customer is transferred within the value chain. By regarding these use cases in this light, we may need to revise their definition which we began in the previous step of the methodology.

- **Clarify the roles performed for each customer-use case to fulfill the use case** A role performs a use case, so roles must implement the accountability to the customer. The roles documented in conjunction with the use cases should be reviewed and updated as necessary to make them specific to the accountability they must implement.

- **Define the roles around "customer teams," which implement customer accountability** Problems often arise by distributing accountability because of the lack of a global view. One way around this problem is to establish a strong sense of customer teams around the customer. Gaps are minimized by defining the roles participating in such a team. Participation in a customer team is implemented by the scripts of the information-processing nodes. In this way, each information-processing node (i.e., in this case, people) will execute a script in which part of its duties is to participate in such a customer team.

♦ **Alternatively, have all accountability flow to a single role** An alternative to the customer team is to put one role of an information-processing node in charge of the customer accountability for the entire ABP.

♦ **Don't factor the customer's view of the enterprise** Customers will expect the enterprise to be knowledgeable about its current and past activities during each of their use cases with the enterprise. Also, the enterprise must have continuity between its individual activities with the customer. That is, during one use case executed by an ABP, knowledge of previous or current use cases (possibly performed by other ABPs) for this customer is important. Not only is it desirable from a customer relations standpoint that the enterprise see the customer as the sum of previous activities, it is also much more efficient. A use case executed now can be made much more efficient if the results of previous use cases are used as the context in which the current use case is executed. Designing use cases and roles around customer teams or single points of accountability will solve this need.

♦ **Define measurements** Measurements of customer accountability must be defined for each ABP. Some typical measurements include:

- Time (i.e., time for each product cycle; overall time)

- Actual outcome: comparing the specifications negotiated with the specifications delivered

- Customer satisfaction: customer surveys and anecdotal evidence

Documenting the abstract business process flows

The ABP flows are documented using the dependency diagrams introduced in the process dependency model described earlier. The factoring of customer responsibility is pointed out in the description of the applicable use cases.

21.9 Hierarchical-multilayer structure of the abstract business processes

In Figure 21.2, we see that the next step of the work flow to construct the enterprise model (stage 4) is the development the hierarchical-multilayer structure of the enterprise. This step is performed iteratively with the step defining the abstract business process (ABP) flows described in the previous section.

There are two components that are intermixed to make this step: the hierarchical definition and the multilayer definition of the enterprise. The hierarchical definition arranges the ABPs into coordination/control hierarchies. An ABP may control other ABPs and be controlled itself. The abstract business process hierarchy will be initially defined in this stage and augmented in the business operations plan (stage 5) and infrastructure objects definition (stage 7) stages of the enterprise modeling methodology.

The multilayer component of this step defines the abstraction layers of the enterprise. This step arranges the ABPs into a vertical series of strata, each of which represents an abstraction of expertise, authority, autonomy, knowledge, etc. The hierarchical definition may be part of this definition of the abstraction layers.

Hierarchical structure of the ABPs

We originally defined the hierarchical structure of the general system in Chapter 3. We refined the definition in Chapter 15 as it relates to the enterprise. Now we can use the ideas from these chapters to define the control/coordination hierarchy of the ABPs of our enterprise. Figure 21.4 shows the basic control/coordination hierarchy of the enterprise as well as its relationship to the subprocess ABPs.

In Figure 21.4, the enterprise is shown decomposed into the standard set of six major ABPs, labeled M&C (management and control), M (marketing), IL (inbound logistics), O (operations), S&S (sales and services) and OL (outbound logistics). As we have noted previously, the decomposition of an actual enterprise may have different names but these six functional areas must be performed by any enterprise. Also, as shown in Figure 21.4, each ABP is decomposed into its own set of six ABPs. The ABPs at any given level of decomposition will form a coordination/control hierarchy. Here are some rules of thumb that can be used to govern the definition of the control/coordination hierarchy of the enterprise or its ABPs:

- The management and control (M&C) ABP subprocess is a peer of the other five ABP subprocesses and its product will be directions delivered to the other five ABPs.

- The M&C ABP gives direction to its other five peer ABPs via their own M&C ABP. Thus the ABP at a higher level only talks to the M&C ABP of the lower levels and never directly to the other lower-level ABPs.

- Each of the other five ABPs gives performance feedback to its own M&C ABP and never directly to the M&C ABP at the higher level.

- Similarly, the marketing ABP (M) also gives direction to its peer ABPs and receives performance feedback from them but never to or from the lower level.

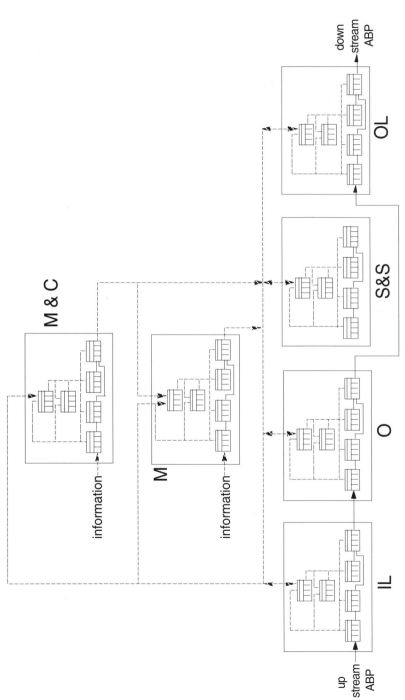

Figure 21.4 *Control/coordination hierarchy of the enterprise.*

Documenting the hierarchical structure of the enterprise

The hierarchical structure is documented in either a hierarchical diagram or an outline; each has its advantages. The hierarchical diagram is good for presenting the structure to an audience. On the other hand, an outline is the easiest to construct and keep up to date. Also, some diagramming tools allow a diagram to be constructed from the outline and vice versa. Here is an example of an outline:

ABP 1.0

    ABP 1.1

    ABP 1.2

    ABP 1.3

ABP 2.0

    ABP 2.1

        ABP 2.1.1

        ABP 2.1.2

    ABP 2.2

Abstraction layering of the ABPs

We originally defined the multilayer structure of the general system in Chapter 3 and refined the definition in Chapter 15 for the enterprise. Here are some rules of thumb that can be used to define the abstraction strata of the enterprise. Keep in mind that an enterprise can have many hierarchical-multilayer structures. Also, a given hierarchical-multilayer structure may apply only to parts of the enterprise:

- ◆ The starter set of structural patterns (Appendix A: Starter Set: Structural Patterns) can be used to guide the definition of the hierarchical-multilayer structures of the enterprise or its parts.

- ◆ The general structural patterns of abstraction, change, and time (see Appendix A) should be used as a starting point for structuring the enterprise into abstraction layers.

- ◆ The information structural patterns of information transfer time and information transfer quantity (see Appendix A) should be used to further clarify the information characteristics of the layering of the enterprise.

- ◆ The planning structural patterns of planning horizon and planning function (see Appendix A) should be used to characterize the planning characteristics of each layer of the enterprise.

◆ The infrastructure structural patterns of Infrastructure and infrastructure-product (see Appendix A) should be used to characterize the layers of an infrastructure-based enterprise, such as a telephone company.

◆ The resource usage structural patterns of allocation and brokerage (see Appendix A) may apply to the abstraction layers of the enterprise.

◆ The software family of structural patterns consisting of software, portability, reusability, and polymorphism (see Appendix A) may apply to the enterprise or help solve specific problems of its structuring.

◆ All enterprises have at least the three layers shown in Figure 15.7 consisting of:

> Level 1: Economics and Goals
>
> Level 2: Market Information Processing and Control
>
> Level 3: Production

Documenting the abstraction layers of the enterprise

The multilayer structure is documented using a layered diagram, such as the ones used in Appendix A. The diagram is accompanied with a text description that includes:

◆ **Name of abstraction layering**   Select a meaningful name for the layering in question.

◆ **Abstraction category**   Categorize the abstraction layering according to the starter set names. Also, expand the starter set as new structural patterns are revealed.

◆ **Layers**   Describe each layer as follows:

> Name of layer
>
> Description of layer

21.10 Metamodel: Enterprise model

The metamodel of the enterprise model (stage 4) identifies the major modeling entities created in this stage and their relations within the model. The metamodel is shown in Figures 21.5 and 21.6 in which modeling entities are shown as rectangles and their relations as diamonds. The modeling entities identified in other stages of the enterprise modeling methodology are shown as gray rectangles. The enterprise modeler invoking the enterprise modeling methodology will create an enterprise model which conforms to Figure 21.5 and 21.6. That is, the business entities and relations of the actual enterprise in question will conform to the modeling entities and relations shown in Figures 21.5 and 21.6.

21.11 Deliverables: Enterprise model

The enterprise model is delivered as a comprehensive document. It should be noted that the table of contents of the enterprise model document shown here is a generic set of deliverables and will change depending on the specific enterprise.

Table of Contents

- 1.0 Business Rule
  - 1.1 Functional Business Rules
  - 1.2 Structural Business Rules
  - 1.3 Behavioral Business Rules
- 2.0 Functional Business Model
  - 2.1 Functional Areas
  - 2.2 Business Functions
  - 2.3 Business Processes
- 3.0 Process Dependency Model
- 4.0 Business Events List
- 5.0 Abstract Business Processes Definition
- 6.0 Use Case Definition
- 7.0 Roles Definition
- 8.0 Abstract Business Process Flow Model
- 9.0 Hierarchical-Multilayer Structure of the Enterprise

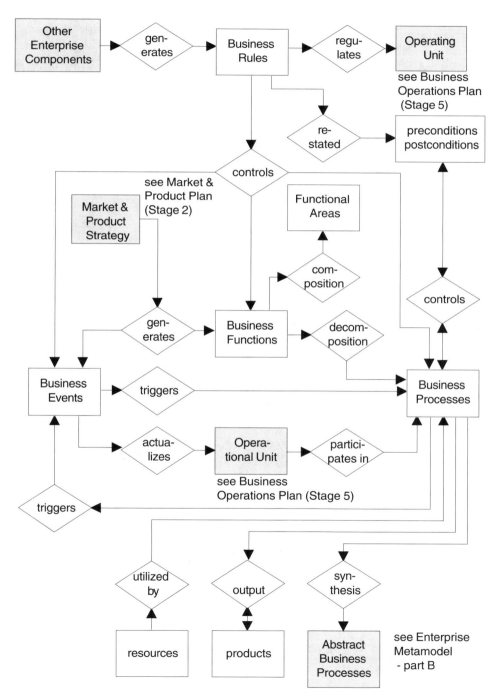

Figure 21.5 *Metamodel of the enterprise model (stage 4)—part A.*

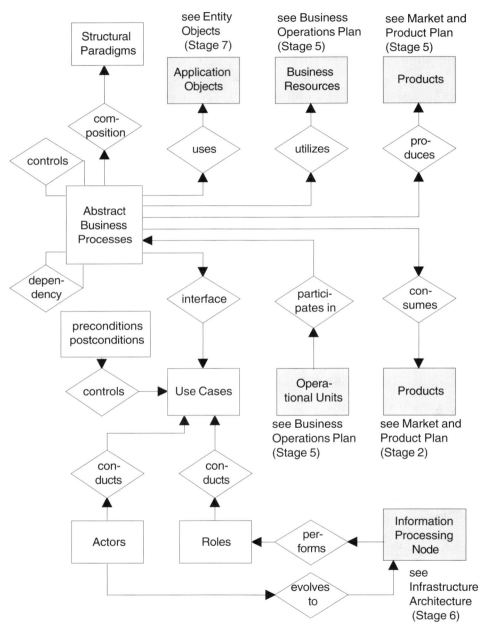

Figure 21.6 *Metamodel of the enterprise model (stage 4)—part B.*

Chapter 22

Business Operations Planning (Stage 5)

22.1 Introduction

Figure 22.1 provides a logical view of the business-operations-planning stage of the methodology.

The purpose of the business-operations-planning stage is to establish a pragmatic, real-world picture of how the business will perform the defined valued-added processes, the resources required to accomplish the processes, and, finally, how the enterprise will get from its present state to this desired future state of operations. In other words, operations planning establishes the details of how the enterprise will operate, what resources are required and how the enterprise will get from its current state to the intended state (a start-up plan for new enterprises, a transition plan for existing ones). The product of this process should be a cookbook for implementing and then running the enterprise.

22.2 Business operations planning methodology summary

Business operations planning is conducted in terms of ongoing or steady-state operations and of initial startup (a new business) or transition (an existing business) operations. The business operations plan is the product of this planning phase and presents the following from the perspectives of initial startup and ongoing activities:

◆ Functional and organizational structure

◆ Defined and prioritized resource requirements

future strategy business plan ®
Stage 5 — "Business Operations Planning"
Development Process

Hierarchal Analysis	Functional Business Structuring	Systems Requirements Definition	Resource Requirements Definitions	Asset Rquirements Definitiion

Mandates & Strategy

Product & Sales Plar

Pocess Model

     Control Structure

Use Cases

	Business Unit Definitions	Process Systems & Requirements	Resource Requirements Definitions	Process Flow Definition

Technolog. Architecture

Philosophy & Values

fsbp
Book 5

Organization & Structure	Operating Unit Structure	Business Systems Definition	Business Resource Requirements	Physical Asset Requirements

The Business Operations Plan

Figure 22.1 *Business operations plan (stage 5) content and development process.*

- ◆ Business support processes and systems and their inter-relationships

- ◆ Transition and growth strategies

The business operations plan is delivered as a document that can be used by managers responsible for actualizing the enterprise engineering plan. The operating plan for the enterprise is developed in two distinct phases. The first phase addresses the way that the business should eventually be operated. After having identified the desired operating approach, the second phase establishes a process for transition into and/or then growing the enterprise operations. The content and the development process associated with the business operations planning stage are shown in Figure 22.2.

22.3 Business operations planning interfaces

In the business operations plan, we finally generate the equivalent of the organization chart. We mention this specifically because efforts to define, or redefine, businesses frequently begin with reorganization or restructuring of the affected business. As noted in Chapter 8, it is only after discovering what value you intend to deliver to whom and how you will create that value that you can establish the organization and control structure appropriately.

Business operations planning depends on the previous results of the business definition (stage 1) and public policy strategy (stage 2). In particular, the business operations plan (stage 5) is the realization of the enterprise model (stage 4). That is the market and product plan (stage 2) proposes a line of business, which is realized by the enterprise model. The enterprise model is, in turn, actualized by the business operations plan.

Business operations planning occurs concurrently with infrastructure architecture planning (stage 6). These two processes are interconnected via an iterative feedback cycle that allows each process to accommodate the needs and capabilities of the other. The actual business operating structure will be dependent upon the capabilities and requirements of the physical infrastructure of the enterprise. The macro-issues of technology and other physical resources available to the enterprise will have been reflected in the aforementioned inputs to these stages. It is now that specific and finite definitions must be established.

The output of these phases is of sufficient depth and detail to support requests for bid for procurement and/or to support implementation. Such awards may be in the form of projects encompassing the discrete engineering, purchasing, and installation of infrastructure supporting a specific process or function.

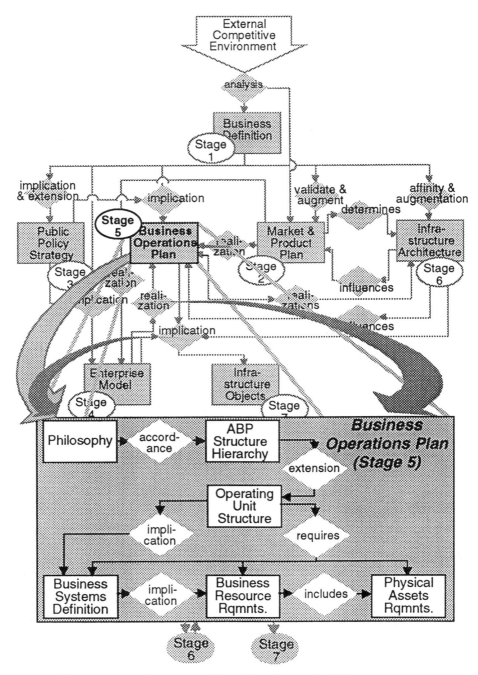

Figure 22.2 *Business operations planning methodology summary.*

22.4 Hierarchical analysis

The development of the enterprise model in stage 4 of the methodology defined the general hierarchy of the abstract business processes for the enterprise. The first step of business operations planning is to evaluate these hierarchical relationships between the functional processes and to interrelate them with a management governance philosophy that optimizes the enterprise's ability to achieve its objectives. These assessments are then used in the next step, which is to establish the operating or functional organization structure for the enterprise. The management governance philosophy will largely be directed by the strategic positions and mandates established in the business definition (stage 1) as well as by the policies established in the public policy strategy handbook (stage 3). The relationships between functional processes are established in the enterprise model from stage 4. We discuss individual procedures for establishing each in turn.

Organizational and structural philosophy

In Chapter 16, we defined *organization* as a group of information-processing nodes interconnected by authority relations. We also identified a list of functions of an organization. Those discussions were necessarily theoretical and derived from the concepts of general systems theory. Now we must establish the human aspects of organization. The next step in this business-operations-planning stage is to define the organizing philosophy of the enterprise. This will not only determine the interrelationships of processes and technology, but it will guide the finite sociologic and political relationships of involved human beings as well (this is another opportunity for finding and applying a fractal abstraction; an organization can sustain efficiency and flexibility when the same hierarchical control and organizing philosophies can be applied to people and machines).

An organizing philosophy is necessary to provide coherence and consistency in the operation of the value adding processes of the business. In addition, where there are more than one individual, there are often diverse opinions regarding appropriate and/or superior approaches to the management of such processes. Accordingly, the value system established for the enterprise must be used to establish and justify such an approach to management of the operations processes.

This involves reviewing the strategic mandates from the business definition stage, the detailed description of customer need in the target marketplace from the market plan, the temporal and logistical relationships between the various functions and processes associated with creating customer value in the use cases established in the enterprise model from stage 4. Ideas or concepts for structure are then introduced and evaluated based upon their ability to achieve desired results over time.

Three examples of philosophic ideas associated with structure and organization are:

◆ Empowerment (at any given time anyone can control the direction of enterprise resources)

◆ Customer control (of the process; he customers' use and consumption directly controls parts or all of the value added process)

◆ Strategic-capability focused (only core competency–derived value is provided by corporate resources; all else is gained via strategic relationships)

Five or six such principles thoughtfully derived from the circumstances and values of the organization will contribute greatly to the process of creating a functional and organizational structure for the enterprise.

Abstract business process structure hierarchy

In the discussion of general business foundations (Chapter 11), we referred to the self-similarity of all levels in an enterprise as an example of an abstraction that retains its validity independent of scale—in other words, a fractal. For example, we use the idea of self-similarity to describe the hierarchical multilayered architecture in the enterprise model process (stage 4). In that case, we define the hierarchical-multilayered architecture as a set of abstract business processes within other abstract business processes. At any level of decomposition, these abstract business processes are a recursion of the general abstract business process.

The business operations planning stage must identify a set of business operating principles that will continue to work at the various scales of the enterprise: the corporation, the business unit, the functional process, the technology infrastructure, the work group. and so on. Such principles will fall into the following two categories:

◆ **Structural** The generic structure of the enterprise introduced in Chapter 16 will be used to guide the definition of business operations structural principles. These structural principles can be used at all levels of enterprise decomposition. For example:

• Empowerment (at any given time anyone can control the direction of enterprise resources)

• Customer control (of the process—the customers' use and consumption directly controls parts or all of the value added processes of the enterprise)

♦ **Functional**   Business operations functional principles that can be used at any scale of the enterprise are closely related to the strategic imperatives and mandates developed during the business definition (stage 1). We synthesize the imperatives and mandates into business operations functional principles that apply to all levels of decomposition of the enterprise. For example:

- Strategic-capability focused (only core competency derived value is provided by enterprise resources—all other value is gained via strategic relationships)

- Distributed management of human resources (HR management is the responsibility of managers throughout the enterprise as opposed to being established as a separate entity or organization)

22.5 Operating unit structure

Given these philosophies, abstractions, and guidelines, an organization's structure is designed around the functional processes and operating strategies as if the business were in a steady-state operating mode. The organization structure will begin by establishing specific operating "units" of the enterprise. This, in turn, implies management requirements that are also identified and defined.

The organization structure is created in terms of business functions and/or processes (from the enterprise model) that will be included in each organizational entity. The degree of responsibility and control for each as well as intended metrics for determination effectiveness will be included as well. The ability to leverage and support the philosophies, abstractions, and guidelines provided are also discussed and presented here.

The specific responsibilities associated with each organizational domain and the functions and/or processes within each domain are developed and explained. This is done in conjunction with the abstract business process(es) that were provided as input from the last step. This facilitates the demonstration of consistent and harmonious governance of assets and resources in the creation and delivery of value to the marketplace.

22.6 Business systems definitions

From this point on, this stage of the methodology becomes one of grinding out the requirements and details necessitated by the preceding steps. The required skills for this stage are generally available and are consistent with what any good project manager exercises while establishing the requirements for a major project. When supported by the inputs and activities defined in the preceding steps, these tasks are readily satisfied by experienced resource managers This is not to say that they are trivial—just the opposite! This is a detail-intensive effort that is critical to understanding and realizing the real potential of the designed enterprise.

The business operations plan proceeds to definition of the business systems necessary to operate the enterprise model established earlier. Business systems are more global than the abstract business processes (although both are examples of general systems as introduced in Chapter 2). A given business system will touch several abstract business processes either directly or indirectly. An obvious example of a business system is an information processing computer system which touches many business processes. However, for business operating purposes, we consider manual or mechanized process or group of procedures to be both business systems.

All operational and managerial systems are highlighted here. These would include such things as accounting systems for asset management, accounts receivables and payables, payrolls; budget management systems; general systems for performance management, market perceptions and assessment, product development; operating systems supporting product maintenance, resource procurement, human resources utilization; and support systems for education and training, general marketing and enterprise image; etc.

Business systems will be supported in the global object space described in the infrastructure objects definition (stage 7). There, business systems are supported *and* implemented as application objects.

For now, we identify the business systems, describe them, and document their requirements. The work here will be revised many times by the other stages of the methodology.

- ◆ **Description** The description of a given business system includes the relationship of the business system to customer value; the intended contribution from each process or system to the enterprise's objectives and strategic mandates; how the system will relate to others, spatially as well as logically; and, most important, how each process will actually function.

- ◆ **Requirements** The requirements of a given business system include: the requirements for its management; the required people resources; any generic methods or process approaches; and the required tools and/or other necessary physical assets.

22.7 Business resource requirements

Given that we now have identified the processes and systems of the enterprise, we are now in a position to establish, in detail, the resources that will be required to perform them. We have divided these requirements into two general categories: human resources and physical assets. Each discussed briefly.

Human resource needs

For our purposes, human resources included everything to do with people within the business. This encompasses the job descriptions, position skill and education requirements, position site locations, quantities by position type, and any physical support requirements. It also includes an enterprise personnel policy.

This policy will include a discrete compensation plan for all employees tailored to maximize success with the strategic mandates, reflect and encourage the values or the enterprise, and accommodate the needs employees. Employee education, personal growth, organizational progression, and succession options are all accommodated and addressed in the human resources plans. Again, the matrix is an excellent tool for validating the effectiveness of developed alternatives in each of these areas.

Brief descriptions of every position are established based upon the requirements for the business processes established earlier in this stage. From these job descriptions, fundamental skill and background requirements are established and listed. These typically consist of one-page descriptions for both the job process and for the requirements.

The availability and acquisition costs of the appropriate human resources is determined and an acquisition plan established. The outlines of nontechnical management and operating management methods are developed, which will maximize the effectiveness of the functional enterprise model developed earlier in stage 4.

Physical asset requirements

Next, the major business resources are defined. Major business resources encompass the capital resources or infrastructure that will support the business processes as well as the consumable resources that are the grist for the process.

The infrastructure, or capital resources, consist of machinery and technology equipment and the real-estate assets within which the business or enterprise functions. The "what and how" of the technology infrastructure is defined in the infrastructure architecture stage (stage 6) of the methodology and occurs concurrent with this operations planning stage. Quantity and location of infrastructure specifics are developed here and correlated with the spatial or geographic aspects of the enterprise. Real-estate assets include buildings, office space, and special structures to house technology infrastructure such as transmission equipment or computer centers and are a special case of the business resource definition. These assets are defined in terms of capacity, siting, and unique functional requirements. Availability and cost are determined and a procurement strategy established. The output of this process is intended to be of sufficient detail that they can serve as the detailed requirements (when combined with the infrastructure architecture from stage 6) for the actual procurement, engineering, and construction of the enterprise's infrastructure facilities.

Consumable resources are used to support operation of the infrastructure or are physical elements or components of enterprise products. Consumable resources, their attributes and requirements, and where they are needed in the process are identified here. Each resource is defined in terms of quality, quantity, cost, and resource maintenance. The resources are placed in context of the procurement process defined earlier in the stage. This will validate that process while establishing tactical plans for the acquisition of each resource.

22.8 Implementation/transition planning

The business operations plan concludes with the startup or transition operating structure of the enterprise and a plan to transition to steady-state operations (this includes all of the elements provided with the steady-state operating plan). The transition or implementation plan consists of as many manageable and achievable programs and projects as are necessary for the defined business. Typically no single program or project will exceed a six-month development and implementation time frame. A general time-line of these activities and their associated resource requirements is developed and included in the business operations plan.

The transition plan requires a second iteration through this stage. The result is often more complex and has greater scale than the ongoing operating plan (this is particularly true of rediscovered enterprises). The tactics and strategies associated with creating or altering a business are frequently completely different from those associated with its eventual steady-state operation. Accordingly, the whole process must be approached as a different and new task from the original effort.

22.9 Metamodel: Business operations planning

The Operations Planning metamodel is illustrated in Figure 22.3.

22.10 Deliverables: Business operations planning

The business operations plans are delivered as a set of comprehensive documents. The following list is representative of the products from this stage. As always, note that this generic list will vary depending upon the specific enterprise being

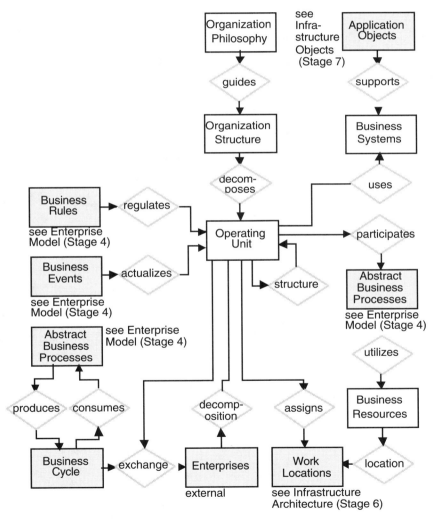

Figure 22.3 *Business operations planning metamodel.*

planned. Note also that there will be two sets of plans. Each contains the same general contents, but one is for a steady-state operating plan and the other is for an implementation or transition plan. The deliverables include:

1.0   Operating Philosophy (often added to Stage 3's Policy Handbook)

2.0   Abstract Business Processes

3.0   Enterprise Organization and Structure

         3.1   Organization Chart

         3.1   Management and Control Structure

4.0   Business Systems Definitions

5.0   Business Resource Requirements

         5.1   Human Resource Requirements

         5.2   Physical Resource Requirements

         5.3   Resource Procurement Plans

Chapter **23**

Infrastructure Architecture (Stage 6)

23.1 Introduction

The graphic representation of the processes and outputs from the infrastructure architecture development process are provided in Figure 23.1.

   This stage of the method establishes the physical characteristics of and relationships between the infrastructure elements of the enterprise. This infrastructure consists of everything that is the physical property of or is under the physical control of the subject enterprise. Every system has physical components and spatial reality. The enterprise system is no different. Accordingly, this stage of the process establishes an architecture defining the desired functional, logical, and spatial relationships and uses of the various infrastructure elements. The infrastructure architecture establishes these physical relationships for inclusion in the object-oriented enterprise model.

23.2 Infrastructure architecture methodology summary

Briefly, this portion of the process provides the following three things:

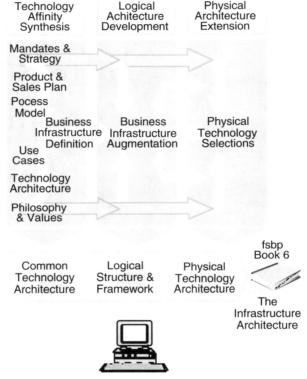

Figure 23.1 *Infrastructure architecture (stage 6) content and development process.*

- ◆ The design principles that have been and will continue to be applied to physical infrastructure elements

- ◆ The logical view of the distributed enterprise functions and conceptual principles for logical relationships between infrastructure elements

- ◆ The general physical view of the distributed enterprise and the spatial relationship constructs applied to infrastructure facilities

The Infrastructure architecture stage defines the technology architecture of the enterprise including its logical and physical views. Recall from Chapter 12 that every enterprise operating in a real physical world must have real and physical assets with which to conduct its business. We called these assets the enterprise's *physical infrastructure*. Remember also that an architecture is both the art or practice of designing and building structures (logical or physical) and a method or style of building. Accordingly, this stage attempts to take advantage of the opportunity to establish a "style" or architecture for this infrastructure that will contribute to an organization's attainment of sustainable competitive advantage.

The requirements of the infrastructure architecture are determined, in part, by the market and product plan and, at the same time, an emerging architecture also influences the market and product plan (phase 2). This will be especially true of an infrastructure-based enterprise. Similarly, the operations-planning phase is also supported by the architecture work. The infrastructure architecture is delivered as a comprehensive document.

The architecture team is most effective when composed of a group of three or four technology generalists—each an expert on a different, relatively broad front of technology. Their mission should be to establish technology design guidelines that will best support the strategic mandates, the fundamental strategies of the enterprise, the intended marketplace, and current and future product sets. Rationale should be required supporting all of the established guidelines. One or more guidelines should directly address every strategic mandate and the fundamental strategies of the enterprise.

This team of technologists should be formed during stage 2, market and product planning. They could even be useful in the business-definition stage. Their role is to provide input and support to those processes on as needed. This part-time support will continue with the operations planning in stage 5. The general constructs and parameters of the design architecture will begin to emerge during that stage. Indeed, decisions regarding product development and, subsequently, operations will be based upon this initial emerging architecture. This stage is about extending and expanding the initial architecture view that always evolves in the earlier stages.

Figure 23.2 shows the content and the development process associated with each of the steps in the infrastructure architecture stage relative to the overall methodology.

23.3 Developing common design principles

The infrastructure architecture begins with a definition of the design principles of the physical enterprise infrastructure. We have found that the most successful

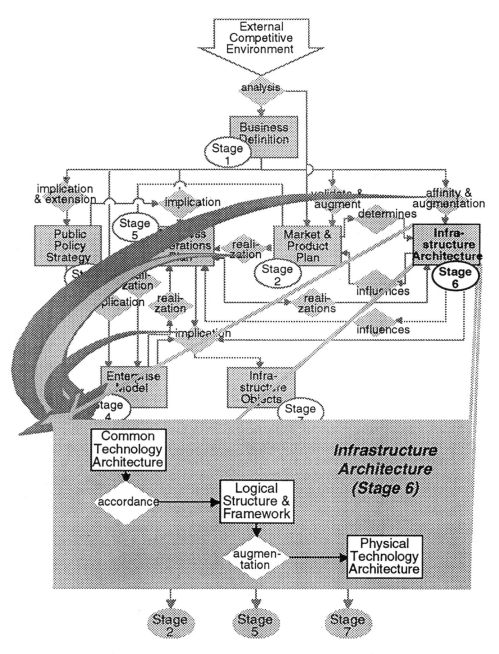

Figure 23.2 *Infrastructure architecture methodology (stage 6).*

design principle is one that stresses a single, unified, infrastructure that is organizationally, logically, and physically integrated. This is consistent with and supports our belief in the systems character of the enterprise environment. This philosophy will be very useful when considering the enterprise as a global object space, a topic of stage 7, infrastructure objects.

Other typical design principles might include such things as the degree of centralization or distribution of specific functional capabilities, the conditions that indicate the appropriate degree of centralization or distribution, and fundamental technology commitments (positive and negative). These are just a few generic examples. The important point to grasp is that the framework provided is just that—a guiding structure. It is not a cookbook that prescribes a solution for every possible situation. As such, the scope and scale of the design principles must be left to the discretion of the architecture team responsible for their development.

23.4 Establishing a logical infrastructure framework

Once the technology design constraints are established, the infrastructure architecture analysis proceeds to the definition of the logical structure (not physical, yet) and framework of the infrastructure of the distributed enterprise. In this view, the distributed enterprise consists of business units spread over geographical areas which may be large (e.g., national, international), or small (e.g., campus, a single building). Therefore, the logical structure and framework of the enterprise must address the infrastructure issues of these complex interconnections, paths, and nodes.

With these guidelines, we are addressing the view of the enterprise as an information processing network (as introduced in Chapter 4). This process results in an architecture for the accumulation, storage, management, and flow of information within the business. The requirements established in this information view differ from the technology design constraints in that these are technology independent. The hierarchical control and management of information is established here. Those fundamental issues associated with the theories introduced in Part 1 of this book are evaluated relative to the unique needs and requirements of the subject enterprise. General rules for information usage that maximize the enterprise's advantages are created by the architecture team.

23.5 Creating the geographic infrastructure architecture

The infrastructure architecture concludes with a physical technology view. This view will define the capabilities, technology families, and actual locations of major components of the physical infrastructure. This is in essence a topology of the infrastructure facilities contained within the business.

Given the guidelines for technology design and logical information structure necessary to maximize the opportunities of the organization, this portion of the methodology begins to look more directly at the actual implementation of the business's physical assets. Considerations of specific technology product alternatives, actual site requirements, general human interface opportunities, and anticipated maintenance demands are assessed independently and as a whole. The architecture team will typically employ support from various technology and infrastructure providers to assist in the synthesis of a physical deployment topology model.

A significant component of the physical technology architecture will be an evaluation of its future evolution and a definition of change capabilities. This is an exercise in understanding the vision created for the enterprise and anticipating its probable future needs. It is not about predicting the future or what technology will or won't offer tomorrow. Establishing the business' future infrastructure needs is essential to assuring that providers can deliver the necessary capabilities when needed.

23.6 Metamodel: Infrastructure architecture definition

The metamodel for the infrastructure architecture process depicts the processes and products of this stage. The metamodel (see Figure 23.3) also shows the interrelationships between these products and the other stages of the overall methodology (the gray rectangles).

23.7 Deliverables and conclusions: Infrastructure architecture definition

The deliverables from the infrastructure architecture stage are provided in two forms. One is a comprehensive internal business document providing the rationale and logic for the guidelines in terms of enterprise strategic mandates and strategy. The other is as a traditional physical requirements guide for vendors and suppliers use in designing specific infrastructure implementation solutions.

The contents of the architecture for either deliverable would appear as follows:

◆ Technology design principles of the enterprise infrastructure

◆ Logical information infrastructure view of the enterprise

◆ Physical infrastructure topology view of the distributed enterprise

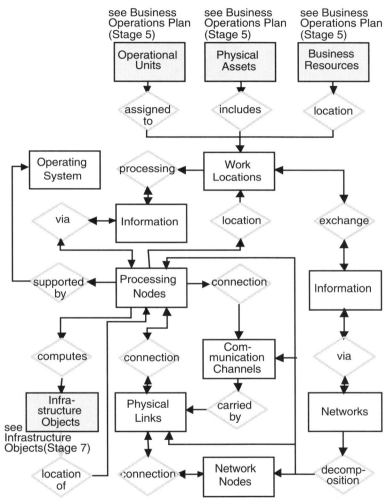

Figure 23.3 *Metamodel of infrastructure architecture definition.*

In conclusion, it is worth noting that this work must be suitable for inclusion in requests for proposals (RFPs) on infrastructure projects from outside and internal organizations. This architecture will provide a significant portion of the requirements for such requests in addition to establishing a infrastructure advantageous to the unique needs of the enterprise.

Chapter 24

Infrastructure Objects Definition (Stage 7)

24.1 Introduction

Once the enterprise model (stage 4), business operations plan (stage 5), and infrastructure architecture (stage 6) are developed, the enterprise modeling methodology enters its last stage, defining the infrastructure objects. This last stage integrates the previous six stages of the enterprise-modeling methodology into a coherent object-oriented environment. Figure 24.1 provides a quick look at the steps, processes, and products from this final stage of our enterprise modeling methodology.

The reason for spending time on the enterprise's object-oriented environment comes from two motivations: a modeling motivation and an information-systems planning motivation of the proposed enterprise. The enterprise modeling motivation arises from our ongoing task in this enterprise modeling methodology to produce an enterprise model using the object-oriented paradigm. At this point, we have completed the first six stages of the enterprise modeling methodology, giving us the details of the enterprise. Now we model the enterprise using the object-oriented paradigm with the constructs implied by these first six stages. This will allow us to finalize the output of our enterprise model in terms of enterprise objects, formally described in this stage. These objects will attempt to capture the enterprise's structural, functional, and behavioral characteristics so that we can better reason about it. The preceding stages of the methodology will have produced the raw material for this definition.

The information systems planning motivation arises because it is our intention that the enterprise will be implemented using object-oriented software technology. In the implementation of the enterprise, the software objects of the enterprise will exist in a global object space (GOS), which is described (i.e., for information-systems planning purposes) in this stage of the methodology.

In producing the work of this infrastructure objects definition stage, these two motivations, enterprise modeling and information systems planning, are intertwined. Keeping these two motivations in mind, the main work of this stage includes the following:

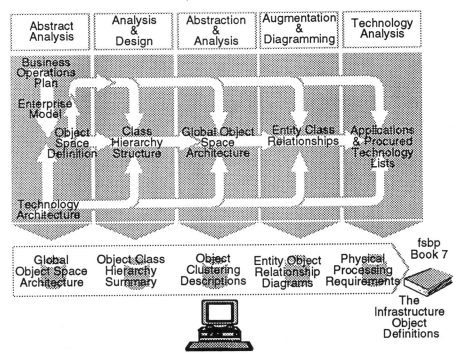

future strategy business plan®
Stage 7 — "Infrastructure Objects Definition"
Development Process

Figure 24.1 *Infrastructure objects definition (stage 7).*

◆ This stage defines the enterprise modeling class hierarchy that will be used to produce an object-oriented model of the enterprise. Later, during software development, these modeling classes will be the forerunners of the software classes which implement the enterprise. For now, they are used to complete the enterprise model and state it in terms of the object-oriented paradigm.

◆ An important component of the enterprise modeling class hierarchy will be the entity class hierarchy. The entity classes used in modeling the enterprise will, for the most part, translate either directly or indirectly into abstract software classes later during the software implementation of the enterprise. The entities of the enterprise are the basis for its information model, which is produced as part of the information systems planning deliverable of this stage. That is, physical enterprise entities will have information surrogates that must be put into a proper information model as a component of information-systems planning. This stage defines the abstract entity classes and their relations as a separate model. In effect, this will serve as the traditional enterprise data model.

◆ This stage also describes the GOS as it will be implemented eventually during software development (i.e., which occurs later as a separate project but uses the object-oriented enterprise model as its starting requirements). We also consider the description of the GOS to be a component of the information-systems planning deliverable. The description of the GOS will include its hierarchical-multilayered architecture, which will also exhibit characteristics of a heterarchy as explained in Chapter 16. The major organizational component of the working GOS will be the software business process objects, which are instantiated from abstract business process (ABP) classes. A description of the major applications needed by the enterprise will be included as well.

◆ Also included will be a description of the major procured-technology components of the GOS such as the foundation classes and distributed object technology.

24.2 Infrastructure objects definition methodology summary

Figure 24.2 summarizes stage 7's step-by-step development of the infrastructure objects definition. This figure can be used as a reference to the material that follows.

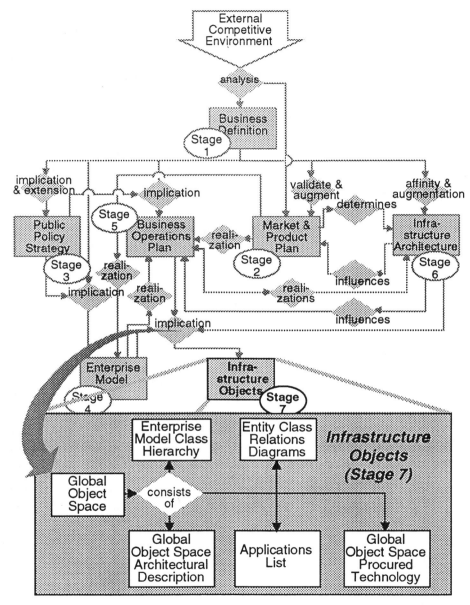

Figure 24.2 *Infrastructure objects definition methodology summary (stage 7).*

24.3 Infrastructure objects definition interfaces

The infrastructure objects definition stage is concerned with the behavioral perspective of the enterprise. In Chapter 2, we presented the three ways of looking at a general system, namely a functional view, a structural view and a behavioral view. The infrastructure objects definition is related to the other stages of the enterprise modeling methodology as shown in Figure 24.2. We see that the infrastructure objects definition (stage 7) uses the work of the enterprise model (stage 4), business operations plan (stage 5), and infrastructure architecture (stage 6) as its initial input. in this final stage of the enterprise modeling methodology, we integrate the other stages.

24.4 Global object space architectural description

The prize we're after is the eventual implementation of the enterprise as a total object-oriented environment. That is, the entire working enterprise, including all of its functions, behavior, and structure, would be implemented using the paradigm of object orientation. The objects of the enterprise will live in the global object space (GOS), which we described in Chapter 16. The architecture of the GOS is one of the important information systems planning deliverables in this last stage of enterprise modeling.

Software objects and physical objects

Recall that there are two flavors of enterprise objects: information-representation objects (software) and physical objects. Both will be intermingled in the GOS. Information-representation objects exist as information and are surrogates for physical or abstract objects. They are the software objects of the enterprise that come about through object-oriented software development. Obviously, the information-representation objects of enterprise modeling can be translated into software objects using an appropriate object-oriented software development methodology in a fairly straightforward manner. However, the GOS will also contain the nonsoftware objects of the enterprise, that is, the physical objects that will also be designed, implemented, and managed as objects using the object-oriented paradigm.

Physically, the GOS of an operational enterprise consists of three components: a software object class library, enterprise objects themselves (both software and physical), and relations among the enterprise objects. In effect, the global object space accounts for the operational object orientation of the enterprise: the enterprise object class library provides the mechanism for generating the enterprise objects, which through time will form and withdraw relations with each other as the

enterprise operates. We refer to this evolution of life cycle of objects and their relations as CRUD (create, read, update, delete). In effect, the operations of the enterprise is completely accounted for by the CRUD of its objects and their relations.

In the case of physical objects, there is not a literal generation of them from
the class library. Rather, when a physical object becomes reality in the enterprise
(i.e., it is procured or constructed), its underlying concept will be defined by an
appropriate class in the class library. However, physical objects and relations will
be described in terms of CRUD, just like software objects and relations.

Architecture of the GOS

Thus an overall deliverable of this stage of the enterprise modeling methodology is
a definition of the architecture of the global object space. Notice that at this point,
we are using the GOS as a conceptual structure for information systems planning.
Later, it will (i.e., could) evolve to the central operational component of the enterprise during implementation, as explained earlier. The importance of the architecture of the GOS is clear: the implementation phase will include both software
development and nonsoftware development, all organized around the architecture
of the GOS. Thus the architecture of the GOS is a critical deliverable.

Developing the GOS architecture

The GOS architecture will be developed iteratively by the interaction of the various
steps of this stage. Here are some rules of thumb and pragmatic advice on developing the GOS architecture:

- ◆ The GOS architecture is essentially a structural description and draws on
  Chapter 15. The GOS will implement the hierarchical-multilayer structure
  of the enterprise. Appendix A presents a starter set of structural patterns
  which can be used in this work.

- ◆ The GOS will be defined in terms of its conceptual layering and functionality
  within each layer. An important part of this layering is the hierarchical
  organization of the abstract business processes (APBs) initially defined in
  the enterprise model (stage 4) and enhanced in the business operations plan
  (stage 5). Recall that the ABPs implement the value chains of the enterprise.

- ◆ The architecture of the GOS will include significant procured technology
  components, which are defined later in this chapter.

Documenting the GOS architecture

The architecture deliverable will be in the form of text and diagrams, which will
include the following:

♦ **Description of the GOS operation**   This will be a text description of the GOS operation intended to convey the concept of the GOS. It will give the flavor of how the GOS will operate and will facilitate the communication of the GOS concept. We presented a description of a generic GOS in Chapter 16, which can be used to get started.

♦ **Description of the GOS hierarchical-multilayer structure.**   The GOS will probably have several hierarchical-multilayer substructures. Each should be documented as a diagram and corresponding text description. The layered diagrams of Appendix A will be useful here.

24.5 Enterprise modeling class hierarchy

Another deliverable of this stage of the enterprise modeling methodology is a description of the enterprise modeling object class hierarchy. Like the GOS architecture, this is also an all-encompassing deliverable that is not constructed as an isolated unit of work. Rather, the development of this deliverable will be done by iteration among the various steps of this stage of the enterprise modeling methodology and other stages as well.

Using the enterprise modeling class hierarchy

The enterprise modeling class hierarchy defines the inheritance hierarchies of classes found in the enterprise model. Inheritance, defined in Chapter 5, is very important because it allows reusability of concepts. In summary, inheritance permits classes to be defined in terms of existing classes in which the definition of attributes and behavior are reused. The new class is called a *subclass* and the existing class is called a *superclass*. A new subclass is given the definition of its superclass, which can then be added to or modified to define the new class. Classes are placed in a enterprise modeling class hierarchy.

The enterprise modeling methodology creates a model of the enterprise, which will later be designed and constructed (e.g., by letting RFPs or commissioning projects within the enterprise). The classes of the enterprise modeling class hierarchy that we define at this early point will find their way into the software development projects as a starting point for the software classes. Thus the work we do now will organize and clarify the future work that is needed to actually build the enterprise.

However, we shouldn't overestimate the usefulness of the classes in the enterprise modeling class library. These classes are used to make a model of the enterprise and to make the work of modeling the enterprise easier and more versatile by permitting the use of standardized building blocks. The concepts behind the modeling classes will hopefully be transferable to the software development class libraries.

Enterprise modeling classes starter set

Appendix B contains a starter set of enterprise modeling classes. The enterprise modeler should update this starter set for the specific needs of the enterprise in question. The following sections define and discuss the families of classes of the enterprise-modeling class hierarchy.

Process classes

The dynamics of the enterprise comes from its processes. In enterprise modeling, we model processes using our hierarchy of process classes, which are defined in the enterprise-modeling class hierarchy. Recall that our enterprise-modeling methodology generalizes the business process into a generic structure we call the *abstract business process* (ABP), as described in Chapter 14. The ABP classes will be used to model the upper-level abstract business processes of the enterprise.

Another branch of the process class hierarchy is the process-element classes intended to represent elementary (i.e., lowest-level) processes. Elementary processes differ from ABPs in that they do not have a complement of the standard set of six ABP subprocesses as described in Chapter 21. In the enterprise modeling class hierarchy of Appendix B, we have identified a number of process element classes that represent useful definitions of finite enterprise activities. These process element classes can be used as the subprocesses of more complex processes until eventually the level of the ABP is built up from reusable parts.

Entity classes

The entity classes we will define are for the real-world objects corresponding to the physical, abstract, and information entities of the enterprise. They are the machines, people, materials, orders, or business records that combine to accomplish the mandates and imperatives of the enterprise. The entity objects can take advantage of inheritance to simplify their definition. The entity classes are revealed by the other stages of the methodology.

Concept of clusters

To simplify the modeling project, the classes and corresponding objects of the enterprise can be organized into clusters. Clustering is a way to partition and abstract the problem domain such as the one proposed here. Clustering is applicable to both the construction of the enterprise modeling class hierarchy as well as to the information-systems-planning deliverable. Thus we will introduce clustering here as it relates to the enterprise modeling class hierarchy but also refer to it later in this chapter when we discuss aspects of the information-systems-planning deliverables.

Clustering takes advantage of the fact that objects in a working object-oriented system tend to fall into groups that are interconnected with one another by many relationships. By contrast, relatively few relationships connect objects in different clusters. Since objects are instantiated from classes, it is the classes and their relations that will be used to define clusters. Clustering gets its intellectual clout from several sources:

◆ First, clustering is the adaptation of H. A. Simon's concept of nearly decomposable systems (Simon, 1981) introduced in Chapter 2. According to Simon, for the generic system consisting of a series of subsystems that, in turn, consist of their own components, the frequency of interaction of the various components within a subsystem is much greater than the interaction between the subsystems themselves. Therefore, we can use Simon's concept of nearly decomposable systems to assert that classes of an object environment ought to fall into clusters of intense interaction as realized by their relations with each other. For now, we are not attempting to define these subsystems referred to by Simon. Rather, we are using the ideas of Simon, to acknowledge the natural relations of objects in any modeling domain including the enterprise.

◆ Second, clustering is the recognition of expertise. That is, a given cluster tends to have its own set of people who are experts in the underlying subjects of the cluster.

◆ Third, clustering is a way of organizing the work of designing and developing an object environment. The classes and corresponding objects of a cluster represent concepts from the same discipline or expertise. Thus the classes of a cluster would be the responsibility of the same modelers, and later, designers or implementors.

Notice that we are not using the idea of clustering as a structural view of the enterprise at this point; we are using clusters as a structural view of the classes of the enterprise, which is very different. We have already discussed at length the main structural organization of the classes of an object environment, that of the inheritance hierarchy of classes and subclasses (i.e., the enterprise class library). Clusters are another way of structuring the classes based on their interrelations. The categorization of a given class into a given cluster is done on the basis of the relative intensity that the class has with the other classes of the cluster. That is, the classes of a given cluster seem to be related to each other and the intensity of these relations is the main criteria for defining a cluster. On the other hand, a given class of a cluster will have relatively fewer relations with classes in other clusters.

Another factor about clusters is that the classes used to create the objects of a cluster will also tend to be related in the class hierarchy. This natural property of clusters helps to organize the work (i.e., project management) of designing, developing, and maintaining the enterprise class library. The classes of a cluster can usually be organized into their own branches of the inheritance hierarchy of the enterprise class library because they tend to deal with the same domain concepts. A given cluster will probably represent several of the branches of the class subhierarchies that can be developed and maintained as a unit from a project-management standpoint. In this way, the classes of a cluster can probably take advantage of inheritance in which related abstract classes are specialized into lower-level classes. This will provide opportunities for reuse of enterprise-modeling concepts.

While we warned earlier that we are not using clusters as another structural view of the enterprise (i.e., for purposes of enterprise modeling), we will use clusters to organize work that will result in artifacts having structural implications. In particular, one of our main uses of clusters is to organize and define the applications of the enterprise. Applications are not a structural view of the enterprise, but they have structural implications. Applications will be discussed later in this chapter, but for now it is easy to see how clusters will help to define applications. By recognizing that if a cluster represents a locus of relations, it must also represent a locus of interaction, we ought to organize our applications in terms of clusters. Also, we will use clusters to help us organize the work of defining the enterprise modeling class hierarchy as well as the enterprise class-relations diagram. All of these will be explained later in the chapter.

Generic enterprise clusters

Most enterprises will have at least the following generic clusters of their enterprise classes. This list can be used as a starting point for defining the clusters of the target enterprise. As noted above, the boundary of a cluster is based on the sparse relations between the classes of the cluster and the classes of other clusters. However, this is an imperfect criteria often requiring good judgment. Also, some of the clusters have classes with relatively more relations with the classes of other clusters which we have pointed out below as applicable. This means that a class might legitimately be classified in either of the clusters and where it actually ends up is a subjective call.

- ◆ **Enterprise cluster**   This represents the cluster of classes that will be used to describe the overall enterprise and its management. This cluster will include classes for the business planning and goal setting of the enterprise. Also included will be classes to define the enterprise's organizational structure and corresponding budgets.

- ◆ **Legal cluster**   This cluster of classes will include classes for the legal and public policy functions of the company such as contracts, permits, licenses, public policies, etc.

- **Marketing cluster**   This cluster will include classes for the marketing function of the enterprise. Included will be classes for product usage history, product service history, product sales history, and customer profiles. Various classes of this cluster will have relations with the production planning classes of the production cluster.

- **Accounting cluster**   This cluster will include the classes for the money accounting to run the business. Included will be classes to manage accounts payables, accounts receivables, cost accounting, payroll accounting, and financial accounting.

- **Customer cluster**   This cluster will include the classes for the enterprise's customers and the sales/service/order/dispatch function of the enterprise. This cluster will include classes for current, past, and prospective customers. Also, this cluster will include classes to define customer business profiles. For an infrastructure company (e.g., a telephone company) this cluster will include classes to define customer deployed products and corresponding consumption data and service results. Various classes of this cluster will have relations with the accounts receivable classes of the accounting cluster.

- **Production cluster**   This cluster would be where the unique classes of the enterprise's operations (i.e., producing its end products) would be placed. From a generic standpoint, this cluster will include classes for production requirements and production planning (i.e., capacity management) as well as production control. Also included will be classes for materials flow within the enterprise.

- **Product cluster**   This cluster will include the classes for the products offered by the enterprise. This cluster will include classes to define product capabilities, product sales statistics, product rate structure, and sales strategies for the product. It will include classes to describe product types (generic products). For an infrastructure company, it will include classes for deployed products with relations to various classes of the infrastructure cluster.

- **Procurement cluster**   This cluster includes classes for the enterprise's vendors and purchasing function. Included will be classes defining current purchase orders, received goods, inspection and storage of goods, and vendor history.

- **Employee cluster**   This cluster includes the classes to manage the human resources of the enterprise. It will be used to manage the past, present, and prospective employees of the company. Included will be classes for employee skills, training, and job assignments, both current and historical. Various classes of this cluster will have relations with various classes of the payroll accounting of the accounting cluster.

- **Infrastructure cluster**   This cluster includes classes for the enterprise's physical infrastructure such as buildings, networks, campuses, and other assets. This cluster will also include related classes such as procedures (to work on the infrastructure units), and activities (historical events that occur to the infrastructure units). For an infrastructure company, this cluster will include both the physical infrastructure as well several closely related classes used to define functional aspects of the physical infrastructure of the enterprise. For an infrastructure company, the later classes will have relations with various classes of the product cluster.

Developing the enterprise modeling class hierarchy

The enterprise modeling class hierarchy will be developed iteratively by the interaction of the various steps of this stage. Here are some rules of thumb and pragmatic advice:

- **Clusters**   The work of defining the enterprise modeling class hierarchy can be organized around the clusters. This may involve discovering and fine-turning the clusters themselves as the work proceeds.

- **Subclassing**   Use the starter set of enterprise modeling classes given in Appendix B to create subclasses of the enterprise modeling classes.

- **Infrastructure stage (stage 6)**   This stage of the enterprise modeling methodology will contain a wealth of information on enterprise modeling classes. Each physical component of the infrastructure architecture will lead to one or more corresponding entity classes. Figure 24.4 at the end of this chapter shows a summary of the classes that can be derived by abstraction from the other stages of the methodology.

- **Business operations planning (stage 5)**   This stage of the enterprise modeling methodology will also imply classes for our budding enterprise modeling class hierarchy as shown in Figure 24.4. These classes will include the organizational and resource entity classes as well as the entities of the business systems (management procedures, job positions, methods, tools, etc.).

Documenting the enterprise-modeling class hierarchy

The enterprise-modeling class hierarchy deliverable will be in the form of text and diagrams that include the following:

◆ **Class hierarchy diagrams**   The easiest way to create a class hierarchy diagram is to draw it in several diagrams, making it as modular as possible. A hierarchy of diagrams is created in which each diagram shows only two or three levels of the hierarchy. Lower-level diagrams take off where upper-level diagrams leave off to show the next couple of levels of specialization.

◆ **Text description**   Each class is described in text form and includes the following:

Name: name of class.

Superclass: name of superclass.

Subclasses: names of subclasses of the class.

Attributes: description of the nature of the information that would be retained by an object instantiated from this class. Where possible, a list of actual attributes and their descriptions would be desirable (but not necessary).

Behavior: description of the major dynamics that objects of this class would have. Where possible, state-transition diagrams (described in Chapter 16) would be desirable (but not necessary).

Cluster: identify the cluster to which the class is assigned

24.6 Entity class-relations diagram

An important part of the definition of the information systems planning deliverable of this stage of the enterprise modeling methodology is the entity class-relations diagram. This diagram was originally presented in Chapter 8 and will, in effect, be a conceptual data model of the enterprise showing the major classes of entities and their relations.

Developing the entity class-relations diagram

The entity class-relations diagram will be developed iteratively by the interaction of the various steps of this stage. Here are some rules of thumb and pragmatic advice:

◆ The entity class-relations diagram is drawn for the working enterprise as if it were in operation. The enterprise, like any general system, will have a characteristic steady state that is captured in this diagram.

◆ The entity class-relations diagram shows only the major entity classes and their relations with other major entities. This is because it is very general and shows only the concepts of the enterprise entities and their relations for information systems planning purposes.

- The entity class-relations diagram is philosophically similar to an entity-relations diagram of classic data modeling except that it shows classes rather than entity types.

Documenting the entity class-relations diagram

The entity class-relations diagram deliverable will be in the form of a diagram as described in Chapter 8. Its characteristics include the following:

- Each major entity is drawn as a node and its relations as lines.

- Clustering can be used to simplify the diagram and, if appropriate, present it hierarchically (i.e., the top diagram shows the clusters that are decomposed into entity class-relations diagrams).

- Arrowheads on the relation lines can be used to show the general cardinality of the relation as either a "many occurrences" (arrowhead) or just "one occurrence" (no arrowhead). Notice that there is no attempt to capture the actual cardinality of the relation or the optional-mandatory nature of the relation since we are only diagramming at the conceptual level.

24.7 Applications list

As part of the information systems planning deliverable, the functionality of the major applications of the enterprise is summarized at this point. Applications were introduced and defined in Chapter 16. In summary, an application is an object in the Global Object Space that provides direct human intervention of the normal automatic workings of the process objects of the enterprise. Humans must always be able to view and change the objects of the working enterprise. Applications allow navigation and updating of the enterprise objects within the discipline of business rules.

Characteristics of applications

Applications are objects in which the services send messages to invoke processing in other objects. Applications provide a user interface that, in effect, gives the user a window into the global object space. Applications will have the following characteristics:

- **Thread of control** Applications are high-level control objects that send various combinations of messages to other objects for setting them into action. Applications have their own thread of control. The thread of control in an application consists entirely of objects interacting through messages. These other objects will, in turn, send messages to yet other objects causing complex processing. However, the thread of control inevitably will return to the application object where ultimate control is vested.

◆ **User interface**   Applications will present the user interface to the external human invoking the application. The user interface will be implemented using the foundation classes described shortly.

◆ **Editing other objects**   Besides being a window, applications are editing tools that change, create, or destroy the objects of the GOS. As an editing tool, an application is used to disturb the natural state (resulting from normal business processes) of the objects in the GOS by either changing their attributes or changing their structural relations.

◆ **Proxy objects**   Applications will send messages to the proxy objects to communicate with the external objects outside of the GOS. Messages will be sent to retrieve information or to cause processing or updating of the external objects.

◆ **Physical objects**   Applications will send messages to the physical objects (e.g., physical information-processing nodes) of the GOS to access or update their information.

Developing the applications list
Here are some rules of thumb and pragmatic advice for developing the applications list:

◆ Applications should be defined to view and change all major enterprise objects of the GOS.

◆ The applications list can be developed by considering the object clusters described previously. An application will fall within a cluster, leveraging the expertise of that cluster.

Documenting the applications
Each application in the applications list should be documented as follows:

◆ **Name**   Name of Application

◆ **Description**   Include a paragraph describing what the application does.

24.8 Global object space–procured technology

The infrastructure objects definition (stage 7) completes the information systems planning deliverable with a description of the procured technology of the GOS.

This will not be a brand-name list but descriptions of generic technology products that will provide key components of the GOS for purposes of technology planning as described in this section.

Foundation classes

The software objects of the GOS can take advantage of industry foundation classes. These object classes represent the utilitarian, or common, components of any enterprise. They are used by other objects and originate as procured libraries or are designed and constructed by the enterprise itself with the intention of building reusable assets. One important set of foundation classes are the user-interface classes summarized earlier. We will define and summarize the foundation classes in the procured technology sections of the delivered documentation.

Distributed object management environment

A component of the infrastructure object environment that must be defined is the technical capabilities of the distributed object management environment. For many enterprises, the distributed object management environment will be implemented using an object-oriented database management system (ODBMS) as an integral component. The ODBMS will allow the objects of the GOS (i.e., the complete set of software objects) to be distributed transparently across the various computer processors of the enterprise defined in the infrastructure architecture (stage 6) stage.

Here are some specific technical capabilities that must be provided by the distributed object management environment. We can assume for now during enterprise modeling (at the minor risk of being proved wrong later) that the distributed object management environment will be provided by an off-the-shelf ODBMS to implement the GOS. The following minimum technical capabilities must be provided by the ODBMS to support the GOS concept:

- **Persistent software objects**   The ODBMS must positively guarantee the safekeeping of software objects.

- **Distribution**   The ODBMS will support distributed objects. Objects can be stored on various computer processors of the hardware substrate of the GOS. The ODBMS must allow them to be accessed transparently. The distributed objects will appear as a single object space to the other objects in the GOS.

- **Object-oriented programming language**   The ODBMS will support a complete object-oriented programming language.

♦ **Transactions**   The ODBMS will provide transactions (keeping the database in a logically consistent state over sequences of updates).

♦ **Versions and configurations**   The ODBMS will support update integrity including object versions (ability to track multiple versions of an object) and object configurations (logical sets of mutually consistent object versions).

♦ **Concurrency**   The ODBMS will provide concurrency control (mediation of simultaneous access). The ODBMS will support object locking. Locks will be placed any time an object is updated to prevent concurrent updates.

♦ **Security**   The ODBMS will support security. Security means that a user cannot access data for which they have no authorization.

♦ **Physical grouping**   The ODBMS will support object physical grouping. This is the capability of optimizing the location of objects on a distributed network for performance reasons.

♦ **Query language**   The ODBMS will provide a query language that may be used for ad hoc operations by humans.

♦ **Fault-tolerant object management**   The ODBMS will support transparent management of critical objects requiring fault-tolerant operation.

Developing the global object space–procured technology
Here are some rules of thumb and pragmatic advice:

♦ The procured technology definition will probably require the use of specialized technical expertise.

♦ The procured technology definition will be related to the definition of computer and network assets defined in the infrastructure architecture (stage 6) stage.

Documenting the global object space–procured technology
The global object space–procured technology deliverable will be in the form of text and will include the following:

♦ **Description of each technology component**   The description of the technology component should include the external (black box) capabilities that it should provide to the GOS.

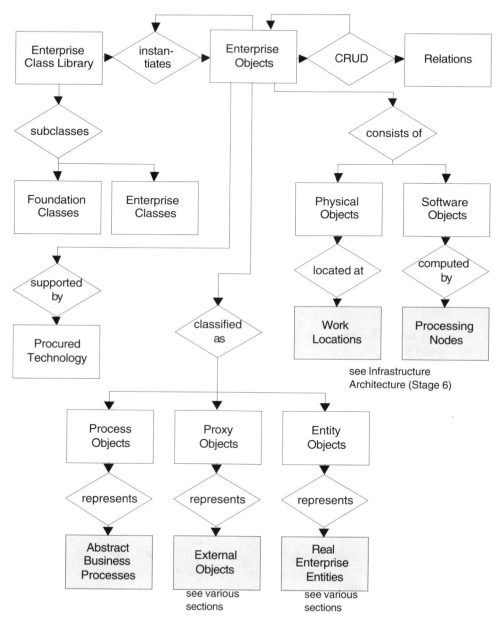

Figure 24.3 *Metamodel: infrastructure objects definition.*

◆ **Description of integration**   The description of the technology component should include how it will actually be integrated into the GOS considering that it is coming from an outside vendor. This description must focus on satisfying the published interface to the technology component from both a systems-integration and a project-management standpoint.

24.9 Metamodel: Infrastructure objects definition

The metamodel of the infrastructure objects definition (Figure 24.3) identifies the major business entities, which are modeled in this stage, and their relations. The metamodel Figure 24.3 represents the relations among the business entities as diamonds. The modeling process will use these entities and their relations to construct the specific infrastructure objects definition of the target enterprise. The business entities identified in other stages of the enterprise modeling methodology are shown as gray boxes, while the entities identified in this stage are shown as clear boxes.

24.10 Deliverables: Infrastructure objects definition

The infrastructure objects definition will be delivered as a comprehensive document with the following generic table of contents:

1.0		Global Object Space Architecture
	1.1	Description of Operation
	1.2	Description of the GOS Hierarchical-Multilayer Structure
2.0		Description of Object Clusters
	2.1	Enterprise Cluster
	2.2	Legal Cluster
	2.3	Marketing Cluster
	2.4	Accounting Cluster
	2.5	Customer Cluster
	2.6	Production Cluster
	2.7	Product Cluster
	2.8	Procurement Cluster

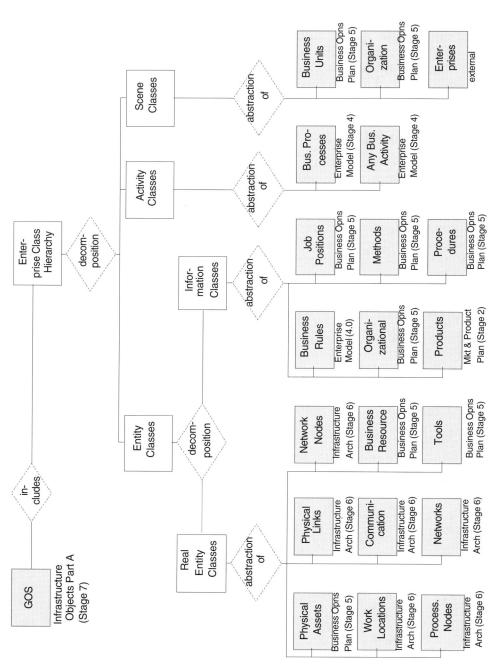

Figure 24.4 *Deriving enterprise classes from the other stages.*

Part 6

Conclusions

Introduction to Part 6

THIS LAST PART IS THE CONCLUSION to the book and consists of two chapters:

- ◆ Chapter 25 attempts to explain the relation between enterprise modeling and software development. We will see that enterprise modeling creates the global "what" and software development creates one aspect of the specific "how" of the enterprise.

- ◆ Chapter 26 is the conclusion of the book. We will attempt to draw together the major points of the book.

Chapter **25**

Enterprise Modeling Meets Software Engineering

25.1 Introduction

This chapter discusses the relationship between enterprise modeling and software engineering and the point of interface between the two where they come together. We have seen in the other parts of the book that the enterprise modeling methodology we are proposing takes a strong object-oriented view of the enterprise to produce an object-oriented enterprise model. Later the resulting enterprise model will be designed and constructed by letting RFPs (request for proposal) or commissioning projects within the enterprise. Notice the clean separation between the enterprise modeling project and the various implementation projects for designing and constructing the proposed enterprise using the enterprise model. Thus the enterprise model must interface with various lower-level engineering methodologies, particularly software development.

Software development is conducted using a methodology. Since our enterprise model produced during the enterprise modeling project will be stated in object-oriented terms, we can assert that an object-oriented software development methodology should be the easiest with which to interface. This chapter begins with an introduction to object-oriented software development methodologies. where we will see that virtually all object-oriented software development methodologies consist of three phases: they begin with object-oriented analysis (OOA), proceed to object-oriented design (OOD), and finish with object-oriented programming (OOP).

It is the initial phase, the object-oriented analysis, with which our enterprise model will interface. This chapter discusses this coming together. We will see how the output of the enterprise model represents requirements that are solved or satisfied by the OOA.

This chapter continues by discussing how some of these object-oriented software development methodologies may be incompatible with our definition of enterprise modeling. Most object-oriented software development methodologies use sound concepts of physical implementation but actually subtly advocate an enterprise model. This is a classic case of putting the cart before the horse. We will focus on several problem areas. First, some object-oriented software methodologies are actually data-focused instead of object-focused; another problem of object-oriented software development methodologies is that they are reluctant to deal with the target system as a hierarchy of processes. We will discuss both points in this chapter.

We will close this chapter with our recommended object-oriented software development methodology, one that is very compatible with the object-oriented constructs of our enterprise model. It is known as object-oriented software engineering (OOSE) and was originated by Ivar Jacobson, a pioneer in object-oriented technology.

25.2 What is an object-oriented software development methodology?

Let's start the chapter by understanding what an object-oriented software development methodology is. A methodology is a planned procedure in which a specified goal is accomplished by a series of steps. In the case of software development, the methodology defines the series of steps to complete the development of a software system. Virtually all object-oriented software development methodologies consist of three activities: object-oriented analysis (OOA), object-oriented design (OOD), and object-oriented programming (OOP). While each individual object-oriented software development methodology has its own definition of OOA, OOD, and OOP, there is a kernel of commonalty outlined in the following section.

Object-oriented analysis

Object-oriented software development methodologies begin with object-oriented analysis. OOA is the process of specification of user requirements and systems functions, independent of the means of implementation. This phase brings together the users and developers to provide a description of the problem domain. One of the major tools of OOA is joint application design (JAD), a series of structured sessions between users and software engineers to define the requirements of the proposed system. The JAD sessions are enhanced with diagramming and functional decomposition tools. During OOA, a model of the domain consisting of a set of collaborating domain objects is constructed. The essential object classes are identified and modeled including their logical relationships and interactions. Requirements are examined from the perspective of the classes and objects found in the vocabulary of the problem domain as jointly discovered in the JAD process. OOA focuses on three types of models jointly developed by users and software engineers. The three models correspond to our three views of a general system introduced in Chapter 2, namely, structural, behavioral, and functional:

- **Structural view: the information model**   The OOA begins with an information model. This is OOA's structural view of the system. An object-oriented information model is constructed using many of the techniques of classic data analysis and modeling. The information model is constructed by identifying the real-world objects of the problem domain and summarizing their attributes and relationships. Since OOA is just the beginning of the development sequence, the information model at this point is fairly general, lacking in detail but strong on concepts. The information model is documented by both text and diagrams. The text is used to describe the objects, attributes relationships, and structures. The diagrams portray the higher-level objects and their relationships.

- **Behavioral view: dynamic model**   Concurrent with producing the information model, OOA analyzes the dynamic behavior of the objects and their relationships. This is the OOA behavioral view of the system. A series of techniques are used to model the dynamic behavior of the objects and to define their life cycles. A good starting point is to communicate the concepts of the systems behavior between the users and the software engineers. A satisfactory way to accomplish this is to begin by constructing an overall description of how the system will operate as if observed externally. Once the big picture of the system is understood, specific aspects of its dynamics can be observed. The life cycle of important objects is defined, the life cycle of an object being the state of the object over time. An object's life cycle is expressed as a state transition diagram (STD), which was introduced in Chapter 2. An STD is constructed for the most important objects from the information model. Again, since we are only at the OOA stage, the dynamic model is general and lacks substantive detail. It is intended to communicate concepts.

◆ **Functional view: the process model** Once the aforementioned information and dynamic models are well underway, the object-oriented analysis proceeds by constructing a process model. This step can use traditional data-flow diagramming (i.e., invented by DeMarco and others) to show the overall flows of the system. The process model defines the major information transformations of the system that implement its purpose. The process model shows how each transformation affects each of the major objects discovered in the information model. Also, the process model correlates the transformations with the corresponding state changes of the major objects discovered in the dynamic model. The process model of OOA, like the information model and the dynamic model, is fairly general and is intended to communicate concepts between the users and the software engineers.

Object-oriented design

Object-oriented design is very close intellectually to object-oriented analysis. This means that the products of OOA are used directly by OOD, which expands and refines them. OOA and OOD are usually intermingled (i.e., a design is proposed based on the current understanding of the problem and is criticized and refined, which in turn causes a greater understanding of the problem and more OOA to occur, etc.). However, OOA is a global view of systems architecture, while OOD is focused on specific parts of the system. In fact, the typical system development project will divide the results of the OOA between more than one team so that each team pursues the OOD of a separate part of the system. Like OOA, OOD focuses on the three views of a system, namely the structural, behavioral, and functional. The OOD phase expands the details of the three models begun in the OOA phase:

◆ **Structural view: information model** During OOD, the information model is expanded to focus on the definitions of the specific classes of the system. While the classes defined in OOA relate to real-world concepts, the classes of OOD are software structures that simulate real-world objects. The classes of OOD are arranged in inheritance hierarchies in which each subclass is specialized to the specific behavior and attributes of its real-world objects. Also, a number of new classes are revealed in OOD, which are required to make the system actually work. During OOD, processing responsibilities are assigned to each class and the attributes (i.e. information contents) are defined for each class. The interface that objects instantiated from a class will present to the outside world are defined for each class. Recall that the interface of an object is the set of services that can be invoked by sending messages to the object.

◆ **Behavioral view: dynamic model** OOD uses a series of modeling techniques to model the detailed behavior of the objects and to define the states of the objects over time. An object's life cycle is expressed as a detailed state transition diagram that uses as a starting point the dynamic model produced in OOA. As a practical matter, state transition diagrams are constructed for only the more important classes.

◆ **Functional view: process model** The processes discovered in the process model of OOA are expanded in detail. The OOA processes describe the overall transformations of the system and are a high level, external description of the system from a user's standpoint. In effect, the transformations are the purpose of the system. During OOD, each process is decomposed into lower-level processes until an elementary level is reached. Then the elementary processes are defined in terms of a sequence of services provided by the various objects of the system. Also, each state change of the objects (i.e., discovered in the dynamic model) is correlated to an elementary process in the process model.

In addition to expanding and completing these three models, OOD focuses on other aspects of the emerging system:

◆ **Technology model** During OOD, for the first time the actual target implementation platform is defined. The implementation platform includes the computer hardware, networks, operating systems, programming languages, and database managers. The technology model defines the software and hardware in which the system will be implemented.

◆ **Structural model** During OOD, the overall system is decomposed into subsystems. This is done both to better understand the system as well as to divide the work among project team members.

Object-oriented programming

The software system is constructed and tested using object-oriented programming (OOP). Software development in an object-oriented environment will consist of writing new classes and pulling together a suite of existing common classes into a solution. The software engineer must have intimate knowledge of the class library and the capabilities of each class.

Object-oriented systems have powerful development environments in which the classes are defined, the source code for methods is written, and the application is tested. An object-oriented development environment will have many tools to enhance the process of software development.

Conclusions

The enterprise model created by the methodology proposed in this book presents three views of the enterprise: a functional view, a structural view and a behavioral view. These three views are specializations of the three views of a general system. The three views of the enterprise will flow into the three major models created in object-oriented software engineering: the information model (structural view), the dynamic model (behavioral view), and the process model (functional view).

25.3 The point of interface between the enterprise model and OOA

As we mentioned earlier, the exact point of interface between enterprise modeling and software development is the OOA phase that starts where the enterprise modeling phase ended. OOA uses the documents produced during the enterprise modeling phase as one of its primary inputs. We have outlined our own enterprise modeling methodology in Part 5 of this book, resulting in a set of documents. Thus it is these documents that would be the input to the OOA that follows our enterprise modeling phase.

Many of the ideas in this section are based on the work of Alan Davis in his book *Software Requirements: Objects, Functions, and States* (Davis, 1993). In this book, Davis describes the early phases of a software development project, commonly called the *requirements phase*. The ideas of Davis can be extended to the development of any human artifact. In a very broad sense, the construction of the enterprise is identical, in format at least, to the construction of any human artifact, such as a software system. In this section, we will use Davis' ideas to describe the relationship between enterprise modeling and OOA.

Relationship between artifact, owner, and engineer

The activity of producing an artifact has two distinctive roles: the owner and the engineer. It has a distinctive entity: the artifact in question. It is the nature of the relationship between these three, the artifact, the owner, and the engineer, that is at the heart of the matter:

- ◆ **Artifact** Davis calls the artifact created by an engineering project a product. That is because this is exactly what its status is: it is human made; it has value to humans; it exists only because of its value; it isn't free, and someone has to pay for it.

- ◆ **Owner** The owner is the one who needs the artifact and pays for it. Paying for the artifact means paying for something that wouldn't otherwise exist or continue to exist. In the most general sense, the artifact can be a one-off or a mass-produced product. In either case, the owner pays for the product, although in the case of the mass-produced product, the owner pays his or her prorated share. In either case, the relationship between the owner and the engineer is identical. The owner determines the value of the artifact and defines what the artifact would have to be to be valuable.

◆ **Engineer**   The engineer is the one who designs and constructs the artifact. The engineer does not define the value of the artifact but starts with the assumption that the owner is willing to pay for the artifact for whatever reason. The engineer uses the requirements created by the owner to design then construct the artifact.

What are requirements?

Any engineering project that creates a human artifact begins with a set of requirements created by the owner. What does this have to do with enterprise modeling? As in any human artifact, the relationship between enterprise modeling and OOA is one of defining requirements and then implementing the requirements. We will return to this point in a moment. For now, we ask the question: just what are requirements?

A requirement is a complete description of the external behavior of the artifact to be built (Davis, 1993). Davis defines the nature of the description of the artifact, which is called a *requirements specification:*

◆ **Functionality**   The requirements specification defines and describes what the artifact will do from an external standpoint. This description of the artifact is from the view of a user who will not care about how the artifact accomplishes its functions, just that it does in fact accomplish them.

◆ **Interfaces**   The owner will use the artifact through the artifact's interface. The interface is the artifact's boundary with its environment, which includes the owner. The requirements specification defines and describes all interfaces between the artifact and its environment.

The "what-how" relationship

The requirements specification can be thought of as specifying "what." The requirements specification describes the external functionality and interfaces that the proposed artifact must have to be valuable. These are aspects of the "what" of the artifact.

On the other hand, the engineer specifies the "how." The engineer designs the internal components of the artifact that will create the external functionality and cause the interfaces with the environment. Thus the owner regards the artifact as a black box, which provides *what* he or she wants while the engineer regards the artifact as a set of internal components that combine to account for *how* the artifact will cause the value required by the owner.

Notice that these two little words, *what* and *how,* capture the essence of the world view of each of the parties as it relates to the artifact in question. In particular, the owner must never cross the line and discuss the "how" since this is the job of the engineer. Also, the engineer is not entitled to choose the "what" or to require a justification of it.

The what-how stack

The artifact may be complex, requiring various specialized engineering disciplines to design and build it. In this case, the engineer acts as a general contractor receiving the requirements specifications from the owner and decomposing them into lower-level requirements specifications intended for various lower-level engineering disciplines.

Davis points out that these specifications to subcontractors are yet a lower-level round of the what-how relationship between an owner and an engineer. The engineer, acting as a general contractor, is the "owner" in relationship to the engineers acting as subcontractors. An interesting sociological aspect of this is that the engineer may not regard himself or herself as an owner *but the engineers at the lower level do.* The engineer acting as a general contractor regards the components being designed and built by the subcontractors as black boxes that must have certain interfaces with the environment and have certain external functionality. In fact, creating a complex artifact causes a chain reaction of what-how relationships that can be arranged in a stack as shown in Figure 25.1 (Davis, 1993).

Figure 25.1 shows the first three layers of a what-how stack (i.e., there could be many more layers). Each layer will first act as an engineer and take the specifications of the requirements of the artifact from the upper layer and then act as an owner to the lower-level engineering disciplines by creating a set of lower-level specifications required to design and construct the various components of the artifact.

The requirements specification

Each layer in the what-how stack produces a requirements specification for the next lower level. According to Davis, a requirements specification is produced by two activities that are performed iteratively (i.e., they are done together and they influence each other) (Davis, 1993):

- ◆ **Problem analysis** Acting as an analyst, the owner performs the problem analysis. The major activities of problem analysis are to understand the

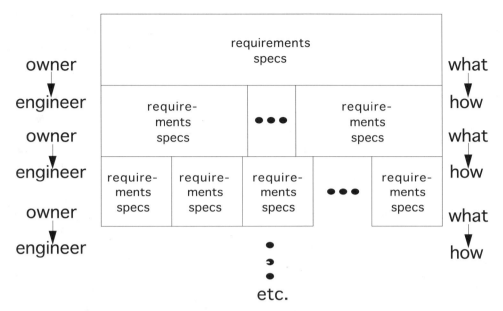

Figure 25.1 *What-how stack.*

problem and to identify the constraints placed on its solutions. At first, this is largely an information-collection-and-organization task. Then the hard part is done. According to Davis, it is the job of the owner to determine what is really needed (Davis, 1993).

Problem analysis identifies all possible constraints and integrates them. At first, the result is probably a negative solution space (i.e., no solution is possible that conforms to all the constraints). The owner makes some judgments and adjusts the constraints, relaxing some, forgetting about others, until a reasonable solution space is revealed. Notice that this is really a design activity in its own right, but more than anything, it is a synthesis activity in which good judgment is critical. The only person who can do this work is the owner.

◆ **Product description** Once the problem analysis is performed, a product space that contains a range of solutions that meet the constraints (i.e., as adjusted) is revealed. The owner congeals and synthesizes the various solutions into one or more products. A product has the external behavior and interfaces to the environment needed by the owner. In particular, a product satisfies the constraints. One of the products is selected by the owner, documented in the requirements specification. and turned over to the engineer. Again, the only person who can do this work is the owner.

Enterprise modeling: What-how stack

We can now construct a generic what-how stack for enterprise modeling. The enterprise modeling process will be conducted by the owners of the enterprise and produce an external view that satisfies their constraints. The resulting enterprise model will be documented, for example, in the series of stages of the methodology proposed in this book. The documents will then be turned over to various engineering groups inside the enterprise or outside of it. The owners will communicate with the various engineering groups formally via RFPs or with a less-formal interface that nevertheless divides the roles of owner and engineer. A what-how stack similar to Figure 25.2 will be created.

In Figure 25.2, we see the what-how stack starting with the enterprise model. The enterprise model is decomposed into various engineering projects. We see in the figure that one of these is software development but there will be others, such as designing and constructing the infrastructure of the enterprise (buildings, communications channels, etc.) The software development projects will be done using the OOA, OOD, and OOP phases as previously explained. Each layer will be a what-how layer of the stack.

25.4 Incompatibilities with software development methodologies

As we saw earlier, our enterprise modeling methodology takes a strong object-oriented view of the enterprise to produce an enterprise model. Our enterprise modeling methodology results in an enterprise-wide requirements specification. The documentation resulting from our enterprise modeling methodology would be suitable for inclusion in RFPs for the systems work implied by the plan. As we saw in the previous section, an enterprise modeling methodology operates at a high level and must ultimately interface with low-level engineering disciplines, especially software development.

As we developed our enterprise modeling methodology described in this book, we reviewed the best of breed of the current crop of object-oriented software development methodologies. In this section, we would like to make some comments on the general compatibility of these software development methodologies with our concepts of enterprise modeling. These software development methodologies are necessarily microviews of various parts of the enterprise and, for the

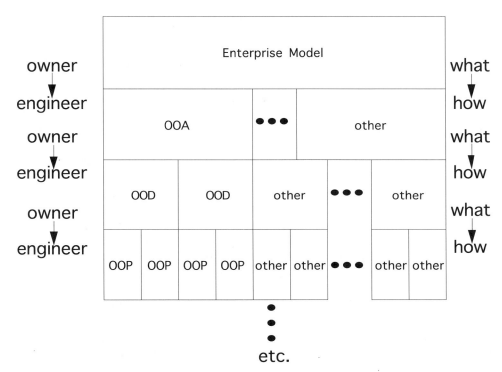

Figure 25.2 *What-how stack of enterprise modeling.*

most part, they do promote the orderly construction of software for those small slices of the enterprise. However, some of the object-oriented software development methodologies are incompatible with our proposed enterprise modeling methodology. We will summarize these incompatibilities in the following sections.

Problem: Centralized database enterprise model

Some object-oriented software methodologies are data focused. A data-focused software methodology emphasizes data and its interrelationships and is intended for designing a centralized database, which happens to be implemented using object-oriented technology. A data-focused object-oriented design methodology contemplates creating an enterprise-wide centralized database consisting of data objects, which are interlocked by relations. While the centralized database may be distributed over many computers, it is still designed to be a logical whole. The data objects of the centralized database have complex interrelationships that are designed using data-modeling techniques and tools. Thus even though the corporate database is distributed among computer sites, it is designed as one centralized database.

There are many advantages to the centralized corporate database. The centralized corporate database is founded on sound principles of eliminating data redundancy, making data independent of its applications and using data as a resource to be shared among the systems of the enterprise. As a management strategy, the centralized database provides enterprise control over data standards, security restrictions, and integrity constraints. All of these are sound concepts of physical implementation.

The problem with the centralized database is that it is advocated as an enterprise model, which results in the separation of the data from the operations of the enterprise. In effect, all of the data is extracted from the operations of the enterprise and placed in the centralized database where it is managed as a single enterprise resource. This is much more than a physical implementation; it is a philosophical proposal for an enterprise model. The result is an enterprise architecture that builds a wall between the data and the operation of the enterprise. The separation is many faceted: the separation is technology-based because it is implemented by computers, which tend to be separate from the enterprise operations. Paradoxically, many modern enterprises use computer technology in their operations so that two competing technology camps are created, the centralized database camp versus the enterprise operations camp. Also, the separation of the data from the operations is sociologically based because it separates the enterprise into a computer culture versus a noncomputer culture. Finally, the separation is management based because it tends to separate the management expertise into a computer/data discipline versus an operations discipline.

The enterprise model that is implied by this datacentric focus has a series of peripheral processes encircling the data reservoir. In reality, the data reservoir is a distributed database that physically exists at many computer sites. The data reservoir leads to an unnatural and unrealistic enterprise model because the data reservoir is not integral to the enterprise operations. That is, the business processes of the enterprise are outside of the data reservoir and when it comes time to use or update data, a business process must be connected to the data reservoir. In an attempt to integrate this reservoir of data with the operations of the enterprise, interfaces are constructed joining the data reservoir with the machines, workers, and systems of the enterprise operations. No matter how efficient these interfaces are, they are still just that, interfaces that separate the two worlds of enterprise operations with the centralized database.

Therefore, we think that datacentric object-oriented software methodologies may lead to the wrong enterprise model. This is because the enterprise modeling methodology proposed in this book results in an object-oriented enterprise model.

Carried to its ultimate conclusion, the enterprise would be equivalent to a global object space (GOS) that accounts for the total enterprise as we discussed in Chapter 16. In a completely object-oriented enterprise, the objects of the enterprise will be members of a society of objects residing in the GOS and include both software objects and physical objects.

In the GOS, no single object will have total information or even access to total information about the enterprise. Rather, each object, whether software or physical, will have its own local data attributes. In the GOS architecture, each object will look after its own data attributes instead of handing them over to a centralized database. The objects will negotiate with other objects in the GOS to perform their goals.

Ideally, the objects in the GOS will know nothing about the internals of other objects. If an object needs access to the data attributes of another object, the first object will have to send messages to the second object asking for the desired data attributes. One huge advantage is that objects can be changed or added with minimum impact on the other objects of the GOS. However, if the objects are interlocked in data relations proposed by the centralized database approach, then changing or adding objects would be difficult.

The need for modeling the business process

We feel that some object-oriented software development methodologies do not properly model the process. This is unfortunate since the enterprise consists of processes. Managers and end users universally describe the enterprise as a set of processes. The process is the target of enterprise design, optimization, and reengineering. However, many object-oriented software methodologies distance themselves from the process concept, favoring instead the data concept. The word *process* conjures up the procedural programming paradigm (i.e., COBOL), which the object-oriented paradigm is committed to replace. But we have to face it, the enterprise is an interlocking network of processes. These processes do indeed have data and the technology of the database is the ideal physical implementation. The point is that the centralized, corporate database discussed earlier is the wrong enterprise model because the enterprise doesn't look like that at all. Let's look at this in more detail.

Not only do users and owners view the enterprise as a series of processes, so do most business consultants, strategists, and authors. In designing our enterprise modeling methodology, we analyzed several of the leading theories on strategic business planning and management. We found that in the theories we analyzed, the enterprise is universally viewed as a series of processes. For example, the Porter value chain, which was defined in Chapter 13, is one of the tools we advocate to analyze the enterprise. Recall that the Porter value chain is a model of the enterprise as a chain of value-adding business processes. According to Porter, every business enterprise is made up of a standard set of generic business processes. A business process takes input in the form of materials, assets, information, and human effort and produces a product (as well as information) which is more valuable than the inputs.

Therefore, an object-oriented software development methodology must support the principle that the enterprise is a series of business processes. Each business process is decomposed into subprocesses that, at their own level, produce value-added products by consuming or controlling various enterprise objects (materials, assets, information or human effort). This brings up the next requirement of a software development methodology.

The need for modeling process hierarchies

As we said many times in this book, the enterprise is a general system. Our enterprise modeling methodology models the enterprise as a hierarchy of abstract business processes (ABPs), which are subsystems of the enterprise. The requirement of a software development methodology is that it must deal with the enterprise considered as a system hierarchy. That is, the enterprise is decomposed into a series of subsystems (business processes), which in turn may also be decomposed into yet lower layers of subsystems (business process).

Unfortunately, many object-oriented software methodologies also distance themselves from any hint of "hierarchical decomposition" (i.e., in the same way as they distance themselves from the word *process* as described earlier). The reason is that structured design methods use hierarchical decomposition, and object-oriented technology is committed to replace the structured design paradigm with the object-oriented paradigm.

Our use of decomposition is not the same as the classic decomposition of structured design that emphasizes the decomposition of fine-grained software functions into yet finer-grained software functions. In our use of decomposition, we are very much at the macroscopic-systems level and we always end up with a decomposition of subsystems that are identifiable as business processes or enterprise objects. As mentioned earlier, these business process subsystems and their enterprise objects are the focus of management and become the subject of management's value engineering efforts, that is, enhancing the value-adding capability of a business process considered as a subsystem.

25.5 Recommendation: Jacobson's OOSE

Ivar Jacobson is a pioneer in object-oriented technology and the author of the object-oriented development methodology he calls Object-Oriented Software

Engineering. OOSE is the software development methodology we recommend. It is ideal because it permits the easy integration of the enterprise modeling methodology proposed in this book. In this section, we will summarize the essential parts of OOSE. For a more detailed view, the reader should refer to (Jacobson, 1992).

Primary objects of OOSE

In OOSE, any software system consists of three distinct dimensions:

- **Information**   This dimension is about the system's internal state.

- **Behavior**   This dimension is about how the system's internal state changes over time.

- **Presentation**   This dimension is about the system's interface to the external environment.

In OOSE the three dimensions represent the three types of objects that a software system must contain. In effect, the objects of a software system are categorized by their tendency to be specialized toward one of these three dimensions. A given object will possess capabilities in all three dimensions but will tend to be specialized toward just one. Figure 25.3 shows the three types of objects and their tendencies toward specialization to one of the three dimensions.

Jacobson makes the point that many other object-oriented software development methodologies recognize only one object type, which then must embody all three dimensions. However, as we'll see, this approach intermixes within each object a higher potential for change so that we are unable to take advantage of change isolation. We will discuss the three types of objects in the following sections.

Interface objects

Interface objects sit on the system boundary between the inner world of the system and the outside world of the environment. Their purpose is to receive information from the environment and to present information to the environment. It is through interface objects that the actors and the target system communicate with each other to implement use cases, a related theory of Jacobson's, which we discussed in Chapter 14. On the receive side of the communications scenario, the interface objects translate the actor's intentions into internal messages or events that the system can understand. Similarly, on the send side, the interface objects translate the systems intentions into messages or events that the actor can understand.

Using the terminology of the Shannon/Weaver model of communications (see

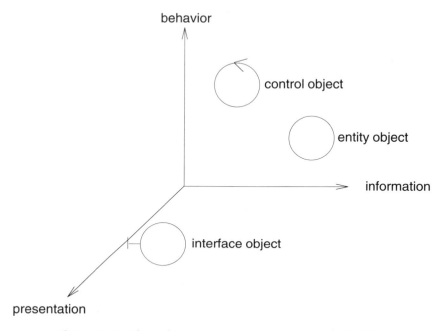

Figure 25.3 *Three dimensions of software objects of OOSE.*

Chapter 4) we recognize the interface objects as performing the lower-level semantic coding/decoding and transmission functions of a communications scenario:

- ◆ On the send side, the interface objects perform the syntactical coding function of converting internal information into a transportable form that the receiver can decode. Also, the interface objects activate the physical phenomena that causes the information to be transmitted to the receiver on the channel.

- ◆ Similarly on the receive side, the interface objects perform the receive function that receives the physical phenomena from the channel. The interface objects then perform the syntactical decoding of the received information into a form usable by the receiving system. Notice that the interface objects know nothing about the meaning (semantics) of the information.

As we mentioned earlier, interface objects are closely associated with Jacobson's use cases. The interactive scenarios of the use case receive and send information between the actor and the system. Each use case will tend to have its own unique set of specialized interface objects although there will be plenty of opportunities for reusability of the interface object classes between the various use cases and within the inheritance hierarchies.

In the most general sense, interface objects are both software components and hardware components. We have used this level of generality in our enterprise modeling methodology. All the following system components would be considered interface objects:

- GUI (software)

- X.25 protocol converter (software)

- Display screen (hardware)

- Bank-card reader (hardware)

In Figure 25.3, we see that interface objects are dominant on the presentation dimension with only minor behavior and information dimensions. Interface objects isolate the system functionality that is directly dependent on the system's environment. The interface objects separate the functionality of the system from its communications with the actors. As a system asset, interface objects are the least valuable of the three types of objects. Also, they have the highest change activity.

Entity objects

The entity objects are the information-bearing objects of a software system. They are used to represent the real-world entities of the system. In the case of an enterprise, entity objects would be the various business object (e.g., products, resources, accounts, orders, etc.) of the enterprise. Entity objects hold the permanent information of the system and are long lived. They are a shared resource and are used by the various use cases. As such, their asset value is the highest of the three types of objects. Also, their change level is the lowest of the three.

In Figure 25.3, we see that entity objects are dominant on the information dimension with only a small behavior dimension and no presentation dimension. The entity objects do include the behavior directly associated with their information. Thus entity objects include the behavior to access and update the information contained in the entity object as well as creating and removing themselves.

The allocation of other system behavior to entity objects is often a point of debate in the design of a system. How much behavior should be built into these objects? The problem is that information is interconnected in a complex network in which information points at dependent information. Entity objects will be arranged into complex networks in which entity objects point at their dependent entity objects. The updating of the information in an entity object will inevitably imply the need for updating the information in other entity objects of the information network. The question is: should the entity object realize this and cause the updates to occur in the dependent entity objects? Jacobson takes a pragmatic approach to this debate as he explains the two extremes: "One extreme case is that an entity object comprises only reading and writing operations (of its data), and the other extreme case is having whole courses of events included in the operations. As always, the right thing is a middle course between these two extremes. The same basic rules (of good design) apply to entity objects as to other objects, that is, everything (behavior and information) that is naturally connected with the entity object should be placed in it" (Jacobson, 1992).

Control objects

Control objects tie together the objects that participate in a use case. The interactive scenario of the use case is manifested as a set of events and messages. As we saw earlier, these events and messages come from the interface objects and have been syntactically translated to be meaningful to the system. The events and messages are directed at the control objects of the system. Control objects manage the sequence of actions of a set of related objects and are a useful way to implement centralized control of a set of objects.

Control objects implement the dynamics of the whole system and represent macro-level behavior. In effect, they implement the functionality of the system. In Figure 25.3, we see that control objects are dominant in the behavior dimension, have some information dimension, but no presentation dimension. The information that a control object retains represents the state of the coordination of the set of related objects which it directs.

A use case will tend to have its own unique control object. The class of a control object will tend to be unique to a use case (although there will be plenty of opportunities for reuse by inheritance). Control objects are used to concentrate the control logic of a use case. Control objects tend to operate on several entity objects, then return the results to the interface objects. As such, control objects are transaction oriented in the computer science sense. Transactions are atomic sequences that the system guarantees as either completely happening or not happening at all. The system is always left in a consistent state with the use of the transaction mechanism. Control objects have medium asset value to the system compared to the interface objects (least valuable) and the entity objects (most valuable). Also, their change level is in the middle compared to the interface objects (most change) and the entity objects (least change).

Separating out the control logic of the complex sequences of a use case tends to enhance reusability of the entity objects. That is, we don't want to encumber the entity objects with global responsibilities or unnecessarily couple them together.

In this way, the entity objects, which are our most valuable system asset, will be much more reusable and, hence, even more valuable. Also, control objects encapsulate interrelated functionality that might otherwise be scattered.

The use of control objects advocated by OOSE is somewhat controversial in the object-oriented community. Jacobson defends the concept of control objects as follows: "It is usually not difficult to find suitable information carrying objects in an enterprise (entity objects). However, it is the dynamics describing how the system is utilized that are difficult to define correctly. Many people assert that the dynamics need no particular modeling: it simply constitutes operations on information-carrying objects (entity objects) and therefore can be included in them. However, systems often exhibit behavior that cannot naturally be said to belong to any particular information-carrying object. For this reason, it is better to model separate dynamic objects (control objects)" (Jacobson, 1992).

Multilayered architecture

Jacobson combines the three types of objects into a multilayered architecture summarized in Figure 25.4. A system will consist of these three layers:

♦ The top layer interfaces with the actors and converts the myriad events and messages coming from the use cases into syntactically correct messages that are understandable to the system. A working use case will have its own interface objects and control object. The control objects respond to the messages from the interface layer but don't know anything about these interface objects. To the control objects, messages come out of the blue.

♦ Control objects, in turn, control the complex interaction of the use case scenario. This complex interaction almost always involves accessing and causing the updating the information of the entity objects. The control objects coordinate this complex processing by sending messages to the entity objects at the bottom of Figure 25.4. In effect, a control object executes a script using the terminology of Chapter 4.

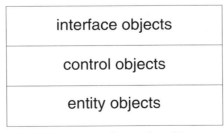

Figure 25.4 *OOSE layered architecture.*

◆ The entity objects respond by updating themselves and possibly sending messages to other strongly coupled entity objects. Once the entity object has completed its response to the message, its state may have changed. The entity object indicates these state changes by informing the control object level.

◆ The control object must be able to interpret and respond to these state changes by sending messages to other objects in the system that need to know about the state changes. The messages that are in response to state changes of entity objects may be directed upward to the interface layer or downward to other entity objects that need to know.

Conclusions

The enterprise modeling methodology proposed in this book presents the enterprise as a hierarchy of business processes beginning with what we termed abstract business processes. The ABPs are, in turn, decomposed into lower layers until the objects of the enterprise are revealed such as people, machines, materials, and information. The ABPs implement the dynamic behavior of the enterprise and are arranged into sequences or networks that exchange information with each other to create the value-added products in the value chain. They control lower-level abstract business processes as well as the objects of the enterprise.

The three object types of OOSE are conceptually identical to the objects used in the enterprise modeling methodology proposed in this book. The object model proposed in this book is stated in terms of complex networks of abstract business processes and their lower-level entity objects (people, materials, machines, etc.). This is equivalent to the interface objects, control objects, and entity objects of OOSE. That is, the message passing interface of an abstract business process becomes the interface object of OOSE; the abstract business process becomes the control object of OOSE; the entity object (people, machines, materials, etc.) becomes the entity object of OOSE.

25.6 Converting the enterprise modeling class hierarchy to a software development class hierarchy

One of the significant deliverables of the enterprise modeling methodology proposed in this book is an enterprise modeling class hierarchy. The enterprise modeling class hierarchy is finalized in stage 7 of the methodology as explained in Chapter 24. Also, Appendix B presents the upper parts of the enterprise modeling class hierarchy. The enterprise modeling class hierarchy deliverable is one of the major inputs to the OOA phase of software development. In this section, we will discuss how the enterprise modeling class hierarchy is used as a starting point for defining the software object classes of OOA.

First, let's remind ourselves of what the classes of the enterprise modeling class hierarchy really are and what they are used for. The enterprise modeling class hierarchy is used to create an object-oriented model of the enterprise. The starter set of enterprise modeling classes found in Appendix B can be adapted and modified to the needs of specific enterprise modeling projects. The enterprise modeling classes standardize and clarify the real-world objects of the enterprise. In this way, the enterprise modelers will have at hand a uniform set of reusable modeling constructs which they can mix and match to create an enterprise model.

Recall that OOA creates an object model of the same real-world domain, namely the enterprise. Therefore, during the enterprise modeling project, an eye will be kept on the ultimate goal of implementing the enterprise with the intent that the classes of the emerging enterprise modeling class hierarchy will be used as a starting point for defining the software classes of the OOA. The translation of an enterprise modeling classes to the OOA classes of software implementation will be done as follows.

Entity classes

Entity classes of the enterprise modeling class hierarchy can be brought largely straight across to the OOA class hierarchy. Recall that during OOA, an information model is constructed by identifying the real-world objects of the problem domain and summarizing their behavior, attributes and relationships. Any entity class of the enterprise modeling class hierarchy certainly meets this requirement of being a class representing real-world objects of the OOA problem domain.

For example, the enterprise modeling class hierarchy will contain classes such as *customer, product, invoice,* or *payment* as well as their subclasses suitable for enterprise modeling. The OOA phase will use these same concepts and will have these same classes (as well as add many new classes). However, in the OOA phase, the enterprise modeling classes will be abstract classes at the top of the OOA class hierarchy and will be specialized to the more specific object model created in the OOA phase.

For example, during enterprise modeling, the *product* class and its subclasses are very high-level concepts. During the OOA phase, the enterprise modeling *product* class and its subclasses will be specialized to the actual products of the enterprise. Even then, the class hierarchy of OOA will be very general and abstract. It will require the work of the OOD to specialize the OOA classes to working software constructs.

Process classes

Process classes of the enterprise modeling class hierarchy define the dynamics of the enterprise. In an enterprise that uses a fully implemented global object space (GOS; see Chapter 16), the classes of the enterprise modeling class hierarchy would translate straight across to OOA classes. In this case, the software process objects living in the GOS would have their own threads of control and implement the dynamics of the GOS. In effect, all the activities of the enterprise would be accounted for by the process objects of the GOS.

What about an enterprise that does not implement a GOS or only partially implements one? In this case, the process classes of the enterprise modeling class hierarchy represent the specifications for traditional applications. In many ways, an enterprise without a formal GOS still has a "virtual GOS," consisting of people and applications in a loosely coupled confederation. The process classes of the enterprise modeling class hierarchy are generic business processes encapsulating useful enterprise functionality. The process descriptions of the enterprise model will be expressed in terms of these process classes. This will be a very precise and useful description of the functional view of the enterprise even if the enterprise is not actually implemented as a GOS. The software developers would use the process descriptions of the enterprise model to construct their own conventional process model.

25.7 Conclusion

In this chapter, we discussed the relationship between enterprise modeling and software engineering. We started the chapter with an introduction to software development methodologies. We reviewed the common characteristics of most object-oriented software development methodologies and found them to have three distinct phases: object-oriented analysis (OOA), object-oriented design (OOD), and object-oriented programming (OOP). Each phase focuses on three models of the emerging system, which correspond to our three views of the general system: the information model corresponds to the structural view; the dynamic model corresponds to the behavioral view; and the process model corresponds to the functional view. Each model evolves as the object-oriented development methodology advances from OOA to OOD to OOP.

In this chapter, we pointed out that the interface between enterprise modeling and object-oriented software development is the OOA phase. We used the work of Alan Davis to clarify this interface. Davis defined the roles of the participants in an engineering project (e.g., building or rebuilding an enterprise) and found that there is the distinct role of the owner, which is different from the engineer. Davis developed the idea of the what-how stack, in which each layer of a complex engineering project consists of these two roles, the owner and the engineer. We used Davis' ideas in this chapter to define the relationship of enterprise modeling to software development as a what-how stack of owner and engineer. The enterprise model produced by the owner's role defines what is required and the software system produced by the engineer defines how the requirements will be satisfied.

Next, we made some comments on object-oriented development methodologies and found that some are not compatible with our enterprise modeling methodology. We commented that many object-oriented development methodologies are datacentric and propose an enterprise model designed around a centralized logical database concept. In our enterprise modeling methodology, we stress that the enterprise should become a global object space (GOS) of distributed software and physical objects. In the GOS, there is no centralized database and each object controls only its own local data, which is not compatible with the centralized database concept. We also discussed the need for implementation of process objects and pointed out that many object-oriented development methodologies distance themselves from processes and process decomposition. However, enterprises consist of business processes that must be decomposed and implemented as software objects that reside in the GOS.

We pointed out that one software development methodology in particular is very compatible with our enterprise modeling methodology. It is Object-Oriented Software Engineering (OOSE) developed by Ivar Jacobson. OOSE defines three types of objects (the interface object, the control object and the entity object) that are very compatible with the object-oriented constructs produced by our methodology.

We closed this chapter with a clarification of the how the enterprise modeling class hierarchy can be leveraged to produce the software class hierarchy of OOA. We warned that the classes of the enterprise modeling class hierarchy are very general and abstract. However, they are classes that model real-world objects from the problem domain. As such, they should be able to be leveraged in OOA.

Chapter 26

Conclusion

26.1 Introduction

In this book, we described an enterprise modeling methodology called Future Strategies Business Planning®, or fsbp® for short. It is a comprehensive methodology that can be used for both starting an enterprise and for reengineering an existing enterprise. The fsbp® methodology begins at the business strategy level and ends with a definition of the object-oriented architecture of the enterprise. The output from fsbp® can be thought of as a statement of requirements that would be used to begin building or reengineering the enterprise. Building or reengineering the enterprise will require a broad spectrum of engineering and professional expertises including business, operations, infrastructure, and computer systems. The results of fsbp® are a set of documents that are used as the basis for issuing RFPs (request for proposal) to the various engineering and professional experts required to build or reengineer the enterprise.

26.2 Academic foundations

In developing fsbp®, the authors of this book have sought to define and interpret the enterprise from an academic point of view. The authors were not interested in accepting any current methodology from the world of reengineering, computer software development, or business planning. While there are many fine methodologies, the authors felt that no enterprise modeling methodologies that define the enterprise in terms of academic formalisms were available. This section summarizes the academic formalisms that the authors used as a foundation to fsbp®.

The enterprise is a general system

The first academic formalism of fsbp® is that the enterprise is an example of the phenomenon known as a *general system*. A general system is defined as a collection of related objects, which together pursue common objectives and exist for the overall good of the whole. The authors developed fsbp® by studying general systems theory and several systems related academic disciplines. The authors asked some basic questions: Just what is a system? What are the abstract properties of systems? How are systems structured? How do systems behave over time? The authors found that the discipline of general systems theory has produced many very powerful concepts and tools that can be used to understand and reason about the enterprise.

One comforting conclusion that the authors came to early in their research for this book is that there is a lot of precedence in analyzing complex domains in terms of general systems theory. General systems theory is so completely general that it can be used to give structure and meaning to virtually any complex domain. The modeler uses general systems theory to map the domain of interest into a set of enduring systems constructs which apply to any general system.

Even more exciting is the phenomena that principles in one general system will tend to be true in a completely different general system. John W. Sutherland refers to this as constructing isomorphisms between abstract models of different systems phenomena to find their similarities: "The systems scientist should explicitly search for (and subsequently exploit) isomorphisms among the 'universe' of phenomena, this in the hopes of increasing the efficiency of science through the generation of broadly significant analogies" (Sutherland, 1975).

The search for underlying isomorphisms between general systems from completely different domains is at the heart of general systems theory. George Klir explains it this way: "certain concepts, principles, and methods have been shown not to depend on the specific nature of the phenomena involved. These can be applied, without any modification, in quite diverse areas of science, engineering, humanities, and the arts, thus, introducing links between classical disciplines and allowing the concepts, ideas, principles, models, and methods developed in different disciplines to be shared" (Klir, 1972). In the fsbp®, the authors have attempted to identify and make use of a core set of general systems concepts, principles, models, and methods referred to by Klir as follows:

- **Modeling** A major part of this book is devoted to describing general systems modeling and how it is used to model the enterprise. Any general system is modeled in terms of three views: a structural view, a behavioral view, and a functional view. This means that any modeling construct of the enterprise can be categorized in terms of these three. We will discuss these three views of enterprise modeling later in the chapter.

- **Hierarchical-multilayer organization** Throughout this book, the enterprise was described as being organized as a hierarchical-multilayered system. This means that the business processes of the enterprise are organized as both a hierarchy and as abstraction layers. The hierarchical aspect of a systems organization relates to the coordination of subsystems by command and control. Any two levels of a hierarchical system consist of a meta-layer above an operations-layer. The meta-layer constrains the subsystems of the operations-layer to accomplish the objectives of the whole. *Constraint* not only means limiting the operations of the subsystems but changing their internal operations.

    The multilayer aspect of a hierarchical-multilayered system relates to the abstraction layering of the subsystems in terms of functional abstraction. Each layer is self-contained but depends on lower layers for services or resources. Each layer has its own concepts, theories, and methodologies. Appendix A presents a starter set of structural patterns that can be used and enhanced in actual enterprise modeling projects.

- **Optimization versus suboptimization** The meta-layer of a hierarchical-multilayered system continuously monitors and fine-tunes its operational subsystems so as to optimize the performance of the whole. This is the first principle of systems management: no subsystem is permitted to suboptimize itself at the expense of the optimization of the whole. The avoidance of suboptimization of components of a business is a well-known principle of enterprise management. We see how a principle of enterprise management is, in fact, a principle of general systems management. In fact, we assert that most principles of enterprise management are really principles of general systems management. Sutherland's isomorphisms between phenomena from different general systems mentioned earlier are very apparent here.

- **Information theory** This book described the enterprise in terms of the specialized general system known as the information-processing network.

The book describes in detail the information-processing nodes that make up the information-processing network. In the book, we found that the enterprise is based on the flow of information and that the purpose of information, according to Herbert Simon, is adaptivity (Simon, 1981). The information-processing network of the enterprise is a vast network of information-processing nodes which may be people, organizations, computers, or other information machines.

Physical information-processing nodes (at the lowest level of decomposition) have at their core an information processing capability that Newell and Simon call a *physical symbol system*. The physical symbol system is their model of a machine that uses information to define its sequence of operations (Newell and Simon, 1987). The information-processing node can be modeled as executing a script. An information-processing node with its physical symbol system is the change mechanism for a low level business process. However, we use the idea of the change mechanism to account for the dynamics of any business process. Also, we have asserted in this book that the change mechanism of any business process is an information-processing node corresponding to that a level of process decomposition. Higher-level business processes have higher-level information-processing nodes (e.g., organizations) while lower-level business processes have lower-level information-processing nodes (e.g., people, computers).

◆ **Conceptual modeling**   A major part of this book is devoted to describing the academic field of conceptual modeling and showing how it is used as a foundation for enterprise modeling. The principal tool of conceptual modeling is the conceptual type hierarchy, which is used to categorize the concepts of any modeling domain into an inheritance hierarchy.

The conceptual type hierarchy proposed in this book for enterprise modeling has four major subtypes: the entity, which models existence; the scene, which models complex arrangements of entities; the situation, which models the evolving snapshots of scenes over time; and the relation, which models the connection between concepts. All concepts we encounter in the real-world of the enterprise must fall into one of these four types. Furthermore, the conceptual type hierarchy will be used as a theoretical foundation for building an object-oriented enterprise modeling class hierarchy discussed later.

Driving force and strategic framework

Another theory that the authors have drawn on is the work of Benjamin Tregoe and John Zimmerman. Tregoe and Zimmerman developed the concept of the "driving force" of an enterprise and this is another important academic formalism used by fsbp®. The enterprise's driving force is its most important business rule and dominates all others. An enterprise's driving force is determined by impartial analysis of the value system (discussed next as an academic formalism) of the enterprise. In the fsbp®, we give a procedure for doing this impartial analysis.

Tregoe and Zimmerman have used the driving force as a unifying concept to develop their ideas of the enterprise's strategic framework. An enterprise's strategic framework determines its products and markets as well as the key capabilities that the enterprise requires. The strategic framework is the glue that keeps the enterprise focused on delivering value to its customer as it faces new challenges.

Tregoe and Zimmerman's concepts of the driving force and the strategic framework have been used throughout the fsbp® but especially in the first three stages of the methodology (i.e., business definition, stage 1; market and product plan, stage 2; and public policy plan, stage 3). The fsbp® identifies the enterprise's strategic framework and driving force by using analytical techniques. The business definition begins by capturing and isolating the issues that cannot be ignored if one is to achieve industry success—fsbp® calls them the *strategic business imperatives.* Typically, 30 to 40 synthesized imperatives are imposed upon an enterprise by its owners, the marketplace, competitors, suppliers, etc. Actually, hundreds of strategic imperatives will be identified during a typical business definition, but they can usually be organized around 30 to 40 major topics.

These strategic imperatives are then synthesized into a handful (6 to 10) of strategic mandates that can be used as operating tenets to lead every aspect of enterprise operations. These strategic mandates are *the* critically important issues to an enterprise. One of these strategic mandates is identified as the driving force of the enterprise.

The strategic mandates and the strategic imperatives are used by fsbp® in all other stages to engineer (or reengineer) the enterprise. Therefore, the effectiveness of all business processes of the enterprise is evaluated by their ability to satisfy the strategic mandates and imperatives. During enterprise modeling, stage 4, the mandates and imperatives are restated as business rules that control the operation and results of the business process of the enterprise. The object-oriented enterprise model that is developed by fsbp® consists of object classes that cross-reference the business rules. In particular, each process object of the enterprise maintains its collection of business rules, which controls the process.

The value system of the enterprise

Throughout this book, there were frequent references to the concepts of the value chain of Michael Porter. Porter's value chain is another important academic formalism used by fsbp®. According to Porter, any enterprise consists of a collection of business processes that add value to products. The word *value* has many interpretations, but Porter stresses the economic definition: value is a measure of the willingness of a customer to use its limited resources to obtain a product. In the flow of products between business processes of an enterprise, the concept of value is critical. A business process can be modeled as an internal customer that is willing to use its limited resources to purchase products from other business processes.

The willingness of a business process to purchase the products of other business processes is caused by the strategic imperatives and mandates of the enterprise discussed earlier. The strategic imperatives and mandates create the mechanisms of a microeconomy within the enterprise in which business processes purchase products from each other in their pursuit of satisfying the strategic imperatives and mandates. The result is that value is naturally added to products as they flow from business process to business process.

Porter's point is that the same value-adding mechanism that operates within the enterprise also operates within the larger system of customers, suppliers, and competitors of the enterprise. Porter calls this larger environment the *value system* of the enterprise. It is the optimization of the value system that is critical. This means that the value chain of an enterprise (i.e., consisting of business processes) must not be suboptimized in any way that is detrimental to the larger value system of customers and suppliers. Ultimately, the value system leads to the definition of the strategic imperatives and mandates of the enterprise as discussed earlier.

The fsbp® uses the ideas of Porter's value system to analyze and clarify the external environment. fsbp® always considers three value systems: market values; industry values; and sociopolitical values:

- ◆ Market values relate to quantitative and qualitative components of product worth.

- ◆ Industry values identify current and future potential opportunity associated with an enterprise's actions and positioning.

- ◆ Sociopolitical values deal with those constraints and expectations that are determined within organized society and its institutions (typically, executive, legislative, and judicial).

The last sociopolitical value system drives a very important stage of fsbp®: the public policy strategy, stage 3. These values constitute the political mores under which the enterprise will operate and the social mores governing the employee's actions, relationships, and reactions. Thus public policies are at the heart of the meaning of human values as opposed to Porter's more restrictive economic values.

During enterprise modeling, stage 4, the public policy values are restated as business rules similar to the various strategic mandates and imperatives. In this way, public policies are cross-referenced in the enterprise object model, and they contribute to the control of business processes.

Object-oriented paradigm in enterprise modeling

Another important academic formalism of fsbp® is the use of the object-oriented paradigm in enterprise modeling. Invented in the 1960s, object-oriented technology was originally conceived and limited to software development. In that domain, its purpose was to ease the process of software development by combining related data and procedures into software packages called objects. In practice, these software objects typically correspond to real-world objects such as customers, vendors, accounts, and purchase orders, allowing object-oriented systems to directly reflect the way one naturally views the business.

In effect, an object-oriented software system is a simulation of a domain of the real world in which the software objects interact with each other analogous to the interaction of the corresponding real-world objects that are being simulated. This ability to model the real world is one of the advantages that object-oriented technology holds over other software-development paradigms. Because software objects can contain other software objects, they can simulate real-world objects of any complexity. Complete products, markets, and even the entire enterprise can be represented as software objects.

Object-oriented technology in enterprise modeling

The preceding paragraphs describe how object-oriented technology is a boon to software development. However, another powerful use of the object-oriented paradigm is in systems modeling, particularly enterprise modeling. When we consider the enterprise, we find that it consists of business processes that are its subsystems. These subsystems usually consist of yet lower-level subsystems. These subsystems are additional examples of the general systems phenomena. We decompose each layer of subsystems until we hit the level of concrete things, that of the people, machines, systems, departments, buildings, information, and energy that are combined to produce products.

The important modeling concept here is that these concrete things of the enterprise are examples of objects. Also of importance is that those various subsystems we encountered when we were decomposing the hierarchy are also objects. There are actually two different types of objects here. The objects representing the subsystems are fundamentally different from the objects representing people or machine or buildings. The subsystem objects are basic process abstrac-

tions that implement the dynamic behavior of the enterprise. In the fsbp®
process, they are called abstract business processes (ABPs). The design of an
enterprise is accomplished by designing and configuring its ABPs. The same can
be said of reengineering the enterprise; that is, it, too, is accomplished by designing and configuring its ABPs.

The ABP is a class in our enterprise modeling class hierarchy and it simulates
the business process at any level of decomposition. The ABP consists of six subprocesses: management, marketing, inbound logistics, operations, sales/service,
and outbound logistics. As the enterprise is decomposed, the ABP object class is
used as a starting point for defining more specialized business processes. In effect,
all business processes have at their core the basic attributes and behavior of the
ABP no matter what level of decomposition. We are reminded of the concepts of
Benoit Mendelbrot's fractals. That is, an ABP is a fractal because it is made from
subprocesses, which are also ABPs. This means that the basic values of the enterprise discussed earlier are part of every business process regardless of the level of
decomposition.

We can conclude that the object-oriented paradigm provides an ideal enterprise
modeling capability in which real world values, meaning, and relationships are
captured in the model. The object-oriented paradigm allows the enterprise "engineers" such as accountants, software engineers, or marketing people to view and
understand the enterprise model in real-world terms and concepts. The model and
the problem domain are in very close intellectual correspondence. The cognitive
wisdom of the domain experts can be easily mapped onto the model of the enterprise, which is represented using objects.

26.2 The three systems' views of the enterprise

Recall that in Chapter 2 we presented three views in which any general system can
be analyzed: functional, structural, and behavioral. The enterprise, being a general
system, can be analyzed in terms of these three. We can put the stages of fsbp® in
perspective by showing the layered structure of the enterprise model for each of
these views.

Functional view
Figure 26.1 presents the three layers that produce the functional view of the enterprise. In the figure, we see that the business definition (stage 1) provides the economics and positioning perspective and drives (from an intellectual standpoint)
the middle layer consisting of the market and product plan (stage 2) and the public
policy strategy (stage 3). The middle layer defines the products, markets, and policies and represents the realization of the business definition (stage 1). The middle

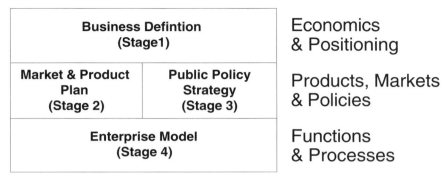

Figure 26.1 *Deriving the functional view of the enterprise.*

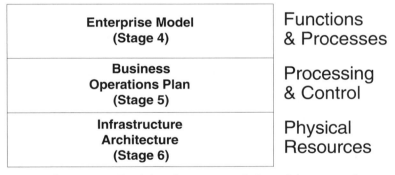

Figure 26.2 *Deriving the structural view of the enterprise.*

layer, in turn, intellectually drives the bottom layer, the enterprise model (stage 4). The bottom layer is the realization of the products, markets, and policies, which now take the form of enterprise functions and processes. The business processes of the enterprise model (stage 4) are controlled by business rules derived from the strategic imperatives and mandates defined in the business definition (stage 1) as well as the public policies defined in the public policy strategy (stage 3).

Structural view
Figure 26.2 presents the three layers that produce the structural view of the enterprise. In the figure, we see the enterprise model (stage 4) defining the functions and processes of the enterprise. The enterprise model (stage 4) drives the intellectual development of the business operations plan (stage 5), which defines the processing

and control of the enterprise. The business and operations plan (stage 5) drives the intellectual development of the infrastructure architecture (stage 6).

Notice that while these three layers are the sequence for deriving the structural view, they also show the operational architecture of the enterprise. That is, when the enterprise is in operation, the top-layer functions and processes defined in the enterprise model (stage 4) are implemented by the processing and control defined in the business operations plan (stage 5) of the middle layer. The processing and control of the middle layer make use of the physical resources of the bottom layer derived from the infrastructure architecture (stage 6). We recognize this operational architecture as an example of the infrastructure structural pattern summarized in Appendix A.

Behavioral view

Figure 26.3 presents the three layers that produce the behavioral view of the enterprise. In the figure, we see the value system (top) influencing the values of the enterprise, which results in the definition of the strategic imperatives and mandates as well as the policies of the enterprise. The values are used to define the processes, entities, and relations of the functional and structural models (middle). These, in turn, are used as a basis for defining the infrastructure objects (stage 7) (bottom). In this way, the objects defined in the infrastructure objects (stage 7) are directly correlated with the values from the value system.

While these three layers are the sequence for deriving the behavioral view, they also show the basic change management system of the enterprise. That is, the value system (top) will result in different values for the enterprise over time. These new values are reflected in the functional model and structural model (middle) by the continual reengineering processes of the enterprise which results in changes to the infrastructure objects (bottom). At any time, the infrastructure objects can be cross-referenced to the values they support.

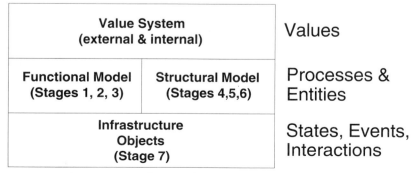

Figure 26.3 *Behavioral perspective of the enterprise.*

26.4 The three people-dimensions of enterprise modeling

While fsbp® is founded on academic formalisms summarized above, it is also founded on the expectations of the people involved in enterprise modeling. In fact, one of the first activities the authors conducted in developing fsbp® was to look pragmatically at the real-world arena where enterprise modeling occurs. The authors found that in any enterprise modeling project, there are three dimensions that must be brought together: the executive dimension, the project-manager dimension, and the engineering dimension.

The problem is that the expectations and requirements of each of these dimensions are different. In modern terminology, we would say they are orthogonal (i.e., each is a different axis in the figure). The expectations and requirements of the three dimensions are not necessarily incompatible, but nothing about them makes them naturally compatible:

◆ **Executive dimension**   First, there are the concerns and influences of the executives who are sponsoring the enterprise modeling project. This level operates in the broader economics environment building strategic plans

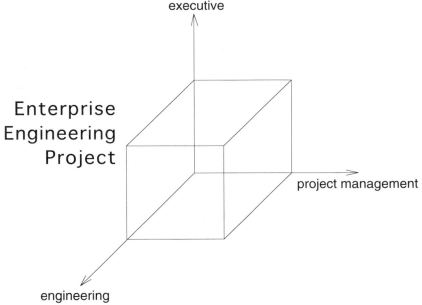

Figure 26.4 *Three dimensions of enterprise development.*

that define the future of the enterprise. The enterprise modeling project becomes a step in that strategic plan. Thus the executive level looks at the enterprise modeling project in terms of future opportunity, that is, in terms of investment and return on investment.

What are the general requirements of the executive level with an enterprise modeling methodology such as fsbp? We can say that the executive level is concerned with identifying its economic goals and guaranteeing the accomplishment of these goals by engineering the enterprise and its various subsystems. Also, the executive level is determined that the engineering project be conducted in a productive and managed sequence though they seldom want to participate directly in that management.

We have seen that the early stages of fsbp® (i.e., business definition, stage 1; market and product plan, stage 2; and public policy strategy, stage 3) address these concerns of the executives of the enterprise.

♦ **Project-manager dimension** Second, there are the concerns and influences of the project manager in charge of the enterprise modeling project. The project manager looks at the project in terms of schedules, quality, and cost, in short aspects that relate to the control of the enterprise engineering project. The project manager must answer to the executive level and is very interested in minimization of risk while meeting the project's objectives.

What are the general requirements of the project manager with an enterprise modeling methodology such as fsbp®? To the project manager, a very good way to conduct the project is to use proven and sound project management techniques that have been tested on previous projects in the enterprise. For the project manager, in order to reuse project management techniques, it is very useful to identify the underlying principles that made a project successful and then abstract and codify these principles into a set of instructions to be used on future projects.

The fsbp® methodology is based on the experiences of the authors through many years of enterprise engineering. The fsbp® methodology abstracts and codifies the principles of successful enterprise modeling and presents a comprehensive step-by-step process. The authors have designed fsbp® with the concerns of the project manager in mind.

♦ **Engineering dimension** Third, there are the concerns and requirements of the engineering professionals who must actually engineer the enterprise. The word *engineering* is important here. We are not restricting ourselves to the collegiate or professional disciplines of engineering such as electrical, civil, or software engineering. We are using the word in a broad sense of any occupation that develops complex human artifact. In the words of H. A. Simon, engineers are "concerned with how things ought to be, with devising artifacts to attain goals" (Simon, 1981).

In the case of enterprise engineering, the development "engineers" would be those who are experts at the various subsystems of the business such as operations, marketing, procurement, software and so on. The engineering professionals who are developing the enterprise will use a set of laws, models, concepts, and ideas from their respective fields of expertise. For simplicity, we will call these the *engineering principles* of the enterprise. Because the enterprise is a general system, the engineering principles always relate to the three system views: function, behavior, structure.

What are the general requirements of these engineering professionals with an enterprise engineering methodology such as fsbp? The engineers regard their work in terms of a professional career path. We can say that the engineering professionals are concerned with the identification and codification of their engineering principles so that the principles can be learned, tested, perfected, and reused in a professional career.

The authors have developed fsbp® using a strong theoretical basis of academic formalisms. These academic formalisms are the foundations for the various engineering principles of which the enterprise engineers are concerned.

As we saw earlier, the three dimensions, the executive, the project manager, and the engineering professionals have concerns and needs in the enterprise engineering process. Each wants to take advantage of previous experience and be guided by principles that will guarantee their success. The fsbp® methodology was designed to meet these requirements of the three dimensions.

Thus we have the major requirement of an enterprise engineering methodology, that of specifying the principles for the three levels. We can assume that there will be three sets of principles, one for each of the dimensions (i.e., executive, project manager, engineer). One big question, is the synergy and compatibility of these three sets of principles. For example, on a typical enterprise engineering project, are the principles used by the executive level to define strategy compatible with the principles used by the engineering professionals to engineer the enterprise?

The authors have found in using fsbp® that there is considerable synergy and compatibility between the three dimensions because the methodology considers the enterprise as a system. The theory of systems is a very powerful paradigm that holds the three dimensions together. This means that all enterprise activities become systems activities: starting an enterprise is really the same as developing a system; strategic planning in an enterprise is just a form of systems planning; managing an enterprise is the same as administering a system; reengineering an enterprise is a systems modification project. Again, we are reminded of Sutherland's isomorphisms between differing phenomena unified by general systems theory introduced earlier in this chapter.

Part 7

Backmatter

Introduction to Part 7

THIS PART OF THE BOOK PRESENTS the backmatter, which consists of the following:

- ◆ **Appendix A**   Appendix A presents a starter set of structural patterns.

- ◆ **Appendix B**   Appendix B presents a starter set of enterprise modeling classes.

- ◆ **Appendix C**   Appendix C describes the Martin-Odell modeling technique known as *object-flow diagramming*.

- ◆ **Appendix D**   Appendix D presents the principal tool of the enterprise modeler: the matrix.

- ◆ **Appendix E**   Appendix E is a list of references cited throughout the book.

Appendix A

Starter Set: Structural Patterns

A.1 Introduction

In Chapter 3, we presented abstraction layering as a structural principle of complex systems such as the enterprise. While there are many different possible abstraction layerings of the enterprise, we can generalize the various abstraction layerings into a series of structural patterns. A structural pattern is a broad-based paradigm, model, or example that can be used to define or reason about the abstraction layers of the enterprise. In this appendix is a somewhat eclectic collection of important structural patterns that can be used and reused in designing any enterprise.

In this appendix, each structural pattern is presented as a series of layers. Each layer of a structural pattern represents a different abstraction strata of the overall structural pattern. The enterprise components that make up a given layer are business processes. Structural patterns are applicable to any level of process decomposition of the enterprise. Thus at the higher levels of process decomposition, structural patterns are used to design the structure of the ABPs while at the lowest level, structural patterns are used to design the structure of process elements.

The following set of structural patterns is presented as a starter set and is intended to stimulate enterprise engineers to create a customized set, which they can use to model a specific enterprise. The structural patterns are placed into categories and are arranged more or less in order of the most general to the specific. The structural patterns can be used in the design of the enterprise including both building new enterprises as well as reengineering existing ones. While the domain of design is intended to be the enterprise, many of the structural patterns apply to the abstraction layering of any general system.

> The authors are very interested in perfecting and expanding this set of structural patterns and to serve as the clearing house for the definition and documentation of enterprise structural patterns. If the reader has any additions, corrections, or suggestions please contact the authors by Internet e-mail at 76635.3346@compuserve.com

A.2 General structural patterns

The following structural patterns are applicable to any domain.

Structural pattern: Abstraction

One of the most important structural patterns is the principle of abstraction itself. Abstraction, as we learned in Chapter 1, means hiding complexity coupled with drawing out the essence of a complex domain. Abstraction is used to present to a user of a system a simplified or focused view of a complex world. The abstraction structural pattern is the underlying principle of many of the other structural patterns presented in this appendix.

Figure A.1 shows the essential parts of the abstraction structural pattern.

The abstraction structural pattern consists of three layers:

- The user layer is the current focus of the design. The designer has determined that this layer needs access to services or resources provided by another part of the system indicated by the bottom layer in Figure A.1. However, this other part of the system is complex, sophisticated, ornate, or intricate. The design problem to be solved is to give the user layer efficient access to this complex world of the bottom layer.

- The designer solves the problem by designing a middle layer between the user layer and the complex world. This middle layer is an abstract world that presents a simplified or focused view of the complex world. This view of the world is oriented to the user layer and is presented using ideas, ter-

Figure A.1 *Abstraction structural pattern.*

Figure A.2 *Change structural pattern.*

minology, and paradigms from the user domain. Thus the detailed, confusing, or sophisticated subsystems of the bottom layer are presented to the user as a simplified, pertinent, and useful subset.

◆ The bottom layer is the complex world. It contains subsystems that require their own expertise and are guided by their own principles or laws.

Structural pattern: Change

A typical problem to be solved by the enterprise designer is that of the potential for change. The designer must make it easy to manage change and implement change in the target enterprise. This problem can often be solved by the layered-architecture approach. In effect, the designer segments the subsystems into layers depending on their change profiles. Most hierarchical-multilayered systems are either already divided into layers with different change profiles or can be naturally partitioned in this way so that using this structural pattern should be fairly easy. The change structural pattern is especially useful in characterizing the layers of the broader system and in deciding where new functionality should be placed.

Figure A.2 shows the essential parts of the abstraction structural pattern.

The change structural pattern consists of three layers arranged by their relative change profiles:

◆ At the top layer are placed subsystems with the least prospect for change.

♦ The middle layer is where the subsystems with medium change activity are placed.

♦ The bottom layer is for subsystems that undergo frequent change.

Structural pattern: Time

A design problem that is similar to the change structural pattern is the time structural pattern. The designer must segment the subsystems into layers by their sense of time. Time becomes a factor in the design of systems, usually in the form of the system's cycle time, which is the period of time in which a complete state transition occurs in the system without need for more input. For example, the conceptual process (as well as all of its subtypes) has a product cycle in which one instance of its product is created by transforming various input entities. Like the change structural pattern, most hierarchical-multilayer systems are usually already divided into layers with different perspectives of time anyway. Thus the time structural pattern should be easy to use and can be effective in characterizing the layers of the system or deciding where proposed system functions belong.

Figure A.3 shows the essential parts of the time structural pattern.

The time structural pattern consists of three layers:

♦ Subsystems with the longest cycle times are placed in the top layer. Typical time horizons might be measured in days, weeks, or years in this layer.

♦ The middle layer is where the subsystems with medium cycle times are placed. For example, time might be measured in hours and days in this layer.

♦ The bottom layer is where subsystems with rapid cycle times are placed (e.g., in seconds or minutes).

A.3 Information structural patterns

The following structural patterns relate to the general information characteristics of a layered structure.

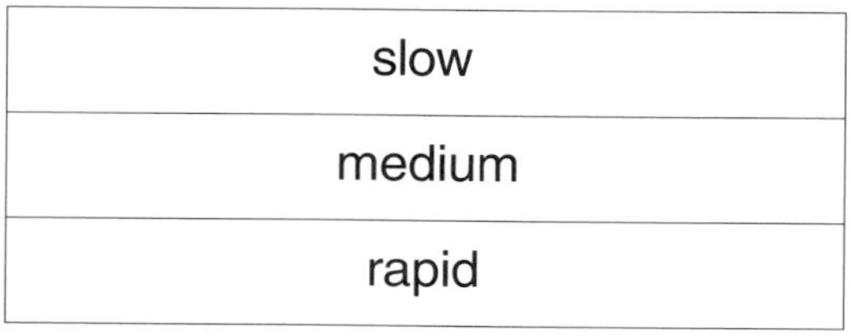

slow
medium
rapid

Figure A.3 *Time structural pattern.*

Structural pattern: Information transfer time

The next two structural patterns relate to information flow. These structural patterns are primarily used to describe or characterize the abstraction layers of a hierarchical-multilayer system, as opposed to providing design guidelines. The first information flow structural pattern characterizes the typical transfer time of information as it is sent from one information-processing node to another. This transfer time is the amount of time it takes information to be communicated and stored.

Figure A.4 shows the essential parts of the information transfer time structural pattern.

The information transfer time structural pattern consists of three layers. Each layer has its own characteristic information transfer time:

- The top layer contains information that has the scope of the entire enterprise. Individual information-processing nodes that operate in the enterprise layer transfer information and store it (internalize it) at a slow rate measured in hours or days (e.g., because the information and ideas are complex).

- The middle layer contains information with the scope of an organization (i.e., several information-processing nodes responsible for one or more abstract business processes). The individual information-processing nodes that operate at this level of scope transfer information and store it in minutes or hours.

- The bottom layer contains information with the scope of a physical information-processing node. This is the internal world of the machine or person in which the information transfer time is measured in seconds (including fractional seconds such as milliseconds, microseconds) to minutes.

Structural pattern: Information transfer quantity

The next information flow structural pattern characterizes the typical amount of information transferred from one information-processing node to another. The

| Enterprise: Hour-Day |
| Organization: Minute-Hour |
| Physical Node: Second-Minute |

Figure A.4 *Information transfer time structural pattern.*

| Enterprise: Kbyte-Mbyte |
| Organization: Byte-Kbyte |
| Physical Node: Bit-Byte |

Figure A.5 *Information transfer quantity structural pattern.*

transfer quantity is the amount of information (number of physical symbols) transferred in a typical message exchange between information-processing nodes.

Figure A.5 shows the essential parts of the information transfer quantity structural pattern.

The information transfer quantity structural pattern consists of three layers. Each has its own characteristic information quantity of the typical message:

♦ The top layer contains information that has the scope of the entire enterprise. Individual information-processing nodes that operate in the enterprise layer transfer kilobytes (thousands of bytes) to megabytes (millions of bytes) in each message exchange.

♦ The middle layer contains information with the scope of an organization (i.e., several information-processing nodes responsible for one or more abstract business processes). The individual information-processing nodes that operate at this level of scope transfer bytes to kilobytes in each message exchange.

♦ The bottom layer contains information with the scope of a physical information-processing node. This is the internal world of the machine or person in which the information transferred is measured in bits or bytes.

A.4 Planning structural patterns

The next two structural patterns relate to planning. Planning means determining a future state based on the current state coupled with a possible sequence of future events. Planning is one of the classic duties of a meta-layer, a layer that creates goals then monitors its operations-layer for the accomplishment of its goals. If necessary, the meta-layer will adjust the operation or products of its operations-layer. These planning structural patterns are primarily used to describe the planning layers of an enterprise (but could be used for any goal-seeking general system, i.e., a type 4 using the classification scheme introduced in Chapter 2).

| Enterprise: Month-Year |
| Organization: Day-Week |
| Physical Node: Second-Day |

Figure A.6 *Planning horizon structural pattern.*

Structural pattern: Planning horizon

The first planning structural pattern characterizes the scope of the planning process as a time horizon.

Figure A.6 shows the essential parts of the planning horizon structural pattern.

The planning horizon structural pattern consists of three layers arranged by their relative time horizons to planning:

- ◆ The top layer conducts planning that affects the entire enterprise. The planning horizon of this layer covers a period of time measured in months to years.

- ◆ The middle layer consists of the planning functions of the various organizations (groups of information-processing nodes assigned the responsibility of one or more abstract business processes). The planning horizon of the middle layer covers a period of time measured in days to weeks.

- ◆ The bottom layer contains planning functions of the individual physical information-processing nodes. The planning horizon of the bottom layer is measured in seconds to days.

Structural pattern: Planning function

The second planning structural pattern characterizes the function of the planning process itself.

Figure A.7 shows the essential parts of the planning function structural pattern.

The planning horizon structural pattern consists of three layers arranged by their relative change profiles:

- ◆ The top layer conducts planning which affects the entire enterprise. This planning would be described as strategic planning.

- ◆ The middle layer conducts planning which affects an organization (groups of information-processing nodes assigned the responsibility of one or more ABP's). This planning would be described as tactical planning.

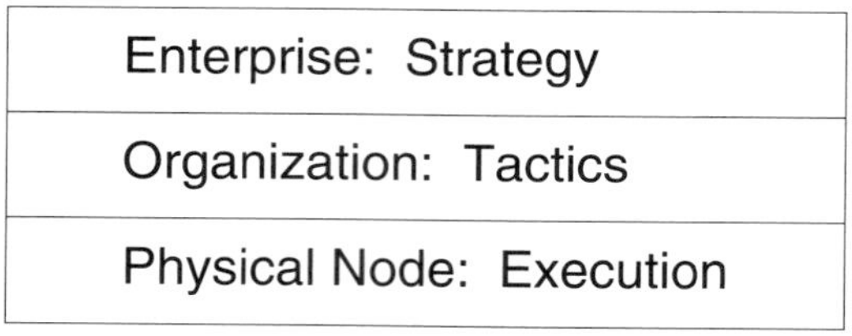

| Enterprise: Strategy |
| Organization: Tactics |
| Physical Node: Execution |

Figure A.7 *Planning function structural pattern.*

♦ The bottom layer conducts planning for an individual physical information-processing node. This planning would be described as execution
   planning.

A.5 Infrastructure structural patterns

The next set of structural patterns relates to the layering of the infrastructure of an
enterprise. An infrastructure is an underlying capital-intensive physical substrate
that provides services to the information-processing nodes of the enterprise. An
infrastructure is usually physically ubiquitous; that is, the substrate covers a geographical area. Some enterprises provide the use of their infrastructure as their
product, such as a telephone system, electrical utility, or highway system. Our own
information-processing network described in this book is an example of an infrastructure. The infrastructure structural patterns presented next are concrete examples of the principle of abstraction.

Structural pattern: Infrastructure

First, we will describe the infrastructure structural pattern itself and then discuss
several other related structural patterns.

Figure A.8 shows the essential parts of the infrastructure structural pattern:

The infrastructure structural pattern consists of three layers:

♦ The customer layer needs the services of the physical substrate. Usually
   this need is frequent or pervasive; the need is not unique to a specific user
   or user function and many, perhaps most, users or user functions need the
   service.

♦ The designer gives the customer layer access to the physical substrate by
   designing an interface layer that sits between the customer layer and the
   physical substrate. This interface layer takes advantage of the abstraction

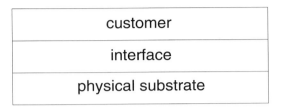

Figure A.8 *Infrastructure structural pattern.*

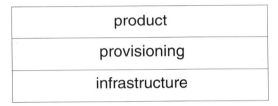

Figure A.9 *Infrastructure-product structural pattern.*

structural pattern by presenting a simplified or useful view of the complex world of the physical substrate.

◆ The bottom layer is the ubiquitous physical substrate. It contains complex subsystems and provides products and services to various subsystems of the general system. It is capital intensive requiring major system investment of resources.

Structural pattern: Infrastructure product

A typical management function of an infrastructure is the design and provisioning of products that the infrastructure provides. An infrastructure product uses the infrastructure substrate in a way useful to the customer by packaging functionality. This is best approached by the three-layer infrastructure-product structural pattern.

Figure A.9 shows the essential parts of the infrastructure-product structural pattern. The infrastructure-product structural pattern consists of three layers:

◆ The product layer presents to the customer a set of useful services provided by the infrastructure.

◆ The designer gives the product layer access to the infrastructure by designing a provisioning layer sitting between the product layer and the infrastructure. The provisioning layer performs the function of binding a product to specific infrastructure components in real time.

◆ The bottom layer is the infrastructure substrate, which consists of physical components organized into subsystems. The subsystems are themselves a layer of abstraction of the physical substrate. The infrastructure is usually single purpose in the sense that it provides a single, very broad fundamental capability such as power (e.g., electrical infrastructure) or communications (e.g., telephone infrastructure).

A.6 Resource usage structural patterns

The following structural patterns relate to the management and usage of resources.

Structural pattern: Allocation

A very useful structural pattern often associated with infrastructures and especially infrastructure products is the pattern of allocation. This means the temporary binding of subsystems of one layer with subsystems of another layer considered as resources. The point is that resources are expensive and can be shared by the various subsystems of the broader system. This sharing is accomplished by using the allocation structural pattern.

Figure A.10 shows the essential parts of the allocation structural pattern.

The allocation structural pattern consists of three layers:

◆ The top layer is the demand layer. It contains multiple, competing users, each of which requires limited resources at unpredictable times.

◆ The designer gives the demand layer access to resources by designing a binding layer that sits between the demand layer and the resource layer. The binding layer performs the function of allocating resources to specific requests. This may involve queuing requests and the use of optimization to

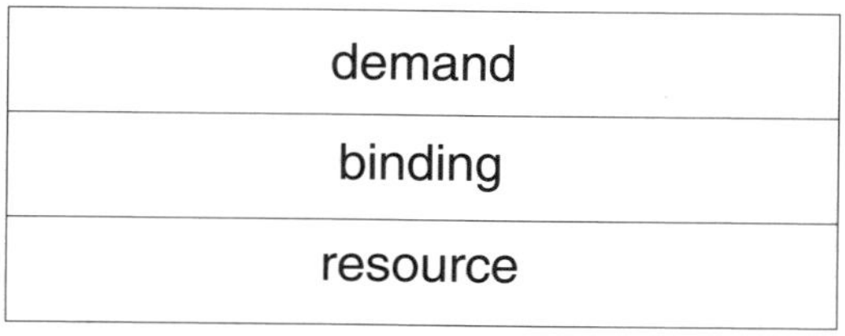

demand
binding
resource

Figure A.10 *Allocation structural pattern.*

select the most efficient use of the limited resources. Two allocation modalities are possible: the long-term allocation and the short-term allocation. The long-term allocation would be used when the resource is being allocated for a relatively long period of time compared to the short-term allocation (e.g., permanently). The short-term allocation modality is used when the allocation of the resource to the user is relatively short (e.g., one product cycle).

◆ The bottom layer is the resources. One of the points of the allocation structural pattern is that these resources are expensive and limited so must be shared.

Structural pattern: Brokerage

This is another very useful pattern for designing the provisioning layer of infrastructure products. Brokerage makes possible the use of different suppliers to provide resources to customers. As such, brokerage tends to be an ABP-oriented pattern that allows customer ABPs and supplier ABPs to be brought together. In this case, the infrastructure is the channeling substrate that connects customers to suppliers. Once brought together, a contract exists between the customer and the supplier. The system has knowledge of this contract and causes future activity of the customer to be channeled into the selected supplier. Notice that a second tier of one or more resource-demand transactions may occur during the life of the contract. That is, the customer and the supplier remain "connected" for an extended session beyond the first transaction in which multiple negotiations and resource consumption occurs.

Figure A.11 shows the essential parts of the brokerage structural pattern.

The brokerage structural pattern consists of three layers:

◆ The top layer is the usual demand layer, but in this case, it takes the form of general customers who have needs and are willing to enter into contracts. This involves expressing the customer demand with an appropriate description language. The description language is able to express the specific requirements of the customer (i.e., specific to the resource domain).

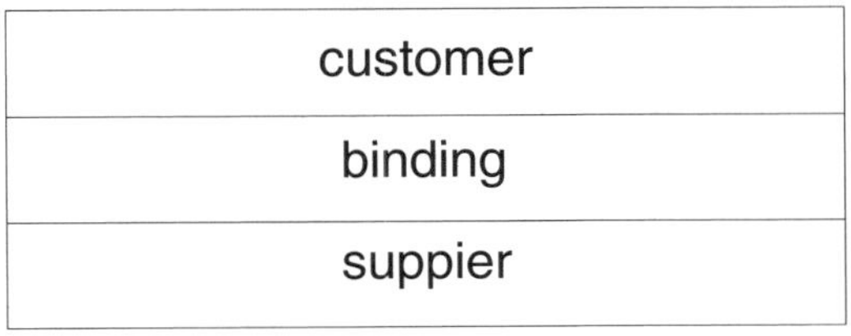

customer
binding
suppier

Figure A.11 *Brokerage structural pattern.*

♦ The designer gives the customer access to supplier-controlled resources by designing a brokerage mechanism as the middle layer. This layer binds the customer to a specific supplier as well as to resources of the supplier. This involves interpreting the customer demand as expressed in the description language. The supplier offers services using this same description language. The binding layer of the brokerage pattern matches the two in an orderly and fair way using algorithms mutually agreed upon by the community of suppliers. A significant component of the binding layer may be shepherding a negotiation process between customer and suppliers. Sometimes a two-stage brokerage scenario is used in which the first stage brings the supplier and the customer together in a general contract and the second stage provides the allocation of specific resources offered by the selected supplier. Once the contract has been negotiated and agreed upon, the system provides channeling between customer and suppliers in which service will be provisioned using the various infrastructure-product patterns discussed elsewhere in this appendix.

♦ The bottom layer contains the suppliers. Suppliers offer their resources to the brokerage layer (i.e., expressed in terms of the description language). Suppliers have heterogeneous resources that provide the various functions useful to the customers. Suppliers always have the right to withdraw or change the resources offered to the brokerage layer.

A.7 Software structural patterns

The next set of structural patterns relate to software. We have already encountered the representation of software in the form of scripts that are sequences of symbols representing instructions. Recall that a script is a sequence of symbols that is interpreted by a physical symbol system proposed by Allen Newell and Herbert Simon. The physical symbol system is the integral information-processing component of people and computers.

However, software is much more general than scripts. Software is purposely constructed by the meta-layer of a hierarchical-multilayered system and loaded into the corresponding operations-layer. The instructions are coded using specific symbols and grammar that follow the restrictive rules of the software definition. Since software is a series of symbols, it can be changed easily. This is one of the points of symbol representation (see Chapter 4). That is, symbol representation is accomplished by using an easily modifiable sequence of codes that may be stored by physical encoding or transmitted by information carrying energy. Thus the sequence of instructions of the software may be easily constructed and modified. Indeed, freedom to construct and modify the instructions easily is the economic value of software. Examples of software are musical scores, company procedures, cookbooks, as well as computer programs. The software pattern is very useful for achieving the middle abstraction layers of several of the structural patterns discussed in this appendix.

Structural pattern: Software

First we will describe the software structural pattern itself, and then we will discuss several other related structural patterns.

Figure A.12 shows the essential parts of the software structural pattern.

The software structural pattern consists of three layers:

- The top layer is where the sequences of symbols representing the software are placed. As explained earlier, software consists of a series of instructions encoded using specific symbols and grammar. The instructions, which are intended for the middle interpreter layer, are imperatives or commands that the middle layer must perform in the order specified. The instructions direct the middle layer to manipulate the lower-level hardware to accomplish the needs of the top layer.

- As usual, the middle layer implements a virtual world. In this case, it is an interpreter, performing the instructions presented from the top layer. We have discussed the interpreter before as an integral component of the physical symbol system. The interpreter is a process that decodes the sequence of instructions and maintains its own state information about the context of the process. It performs its useful work by presenting commands to the lower hardware level. For example, in the case of a musical score, the middle layer is the human player who interprets the musical score of the top layer. In this case, the hardware level is the musical instrument. The human interpreter manipulates the musical instrument (presents commands) to produce music.

Figure A.12 *Software structural pattern.*

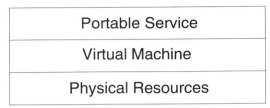

Figure A.13 *Portability structural pattern.*

- ◆ At the bottom is the hardware layer. The hardware has capabilities but lies inert until activated by the commands from the middle interpreter layer.

Structural pattern: Portability

One use of the software structural pattern is to solve a very common design problem, that of the need for portability of parts of the system. Portability means that a system function must be capable of being moved and implemented in another environment. This design problem is solved by using the portability structural pattern. The portability structural pattern is used by designers to design a system so that a system function is not dependent on a specific environment by creating an abstraction of that environment.

Figure A.13 shows the essential parts of the portability structural pattern.

The portability structural pattern consists of three layers:

- ◆ At the top layer are placed subsystems that may be ported into or out of this system. The point is that components of the top layer can be easily moved and implemented on top of another set of resources using the portability structural pattern.

- ◆ The middle layer is the usual abstraction layer. It creates a virtual machine that presents generic services to the top layer. The middle layer abstracts the essence of the capabilities of the lower layer into a standardized set. If a subsystem of the top layer is to be ported in or out, then as long as it continues to use this standard set, no changes to it are needed. If changes are needed because of unique needs of the ported subsystems, this is the only layer that needs to be changed, if at all. Also, if the bottom layer changes due to new physical resources, again, this is the only other layer that needs to be changed leaving the top layer unaffected.

- ◆ The bottom layer is the complex world of the unique system resources. It accepts the commands from the middle layer to perform its primitive operations.

Figure A.14 *Reusability structural pattern.*

Structural pattern: Reusability

The software structural pattern is also used to solve a very common design problem, that of the need for reusability of enterprise resources. The primary objective of reusability is to meet future demand by using resources all ready owned by the enterprise. A secondary objective of reusability is to find alternative uses for the expensive resources owned by the enterprise.

Figure A.14 shows the essential parts of the reusability structural pattern.

The reusability structural pattern consists of three layers:

◆ The top layer represents the resource demands that come from other subsystems in the system. Ideally, we hope to satisfy these demands with resources we already have. This demand comes from the operation of the various subsystems of the system. Notice that in goal-seeking, adaptive systems (level 4 in Chapter 2), a significant part of the operation of the system is spent adapting the system to the future. In our modern terminology, we would call this *reengineering*. Thus, the demand referred to in this top level may be anything from simple resource consumption to demands for major restructuring of the system itself.

◆ The middle layer is, as usual, the abstraction layer. This time it is used by the system designer to create reusable components made up of various configurations of resources from the lower level. This is usually accomplished in software. Ideally, a reusable component would already exist prior to the time it is needed. The middle layer would anticipate future demand. This means that the reusable component is general enough to satisfy future needs. To make a component general enough for unspecified future use, the system designer must abstract the value of the underlying resources. That is, the underlying resources have immutable economic value that arises from their own intrinsic properties. The designer of the middle layer must abstract that value from the lower-level resources and design generalized components using various configurations of those resources. The reusable components so designed will be characterized as useful and pertinent to the current and future system when they are used in the future.

♦ The bottom layer is the complex world of the system resources. They are expensive capital items representing not only financial investment but expertise investment by the system.

Structural pattern: Polymorphism

Polymorphism is a very useful pattern for designing the provisioning layer of infrastructure products. Polymorphism takes advantage of the abstraction of functionality of the substrate to provide flexible real-time binding. The infrastructure is often managed as a resource pool. New units are added to the resources pool to increase the resource capacity of the infrastructure. The new units come from the latest generation of technology and have their own operations, which are usually similar but more sophisticated when compared with the existing units already installed in the infrastructure. Thus the polymorphism pattern is very useful in cases where the infrastructure is heterogeneous due to historical deployment, technology generations, or multiple vendors. The polymorphism structural pattern is typically implemented by software.

Figure A.15 shows the essential parts of the polymorphism structural pattern. The polymorphism structural pattern consists of three layers:

♦ As usual, the top layer is the demand layer. However, in this case it is presented as a catalog of useful functions. The functions are consistently defined and present a unified view of the infrastructure considered as logical services. For example, the user would invoke a function on a resource (i.e., that has been allocated to it). The resources are heterogeneous but can be abstracted into a set of meaningful functions. In effect, the top layer defines what will happen but not how.

♦ The designer gives the top layer consistent logical functions implemented by the resource-pool layer by designing a flexible binding layer that sits between them. This layer performs the translation from the "what" to the "how" in real time, thus shielding the user from this translation. The point of the binding layer is that it implements the function catalog of the top layer and hides the many differences of the units in the heterogeneous resource pool.

♦ The bottom layer contains the resources. It consists of heterogeneous units that provide similar functions but are subtlety different because, for example, they are from different vendors or technology generations.

| catalog of functions |
| flexible binding |
| hetrogeneous resource pool |

Figure A.15 *Polymorphism structural pattern.*

| economics & goals |
| market information processing |
| production |

Figure A.16 *ABP meta-layer pattern.*

A.8 Abstract business process structural patterns

The final set of structural patterns relate to the abstract business process (ABP).

Structural pattern: ABP meta-layers

We have already encountered this structural pattern in our discussion of the ABP in Chapter 15. The ABP has a hierarchical-multilayer structure consisting of three layers: an operations-layer at the bottom with two meta-layers above it.

Figure A.16 shows the essential parts of the ABP meta-layers structural pattern. The ABP meta-layer structural pattern consists of three layers:

- ◆ **Economics and goals**   This is the meta-layer that transforms input information into economic knowledge and produces the goals of the ABP.

- ◆ **Market information processing**   This is the meta-layer that transforms environmental marketing information into the definition of products as well as the definition of the technology and processes to produce the products.

- ◆ **Production**   This is the operations-layer, which transforms input products from suppliers to final products that are sold to customers. This layer also services the products once they are sold to customers.

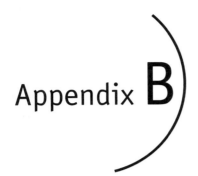

Appendix B

Starter Set: Enterprise Modeling Classes

B.1 Introduction

This appendix gives a starter set of the major abstract classes of the enterprise modeling class hierarchy. This starter set of enterprise classes is arranged into an object class hierarchy as discussed in Chapter 5. The purpose of this starter set of enterprise modeling classes is to define a library of enterprise modeling concepts. The enterprise modeling classes can be used by enterprise modelers to build an object-oriented enterprise model by selecting classes from the hierarchy for use in an enterprise model. Also, enterprise modelers can expand this starter set by defining subclasses corresponding to the unique concepts in their own enterprise model. In this way, the enterprise model will be made up of a set of uniform concepts that are used and reused in the enterprise modeling project and defined formally in the enterprise modeling class hierarchy.

There are three major branches of the enterprise modeling class hierarchy: the entity classes, the scene classes, and the activity classes. Entities represent structure, scenes represent complex arrangements, and activities represent dynamics. In our description of the various classes of the enterprise modeling class hierarchy, we will describe only the upper parts of the inheritance hierarchy.

B.2 Enterprise class hierarchy

Figure B.1 shows the highest level of the enterprise modeling class hierarchy, the level containing the three major branches of the class hierarchy. In later sections we will show the class hierarchies under each of these major branches.

Enterprise root class

This is a place holder that anchors the enterprise modeling class hierarchy. It is the ultimate abstract class and could be used to place attributes and behavior which every class would inherit.

Entity class

This represents the abstract class that anchors the entity class subhierarchy. Entities are the "things" of the enterprise and represent anything that is defined, treated, or evaluated as a whole. We gave the details of this class in Chapter 8. To summarize, this abstract class contains the properties (i.e., attributes and behavior) inherited by all entity objects. For example, this abstract class (see Figure 8.1) contains the attributes for the parent-child relations with other entity objects (part of, consists of). This abstract class contains the behavior inherited by all entity objects, such as maintaining its relations with its parent object or its collection of children objects. We will define the subclasses of the entity class further in a later section.

Activity class

This represents the abstract class that anchors the activity class subhierarchy. Activities represent dynamic behavior involving a collection of entities. This abstract class contains the attributes inherited by all activities, including metrics

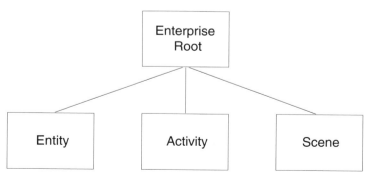

Figure B.1 *Upper classes of the enterprise class hierarchy.*

(start time/date, end time/date), the collection of activities with which it is temporarily related, and the collection of entities it affects. This abstract class contains the behavior to maintain its metrics and maintain its collection of entities and activities. We will define the activity classes further in a later section.

Scene class

This represents the abstract class that anchors the scene class subhierarchy. Scenes represent complex arrangements of objects (including entity objects and other scene objects). This abstract class contains attributes of its collection of objects as well as its collection of scenes of which it is a member. This abstract class contains the behavior to maintain its collections of objects. We will define the subclasses of the scene class further in a later section.

B.3 Entity classes

The entity class hierarchy is a subhierarchy of the enterprise modeling class hierarchy introduced earlier and will contain the classes representing the various entities of the enterprise. Figure B.2 shows the upper parts of the enterprise modeling class hierarchy, which will be referenced in the text below:

Real entity class

This is a place holder for anchoring the real entity class subhierarchy. This abstract class contains the attributes inherited by all real entities, such as physical properties, location, and cost (both initial cost and a collection of maintenance costs). It contains a collection of capability objects (defined shortly) that describe its characteristics. Its behavior consists of maintaining these attributes:

- **Product class**   This is the generic product entity class of a real product. It would serve as the abstract class to various product entity subclasses. It contains behavior corresponding to the product's life cycle and maintains its product capabilities.

- **Various product subclasses**   This is where the various enterprise entity product subclasses would be placed.

- **Resource class**   This is the abstract resource entity class. Notice that it is a subclass of the product class because all resources are at one time a product; they are created by upstream business processes. The resource class contains attributes describing its use as a resource such as allocation attributes and a collection of its usage history. The resource class contains

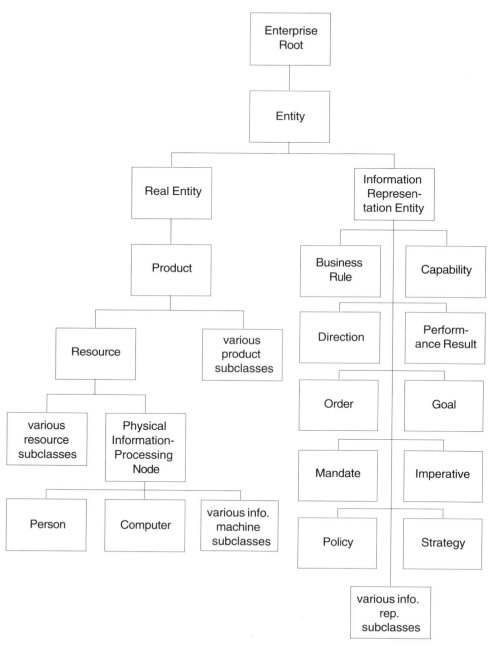

Figure B.2 *Upper classes of the entity class hierarchy.*

behavior to keep track of its resource usage (e.g., allocation, depletion) and to maintain its resource capabilities.

◆ **Information-processing node class**   This is the abstract physical information-processing node class. Physical information-processing nodes are one of the most important resources of the enterprise and have been discussed at length throughout the book. The information-processing node class contains attributes describing a node in an information-processing network such as connections to channels of one or more information-processing networks. The information-processing node class also contains attributes for describing memberships in organizations, assignments to processes as a change mechanism, etc. It contains behavior for participating in the network (sending, receiving, and storing information) as well as participating in an organization (membership, reporting, payment). Its major subclasses (not shown) are the Person class, Computer class and any other information machine subclasses identified by the enterprise.

The person class is an abstract class that models a human being for purposes of enterprise modeling. It is a place holder for the various subclasses of workers, managers, or executives of the enterprise as well as people associated with the enterprise such as people in the customer or supplier enterprises.

The computer class is an abstract class that models a computer. It is a place holder for the various general-purpose computers, intelligent network nodes, embedded processors, etc.

The box labeled "various information machines" subclasses is a place holder for other machines that have the physical symbol system capabilities to receive, store, and process information such as numerical controlled milling machines, etc.

◆ **Various resource subclasses**   This is where the various other enterprise entity resources subclasses would be placed. Enterprise resources were discussed in Chapter 24 (Figure 24.4).

Information representation entity class

This represents the abstract class that anchors the information representation entity class subhierarchy. Information representation entities are also "things" of the enterprise, but they do not have the same sense of physical reality. Their corporal reality is as physical information, a lesser characteristic. More importantly, information representation entities are used as surrogates for other objects, including scenes, activities, and physical entities. Thus, if we ever want to consider these other objects as information abstractions (which is extremely likely), we would have appropriate surrogates in the information representation entity class hierarchy. Notice that we do not have a class for the abstract entities as our conceptual type hierarchy does (described in Chapter 6, Figure 6.1). This is because abstract entities represent thoughts and ideas and would always be represented by a corresponding information representation entity in any analysis. There's no reason to have an abstract entity subhierarchy since we would always represent an abstract entity as an information representation entity anyway.

We have already encountered several information-representation entities that we can place in the hierarchy. This hierarchy would also be where software objects are placed when the time comes to build the object-oriented software of the enterprise. The entities include:

- **Business rule** This is an abstract class representing the hierarchy of business rules. It has attributes of the declaration of its rule as well as a list of other objects which are controlled by the business rule. Its behavior would include the rule-oriented processing of testing and enforcement. Subclasses (not shown) would include the three subtypes of business rules: the functional business rule class, structural business rule class, and behavioral business rule class corresponding to the three subtypes of business rules we encountered in Chapter 13.

- **Capability** This is an abstract class representing a description of a capability. Recall that a capability (introduced in Chapter 8) is the ability of an object to perform actions (typically associated with process objects) or be used to perform actions (typically associated with entity objects). It has attributes describing the specifics of the capability as well as the collection of objects that possess this capability. Its behavior will include answering if its owner meets a requirement or request for a capability from some other object which needs it. Examples of subclasses (not shown) of the capability class would include product-functional property classes, market-functional requirements classes, or customer-functional needs classes.

- **Direction** This is the abstract direction class. It is used by a superior process to communicate with a subordinate process. It contains attributes describing the directions, such as what to do, when, and the expected results.

- **Performance result** This is the abstract performance-result class. It is used by a subordinate process to communicate with a superior process concerning the status of directions. The performance-result class contains attributes describing the original directions and the actual results or status so far.

- ◆ **Order**   This is the abstract-order class. An order is a solicitation sent to other objects typically to process objects to obtain products or services. The order class contains attributes describing the order, such as issue date/time, due date/time, description of what is being ordered, etc. It contains behavior corresponding to the order life cycle.

- ◆ **Goal**   This is the abstract goal class. It is used by a process to define its goals. It contains attributes describing the goal, which consists of the proposed future state of a collection of objects. For example, typical goals might be the enterprise's desires relative to: size and growth, and return or profit. The goal class contains behavior to manage its collection of objects and to report the status of the accomplishment of the goal. A subclass of the goal class (not shown) is the objective class.

- ◆ **Imperative**   This is the abstract imperative class. Imperatives were described in Chapter 18 and are statements representing a broad agenda for achieving successful entry and/or long-term viability in a market (a typical enterprise will have a few hundred imperatives). Imperatives state the things that are fundamental to competitive success and with which any business must be able to deal in order to succeed within the target industry. Imperatives include both positive opportunities to pursue as well as pitfalls to be avoided. An Imperative objects includes a collection of mandate objects that cover the imperative in the sense of "if imperative, then mandate." An imperative object also includes a collection of business rule objects, which are implied by the imperative.

- ◆ **Mandate**   This is the abstract mandate class. Mandates were described in Chapter 18 and are statements of critically important issues to the enterprise. The mandates should comprise all of the values and motivating logic behind every enterprise decision. Imperatives are synthesized into a small set of mandates. A typical enterprise will have 6 to 10 mandates. A mandate object includes a collection of imperative objects, which the mandate covers in the sense of "if imperative, then mandate."

- ◆ **Policy**   This is the abstract policy class. Policies were described in Chapter 20 and represent decisions of the enterprise that are typically public in nature but also include any non–market-based or non–economic-based decision. A policy object has an associated collection of business rule objects, which are implied by the policy. Also, a policy object has a corresponding collection of mandate objects, which the policy leverages.

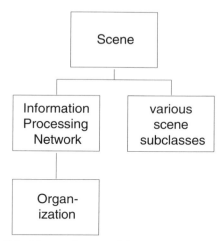

Figure B.3 *Upper classes of the scene class hierarchy.*

♦ **Strategy** This is the abstract strategy class. A strategy is a proposed sequence of state changes of a collection of objects. A strategy object has a corresponding collection of mandate objects, which the strategy supports (directly or indirectly). A major subclass of the strategy class is the plan class (not shown).

♦ **Various information representation subclasses** This is where the various other enterprise entity information representation subclasses would be placed.

B.4 Scene class hierarchy

The scene class subhierarchy will contain the classes representing complex arrangements of entity objects or other scene objects. Figure B.3 shows the upper parts of the scene class subhierarchy, which will be discussed in the text following.

Information-processing network class

This is the abstract information-processing network class. It contains attributes describing a network of communicating information-processing nodes, including attributes for the collection of member information-processing nodes, the collection of communication channels, and the arrangement of the communications channels. It contains behavior to manage the communication network as an infrastructure including resource allocation, usage recording, billing, repair and recovery. Also, it contains behavior to manage its collection of member nodes including membership, reporting, and payment.

Notice that this class must contain attributes and behavior similar to the information-processing node (discussed previously). This is because the information-processing network can be abstracted as an information-processing node.

Organization class

This is the abstract organization class. It is a subclass of the information-processing network class. It contains attributes describing an organization, such as its collection of resources and assigned business processes. It contains behavior representing various global functions of the organization described in Chapter 15. These include:

- ◆ Allocation function: provides resources for business processes

- ◆ Membership function: keeps track of membership in the organization

- ◆ Reporting function: provides organizational information to other organizations

- ◆ Boundary function: controls the organization's boundary

- ◆ Management function: controls the integrity of the organization

Subclasses of the organization (not shown) include various groupings of information-processing nodes (e.g., team class, department class, enterprise class, etc.).

Various scene subclasses

This is where the various other enterprise scene subclasses would be placed.

B.5 Activity class hierarchy

The activity class hierarchy will contain the classes which cause enterprise change. Figure B.4 shows the upper parts of the activity class hierarchy, which can be referenced in the text following.

Process class

This is the abstract process class we described in detail in Chapter 8.This class is one of our main concerns in enterprise modeling. The process class has the following subclasses:

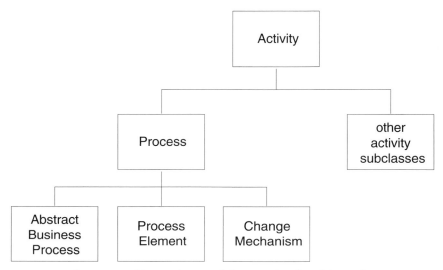

Figure B.4 *Upper classes of the activity class hierarchy.*

- **Abstract business process**   This is a subclass of the process class that represents the abstract business process (ABP) introduced in Chapter 14.In addition to the attributes it inherits, the ABP contains the six specialized subclasses (management and control, marketing, inbound logisitics, operations, sales and services, and outbound logistics). The subclasses (not shown) of this class include classes representing these six, namely: management and control class, marketing class, inbound logistics class, operations class, sales and service class, and outbound logistics class.

- **Process element**   This is the elementary process that is not (by definition) an abstract business process and thus does not have the standard set of six subprocesses. We will give a starter set of the subclasses of the process element class in the next section.

- **Change mechanism class**   This is the abstract change mechanism class. We described this class in detail in Chapter 8. Recall that every process has a change mechanism that is physically implemented by an information-processing node. We define it here as a class primarily for completeness. In actual enterprise modeling, the change mechanism class is not significant since the much more dominant and visible information-processing node is usually the focus of modeling.

In effect, the change mechanism class models the process of executing a process. We say that the change mechanism is itself a process because it is a purposeful sequence of actions that creates events, which in turn results in the execution of a process. Also the change mechanism must receive events (from other change mechanisms). Notice that we are not talking about the actual meaning of either its actions or what it does to respond to a given event. Instead, we are talking about the process of blindly executing actions or receiving events. That is, an information-processing node has a physical reality which would remain inert if it weren't for its change mechanism process. A familiar example of a change mechanism is the process of executing a program in a computer. The computer is an information-processing node that contains a process within its central-processing unit to execute a computer program. The process of actually executing the computer program is its change mechanism.

Various activity subclasses

This is where the various enterprise activity subclasses would be placed.

B.6 Process element classes

The following describes some of the major process element classes that will find wide use in enterprise modeling. Recall that a process element is the lowest level of process decomposition where physical information-processing nodes transform input products into output products. Thus process elements represent the lowest level, consisting of the atomic processes of the enterprise. All other higher-level processes are ultimately composed of process elements. Thus process elements represent the level of greatest possible reusability and the enterprise modeler can obtain the greatest leverage of reusability at this level. The following list of process elements should be regarded as a starter set to stimulate the development of an enterprise-unique set of process element classes.

Interface process class

This process element class provides generic business process interface processing. Interface processes are used to implement use cases described in Chapter 14. Interface processing consists of first providing the means to contact the host process followed by starting the sequence of the contact scenario itself. The interface process element also logs the contact. The actual contact scenario is provided by subclasses that make use of this abstract class:

- **Supplier interface process class**   This abstract class provides generic supplier interface processing and is a subclass of the interface class where much of the generic processing is defined. Supplier interfacing is specialized to conducting use cases with suppliers and making available information representing the current context of the enterprise's relationship with the supplier. Other information is also made available, such as fixed information about the supplier.

- **Customer interface process class**   This abstract class provides generic customer-interface processing. Customer interfacing is specialized to conducting customer use cases and making available information representing the current context of the enterprise's relationship with the customer. Other information is also made available, such as fixed information about the customer.

- **Superior interface process**   This abstract class provides generic superior interface processing. Superior interfacing is specialized to conducting use cases with lower-level business processes including giving direction to lower-level business processes and receiving performance feedback from them.

- **Subordinate interface process**   This abstract class provides generic subordinate interface processing, which is specialized to receive direction from upper-level business processes and giving performance feedback to them.

Management process class

This abstract business process provides generic management processing. Management processing is conducted by creating the direction product that is sent to other business processes using the superior and subordinate interface processes:

- **Planning process**   Planning will be an important component of most management activities. This abstract class will provide generic planning processing. The primary output of planning is a proposed sequence of future events and corresponding future states of a target set of objects. The main activity during planning is what-if analysis, seeing what happens if the attributes of the target objects are changed in certain ways. This class will be subclassed whenever there is a need for the capability of planning in a business process. There will be many opportunities to use this class, such as product planning or infrastructure strategy planning.

- **Forecasting process**   Forecasting is the process of predicting a future state of a collection of objects as defined by the values of their attributes. The primary activity is prediction, starting with the current values of the attributes of the objects in question, which are changed by a scenario (sequence of simulated events) to arrive at a new state of the objects. This abstract class can be subclassed whenever there is the need for the capability of forecasting in a business process. There will be many opportunities to use this class, such as infrastructure capacity forecasting or skills forecasting.

◆ **Controlling process** Controlling is the process of sending directions to other process objects. Directions are information objects that contain what to do when and the expected results. This abstract class can be subclassed whenever there is a need for the capability of controlling in a business process. Controlling also includes receiving performance reports back from the controlled process describing the results of the process. The controlling process is closely associated with the superior and subordinate interface processes described earlier.

◆ **Monitoring process** Monitoring will be an important component of most resource and process management activities of various business processes. This abstract class will provide generic monitoring processing. It can be subclassed whenever there is the need for the capability of monitoring in a process. The primary action of monitoring is an action trigger, occurring when a predefined condition becomes true. Monitoring is performed by continual sampling, looking, polling, and testing for the trigger condition. There will be many opportunities to use this class, such as monitoring network use or business performance.

◆ **Reporting process** Reporting is the process of sending performance results to other process objects. Performance results are information objects that contain the original directions and the actual results. This abstract class can be subclassed whenever there is a need for the capability of reporting in a business process.

Assessment process class

This process element provides generic assessment processing. It provides the structure of a three-step assessment process consisting of determining assessment categories, developing assessment criteria or measurements, and performing the actual assessment. This abstract class will consist of the following subclasses:

◆ **Quality assessment process** This abstract class provides generic quality assessment processing. Since it is a subclass of the more general assessment process, it inherits the structure of the assessment scenario. This abstract class specializes the assessment scenario to the domain of quality. The three-step assessment scenario is specialized as follows: first, the determination of the assessment categories are specialized to become quality measurement categories; second, the assessment levels are developed as quality performance measurements (numerical); and third, the assessment evaluation becomes a process of accumulating data and comparing it to the performance levels.

◆ **Auditing process** This abstract class provides generic auditing. Auditing is the process of evaluating the state of the target object using the specified test scenarios, which provide the semantic context of the test. Auditing will produce exception alerts to a collection of registered objects who have requested to be notified.

Inventory management process class

This process element class will provide generic inventory processing of an inventory (collection) of generic objects. The primary product of inventory management is the management of a collection of resources. Inventory processing deals with managing the collection of resources as it relates to the life cycle of the individual objects. The life-cycle management will be generic but useful and will include generic services to

- ◆ Determine probable requirements of inventory objects
- ◆ Secure an adequate supply of the inventory objects
- ◆ Store inventory objects
- ◆ Issue and deliver inventory objects
- ◆ Record transactions and maintain history
- ◆ Prepare and furnish data for cost and financial accounting

This class may be subclassed to support a specific inventory business process. Several inventories must be maintained by an enterprise. For example:

- ◆ Employee inventory
- ◆ Heavy-equipment inventory
- ◆ Skills inventory
- ◆ Training records
- ◆ Vendor inventory

Financial management process class

This process element class will provide generic financial account processing. This class is closely associated with the financial transaction process (discussed next). This class may be subclassed to construct the various financial accounting processes of the enterprise including budget process classes, journals process classes, cash management process classes, or debt management process classes.

Financial transaction process class

This abstract class provides generic financial transaction processing. A financial transaction is a unit of processing in which the specified account is debited or credited. This class is closely associated with the financial management process classes (above) and may be subclassed to provide specific transaction processing depending on the corresponding financial management process.

Allocation process class

This process element class will provide allocation services on queues of generic objects waiting to be assigned a generic resource object. The primary product of allocation is orderly use of a scarce resource by providing a single point of control through which competing requests are serialized. Allocation processing typically involves associating a designated object considered the resource to a client that may have to wait in a queue before being serviced. The set of client objects are in competition with each other for use of the scarce resource object. Thus the allocation classes will permit the definition of the enterprise's selection policy (criteria to be used to select an object from the waiting queue of objects). The allocation classes will have a monitoring process (discussed above) to wake up and see if the scarce resource has become available for allocation. This class may be subclassed to develop specific allocation capabilities in business processes that do allocation.

Scheduler process class

Closely coupled to the allocation process class is the scheduler process class. This process element class will provide generic scheduling services to provide orderly future activity against the target object. The primary output of scheduling is the association of future time-slot objects to the object in question. Scheduling involves comparing calendars (collections of time-slot objects) to see if the given time slot is available or not. For example, if the time slot is available, it is placed in the calendar collection. If the time slot is not available, another time slot can be sought or a negative response can be returned, depending on the context. This class may be subclassed to develop specific scheduling capabilities. There will be many opportunities to use this class because the use of scheduling in the business flows will be a common requirement. Some examples are scheduling expensive one-of-a-kind tools or scheduling heavy equipment.

Classification process class

This process element class performs generic classification processing consisting of classification, reclassification, and declassification of the target input object. Classification consists of examining the collection of capability objects of the input object. These capabilities represent pertinent properties to be used in the classification process. The process of classification consists of evaluating the capability objects and selecting another object called the classification abstraction object, which serves as the classification abstraction. The actual classification algorithm is implemented in the subclasses to this abstract class. The classification abstraction object is a collection object and the input object being classified is added to the collection. Reclassification is similar but starts with the removal of the input object from the specified classification abstraction collection. Declassification is just the removal of the input object from the specified classification abstraction.

Selection process class

This abstract class will provide generic selection services. This process element is similar to the classification process element described above. The classification is performed to produce a classification abstraction object but there is no retention of the classification knowledge by adding the input object to the classification abstraction object collection as is done in the classification process. Rather, the classification abstraction object is returned as the selection.

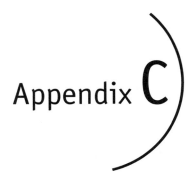

Appendix C

Object-Flow Diagrams

C.1 Introduction

In their book, *Object-Oriented Analysis & Design*, James Martin and James Odell proposed a useful process-modeling technique (Martin and Odell, 1992). Their object-flow diagramming is used for analyzing and documenting process dependencies based on the concepts of the Porter value chain (described in Chapter 13). In this appendix, we will explain this technique.

C.2 Overview of object-flow diagramming

The object-flow diagram (figure C.1) is a process model of the Porter value chain. In effect, an object-flow diagram combines the concepts of the business process and Porter's value activity. Recall that we stated in Chapter 13 that the ABP and the Porter value chain are equivalent. The object-flow diagram represents key enterprise activities as business processes linked by the products that are produced and consumed.

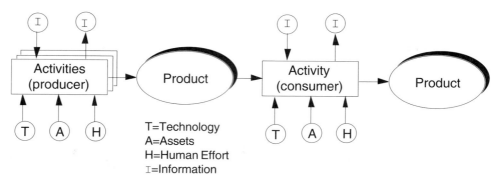

Figure C.1 *Object-flow diagram.*

C.3 Activities

The activities shown in Figure C.1 are continuous processes. They are persistent, and we are not concerned with when they are activated or when they are terminated. Activities can be thought of as small businesses that maintain their own black box world.

Input-output
An activity consumes products and, in turn, produces a product and possibly some associated information. The product is then consumed by a downstream activity:

♦ **Outputs**   An activity produces the following:

        Product

        Information (I)

♦ **Inputs**   An activity consumes the following:

        Information (I)

        Technology (T)

        Assets (A)

        Human effort (H)

        Products from upstream stream activities

Decomposition of activities

Activities are decomposed into more detailed object-flow diagrams. The decomposition can continue until a level of detail is reached at which the activity can be modeled as an event schema. An event schema can be expressed as

- ◆ A state-transition diagram (we originally introduced it in Chapter 2)

- ◆ Script expressed as a series of steps that cause state changes (we originally introduced scripts in Chapter 4)

C.4 Products

The product shown at the center of Figure C.1 is an asset produced by an activity. It fulfills the purpose of the activity and represents the manifestation of its purpose.

Characteristics

A product has the following characteristics:

- ◆ Input products are consumed by activities in the sense that they become an integral part of the output product in some way. Thus all the products along the value chain somehow become part of the final product at the end of the value chain.

- ◆ The product must be salable either to the next activity or to the outside market.

- ◆ The product must have measurable quantity and quality. Unless the product can be counted and graded, the reason for producing it is questionable.

Single output product

The object-flow diagramming technique can result in complex interrelationships of the diagram activity nodes. To simplify the diagram and the conceptual model, the following convention is used:

- ◆ An activity can take in many products but produce only one product.

- ◆ Where large activities produce several products, the activity should be broken down into several smaller, single-product activities.

Producer/consumer relationship

The flow of products from producer to consumer takes place because of the relationship between the producer and the consumer. This relationship is actually a mutual agreement between the two parties:

- **Communications protocol**   The first point on which the producer and the consumer must agree is the format and syntax of the information exchange itself. This requires the exchange of information back and forth to establish this agreement. Once agreed upon, it becomes part of the reusable state information of the two parties and doesn't have to be reestablished.

- **Relationship information**   Both the consumer activity and the producer activity maintain state information about their mutual relationship, such as historical or performance information about their past exchanges.

Producer/consumer scenario

The producer activity and consumer activity must exchange messages during the life of the contract. These message exchanges use the communications protocol. They occur at predictable points of time and are performed using well-defined message exchange scenarios, which we call *use cases*. We discussed use cases at length in Chapter 14. In object-flow diagramming, we are interested only in a summary definition of the use cases to portray process dependencies. Here is a brief list of abridged use cases that a consumer activity and producer activity exchange:

- ◆ Negotiate price quality level, delivery schedule (consumer to producer)

- ◆ Place order (consumer to producer)

- ◆ Respond to order (producer to consumer)

- ◆ Communicate product specifications (consumer to producer)

- ◆ Ship product (producer to consumer)

- ◆ Receive product (consumer to producer)

- ◆ Communicate problems (consumer to producer)

- ◆ Respond to problems (producer to consumer)

- ◆ Return product (consumer to producer)

C.5 Porter value chain

Porter's generic value chain (see Chapter 13) can be readily modeled using the object-flow diagramming techniques described earlier. Recall that the generic value chain consists of primary activities and secondary activities.

Porter value chain: Primary activities

The primary activities of the generic enterprise would be modeled as shown in Figure C.2. Figure C.2 shows the generic activities and products that make up the primary activities of an enterprise. See Chapter 13 for a detailed explanation of their meaning.

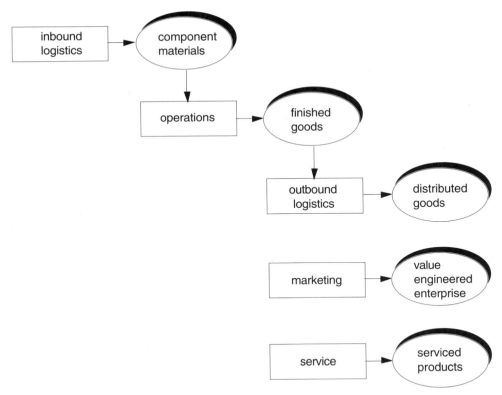

Figure C.2 *Porter value chain: primary activities.*

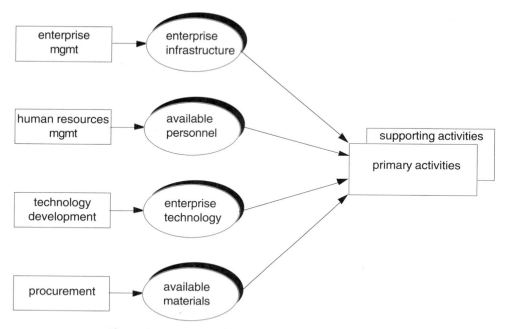

Figure C.3 *Porter value chain: supporting activities.*

Porter value chain: Supporting activities

Similar to the primary activities, the secondary activities of the Porter's generic value chain (see Chapter 13) can be readily modeled using object-flow diagramming. Recall that the support activities support the rest of the enterprise, including the primary and supporting activities. Figure C.3 shows the generic activities and products that make up the supporting activities of an enterprise.

Object types

As it relates to object-oriented terminology, the object-flow diagramming technique leads to the identification and definition of the objects of the enterprise:

- **Process object**   An activity is an executing process object.

- **Entity objects**   The process object representing the activity accesses or uses entity objects, including:

    Input products

Output product

Technology components used

Assets used (i.e., other than technology components)

People (input human effort)

Input information entities

Output information entities

Suppliers (organizations)

Customer (organization)

C.6 Value measurements

To measure the value and performance of an activity, we focus on the cycle of the activity, the transformations that takes place within a designated measurement interval. The cycle's designated measurement interval corresponds to the natural cycle of the process, such as the interval to produce one unit of product (or a designated number of product units).

Value metrics

We can develop useful performance-oriented value metrics around the average cycle including:

- ◆ Average elapsed time per cycle of activity

- ◆ Average cost per cycle of activity

- ◆ Average number of products per cycle

- ◆ Average cost per product

Alternatively, the cycle's designated measurement interval can be fixed; that is, it can be chosen as any meaningful fixed length of time that makes sense for the process, such as one day. We can then develop meaningful performance metrics centered around the fixed-time interval:

- ◆ Average cost per cycle of activity

- ◆ Average number of products per cycle

- ◆ Average cost per product

Value chain concept

An activity transforms its inputs (products, technology, information, human effort) into an output product. This output product must be more valuable (or at least as valuable) as the sum of the costs of the constituent inputs. The meaning of value is centered around the idea of usefulness to the customer of the activity. That is, a product must be useful to downstream activities and must contribute directly to the corresponding activity of producing the downstream product. Therefore, the enterprise is made up of a series of value activities, each of which produces something more important and useful out of something that is less so. Thus, the value V of an activity must meet the following relationship with the cost C of the activity:

$$C_a \leq V_a + I_a$$

where

C_a = cost of the product produced by the activity

V_a = value of the product produced by the activity

I_a = the value of the output information produced by the activity

$$C_a = \Sigma C_p + \Sigma C_t + \Sigma C_a + \Sigma C_h + \Sigma C_i$$

where

ΣC_p = sum of the costs of the input products

ΣC_t = sum of the costs of the technology used

ΣC_a = sum of the costs of the other assets used (in addition to technology)

ΣC_h = sum of the costs of the human effort

ΣC_i = sum of the costs of the input information

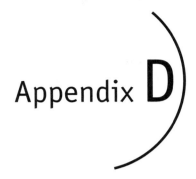

Appendix D

Comparative Evaluations Using Matrices

D.1 Introduction

The scale of information accumulated in the business planning process can be daunting. An excellent approach for accomplishing the necessary comparative analysis of this much information is to use simple two-dimensional matrices. Aside from the analytical advantages this approach presents, it also provides an excellent tool for communicating the rationale behind analytical observations and choices.

If the scope of subject information is too diverse, more than one two-dimensional matrix is used rather than attempting to establish multidimensional models. The quantization of qualitative and or quantitative values associated with the information is kept as simple as possible, and the value scale is only as granular as necessary to establish clear differentiation between the entities being compared. Since this is generally a relative thing—comparisons usually are—this is all that is necessary to gain the appropriate knowledge from the gathered information.

These matrices can provide very rich and interesting relationships between and among the gathered information. What follows is an example of how to use matrices to evaluate and compare some rather broad and diverse sets of information. In this case, taken from an actual study, we were looking for a determinant of the amount of communication required within various industries.

D.2 Example: Information content

A review of fundamental information theory establishes a direct correlation between the information intensity of a process and the need to communicate that information. This *intensity* refers to the mass or volume of information, the degree and complexity of interrelationships in the information, and the velocity and scope of information movement within a company. All companies process information within their internal systems. If a company is characterized as information intensive, its information processing consists of frequent updating in which the information itself has complex relationships. Companies with this profile might be stock brokerages or hospitals, as opposed to other types of companies, which tend to have plenty of typical business information (accounts, payroll, etc.), but the information is neither frequently updated nor especially complex when compared to the information-intensive company. Examples of these types of businesses include electric power utilities or wholesale distributors.

Figures D.1 and D.2 present a preliminary look at various industry markets from the perspective of the information intensity in the three operational aspects of business: procurement, process, and distribution. The generic industry market segments are grouped by large players and small players. For our purposes, major players are considered to be those with annual gross revenues of $1 billion or more.

On both the large and small industry matrices, the cumulative communications expenditure is evaluated for each category. Segment size in dollars are rated in both matrices as follows:

1 = less than $10 billion annual revenue

2 = from $10 to $100 billion per year

3 = $100 billion or more per year

The number of participants in each segment is also displayed. This strongly affects market strategy: A business depending on a segment with few participants is very vulnerable to share (and revenue) erosion. The defection of even one buyer to a competitor results in a significant percentage loss of the total business. Conversely, a segment with many customers is more susceptible to competitive entry or expansion. Given large numbers of alternative buyers, at least a few will always be willing to try a new alternative supplier.

At the same time, however, having many players also helps incumbent providers defend their position. Initial competitor successes do not have significant impact upon market share and revenues. This leaves incumbents with both time and resources for mounting an effective response. The number of participants in each segment is counted in both matrices as follows:

1= fewer than 1000 participants

2 = between 1000 and 100,000 participants

3 = 100,000 participants or more

When studying the matrices, keep in mind that

- ◆ industry segment (shown in columns) refers to a market partition based on commonly accepted criteria. Industry segmentation is used because it encompasses all inter- and intra-enterprise communication opportunities,

- ◆ information Intensity is made up of operational areas (top three rows) and measurements of size (bottom two rows),

- ◆ operational areas (first three rows) are the three major flows in a business, which tend to be useful categories for determining information intensity,

- ◆ size in dollars and number of players(bottom two rows) show the relative industry opportunity size in dollars and customers,

- ◆ rating system (shading) consists of echelons as explained earlier.

The view shown by the information content of industry markets matrices demonstrates multiple aspects of the marketplace when values are applied and added by each row and column:

- ◆ Opportunity relative to each industry (columns)

- ◆ Operational area(s) (rows) around which you may wish to leverage

- ◆ Relative size of the industry opportunity in dollars and customers (rows)

- ◆ Segments (columns) in which products may be highly leveraged

From a pure market perspective and according to this matrix, the three large industries to pursue as information intensive would be education, health services, and finance. The most attractive small industry segments would be communications providers, government, and finance. Finance emerges as the leading contender on both the large and small industry segment matrices and would be an

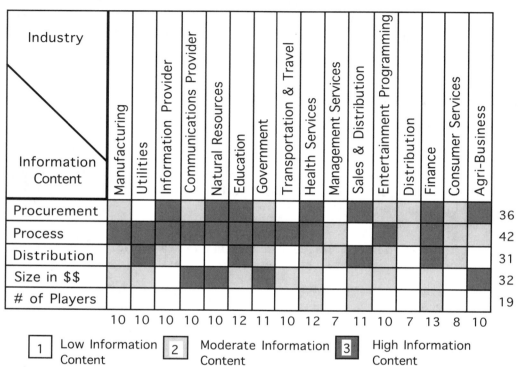

Figure D.1 *Information content of large industry markets.*

obvious first target segment. However, results from matrices on competitive alternatives, technology trends, and general consumer trends must also be considered before selecting target markets.

This analysis approach demonstrates the degree of universal information intensity within the business domains of procurement, process, and distribution. When considering the results of this matrix alone, the specific functional and physical attributes of the proposed business' infrastructure environment should be constructed with maximum ability to support the business process operational area of any industry segment. The process area has the highest aggregate information intensity of the three business domains for both large and small segments.

This example used two matrices to illustrate the same characteristics for entities (industries) that are separated based upon a fundamental differentiation (size), which cause them to have significantly different or not easily comparable metrics.

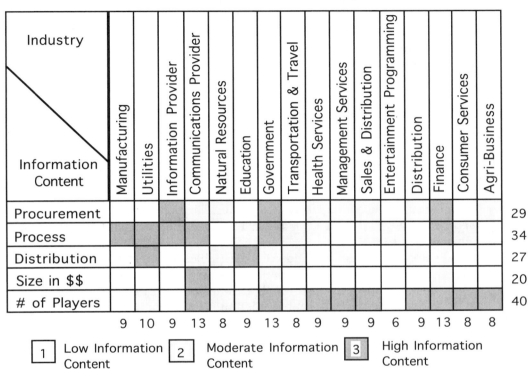

Figure D.2 *Information content of small industry markets.*

In other cases, you might use multiple matrices in the same subject area handle complexities in the scope of information. Competitor analysis is an example in which four separate matrices are produced and then the results of these are compared in still another matrix. The following is another actual case demonstrating this approach.

D.3 Example: Competitor analysis

The following five competitive analysis matrices present an evaluation of current or expected competitors in a major midwestern city. We have evaluated their goals and objectives, assumptions and internal beliefs, capabilities, and their strategies. They are assessed by category from the perspective of a new communications transport business intending to subsume access. That is to say, we have assessed the degree of threat that they pose to the new business. Given the results of the four analyses, we then provide an overall competitive analysis matrix that demonstrates the degree of competitiveness within the proposed geographic area.

The first matrix evaluates and ranks competitors' goals and objectives in 10 areas. Table D.1 provides definitions for each area and the rating criteria applied.

Among other things, this exercise demonstrates who is most closely focused upon the same target market as the competitive telecommunications carrier. It also gives a feel for the degree or intensity of that focus. The results demonstrate that MCI's goals relate strongly to those of the new business. MCI is followed closely by AT&T and Cellular One. The objectives of MFS are also strongly linked to the same business area, though not as strongly as the others.

From an intensity standpoint, these three players' strategies are rated as being very highly competitive with the strategy of the proposed business. It should also be noted that the current leader in this Midwestern market, U S WEST, has goals that conflict least with the competitive telecommunications carrier's goals.

Remember that we should keep these results in context with those of the remaining competitive analyses.

The final category column, which isn't on the tables, is consistency. This is used in the same manner for all of the competitive assessments. Consistency is the degree to which a competitor's position in all matrix categories are consistent and leverage together to achieve the stated mission. Consistency is evaluated as follows:

> 1 = inconsistent
>
> 2 = consistent but little dynamic synergy
>
> 3 = extremely leveraged

Figure D.3 is the competitor goal analysis matrix.

Next, the strategies of the competitors are evaluated based upon their apparent viability relative to the current environment, the current state of their business, and emerging trends. The categories assessed are fairly straightforward and the ratings are similar to those in the goal analysis. The results of the competitor strategy analysis are represented in Figure D.4.

From this matrix, we can see that MCI and AT&T are again strongly positioned. Their strategic approaches are rated as being very appropriate to achieving their goals. While MFS has moved up compared to the last perspective, and Cellular One has fallen off, the others remain relatively weak. Looking at the columns, the categories of industry product, business management, and financial strategies appear to be particularly effective. On the other hand, there is a pronounced weakness in the industry relative to handling the emerging industry transition. Other categories

---

Table D.1   Competitor goal analysis categories and ranking criterion

Mission—the overriding purpose for being in business.
   1 = strong and directly competitive
   2 = strong but indirectly competitive, or weak and directly competitive
   3 = weak and not directly competitive

Business Management Capability—how competitive, effective, and pragmatic is
   leadership provided and articulated. Includes executive management and board.
   1 = conservative and tactical
   2 = moderate
   3 = flexible and effective

Generic Strategy—positioning and market strategy aptness relative to goals.
   1 = inconsistent with goals or unrealistic
   2 = moderately appropriate
   3 = appropriate and effective

Technology Deployment—ability of existing and planned base relative to goals,
   includes extent of current and planned deployment in the target market.
   1 = not leveragable to or consistent with plans and objectives
   2 = base combines applicable and non-applicable facilities in plans
   3 = appropriately deployed and highly leveragable

Constraints—regulatory, anti-trust, or other government or social limitations.
   1 = prohibited from or impeded in realizing plans and goals
   2 = sensitive gray areas and/or sensitivity exists around goals
   3 = there are no constraints

Values—beliefs which significantly affect goal establishment or attainment.
   1 = strongly limiting or inconsistencies with objectives
   2 = neutral effect or non-existent
   3 = strongly empowering - supportive of goal attainment

Profitability—gross margin goals.
   1 = less than 5%
   2 = 5% to 15%
   3 = more than 15%

Size—market share (revenue basis), cash, and book value objectives.
   1 = under 2% of market and $1 million in revenue
   2 = under 10% of market and $100 million in revenue
   3 = more than 10% of market and $100 million revenue

Growth—the desired rate of business growth.
   1 = flat growth—less than 5% per year
   2 = moderate growth—5% to 8% per year
   3 = exceptional growth—more than 9% per year

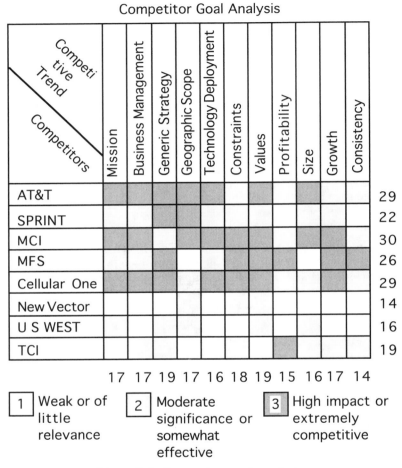

Figure D.3 *Competitor goal analysis.*

of industry weakness include mission, market, and technology strategies. Perhaps more important is that the industry as a whole does not have strategies that leverage well across these specified categories.

The third competitor analysis component deals with competitors' views and beliefs about themselves and the industry environment (Figure D.5). In this analysis, some of the same categories are addressed as in the other three competitor assessments. However, this evaluation looks at the categories from the perspective of competitors' subjective beliefs about each category.

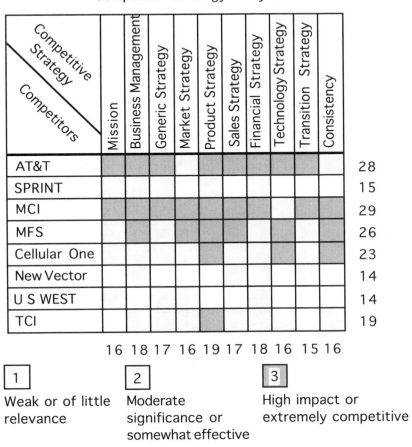

Figure D.4 *Competitor strategy analysis.*

Two things stand out when considering the results of the matrix in Figure D.5. The first is that MCI, MFS, Cellular One, and AT&T have a fairly realistic grasp of the world. Second, when looking at the category results, one sees that the influence of conventional wisdom is a significant industry weakness.

The final component analysis deals with competitors' capabilities to initiate and react to events. The first three diagnoses dealt with competitors' likely competitive activity, the nature of that activity, and its probable intensity. This area deals with competitors' abilities to exert their individual wills upon the industry.

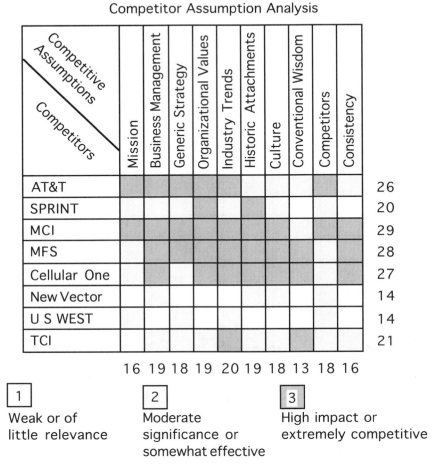

Figure D.5 *Competitor assumption analysis.*

The categories addressed in the capability matrix deal with operational resources, skills associated with their management and use, and the degree to which they complement each other (Figure. D.6).

Again, MCI, AT&T, and MFS dominate the matrix. They appear to be quite powerful. While the industry's weakness seems to be in the categories of profit and operating management, these three are strong or moderate in both. In this assessment, U S WEST, with the largest share of the relevant local market, appears to be among the least capable in the local industry.

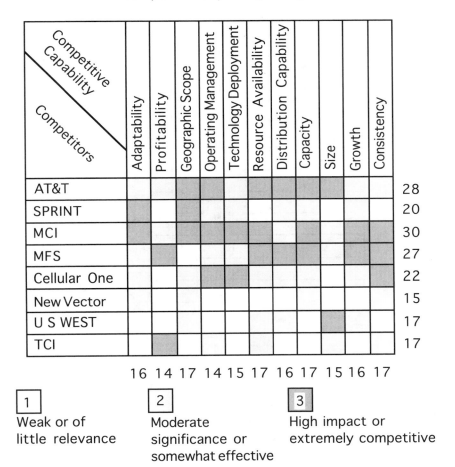

Figure D.6 *Competitor capability analysis.*

The final step in the competitor analysis process is to accumulate the results of the individual assessments into one overall matrix. Consistency and leverage between results from the four phases are evaluated for each competitor. By multiplying the total ratings from goals, assumptions, strategy, and capability by the consistency rating, we derive an overall competitiveness value for each player (Figure D.7).

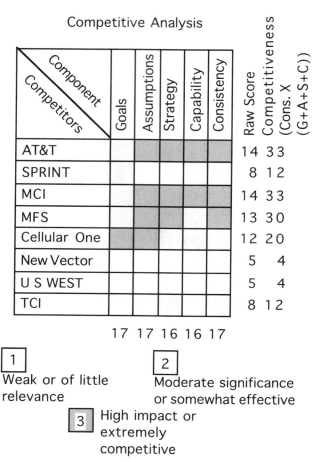

Competitive Analysis

Competitors \ Component	Goals	Assumptions	Strategy	Capability	Consistency	Raw Score	Competitiveness (Cons. X (G+A+S+C))
AT&T		▓	▓	▓	▓	14	33
SPRINT						8	12
MCI		▓	▓	▓		14	33
MFS			▓		▓	13	30
Cellular One	▓	▓				12	20
New Vector						5	4
U S WEST						5	4
TCI						8	12

17 17 16 16 17

| 1 | Weak or of little relevance
| 2 | Moderate significance or somewhat effective
| 3 | High impact or extremely competitive

Figure D.7 *Competitive analysis.*

The median competitive value with this approach is 20. Average competitive potential in each component (column) would aggregate to 16. Rows or columns which vary from these averages signal higher than usual sources of risk or opportunity. For example, a column total of 11 would represent a significant industry weakness to be exploited. A 33 would show significant proficiency which must be equaled, exceeded, or avoided. Similarly, row totals identify weak competitors, which can be exploited, or strong ones, against which defensive strategies can be deployed.

The competitive analysis matrix shows a mediocre competitive environment. However, in looking specifically at the competitors who are focusing upon the same Midwestern market, primarily US WEST and MFS, it can be seen that MFS is an extremely significant threat. The power competitors, AT&T and MCI, are primarily interested in local transport from the perspective of more efficient access to their customers. They might easily be managed with a strategy that provides them complimentary access to their markets. A strategy with comparable effect must be established to offset the competitive position of MFS.

Collectively, these matrices also demonstrate areas of industry weakness. Low total valuations of strategies and capabilities around product, transition and technology strategy, technology and distribution capability, represent competitive weaknesses. A new entrant should take advantage of these areas of opportunity.

D.4 Conclusion

These are two relatively simple applications of the matrix approach to knowledge synthesis. Hopefully, one can see that by applying some thought to the relationships between the elements of information and their attributes, simple matrix structure can be devised, which will present the relationships among and leverage between the information content of the elements.

This matrix approach will be used repeatedly in the analysis and instantiation of information relationships within the methodology.

Bibliography

(Ackoff, 1971) R. L. Ackoff, "Towards a System of Systems Concepts," in *Management Science*, No 17, July 1971.

(Agha, 1986) G. A. Agha, *ACTORS: A Model of Concurrent Computation in Distributed Systems*, The MIT Press, Cambridge, MA, 1986.

(Angyal, 1969) A. Angyal, "A Logic of Systems," in *Systems Thinking*, Harmondsworth 1969.

(Aoki, 1993) T. Aoki, "Future Switching System Requirements," in *IEEE Communications Magazine*, January, 1993, pp. 34–38.

(Appeldorn et al., 1993) M. Appeldorn, R. Kung, R. Saracco, "TMN + IN = TINA," in *IEEE Communications Magazine*, March, 1993, pp. 78–85.

(Apple Computer, 1992) Apple Computer Eastern Research and Technology, *Dylan, An Object-Oriented Dynamic Language*, Apple Computer, Inc., Cupertino, CA, 1992.

(Athey, 1982) T. H. Athey, *Systematic Systems Approach: An Integrated Method for Solving Systems Problems*, Prentice Hall, Englewood Cliffs, NJ, 1982.

(Atkinson, 1991) C. Atkinson, *Object-Oriented Reuse, Concurrency and Distribution: An ADA-Based Approach,* Addison-Wesley Publishing Company, Reading, MA, 1991.

(Bacon, 1993) J. Bacon, *Concurrent Systems: An Integrated Approach to Operating Systems, Database, and Distributed Systems,* Addison-Wesley Publishing Company, New York, NY, 1993.

(Bailin, 1989) S. C. Bailin, "An Object-Oriented Requirements Specification Method," in *Communications of the ACM,* Vol. 32, No 6, May 1989, pp. 608–623.

(Bapat, 1994) S. Bapat, *Object-Oriented Networks: Models for Architecture, Operations, and Management,* Prentice Hall, Englewood Cliffs, NJ, 1994.

(Barr et al., 1993) W. J. Barr, T. Boyd, Y. Inoue, "The TINA Initiative," in *IEEE Communications Magazine,* March, 1993, pp. 70–76.

(Bence, 1993) A. T. Bence, "ANSA–Industry Collaboration in Distributed Systems," in *BT Technology Journal,* Vol. 11, No 1, January, 1993, pp. 61–70.

(Bennett and Policello, 1993) R. L. Bennett, G. E. Policello II, "Switching Systems in the 21st Century," in *IEEE Communications Magazine,* March, 1993, pp. 24–28.

(Berard, 1993) E. V. Berard, *Essays on Object-Oriented Software Engineering,* Prentice Hall, Englewood Cliffs, NJ, 1993.

(Biggerstaff and Perlis, 1989a) T. J. Biggerstaff, A. J. Perlis, Editors, *Software Reusability, Volume 1: Concepts and Models,* ACM Press, Addison-Wesley Publishing Company, Reading, MA, 1989.

(Biggerstaff and Perlis, 1989b) T. J. Biggerstaff, A. J. Perlis, Editors, *Software Reusability, Volume 2: Applications and Experience,* ACM Press, Addison-Wesley Publishing Company, Reading, MA, 1989.

(Black, 1992) U. Black, *Network Management Standards: the OSI, SNMP, and CMOL Protocols,* McGraw-Hill Book Company, New York, NY, 1992.

(Bohm, 1980) D. Bohm, *Wholeness and the Implicit Order,* Ark Paperbacks, London, England, 1980.

(Booch, 1991) G. Booch, *Object-Oriented Design with Applications,* The Benjamin Cummings Publishing Company, Redwood City, CA, 1991.

(Bounding, 1956), K. E. Bounding, "General System Theory—the Skeleton of Science," in *General Systems I,* 1956.

(Boynton et al., 1993) A. C. Boynton, B. Victor, B. J. Pine, II, "New Competitive Strategies: Challenges to Organizations and Information Technology," in *IBM Systems Journal,* Vol. 32, No 1, 1993, pp. 40–64.

(Brathwaite, 1993) K. S. Brathwaite, *Object-Oriented Database Design: Concepts and Application,* Academic Press, Inc., San Diego, CA, 1993.

(Brown, 1991) A. W. Brown, *Object-Oriented Databases: their Applications to Software Engineering,* McGraw-Hill Book Company, Maidenhead, England, 1991.

Buaron, 1981] Roberto Buaron, "New-Game Strategies," *The McKinsey Quarterly* (Spring, 1981), pp. 22–40, The McKinsey Foundation for Management Research, New York, New York

(Burkhart, 1992) R. Burkhart, "Process-based Definition of Enterprise Models," in *Enterprise Integration Modeling: Proceedings of the First International Conference,* C. J. Petrie, Jr, editor, The MIT Press, Cambridge, MA, 1992, pp. 229–238.

(Bußler, 1992) C. Bußler, "Capability Based Modeling," in *Enterprise Integration Modeling: Proceedings of the First International Conference,* C. J. Petrie, Jr, editor, The MIT Press, Cambridge, MA, 1992, pp. 389–398.

(Campbell, 1982) J. Campbell, *Grammatical Man: Information, Entropy, Language, and Life,* Simon and Schuster, New York, NY, 1982.

(Cattell, 1991) R. G. G. Cattell, *Object Data Management: Object-Oriented and Extended Relational Database Systems,* Addison-Wesley Publishing Company, Reading, MA, 1991.

(Caudill and Butler, 1990) M. Caudill, C. Butler, *Naturally Intelligent Systems,* The MIT Press, Cambridge, MA, 1990.

(Chapman et al., 1993) M. Chapman, M. Bagley, A. Oshisanwo, M. Key, "ROSA–the European Community's Open Service Architecture," in *BT Technology Journal,* Vol. 11, No 1, January, 1993, pp. 48–60.

(Chen, 1976) P. P. S. Chen, "The Entity-Relationship Model: Toward a Unified View of Data," in *ACM Transactions on Database Systems,* Vol. 1, No 1, March 1976, pp. 9–36.

(Cheng, 1993) W. K. Cheng, "Distributed Object Database Management Systems," in *Journal of Object-Oriented Programming,* March-April, 1993, pp. 69–74.

(Chiu and Sudama, 1992) D. M. Chiu, R. Sudama *Network Monitoring Explained: Design and Application,* Ellis Horwood Limited, Chichester, England, 1992.

(Chorafas and Steinmann, 1993) D. N. Chorafas, H. Steinmann, *Object-Oriented Databases,* Prentice Hall, Englewood Cliffs, NJ, 1993.

(Coad and Yourdon, 1991a) P. Coad, E. Yourdon, *Object-Oriented Analysis, 2e,* Yourdon Press, Englewood Cliffs, NJ, 1991.

(Coad and Yourdon, 1991b) P. Coad, E. Yourdon, *Object-Oriented Design,* Yourdon Press, Englewood Cliffs, NJ, 1991.

(Coad, 1992) P. Coad, "Object-Oriented Patterns," in *Communications of the ACM,* Vol. 35, No 9, September 1992, pp. 152–159.

(Cockburn, 1993) A. A. R. Cockburn, "The Impact of Object-Orientation on Application Development," in *IBM Systems Journal,* Vol. 32, No 3, 1993, pp. 420–444.

(Connell and Shafer, 1989) J. L. Connell, L. Shafer, *Structured Rapid Prototyping,* Yourdon Press, Englewood Cliffs, NJ, 1989.

(Courtois, 1985) P. J. Courtois, "On Time and Space Decomposition of Complex Structures," in *Communications of the ACM,* Vol. 28, No 6, June 1985, pp. 590–603.

(Curtis et al, 1992) B. Curtis, M. I. Kellner, J. Over, "Process Modeling," in *Communications of the ACM,* Vol. 35, No 9, September 1992, pp. 75–90.

(Daniels and Cook, 1993) J. Daniels, S. Cook, "Strategies for Sharing Objects in Distributed Systems," in *Journal of Object-Oriented Programming,* January, 1993, pp. 27–36.

(Davenport, 1993)T. H. Davenport, *Process Innovation: Reengineering Work through Information Technology,* Harvard Business School Press, Boston, MA, 1993.

(Davidson, 1993) W. H. Davidson, "Beyond Re-engineering: The Three Phases of Business Transformation" in *IBM Systems Journal,* Vol. 32, No 1, 1993, pp. 65–79.

(Davis, 1993) A. M. Davis, *Software Requirements: Objects, Functions, States,* Prentice Hall, Englewood Cliffs, NJ, 1993.

(Decker et al, 1992) K. S. Decker, V. R. Lesser, A. J. Garvey, M. A. Humphrey, "An Approach to Modeling Environment and Task Characteristics for Coordination," in *Enterprise Integration Modeling: Proceedings of the First International Conference,* C. J. Petrie, Jr, editor, The MIT Press, Cambridge, MA, 1992, pp. 379–388.

(DeMarco and Lister, 1987) T. DeMarco, T. Lister, *Peopleware: Productive Projects and Teams,* Dorset House Publishing, NY, 1987.

(Dickerson and Fogarty, 1993) K. R. Dickerson, K. D. Fogarty "The Contribution of the RACE Programme to International Standards," in *BT Technology Journal,* Vol. 11, No 1, January, 1993, pp. 177–182.

(Dillon and Tan, 1993) T. Dillon, P. L. Tan, *Object-Oriented Conceptual Modeling*, Prentice Hall, Englewood Cliffs, NJ, 1993.

(Drucker, 1973) P. F. Drucker, *Management: Tasks, Responsibilities,* Practices, Harper & Rowe, Publishers, Inc., New York, New York, 1973

(Drucker, 1992) P. F. Drucker, *Managing for the Future: The 1990s and Beyond*, Truman Talley Books / Plume, Inc., New York, New York, 1993

(Elbert and Richards, 1993) I. Ebert, P. Richards "Technology's Role in Switching Systems Evolution," in *IEEE Communications Magazine*, January, 1993, pp. 26–32.

(Firesmith, 1993) D. G. Firesmith, *Object Oriented Requirements Analysis and Logical Design: A Software Engineering Approach*, John Wiley & Sons, New York, NY, 1993.

(Forrester, 1961) J. W. Forrester, *Industrial Dynamics*, Boston, 1961.

(Frick and Riis, 1990) J. Frick, J. O. Riis, "Activity Chains: A Method for Identifying and Evaluating Key Areas of Integration in SME's," in *Computer Integrated Manufacturing: Proceedings of the Sixth CIM-Europe Annual Conference, 15–17 May 1990*, L. Faria and W. Van Puymbroeck, editors, Springer-Verlag, London, England, 1990, pp. 119–130.

(Garrahan et al., 1993) J. J. Garrahan, P. A. Russo, K. Kitami, R. Kung, "Intelligent Network Overview," in *IEEE Communications Magazine*, March, 1993, pp. 30–36.

(Gielingh, 1992) W. Gielingh, "Requirements for the Development of Layered Information Models," in *Enterprise Integration Modeling: Proceedings of the First International Conference*, C. J. Petrie, Jr, editor, The MIT Press, Cambridge, MA, 1992, pp. 270–277.

(Glazer, 1993) R. Glazer, "Measuring the Value of Information: The Information-Intensive Organization," in *IBM Systems Journal*, Vol. 32, No 1, 1993, pp. 99–110.

(Gleick, 1987) J. Gleick, CHAOS: Making a New Science, Viking Penguin, Inc., New York, New York, 1987

[Gluck, 1980] F.W. Gluck, "Strategic Choice and Resource Allocation," *The McKinsey Quarterly* (Winter, 1980), pp. 22–23, The McKinsey Foundation for Management Research, New York, New York

(Godfrey and Hendry, 1993) M. D. Godfrey and D. F. Hendry "The Computer as von Neumann Planned It," in *IEEE Annuals of the History of Computing*, Vol. 15, No 1, 1993, pp. 11–21.

(Goldberg and Robson, 1989) A. Goldberg, D. Robson, *Smalltalk-80: the language,* Addison-Wesley Publishing Company, Reading, MA, 1989.

(Goldberg, 1994) A. Goldberg "Keynote Address: Object-Oriented Systems, Not Object-Oriented Programming", Object Expo Conference, SIGS Conferences, Inc., NY, June 6–10, 1994.

(Goranson, 1992a) H. T. Goranson, "Dimensions of Enterprise Integration," in *Enterprise Integration Modeling: Proceedings of the First International Conference,* C. J. Petrie, Jr, editor, The MIT Press, Cambridge, MA, 1992, pp. 101–113.

(Goranson, 1992b) H. T. Goranson, "The CIMOSA Approach as an Enterprise Integration Strategy," in *Enterprise Integration Modeling: Proceedings of the First International Conference,* C. J. Petrie, Jr, editor, The MIT Press, Cambridge, MA, 1992, pp. 167–178.

(Goranson, 1992c) H. T. Goranson, "Services in the SIRIUS-BETA Inter-Integration Domain," in *Enterprise Integration Modeling: Proceedings of the First International Conference,* C. J. Petrie, Jr, editor, The MIT Press, Cambridge, MA, 1992, pp. 341–355.

(Graham, 1991) I. Graham, *Object-oriented Methods,* Addison-Wesley Publishing Company, Reading, MA, 1991.

(Hall and Fagen, 1956) A. D. Hall III and R. E. Fagen, "Definition of a System" in *General Systems I,* 1956.

(Hall, 1989) A. D. Hall III, *Metasystems Methodology: A New Synthesis and Unification,* Pergamon Press, New York, NY, 1989.

(Hammer and Champy, 1993) M. Hammer & J. Champy, *Reengineering the Corporation: A Manifesto for Business Revolution,* Harper Collins Publishers, New York, NY, 1993.

(Handel and Huber, 1991) R. Handel, M. N. Huber, *Integrated Broadband Networks: An Introduction to ATM-Based Networks,* Addison-Wesley Publishing Company, New York, NY, 1991.

(Harmon and Taylor, 1993) P. Harmon, D. A. Taylor, *Objects in Action: Commercial Applications of Object-Oriented Technologies* Addison-Wesley Publishing Company, Reading, MA, 1993.

(Hars and Scheer, 1992) A. Hars, A. W. Scheer "Reference Models for Enterprise-wide Data Engineering," in *Enterprise Integration Modeling: Proceedings of the First International Conference,* C. J. Petrie, Jr, editor, The MIT Press, Cambridge, MA, 1992, pp. 180–188.

(Henderson and Venkatraman, 1993) J. C. Henderson, N. Venkatraman, "Strategic Alignment: Leveraging Information Technology for Transforming Organizations," in *IBM Systems Journal*, Vol. 32, No 1, 1993, pp. 4–16.

(Hewitt and Inman, 1991) C. Hewitt, J. Inman "DAI Betwixt and Between: From 'Intelligent Agents' to Open Systems Science," in *IEEE Transactions on Systems, Man, and Cybernetics*, Vol. 21, No 6, November/December 1991, pp. 1409–1419.

(Hitchins, 1993) D. K. Hitchins, "A Unified Systems Hypothesis," in *Systems Practice*, Vol. 6, No 6, 1993, pp. 613–645.

(Hitson, 1991) B. L. Hitson, "Distributed Systems Infrastructure for a Prolific Manufacturing Enterprise," in *Proceedings of the Twenty-Fourth Annual Hawaii International Conference on Systems Sciences*, B. D. Shriver, editor, IEEE Computer Society Press, Los Alamitos, CA, 1991, Vol. 2, pp. 292–301.

(Hoare, 1972) C. Hoare, "Notes on Data Structuring" in *Communications of the ACM*, 1972.

(Honiden et al., 1993) S. Honiden, N. Kotaka, Y. Kishimoto, "Formalizing Specification Modeling in OOA," in *IEEE Software*,, January, 1993, pp. 54–66.

(Iggulden, 1992) D. Iggulden, "The ANSA Architecture as a Framework for Heterogeneous Execution Environments," in *Enterprise Integration Modeling: Proceedings of the First International Conference*, C. J. Petrie, Jr, editor, The MIT Press, Cambridge, MA, 1992, pp. 503–512.

(Jacobson et al., 1992) I. Jacobson, M. Christerson, P. Jonsson, G. Overgaard, *Object-Oriented Software Engineering: A Use Case Driven Approach*, Addison-Wesley Publishing Company, New York, NY, 1992.

(Jacobson, 1994) I. Jacobson, "Using Objects to Develop Your Business & IT Support—The Use Case Driven Approach," Object Expo Conference, SIGS Conferences, Inc., NY, June 6–10, 1994.

(Jones, 1986) C. Jones, *Programming Productivity*, McGraw-Hill Book Company, New York, NY, 1986.

(Jorgenson, 1992) B. R. Jorgenson, "Model Repository Technology for Model Integration," in *Enterprise Integration Modeling: Proceedings of the First International Conference*, C. J. Petrie, Jr, editor, The MIT Press, Cambridge, MA, 1992, pp. 419–429.

(Katz, 1990) R. L. Katz, "Business/Enterprise Modeling," in *IBM Systems Journal*, Vol. 29, No 4, 1990, pp. 509–525.

(Keen, 1993) P. G. W. Keen, "Information Technology and the Management Difference: A Fusion Map," in *IBM Systems Journal*, Vol. 32, No 1, 1993, pp. 17–39.

(Khoshafian and Abnous, 1990) S. Khoshafian, R. Abnous, *Object Orientation: Concepts, Languages, Databases, User Interfaces,* John Wiley & Sons, New York, NY, 1990.

(Kilov and Ross, 1994) H. Kilov, J. Ross, *Information Modeling: an Object-Oriented Approach,* Prentice Hall, Englewood Cliffs, NJ, 1994.

(Kim, 1990) S. H. Kim *Designing Intelligence: A Framework for Smart Systems,* Oxford University Press, New York, NY, 1990.

(Klir, 1972) G. Klir, *Trends in General Systems Theory,* John Wiley & Sons, New York, NY, 1972.

(Konsynski, 1993) B. R. Konsynski, "Strategic Control in the Extended Enterprise," in *IBM Systems Journal,* Vol. 32, No 1, 1993, pp. 111–142.

(Kosanke, 1991) K. Kosanke, "The European Approach for an Open System Architecture for CIM (CIM-OSA)–ESPRIT Project 5288 AMICE," in *Computing and Control Engineering Journal,* Vol. 2, No 3, May 1991, pp. 103–108.

(Kosanke, 1992) K. Kosanke, "CIMOSA–A European Development for Enterprise Integration, Part 1: An Overview," in *Enterprise Integration Modeling: Proceedings of the First International Conference,* C. J. Petrie, Jr, editor, The MIT Press, Cambridge, MA, 1992, pp. 180–188.

(Kowalkowski, 1994) F. F. Kowalkowski, "The Business Use of Objects", Object Expo Conference, SIGS Conferences, Inc., NY, June 6–10, 1994.

(Kramer and de Smit, 1977) N. J. T. A. Kramer and J. de Smit, *Systems Thinking,* Martinus Nijhoff Social Sciences Division, Leiden, The Netherlands, 1977.

(Krasner, 1983) G. Krasner, Editor, *Smalltalk-80: Bits of History, Words of Advice,* Addison-Wesley Publishing Company, Reading, MA, 1983.

(Kuhn, 1970) T. S. Kuhn, *The Structure of Scientific Revolutions,* The University of Chicago Press, Chicago Illinois, 1970.

(Küppers, 1990) B. Küppers, *Information and the Origin of Life,* The MIT Press, Cambridge, MA, 1990.

(Lantz, 1989) K. E. Lantz, *The Prototyping Methodology,* Prentice-Hall, Englewood Cliffs, NJ, 1989.

(Livesley, 1992) W. A. Livesley, "Object Resource Systems–a Complete Integration Approach," in *Computing and Control Engineering Journal,* November, 1992, pp. 269–274.

(Luftman et al., 1993) J. N. Luftman, P. R. Lewis, S. H. Oldach, "Transforming the Enterprise: The Alignment of Business and Information Technology Strategies," in *IBM Systems Journal,* Vol. 32, No 1, 1993, pp. 198–221.

(Malamud, 1992) C. Malamud, *Stacks: Interoperability in Today's Computer Networks,* Prentice Hall, Englewood Cliffs, NJ, 1992.

(Martin and Odell, 1992) J. Martin, J. J. Odell, *Object-Oriented Analysis and Design,* Prentice Hall, Englewood Cliffs, NJ, 1992.

(Martin, 1989) J. Martin, *Information Engineering, Book 1: Introduction,* Prentice Hall, Englewood Cliffs, NJ, 1989.

(Martin, 1990) J. Martin, *Information Engineering, Book 2: Planning and Analysis,* Prentice Hall, Englewood Cliffs, NJ, 1990.

(Martin, 1991) J. Martin, *Rapid Application Development,* Macmillan Publishing Company, New York, NY, 1991.

(Martin, 1993) J. Martin, *Principles of Object-Oriented Analysis and Design,* Prentice Hall, Englewood Cliffs, NJ, 1993.

(McFadden and Hoffer, 1988) F. McFadden, J Hoffer, *Data Base Management, 2e,* The Benjamin Cummings Publishing Company, Menlo Park, CA, 1988.

(Medina, 1981) B. F. Medina *Structured Systems Analysis: A New Technique,* Gordon and Breach Science Publishers, New York, NY, 1981.

(Mertins et al, 1992) K. Mertins, W. Sussenguth, R. Jockem, "An Object Oriented Method for Integrated Enterprise Modeling as a Basis for Enterprise Coordination," in *Enterprise Integration Modeling: Proceedings of the First International Conference,* C. J. Petrie, Jr, editor, The MIT Press, Cambridge, MA, 1992, pp. 249–258.

(Mesarovic and Takahara, 1989) M. D. Mesarovic, Y. Takahara *Abstract Systems Theory,* Springer-Verlag, Berlin, 1989.

(Mesarovic et al., 1970) M. D. Mesarovic, D. Macko, Y. Takahara, *Theory of Hierarchical, Multilevel, Systems,* Academic Press, New York, NY, 1970.

(Miller and Rice, 1967) E. J. Miller and A. K. Rice, *Systems of Organizations,* London England, 1967.

(Mimno, 1991) P. Mimno, "What is RAD?" in *American Programmer,* January, 1991.

(Minsky, 1985) M. L. Minsky, *The Society of Mind,* Simon and Schuster, New York, NY, 1985.

(Monarchi and Puhr, 1992) D. E. Monarchi, G. I. Puhr, "A Research Typology for Object Oriented Analysis and Design," in *Communications of the ACM,* Vol. 35, No 9, September 1992, pp. 35–47.

(Montgomery, 1994) S. Montgomery, *Object-Oriented Information Engineering: Analysis, Design, and Implementation,* Academic Press, Inc., Boston, MA, 1994.

(Mullin, 1989) M. M. Mullin, *Object-oriented Program Design with examples in C++*, Addison-Wesley Publishing Company, Reading, MA, 1989.

(Mullin, 1990) M. M. Mullin, *Rapid Prototyping in Object-Oriented Systems*, Addison-Wesley Publishing Company, Reading, MA, 1990.

(Nerson, 1992) J. Nerson, "Applying Object-Oriented Analysis and Design," in *Communications of the ACM*, Vol. 35, No 9, September 1992, pp. 63–74.

(Newell and Simon, 1972) A. Newell, H. A. Simon *Human Problem Solving*, Prentice Hall, Englewood Cliffs, NJ, 1972.

(Newell and Simon, 1987) A. Newell, H. A. Simon "1975 Turing Award Lecture: Computer Science as Empirical Inquiry: Symbols and Search", in *ACM Turing Award Lectures: The First Twenty Years*, ACM Press, Addison-Wesley Publishing Company, Reading, MA, 1987, pp. 287–317.

(Nierstrasz et al, 1992) O. Nierstrasz, S. Gibbs, D. Tsichritzis, "Component-Oriented Software Development," in *Communications of the ACM*, Vol. 35, No 9, September 1992, pp. 160–165.

(Norden, 1993) P. V. Norden, "Quantitative Techniques in Strategic Alignment," in *IBM Systems Journal*, Vol. 32, No 1, 1993, pp. 180–197.

(O'Sullivan, 1994) D. O'Sullivan, *Manufacturing Systems Redesign: Creating the Integrated Manufacturing Environment*, P T R Prentice Hall, Englewood Cliffs, NJ, 1994.

(Olson, 1993) D. Olson, *Exploiting Chaos: Cashing in on the Realities of Software Development*, Van Nostrand Reinhold, New York, NY, 1993.

(OMG, 1990) Object Management Group, *Object Management Architecture Guide Revision 1.0*, Framingham, MA, 1990.

(OMG, 1991) Object Management Group, *The Common Object Request Broker: Architecture and Specification Revision 1.1*, Framingham, MA, 1991.

(Osher, 1991) H. Osher, "Distributed Object Management," in *Object Magazine*, September/October, 1991.

(Oshisanwo et al., 1992) A. Oshisanwo, M. Chapman, M. Key, A. Mullery, J. Saint-Blancat, "The RACE Open Services Architecture Project," in *IBM Systems Journal*, Vol. 31, No 4, 1992, pp. 691–710.

(Oxford, 1986) *Dictionary of Computing*, Oxford University Press, New York, NY, 1986.

(Pan and Tenenbaum, 1991) J. Y. C. Pan, J. M . Tenenbaum, "An Intelligent Agent Framework for Enterprise Integration," in *IEEE Transactions on Systems, Man, and Cybernetics*, Vol. 21, No 6, November/December 1991, pp. 1391–1408.

(Parsaye et al., 1989) K. Parsaye, M. Chignell, S. Khoshafian, H. Wong, *Intelligent Databases: Object-Oriented, Deductive, Hypermedia Technologies,* John Wiley & Sons, New York, NY, 1989.

(Pascale, 1990) R. T. Pascale, *Managing on the Edge: How the Smartest Companies use Conflict to Stay Ahead,* Simon and Schuster, New York, New York, 1990

(Peat, 1987) F. D. Peat, *Synchronicity: the Bridge between Matter and Mind,* Bantam Books, NY, 1987.

(Personick, 1993) S. D. Personick, "The Evolving Role of Telecommunications Switching," in *IEEE Communications Magazine,* January, 1993, pp. 20–24.

(Pfeiffer and Hartley, 1992) H. D. Pfeiffer, R. T. Hartley, "The Conceptual Programming Environment, CP," in *Conceptual Structures: Current Research and Practice,* T. E. Nagle et al, editors, Ellis Horwood Limited, Chichester, England, pp. 87–107.

(Pinson and Wiener, 1988) L. J. Pinson, R. S. Wiener, *An Introduction to Object-Oriented Programming and Smalltalk,* Addison-Wesley Publishing Company, Reading, MA, 1988.

(Porter, 1980) M. E. Porter, *Competitive Strategy: Techniques for Analyzing Industries and Competitors,* The Free Press, New York, NY, 1980.

(Porter, 1985) M. E. Porter, *Competitive Advantage: Creating and Sustaining Superior Performance,* The Free Press, New York, NY, 1985.

(Porter, 1990) M. E. Porter, *The Competitive Advantage of Nations,* The Free Press, New York, New York, 1990

(Pye, 1988) C. Pye, *What is OSI?,* NCC Publications, Manchester, England, 1988.

(Querenet, 1991) B. Querenet, "The CIM-OSA Integrating Infrastructure," in *Computing and Control Engineering Journal,* Vol. 2, No 3, May 1991, pp. 118–125.

(Querenet, 1992) B. Querenet, "CIMOSA–A European Development for Enterprise Integration, Part 3: Enterprise Integrating Infrastructure," in *Enterprise Integration Modeling: Proceedings of the First International Conference,* C. J. Petrie, Jr, editor, The MIT Press, Cambridge, MA, 1992, pp. 206–215.

(Robertshaw et al, 1978) J. E. Robertshaw, S. J. Mecca, M. N. Rerick, *Problem Solving: A Systems Approach, Petrocelli Books, Inc., New York, NY, 1978.*

(Rook, 1994) F. W. Rook, "Business Process Reengineering & Automation with OT", Object Expo Conference, SIGS Conferences, Inc., NY, June 6–10, 1994.

(ROSA-L, 1992) ROSA (RACE Open Service Architecture) *The ROSA Handbook, Release Two, ROSA Workpackage L, Deliverable 93/BTL/DNR/DS/A/013/b1*, BT Laboratories, Ipswich, England, December, 1992.

(ROSA-W, 1992) ROSA (RACE Open Service Architecture) *The ROSA Case Study, ROSA Workpackage W, Deliverable 93/BTL/DNS/DS/A/011/b1*, BT Laboratories, Ipswich, England, May, 1992.

(ROSA-X, 1992) ROSA (RACE Open Service Architecture) *Foundation of Object-Orientation in ROSA, Release Two, ROSA Workpackage X, Deliverable 93/BTL/DNS/DS/A/010/b1*, BT Laboratories, Ipswich, England, May, 1992.

(ROSA-Y, 1992) ROSA (RACE Open Service Architecture) *ROSA Architecture, Release Two, ROSA Workpackage Y, Deliverable 93/BTL/DNR/DS/A/005/b1*, BT Laboratories, Ipswich, England, May, 1992.

(ROSA-Z, 1992) ROSA (RACE Open Service Architecture) *Specifying IBC Services Using the ROSA Architecture,ROSA Workpackage Z, Deliverable 93/BTL/DNR/DS/A/003/b1*, BT Laboratories, Ipswich, England, May, 1992.

(Rubin and Goldberg, 1992) K. S. Rubin, A. Goldberg, "Object Behavior Analysis," in *Communications of the ACM*, Vol. 35, No 9, September 1992, pp. 48–62.

(Rumbaugh et al., 1991) J. Rumaugh, M. Blaha, W. Premerlani, F. Eddy, W. Lorensen, *Object-Oriented Modeling and Design*, Prentice Hall, Englewood Cliffs, NJ, 1991.

(Rumbaugh, 1993a) J. Rumbaugh, "Controlling Code: How to Implement Dynamic Models," in *Journal of Object-Oriented Programming*, May, 1993, pp. 25–30.

(Rumbaugh, 1993b) J. Rumbaugh, "Objects in the Twilight Zone: How to Find and Use Application Objects," in *Journal of Object-Oriented Programming*, June, 1993, pp. 18–23.

(Russell, 1991) P. J. Russell, "Modeling with CIM-OSA," in *Computing and Control Engineering Journal*, Vol. 2, No 3, May 1991, pp. 109–117.

(Sandquist, 1985) G. M. Sandquist, *Introduction to System Science*, Prentice Hall, Englewood Cliffs, NJ, 1985.

(Savic, 1990) D. Savic, *Object-oriented Programming with Smalltalk/V*, Ellis Horwood Limited, Chichester, England, 1990.

(Scheer and Hars, 1991) A. W. Scheer, A. Hars, "Enterprise-Wide Data Modeling–the Basics for Integration," in *Computer Integrated Manufacturing: Proceedings of the Seventh CIM-Europe Annual Conference, 29–31 May 1991*, R. Vio and W. Van Puymbroeck, editors, Springer-Verlag, London, England, 1991, pp. 331–342.

(Scheer and Hars, 1992) A. W. Scheer, A. Hars, "Extending Data Modeling to Cover the Whole Enterprise," in *Communications of the ACM*, Vol. 35, No 9, September 1992, pp. 166–172.

(Scherr, 1993) A. L. Scherr, "A New Approach to Business Processes," in *IBM Systems Journal*, Vol. 32, No 1, 1993, pp. 80–98.

(Senge, 1990) P. M. Senge, *The Fifth Discipline: The Art & Practice of the Learning Organization*, Doubleday/Currency, New York, New York, 1990

(Shafer and Ritz, 1991) D. Shafer, D. A. Ritz, *Practical Smalltalk: Using Smalltalk/V*, Springer-Verlag, NY, 1991.

(Shafer and Taylor, 1993) D. Shafer, D. A. Taylor, *Transforming the Enterprise through Cooperation: An Object-Oriented Solution*, Prentice Hall, Englewood Cliffs, NJ, 1993.

(Shelton, 1994) R. Shelton, "O-O Business Engineering: Delivering the Distributed Enterprise", Object Expo Conference, SIGS Conferences, Inc., NY, June 6–10, 1994.

(Shlaer and Mellor, 1988) S. Shlaer, S. J. Mellor, *Object -Oriented Systems Analysis: Modeling the World in Data*, Yourdon Press, Englewood Cliffs, NJ, 1988.

(Shlaer and Mellor, 1992) S. Shlaer, S. J. Mellor, *Object Lifecycles: Modeling the World in States*, Yourdon Press, Englewood Cliffs, NJ, 1992.

(SIGS, 1992) SIGS Publications, *JOOP Focus on ODBMS*, SIGS Publications, New York, NY, 1992.

(Simon, 1981) H. A. Simon, *The Sciences of the Artificial, 2 e*, The MIT Press, Cambridge, MA, 1981.

(Smith, 1991) D. N. Smith, *Concepts of Object-Oriented Programming*, McGraw-Hill Book Company, New York, NY, 1991.

(Smith, 1991) M. F. Smith, *Software Prototyping: Adoption, Practice and Management*, McGraw-Hill Book Company, London, England, 1991.

(Snyder, 1993) A. Snyder, "The Essence of Objects: Concepts and Terms," in *IEEE Software*, January, 1993, pp. 31–42.

(Snyder, 1993) A. Snyder, "The Essence of Objects: Concepts and Terms," in *IEEE Software*, January, 1993, pp. 21–42.

(Soergel, 1985) D. Soergel, *Organizing Information*, Academic Press, San Diego, CA, 1985.

(Soley, 1992) R. M. Soley, "Using Object Technology to Integrate Distributed Applications," in *Enterprise Integration Modeling: Proceedings of the First International Conference,* C. J. Petrie, Jr, editor, The MIT Press, Cambridge, MA, 1992, pp. 445–454.

(Sowa and Zachman, 1992a) J. F. Sowa, J. A. Zachman, "Extending and Formalizing the Framework for Information Systems Architecture," in *IBM Systems Journal,* Vol. 31, No 3, 1992, pp. 590–616.

(Sowa and Zachman, 1992b) J. F. Sowa, J. A. Zachman, "A Logic-Based Approach to Enterprise Integration," in *Enterprise Integration Modeling: Proceedings of the First International Conference,* C. J. Petrie, Jr, editor, The MIT Press, Cambridge, MA, 1992, pp. 153–163.

(Sowa, 1984) J. F. Sowa, *Conceptual Structures: Information Processing in Mind and Machine,* Addison-Wesley Publishing Company, Reading, MA, 1984.

(Sowa, 1992) J. F. Sowa, "Conceptual Graphs Summary," in *Conceptual Structures: Current Research and Practice,* T. E. Nagle et al, editors, Ellis Horwood Limited, Chichester, England, pp. 3–51. (Stecher, 1993) P. Stecher "Building Business and Applications Systems with the Retail Application Architecture," in *IBM Systems Journal,* Vol. 32, No 2, 1993, pp. 278–306.

(Stecher, 1993) P. Stecher, "Building Business and Applications Systems with the Retail Application Architecture," in *IBM Systems Journal,* Vol. 32, No 2, 1993, pp. 278–306

(Stone, 1992) C. Stone, "Object Request Broker: the End of the Beginning," in *Object Magazine,* March/April 1992.

(Strang et al., 1993) C. J. Strang, J. G. Callaghan, A. Walles, "An Integrated Approach to Communications Management," in *BT Technology Journal,* Vol. 11, No 1, January, 1993, pp. 71–77.

(Sully, 1993) P. Sully, *Modeling the World with Objects,* Prentice Hall, Englewood Cliffs, NJ, 1993.

(Sutherland, 1975) J. W. Sutherland, *Systems: Analysis, Administration, and Architecture,* Van Nostrand Reinhold, New York, NY, 1975.

(Sventek, 1992) J. Sventek, "The Distributed Application Architecture," in *Enterprise Integration Modeling: Proceedings of the First International Conference,* C. J. Petrie, Jr, editor, The MIT Press, Cambridge, MA, 1992, pp. 481–492.

(Taylor, 1991) D. A. Taylor, *Object-oriented Technology: A Manager's Guide,* Addison-Wesley Publishing Company, Reading, MA, 1991.

(Taylor, 1992) D. A. Taylor, *Object-Oriented Information Systems: Planning and Implementation,* John Wiley & Sons, New York, NY, 1992.

(Taylor, 1994) D. A. Taylor, "Business Engineering with Object Technology", Object Expo Conference, SIGS Conferences, Inc., NY, June 6–10, 1994.

(Tepfenhart, 1992) W. M. Tepfenhart, "Using the Situation Data Model to Construct a Conceptual Basis Set," in *Conceptual Structures: Current Research and Practice,* T. E. Nagle et al, editors, Ellis Horwood Limited, Chichester, England, pp. 253–267.

(Thurow, 1992) *L. Thurow, Head to Head: The Coming Economic Battle Among Japan, Europe, and America,* William Morrow and Company, Inc., New York, New York, 1992, pp. 27–56

(Tregoe & Zimmerman, 1980) B. B. Tregoe & J. W. Zimmerman, *Top Management Strategy: What it is and how to make it work,* Simon & Schuster, Inc., New York, New York, 1980

(Tregoe et al, 1989) B. B. Tregoe, J. W. Zimmerman, R. A. Smith, P. M. Tobia, *Vision in Action: Putting a Winning Strategy to Work,* Simon & Schuster, Inc., New York, New York, 1989

(Tung et al, 1992) S. L. Tung, R. T. Keim, R. G. Ramirez, "Modeling the Business via Object-Oriented Techniques," in *Proceedings of the Twenty-Fifth Annual Hawaii International Conference on Systems Sciences,* B. D. Shriver, editor, IEEE Computer Society Press, Los Alamitos, CA, 1992, Vol. 4, pp. 557–567.

(Turban, 1992) E. Turban, *Expert Systems and Applied Artificial Intelligence,* Macmillan Publishing Company, New York, NY, 1992.

(Vernadat, 1992) F. B. Vernadat, "CIMOSA–A European Development for Enterprise Integration, Part 2: Enterprise Modeling," in *Enterprise Integration Modeling: Proceedings of the First International Conference,* C. J. Petrie, Jr, editor, The MIT Press, Cambridge, MA, 1992, pp. 189–204.

(von Weizsacker, 1980) *The Unity of Nature,* (English Translation, F. Zucker, ed.), Farrar–Straus–Giroux, NY, 1980.

(Voss, 1991) G. Voss, *Object-Oriented Programming: An Introduction,* McGraw-Hill Book Company, Berkeley, CA, 1991.

(Waldrop, 1992) M. M. Waldrop, *Complexity: The Emerging Science at the Edge of Order and Chaos,* Simon and Schuster, New York, NY, 1992.

(Wand and Woo, 1991) Y. Wand and C. C. Woo, "An Approach to Formalizing Organizational Open Systems Concepts," in *Conference on Organizational Computing Systems,* P. de Jong, editor, ACM Press, New York, NY, 1991, pp. 141–146.

(Wand, 1989) Y. Wand, "A Proposal for a Formal Model of Objects," in *Object-Oriented Concepts, Databases, and Applications*, W. Kim and F. Lochovsky, editors, Addison-Wesley Publishing Company, Reading, MA, 1989, pp. 537–559.

(Way, 1992) E. C. Way, "The Dynamic Type Hierarchy Theory of Metaphor," in *Conceptual Structures: Current Research and Practice*, T. E. Nagle et al, editors, Ellis Horwood Limited, Chichester, England, pp. 543–557.

(Wegner, 1989) P. Wegner "Capital-Intensive Software Technology", in *Software Reusability, Volume 1: Concepts and Models*, T. J. Biggerstaff, A. J. Perlis, Editors, ACM Press, Addison-Wesley Publishing Company, Reading, MA, 1989.

(Wegner, 1990) P. Wegner, "Concepts and Paradigms of Object-Oriented Programming," in *ACM SIGPLAN OOPS Messenger*, ACM Press, New York, NY, 1990, pp. 7–87.

(Whyte et al., 1969) L. L. Whyte, A. G. Wilson, D. Wilson, *Hierarchical Structures*, American Elsevier, New York, NY, 1969.

(Williamson and Azmoodeh, 1991) G. I. Williamson, M. Azmoodeh, "The Application of Information Modeling in the Telecommunications Management Network," in *BT Technology Journal*, Vol. 9, No 3, July, 1991, pp. 18–26.

(Winblad et al., 1990) A. L. Winblad, S. D. Edwards, D. R. King, *Object Oriented Software*, Addison-Wesley Publishing Company, Reading, MA, 1990.

(Wirfs-Brock et al, 1990) R. Wirfs-Brock, B. Wilkerson, L. Wiener, *Designing Object-Oriented Software* Prentice Hall, Englewood Cliffs, NJ, 1990.

(Wood and Silver, 1989) J. Wood, D. Silver, *Joint Application Design: How to Design Quality Systems in 40% Less Time*, John Wiley & Sons, New York, NY, 1989.

(Work and Balmforth, 1993) G. Work, A. Balmforth, "Using Abstractions to Build Standardized Components for Enterprise Models," in *Proceedings of the 1993 Software Engineering Standards Symposium*, IEEE Computer Society Press, Los Alamitos, CA, 1993, pp. 154–162.

(Young, 1964) O. R. Young, "A survey of General Systems Theory," in *General Systems IX*, 1964.

(Yourdon, 1992) E. Yourdon, *Decline and Fall of the American Programmer*, Yourdon Press, Englewood Cliffs, NJ, 1992.

(Zachman, 1987) J. A. Zachman, "A Framework for Information Systems Architecture," in *IBM Systems Journal*, Vol. 26, No 3, 1987, pp. 276–292.

Index

I